THE VIDEO GAME EXPLOSION

A History from PONG to PlayStation® and Beyond

Edited by Mark J. P. Wolf

Greenwood Press
Westport, Connecticut · London

Library of Congress Cataloging-in-Publication Data

The video game explosion : a history from Pong to Playstation and beyond / edited by Mark J.P. Wolf.
    p. cm.
  Includes bibliographical references and index.
ISBN 978–0–313–33868–7 (alk. paper)
1. Video games—Social aspects. 2. Video games—History. I. Wolf, Mark J. P.
GV1469.34.S52V52 2008
794.809—dc22   2007033893

British Library Cataloguing in Publication Data is available.

Library of Congress Catalog Card Number: 2007033893
ISBN: 978–0–313–33868–7

First published in 2008

Greenwood Press, 88 Post Road West, Westport, CT 06881
An imprint of Greenwood Publishing Group, Inc.
www.greenwood.com

Printed in the United States of America

The paper used in this book complies with the
Permanent Paper Standard issued by the National
Information Standards Organization (Z39.48-1984).

10 9 8 7 6 5 4 3 2 1

CONTENTS

Illustrations   ix

Acknowledgments   xi

Introduction   xiii

A Brief Timeline of Video Game History   xvii

Part I   Looking at Video Games   **1**

   Chapter 1   What Is a Video Game?   3
        Mark J. P. Wolf

   Chapter 2   Imaging Technologies   9
        Mark J. P. Wolf

   Chapter 3   Modes of Exhibition   13
        Mark J. P. Wolf

   Chapter 4   Influences and Precursors   17
        Mark J. P. Wolf

   Chapter 5   The Study of Video Games   21
        Mark J. P. Wolf

Part II   The Early Days (Before 1985)   **29**

   Chapter 6   Mainframe Games and Simulations   31
        David H. Ahl

   Chapter 7   Arcade Games of the 1970s   35
        Mark J. P. Wolf

Chapter 8   Video Games in Europe: The Early Years   45
              David Winter
Sidebar   System Profile: The Magnavox Odyssey   50
              David Winter

Chapter 9   Early Home Video Game Systems   53
              Leonard Herman

Chapter 10   Company Profile: Atari   59
              Leonard Herman

Chapter 11   System Profile: The Atari Video Computer System (VCS)   63
              Leonard Herman

Chapter 12   Vector Games   67
              Mark J. P. Wolf

Chapter 13   Video Game Stars: Pac-Man   73
              Mark J. P. Wolf

Chapter 14   The Rise of the Home Computer   75
              Bob Rehak

Chapter 15   Genre Profile: Adventure Games   81
              Mark J. P. Wolf
Sidebar   Company Profile: Electronic Arts   89
              Alison McMahan

Chapter 16   Arcade Games of the 1980s   91
              Mark J. P. Wolf

Chapter 17   Laserdisc Games   99
              Mark J. P. Wolf

Chapter 18   The Video Game Industry Crash   103
              Mark J. P. Wolf

Part III   The Industry Rebounds (1985–1994)   **107**

Chapter 19   System Profile: The Nintendo Entertainment System (NES)   109
              Dominic Arsenault
Sidebar   Company Profile: Nintendo   113
              Dominic Arsenault

Chapter 20   A New Generation of Home Video Game Systems   115
              Leonard Herman

Chapter 21   CD-ROM Games   121
              Carl Therrien

Chapter 22   Genre Profile: Interactive Movies   127
              Bernard Perron

Chapter 23   Arcade Games of the 1990s and Beyond   135
              Mark J. P. Wolf

Chapter 24   Handheld Video Game Systems   143
              Leonard Herman
Sidebar   Company Profile: Sega   149
              Alison McMahan

Chapter 25   Shareware Games: Between Hobbyist and Professional   151
              Brett Camper

Part IV   Advancing to the Next Level (1995–Present)   **159**

Chapter 26   The Later Generation Home Video Game Systems   161
              Leonard Herman

Chapter 27   Online Role-Playing Games   173
              Kelly Boudreau

Chapter 28   System Profile: Sony PlayStation   177
              Dominic Arsenault
Sidebar   Company Profile: Sony   181
              Mark J. P. Wolf

Chapter 29   Video Game Stars: Lara Croft   183
              Alison McMahan

Chapter 30   Genre Profile: First-Person Shooting Games   187
              Bob Rehak
Sidebar   Retrogames   194
              Bob Rehak

Chapter 31   Independent and Experimental Video Games   197
              Brett Camper

Chapter 32   Video Games in Europe   203
              Lars Konzack

Chapter 33   Video Games in Asia   211
              Benjamin Wai-ming Ng

Chapter 34   Video Games in Australia   223
              Thomas H. Apperley

Part V   A Closer Look at Video Games   **229**

Chapter 35   The Video Game Development Process   231
              Feichin Ted Tschang

Chapter 36   Graphics in Video Games   239
              Carl Therrien

Chapter 37   Sound in Video Games   251
              Eric Pidkameny

Chapter 38   Video Game Genres   259
              Mark J. P. Wolf
Sidebar   Best-Selling Video Games   275
              Mark J. P. Wolf

Chapter 39   The Video Game as an Object of Controversy   277
              Dominic Arsenault
Sidebar   Video Games Rating Systems   281
              Mark J. P. Wolf

Chapter 40   Morals, Ethics, and Video Games   283
              Mark J. P. Wolf

Chapter 41   Video Games and Their Relationship with Other Media   293
              Martin Picard
Sidebar   How to Get a Job in the Video Game Industry   301
              Mark J. P. Wolf

Chapter 42   The Future of Video Games   303
              Mark J. P. Wolf

Glossary of Video Game Terminology   311

Resource Guide   317

Notes   329

Index   343

About the Contributors   377

ILLUSTRATIONS

Figure 7.1 The eight-player game *Indy 800* (1975).   38
Figure 7.2 An early attempt at a 3-D look.   42
Figure 8.1 The Magnavox Odyssey.   46
Figure 8.2 Interton Video 2000 (Germany, 1975).   47
Figure 8.3 The Ping-O-Tronic.   48
Figure 8.4 The VideoSport MK2.   49
Figure 15.1 Examples of different graphics standards.   85
Figure 15.2 An advancement in interactivity.   86
Figure 15.3 The Quiki-Mart in 1987 and 1991.   87
Figure 16.1 Gottlieb's *Exterminator* (1989).   97
Figure 25.1 Adversaries in *Beast* (1984).   153
Figure 25.2 *Sopwith* (1984–1986).   154
Figure 25.3 Tiny turn-based tanks with a big bang from *Scorched Earth*.   154
Figure 25.4 *One Must Fall 2097* (1994).   157
Figure 31.1 Falling downstairs in *Porrasturvat* (2002).   199
Figure 31.2 Building up a makeshift ship in *TUMIKI Fighters* (2004).   200
Figure 31.3 Scenes from experimental games.   202
Figure 36.1 Two screen images from *Adventure* for the Atari 2600.   240
Figure 36.2 Isometric perspective in *Zaxxon* (1982).   241
Figure 36.3 Close-ups in *King's Quest V* (1990) and *Loom* (1990).   242
Figure 36.4 *King of Chicago* (1987).   243
Figure 36.5 Decomposed running animation.   244
Figure 36.6 Full-motion video evolves.   244
Figure 36.7 Atari's arcade game *Battlezone* (1980).   247
Figure 36.8 Two images from Atari's arcade game *I, Robot*.   247
Figure 36.9 Light maps and textured 3-D creatures in id Software's *Quake* (1996).   248
Figure 36.10 Valve Software's *Half-Life 2* (2004).   249

ACKNOWLEDGMENTS

I would first like to thank all the contributors to this volume, who are some of the best people writing about video game history today: David H. Ahl, Thomas H. Apperley, Dominic Arsenault, Kelly Boudreau, Brett Camper, Leonard Herman, Lars Konzack, Alison McMahan, Benjamin Wai-ming Ng, Bernard Perron, Martin Picard, Eric Pidkameny, Bob Rehak, Carl Therrien, Feichin Ted Tschang, and David Winter. Without their work, this volume could not have appeared. Thanks also to Kristi Ward at Greenwood Press, who initiated the project. Earlier versions of some of my essays in this book appeared in my books *The Medium of the Video Game* (2001), *Virtual Morality: Morals, Ethics, and New Media* (2003), and *The World of the D'ni: Myst and Riven* (Italian version, 2006), and in Paul Messaris and Lee Humphreys, editors, *Digital Media: Transformations in Human Communication* (2006); I am thankful for these presses' interest in my work. Thanks to Keith Feinstein, Sascha Scheuermann, Adrian Purser, Cody Johnson, Bill Esquivel, Andreas Kraemer, Henry Jenkins, and Tom Krenzke, who also provided assistance for which I am grateful. Thanks also to Concordia University Wisconsin for the sabbatical in spring of 2006 that gave me additional time to work on this book, and to my wife, Diane and my sons, Michael, Christian, and our dear departed Edward. And, as always, thanks be to God.

INTRODUCTION

Mark J. P. Wolf

Video games have now been around long enough that an interest in their history is growing. Many who grew up with the games as they developed are looking back fondly on those early days, and some of them are still active gamers. Others have become game collectors, trying to preserve the history along with the games themselves. And some who are too young to remember the first generations of video games are curious about them, and are perhaps dismayed at how difficult it can be to find older games (or they may dismiss them as too simplistic and graphically unsophisticated, without realizing their importance or understanding how they were seen when they first appeared). Still others may look upon games as a part of popular culture and ask how they fit into the broader cultural scheme of the past few decades.

As a history of video games, this book owes much to its predecessors. Before there were books on video game history, there were detailed magazine essays, like the multipart "Electronic Games: Space Age Leisure Activity" by Jerry and Eric Eimbinder, which appeared in several months' issues of *Popular Electronics* and chronicled the industry and technology up to 1980, when it was written. Not only are these early histories valuable for research, but they also embody the enthusiasm of the time as well, and provide some insight into how the games were received when they appeared. The first history book appeared a few years later, George Sullivan's *Screen Play: The Story of Video Games* (New York: F. Warne, 1983), a 93-page book for a juvenile audience. Perhaps publishers had to be persuaded in undertaking a history for an adult audience, since the first such book, Leonard Herman's *Phoenix: The Fall and Rise of Home Videogames,* did not appear until 1994 (Springfield, NJ: Rolenta Press), and was initially self-published when no commercial publisher could be found (the book was a success and is now in its fourth edition). Steven Kent's *The First Quarter* (Colorado Springs, CO: BDW Publishing, 2001) and its enlarged revision, *The Ultimate History of Video Games* (New York: Three Rivers Press, 2001), focuses on the industry and the men and women behind it, while Rusel DeMaria and Johnny L. Wilson's *High Score! The Illustrated History of Electronic Games* (San Francisco: McGraw-Hill Osborne Media, 2003) and Van Burnham's *Supercade: A Visual History of the Videogame Age, 1971–1984* (Cambridge, MA: MIT Press, 2003) are both mainly visual histories rather than scholarly works. Some reference works are available, like Bill Kurtz's *Encyclopedia of Arcade Video Games* (Schiffer Book Farm, PA: Schiffer, 2003), or the online *Killer List of Video Games* (www.klov.com). And then there are books about individual companies, like Scott Cohen's *Zap! The Rise and Fall of Atari* (New York: McGraw-Hill, 1984) or David Sheff's *Game Over: How Nintendo Zapped an American Industry, Captured Your Dollars, and Enslaved Your Children* (New York: Random House, 1993).

This book differs from its predecessors in several ways. It is intended both for the general reader interested in video game history as well as for students with chapters thematically organized around various topics, which are generally arranged in chronological order and tell the story of video games from their earlier inception to the present day. Other features of the book include sidebars and profiles that highlight various aspects of video game history and a glossary of terminology relating to video games and their technology. Some of the best people writing on video games today have contributed their scholarship to form this comprehensive history. While other books on video games have been written from a journalistic, sociological, psychological, or nostalgic point of view, here the video games themselves occupy a central position. Other aspects of history, such as the companies, game designers, technology, merchandising, and so forth, provide a necessary background, but games always remain in the forefront.

The book is divided into five parts. The first part, "Looking at Video Games," begins with the question of what video games are, where they came from, and what influenced their development. Imaging technologies and the modes of exhibition are also examined. Finally, the ways in which the study of video games differs from the study of traditional media are explored. Together, these chapters serve to introduce video games as the complex, unique, and interesting medium that they are.

The second part, "The Early Days (Before 1985)," looks at the formative years of video game history during which time games developed from a novelty into an industry. In the early 1970s, games were being made on mainframe computers and were available in arcades alongside pinball games. Relatively simple home systems were appearing and gaining in popularity, in both the United States and Europe, along with home computers. The most prominent company of this era was Atari, which also became the only company to produce arcade games, home console systems, and home computers. Various types of new technology, like vector graphics and laserdiscs were incorporated into games during the late 1970s and early 1980s. Finally, a glut of cheap product and changing consumer demand helped to bring about an industry crash in the mid 1980s, ending what we now think of as the early days of video games.

The third part, "The Industry Rebounds (1985–1994)," begins with a look at the Nintendo Entertainment System (NES), the success of which helped to end the crash and show that the video game industry was still a viable one. After Nintendo's success, other companies followed suit, releasing a new generation of home video game console systems. Arcade games found themselves competing with home games and began offering three-dimensional graphics and innovative interfaces to lure players back to the arcades. Hand-held games became more sophisticated, and consequently more popular during this time. New technologies like the CD-ROM helped rejuvenate the industry, and shareware games also brought new ideas into gaming.

The fourth part, "Advancing to the Next Level (1995–Present)," covers the rise of another new generation of even more powerful home game systems, including the Sony

PlayStation, Sega Saturn, and Nintendo 64. Online role-playing games grew into big business during this time, attracting hundreds of thousands and later millions of players. Today video games are a worldwide phenomenon, and because much video game study tends to focus on the industry in North America, several chapters cover video games in Europe, Asia, and Australia as well.

The last part of the book, "A Closer Look at Video Games," examines the video game design process, the development of graphics and sound in games, and video games' relationship with other media. Other chapters explore video game genres, the video game as an object of controversy, the moral and ethical aspects of video games, and finally the future of video games. Also included in the book are a brief timeline of video game history, a glossary of video game terminology, and a resource guide for video game research, which includes print and online sources as well as organizations which researchers may find useful.

A wide variety of contributors have made this volume possible. Offering their knowledge of early games are David H. Ahl, the founder of *Creative Computing* magazine, author of 22 books and over 50 computer games, and David Winter, whose website, www.pong-story.com, has extensive information on early games culled from his personal collection of over 800 early game systems. Leonard Herman, author of *Phoenix: The Fall and Rise of Videogames,* traces the history of home video game systems and handheld games through a number of essays. Lars Konzack, Benjamin Wai-ming Ng, and Thomas H. Apperley give the book a global perspective, writing about video games outside of North America. Looking outside the commercial video game industry, Brett Camper examines the history of shareware and experimental video games, and other authors, including Bernard Perron, Bob Rehak, Alison McMahan, Ted Tschang, Dominic Arsenault, Martin Picard, Carl Therrien, Kelly Boudreau, and Eric Pidkameny, touch on a range of topics from their expertise, from video games' graphics, sound, technology, and production process, to home computers, retrogaming, and other media, as well as various genre, company, and system profiles.

The history of video games now spans over four decades, and while this is a relatively short time compared to the histories of other more traditional media, it is fast moving and exciting, with innovations and advances occurring at a rate unparalleled in other media. The history of video games is dense and multifaceted, as it coincides with other areas such as film, television, the Internet, and other interactive media; storage technologies such as diskettes, laserdiscs, CD-ROMs, DVDs, and computer technology in general; various transmedia entertainment franchises, popular fads, and of course, merchandising. In the past decade or so, people have begun to study various aspects of video games, approaching them from a variety of disciplines, while a discipline specific to video game study is also developing. While an increasing amount of historical information has been appearing, particularly on the Internet, in scholarly work more attention has been paid to theory than to history, and newer games are discussed more than the earlier ones that preceded, and in many cases, inspired them. A broad knowledge of video games' origins and development, then, is necessary and crucial to the understanding of their current state, and this book hopes to provide that.

A Brief Timeline of Video Game History

1958 William Higinbotham's *Tennis for Two* experiment shown at Brookhaven Laboratory. The experiment demonstrates interactive control of on-screen game play, though many today do not consider this to have been a real video game.

1962 The finished version of the mainframe computer game *Spacewar!* is written at MIT. It will later inspire Nolan Bushnell to create *Computer Space* (1971).

1966 Ralph Baer writes a four-page paper describing his ideas for playing interactive games on ordinary television sets.

1971 The first coin-operated arcade video game, Nolan Bushnell's *Computer Space,* appears.

1972 Ralph Baer's Magnavox Odyssey, the first home video game system, is released. Nolan Bushnell's *PONG* appears in the arcade becoming the first hit game.

1973 The arcade video game industry takes off, as many companies begin producing video games, including Chicago Coin, Midway, Ramtek, Taito, Allied Leisure, and Kee Games, which was secretly owned by Atari.

1974 Kee Games's *Tank* is the first game to store graphics data on a ROM chip. Midway's *TV Basketball* is the first arcade game to use human figures as avatars, instead of blocks or vehicles.

1975 Midway's *Gun Fight* is the first game to use a microprocessor. Atari's *Steeplechase* is the first six-player arcade video game, and Kee Games's *Indy 800* is the first eight-player game, complete with a steering wheel and foot pedals for each of eight players (it also used a color CRT).

1976   General Instruments's AY-3-8500 chip is released, which had all the circuitry necessary for a video game on a single chip. The Fairchild/Zircon Channel F, the first cartridge-based home game system, is released. Atari's *Night Driver* is the first game to simulate a first-person perspective, though it did not have true 3-D graphics. Atari's *Breakout* is released.

1977   The home video game industry suffers its first crash, and many companies quit the industry. Atari's VCS home console system (later renamed the 2600) is released. In Japan, Nintendo releases its first home video game, Color TV Game 6. Kee Games's arcade game *Super Bug* introduces 4-directional scrolling.

1978   Taito's *Space Invaders* appears and becomes the inspiration for many vertical shooting games to follow. Atari's arcade game *Football* introduces 2-directional scrolling.

1979   Vectorbeam releases *Warrior,* the first one-on-one fighting game. Atari's *Asteroids* and *Lunar Lander,* both vector graphics games, are released. Namco's *Galaxian* is the first game to have 100 percent of its graphics in RGB color (a standard used for color video using red, green, and blue signals). Namco's *Puck-Man* (later renamed *Pac-Man*) is released in Japan.

1980   *Pac-Man* is released in North America, and other influential games *Battlezone, Defender* also appear. Atari's *Battlezone* is the first arcade game to feature a true 3-D environment. *Ultima* becomes the first home computer game with 4-directional scrolling. *Star Fire* is the first cockpit game, and the first arcade game to feature a high-score table using players' initials.

1981   Nintendo's *Donkey Kong* and Atari's *Tempest* are released. The United States arcade game industry reaches $5 billion.

1982   Gottlieb's *Q*bert* is released. Sega's arcade game *Zaxxon* becomes the first arcade game to be advertised on television. Late in the year, arcade game income drops, and it appears that another video game industry crash is coming, one that is larger than the 1977 crash.

1983   The video game industry crash affects the home video game industry. Nintendo's Famicon system is released in Japan. Atari's *I, Robot* is the first raster video game with filled-polygon three-dimensional graphics. Atari's vector game *Star Wars* is released.

1984   The video game industry crash continues. Nintendo releases the Famicom system in Japan. RDI releases the Halcyon, a laserdisc-based home video game system.

1985   Nintendo releases a new version of its Famicon, renamed the Nintendo Entertainment System (NES), in America. Its popularity helps to bring an end to the industry crash. Nintendo also releases *Super Mario Bros.,* which becomes one of the best-selling games of all time. Alex Pajitnov designs *Tetris.*

1986 *The Legend of Zelda* appears (for the Nintendo Famicom), the first in a long series of Zelda games. Taito's *Arkanoid* and *Bubble Bobble* appear in arcades. Sega releases the Sega Master System (SMS).

1987 Cyan's *The Manhole* becomes the first computer game to be released on CD-ROM. Yokai Douchuuki, the first 16-bit arcade game, is released in Japan. LucasArts's *Maniac Mansion* is the first adventure game with a point-and-click interface. Incentive Software releases *Driller,* a home computer game with breakthrough 3-D graphics. Taito's arcade game *Double Dragon* is released.

1988 Namco's *Assault* is released. Williams's *NARC* is the first game to use a 32-bit processor. Nintendo releases *Super Mario Bros. 2.*

1989 Atari releases the arcade games *Hard Drivin'* and *S.T.U.N. Runner.* Gottlieb's *Exterminator* is the first game to use all digitized imagery for its backgrounds. Two handheld video game consoles are released: Nintendo's Game Boy and Atari's Lynx. The Sega Genesis home console system appears.

1990 Maxis releases Will Wright's *SimCity,* the first in a long line of Sim games. Nintendo releases *Super Mario Bros. 3.* Sega Game Gear is released in Japan. Squaresoft's *Final Fantasy* series is introduced to North America.

1991 Nintendo releases the Super Nintendo Entertainment System (SNES) in North America. Capcom releases *Street Fighter II.* Sega releases the home video game *Sonic the Hedgehog,* the main character of which would go on to become Sega's mascot. Philips Electronics releases the CD-i (compact disc interactive) system which uses compact discs.

1992 Midway releases the arcade game *Mortal Kombat.* Virgin Games's *The 7th Guest* is released and becomes the best-selling home computer game. Sega releases *Virtua Racing,* a 3-D racing game. id Software releases *Wolfenstein 3D,* a 3-D home computer game. Virtuality releases *Dactyl Nightmare,* an arcade game with a VR (virtual reality) headset and gun interface.

1993 Cyan's *Myst* is released and becomes the best-selling home computer game of all time, a title it will hold until 2002. id Software releases *Doom.* The World Wide Web goes worldwide. Sega releases *Virtua Fighter,* a 3-D fighting game. New home systems include the Pioneer LaserActive CLD-A100 and the Atari Jaguar.

1994 Nintendo releases the home game *Donkey Kong Country.* The Sega Saturn and the Sony PlayStation are released in Japan. Ernest Adams forms the Computer Game Developers Association. Blizzard releases the real-time strategy game *Warcraft.* Sega releases the arcade game *Daytona USA,* a racing game with texture-mapping. SNK's Neo•Geo home console system appears.

1995 The Sony PlayStation and Sega Saturn make their North American debut. Nintendo releases *Donkey Kong Country 2: Diddy's Kong Quest.* Blizzard releases *Warcraft II.*

1996 The Nintendo 64 appears in Japan and North America. Nintendo also releases the Virtual Boy, a portable game system with a separate screen for each eye which when combined creates a three-dimensional image. Digipen Institute of Technology becomes the first school to offer college degrees in video game development.

1997 The Nintendo 64 is released in Europe and Australia. DreamWorks, Sega, and Universal open the first GameWorks arcade in Seattle. Bandai's Tamagotchi appears. Cyan's *Riven,* the sequel to *Myst,* appears. Sega releases *Top Skater,* an arcade game with a skateboard interface. Nintendo releases *Mario Kart 64.* The MMORPG *Ultima Online* begins.

1998 Konami releases *Dance Dance Revolution* and the first games in its *Beatmania* series and *GuitarFreaks* series. The Nintendo Game Boy Color appears. Sierra Studios releases *Half-Life.* SNK releases the Neo•Geo Pocket handheld video game system. Rockstar Games releases *Grand Theft Auto.*

1999 The Sega Dreamcast is released. The MMORPG *EverQuest* begins. Nintendo releases *Donkey Kong 64.* The Game Developers Conference holds the first Independent Games Festival. *Tony Hawk's Pro Skater* is released. The MMORPG *Asheron's Call* begins.

2000 Sony's PlayStation 2 appears. Nintendo sells its 100 millionth Game Boy console. Maxis's *The Sims* is released. The United States Post Office issues a stamp depicting video games.

2001 Microsoft's Xbox and the Nintendo GameCube appear. Midway Games leaves the arcade video game industry. Bungie Studios's *Halo: Combat Evolved* appears. Sega announces that it will no longer develop home video game consoles.

2002 *The Sims* overtakes *Myst,* and becomes the best-selling home computer game of all time. The MMORPG *Sims Online* begins. Sega releases *Rez* for the PlayStation 2. Microsoft's Xbox Live online gaming service begins.

2003 The MMORPG *Star Wars Galaxies* begins. Nintendo stops production of the NES and SNES. Atari's *Enter the Matrix* is released. Cell phone company Nokia releases the N-Gage handheld video game system.

2004 Sony releases the PlayStation Portable in Japan, and the PlayStation 2 in China. Nintendo releases the Nintendo DS (dual screen) handheld video game system. Bungie releases *Halo 2.*

2005 Sony releases the PlayStation Portable in North America. Nintendo releases the Game Boy Micro. Microsoft releases the Xbox 360. Tiger

Telematics releases the Gizmondo in England and North America. *The Sims* appears on postage stamps in France.

2006 The Nintendo Wii and Sony's PlayStation 3 are released. Microsoft releases the Xbox 360 in Australia.

2007 The MMORPG *World of Warcraft* is estimated to have more than 9 million players worldwide.

PART I

Looking at Video Games

In less than four decades video games have gone from simple bouncing block graphics to a global industry of enormous proportions. In 2006 alone, the U.S. video game industry made a record $12.5 billion. Video games have a growing influence on other media like film, television, and the Internet and are played by hundreds of millions worldwide. And yet the study of video games has only recently gained acceptance in academia, and most of the writing that exists is mostly about newer games, and typically home computer games at that. Relatively little has appeared regarding older games and game systems, arcade games, or video game history in general. Part of the reason is that many of the old games are already gone or very hard to find and play; although this may make writing about them more difficult, it also suggests a greater need for historical research, before it is too late.

Before we look at the history of video games, it is useful to ask what exactly we mean by the term "video game," and how it is distinct from other media forms. At the same time, we also can look at the precursors and influences that shaped the video game and gave it the form that it has. As the video game is very dependent on different types of technology, these will be examined as well, including imaging technologies and modes of exhibition through which video games are brought to the public. Finally, an examination of the study of video games itself, and how it differs from the study of traditional media forms, is included. Together, these chapters provide the necessary background from which a study of video game history can begin.

CHAPTER 1

WHAT IS A VIDEO GAME?

Mark J. P. Wolf

What exactly constitutes a "video game"? Although the term seems simple enough, its usage has varied a great deal over the years and from place to place. We might start by noting the two criteria present in the name itself; its status as a "game" and its use of "video" technology. (These two aspects of video games may be reason for why one finds both "video game" (two words) and "videogame" (one word) in use: considered as a game, "video game" is consistent with "board game" and "card game," whereas if one considers it as another type of video technology, then "videogame" is consistent with terms like "videotape" and "videodisc." Terms like "computer games" and "electronic games" are also sometimes used synonymously with "video games," but distinctions between them can be made. "Electronic games" and "computer games" both do not require any visuals, while "video games" would not require a microprocessor (or whatever one wanted to define as being essential to being referred to as a "computer"). Thus, a board game like *Stop Thief* (1979), for example, which has a handheld computer that makes sounds that relate to game play on the board, could be considered a computer game, but not a video game. More of these kinds of games exist than games that involve video but not a computer, making "video games" the more exclusive term. The term "video games" is also more accurate in regard to what kinds of games are meant when the term is used in common parlance, and so it will be the term used here.

Although even definitions of "game" can vary, elements one would expect to find in a game are *conflict* (against an opponent or circumstances), *rules* (determining what can and cannot be done and when), use of some *player ability* (such as skill, strategy, or luck), and some kind of *valued outcome* (such as winning vs. losing, or the attaining of the highest score or fastest time for the completing of a task). All these are usually present in video games in some manner, though to differing degrees. In video games, the scoring of points, adherence to the "rules," and the display of the game's visuals are all monitored by a computer instead of by human beings. The computer can also control the opposing characters within a game, becoming a participant as well as a referee.

Most video games are one-player games in which the player faces computer-controlled opponents and situations. Due to the almost instantaneous speed at which a computer can process user input, respond with reactions, and display the action on-screen, video games are often designed to require fast action and reflexes, much like sports or games like pinball or table tennis. Fast action is, for some, so important to the gaming experience that narrower definitions of video game exclude text adventures, adaptations of card games and board games, contemplative puzzle-based programs like *Riven* (1997) or *Rhem* (2002), or any of the *Ultima* or *Zork* series, all of which generally do not require quick reflexes, and some of which are more like puzzles and arguably not "games" in the classic sense. Another element is the *identity* of the computer as a player. Keith Feinstein, the owner of the video game museum Videotopia, has suggested that the playing of a video game has a necessarily emotional element to it, similar to that of struggling against a playmate of comparable skill and ability. In his view, the computer must be more than a referee or stage manager controlling the video game's world, but an active opponent who competes with the human player. By assigning an identity to the computer player and creating a "one-on-one" situation within the game, competition becomes possible and emotional stakes are raised, just as they might be in a two-player game in which human beings compete against one another.

The programs mentioned above, however, are all marketed as games, and would be included in the broader definition of the term found in popular culture. Almost all programs designated as games by their makers contain the criteria mentioned above, albeit to varying degrees. For example, in *SimCity* (1989) and other "Sim" programs from Maxis Software, outcomes are ongoing, as conditions of the simulated world improve or worsen depending on the player's decisions. Conflict occurs between the player (who is trying to provide order to the city) and circumstances or situations (such as natural disasters, taxpaying citizens, crime, pollution, and occasional wandering monsters). The "rules" are built into the game's responses; tax the citizens too much and they will move away, cut funding to the police station and the crime rate will rise, and so on. In puzzle-based games like *Myst* (1993) or *Riven,* conflict may arise from the difficulty of puzzle-solving, pitting the player's mind against the game-designer's mind. Outcomes are also valued in these games; in each, several different endings or outcomes are possible, one of which is more desirable than the others.

A still broader (and less accurate) definition of the term "video games" sometimes includes educational or utility cartridges made for dedicated game consoles. Some of these, like *Mario Teaches Typing* (1991) incorporate gameplay into learning, although many do not. Still, educational cartridges [like Atari 2600 cartridges *Basic Programming* (1979) and *Fun With Numbers* (1977)] and utility cartridges (such as diagnostic and test cartridges) often appear in lists of game cartridges, are sought by collectors, and are included within the popular and very loose usages of the term video games found in stores and Internet discussion groups. Even though these programs are not games (according to the above criteria), the read-only memory (ROM) cartridges containing them are the same as those used for games; they are also given identification numbers similar to the games; and they receive much the same treatment as game cartridges in the marketplace. Thus, the grouping of educational and utility programs together with games reflects their status as commercial and cultural artifacts more than they reflect actual considerations of the program's content or the player's experience of that content.

While the degree to which a program can be considered a game depends on varying criteria, its status as "video" is less problematic. By the strictest definition, "video" refers to the use of an analog intensity/brightness signal displayed on a cathode ray tube (CRT), the kind of picture tube used in a television set or computer monitor, to produce raster-based (filled-area images, as opposed to wireframe ones) imagery. The father of video games, then, is Ralph Baer, who was the first to create games that used television sets as their display devices, and the creator of the first home game system, the Magnavox Odyssey, which appeared in 1972.

But popular use of the term "video game" in society, culture, and the industry itself has grown much looser and broader than the original technical definition. Arcade games and home game systems used CRTs as their displays, but not all of them were used to produce raster imagery. Some displayed vector graphics, using a different signal and method of creating screen images. Because both vector and raster games used CRTs, vector games became included in the term "video games," and later as the same games appear on different imaging technologies, popular use of the term came to include games using *liquid crystal display* (LCD) screens, like Milton Bradley's Microvision or Nintendo's Game Boy, and an even *light-emitting diode* (LED)-based screen in the case of Nintendo's short-lived Virtual Boy system. Indeed, with many games ported across many systems, from arcade versions to versions for home consoles, home computers, and handheld game systems, and games becoming available for new technologies like plasma HDTV screens, the idea of a video game has become something more conceptual and less tied to a specific imaging technology, at least in its popular usage.

The term "computer games" is sometimes used, though it covers a wider range of games (including those without any graphical displays), and it is arguably more accurate, since the majority of video games depend on a microprocessor. But by the mid-1980s, "video game" seemed to have become the general term most used in both popular culture as well as the commercial game industry itself, while "computer game" was often reserved specifically for versions of games released for home computers. This may be due to the central place of the image and screen in the gaming experience, while the computer itself remains behind the scenes, quietly controlling all that goes on within the game. Such a demarcation might also have been encouraged by the fact that the computers present in arcade games and game consoles during the 1980s and 1990s were usually dedicated machines that only played games, unlike home computers which had other uses.

On the other hand, the use of a CRT with raster graphics is not enough to make a game a video game; one would expect the action of the game to take place interactively on-screen. Thus, certain games, like the *Clue VCR Mystery Game* (1985), a version of the board game *Clue* which uses video clips on videotape, would not qualify since the video image is not interactive, nor does the action of the game—such as the moving of a player's pieces— occur on-screen. Some games walk the line between board game and video game, involving elements of both. Three games for the Philips Videopac video game system, *Conquest of the World* (1982), *Quest for the Rings* (1982), and *The Great Wall Street Fortune Hunt* (1982), all involved on-screen video game play as well as a game board with movers, combining video game and board game play. As the other cartridges available for the Videopac system were all on-screen games, the three video/board games are usually listed along with them, although they are really hybrid games. There are also games which used plastic overlays placed on the screen, such as the early games for the Magnavox Odyssey 100 system or the GCE/Milton Bradley Vectrex system. These overlays contained background images, while the screen provided the moving elements of the player-characters and provided color to black-and-white screen graphics. A number of early arcade games also added non-video elements to their game screens, such as *Warrior* (1979), which featured two vector-graphics knights in top view moving through scenery on the screen's overlay. As long as the action itself takes place on-screen, such games are generally considered to be video games.

Some adaptations of games occur on systems whose screens have far less resolution than a television screen. Nintendo's Virtual Boy system, for example, uses twin monochrome screens (one for each eye), which are high-resolution LED displays of 384 x 224 pixels. Sega's Game Gear, a handheld system, has an LCD screen of 160 x 144 pixels. Nintendo's Game Boy system uses a reflective LCD screen of 160 x 144 pixels, but with the Super Game Boy, a converter that plugs into the Super Nintendo Entertainment System (SNES), Game Boy games can be played on a television screen through the SNES. And with even lower resolution screens, there is the Atari Lynx, with an LCD screen of 160 x 102 pixels, and the Milton Bradley Microvision system, with an LCD screen of only 16 x 16 pixels.

As we move beyond games using CRTs and screen resolution decreases, the question arises as to how much resolution is needed for inclusion in even the loosest definition of a "video" game. The handheld game systems mentioned above are included in many lists of video games because they are produced by the same companies (Atari, Nintendo, Sega, etc.) who produce video game systems that use television screens, and because they are all cartridge-based systems (as opposed to handheld electronic games which are hardwired to play one game only).

One of the most important questions regarding the game's visual display is whether or not the game's screen is pixel-based and capable of imaging (see next chapter). Many handheld electronic games use LED and LCD displays but are not based on a grid of pixels. Games such as Parker Brothers' *Merlin* (1978) or Mattel *Electronics Basketball* (1978) have banks of lights which can be turned on or off, and while in some cases the lights may be said to represent "players" (as in Mattel *Electronics Basketball*), the lights are not used together as imaging elements. Similarly, in games with LCD displays like Bandai's *Invaders of the Mummy's Tomb* (1982) and *Escape from the Devil's Doom* (1982) or Mega Corp's *Fireman Fireman* (1980) or *The Exterminator* (1980), the LCD elements or cells that are turned on and off are often shaped like the game's characters in different poses and positions. These poses are laid out across the screen in such a way that they do not overlap, since the cells must be discrete to function independently. Thus, the positions that characters can occupy are limited to a few non-overlapping poses, which are turned on and off in sequence to suggest motion through a marquee-like effect. In other words, whole images of characters are turned on or off, as opposed to pixels arranged in a grid which work together to create imagery.

The concept of a grid of pixels used for imaging, then, can be one criterion dividing the video game display from those used in other forms of electronic games. Pixels, as abstract picture elements (usually squares, rectangles, or dots), are all identical in shape and size and can be used in any part of an image. Only collectively do they produce a design which is recognizable as a character or object. (Pixels, of course, must also turn on and off and use the same marquee effect to suggest movement, but the overall effect of movement it produces is a much more subtle one and improves with resolution.)

The screen which is a grid of pixels is a useful way to draw the line between the video game and many handheld electronic games. Yet even some handheld games are occasionally included in the widest, loosest definition of "video game" because they contain versions of arcade video games, for example Nintendo's LCD handheld versions of *Donkey Kong Jr.* (1982), or Nelsonic's *Q*bert* wristwatch game of 1983. In both cases the game appears on a screen and play is analogous to the arcade game of which it is a version, even though it is highly simplified and the imaging technology is quite different.

So while video games began as games played on a television screen with raster imagery, advances in imaging technologies, the porting and adapting of game titles to hardware with a variety of imaging technologies, and commercial marketing which tends to use the term video game to describe all of these things have resulted in a broad, popular definition of the term, the boundaries of which remain as blurred as ever as new software and hardware continue to appear.

CHAPTER 2

IMAGING TECHNOLOGIES

Mark J. P. Wolf

Video games require displays whose images can be changed quickly. A variety of different imaging technologies are used to produce video game imagery, and the vast majority of video games use either raster graphics, vector graphics, liquid crystal displays, light-emitting diodes, or prerecorded video imagery on laserdisc or compact disc or DVD-ROM. How the actual images are controlled by the computer and rendered on-screen depend on the graphics techniques used.

Screen Technologies

The most common kind of screen that is used, a cathode ray tube, is used to produce both vector graphics and raster graphics. The CRT, used in televisions and computer monitors, contains an electron gun at the narrow end of a funnel-shaped glass tube. The electron gun generates a very narrow, focused beam of electrons which is fired at the screen, located at the wide end of the tube. En route to the screen, the electron beam is deflected by electromagnetic means (such as coils or electrodes), which are controlled by an external signal. The deflected electron beam hits the inside of the screen, which is coated with phosphorescent (light-emitting) material of red, green, or blue. The electrons cause the material to fluoresce, or glow, producing the pixels of the image on-screen.

Vector graphics and raster graphics differ in the way they use the electron gun to produce an image on-screen. Vector graphics are made up of points and straight line segments, which are stored as coordinates in a set of display commands. The display commands are sent to a *vector generator*, which converts the commands into a signal that is sent to the monitor's beam-deflection circuits. Using this signal, the electron beam is deflected from one line segment endpoint to another, causing the beam to draw the vector lines onto the screen one by one. In vector graphics, all images are made up of line segments and points, and text characters are made up of collections of line segments. Because the path of the electron beam follows the command list instead of a preset scanning pattern, this process is also referred to as *random scan*. Vector graphics were the earliest CRT-based computer graphics and were widespread by the late 1960s. Vector graphics appeared in a number of arcade video games in the late 1970s and early 1980s, and in one home game system, the GCE/Milton Bradley Vectrex, which appeared in 1982. The best-known arcade games using vector graphics include *Asteroids* (1979), *Battlezone* (1980), *Defender* (1980), *Tempest* (1981), and *Star Wars* (1983) (see Chapter 12, "Vector Games" for more on these games).

Raster graphics use the electron gun to draw an image onto the screen in much the same way that a television set does. Unlike vector scanning, raster scanning guides the electron beam back and forth, scanning the entire screen row by row across the screen from top to bottom, making an image from the glowing phosphors. By producing almost 30 images a second, the image is made to appear continuous. This kind of imaging produces raster graphics, and is the kind of imaging to which the word "video" refers. Raster images are usually full screen and full color, since the raster signal causes the electron gun to cover the entire screen during its scanning. Since raster scanning uses the same electron beam deflection path for every image, the preset path can be hardwired into the hardware. Filled shapes, text, and complex images are also easier to produce with raster scanning, and it is the method used in almost all arcade video games, home games, and computer graphics produced today.

Laserdisc games and many CD-ROM- and DVD-ROM-based games use prerecorded video imagery in their games. While the images for these games are rendered on-screen through the use of raster scanning, images are stored and read from a disc, rather than calculated from mathematically represented computer models. Stored imagery is not as flexible to use as imagery generated interactively during gameplay, and its use has declined as computer-generated imagery has improved (see Chapter 17, "Laserdisc Games," for more on these games).

Some imaging technologies do not involve CRTs. A number of handheld games and game systems use liquid crystal display technology. An LCD contains a thin layer of long, crystalline molecules that polarize light, sandwiched between grids of fine wires and polarizers. The polarizers (which can reflect certain kinds of light) are lined up in such a way so that light passing through the crystals is polarized and reflected back to the viewer, resulting in a bright, clear square. When current is applied to the grids, the molecules line up together in the same direction and have no polarizing effect, and light is absorbed, resulting in a darkened square. Early LCD screens were black and white and can be found in games from the early 1980s and game systems such as Milton Bradley's Microvision or Nintendo's Game Boy. Color LCD screens are now common, appearing in game systems like the Atari Lynx or Game Boy Color, as well as in laptop computer screens.

Far less common are displays using light-emitting diode technology. LED displays use diodes that produce light when a current is applied to the diode. LEDs can come in red, yellow, or green, but red LEDs are the most common. Although many handheld electronic games use LED displays, Nintendo's Virtual Boy is the only pixel-based imaging system to use one.

Another imaging technology gaining popularity is the plasma screen, which is used for flat-screen HDTVs. The method of transducing the signal into an image is different than that of a CRT; instead of an electron beam, the red, green, and blue phosphor components of each of the plasma screen's pixels are controlled separately, resulting in a flicker-free, glare-free, sharp image, as opposed to one scanned onto the screen row by row.

Computer-Generated Imagery

While imaging hardware is certainly a determining factor, the look of a game's graphics also depends on such things as the amount of processor speed and memory, and the way the computer program generates the imagery.

Early computer graphics were generally either wireframe or bitmaps. Wireframe graphics are built of geometrical figures such as points and line segments drawn between points, and the objects it depicts are stored as sets of coordinates and the mathematical relationships between them. Vector graphics were typically wireframe due to the way in which the images were drawn on the screen line by line. An advantage of wireframe graphics was the speed at which they could be drawn on-screen, and also the fact that the graphics being generated could be three-dimensional in nature (as games like *Asteroids* show, they were not always three-dimensional, and sometimes appeared as flat graphics).

While they were good for drawing large geometric figures, wireframe graphics could not easily be used to depict small, detailed figures like game characters. Bitmaps, on the other hand, are grids of pixels which are used to define an image. Small bitmapped images that are moved about the screen by being redrawn at different coordinates are known as *sprites*. Examples of sprites are the individual space invaders in *Space Invaders* (1978), or the Pac-Man or ghost characters in *Pac-Man* (1980), or the bouncing balls or bullets used in shooting games.

Two-and-a-half-dimensional graphics, as they are sometimes called, involve overlapping planes of two-dimensional graphics; this also is referred to as *priority* (referring to the determination of which plane is drawn over the others). Through the use of multiple planes of imagery—one behind the other—which scroll through the screen at different rates, a sense of depth can be achieved; this is called parallax scrolling, since it simulates the varying of parallax with distance. Objects can be made to appear to float over backgrounds and the effect of multiple layers can be achieved. Yet, while the image is more than a single 2-D plane, it is not real 3-D either, thus the "and-a-half" is added to denote something in between. Two-and-a-half-dimensional graphics appear in the arcade games *Moon Patrol* (1982) and *Zaxxon* (1982), and in home video games like *Super Mario Bros. 3* (1990) and *Warioland* (1995). Some games, like *Pole Position* (1982), simulated a 3-D space through the careful use of scaling (zooming larger or smaller) sprites, enlarging them as they move away from the vanishing point in the game's background. Sega's *Space Harrier* (1985) could quickly scale and rotate 32,000 colored sprites at once. Sprite-based graphics dominated arcade games throughout the 1980s but began to fade in the 1990s as games with true three-dimensionally rendered graphics began to make them look outdated.

Three-dimensional graphics are those which have been encoded as 3-D objects in the computer's memory, for example, cubes, cylinders, spheres, pyramids, or other polyhedra. These objects can be turned and rotated and appear at different angles, unlike the flat grids of pixels in 2-D graphics. Interactive 3-D filled-polygon graphics first appeared in Atari's arcade game *I, Robot* (1983) though they did not reappear until the late 1980s, and it was not until the mid-1990s that they became the standard types of graphics used in arcade video games, and later in home game systems including the Sony PlayStation, Sega Saturn, and Nintendo Ultra 64. Some games, like *Doom* (1993), mixed the two types of graphics; while background hallways were generated in three dimensions, the monsters encountered in the hallways were still sprite-based. Other games, like *Myst*, *Gadget* (1993), and *Riven*, used prerendered three-dimensional imagery rather than imagery generated in real time during gameplay (it is interesting to compare the original version of *Myst* with the remake *realMyst* [2000] which generated all of its imagery as real-time interactive 3-D imagery[1]). Still other games, like the laserdisc games *Astron Belt* (1983) and *Firefox* (1984) had sprites overlaid on top of video imagery, combining two types of graphics into one image.

Finally, some games like *Johnny Mnemonic* (1995) and *Star Trek Borg* (1996) rely almost entirely on video clips for their graphics, resulting in 3-D graphics which are for the most part not interactive; what is gained in image quality is lost in player input. Many laserdisc games and interactive movies (see Chapters 17 and 22, respectively, on each) fall into this category, and are often more like branching stories than interactive games. Other games, like *The 7th Guest* (1993) and *Riven* incorporate video clips into their computer-generated graphic environments.

Now that computers and game systems have increased memories and processing speeds, such hybrid combinations of graphics are no longer as necessary, as most systems can now generate fully 3-D graphics in real time. Advances are now in the ways that game's worlds are designed, where increasing numbers of polygons provide more detail and subtlety, more interactive lighting and simulated physics are possible, and artificial intelligences control characters that interact with the player's character. Graphical advances also open up possibilities outside of photorealism, and narrative development, less hindered now by graphical restrictions, will be able to expand into new territory.

CHAPTER 3

MODES OF EXHIBITION

Mark J. P. Wolf

Over the years video games have appeared in a number of different venues, each with their own technologies, capabilities, market sector, and integration into the cultural production surrounding them. These different modes of exhibition include mainframe games, coin-operated arcade video games, home video game systems, handheld portable games and game systems, and home computer games.

The games created on the giant mainframe computers of the 1960s were limited to the large, refrigerator-sized computers found only in laboratories and research centers (see Chapter 6, "Mainframe Games and Simulations"). These games were experiments and were neither sold commercially or generally available to the public. Some were quite simple, for example, games that played tic-tac-toe. The most famous mainframe game, however, is *Spacewar!* created around 1962 at the Massachusetts Institute of Technology. Written by Steve Russell, J. Martin Graetz, and others for the PDP-1 mainframe computer, *Spacewar!* consisted of two spaceships (the "needle" and "wedge") that could fly about the screen and fire missiles at each other. Other additions to the game included a starfield background, a star with gravity that pulled the spaceships into itself, and a "hyperspace" feature allowing ships to disappear and reappear elsewhere on the screen. *Spacewar!* was copied and adapted to other computers throughout the 1960s and influenced other programmers. In 1971 it was adapted by Nolan Bushnell into the first arcade game, *Computer Space,* and later a version of it appeared among the first cartridges for the Atari 2600 home video game system.

Arcade Video Games

Coin-operated arcade games are perhaps the best known variety of video games, and were the first and foremost mode of exhibition which brought video games to the public. There are several different forms of arcade games, each allowing for a different type of interaction: standalone consoles, cocktail consoles, sit-inside games, and virtual reality-style games.

A standalone console, the most common kind, has a tall, boxlike cabinet (also referred to as an "upright") which houses the video screen and the control panel for the game.

The game's controls might include joysticks, a trackball (also spelled "track-ball" or "trak-ball"), paddles (round, rotating knobs), buttons, guns with triggers, steering wheels, and so forth. Occasionally there are controls for more than one player, although single-player games are the most common. Smaller versions of these cabinets are sometimes referred to as "cabaret" cabinets or "mini" cabinets.

The cocktail console is designed like a small table, with the screen facing upward through a glass table-top. Often such games are designed for two players, and controls are set on both ends of the table, with the screen between them. This type of console was popular in bars or restaurants where patrons could sit and play a video game while setting their drinks on the table-top. Two-player games in cocktail consoles are often designed so that the screen can be viewed from either side, and usually contain games with an overhead view of a playing field (for example, a football game which is viewed from above) so that neither player has an upside-down view.

Sit-inside, ride-in, or ride-on consoles can even involve physical movement of the player's body, usually to simulate the driving or flying of a vehicle in the game, typically with a first-person perspective point of view. These games range from merely having a seat in front of the screen, to enclosing the player in a box, or even moving the seated player around during the game. In driving and racing games, foot pedals and stick shifts are sometimes included as well. Other types of interaction are possible; *Prop Cycle* (1993) for example, has the player pedaling a bicycle, while *Alpine Racer* (1995) has the player holding ski-pole handles and standing on movable skis. In Sega's *Top Skater* (1997), the player rides on a skateboard, while in Namco's *Final Furlong* (1997) the player rides a "horse." These games tend to be more expensive than other types of games, sometimes requiring as many as four or five quarters per game (instead of only one or two).

Although virtual reality style games are often hyped in movies, they have yet to become popular at the arcade; *Dactyl Nightmare* (1992) was the only one available throughout the 1990s, possibly because of its higher cost and need for an attendant. Each player stands inside a circular railing on a raised platform, wearing headsets with miniature screens for each eye while holding a gunlike device with a trigger, an image of which also appears on-screen. The game consists of two players wandering around an abstract setting composed of platforms, walls, and stairs, trying to find and shoot each other. Adding to the action is a green pterodactyl that occasionally picks up players and drops them. The players' views are sometimes shown on two monitors so that bystanders can watch the game from both points of view. Although the novelty of the game was its virtual reality interface, the game cost about $4 for four minutes, and the setup required an attendant to be on duty, raising the cost of exhibition. Besides appearing in arcades, *Dactyl Nightmare* has also traveled as a fairground exhibit, its monitors often successfully drawing a crowd of bystanders.

Home Video Games

Contemporaneous with arcade games, home video game systems appeared in 1972 with the release of the Magnavox Odyssey Model ITL-200 system designed by Ralph Baer. Home video game systems typically use a television for their graphic displays, although some systems, such as the GCE/Milton Bradley Vectrex or Nintendo Virtual Boy, are designed to sit on a table-top and come complete with their own screens. Home game systems which display their graphics on a television can be console-based, cartridge-based, or laserdisc-based systems.

Console-based systems, like PONG, Wonder Wizard, or Atari Tank, have their games hardwired into them and are ready to go when the console is turned on. Many of the very early home video game systems were console based and had games such as tennis, hockey, and table tennis, most of which were variants of ball-and-paddle games. (Magnavox television model 4305 even had a built-in color *PONG*-like game with controllers that connected to the TV.)

Cartridge-based game systems have their games hardwired into cartridges which are plugged into the game console, allowing new games to be made for the console and sold separately. The first cartridge-based system was the Fairchild Channel F (which was first released as the Video Entertainment System) in 1976. The Fairchild Channel F came preprogrammed with *Hockey* and *Tennis*, in addition to having a cartridge slot for which 26 cartridges were eventually made. The best-known early cartridge-based system is, of course, the Atari 2600 released in 1977. Cartridge-based systems could provide more games than purely console-based systems (some systems, like the Atari 2600 and the Nintendo SNES had hundreds of cartridges available for them) and soon became the main kind of system produced, until the coming of the CD-ROM.

Although most systems used the cards or cartridges with read-only memory hardwired into them, one system, Rick Dyer's Halcyon system, used laserdiscs, which could store video images. But at a cost of around $2,000, this system was too expensive for most consumers and was not a success.

Handheld portable games and game systems give players more flexibility than home video game systems, since they run on batteries and can be carried along with the player. Handheld games are usually small enough to fit in the palm of one's hand and have small LED or LCD screens with buttons and controls beneath the screen or to the sides of the screen. Some of these games (although perhaps not always technically video games themselves) are simplified versions of video games from other systems, such as Nintendo's LCD handheld *Donkey Kong Jr.,* or games using the same characters, such as *Mario's Cement Factory* (1983). While most of these games are self-contained, there are handheld cartridge-based systems as well, including Milton Bradley's Microvision, Nintendo's Game Boy, Game Boy Color, and Atari Lynx. Today, "handheld games" could also refer to digital games played on a number of portable media devices, including cell phones and personal digital assistants (PDAs).

Although many arcade games and home video game systems have computers built into them, they are dedicated systems whose only purpose is that of gameplaying. Beginning in the late 1970s and throughout the 1980s, home computers became available and their numbers grew quickly. Early video game systems helped to usher them in, as early home game systems like PONG and the Atari 2600 were often the first computer products to enter into people's homes. Practically every type of home computer had game software available for it—on floppy disk, tape drive, cartridge, diskette, or CD-ROM. Systems like the Texas Instruments 99/4a computer had a built-in slot for game cartridges, and other computers like Coleco's Adam and the Atari 400 and 800 were even made by game companies. While cartridges for the Atari 2600 contained small amounts of ROM, computer games stored on floppy disks could be several times larger in size. Storage media like magnetic disks could also be written on, allowing games in progress to be saved, which in turn meant that more complex games, taking more than an afternoon to play or solve, could be produced.

Today most home computer games have moved to CD-ROMs (compact disc, read-only memory) or DVD-ROMs (digital video disc, read-only memory). While a typical 5.25-inch floppy disk held around 164 kilobytes, and a 3.25-inch diskette held a little over a megabyte, a CD-ROM holds around 650 to 700 megabytes (a megabyte is 1,000 kilobytes). The increased amount of storage on a CD-ROM allowed longer and more detailed games, as well as higher-resolution graphics which added to a game's verisimilitude. Yet during the 1990s games were expanding so fast that even a single CD-ROM was not enough; even some relatively early CD-ROM games, such as *Riven* and *Star Trek: Borg,* took up multiple CD-ROMs. Newer technologies such as DVD-ROMs, which hold several gigabytes of data, contain even larger games, and networked games played online are often so enormous that they take up several computer servers and terabytes of data (a terabyte is 1,000 gigabytes, or 1,000,000 megabytes).

Networked games, which are often typically role-playing games (RPG), are games in which multiple participants are connected via modem to a video game world on a server and can interact with users around the world and with each other's characters. These games can be run locally, over a LAN (local area network), or on the Internet from anywhere in the world. Because many offices have computers networked together, gameplay has entered the workplace with games like *Quake III* (1999), *Unreal Tournament* (1999), and *Half-Life* (1998) occurring during lunchtime and after hours (and, no doubt during the workday as well). Networked games grew in popularity and size, from games like *Sceptre of Goth* (1983) in the mid-1980s, which could have a maximum of 16 players online at once, to *Everquest* (1999), which has thousands of characters and requires multiple servers. Networked games are some of the largest and most detailed video games [for example, *Ultima Online* (1997) is said to have more than 189 million square feet of virtual surface in its world] and have the largest numbers of players playing together. Most of these games run 24 hours a day, with players logging on and off whenever they want.

Although some people make distinctions between "video games" and "computer games," games are often "ported" (rewritten into different computer languages or systems) from one platform to another, broadening their markets and appearing in multiple modes of exhibition. Many dedicated game systems now have larger memories, faster speeds, and use CD-ROMs instead of cartridges. Computer emulation programs can simulate different game systems on a computer, with varying degrees of success. Even the notion of a "dedicated system" may soon be a thing of the past; Sony's PlayStation consoles, for example, are designed primarily as game systems, but they also can play DVDs and audio CDs, connect to the Internet, and download and store digital music and video from the World Wide Web.

The wide range of modes of exhibition have contributed both to the size and success of the video game industry, and today games are created for practically any computer-based technology with a screen.

CHAPTER 4

INFLUENCES AND PRECURSORS

Mark J. P. Wolf

The video game was the product of many researchers, experimenters, inventors, and entrepreneurs, and its initial form was influenced by other media and technology already in existence. The various forces that converged to produce the video game tended to gravitate around the two poles of art and technology. The period of the 1960s and 1970s saw a convergence of art and technology, and the spirit of experimentation that existed provided a fertile ground for interest in and acceptance of new media.

Technology

Apart from the computer itself, much of the technology used by the video game was already firmly in place by the 1960s. Television was well established in the majority of American homes, and as the size of its cabinet shrank and its screen grew, it became more of an appliance and less of a piece of furniture (except for the sets with the largest screens, which were available in wooden floor-standing cabinets into the late 1970s). All that remained to be added was the microprocessor (in the video game console) to supply the television with image and sound, and it was a company that made televisions, Magnavox, that would purchase and market the first home video game system, Ralph Baer's Magnavox Odyssey Model ITL 200.

By the 1960s, computer graphics were already into their second decade of development. In 1949, the Whirlwind mainframe computer at the Massachusetts Institute of Technology became the first computer to use a CRT as a graphic display. The Whirlwind was shown to the general public on a 1951 episode of Edward R. Murrow's *See It Now* and demonstrated a bouncing ball program and calculation of a rocket trajectory. Mainframes continued to be produced during the 1950s, and became more accessible outside the military establishment. In 1962, around the same time *Spacewar!* was being written, Ivan Sutherland completed his Sketchpad system as a doctoral thesis at MIT. The program allowed a user to create graphics on-screen interactively, using a light pen to draw directly on the CRT screen. By 1963, the trade periodical *Computers and Automation* was already sponsoring a competition for computer art, and the late 1960s saw a number of museum exhibitions displaying computer graphics.

Once interactive display graphics were wed to the cathode ray tube, the only remaining barriers to the commercial production of video games were public access and affordability. During the 1960s, minicomputers were starting to replace mainframes in some areas, but they were still neither small enough nor cheap enough for efficient mass production. These problems were solved in 1971 with the microprocessor, invented by Marcian E. Hoff, an engineer at the Intel Corporation. By placing a central processor on a chip, computer components could be produced more cheaply and in greater quantity, allowing for the development of the home video game and the personal computer, as well as cheaper and smaller electronic calculators. Using the new technology, Nolan Bushnell translated *Spacewar!* into a smaller unit containing the electronic circuitry necessary to deliver interactive graphics, which he set, along with a monitor and a control panel, into a tall, floor-standing plastic cabinet. The game was renamed *Computer Space,* and appeared in 1971. The following year he used his profits to produce a second game, *PONG,* which was more successful and widespread, and became many people's first experience of a video game.

One of Bushnell's most important contributions to the video game was the addition of a coin slot, making the video game a profitable venture and soon a commercial industry. Video games were exhibited in arcades, where they joined a long line of coin-operated machines reaching back into the 1880s, when saloon owners began installing coin-operated machines for bar patrons to compete on, or place bets on, as well as vending machines. Due to their success, there was soon a wide variety of coin-operated machines —strength testers, slot machines, card machines, racing games, and other "trade stimulators" as well as the coin-operated mutoscopes and kinetoscopes, the early moving-picture machines—that paved the way of the cinema.[1]

Free-standing and countertop coin-operated machines could be found in saloons, parlors, and shop-lined arcades and continued to flourish into the 1930s and early 1940s. The pinball machine developed out of these machines during the 1930s and was produced by companies that produced other games, like the Bally Corporation or the Bingo Novelty Company. Through a series of innovations, the pinball machine gradually evolved into the form players are familiar with today. In 1933 electricity was added, and lights and backglasses were added in 1934. The pinball bumper was added in 1937, and the flipper in 1947.[2] After World War II, the pinball game saw its golden age during the period 1948 to 1958.

Costing only a nickel a play, pinball games flourished as a source of cheap entertainment during the Depression and the Second World War, and they were popular enough that their prices rose to a quarter (today some even charge 50 cents or more). Other arcade games that were even closer to video games were electromechanical games like Sega's first game, *Periscope* (1968), and Chicago Coin Machine Company's *Apollo Moon Shot Rifle* (1969), which featured upright cabinets and game controls under a screen (but no video monitors). These games were coin-operated and relied on mechanical figures staged inside the game's cabinet, some with mechanical sound effects as well. These games, perhaps more than any others, helped to pave the way for video games, which were, for arcade players, yet another technological development in the world of arcade coin-operated gaming.

During the early 1970s, the video game was able to achieve commercial success through its integration into the same market venues as the pinball game (also a quarter a play).

In the years that followed, video games quickly grew into an industry, until they replaced pinball games as the main games found in arcades. Besides new companies like Nutting Associates and Atari, companies producing pinball games such as Bally and Gottlieb also became producers of video games.

The early games' content was also influenced by technology. The explosion of techno-logical developments in the United States following the Second World War, and particu-larly the space program, renewed the public's interest in science and science fiction. J. Martin Graetz acknowledges that science fiction novels, by authors such as E. E. Smith, and the science fiction films of Japan's Toho Films Studios (best known for Godzilla movies) were the main influences on the writing of *Spacewar!*[3] Throughout their entire history, video games have maintained a solid tradition of spaceships, shooting, and monsters, and science fiction themes have dominated the market. Computer graphics of the late 1960s and early 1970s, however, were not sophisticated enough to easily and cheaply produce detailed, representational moving imagery in real time, so simple geometric figures, made from dots, lines, squares, and rectangles, had to suffice. Detail and complexity were sacrificed for immediate and interactive action; a player could imagine the details, but action had to happen on-screen, and fast.

Art

Although their simplicity was due to technological limitations and not the result of deliberate artistic choices, the minimal, often abstract graphics of early video games fit in rather well with trends in the art world during the 1960s. During the 1950s, abstract art came to dominate the New York City art scene, and many strands of it developed into the 1960s. There were color-field painters, like Barnett Newman and Mark Rothko, and the "hard-edge" painting style of painters like Ellsworth Kelly and Alexander Liberman, emphasizing simple forms and geometric simplicity. Influenced by these and other abstract movements, minimalist art developed in the mid-to-late 1960s. Artists such as Donald Judd, Sol Lewitt, Tony Smith, and others worked with squares, cubes, stripes, and geometric shapes, and other minimal forms to create abstractions. Early video game graphics, with their points, lines, and blocks of color, often on a black background, coincided with minimalist, abstract styles of art. Likewise, electronic music developed during the 1960s and came to be known for its new, computer-generated sounds and sometimes repetitious compositions. Electronic sounds could be generated and repeated by a computer and soon synthesized beeps and boops became the computer-generated soundtracks for video games.

The time-based and interactive nature of the video game also fit in with trends in 1960s art. The "happenings" of artists like John Cage and Allan Kaprow emphasized experience and process over product (sometimes including the audience's participation), and Sol Lewitt's famous essay of 1967, "Paragraphs on Conceptual Art,"[4] placed more importance on concept than a tangible art object. There also were performances known as "light shows," like Jordan Belson's Vortex Concerts, or the light works of The Single Wing Turquoise Bird, a Los Angeles group who created abstract projections of light and color for rock concerts in the late 1960s. These shows were huge projections of shifting, moving light and color patterns which were designed primarily as experiences that could never be repeated exactly; chance often played a part in their making. Art installations using video cameras and monitors also appeared around this time. In 1970, Gene Youngblood's book

Expanded Cinema explored the merger of art and technology of the time and included sections entitled "Television as a Creative Medium" and "Cybernetic Cinema and Computer Films," acknowledging the growing role of television and computer graphics in the visual arts.[5]

Further Refinements

The video game, then, was perhaps the most commercially successful combination of art and technology to emerge in the early 1970s, and in many cases, the first computer technology widely available to the public and the first to enter homes. As entertainment, it would soon come to compete with film and television, providing another source of on-screen "worlds" of sight and sound, and the only ones with which a player could directly interact. As its memory and processing speeds grew, and its graphics capabilities improved, more games appeared which licensed franchises from film and television hoped to play on their appeal. Not only content, but cinematic styles of composition and editing, storytelling devices, and other conventions from film and television made their way into video games. Games became more character-centered, backgrounds had more scenery and became locations, and there was often more narrative context surrounding the action of the game. By the 1990s, video games had title screens, end credits, cutting between different sequences, multiple points of view, multiple locations, and increasingly detailed storylines. Many films and television shows were adapted into video games, and during the 1990s, a number of video games became theatrical motion pictures.

But alongside these influences from outside, interactivity and the ability to depict a navigable space have forced video games to develop their own styles and conventions, with new ways of structuring space, time, and narrative that are unique to video games. As an established cultural force and a vast commercial industry, video games continue to carve out their niche among other media and act as an influence upon their form and content as well.

CHAPTER 5

THE STUDY OF VIDEO GAMES

Mark J. P. Wolf

It is strange to think that there was a time when people debated whether or not film was an art, but during its first two decades, when the average film was quite short and slapstick was popular, some people wondered if the medium could ever achieve more. Today there are still some who question whether video games are an art, or worth studying academically, but, like film, video games are wide ranging in their content and styles, video game designers continue to explore their artistic potential, and games are finally gaining some respect within academia.

Today video games are a multibillion-dollar-a-year industry, bigger than the film industry, and occasionally using the same actors, storylines, and special effects that films use. Video games compete in all the places where film is found, including movie theaters (many of which have arcades), the television at home, and in video rental stores, which rent games and game systems. Film, television, and video games also share some of the same franchises, those programs whose characters and stories appear in all three media. Furthermore, video games are rated just as films and television programs are, due to violence, nudity, and adult themes. Whereas films are rated by the MPPDA (Motion Picture Producers and Distributors Association), many video games are now rated by the ESRB (Entertainment Software Ratings Board) or the AAMA (American Amusement Machine Association).

The video game has an important place in cultural history. The video game was the first medium to combine moving imagery, sound, and real-time user interaction in one machine, and so it made possible the first widespread appearance of interactive, on-screen worlds in which a game or story took place. It was also the first mass medium to require hand-eye coordination skills (except for pinball, which was much more limited and not as complicated). During the early 1970s, video arcade games were the first computers that could be used by the general public, and home game systems became the first computers to enter people's homes. Games helped build a positive, fun, and user-friendly image of the home computer, introducing it as a recreational device instead of a merely utilitarian one, and would remain a driving force behind home computer sales from the late 1970s onward.

Although video games have been around for several decades, serious academic study of them was slow to develop.[1] At first there were mainly just essays for hobbyists in electronics and books for gameplayers with playing advice. Some writings appeared from designers, but only around the late 1990s did scholarly analysis really begin to appear, when the generation who grew up with video games began entering academia and writing about them. The Internet and the World Wide Web also helped to form online communities of video game enthusiasts and collectors, who collaboratively produced some of the best reference resources on video games [like the "Killer List of Videogames" (KLOV)[2]], many of which are still available online today. After 2000, academic writing about video games gradually grew more fashionable as scholars who grew up with video games began writing about them for a large audience who were familiar with the games. Today there are a number of academic journals (like Sage's *Games and Culture*) as well as online journals (like *Game Studies*[3]) devoted to the study of video games. A growing number of schools now offer degrees in the area of game studies, and there are even several annual conferences [like DiGRA (Digital Games Research Association) or the International Game Developers' Association (IGDA) conferences] organized around the study of video games.

Studying Video Games

As audiovisual entertainment that often involve some kind of narrative structure, video games share a number of similarities with film and television, especially the later ones that are designed to resemble films, with opening sequences, end credits, continuity editing, cinematic camera moves, and other visual conventions borrowed from the cinema. At the same time, the study of video games adds new elements that do not exist in traditional media, like interactivity, spatial navigation of an on-screen world, and the algorithmic structures governing the behavior of the characters and events of a game's world (for example, a character's reactions will often be based on what the player does during the game). There is also the interface, which connects the player to the game, which can include a mouse, joystick, trackball, gun, head-mounted display, keyboard, footpad or pedal, or specialized game controller. All these things should be considered when analyzing a video game.

Studying video games is, in some ways, harder than studying other media like film or television. First, there is the availability of the games themselves. Whereas a growing number of films and television programs are now available on videotape and DVD, old video games can be harder to find. Some home games can be found in online auctions, but less common and rare games will either be expensive or not for sale. Also, the person wishing to study old home games will need a game system to play them on, which also may be expensive or difficult to find. Arcade games are even more difficult to find and can be very expensive to buy, and owners often need to know specialized technical knowledge to keep them running. Even more common arcade games like *Pac-Man* or *Defender* may be difficult to locate, since most arcades tend to feature newer games. Since the growth of the World Wide Web, versions of many home games and arcade games can be played by emulators [like MAME (Multiple Arcade Machine Emulator)] on home computers; however, emulations can differ somewhat from the original games they are emulating, so the experience of playing them may not be accurately recreated, which can limit their usefulness for certain types of research.

Even when a copy of the original game is available, video games can be more difficult to study than traditional media. Whereas someone can listen to a piece of music, read a novel, or sit and watch a film from beginning to end and be satisfied that he or she has seen all there is to see of it, this is usually not the case with a video game. Gameplaying skills may be required to advance beyond the first few levels, or some puzzle-solving ability may be needed just to enter a locked door encountered early on in the game. Instead of fixed, linear sequences of text, image, or sound which remain unchanged when examined multiple times, a video game experience can vary widely from one playing to the next. Even if a player has the right skills, there are often courses of action and areas of the game which are still left unexplored even after the game has been played several times. Mastery of the video game, then, can be more involved (and involving) than mastery of a film; in addition to critical skills, the researcher must possess gameplaying or puzzle-solving skills, or at least know someone who does. Guides and cheat books are also sometimes available.

More time is also needed when studying a video game. Whereas movies are generally no more than a few hours in length, video games like *Riven, Tomb Raider* (1996), *Final Fantasy* (1987), *Icewind Dale* (2000), and so on, can average 40 or more hours to complete, not including all the possible endings they may contain. Sometimes it is not even clear how many choices a player has, and discovery of alternate narrative paths or hidden features (known as "Easter eggs") are themselves a part of game play. It make take a good amount of playing time and attention to detail to say for certain that one has seen and heard everything a game has to offer (that is, all the screens, sounds, and video clips), and there is often an underlying logic that must be uncovered as well in order to do so. There are some games, like the massively multiplayer online role-playing games (MMORPGs) which run continuously 24 hours a day, 7 days a week, and which are so large, that no one can ever see all the events occurring, nor can the game be restarted and replayed; they can only be experienced once in real time just like historical events, and each player's experiences will be unique.

Finally, the way a game is experienced is different from other media. Although one can refer to film viewing as "active," meaning that the viewer is attentive to what is being shown and is applying imagination and critical thinking to make sense of or "read" a film, video game play requires input—physical action of some kind—from the player in order to function, and often quick reactions within a very limited timeframe. Only when a player becomes attuned to the way in which a game operates will success be possible; thus a certain manner of thinking and reacting is encouraged, sometimes at the reflex level. In a film, all the steering of on-screen events is done for us by the filmmaker, whereas a video game leaves more possibilities open. The manner and the degree to which a film or a video game is a vicarious experience differ greatly.

While studying video games we should also consider the time in which the game was made. Game design is always limited by what is technologically possible, and some knowledge of the software and hardware available at the time when the game was made is essential to appreciating the games themselves. The Atari VCS 2600, for example, which appeared in 1977, had only 128 bytes of random-access memory (RAM) (and no disk storage), a graphics clock which ran at roughly only 1.2 MHz, and plenty of other programming limitations which had to be overcome with a limited amount of code, since early cartridges had only 2 or 4 kilobytes of ROM. Knowing this, some of the early games for the system are rather impressive, considering the restraints faced by the games' programmers. Cultural constraints also existed: early games had to have simpler controls, because players had to learn how to use them. For example, the controls of the first arcade game *Computer Space* were thought to be confusing at the time, whereas today they would be intuitively understood by players. After the various general restraints and limitations, there is also the background specific to the individual game being studied to consider.

Analyzing Video Games

When analyzing a video game, one should examine the four elements that are common to all video games: *graphics,* an *interface,* an *algorithm,* which is the computer program that is running the game, and some kind of player-controlled activity occurring on-screen, which is also sometimes referred to as *interactivity.*

Graphics involves a changeable visual display on a screen, with pixel-based imaging. (See Chapter 2, "Imaging Technologies," for more detail on the different kinds of screens.) An analysis of a game's graphics would include an examination of many of the same elements that are found in other media—visual design, color, lighting effects, point of view, and so on—as well as character design and other graphical elements such as title sequences, cut-scenes (scenes in between game levels), and credits.

The interface is at the boundary between the player and the game itself and includes such things as the screen, speakers, and input devices like a joystick, keyboard, or game controller, as well as on-screen elements like menus, buttons, and cursors. How the interface is designed influences the player's experience of the game, for example, a driving game using a steering wheel will be quite different from one using a paddle or a keyboard. Likewise, on-screen tools like menus and informational graphics may be designed to be integrated into the game to some degree, and will also affect how the game is experienced.

An algorithm is a computer program that controls the game, and responds to the player's input. It controls all the graphics, sound, and events of the game, and all the computer-controlled players within a game (it also controls the player-character, but with input from the player). Since the algorithm is made up of computer code, we cannot read it directly (without hacking into a game), but we can come to know it through the playing of a game, as we notice what responses are given for what player actions, and what rules seem to govern the gameplay. A good analysis of the game's algorithm may reveal the workings of a game, and ways that a game can be beaten.

Finally, there is the interactivity of the game. This can be divided into two areas: what the player does with the interface during gameplay (like hitting buttons or moving joysticks), and what the player's character is doing on-screen (for example, running through mazes or shooting). The second of these areas is one which we can examine in detail as we consider what kind of choices the player must make during a game, and how those choices are structured and make up the game.

Looking at Interactivity

The smallest unit of interactivity would have to be the choice, which consists of two or more options from which the player chooses. For any given moment in a game, there are a number of choices facing the player, and in every game there is a sequence of choices made by the player over time until the end of the game. A game's replayability often depends on its having a good number of options and choices, in at least one of the two dimensions just mentioned. Simple action games, for example, have large grids along the time dimension, while the number of options offered simultaneously may be small [at any given moment in *Space Invaders,* the player has only four options: move left, move right, fire, or wait (do nothing)]. Puzzle games, on the other hand, may have a wide variety of options open at any given moment but need only a few dozen correct choices to be made for the game to be won.

The speed at which options must be considered and choices must be made is also crucial to an examination of a game's interactive structure. Action games have a near-continuous stream of choices for the player, who may be in constant motion battling opponents while avoiding danger. Although the sequential choices are made one after another so quickly that they appear to be continuous, they are in fact still made in discrete fashion due to the nature of the computer clock which regulates the game (and number of choices made per second can depend on the speed of that clock). In the genre of interactive movies, a players' choices are often spread out in time, in between video clips which may be as long as several minutes each. Some games involving navigation or the solving of puzzles may accept a fast series of choices to be input (for example, a player moving through a location quickly) but at the same time not require quick decisions. The time pressure under which a player must play determines whether the choices made by the player are made as a result of reflex action or reflection (at least during the initial playing; in fast-action games, more reflection can occur on subsequent playing once the player knows what to expect).

Games requiring both reflection and reflex action may also increase their replayability since players will need more playing experience and a foreknowledge of what they are facing in order to make the right choices at a fast enough rate. Even in some early arcade games and Atari 2600 games [like Activision's *Stampede* (1981), which features a horizontally scrolling track of cattle to be roped], a player always encountered the same scenarios or patterns of opponents, so that it was possible to memorize where they would appear next and anticipate their presence; indeed, at higher speeds, this would be the only way to keep from getting defeated. Whether or not the conditions of the game include a series of events or character positions which differs from one playing to the next should also be considered in the analysis of a game, since it affects how prior knowledge of a game changes gameplay.

Prior knowledge of a game, gained from multiple playings, may also be crucial if some of the choices available to the player at a given time are hidden choices. The options that are included in a choice can occur anywhere on a spectrum from apparent or obvious ones to hidden options of which the player is completely unaware (for example, a character might have three hallways to choose between, but not know about a hidden trapdoor beneath their feet). Certain navigational paths, such as roadways, indicate an obvious course of action, while hidden doorways, chambers, or objects may require thorough searches to be found, or even an elaborate sequence of actions which the player is unlikely to perform inadvertently and must learn from the game or some outside source. Such inside knowledge of a game encourages players by rewarding them for their efforts, and invites them to search further for more. The intentionally hidden "Easter eggs" and unintentional bugs found in games also may add to a gaming experience as a player finds them and learns to exploit them (or becomes frustrated by them). Such hidden features add to the replayability of a game, as well as the playing of a game not to win or complete an objective, but rather to explore the game's world and the ways in which the game functions.

The above discussion of the timing given for the making of choices suggests that there can be several layers of choices present at different scales in the game. Some fast-action reflex decisions, like those in a fight or shoot-out, are made quickly and instantly and are determined by other more large-scale choices which the player considers and executes over a longer period of time, such as where to go or what strategy to use. Some choices affecting all aspects of a game may even be made before the gameplay itself begins [for example, in some adventure games, the choosing of an avatar (a player-character) and the various attributes of that avatar]. Depending on the speed of the action, a player may need to engage in short-term and long-term decision-making almost simultaneously, as the player switches back and forth between different objectives (for example, fending off attackers, finding certain treasures or supplies, and managing health levels) all while navigating through locations and gaining information which may be needed for larger decisions which determine the narrative direction of the game.

This leads to the next important area in analyzing the choices a player makes in a game: what are the consequences of the choices made? Some choices may be trivial and have little or no consequences (for example, wandering in a well-known area where there are no dangers, without any time pressure), while others may determine whether or not the game ends immediately (for example, when a player's character gets killed). Looking at the interactive structure of a game, then, each choice can be considered for its importance (what are the consequences of the choice made?), its difficulty (fending off attackers rather than letting them kill you is an easy choice to make, whereas deciding what to do to get into a locked room or which character to trust may be much more difficult to decide), and the amount of time given for the player to decide (reflex action versus reflection, and how much time for reflection). One could also consider how much information the player is given on which to base a choice, and sometimes only in retrospect does the player realize whether all of the available pertinent information was collected or even recognized.

The importance of consequences also depends on the irreversibility of the actions that caused them. After a choice is made, can whatever has been done be undone, and can the game return to the same state as it was before the choice was made? Irreversibility may play a greater role in more narrative-based games or games involving strategy, where a return to a previous game state is more unlikely or difficult. Many turn-based games, like adaptations of board games, may feature an "undo" command similar to what one might find in utility-based software; or like the games of the *Blinx* series, even allow the player to "rewind" action sequences and go back in time, allowing for more exploration and experimentation even in situations harmful to the player-character.

Every arcade game, console-based game, and cartridge-based game can of course be restarted and replayed from its beginning, returning the game to its initial state. This, however, is not true of large-scale networked games (MMORPGs), which contain persistent worlds with thousands of players. The ongoing nature of these games and their continually developing worlds make the consequences of players' actions much more long lasting, and the time and money investing in them raise the stakes of play and the seriousness of player termination. Many MMORPGs have areas which do not allow player-characters to be killed, and the acquisition of experience and game-world objects and abilities, as well as the building of virtual communities within the game's world, are pursued as long-term objectives stretching over months or even years. The irreversibility of players' actions and their consequences weighs heavily in the consideration of the choices faced by the MMORPG player.

Finally, an analysis of a game's interactivity would have to include a look at the motivation and the basis by which choices are made within a game. What are the game's objectives and how are they linked to the choices that the player is asked to make? Which options within choices are considered to be the correct ones, and why? In many fast-action games, the majority of choices are made in order to keep the player-character from getting killed, including the dodging of projectiles and the evading or killing of attackers and opponents. The motivation behind the decision-making required in a game can be complex and hierarchical, as the player must complete a number of smaller objectives in order to complete other larger ones. Sometimes this can result in actions which appear to run counter to the larger objectives of which they are a part (for example, killing large numbers of people and destroying property in order to save the world). In almost all cases, the overall motivation behind gameplay is the completion or mastery of the game, either by solving all the puzzles in a game, or by having the highest score, fastest time, or seeing all the possible endings and outcomes. In short, the goal of the player is the exhaustion of all the challenges the game has to offer.

The structure of a game's interactivity and the nature of the choices that make it up is at the heart of the gaming experience and often determines whether or not a game is considered fun. Games that are too easy may bore a player, while games that are too difficult may cause the player to give up in frustration. As players vary greatly in their skill levels, problem-solving ability, hand-eye coordination, and amount of patience, games must either contain a variable level of difficulty or have carefully designed puzzles and interactivity which balance the advances and obstacles that players encounter in a game. This balance then becomes a part of the game and should be included in any analysis of the game.

While specific analytical tools are being developed for the study of video games and their interactivity, some of these tools may prove useful in other areas of media studies, and may reveal new insights there.

Wider Applications for Video Game Studies

As video games are studied, new theories of interactivity will appear that will be useful beyond video game studies. More often than not today, media technologies include interactivity, in everything from computer software of all kinds and almost all Internet websites, to such things as cell phones, answering machines and their automated touch-tone interactive branching structures, CD-ROMs, DVD menus, touch-screen kiosks in malls, ATMs, and a growing number of gadgets for adults and children. While most of these technologies are not games, they do center on user interaction, and often rely on established conventions from other media. On the other hand, many of them are gamelike or even contain games, or at least try to capture the same sense of playfulness and "fun" associated with gaming. Far less flashy and sensational than video games, these media make up a large part of people's lives, including people who do not play video games.

Of all the various aspects of interactive media, it is probably interactive imagery which will provide the most (and most interesting) fruits of analysis. With the appearance of Renaissance perspective, the image was no longer just a surface, it became a window looking into another space or world. With the addition of interactivity, the image is not just a window but a tool, which allows one to (metaphorically) reach through the window frame to find things and manipulate and interact with them instead of just viewing them, and in some cases interact with other people and parts of the world. Unlike a photograph which always depicted the past, no matter how recent, or the live television image which depicted a geographically distant present (although it, too, was already microseconds into the past), the time depicted in the interactive image of the video game is that of the user, a continuous now that invites involvement and offers a potential to be explored through use. Even when one plays an old video game, like an old Atari cartridge from the 1970s, there is a sense in which the events depicted in the game are occurring for the player in the present.

The above description suggests two different areas to consider when analyzing interactive imagery: the interior world of the image and the image's connections to the exterior world. Both can be found in video games. By the "interior world," I mean the self-contained on-screen world of the game itself, and the way the player is (or can be) involved within it. Most existing methods of image analysis deal with two-dimensional images and were not designed to deal with three-dimensional worlds seen through the window of the image, much less interactive ones. Film theory perhaps comes the closest, as areas of it deal with the on-screen world and its construction, but it, too, falls short. The on-screen world seen in a film differs from that of a game in that all the events, camera angles, and storyline are limited to those seen during the duration of the film; one cannot look around a corner or change the course of events as is possible in most games. Video game studies will have to propose new methods for the analysis of the worlds seen through the window of the image, and the way in which the image becomes a tool in the hands of the person controlling its point of view.

Game studies will almost certainly provide insights into interaction that will be of use to the designers of interfaces, wherever they are used, and many of the experiences found in gaming, such as navigation, puzzle-solving, hand-eye coordination and so on, will also make their way into other media and need to be examined thoroughly. The study of video games itself is still very young, and there is much left to be discovered and discussed. It is a unique field of study, and one that is expanding quickly and will continue to expand for many years to come.

PART II

The Early Days (Before 1985)

When Nolan Bushnell added a coin slot to the arcade game *Computer Space* in 1971, the video game industry was born. Before the arcade brought video games to the public, mainframe games were available only to those who had access to computer labs at universities or corporations. Beginning with *PONG* in 1972, video games found success alongside pinball games in arcades. Home game systems also found popularity in the United States and Europe; the Atari VCS, later named the 2600, had over a thousand different cartridges produced for it by dozens of companies. Arcade games were produced mainly in the United States and Japan, and hit games like *Space Invaders*, *Pac-Man* (released in 1979 in Japan and 1980 in North America), and *Defender*, helped to cement their popularity and usher in a golden age of arcade video games in the early 1980s.

As the arcade game industry grew, the home game industry followed suit, spurred on with the rise of home computers, many with gameplay capabilities. Companies like Atari, Intellivision, and Coleco produced multiple home console systems, and third-party developers arose to produce games for them as well. Success gave rise to excess, and soon all kinds of companies were producing games, many of which were low quality, and the market was glutted with product. Interest flickered at the arcades, and soon the home game industry found itself in the midst of an industry crash, as prices fell and consumer demand waned.

The crash forced the video game industry to pause and reassess itself, and new technologies were tried at the arcade to attempt to revive business. A new system developed in Japan in 1983, the Nintendo Famicom, was renamed the Nintendo Entertainment System (NES) in 1985 and came to the United States where it found immediate popularity. A technological leap beyond all existing home game systems, it proved that the industry was still viable and ushered in a new era in video game history.

Today, the great popularity of retrogaming suggests that many look back on the early days of video games with nostalgia. The period from 1971 to 1985 saw video games change from an electronic novelty into a worldwide industry and set the stage for all the developments that were to follow.

CHAPTER 6

MAINFRAME GAMES AND SIMULATIONS

David H. Ahl

In the 1950s and 1960s, computer time was both scarce and expensive and writing games for the fun of it was actively discouraged at most computer centers. Nevertheless, there were many other reasons than just plain fun for writing computer games. Common reasons included exploring the power of the computer, improving understanding of human thought processes, producing educational tools for managers or military officers, simulating dangerous environments, and providing the means for discovery learning.

In some sense, the association of computers and games started in 1950 when Alan Turing, a British mathematician often considered the father of modern computer science, proposed his famous *imitation game* in the article "Computing Machinery and Intelligence," published in *Mind* magazine. In the imitation game a human judge engages in a natural language conversation with two other parties, one a human and the other a machine; if the judge cannot reliably tell which is which, then the machine is said to pass the test. Never programmed by Turing himself, a variation of Turing's game called *Eliza* was put in the form of a computer program 13 years later by Joseph Weizenbaum, a professor of computer science at MIT. In this game, the user could "converse" with the computer using real phrases and sentences. The computer would reply with a question to clarify the user's statement gradually learning more and more about the user until it seemed that the computer was actually carrying on an intelligent, human-like conversation.

In 1952, behind a cloak of secrecy, the first military simulation games were programmed by Bob Chapman and others, researchers at Rand Air Defense Lab in Santa Monica. That same year, a number of "formula" games (*Nim,* etc.) and "dictionary look-up" games (*Tic-tac-toe,* etc.) were programmed for several early computers. Also in 1952, a computer was specially designed to play *Hex,* a game with no exact solution, by E. F. Moore and Claude Shannon at Bell Labs in New Jersey.

In 1953, Arthur Samuel, a researcher in artificial intelligence at IBM, first demonstrated his *Checkers* program on the newly unveiled IBM 701 computer at IBM in Poughkeepsie, New York. Later that year, the book *The Complete Strategyst* by J. D. Williams was published by the RAND Corporation (Santa Monica, California). This was the first primer on game theory and provided the theoretical foundation for many early computer game programs.

The first computer game of blackjack was programmed in 1954 for the IBM 701 at the Atomic Energy Laboratory at Los Alamos, New Mexico. Also in 1954, a crude game of pool—perhaps the first nonmilitary game to use a video display—was programmed at the University of Michigan.

The military set the pace for simulation games for many years, and in 1955, *Hutspiel,* the first theater-level war game (NATO vs. USSR) was programmed at the Research Analysis Corporation in McLean, Virginia.

Although Allen Newell, J.C. Shaw, and Herbert Simon, three computer science professors at Carnegie Institute of Technology (now Carnegie-Mellon University) are frequently credited with the first chess game—probably because they stayed at it for over 20 years—the first version of computer chess was actually programmed in 1956 by James Kister, Paul Stein, Stanisław Ulam, William Walden, and Mark Wells on the MANIAC-1 at the Los Alamos Atomic Energy Laboratory. The game was played on a simplified 6 x 6 board and examined all possible moves two levels deep at the rate of 12 moves per minute. It played at a similar level as a human player with about 20 games worth of experience. In contrast, *Deep Thought,* the 1990 computer chess champion, examined about 1.5 million moves per second and used a combination of brute force and intuitive play on a standard board. Although *Deep Thought* was rated at about 2600 on the FIDE system (tournament chess players are rated by the Federation Internationale des Eches, which orders players who participate in international games under strict tournament rules), which places it among the top 40 human players in the world, the program was decisively defeated by Garry Kasparov in a two-game match in October 1989. Except for a small band of enthusiasts, the interest in computer chess has waned somewhat, probably because the computer programs are so good that playing them is discouraging for all but a small handful of championship-level players.

In 1958, a tennis game, *Tennis for Two,* was designed for an analog computer at Brookhaven National Lab by Willy Higinbotham. This game, played on an oscilloscope display, was significant in that it was the first game to permit two players actually to control the direction and motion of the object moving on the screen (the ball). The object of the game was to maintain a volley for as long as possible by hitting the ball with one of the two rackets at each side of the screen. A line down the middle indicated the net; gravity, bounce, and even wind speed were calculated into game play.

In 1959, large-scale simulation games moved into the private sector with the programming of *The Management Game* by Kalman J. Cohen, Richard M. Cyert, and William R. Dill, and others at Carnegie Tech in Pittsburgh. This game simulated competition between three companies in the detergent industry and integrated modules on marketing, production, finance, and research. Modified and updated for newer computers, but still in use at many graduate schools of business today, this game may well have set the record for the longest life of any computer game ever written. In this two-semester-long game, players make decisions about manufacturing, advertising, distribution, finances, personnel research and development, and all the aspects of running a real business over a simulated period of three years. Each week of play corresponds to a calendar quarter of business and the competition is fierce to have the highest profit and market share at the end of three years. (It is interesting to note that the Bendix G-15 computer with its rudimentary high-level GATE language, on and in which this game was initiated, is a direct descendent of the very first electronic digital computer, Colossus, invented by Tommy Flowers in 1943 for codebreaking at Bletchley Park, United Kingdom.)

With the delivery in 1959 of the first Digital Equipment Corporation (DEC) PDP-1 computer with its 15-inch video display, the continuing evolution from text-only games to video games was dramatically hastened with the demonstration at an MIT open house in 1962 of *Spacewar!,* an interactive game written by Stephen R. Russell, J. Martin Graetz, and Alan Kotok. In this game, two crude spaceships orbited around a star that exerted a powerful gravitational pull on each ship. Each opponent controlled his ship and attempted to shoot the other ship while also trying to avoid being pulled into and burned up by the star.

Also in 1962, but in a completely different area, Omar K. Moore at Yale built a device called "The Talking Typewriter" for teaching reading to young children. In the device, built by Edison Electric, a computer controlled a CRT display, slide projector, and audio recorder. In 1964, a more general-purpose computer-assisted instruction (CAI) system using IBM hardware, including a CRT with graphics, light pen, and audio, was developed by Patrick Suppes at Stanford. Military research kept pace, and in 1964 the Bunker-Ramo Corporation demonstrated a CRT display that simultaneously combined computer data with a projected background.

Artists began to realize the potential of the computer in 1964 when A. Michael Noll at Bell Labs produced the first computer art on a CRT display. Many years later, spurred by such companies as Activision, Lucasfilm Games, and Cinemaware, artists began to play a much larger role in the creation of games through computer animation.

Rounding out the landmark year of 1964, the language Basic was developed by John Kemeny and Tom Kurtz on the GE 225 timesharing system at Dartmouth College. Within a few months, the first interactive educational games and simulations began to appear on the Dartmouth system.

Various types of graphics displays from many manufacturers were introduced in the mid-1960s, opening the door to new video effects. Thus, we find a video pool game developed at RCA (1967), a ball-and-paddle game by Ralph Baer at Sanders Associates (1967, later to become the Magnavox Odyssey home video game in 1972), a rocket car simulation by Judah Schwartz at MIT (1968), a graphic flight simulation by the computer firm Evans & Sutherland (1969), a lunar lander game at DEC (1969), and a device to permit computer output and standard television video on the same display at Stanford (1968).

In the October 1970 issue of *Scientific American,* Martin Gardner devoted his "Mathematical Games" column to a description of John Conway's *Game of Life.* Easily programmed, it began to appear on virtually every video computer terminal in the country within weeks. In this game, colonies of figures reproduce, move around, and die off according to certain rules with the object of the game being to devise patterns that can sustain life for as long as possible.

In the late 1960s, the National Science Foundation was attempting to encourage the use of computers in secondary schools to improve science education. One of the notable NSF-funded projects that produced scores of simulation games in science and social studies was the Huntington Computer Project directed by Ludwig Braun at Brooklyn Polytechnic Institute (later at SUNY, Stony Brook). In the project's *Malaria* simulation game, for example, students must try to control an outbreak of malaria in a Central

American country using a combination of various pesticides, inoculations, and treatment of the ill—all without bankrupting the country.

Also in the late 1960s, both DEC and Hewlett-Packard started major marketing efforts to sell computers to secondary and elementary schools. As a result, both companies sponsored a number of small-scale projects to write computer games and simulations in various fields, many of which were released in the early 1970s. In DEC's *King* game (later called *Hammurabi*), for example, players must decide how much land to buy, sell, and cultivate each year, how much to feed the people, etc., while dealing with problems of industrial development, pollution, and tourism.

In 1972, William Crowther and Don Woods wrote a game for the DEC PDP-10 time-sharing system that they simply called *Adventure.* The game, the first in the interactive role-playing fantasy genre, was unbelievably popular and players consumed vast amounts of timeshared computer time on whatever system it was loaded.

By the mid-1970s, computer games had successfully made the transition to commercial arcade games and the rapidly expanding field of home computers, where their growing popularity helped them become the basis of an industry and a mass medium.

CHAPTER 7

ARCADE GAMES OF THE 1970S

Mark J. P. Wolf

Arcade games were around for decades before video arcade games appeared. By the late 1960s, pinball games had already seen their peak but were still common and popular, and other electromechanical arcade games were gaining new ground. Electromechanical games were coin-operated games that had no microprocessors or monitors, but ran by the use of motors, switches, relays, and lights.[1] Many of them were housed in upright wooden cabinets with their controls on the front, located just below a viewscreen behind which the game's action occurred, and became the style of housing adopted by arcade video games. Examples of these games from the late 1960s include Midway Manufacturing's bowling game *Fantastic* (1968), Chicago Coin Machine's shooting game *Carnival Rifle* (1968) and driving game *Drive Master* (1969), and Sega's submarine game *Periscope* and shooting game *Duck Hunt* (1969). Because of all their moving parts, electromechanical games broke down often, frustrating arcade operators and cutting into their profits. The industry was looking for a way to make more reliable games.

A number of companies, like Gottlieb, Bally, Williams, Midway, Sega, and Allied Leisure, made pinball games and other eletromechanical games before joining the video game industry. One such company, Nutting Associates, was started in 1968 by Bill Nutting, and its first game was *Computer Quiz* (1968). Despite its name, *Computer Quiz* did not have a computer in it; the text that appeared in its window was actually projected from frames of movie film inside the game. The game did not do well, and the company was in trouble. A new employee of the company, Nolan Bushnell, had the idea of making an arcade game from the mainframe game *Spacewar!*. They gave it a name that matched *Computer Quiz,* and the result was *Computer Space,* which came out in both one-player and two-player versions. The controls for *Computer Space,* although simple by today's standards, were much more complicated than those of electromechanical games, and the game did not do well commercially. But *Computer Space* was innovative in that it was electronic instead of electromechanical; although it had no microprocessor, RAM, or ROM; it did have a specially modified 15-inch television screen on which it produced simple game graphics from moving dots. Today *Computer Space* stands as the first video game to have a coin slot, making it the first commercial video game and the start of a new industry, which would soon eclipse the electromechanical game industry from which it arose.

A New Industry Is Born (1971–1974)

Bushnell left Nutting Associates and, along with Ted Dabney and Al Alcorn, went on to adapt the Magnavox Odyssey's table-tennis game for the arcade, resulting in *PONG*, the first hit video game, and incorporated Atari in June 1972. *PONG*'s success spawned a number of sequels, including *Barrel PONG* (1972) and *PONG Doubles* (1972), both by Atari, and even Nutting Associates copied *PONG* and released *Computer Space Ball* that same year. Another game even copied *Computer Space*, For-Play's unlicensed *Star Trek* (1972).

The following year, 1973, saw the release of more than two dozen arcade video games, most of which were copies or variations of *PONG*, some with additional paddles and renamed as hockey, tennis, or soccer: Allied Leisure's *Paddle Battle* and *Super Soccer;* Williams's *Paddle-Ball* and *Pro Tennis;* Taito's *Davis Cup, Elepong,* and *Pro Hockey;* Chicago Coin Machine Manufacturing Company's *TV Hockey, TV Ping Pong, Olympic TV Football,* and *Olympic TV Hockey;* See-Fun's *Olympic Tennis;* For-Play's *Rally;* Bally's *Crazy Foot* (sold in Europe); Ramtek's *Hockey, Volly,* and *Soccer;* Midway's *Winner;* and Sega's *Hockey TV, Pong Tron,* and *Pong Tron II.* Following the lead of Atari's *PONG Doubles,* some were 4-player games, including Allied Leisure's *Tennis Tourney,* Midway's *Leader,* US Billiards's *T.V. Tennis,* Nutting Associates's *Table Tennis,* and Midway's *Winner IV.* Atari even came out with two more ball-and-paddle games that year, *Puppy Pong* and *Snoopy Pong.* Finally, Magnavox sued Atari for stealing the *PONG* game idea from Magnavox's Odyssey, but Atari settled out of court, paying a licensing fee close to $800,000. The agreement still ended up to Atari's advantage; Atari had an exclusive license, while Magnavox went after all of Atari's competitors who had also indirectly copied Magnavox's game.[2]

Atari also innovated two new game forms in 1973: a maze game, *Gotcha,* and a space racing game, *Space Race,* which was licensed to Midway under the name *Asteroid,* and imitated by Taito's *Astro Race.* Chicago Coin also released *TV Pin Game,* the first video pinball game, and Nutting Associates released a shooting game, *Missile Radar,* and a codebreaking game, *Watergate Caper,* whose flyer advertised, "You Watched It On TV / You Read About It In Papers / Now—Discover The Secret Combination And Break Into The Watergate Yourself" and "Watergate Caper stimulates the larceny in us all to see if we can break in and not get caught."

Bushnell had a cover-up of his own to conceal in 1973. The pinball industry was set up in such a way that arcade distributors wanted the exclusive rights to distribute games, and Atari wanted to market the same games to multiple distributors. So Bushnell started another company, Kee Games (named after his next-door neighbor Joe Keenan, who became the company's president) to attempt to grab a larger market share. Thus a number of games released in 1974 appeared under two titles, one for Atari and one for Kee Games, including Atari's *Rebound* (Kee Games's version was *Spike*), *Quadrapong* (Kee Games's version was *Elimination*), and *Gran Trak 10* (Kee Games's version was *Formula K*). Finally, in November of 1974, Kee Games released *Tank* which was successful enough that distributors no longer demanded exclusivity, and Atari and Kee were merged together the following month.[3] (*Tank* would later become the basis for *Combat,* the cartridge that came packaged with the Atari 2600.)

Ball-and-paddle games continued to be released throughout 1974, many of which were four-player games that were just variations on the ball-and-paddle theme, including Atari's *Superpong* and *Quadrapong.* One game, Nutting Associates's *Wimbledon,* was among the first arcade video games to use a color monitor, and its four tennis racket avatars were different colors. Atari's *Rebound* (and Kee's *Spike*) featured a twist on the usual ball-and-paddle design; a "volleyball" traveled in parabolic paths as it was hit back and forth over a net.

Other sports were beginning to be adapted to games. Three basketball games came out in 1974: PMC's *Basketball,* Taito's *Basketball,* and Midway's *TV Basketball.* The last two of these games had little blocky players with heads and feet, the earliest graphics representing human characters to appear in an arcade video game. Chicago Coin's *TV Goalee* had its monitor housed inside a model scene within the game's cabinet, so that the screen was the floor of a little stadium. Atari's *Qwak!* was a duck hunting game with a light-gun rifle tethered to the game that players could remove and use to shoot at the screen. Another novel input device to appear that year was a steering wheel, found in Atari's *Gran Trak 10* (and Kee's *Formula K*) and *Gran Trak 20* (introduced in 1974 but released the following year), a two-player version with a steering wheel for each player, and Taito's *Speed Race.* Atari also released a plane-flying game, *Pursuit,* and a video pinball game, *Pin-Pong,* which had a "gravity algorithm" that could speed up the ball as it rolled downscreen.

Gran Trak 10 was among the first games to use a form of ROM, and fixes to the game during production, along with an accounting error that allowed the game to sell for less than it cost to be made, set Atari back and into hard financial times. It was Kee Games's *Tank,* which would restore Atari's fortunes. *Tank* and *Tank II* both used ROM and had better sprites, which were small blocky images of tanks, and double-joystick controls for each player. The use of ROM would allow graphical improvements, which in turn would allow games more variety and move them away from the simple blocks or lines that were used to represent everything on the screen.

Better Graphics and Memory (1975–1977)

By 1975, interest in ball-and-paddle arcade video games was waning, though several companies were still making them; Allied Leisure released three of them that year and even Atari released *Goal IV* (the "IV" designation meant four players, as it did for other games like *Winner IV;* it would be some time until any game had three sequels to it). One ball-and-paddle game, Exidy's *TV Pinball,* advertised in its flyer that the "GAME PLAYS ITSELF to attract attention when not in use"; this came to be known as an "attract mode," and was commonly used by arcade games by the 1980s.

Driving and racing games had surpassed ball-and-paddle games in popularity, and 1975 saw the release of at least a dozen of them, including Capitol Projector Corp.'s *Auto Test,* Allied Leisure's *Pace Car Pro* and *Street Burners,* Midway's *Wheels* and *Wheels II,* Exidy's *Alley Rally* and *Destruction Derby,* and Atari's *Stock Car* and *Crash 'N Score.* These games usually had steering wheel interfaces, some had foot pedals, and two-player games featured two sets of controls. Two single-player games, Midway's *Racer* and Atari's *Hi-Way,* both had seats for the player to sit on while playing, to make playing the game more like the experience of driving. Perhaps the most unusual racing game of 1975 was Kee Games's eight-player *Indy 800,* a color game which had a steering wheel and two pedals for each player, all arranged in a square with the screen in the middle (see Figure 7.1).

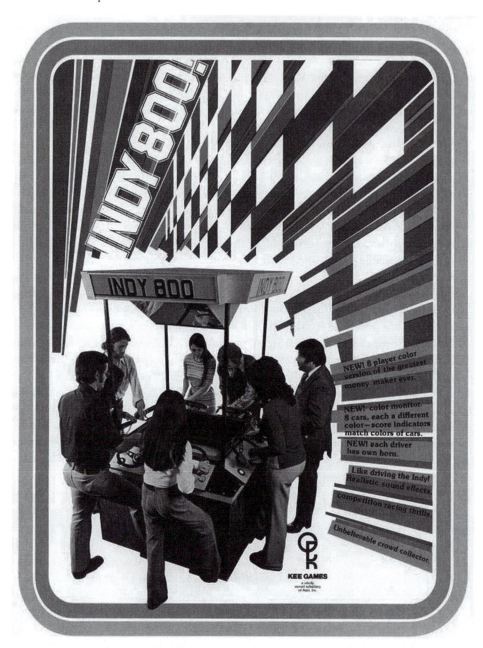

Figure 7.1   The eight-player game *Indy 800* (1975). *Indy 800* had a steering wheel and two pedals for each player, arranged with two players on each side of the screen, which faced upward in the middle beneath the canopy.

Most of the other games released in 1975 were sports related, including several shooting games, some of which, like Sega's *Bullet Mark* and *Balloon Gun,* had either mounted or tethered guns that players used. While some games were patterned after a shooting gallery, others involved vehicles that could shoot, like planes in Atari's *Anti-Aircraft II,* Electra's

Avenger, or Allied Leisure's *Fire Power;* or spaceships, like in Electra's *UFO Chase;* or tanks, as in Fun Games's *Tankers* or Kee Games's *Tank III* (the first game to be the third in a series). One game, Midway's *Gun Fight,* became the first to include detailed human figures; the avatars were cowboys with discernible features such as hats, spurs, and eyes (Taito's *Western Gun,* a copy of *Gun Fight,* came out the same year). Other sports appearing for the first time were pool, in US Billiards's *Video Pool;* skiing, in Allied Leisure's *Ski;* and horse racing, in Atari's *Steeplechase,* which had horses for six players and one computer player, making it the first seven-player game. Three video pinball games also appeared, Volley's *Flip-Out,* Midway's *TV Flipper,* and Chicago Coin's *Super Flipper,* which had a ball puller on it and housed its monitor in a cabinet shaped like a pinball game. Finally, three games of 1975 sought to cash in on Steven Spielberg's popular film *Jaws* released that year: Project Support Engineering's *Maneater,* Atari's *Shark Jaws,* and US Billiards's *Shark.* In the first two games, the player controls a diver who must avoid a shark, while the third is a four-player game in which the players control sharks, and the first shark to eat five divers wins. Human beings had just barely appeared in video games, and already they were targets to be killed and eaten.

The use of human figures as targets to be killed continued in Exidy's 1976 game *Death Race,* based on Paul Bartel's film *Death Race 2000* (1975); in both game and film, competitors gain points by running over pedestrians. As the people (called "gremlins") are run over in the game, they scream and are replaced by crosses. Whereas the violence in *Shark* apparently generated no protest, Exidy's *Death Race* became the object of controversy and began a debate about violence in video games which continues to this day (see Chapter 39, "The Video Game as an Object of Controversy").

The year 1976 also saw many new releases in the now-established genres of ball-and-paddle games (or table-top games), shooting games, driving games, racing games, video pinball, and sports games, some with improved graphics and occasionally innovative additions. Atari's *Breakout* (and its imitator, Mirco Games's *Block Buster*) took the ball-and-paddle game and added a field of blocks that disappeared when hit, creating a new kind of game. Most shooting games now involved airplanes of some kind, though there were also bombing games like Meadows Games's *Bombs Away,* target shooting games like Model Racing's *Clay Buster* which featured clay pigeon shooting, western-themed shooting games like Atari's *Outlaw,* tank shooting games like Kee Games's *Tank 8* in which eight players could all play on one screen, and even Atari's *Starship I,* a *Star Trek*-inspired space shooting game. Midway's *Sea Wolf* even had a periscope viewer and combined a video screen with backlit transparencies that alerted players of various events during the game.

Atari's *Cops 'N Robbers,* with foot pedals and pistol grips, combined shooting and driving and allowed players to play as either the cops or robbers. Other driving and racing games of 1976 included those in which players avoided crashing into other cars, and games like Taito's *Crashing Race* where the idea was to crash into as many cars as possible. Four motorcycle driving games appeared, which had handlebars instead of steering wheels for controllers: Atari's *Stunt Cycle,* Digital Games Incorporated's *Heavy Traffic,* and Sega's *Moto-Cross* and *Fonz.* The *Fonz* handlebars even vibrated when the player's bike collided with another, one of the earliest examples of haptic feedback equipment being used in an arcade video game.

Two other driving games of the year marked the first time first-person perspectives were used in video games; Atari's *Night Driver* and Midway's *Datsun 280 Zzzap* had series of white driving pylons that appeared to be coming towards the viewer, simulating a road ahead seen in perspective, even though no real 3-D computation was involved. At the bottom of its screen, *Datsun 280 Zzzap* also had an information bar showing the time, score, and a zero to 200 speedometer showing the speed, giving the game some of the most advanced informational graphics of its day.

Baseball games like Midway's *Tornado Baseball* and Ramtek's *Deluxe Baseball* featured better graphics that included small player figures whose arms, legs, and head were discernible details. Other new games included Ramtek's card game *Hit Me,* Project Support Engineering's jousting game *Knights in Armor* in which knights rode on galloping horses, and Sega's *Heavyweight Champ,* which had unique boxing glove-like controls for punching, and was probably the earliest one-on-one fighting arcade video game.

A few other games of 1976 are worthy of notice. Three games, UPL's *Blockade,* Ramtek's *Barricade,* and Meadows Games's *Bigfoot Bonkers* had players moving around on a playing field and leaving a trail of blocks behind them, which formed walls in which they would try to trap other players [an idea that would later reach a wider audience in the form of Atari's *Surround* (1978) for the Atari VCS]; this was a new game idea that was specific to video games rather than an adaptation of some other kind of existing game or event. Finally, two games, Kee Games's *Quiz Show* and Ramtek's *Trivia,* were both trivia question based games which read questions stored on magnetic tape systems. Ramtek's game stored 2,000 questions on an 8-track audio tape, and the company made several tapes, allowing operators to change the tape and load new questions, an idea that was ahead of its time and would later be revisited by the DECO cassette system in the 1980s (see Chapter 16, "Arcade Games of the 1980s."

One of the biggest graphical advances of the late 1970s appeared in a relatively unknown game, Kee Games's *Super Bug* of 1977. Whereas previously all games took place on a single screen, *Super Bug* was a driving game that had a Volkswagen Bug that stayed on-screen while the background scrolled behind it and could move in all four directions (up, down, left, right), making it very likely the first video game to feature scrolling. [Electra's *Avenger* (1975) may have been an even earlier scrolling game, but it is unclear whether it really was, and if so, whether the scrolling effect was merely simulated by moving sprites downscreen instead of actually moving the background graphics.] The first well-known game with scrolling was Atari's *Football* (1978), and since Atari had merged with Kee Games, they were able to patent scrolling and require other companies to license it from them.

The other big graphical advance of 1977 was the appearance of vector video games in the arcade, with the arrival of Cinematronics's *Space Wars* and Vectorbeam's *Space War,* which were both copies of the mainframe game *Spacewar!*. Both games had rather sparse wireframe graphics on a black screen, tiny spaceship shapes and a small "sun," and they were still two-dimensional games.

By 1977, ball-and-paddle games had just about disappeared (except for a few, like Rene Pierre's *Special Break* or Sega's *World Cup*). A large number of shooting games were being produced, including hunting games like Amutech's *The Great White Buffalo Hunt,* Midway's *Desert Gun,* and Atari's *Triple Hunt* which had a two-part cabinet which placed the player some distance away from the targets. There were western-themed games (like Taito's *Gunman* and Midway's *Boot Hill*), tank shooting games (like Midway's *M-4* and Ramtek's *M-79 Ambush*), plane shooting games (like Project Support Engineering's *Desert Patrol* and Model Racing's *Flying Shark*), games with mounted bazookas on their cabinets (like *U.N. Command* and *Bazooka,* both by Project Support Engineering, and Taito's *Cross*

Fire), and sea battle and space battle games. In one game, Atari's *Subs,* each player had a separate screen on opposite sides of the cabinet; players could not see each other's screens, and each had a different view of the game's action, which involved trying to figure where a player's sub was located, and torpedo it. Players had to rely on sonar and only had quick glimpses of each other's subs during torpedo hits. [Exidy would later release *Fire One!* (1979) based on the same idea, but with a single screen with a partition down the middle so that each player could only see half the screen while playing.]

There were also some new variations on the shooting theme that year: missile launching games (like Midway's *Guided Missile* and Taito's *Missile-X*) in which the player launched missiles from the bottom of the screen to hit targets appearing above, and their opposites, bombing games (like Atari's *Canyon Bomber,* Taito's *Sub Hunter,* and Sega's *Bomber*) in which the player's avatar moved at the top of the screen dropping bombs on the targets below.

Racing games were also popular and included Taito's *Super High-Way,* Sega's *Main T.T.,* and Atari's *Sprint 4* and *Sprint 8* (for four and eight players, respectively). A few games, like Atari's *Sprint 4* and Taito's *Cisco 400,* came in color. More baseball and football games appeared (Midway's *Double Play,* Meadows Games's *Gridiron,* and Sega/Gremlin's *Super Bowl* among them), as well as two bowling games, Meadows Games's *Meadows Lanes* and Exidy's *Robot Bowl,* both of which featured on-screen scoring boxes for all 10 frames, just like those used in real bowling.

And, finally, 1977 saw a number of games that were sequels or copies of earlier games. Some copied the previous year's games in which player's moving squares left trails that were used to surround and trap other players (Taito's *Barricade II,* Midway's *Checkmate,* UPL's *Comotion* and *Hustle,* Sega's *Crash Course,* and Atari's *Dominos*); there were several *Breakout* clones (Video Games GmbH's *Super Crash,* Subelectro's *Super Knockout,* and Taito's *T.T. Block*), and games which were a variation on *Breakout,* using men bouncing on a seesaw to break balloons instead of blocks (Exidy's *Circus* and Subelectro's *Springboard*). Clones of these games would continue to come out in the years ahead, until new and even more popular games would oust them from the spotlight; and some of these were just around the corner.

Growing Prosperity, Growing Competition (1978–1979)

By the time of the October 1977 release of the Atari VCS (later known as the 2600), home video games had improved, with colorful offerings that were loose adaptations of arcade game ideas, like those found in the 1977 Atari cartridges *Combat, Air-Sea Battle, Indy 500, Starship,* or the 1978 cartridges *Outlaw, Canyon Bomber,* and *Surround.* More color arcade games began to be produced, and sales of the Atari VCS would pick up when the company released a cartridge of a game licensed from the most popular game of 1978, *Space Invaders.*

Space Invaders was made by Taito and later licensed to Bally/Midway for release in the United States. After a slow start, *Space Invaders* grew in popularity in Japan to the extent that it caused a shortage in 100-yen coins, causing the government to triple its production of them.[4] In the United States as well, *Space Invaders* brought money and players into the arcade and was the biggest hit game of its day. At least a dozen games were released that year that were either direct copies (bootlegs) of the game, or very close equivalents, and the following year brought more than another dozen imitators, bootleg games, and games that were clearly inspired by the design of *Space Invaders.* Other games took their variations farther, like *Galaxian* (1979) and *Galaga* (1981), and many other vertically oriented shooting games would come out in the years following *Space Invaders,* so in a sense the game was in large part responsible for an entire subgenre of shooting games.

Other games of 1978 included Atari's *Football,* mainly popular during the football season, which used a scrolling screen for its playing field. Having patented scrolling, Atari made good use of it and released other scrolling games that year. *Sky Raider* was a plane bombing game, with scrolling scenery that the player viewed from above. The game also demonstrates the growing importance of the international market for arcade games, since the game's message text could be set by the arcade operator to appear in English, French, German, or Spanish as desired. Another Atari scrolling game, *Fire Truck,* was unusual in its design; it was a two-player cooperative game, with one player seated in front of a steering wheel that steered the front of the truck, while the other stood behind the first player, using a steering wheel on the back of the first player's seat to control the back of the fire truck. Players would have to work together to navigate the truck through the neighborhood streets without crashing it (the game was all about driving; there was no fire or final destination). A one-player version of the game, *Smokey Joe,* was also released that year (according to the game's flyer, players chose to drive either the cab or trailer portion of the truck, while the computer drove the other part). Cinematronics's second vector graphics game, *Starhawk,* had larger spaceships and a background that looked like the trench on the Death Star from the movie *Star Wars* (1977) (see Figure 7.2). Although it

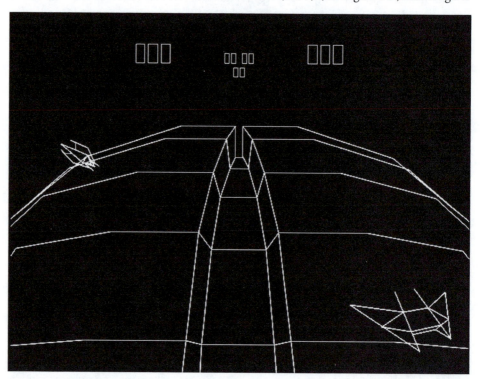

Figure 7.2   **An early attempt at a 3-D look.** *Star Hawk* **was an early vector graphics game which attempted a 3-D look, even though it did not involve any real 3-D computation. Image from www.klov.com.**

was not true 3-D, it looked more like 3-D than any other game of the time, and it would not be too long before vector games moved into the 3-D realm (see Chapter 12, "Vector Games").

Other derivative games appeared in 1978; clones of Atari's *Breakout* and games which were a variation of *Breakout*, plane games, tank games, and a variety of other shooting games, some with mounted guns (Sega/Gremlin's *Cartoon Gun*), mines (UPL's *Blasto*), a spear gun (Bally/Midway's *Blue Shark*), and one, Ramtek's *Dark Invader*, that even featured a real neon laser. Two nonviolent shooting games even appeared; Bally/Midway's *Dog Patch* and Meadows Games's *Dead Eye* had player-characters (hillbillies and a cowboy, respectively) who simply shot at objects tossed in the air. Several racing games also were produced, and one vector game, Vectorbeam's *Speed Freak*, even had a first-person perspective and more detailed graphics which included a highway with a dividing line, oncoming cars, and objects off to the side of the road.

Along with more baseball, bowling, boxing, diving, and video pinball games, sports games expanded into a few other sports in 1978, including those of Taito's *Trampoline*, Midway's *Shuffleboard*, Atari's *Sky Diver*, and Meadows Games's *Gypsy Juggler*. Atari's Tournament Table even offered 12 different games in a single cocktail-style cabinet, including multiple versions of *Breakout, Foozpong, Quadrapong, Handball, Soccer, Hockey, Volleyball,* and *Basketball.* Despite the unusually large selection, they were all ball-and-paddle games, which had long since seen their peak in player interest.

A few other games of 1978 are worth mentioning. UPL's *Frogs* had frogs jumping on lily pads and competing at catching flying insects with their tongues and was a game which was not afraid to be cute ("cute" games would later become almost a genre unto themselves in Japan). Two strategy games also appeared; Nintendo's *Computer Othello,* based on the popular board game of the day, and Universal's *Computer—R-3,* which was essentially a copy of Othello using "X"s and "O"s. Although strategy games would appear in the arcade from time to time, they favored contemplation over action and their games lasted longer than the few minutes typical in action games, meaning fewer quarters taken in per hour. Strategy games, along with games of other more time-consuming genres like adventure games, would eventually find their niche on home computers in the 1980s.

By 1979 arcade video games had grown into a stable and successful industry, displacing pinball games and almost completely replacing electromechanical games at the arcade. Competition from home games was beginning to provide an impetus for innovation, though they also raised interest in video games in general. An increasing number of arcade video games were being made in color, and color games outnumbered black and white games for the first time. One game of 1979, Namco's *Galaxian*, was the first game to have all of its graphics in true RGB color. Inspired by *Space Invaders,* Namco's *Galaxian* was an improvement on the design, with more detailed graphics and ships that flew in varying patterns as they descended. Besides the *Space Invaders* clones that continued coming out in 1979, *Galaxian* had its share of imitators as well, including Subelectro's *Exodus* and *Swarm,* Midway's *Super Galaxians,* Petaco S.A.'s *Zero Time,* Nichibutsu's *Galaxian Part X,* and others.

With a number of other trends continuing from the year before, 1979 saw more baseball games, shooting games (many of which now included aliens), missile-launching games, racing games, and still more *Breakout* clones, including ones made in Japan and Italy, and two *Breakout*-inspired games with elements of pinball integrated into them, Namco's *Bomb Bee* and *Cutie Q.* Through such games, one can see how ideas evolve and genres are hybridized until new types of games and game genres are created. One shooting game of 1979, SNK's *Yosaku,* had players shooting up at birds while dodging their droppings, a creative scenario with a structure essentially the same as *Space Invaders* (you shoot up at an enemy shooting down at you). Atari released two sports games that year, *Atari Baseball* and *Atari Soccer,* which were, along with *Football* from the year before, all two-player games in a cocktail-style cabinet designed so that players stood on opposite sides of the screen, sharing an overhead view with text oriented towards them at either end of the screen, something that could only be done in cocktail format. And other cabinet styles were emerging. Extending the idea of a sit-on console to a sit-in console, Exidy's *Star Fire* (1979) was the first game with an enclosed cockpit (advertised as a "TOTAL ENVIRONMENT" on the game's flyer) although an upright version was also released. *Star Fire* was also the first game to feature a high-score table with players' initials.

Amidst the driving and racing games released in 1979 were games which involved driving within a series of concentric lanes which contained dots to be run over by the cars. Zaccaria's *Dodgem,* Sega/Gremlin's *Head On,* Nichibutsu's *Rolling Crash,* SNK's *Safari Rally,* and Exidy's *Crash!* all were of this design, which appears to have originated with an arcade game, Atari's *Dodge 'Em,* produced sometime between 1975 and 1978; sources do not agree on the date, and no collector is known to have the game if it exists (Atari later came out with a cartridge of the game). Another interesting game involving driving of some kind was Exidy's *Side Track,* a train game which involved tracks that rerouted when the player switched tracks.

More vector games appeared in 1979, including Atari's *Asteroids,* which went on to become a classic arcade game; Cinematronics's *Sundance,* a space game with bouncing suns, and *Tail Gunner,* a space shooting game; Vectorbeam's *Warrior,* which featured an overhead view of two swordfighting knights; and Atari's first vector game, *Lunar Lander. Lunar Lander* was adapted from a mainframe game from 1973, in which players had to safely land a spaceship on the moon's surface without crashing it. The game included a thruster with a proportionate throttle control and a limited fuel supply, which added time pressure to the game. Atari was not the only one adapting an arcade version of *Lunar Lander* in 1979; other variations included Taito's *Galaxy Rescue* and *Lunar Rescue,* and *Destination Earth,* a bootleg version of *Lunar Rescue.*

Finally, two innovative maze games appeared in Japan in 1979. Denki Onyko's *Heiankyo Alien,* in which aliens chased a man through a maze while the man avoided them and inflated bubble traps in which to catch the aliens. The other maze game of the year was Namco's *Puck-Man,* which involved a yellow circle with a mouth that ate dots and was chased by colored "ghosts" or "monsters." The game was released in North America the following year, where its name was changed to *Pac-Man,* and it would become one of the most popular arcade games of all time, ushering in what many consider to be arcade video games' golden age.

CHAPTER 8

VIDEO GAMES IN EUROPE: THE EARLY YEARS

David Winter

1972: Born in the USA...

If 1972 marked the beginning of the American home video game industry, a couple of years would pass until video games reached homes in Europe. In May 1972, Magnavox released the first home video game, the Odyssey, in the United States; sales began in September the same year. Odyssey was a big success in the USA, but Europe was not yet ready for disputing tennis matches on TV. Video games reached the arcades earlier than people's homes (Atari exported *PONG Doubles* around 1973 or 1974, *Computer Space* machines were also put in a few bars, and many *PONG* clones appeared at around the same time.)

The home video game was a very new concept; people were not used to playing games on their TV sets. Also, the video game market was neither dominated by large manufacturers (like Magnavox, Coleco, and Atari in the United States) nor governed by money as it is today. Back in 1974, European home video games were almost nonexistent; they were expensive and produced in a limited amount by small manufacturers, making their promotion difficult.

1973–1974: In the USA, Why Not in Europe?

The first attempts at bringing video games into Europe were the importation of the Magnavox Odyssey and the creation of clones. Thus, the Odyssey was imported into the United Kingdom in 1973, and into 12 European countries in 1974 in very limited numbers. The same year, ITT Schaub-Lorentz released the "Odyssee" in Germany. The German ITT had every word translated in German. The Magnavox version replaced it in late 1974 or very early in 1975. The French ITT version was announced in French magazine *Sciences Et Vie* (January 1974) as being released by ITT-Océanic and Schaub-Lorentz for the first half of 1974. Later, a "Kanal 34" clone was advertised in Sweden in 1975. One ITT was found in Sweden, which may have been an alternative solution to the Kanal 34, as it had two Swedish manuals in addition to the German ones.

Back in 1974, less than five manufacturers were distributing home video games in Europe. Magnavox exported the Odyssey in a slightly modified version that played 10 games (instead of 12 like the U.S. release), while Videomaster released their "Home T.V. Game," a British system which originally sold for £20. This latter is the most interesting as it marked the beginning of the European home video game industry. Videomaster's Home TV Game played only three games: *Tennis, Football,* and *Squash.* There was no on-screen scoring. But for the technology of the day, it was quite advanced. Seleco, a trademark of Zanussi (Italy), released the Ping-O-Tronic in late 1974 (possibly for Christmas).

At the same time, hobbyist construction articles began to appear in electronics magazines. Nowadays, it would be impossible to build a modern video game system on one's own since technology has changed considerably. However, it was not difficult for a hobbyist to build a video game in the 1970s, since such games were mostly designed with discrete components (as opposed to chips containing entire games). The earliest European construction articles, dated July 1974, were published by *Practical Wireless* and *Television Magazine.* One article, split over seven issues because of its length, proposed not only a video game project, but also a color video game project that could be upgraded (color television sets were still very expensive in Europe in 1974). The system used discrete components and initially played only one game: *Football.* Special improvements could be made to add sound effects, on-screen scoring, and game variants. The last section of

Figure 8.1   **The Magnavox Odyssey. Originally developed by Ralph Baer at Sanders Associates between 1967 and 1969, and finalized by Magnavox between 1971 and 1972, the first commercial home video game console was sold between fall 1972 and mid-1975.**

the article was a discussion of the most interesting aspect of the project: "Superman" was a plug-in module that replaced one player to give the impression of playing against the machine. This was the first home video game to offer this feature. A few arcade games did this, but no commercial system would offer this feature before 1976. A hobbyist who read the entire article could easily modify his system to add more players, change the game rules, and why not, add more graphics!

1975: Early Yet, But Ruling!

Videomaster understood that there was something to do in the video game domain, so they released 15 systems between 1974 and the late 1970s. Their next attempt was to improve the 1974 Home T.V. Game in an inexpensive manner, which gave birth to two systems in 1975: the Rally Home T.V. Game and the Olympic Home T.V. Game. Both used very simple electronic circuits [discrete components including a couple of complementary metal oxide semiconductor (CMOS) chips, which consumed less power and were more tolerant to voltage drops, allowing the games to be played even with weak batteries]. The former played two game types (more by creating different game rules). The latter played four game types and came with two metal balls to place on the system case for marking the scores; archaic, but cheap. These three Videomaster systems marked the beginning of the video game industry in the UK.

Another obscure system appeared in the UK the same year: the VideoSport MK2. This system, supposedly released in 1974 and advertised in 1975 used a very basic design: two CMOS chips and discrete components. Transistor circuits generated everything displayed on the screen. The VideoSport MK2 played three games: *Tennis, Football,* and *Hole-in-the-Wall.* In release until 1977, it is believed that only a couple thousand units were sold. Mecstron released a clone of this system in 1976, which played three additional games. In Argentina, another clone called Teyboll Automatico appeared in 1975–1976 but played only the three initial games. Finally, one U.S. company advertised a game which used the same case as the Mecstron but played only the three initial games. It is possible that this one preceded the Mecstron or that Mecstron imported the U.S. game and improved it.

Figure 8.2   Interton Video 2000 (Germany, 1975). The first ball-and-paddle game to use cartridges after the Magnavox Odyssey, the Interton Video 2000 used discrete components and several logic gates; it had no dedicated chips and no processor. Only five cartridges were designed for it. This system also was cloned in Spain around 1976 under the TeleTenis name.

Germany was another place where a more advanced video game system appeared: the Interton Video 2000. This system had a feature that no other *PONG* system had: the use of cartridges. Believed to be the first European *PONG* system to use this technology, the Interton Video 2000 contained the circuits used by every game, and the cartridges contained additional components that set the players' shapes, game rules, and drew additional graphics. Although the system box shows 10 different games, only five are known to exist. The most successful were *Tennis* and *Super Tennis* (*Super Tennis* even displayed on-screen scoring using squares, which was novel for the time since no other system did so). Another cartridge played the first two-player video game constructed by Ralph Baer in 1967: the *Chase Game,* in which two spots representing the players could be moved about the screen.

Italy also showed some interest in the video game market. Seleco, a trademark of Zanussi, released a strange system called the Ping-O-Tronic. This was one of the most basic systems, with only three chips and discrete components. It also played three games: *Tennis, Squash,* and *Attract.* Surprisingly, *Attract* used two vertical lines instead of paddles so that the ball kept bouncing forever; this could have served as a demo mode in stores (the only other game known to do this is *Table by Television*). The Ping-O-Tronic had other interesting features such as a way of adjusting the player's sizes (from very small to enormous) and centering the game field. It was improved many times: a Gun-O-Tronic light gun was even added for models PP-5 and later (Ping-O-Tronic is believed to have had 10 different models, ranging from PP-1 to PP-10).

1976: Still Analog, But Not for Long

Analog systems (those made with discrete components) were still popular in 1976 and more construction articles appeared in magazines. Several systems were released and played almost the same games, and some manufacturers imagined more variants of the

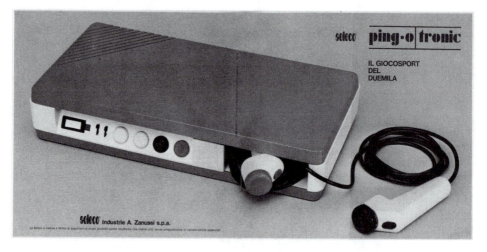

Figure 8.3   The Ping-O-Tronic. Advertised during Christmas of 1974, this system was one of the first European game systems and the first to be released in Italy (not including Magnavox Odyssey imports and clones). It also was designed with discrete components and only three very simple chips. The Ping-O-Tronic was sold by Seleco, a trademark of Zanussi.

popular ball-and-paddle games. Philips released the Tele-Spiel ES-2201—a small cartridge system that played strange games like *Pigeon Shooting* and *Auto-Slalom* (the games were very different from what almost all similar systems played; tennis was supplied with the system but you could buy four other cartridges offering games derived from the ball-and-paddle concept, which used the same characters differently so as to provide games outside of sports). Clones also appeared, for example. the Spanish TeleTenis Multi-Juegos system (in English: TV Tennis Multi-Games) based on the Interton Video 2000 released in 1975 in Germany. Cartridges had the same case, but almost every game was different because the system used a simpler electronic design. Eight games were announced for this system, and two of its games, *Car Racing* and *Naval Battle,* neither of which was ever produced, would have been the most advanced games designed for an analog system. In France, Lasonic released the Lasonic 2000, which played three games. Orelec released the PP 2000, with two games, and some manufacturers sold video game kits that played advanced games such as *Breakout* variants and *Car Race,* still using discrete components. As the technology improved, a few systems started displaying on-screen scoring using squares, lines, and even digits. However, this required additional components, hence a higher cost. An additional board was sold which could be added to the MK3 model to provide on-screen scoring and sound effects.

Figure 8.4 **The VideoSport MK2. Advertised by Henry's in early 1975 in England, the VideoSport MK2 is believed to be the second oldest system from the United Kingdom and remains one of the earliest European games after the first Videomaster Home T.V. Game (1974–1975). Almost entirely analog, it uses discrete components and only two very simple chips.**

SYSTEM PROFILE:
THE MAGNAVOX ODYSSEY

David Winter

In 1966, Ralph Baer, an electronics engineer working at Sanders Associates, thought again about an idea he had in 1951 when he was asked to build a television set: the possibility of using a television set to do something else than watch broadcasts. After writing his TV game ideas on paper, he started building a prototype to see whether something could be drawn electronically on a TV screen. Soon after, a chase game was designed. After many improvements, several other prototypes were built between 1966 and 1968, the most complete being the Brown Box, a double-chassis box covered with wood grain adhesive paper. The best game designed in 1968 was *Tennis,* a ball-and-paddle game which Atari later improved and sold under the name of *PONG.* After calling the most important television manufacturers in late 1968, Sanders Associates signed a first agreement with RCA in 1970, but it was cancelled. Later in 1971, an agreement was signed with Magnavox and Odyssey, and the first home video game console was released in September 1972 after two very successful market surveys in late 1971.

Technically, the Odyssey was a very primitive system. It had no electronic chip, no software, and no microprocessor, and it did not produce sound or color graphics. It could only display two players represented by two squares, one ball, and one center line which could be moved to the left of the screen or reduced to a third of its size. The cartridges provided with the console connected the circuits together so as to display what was necessary for each game, and manage collisions according to the game's rules; for example, the ball bounced when it touched a player's square. In another game, a player's square could disappear when the ball touched it. So the cartridges only contained wires to interconnect the Odyssey circuits.

Only two players could use the system using the big controllers provided, which contained three knobs and one button. One knob moved the player horizontally, one moved it vertically, and the last one gave the ball "English," changing its angle, because the system did not manage proper bounces according to the angle between the ball and a paddle when a collision occurred.

Because of its limited graphics, the Odyssey required the use of plastic overlays which were put on the television screen. They simulated the graphics that later systems could display themselves. Some games were educational: one could learn the states in America or learn basic calculations. Some were casino games like Roulette, or primitive car racing games, or play *Tennis.* Similar sports games were also available: *Volleyball, Basketball, Handball,* and *Baseball,* all based on the ball-and-paddle graphics. Most games required special accessories provided with the Odyssey: plastic chips, dice, carton boards, game cards, paper money, and so on.

Magnavox also released additional games which could be ordered individually or in packs of six. Each game contained its accessories: overlays, chips, and so forth, or even a cartridge (some used one of the six cartridges originally provided with the console). An additional shooting gallery pack also was made available to play two target-shooting games. It consisted of an electronic rifle and all game accessories.

Finally, Magnavox sold a special carrying case which allowed transport of the whole system easily.

The Odyssey was very successful and over 350,000 units were produced between mid-1972 and mid-1975. It was even exported to several countries in Europe, and a couple of pirated versions appeared in Argentina and Spain. The Odyssey remained successful until 1975 when better home systems and more advanced games appeared. By the late 1970s, technology had improved so much that the Odyssey and all similar ball-and-paddle games were replaced by software-programmed systems like the Atari 2600.

But a major advancement would kill this fragile gaming world made of discrete components within the next year: the appearance of video game chips which became available to every manufacturer. Commonly called "PONG-in-a-chip," these devices contained the equivalent of the discrete components of an entire system, and had more advanced features such as digital on-screen scoring, more game variants, and difficulty levels. Atari used its own *PONG* chips, but did not sell them to other manufacturers, as they would have dominated most of the worldwide market in a few years. Texas Instruments released several chips that could be used together to form different games, but these were not successful. The main force of the new *PONG* market was General Instruments (GI). GI started the development of a revolutionary single-chip video game device in mid-1975: the AY-3-8500. A complete video game system could be built with this chip and a few additional components. Since the chip was available to every manufacturer at low cost, it was no longer necessary to design a whole and expensive electronic circuit (GI provided the schematics for using the chip). This drastically changed the video game industry. Between 1976 and 1977, hundreds of manufacturers released their video game systems all over the world, and other chips appeared, some with color graphics, some with more games, and so on. The period of early video game history was over and the market was open to everybody. *PONG* stayed popular for a few years until more advanced cartridge consoles like the Atari 2600, Odyssey[2], and Intellivision appeared in the market at affordable prices.[1]

CHAPTER 9

EARLY HOME VIDEO GAME SYSTEMS

Leonard Herman

Whenever the history of video games is discussed, there is always disagreement about who did what and who actually invented video games. Most historians play it safe without committing themselves and naming the actual inventor. However, when debate switches to the history of video game consoles, there is no argument at all. Instead, we have an actual starting place where video game consoles began.

The well-documented history of video game consoles began in late August 1966, when a television engineer named Ralph Baer sat at a New York bus station waiting for a colleague. Although he worked for Sanders Associates, a defense contractor, Baer's thoughts were on practical uses for televisions. He thought that there might be a way that the TV could be used for interactive purposes, rather than being just a passive device that hypnotized viewers. It was then that Baer had one of his eureka moments and the idea that came to him seemed rather simple—build a device that would attach to a TV and act as a transmitter that would deliver signals to the TV. It would differ from normal transmitters because users would be able to respond and send signals back to it. The practical use for this was a game.

Upon his return to his office in Nashua, New Hampshire, Baer quickly wrote a four-page treatise explaining his idea. He then presented the treatise to his management. Although Sanders was a defense contractor, they decided to supply Baer with $2,000 to take his project forward.

Within three years, Baer and his team had made the four-page treatise a reality. They were able to move spots around a standard television screen in a game they called *Fox and Hounds.* They built several prototype game machines, each containing more sophisticated games than the one before it. By 1968 they were on their seventh prototype. The outside of the small box filled with solid state components was lined with wood-grain contact paper. It was dubbed the "Brown Box" and it could play a number of games including *Ping-pong* and *Volleyball.* Never mind that the crude graphics consisted merely of several light dots of varying sizes. Baer and his team realized they had invented something fun but they did not know what to do with it. Sanders was a defense contractor with no experience in consumer products. The Brown Box had to be licensed.

After the Brown Box was shown to several TV manufacturers, Magnavox decided to license the product in 1971. A year later they introduced the world's first TV game, the Odyssey. Unfortunately, the Odyssey was sold only in Magnavox shops so most people never even heard of the unit. But when the world took notice of Atari's *PONG* in October 1972, Odyssey suddenly became sought after. It was the only way people could play *PONG* at home.

Although the public did not differentiate between the arcade *PONG* and the version of video table tennis that came with the Odyssey, the two were vastly different. For one, the Odyssey could not keep score. Players tallied the scores themselves and games ended at a predetermined limit.

Home *PONG*

While sales for the Odyssey increased with the arrival of *PONG,* the Odyssey was capable of playing games other than forms of video ping-pong. Despite the fact that the console could not generate detailed graphics, the system was packaged with 12 separate games. On Baer's original Brown Box, the different games could be selected by changing the settings of 12 switches. Magnavox opted to include 12 "circuit cards" with the console (see "System Profile: The Magnavox Odyyssey" sidebar). Consumers could change the prepackaged games by merely changing the cards. Magnavox even sold additional cards that allowed consumers to unlock and run more games that were built into the machine. While a similar marketing technique helped ensure the success of the Atari VCS several years later, it did not help Magnavox at all since they were the sole supplier of the Odyssey, making the unit itself hard to find. The additional circuit cards were hidden under the counter and rarely pushed by the salesmen.

In three years Magnavox managed to sell over 300,000 Odysseys.[1] Historical records cannot claim how many of those sales were because of the arcade *PONG* but the number was probably high. Estimates could not even begin to set a number on how many units Magnavox could have sold if they simply distributed the product through traditional means outside of their own stores. And while history does not let us know if the Odyssey had any impact on Atari's decision to sell a home unit of *PONG,* in 1974, an Atari engineer named Bob Brown had aspirations of bringing *PONG* to the home. Most of the top management was against Atari entering the consumer market. Their fears were justified because they knew nothing at all about distributing consumer goods. They also felt that Atari's cash flow would be tied up in inventory that would sell primarily at Christmas. Nolan Bushnell, the founder of Atari, thought that *PONG* for the home was a good idea and he gave Brown the go-ahead.

Brown began work on a home version of *PONG* in the fall of 1974 and completed it in a matter of months. He was aware of problems that Magnavox had with the Odyssey and he was careful not to make the same mistakes. Although *PONG* could only play one game against the Odyssey's 12, *PONG*'s resolution was superior; its controls were more responsive; it displayed color graphics on color televisions, and it could keep score. The best part was the price. Thanks to the declining cost of microchips, *PONG* cost less than the Odyssey.

Bushnell and his team tried selling home *PONG* on their own in January 1975 but were not successful. They believed that the product should be sold in a toy store but they could not find any that were interested. They then decided to try major department stores starting with Sears. The toy buyer was not interested so then they tried sporting goods, with the belief that a computer version of tennis would sell alongside the real thing. The sporting goods buyer, Tom Quinn, was interested. Quinn offered to buy all the home *PONG* games that the company could put together. After being told that Atari could only manufacture 75,000 units, Quinn told Bushnell to double the production and Sears would finance it. In return, Sears wanted the exclusive selling rights of the game throughout 1975.

Bushnell jumped at the offer. Since Sears promised to pay for all of the advertising and to assume complete control, Atari had little to risk. Because Atari had exposure in over 900 stores across the country, it gained a reputation in home games as well as arcade games. Thanks to the Sears deal, Atari sold $40 million worth of home *PONG* games in 1975, netting $3 million.[2]

Other Early Consoles

With the success of home *PONG,* dozens of other companies decided to jump on the video ping-pong bandwagon by releasing their own versions of the game. But only Atari, Magnavox, and Coleco proved they were going to be in for the long haul by releasing more than one type of console and by advancing the technology.

Despite selling approximately 300,000 Odysseys between 1972 and 1973, Magnavox realized that they could not keep marketing the unit. Because it had been built from solid-state circuits, and came with literally hundreds of extra pieces, the unit was expensive to manufacture and sell. Magnavox realized early that it had to figure out a way to reduce costs in order to stay in the game. Baer realized this as early as 1973 and began researching the use of integrated circuits. In May 1974, Magnavox signed an agreement with Texas Instruments to design chips that would reproduce some of the Odyssey games.

The company released two new consoles in 1975. The first, the Odyssey 100, played two simple games: *Tennis* and *Hockey.* Unlike its competitor home *PONG,* it did not feature on-screen scoring or color. The controllers, while built into the unit, were reminiscent of the original Odyssey which contained separate knobs for horizontal, vertical, and "English."

Following closely behind the 100 was the *Odyssey 200.* The 200 looked exactly like the 100 but it featured an additional game called *SMASH.* It also allowed up to four players to compete at once—the first system to do so—and it included a rudimentary on-screen analog scoring system consisting of a series of small rectangles that advanced across the top of the screen whenever someone scored.

The year 1976 was a real turning point in the history of home video games. At this time General Instruments introduced chips that had several games built into them. Coleco was the first to utilize the chip, and it had Baer to thank. Since all home video games had to be licensed by Baer's company, Sanders Associates, and Magnavox, Baer learned early about the development of the new chip. He quickly called Arnold Greenberg, president of Coleco Industries, and told Greenberg that Coleco should look into these chips and build a console around them. Greenberg agreed and Coleco became the first customer to order General Instruments's video game chip. The result was the Telstar, a system which contained three games: *Tennis, Hockey,* and *Handball,* all with on-screen scoring.

Magnavox quickly followed Coleco's lead and released its own console that used the General Instruments chip. The Odyssey 300 played the same three games as the 200, but players only had to contend with one knob, not three. Whether this was a good thing or not is anybody's guess since the three-knob configuration returned with the Odyssey 400. In fact, the Odyssey 400 was basically the same as the 200 except that it contained an additional chip that allowed on-screen scoring.

Magnavox followed the 400 with the Odyssey 500 in 1976. Externally, it was the same as the 400 and it played the same games. However, on the 500 the games were in color, whereas they were only in black and white on all the prior Magnavox systems. But the biggest breakthrough was in the graphics. Instead of utilizing white squares for paddles, the 500 actually had graphics of human characters. This was the first time human characters appeared in a home video game.

The Odyssey 500's contribution was quickly lost in the annals of video game history. This was because Fairchild Electronic introduced a console that same year, 1976, that was far more innovative than the 500; it had cartridges.

The simple concept dated back to 1972 with the original Odyssey that played 12 games and players exchanged small circuit cards to choose the game they wanted to play. Naturally, everyone thought that the individual games were housed on the circuit cards but they were wrong. It was not until a January 2000 interview in *Electronic Gaming Monthly* magazine[3] that Baer revealed that all of the games on the Odyssey were hardwired into the machine. The circuit cards were used to unlock the individual games. Magnavox had the marketing sense to sell additional circuit cards but the number of games that the Odyssey could play was limited.

Programmable Video Game Systems

Jerry Lawson, an engineer with the Fairchild Camera and Instrument Company, took this idea and rethought it. The problem with the latest generation of video games was that people tired of them quickly. They played a few rounds of tennis and hockey and squash and then relegated the console to the closet. While many consumers would buy the next generation console as it was released, people most likely tended not to buy a new console because of the cost. Lawson realized that the only difference between the old consoles and the new ones was the chip that contained the games. If the manufacturers could sell the chips directly to the public and the different chips could be played on one console, people would be more apt to buy new games as they became available.

Lawson designed a system in which the individual chips were housed in large yellow cartridges that resembled audio 8-track cartridges. The company then released a console that they called the Fairchild Video Entertainment System (later renamed Channel F). The Channel F also sported an unusual controller that was different from the paddle and joystick controllers of the day. The controllers resembled plungers on bomb detonators. Atop each was a triangular piece that could be pushed forward, backward, left, or right. It also could rotate like a dial controller or press down into the base of the stick.

The console itself featured an array of controls. Players could control the speed of the ball and the length of a game. They also could pause the game at the press of a button; this was the first time a "pause" function appeared in a home video game.

Although cartridges gave consumers the ability to upgrade their console without buying a new console, people did not go out and buy the Channel F in droves. The company did not aggressively advertise the unit and people did not find the games particularly interesting. Still, the future of video game consoles had arrived and it was not long before other manufacturers followed Fairchild's lead.

Also in 1976, RCA, the company to which Baer first brought his Brown Box prototype, finally decided to enter the fray. Their Studio II, while utilizing game cartridges, represented modern technology at its worst. The games were played in black and white and the controllers were nonexistent; instead, players used two sets of numeric keyboards to control the action. Needless to say the system disappeared quickly.

In 1977 Magnavox released three systems and their boxes had the tagline "The Originator of Home Video Games" under the Magnavox name to let consumers know about the company's video game heritage. The new consoles themselves were nothing special; the Odyssey 2000 was the same as the 300 with an additional game. The 3000 was the same as the 2000 except that the console was restyled and had detachable dial controllers. Magnavox's final dedicated system, the Odyssey 4000, had eight new built-in games and detachable joystick controllers. Magnavox planned an Odyssey 5000, which was to contain 24 games, but the system was never released.

The other major video game companies released new types of game systems, quickly moving away from the old-fashioned ball and paddle games. Coleco released the Telstar Combat, a console that contained two pairs of tank-like controllers. The system itself played tank games so the controllers added the realistic effect of controlling an actual tank.

Atari released a pair of new consoles, in which the hardware was an integral part of the games themselves. *Video Pinball* contained a set of pinball games and the console had flippers buttons built into its side. Stunt Cycle gave players the ability to drive a motorcycle and jump over buses. The console featured motorcycle-type controllers that players could rotate to accelerate.

Atari followed this with the Video Computer System (VCS) (later renamed the 2600). This was Atari's answer to the Fairchild Channel F, a programmable system that allowed players to play different games by changing game cartridges. But Atari had something that Fairchild did not, a library of arcade games that were familiar to players. Another innovative feature was interchangeable controllers. The system was sold with a pair of joystick controllers and a pair of paddle controllers so there was no limit to the type of games that could be played.

In 1978 Magnavox released the Odyssey^2, a cartridge-based system to compete against the VCS. Although Magnavox did not have any arcade titles to offer, they tried to distinguish the system by including a flat membrane keyboard. The allure was that the Odyssey^2 resembled an inexpensive computer.

Coleco released the Telstar Arcade, a system designed by Baer. The Arcade came in a unique three-sided triangular console. One side played standard ball-and-paddle games; one side had a built-in pistol for target games; and the third side had a built-in-steering wheel for driving games. This was the first time a steering controller became available for a home game. Coleco also made additional games in triangular cartridges but only four were ever released and the system disappeared quickly.

Another arcade company entered the fray in 1978. Bally released its Bally Arcade, a system that used cartridges that resembled audiocassettes. Priced $100 more than the VCS, the Arcade had limited distribution and was no match against the VCS, which itself had not yet reached mass popularity.

That was to change in 1980. Toy giant Mattel released its Intellivision, a $300 system that featured exceptional graphics. While the VCS excelled in arcade-type games, its library of sports games were weak at best. The Intellivision offered two-player sports games which were as close to the real thing as was possible with the technology of the time.

Mattel would have reigned supreme except for two things that happened. First, Atari released a home version of *Space Invaders* for the VCS. At the time, *Space Invaders* was the most popular arcade game in history and Atari scored a coup by licensing the home console rights for it, the first time this was ever done. People rushed to buy the VCS just so they could play it at home. But one game does not make a system, and the Intellivision still looked better. Second, in 1979 when four distraught Atari programmers left to form their own company, Activision, things changed. Activision was the first third-party company to release software for the VCS, or any other console. And the games that Activision released played and looked better than almost anything Atari ever released. Their graphics gave the Intellivision a run for its money.

The threat of the Intellivision scared Atari enough that they designed a new system to compete with it. Based on its Atari 400 computer, Atari released the 5200, a system with arcade-style graphics. But before the 5200 could come out, Coleco came out with a system that put the Intellivision threat to rest once and for all.

The Colecovision offered arcade-quality graphics and Coleco licensed games from Sega and Nintendo including *Donkey Kong*. Two expansion modules were also available, one which played all of the games in the VCS (now called the 2600) library.

And the 2600 library was growing rapidly. With the success of Activision, dozens of companies jumped on the software bandwagon. Only a few companies actually spent money on development; the rest merely took well-known games and made their own versions of them. The stakes were high. Game cartridges only cost a few dollars to manufacture and could be sold for many times that.

By the end of 1983 there was too much product available. Between the Intellivision, Odyssey^2, Atari 5200, and Colecovision, people had to decide how they were going to spend their limited disposable income. And owners of the Atari 2600 had to contend with literally hundreds of cartridges that were available. Stores had limited space and could not stock everything and the smaller companies with the less desirable products got hit first. As the smaller companies began to go bankrupt, they unloaded their games at fire-sale prices. Pretty soon $5 Data Age cartridges were selling alongside $25 Atari cartridges. Regardless of the fact that the cheap games were usually unimpressive or that companies like Atari needed to charge higher prices because of their high development costs, people went and bought the less expensive cartridges because they could purchase five games for the price of one Atari game. A domino effect ensued. As the larger companies found their profits shrinking due to the competition from the discounted titles, they too had to discount their own products.

The casualties were high. By 1984 most of the third-party software vendors were history. And while the crash had been caused by an oversaturation of games for the Atari 2600, because it was the market leader, the entire industry suffered. Mattel and Magnavox abandoned the gaming market when their consoles could not compete against the 2600. And Coleco, which did have a system that most gamers admired, decided to go one step ahead and develop their Adam home computer, and actually stopped manufacturing their popular Colecovision so they could concentrate on the Adam. When that turned into a failure, the company nearly went bankrupt.

This left only Atari, whose new owner, Jack Tramiel, decided to abandon the game business in favor of 16-bit computers (see Chapter 10, "Company Profile: Atari"). For all intents and purposes, the American home video game industry had crashed, and the era of early home game systems was over.

COMPANY PROFILE: ATARI

Leonard Herman

No video game company has made a bigger impact than Atari, the company that started the video game industry, and the only company with interests in all three industry sectors: home gaming, arcade gaming, and computer gaming. Atari was founded in June 1972 by Nolan Bushnell and Ted Dabney, using the $500 in royalties from their earlier game, *Computer Space,* released by Nutting Associates in August, 1971. *Computer Space* was ultimately deemed too complex so Bushnell sought out a much simpler game. After witnessing a video table tennis demonstration on Magnavox's new Odyssey in May 1972, Bushnell came up with the idea for *PONG.* He hired Al Alcorn to assemble the device and *PONG* was released in October 1972. It took the world by storm.

Atari began releasing variants of *PONG,* including a home version in 1975, and became the market leader. Warner Communications bought Atari in 1976 for $28 million and with this new surge of capital, Atari released the VCS in 1977. The system took off in 1980 when Atari acquired the license to release a home version of *Space Invaders,* the world's most popular arcade game at the time. The unit sold respectfully for four years, releasing adaptations of Atari's arcade games such as *Outlaw, Night Driver, Super Breakout, Video Pinball, Asteroids, Battlezone, Missile Command, Centipede, Warlords,* and *Pole Position.*

One early employee of Atari named Steve Jobs wanted to create home computers and approached Bushnell with the prospect. Although Bushnell was not interested, he pointed Jobs in the right direction to obtain funding with which Jobs co-founded a company called Apple Computers. By 1978 Atari decided to compete against Apple and entered the home computer field with new personal computers dubbed the 400 and the 800. But Atari's computer division could not evade the stigma of the Atari name, and the computers were thought of as high-quality game machines. Competing with Mattel and Coleco, Atari decided to release a high-end game machine based on the 400. They doubled the VCS's product number (CX-2600) and called the new system the 5200. The VCS was renamed the 2600.

In 1984 Atari announced another new machine, which they called the 7800. But before the system could be released, the company was sold. The arcade division was retained by

Warner Communications and renamed Atari Games. A year later the controlling interest of Atari Games was sold to Japanese arcade manufacturer Namco, who quickly lost interest in its new division by the end of the year. In 1986 a group of Namco employees bought out Namco's share of Atari Games. In 1993, Warner Communications, now Time-Warner Inc., bought a controlling interest in Atari Games and renamed the arcade company Time-Warner Interactive. Arcade giant Williams Electronics purchased Time-Warner Interactive in 1996 and the company's name was changed back to Atari Games, until 1998, when it became Midway Games West. In 2000 Midway released *San Francisco Rush 2049,* the last arcade game to be released under the Atari Games brand name. Midway finally left the arcade business altogether in 2001 and Atari's long legacy as an arcade company finally came to an end.

Returning to 1984's split of the old Atari Inc., the computer and game divisions were sold to Jack Tramiel, who recently had been fired from Commodore Computers, the company he founded. Tramiel's plan was to use Atari to compete against his old company.

Tramiel decided to scrap the game division and concentrate on computers. The company released two computers that were compatible with the 400 and 800 and were dubbed the XE series. The 65XE featured 64 kilobytes of memory while the 130XE boasted 128 kilobytes. However, Tramiel's plan of revenge against his old company included a new 16-bit computer built by a small company called Amiga, which Atari helped fund. But before Atari could secure the rights to it, Commodore wound up gaining the license. Atari quickly obtained the rights to a competing 16-bit machine, which it labeled the ST.

The ST gained a fair following, although most of it was in Europe. Still, the Amiga outsold the ST by about 3 to 2. Surprisingly, it was the video game market that helped keep the Atari Corporation afloat. Following the success of the Nintendo Entertainment System, in 1986 Tramiel released two consoles that had been sitting in warehouses for nearly two years. The 7800 had graphics that could rival the NES and could play the 2600's huge library of cartridges, but by the time it was released, Atari's reputation as an innovator was over. The other console was the 2600jr—a pint-size version of the console that ruled store shelves only a few years earlier. Though its games were primitive compared to the newer Japanese systems, the 2600jr had a retail price of only $50 and was targeted towards lower income households that could not afford the Japanese consoles. The marketing gambit paid off and while the 2600jr was never the show-stopper that it's larger brother was during Atari's heyday, it still managed to net Atari Corporation $25 million in profits. The 2600jr would continue until 1991, but by then Atari would move on to smaller things.

Atari confused everybody in 1987 when it released its first new video game console, the XEGS (XE Game System). The system was basically an XE computer with a detachable keyboard. Atari even released old 800 games for the XEGS such as *Asteroids* and *Space Invaders* but instead of repackaging them, the games were sold in the old packages that claimed that they were for the Atari 400 and 800. A sticker was placed on each box saying the games could also be played on the XEGS. The XEGS was a failure and disappeared rapidly.

Atari's next console came in 1989 with the Lynx, a handheld color system. The Lynx enjoyed a small success. Unfortunately, it was released shortly after Nintendo's Game Boy, which, despite its monochrome screen, proved more popular thanks to its lower price and its being packaged with *Tetris.* Still, the Lynx sold well enough to stick around for a few years and in 1991 Atari released a smaller and less inexpensive version called the Lynx II.

In 1993 Atari once again focused on game consoles, rather than its computers which still enjoyed some success in Europe. The company released a 64-bit console called the Jaguar, which actually contained two 32-bit processors (32-bit and 64-bit refer to the size of the "words" used by the computer's processor, and partly determine the speed at which programs can run). While some of its games such as *Tempest 2000* became instant classics, others, such as *Club Drive,* had graphics that would have looked inferior on the 2600. Without third party support the Jaguar did not have a chance to compete against the Sony PlayStation and Sega Saturn.

By 1996 Tramiel decided to quit. Atari Corporation was merged with JT Storage (JTS) Inc., a manufacturer of hard drives of which Tramiel was a minor shareholder. The new company became JTS Corp. and Atari's role was to simply take care of its intellectual property and to supply badly needed funds to the cash-stricken drive manufacturer. Most of the Atari employees were laid off and, basically, Atari ceased to exist.

In 1997 Hasbro Interactive released an updated version of the classic game *Frogger* for the PlayStation. The game was such a success that Hasbro Interactive executives decided to look into licensing more retro titles. They discovered they could buy Atari, and its large catalog of well-known games, for a mere $5 million and jumped at the chance.

Atari became a division of Hasbro Interactive in 1998, alongside other former companies such as MicroProse and Avalon Hill, as well as Hasbro Interactive itself which was busy releasing electronic editions of as many Milton Bradley and Parker Brothers board games as possible. In a short period of time, old Atari titles such as *Asteroids, Missile Command, Centipede,* and even *PONG* were updated and released for the new modern consoles and personal computers. Even the original Atari 2600 games were released for the modern systems, in anthologies containing dozens of games and pre-1984 arcade hits.

But the large number of titles that Hasbro Interactive released under the Atari brand name was not enough to keep the entire company afloat. In January 2001, Hasbro Interactive was sold to the French software giant Infogrames Inc., which became the second largest video game publisher in the United States and one of the largest in the world. Although Hasbro Interactive was renamed Infogrames Interactive, little else changed. The company still worked out of the same Beverly, Massachusetts, office building that had been home to Parker Brothers for nearly a century and Atari was still merely a brand name.

That was to change two years later. On May 7, 2003, Infogrames Inc. officially renamed its worldwide operations and all of the company's games were sold under the Atari brand name. The U.S. division was renamed Atari, Inc., a name that was near and dear to many fans of the original Warner Communications subsidiary. After seven years, Atari was a company again.

The new Atari's first milestone occurred just a week later when the company released *Enter The Matrix* (a game based on the *Matrix* movies). Within one month of its release more than 2.5 million copies of the game were sold worldwide (excluding Japan), making it the fastest-selling title in the company's history.

While the new Atari was primarily a software company, many Atari fans hoped the company would return to its former glory and release consoles. That wish came true in November 2004, when Atari introduced the Flashback. This console, which resembled a smaller version of the 7800, featured 20 of the 2600 games built into the system. A year later Atari followed this with the Flashback 2 which resembled a small 2600 and came complete with 40 built-in games. As Atari reached its 35th anniversary, it was once again a force in the video game industry.

CHAPTER 11

SYSTEM PROFILE: THE ATARI VIDEO COMPUTER SYSTEM (VCS)

Leonard Herman

In late 1975 Atari began a lucrative business converting its arcade hits into standalone versions for the home. After a succession of consoles which included PONG, Video Pinball, and Stunt Cycle, the Atari executives eagerly anticipated which arcade game should get the home treatment next. The problem was that it took $100,000 and over a year to develop a new home game. In that time a hit arcade game could lose popularity rapidly and Atari did not want to invest a great sum of money on a game console that would have limited appeal.

Atari decided that the solution lay in a programmable system; one that could play many different games. Atari assembled a team of engineers consisting of Joe Decuir, Steve Mayer, Ron Milner, and Jay Minor to create a simple and inexpensive programmable system. The project was code-named "Stella" after Decuir's bicycle.

The console that the team devised was simplicity itself because the software would do most of the work. The heart of the system, which contained 128 bytes of internal RAM, was a 6507 processor which ran at a breathtaking (for the time) 1 MHz.

The graphics chip, commonly referred to as "Stella" but properly named the television interface adapter (TIA), generated all of the sounds and video displays such as high-resolution objects, colors, and low-resolution backgrounds. Stella could line objects up in a row but not in a column. And because of the primitive way that Stella sent data to the screen (one scan line at a time, in sync with the TV's electron gun) the main part of each game program had to constantly write to Stella in order to refresh the graphics correctly.

To make it even harder on the programmer, the programs (or kernels) themselves could not be any larger than 4 kilobytes. Since the unit had been designed to only play *PONG* and *Tank* type games, the design team never anticipated that any game would go beyond a 2 kilobyte boundary.

Before the original prototype was completed, Fairchild Electronics released their own programmable system, the Channel F. In light of the new unexpected competition,

Atari engineers and executives realized they were on the right track with the new programmable system. Unfortunately, Atari did not have enough capital to put the product into production. In order to raise the money to complete the project, Atari was sold to Warner Communications in 1976 for $28 million.

With a great influx of cash behind it, Atari released the VCS in October of 1977. The $199 console was sold with "paddle" and "joystick" controllers. Also included was a cartridge, *Combat,* that featured several variations of Atari's hit arcade game, *Tank* as well as biplane and jet plane games. Eight additional cartridges were available optionally including home versions of popular arcade games like *Surround* and *PONG.*

Although the VCS outsold the Channel F forcing Fairchild to subsequently abandon it, Atari's console did not sell in the numbers that was needed to sustain it. Even new releases in 1978 like *Breakout* and a pair of games, *Hunt & Score* and *Codebreaker.* which incorporated a new keyboard controller, did not stir much interest in the VCS.

Shortly after the release of the VCS, Taito's *Space Invaders* invaded arcades around the world. Atari executives realized that having *Space Invaders* available on the VCS would be a major marketing coup. Without precedent, Atari quickly licensed the home rights for *Space Invaders* and released it for the VCS in January 1980. This resulted in skyrocketing VCS sales as millions were bought just so *Space Invaders* could be played at home. Atari grossed $415 million that year; more than twice the gross from the previous year.[1] They followed up by licensing other arcade hits such as *Defender* (1980) and *Berzerk* (1980), as well as releasing its own hits *Asteroids* and *Missile Command* for the VCS.

Because of its limitations, it was very difficult to write programs for the VCS. Steve Mayer remarked in a 1983 interview with *IEEE Spectrum:*

> Writing the kernels that make up the game programs is like solving acrostic puzzles with lots and lots of possibilities. There's a certain class of programmer that can deal in the microcode like that. If it were easier to program, we wouldn't have these programmers, because they'd be bored. The VCS is an absolute challenge.[2]

One such programmer was Tod Frye, who was given the task to design a VCS adaptation of Atari's monster arcade hit, *Asteroids.* Frye discovered early that he could not create a faithful rendition of the game within the confines of the allotted 4K of memory. Frye decided to use a technique called "bank-switching" which had been developed, but never used commercially, by an Atari programmer named Larry Wagner. The technique involved dividing memory into disjointed sections or banks. Although all banks were available to the program, only one could be accessed at a time. In the case of the VCS, an instruction within the first 4K bank branched to an address in a second 4K bank from which processing continued. The branch to the second bank of 4K was transparent to the CPU. In effect this allowed the VCS to process games that were larger than 4K. Before long 8K and even 16K games (usually using four banks of 4K chips) became the norm for the VCS.

Ultimately, the Atari programmers grew restless. They resented that their creations earned hundreds of millions of dollars for Atari while they were merely treated as employees and were not even entitled to royalties. In addition, Atari kept them anonymous fearing that competitors might lure them away. Atari programmer Warren Robinett decided to do something about it. While writing *Adventure* (1979), he decided to program a hidden room into the game which would cause his name to flash on the screen if it was discovered. When it was announced that a 12-year-old Utah boy found the hidden room, it was too late for Atari to correct the code. One executive called the hidden message an "Easter egg," a term which has remained to this day. Today's games purposely have Easter eggs designed into them.

Four other Atari programmers were not satisfied with hiding their names in games. They teamed up with ex-record company executive, Jim Levy, and formed Activision in 1980, the first company to develop third-party software for video game consoles.

Activision games featured graphics that nearly rivaled those of the competing Intellivision system and showed that the VCS was indeed capable of supplying both good-looking screens and entertaining game play. However, Activision was a direct threat against Atari. Previously, Atari could always depend that its releases, no matter how mediocre, would be best-sellers as consumers hungered for new games. Now Atari's profits were in trouble because the company did not earn a dime when consumers bought Activision cartridges. Atari sued Activision but all it won was a disclaimer on every Activision box stating that the game was compatible with the VCS.

With the success of Activision, many other companies began forming with the express purpose of developing software for the video game systems. Some, like Imagic, were made up of old Atari and Mattel programmers. By 1983 there were more than three dozen companies offering software for the VCS (renamed the 2600 in 1982 after its model number, CX-2600).

Competition did not only attack the software side. The 2600 also battled for survival against Mattel's Intellivision and Coleco's Colecovision, both of which offered adapters which allowed them to play the entire library of 2600 compatible games. Atari fought back with the 5200, a super console of its own. Although the newer consoles were technologically superior to the 2600, their higher price tags kept Atari's humble little machine popular.

The 2600's immense popularity inevitably made it a magnet for a slew of add-on peripherals. Although some were released, others never made it past the prototype stage. Among them was CVC Gameline (1983), a modem that plugged into the cartridge slot and marked the first time that video games could be download through the telephone lines. Starpath's Supercharger (1982) and Amiga's Power Module (1983) also plugged into the cartridge slot but had games loaded into them from inexpensive cassette tapes. Amiga also developed the Joyboard (1982), a stand-on controller that was sold with a skiing game. Other controllers which never made it to market were a voice controller from Milton Bradley, and Atari's Mindlink (1984) a controller which sensed a player's head muscles. Finally, several companies, including Atari, raced to release a peripheral that would turn the 2600 into a personal computer.

Unfortunately, the popularity of the 2600 indirectly led to the infamous video game industry crash of 1983. More and more companies jumped onto the 2600 bandwagon. Before long there were hundreds of games available for the 2600, most of them badly designed with little play value. Even Atari managed to release inferior games. Their 2600 rendition of *Pac-Man* bore little resemblance to the arcade mega-hit from which it was derived. All of these companies competed to occupy a limited amount of shelf space. The first companies to go bankrupt sold their inventory to salvage firms who then sold them to retailers at very low prices. Consumers could then buy cheap games from clearance bins or expensive games from the companies still in business. Most chose the bargain games and this created a vicious circle which bankrupted more companies and forced more salvaged games onto an already crowded clearance table. The remaining companies, like Atari, discounted their games to compete against the low-cost games but wound up losing money in the process. By 1984 only a handful of companies still survived and they no longer had any justification to spend the money needed to develop new games. By all accounts the 2600, as well as the video game industry, was dead.

After Nintendo gambled on video games in 1985 and won, the Atari Corporation, no longer owned by Warner Communications, decided to share in the riches. In 1986 the company released a smaller inexpensive version of the 2600 which it called the 2600jr. The new $50 unit became a hit in households that could not afford a $125 Nintendo. New software also was offered but it was too little to late. Atari's magic was gone. Even with the release of the technologically advanced 7800 which played all of the 2600 games, Atari could not duplicate the enthusiasm that it had created at the beginning of the decade. Before long stores stopped offering the Atari titles, relegating Atari to mail order before finally ending the 2600's life cycle in 1991.

Surprisingly, the console still enjoys a healthy life within the classic gaming community to this day. In 1995, independent programmer Ed Federmeyer wrote *SoundX,* a brand new release for the 2600. He followed this with *Edtris 2600,* a *Tetris* clone. Since then dozens of brand new games for the 2600 have been written and released. In addition, many older games that had been written in the early 1980s but never released such as *Elevator Action* and *Stunt Cycle* have been rediscovered and sold in limited editions at gaming events such as the Classic Gaming Expo and PhillyClassic.

But the enjoyment of the old 2600 games is not left only to the classic gamers. Even modern gamers are now enjoying the old games too as collections of 2600 games have been made available for the modern consoles and PC. Jakks Pacific marketed both an Atari joystick and a paddle controller that plugged directly into a TV and played classic 2600 games. Even Atari got into the act and released the Flashback 2, a standalone system that looked exactly like a small 2600, complete with a pair of joystick controllers, which plugged directly into the TV and played 40 games, several of which never had been released before.

The 2600 may be gone but it certainly has not been forgotten. By being in production for 14 years, the 2600 enjoyed an availability record that still reigns among all consoles and is only second to the Game Boy in home video game systems overall.

CHAPTER 12

VECTOR GAMES

Mark J. P. Wolf

The era of vector arcade video games was a short one, beginning in 1977 and lasting less than a decade. Invented during the 1950s, vector graphics displays (also known as XY monitors) created their imagery differently than raster monitors, like those used in televisions. Whereas the electron beam covers the entire screen in raster-scan monitors, in vector-scan monitors it draws only the line segments that make up the image and leaves the rest of the screen black (see Chapter 2, "Imaging Technologies," for more explanation of vector and raster technologies). Because vector monitors had less to draw, vector graphics were faster with thinner, sharper lines that could be moved smoothly across the screen, as opposed to the solid, blocky graphics of raster games for which movement was more difficult to program. Since objects were drawn individually, more moving objects were also possible; according to Steve Kent, even early vector games could have as many as 40 independent objects, compared to only 10 or so in raster games.[1] The main disadvantage of vector graphics was that bitmaps were not available; everything was constructed from a series of line segments, so creating small, detailed graphics for characters or objects was more difficult than it was in raster graphics. As a result, vector games tended to be less character based and mainly consisted of wireframe imagery on a black background.

Vector graphics came to the arcade when Larry Rosenthal, who had done a master's thesis on the mainframe game *Spacewar!* (1962) at MIT, developed vector technology that could be used in arcade games, which he called the Vectorbeam monitor. Rosenthal licensed his Vectorbeam equipment to the game company Cinematronics. After a dispute, Rosenthal left the company and created his own, which he also called Vectorbeam. Both companies produced games based on *Spacewar!;* Cinematronics's was called *Space Wars* (1977), while Vectorbeam's was called *Space War* (1977). (Instead of continuing to license technology from Vectorbeam, Cinematronics would later buy the company in 1979.)

Cinematronics's next release was *Starhawk,* which had visuals inspired by the Death Star trench scenes in the film *Star Wars* (1977) (see Chapter 7, "Arcade Games of the 1970s," for an image from *Starhawk*).[2] Vectorbeam's next game, *Speed Freak* (1978) was a driving game with a first-person perspective similar to Atari's *Night Driver.* except that instead of the periodic poles that demarcated *Night Driver*'s roadway, *Speed Freak* drew its roadway's edges, as well as the dividing line between lanes. *Speed Freak's* oncoming cars were more three dimensional and resized more smoothly as they approached, unlike *Night Driver's* blocky cars. And when the player crashed into an oncoming car, it exploded into line segments that scattered across the scene, adding a more dynamic feeling of a crash, making *Speed Freak* the best driving game of its day.

In 1979, the success of vector games led Atari to join in. Atari's first vector game, *Lunar Lander,* was an adaptation of the mainframe game of the same name, in which players tried to fly and land a spaceship without crashing it. In November of that year, Atari also released *Asteroids,* which became an arcade classic and one of the best-known vector games, exceeding 70,000 units[3] produced (the production line for *Lunar Lander* was eventually switched over to producing *Asteroids* units). *Asteroids* spawned sequels, imitators, and a bootleg version [Alpha Denshi's *Planet* (1979)], and arcade operators had to make larger coin boxes because the game was taking in so much money.[4] Atari made another version of the game, *Asteroids Deluxe* (1981) with new additions including a shield that could be turned on around the spaceship, and a killer satellite that came after the player, and when fired upon, broke into smaller satellites that had to be destroyed. Other games of the year included Cinematronics's *Sundance,* in which players opened panels in grids to catch bouncing suns; Vectorbeam's *Warrior,* in which two knights seen in overhead view engaged in a swordfight, one of the first one-on-one fighting games [perhaps the second one, after Sega's *Heavyweight Champ* (1976)]; and *Tail Gunner,* a space shooting game which began development under Vectorbeam and finished at Cinematronics after they bought Vectorbeam. *Tail Gunner* was different in that its starfield movement was reversed; instead of flying into the depicted space like other games, the viewer was moving away from it, looking out the back of a spaceship at the ships chasing it; hence the name *Tail Gunner.* Exidy purchased the rights for a cockpit version of the game and released *Tail Gunner II* in 1980.

Other games of 1980 included Cinematronics's *Star Castle,* in which players fired at an enemy ship surrounded by rotating rings that can be destroyed; *Rip Off,* a tank shooting game where pirate tanks are stealing the player's fuel canisters and hauling them off-screen; and *Armor Attack,* which featured jeeps, tanks, and helicopters from a bird's eye view. Also released that year was Atari's *Battlezone,* probably the best-known vector arcade game of all time. *Battlezone* had a first-person perspective view, but unlike *Starhawk* and *Speed Freak,* it had new hardware which could do more 3-D computation. A radar screen showed a schematic overhead view with enemy tanks represented as dots, making *Battlezone* the first arcade video game in which players had to keep track of off-screen events and could be killed by off-screen enemies [similar to the mainframe game *Panther* (1975) developed at Northwestern University]. A version of *Battlezone,* known as the *Bradley Trainer,* also was created for the U.S. military for tank training.

Using the same technology behind *Battlezone,* Atari produced another game, *Red Baron,* in 1981.[5] *Red Baron* was essentially a flying version of *Battlezone* with biplanes, with rounds of shooting in the air as well as from on the ground. Another Atari vector game of 1981 was the arcade classic *Tempest,* an abstract game with shapes moving up a well that the player had to shoot at and stop before they got to the top, an idea that began as a first-person version of *Space Invaders.*[6] (Although *Tempest's* title screen lists "MCMLXXX"—1980—as the copyright date, the game was actually released in 1981.) The scaling imagery used in *Tempest* was easy for vector graphics and was something that could not be done well in raster games. Vector games made good use of scaling and quick, smooth movement, and around 1981 they began to appear in color, including *Tempest.* Games before 1981 were typically either black and white or monochrome (*Battlezone,* for example, had green lines on a black background). Some games, like *Star Castle,* had color overlays on the screen to make the game's lines appear to be different colors, but the monitors themselves were not color.

Sega began production of vector games in 1981. (In 1979, Sega had merged with the game company Gremlin, and so the games it produced are sometimes identified as Sega/Gremlin games.) The company released two vector games in 1981: *Eliminator* and *Space Fury.* Like *Star Castle, Eliminator* had its enemy spaceship situated inside a circular enclosure, although *Eliminator*'s enclosure had a narrow tunnel which the player could try to shoot down to destroy the enemy ship (reminiscent of the shots down the exhaust port that destroyed the Death Star in the film *Star Wars*). Players attempted to destroy the circular enclosure and the enemy ship (which came out after the players as the game progressed), and shot at other players in the multiplayer versions. *Eliminator* was released in a one-player upright version, a two-player cocktail version, and a four-player version (with one player on each side of the screen, which faced upwards in the middle), making it the only four-player vector game ever made. *Space Fury* was another space shooting game, known mainly for its attract mode, which featured a one-eyed big-brained alien commander that taunted players in synthesized speech with lines like "Is there no warrior mightier than I?" and "So, a creature for my amusement. Prepare for battle!"

Other games of 1981 were different variations on shooting games. In Cinematronics's *Boxing Bugs* the player controlled a cannon that fired from one end and had a boxing glove on the other; both were used to knock out bugs that placed bombs near the octagonal protective wall around the cannon. Cinematronics's *Solar Quest* was a space shooting game around a sun with gravitational pull (similar to some versions of *Spacewar!*) but with an odd twist; when enemy ships were destroyed, they left "survivors" floating in space, and players were awarded more points for "rescuing" the survivors than for destroying them; an early instance of players being rewarded for ethical behavior. Midway's *Omega Race,* a space shooting game, had an information box in the middle of the screen around which the action of the game took place, though the object of the game involved shooting alien ships rather than racing around the track.

1982 was another big year for vector gaming, with at least six new arcade games appearing along with the only vector home game console system. Three arcade games were from Atari: *Space Duel, Gravitar,* and *Quantum. Space Duel* was Atari's only vector game which two players could play simultaneously and was similar to *Asteroids* but with 3-D color asteroids and either cooperative or competitive play. *Gravitar,* for two alternating players, combined skills from *Asteroids* and *Lunar Lander,* and was made up of four "universes" (with gravity that was either negative or positive, and landscapes that were either visible or invisible); each "universe" had three solar systems; each solar system had four or five planets (and a "Home Base" and a "Death Star"); and each planet had its own unique terrain to navigate, giving players several dozen different screens to see. *Quantum,* inspired by particle physics, was an abstract game in which players use a trak-ball controller to encircle particles (capturing them) while avoiding hitting other particles.

Sega also had three new vector games in 1982; *Zektor, Tac/Scan,* and *Star Trek* (another game, *Battle Star,* appeared in a flyer from Sega, though it may not have been released). *Zektor* involved freeing eight cities from waves of attacking enemy fighters and "roboprobes." *Tac/Scan* was a three-stage space shooting game in which the player controlled a squadron of seven ships that all flew in formation and moved as one. A unique feature of the game was its change in perspective. *Tac/Scan*'s first stage was two dimensional and similar to games like *Galaxian* and *Space Invaders,* but its second stage was three dimensional, with players firing into the screen instead of up or down it. The third stage, the "Space Tunnel," was a series of concentric rings leading into the screen through which players had to navigate. Unlike the 1972 game of the same name, Sega's *Star Trek* was licensed from Paramount, and the game was released the same year as the film *Star Trek II: The Wrath of Khan* (1982). *Star Trek* had five different controls to learn, six different enemies, and 40 different simulation levels of play, making it one of the most elaborate vector game ever made (along with possibly *Gravitar*).

The release of the only home game system with vector graphics, GCE/Milton Bradley's Vectrex, came in November 1982. Because television sets used raster graphics, the Vectrex came with its own vector monitor. The screen was monochrome, and colored overlays were used to color games' graphics. Games released for the Vectrex included original games (*Bedlam, Blitz!, Fortress of Narzod, Minestorm, Hyperchase,* and others), adaptations of Cinematronics's vector arcade games (*Space Wars, Starhawk, Star Castle, Armor Attack, Rip Off, Solar Quest, Cosmic Chasm*), adaptations of raster arcade games (*Berzerk, Pole Position, Scramble*), games that used a light pen (*AnimAction, Art Master, Melody Master*), and even some 3-D games (*3D Crazy Coaster, 3D MineStorm, 3D Narrow Escape*) which involved an additional special 3-D viewer. Since the system has ceased production, Smith Engineering, the manufacturers of the Vectrex, have allowed Vectrex materials to be copied for noncommercial purposes. This has allowed a community of Vectrex fans to continue creating homebrew games for the Vectrex, and there are now more of these games than there were originally released for the system.

A few more vector games appeared in 1983: GCE/Cinematronics's *Cosmic Chasm,* Centuri's *Aztarac,* and Atari's *Black Widow, Major Havoc,* and *Star Wars.*[7] In *Cosmic Chasm,* the player had to fly through tubes inside a space station to fire at its core and then fly out again before it blew up, an idea probably inspired by the film *Return of the Jedi* (1983) released in spring of that year. *Aztarac,* another space game, had players defending a star base from attacking ships. In *Black Widow,* players controlled a spider on a spider web that it defended from invading bugs by shooting at them. (Self-defense seems to be a popular way of justifying a game's violence.) *Major Havoc* was a detailed multistage adventure game that involved shooting enemy ships, landing in a space station, and navigating a scrolling maze of hallways with a variety of objects (such as robot guards and electrified barriers) which the player passed through on the way to destroying the station's reactor. The game was rather difficult and has a cult following to this day. Finally, the best-known vector game of 1983 was Atari's *Star Wars,* which was licensed from Lucasfilm and was a colorful, 3-D take on the space battles and Death Star trench chase scenes from the film, and even included digitized voice samples from the film's soundtrack.

1983 was the last year Cinematronics would produce vector games. That same year they released their first laserdisc game, and its success redirected their efforts to the new technology (see Chapter 17, "Laserdisc Games"). No company appears to have released vector arcade games in 1984, although work on a few games continued. Occasionally prototypes of games would be produced but not released, or ideas might be reworked and appear in later games (for example, Atari Games's *Tomcat,* which does not appear to have been released, even though screenshots for the game can be found on the Internet).

In 1985 another *Star Wars*-based game, *The Empire Strikes Back,* was released by Atari Games (see Chapter 11, "System Profile: The Atari Video Computer System," for the difference between Atari and Atari Games) and was the last major vector game released. Only one other game may have been produced that year, Exidy's space game *Vertigo* (1985, although some sources claim 1984). Probably the last vector arcade game ever made, which may or may not have actually been released, is Exidy's *Top Gunner* (1986), a sit-in game that is said to be a modification to *Vertigo.*

By the late 1980s, sprite technology had improved greatly and three-dimensional filled-polygon graphics were beginning to return to the arcade after their failed debut in Atari's *I, Robot.* Raster games had improved graphically, the rise of three-dimension raster graphics games in the 1990s was just around the corner, and in the eyes of many players (and game companies), wireframe graphics could no longer compete with them. The unique look and playing experience of vector games, however, has attracted a following and vector games live on as arcade collectibles and in adaptations for emulators, and they are remembered as an important part of the Golden Age of arcade video games.

CHAPTER 13

VIDEO GAME STARS: PAC-MAN

Mark J.P. Wolf

During the 1970s, video game graphics were limited, and player-character graphics were usually no more than colored blocks or simple vehicle designs such as tanks, cars, planes, horses, or spaceships. Midway's *Gun Fight* and Project Support Engineering's *Maneater* had featured human figures as player-characters, but even these characters remained nameless, as did the few other characters in games of the time. But a video game released by Namco in Japan in late 1979 and distributed by Midway in North America a year later, would have named characters with individualized behaviors, and the first video game star: Pac-Man. It would go on to become arguably the most famous video game of all time, with the arcade game alone taking in more than a billion dollars, and one study estimated that it had been played more than 10 billion times during the twentieth century.[1]

Pac-Man was the invention of Namco Limited game designer Toru Iwatani, who joined the company at the age of 22 in 1977. He described the creation of the game in an interview in Susan Lammers's 1986 book, *Programmers at Work*:

> All the computer games available at the time were of the violent type—war games and space invader types. There were no games that everyone could enjoy, and especially none for women. I wanted to come up with a "comical" game women could enjoy. The story I like to tell about the origin of Pac-Man is that one lunchtime I was quite hungry and I ordered a whole pizza. I helped myself to a wedge and what was left was the idea for the Pac-Man shape....
>
> In Japanese the character for mouth (kuchi) is a square shape. It's not circular like the pizza, but I decided to round it out....Food is the other part of the basic concept. In my initial design I had put the player in the midst of food all over the screen. As I thought about it. I realised the player wouldn't know exactly what to do: the purpose of the game would be obscure. So I created a maze and put the food in it. Then whoever played the game would have some structure by moving through the maze. The Japanese have a slang word—paku paku—they use to describe the motion of the mouth opening and closing while one eats. The name Pac-Man came from that word.[2]

(When it was finally designed, the game was originally named "Puck-Man," but changed for its North American release when it was thought that kids would scratch away the middle part of the "P" and make the name offensive.)

Pac-Man had characters with names, including Pac-Man's enemies, the four "ghosts" or "monsters": a red one named Shadow (nicknamed "Blinky"), a pink one named Speedy (nicknamed "Pinky"), a cyan one named Bashful (nicknamed "Inky"), and an orange one named Pokey (nicknamed "Clyde"). Each had a different algorithmic (preprogrammed) behavior, to keep them from all lining up behind Pac-Man and moving in exactly the same way. Pac-Man and the ghosts also appear in three animated cut-scenes or "intermissions" between levels, adding humor to the game as well as giving players a short break between levels.

Before *Pac-Man*, the biggest hit games were *Space Invaders* and *Asteroids*. *Pac-Man* was humorous and nonviolent and represented a departure from space themes and shooting games. It was also one of the first crossover games, reaching a wide audience including women and players of various ages who might otherwise not have played video games. Its success also inspired game designers to innovate, and showed that there was a market for "cute" games, and that a wide variety of game designs were possible.

Over the years, *Pac-Man* was ported to over a dozen different platforms, including a variety of home game systems, and even to mobile phones and the iPod. Over a dozen sequels were released in the arcade, including *Ms. Pac-Man* (1981), *Ms. Pac-Man Plus* (1981), *Super Pac-Man* (1982), *Pac-Man Plus* (1982), *Baby Pac-Man* (1982), *Jr. Pac-Man* (1983), *Pac & Pal* (1983), *Professor Pac-Man* (1983), *Pac-Man & Chomp Chomp* (1983), *Pac-Land* (1984), *Pac-Mania* (1987), *Pac-Man World* (1999), *Pac-Man World 2* (2002), and even a three-dimensional first-person perspective game from Pac-Man's point of view, *Pac-Man VR* (1996). Over the years more than two dozen licensed sequels appeared for home game consoles and cell phones, as well as many clones, pale imitations, and illegal bootleg versions of games.

Pac-Man was also the first video game character to be heavily merchandised in areas outside of video games. There was a song and album entitled "Pac-Man Fever" (the song even made it to the number 9 spot on *Billboard*'s charts in 1982), an animated television series that ran two seasons (1982–1984), the animated Christmas television special *Christmas Comes to Pac-Land,* two board games by Milton Bradley (based on *Pac-Man* and *Ms. Pac-Man*), T-shirts, hats, handheld games, plush toys (some battery operated), children's books and comics, banks, backpacks, seat cushions, clocks, watches, jewelry, keychains, back-scratchers, basketballs, Chinese yo-yos, bubble soap, gumball dispensers, pens, pencils, erasers, stickers, pinwheels, purses, jigsaw puzzles, playing cards, Rubik's Cubes, needlepoints and crosstitch kits, magnets, stationery and paper goods, party supplies, bumper stickers, air fresheners, license plates, trash cans, rugs, table lamps, night lights, telephones, cigarette lighters, glasses, dishes, lunchboxes, pastas, cereal, candy, gum, vitamins, a macaroni and cheese dinner, and other products.[3] Finally, 2002 saw the appearance of the 160-page book *Pac-Man Collectibles* by Deborah Palicia (Schiffer Book Farm, PA: Schiffer, 2002), who is also planning a second book on the topic.

Pac-Man had its 25th anniversary in 2005, which was commemorated by a new arcade video game, the *Pac-Man 25th Anniversary Model* which featured *Pac-Man, Ms. Pac-Man,* and *Galaga* all in one cabinet. More *Pac-Man* games are planned, and games continue to be made for every new home console system that appears. Pac-Man remains popular to this day and will likely remain an iconic figure synonymous with the video game industry for years to come.

CHAPTER 14

THE RISE OF THE HOME COMPUTER

Bob Rehak

Nowadays it would be difficult to find a middle- to upper-class household in the United States that lacks a personal computer. Many homes, in fact, own more than one: iMacs and Dells and Gateways, home-built PCs and brand-X clones sit on our desktops, countertops, and kitchen tables. Outside the home, laptop computers, one to a person, crowd the tables at coffee shops and schools and libraries. These computers run word processors and web browsers, programs for playing games, editing digital photos, balancing checkbooks, and charting family genealogies. Software tailored for entertainment and productivity rides atop operating systems designed to be accessible to a general public: simple icons, point-and-click interfaces, mice and trackpads (used in laptops) that anyone from a child to a senior citizen can operate. Increasingly, computer processors and storage devices are encroaching on that most hallowed shrine of American domestic life—the living room TV—as well as the smaller end of the scale, the pocket devices of phone, camera, calendar, and address book. In sum, personal computers and computing devices constitute a suite of technologies that work with us in our most intimate, mundane, everyday spaces and actions.

But it was not always this way. Only a few decades have passed since the personal computer's hulking ancestors squatted low to the earth like immobile dinosaurs: computers that were themselves the size of living rooms, of entire houses. And the uses these machines were put to had nothing to do with personal finances or instant-messaging friends; instead, they calculated missile trajectories, chemical interactions, mathematical simulations—concerns specific to the places, and populations, where these early computing machines existed. Since then, however, the behemoths found in military bases and research labs have undergone a radical change. This transformation involved breathtakingly rapid advances in miniaturization, memory storage, graphics displays, and power supplies: a string of breakthroughs so regular and seamless they scarcely deserve to be labeled as such. However, equally important was the *social* dimension of the personal computer's rise. The personal computer sprang in equal part from the counterculture 1960s and the commodity-mad 1970s, bringing together both a populist impulse that proclaimed *Computers should be available to everyone!* and a commercial imperative that said *Computers are the next big consumer market!* The result was a cultural as much as a technological revolution, responsible for new directions in hardware and software design, new audiences for computer use and programming, that characterize the modern computing landscape.

Among all of these changes, perhaps no element was more emblematic than the video game. As the first purely recreational use of computer hardware, video games represented a redefinition of what—and who—computers were really "for." A generation of programmers honed their software skills writing games; home users built their own computers in order to make and play games; entire companies were started in order to market games to a new audience of personal computer owners; and the needs of gaming (better and faster graphics and sound, input devices like the trackball and joystick, networked computing environments for head-to-head play) drove technological innovation in the computer industry. In a real sense, video games were the "killer app" that transformed the giant machines of the 1940s and 1950s into the sleek plastic boxes that currently can be purchased at Best Buy and brought home in the back seat of an SUV.

The earliest electronic computers, like the 40-ton ENIAC of World War II, used vacuum tubes to switch bits of binary data—the operation at the heart of all digital computers—on and off. But the tubes were large and hot, preventing them from being placed too closely together, which imposed a maximum size and power limit on the first generation of thinking machines. Technical advances over the next several years made it possible for computers to become much smaller, cooler, and faster. The vacuum tube begat the transistor, the transistor begat the integrated circuit (IC), and the integrated circuit begat the microprocessor. Each innovation packed more binary switches and logic gates into a smaller space, increasing computer power by orders of magnitude while reducing their physical "footprint." By the 1960s, a small cadre of minicomputers had emerged, taking up residence in college research labs and making inroads in the world of business. It was here, using the refrigerator-sized LINCs, PDP-8s, and VAXes, that an early generation of programmers began putting computers to recreational use, creating the first computer games and designing ever more elaborate graphical "hacks." Access to the minicomputers was generally guarded by a priesthood—an inner circle of authorized users who stood between the burgeoning population of enthusiasts and the machines that so fascinated them. Hackers engaged in a perpetual contest to gain access to the machines and run programs written in their spare time, outside the strictures of class assignments and business projects. In pushing against the priesthood's authority and the interdiction that computers were only for serious, public use, 60s hackers laid the groundwork for a computing culture that would truly be open to all comers—small, cheap, privatized computers.

In the early 1970s, the development of Intel's 8008 "computer on a chip"—thousands of logic circuits imprinted on a single piece of silicon—made it possible, for the first time, for home users to build computers for their own enjoyment. Yet none of the big companies like IBM and DEC that had dominated the 1960s seemed interested in exploiting the home market. This oversight can be attributed in part to a cultural misperception: a belief, possibly unconscious, that the values and passions of domestic space were incompatible with the institutional definition of computers as tools for large-scale, serious computation. While this was perhaps understandable given where computers had "evolved," it failed to take into account a generational logic by which those who had been teased with computers in the 1960s came into the 1970s ready to make such a thing happen. The first personal computers would come from hobbyists and fanatics, not from big corporations.

The first machine that can properly be called a personal computer, the MITS Altair 8800 released in 1975, may look primitive to us now, but it was by no means a simple device. Rather than spreading its processor demands across a flotilla of circuit boards, the Altair made use of Intel's single-chip microprocessor. It arrived not as a finished machine but a kit, a box of pieces that users had to assemble themselves—a laborious process that often took months and encouraged hobbyists to communicate with each other, pooling resources in order to answer questions and solve technical problems. Once assembled, the Altair had to be programmed through a tedious process of flicking individual switches, literally setting on/off registers in the computer's 256-byte memory. There was no storage capacity, so even the act of loading an operating system had to be performed anew each time the Altair was switched on. And there was no display, so the unit could only communicate through flashing the lights on its front panel. Nevertheless, the Altair was a success beyond anything its creators planned, eventually selling 10,000 units.[1]

The Altair is significant not just because it represents the first time computers had fallen within reach of the home user, but because the social and commercial trends it kicked off directly fed into the next phase of the personal computer explosion. The technically advanced community of Altair builders came together to form a grass roots organization known as the Homebrew movement. As other kit computers joined the marketplace, these groups found common ground in the Homebrew Computer Club, holding periodic meetings in which announcements were shared and technical problems solved. Homebrew also seeded an interest with many individuals who would go on to play integral roles in the personal computer's development, including a young Steve Wozniak, Paul Allen, and Bill Gates.

Without a doubt, the most significant year of the decade was 1977, which saw the launch of three separate machines—each different from the other in terms of technical capability, audience, and brand identity, but equally epochal. The Commodore PET was one of the first computers to incorporate a monitor, keyboard, and cassette-tape storage device in the same case as the motherboard (the board with all the computer chips on it). Pyramidal and white, PETs quickly began to appear in schoolrooms across America. The TRS-80 was the first computer to be sold by the ubiquitous, low-end hardware store Radio Shack. Developed by parent company Tandy, the TRS-80 packaged a combination keyboard/motherboard, a cassette storage unit, and a black-and-white display for $599. In its base configuration, it came with 4K of RAM (16 times that of the Altair 8800), which could be expanded to 16K or 48K for an additional cost. The TRS-80 was a best-seller, shipping 250,000 units[2] before its discontinuation in January 1981. However, Tandy's vanguard machine never lost its air of essential cheapness, and this, along with its affiliation with the little-respect Radio Shack, led many to dub it the "Trash-80."

1977 was also the year that the Apple II hit the market. Steve Jobs and Stephen Wozniak, two scruffy college kids who were part of the Homebrew culture, assembled the first Apple in a suburban California garage, selling their Volkswagen to finance the project. While the Apple I, in its wooden case, was built primarily to impress other hackers and hobbyists, its followup—the Apple II—was an immediate and unmitigated success, the first true personal computer and the first commercial blockbuster. By 1980, only three years after its introduction, Apple had become a billion-dollar company.

The Apple II's streamlined beige case contained a motherboard, keyboard, and expansion slots. Wozniak's clever engineering placed 6502 microprocessor at the heart of a complex circuit board that held a maximum of 48K of RAM. More significantly for home enthusiasts, the Apple II boasted a colorful display (both in blocky "lo-res" graphics and a separate "hi-res" mode). The problem faced by the Altair 8800 only a few years earlier, of limited memory and an almost completely inscrutable input-output scheme, was decisively resolved by the Apple II, whose open architecture and multiple expansions slots encouraged the home users' creation of software and hardware. The Apple II came with a programming language, Integer BASIC, prestored in ROM. The machine also shipped with reference manuals laying out every detail of the circuit board and ROM architecture. All of this contributed to a robust community of developers whose innovations supplied the Apple II with programs and peripherals to meet many needs.

What kinds of software did these early personal computers run? Overwhelmingly, the answer was video games. Machines like the Apple II were a gamer's dream, offering color graphics and sound capable of emulating the video games found in public arcades. Conversions of games such as *Space Invaders* and *Pac-Man* existed alongside embryonic versions of many of today's popular software genres, including flight simulators and even rudimentary first-person shooters. Even computers like the TRS-80, whose graphics were limited to the ASCII character set, thrived on a diet of text-based adventures. Other text-based games written for teletype terminals—titles like *Star Trek, Eliza, Hunt the Wumpus,* and *Colossal Cave Adventure*—found their way into homes through the publication of David H. Ahl's *Basic Computer Games* in 1978. Outside the world of gaming, Visicalc, an accounting spreadsheet, became the first "killer app" for the Apple II, serving both as a home tool to manage finances and as a business tool for companies brave enough to break with the minicomputer tradition and use microcomputers in the workplace. But it was video games that introduced the notion of the personal computer as a plaything and more importantly an interactive playmate: a logic that often motivated the computer's purchase by parents who saw in the machine a tool that would intrigue and entertain their children.

A large factor in the proliferation of video games, both legal and illegal, was the development of cheap, fast storage media. Ever since the days of punchcard storage, software had been copied and modified by one user after another, spreading virally throughout the technical community. Now a similar practice emerged, first around paper printouts of BASIC listings, then around electronic storage media. And here one of the personal computer's early limitations came into sharp relief. The first personal computers used audiocassette players and tapes to read and write programs to memory. The tape drives were slow and often unreliable. A faster alternative was the floppy disk drive, which wrote data onto flat floppy disks in plastic sleeves, 5 ¼ inches across. Though floppies had been in use for years as a storage medium for minicomputers, the Apple II was one of the first computers to make this mode of storage practical on a home budget, utilizing a controller card plugged into the motherboard. The TRS-80 and PET also featured floppy drives as expensive upgrades. Once a computer made the move to DOS (disk operating system), programs could be loaded and saved much more quickly and conveniently. Floppies also enabled software to be copied more efficiently, leading to a spread of shared software and the flourishing of piracy.

The troika of Apple, Commodore, and Tandy dominated the market throughout the late 1970s. As the decade turned, however, several competitors appeared. Texas Instruments, heretofore a maker of calculators, introduced a color computer called the TI-99/4a in 1979. Commodore offered a low-cost followup to the PET, the VIC-20, followed in 1982 by the Commodore 64, which went on to become the best-selling personal computer of the twentieth century. Also of note were the game-maker Atari's entries in the field, the Atari 400 and 800. Like the TI-99/4a, the Atari computers featured add-on slots for game cartridges, an alternative to floppies. All of the machines featured color graphics, sophisticated sound, and chip sets specialized for the delivery of dazzling audiovisuals, a sign of the important role played by video gaming in setting performance agenda.

But this crowded field thinned out with the introduction of two machines that quickly came to symbolize divergent trends in personal computer design. In 1981, IBM released its Personal Computer, effectively branding the letters "PC" for any machine working to IBM specifications and running an operating system known as PC-DOS. Initially too expensive to make inroads on the home market, the IBM PC proved successful as a low-end business machine. Significantly, the DOS operating system was sold under the name MS-DOS by its creator, the software company Microsoft, leading to a wave of PC clones—functionally equivalent computers released by different companies. Throughout the 1980s and 1990s, PCs and their descendents became a dominant sector of the personal computer market.

The other landmark computer launched at the time was Apple's Macintosh, released in 1984 amid an advertising campaign that stressed the Mac's difference from the PC. The Mac marked a major turn in Apple's philosophy of computer aesthetics and set forth a paradigm for the interface that profoundly shaped computer design from that point onward. Molded into an all-in-one unit of off-white plastic, the Mac comprised a black-and-white monitor and a 3.5-inch floppy drive. A keyboard connected to it, but the real innovation was a second device which attached to the keyboard: a small, square pointing device known as a mouse. The mouse was essentially a trackball, like that on the arcade game *Missile Command,* but turned on its belly: moving the mouse caused an arrow-shaped cursor to move on-screen. This was the key to the Macintosh's interface, an all-encompassing graphic environment modeled on the metaphor of a desktop, complete with folders and a trash can for deleting documents. Users could point and click objects on-screen—represented by icons—and drag them to new locations as though they were physical objects. The cartoonish, simple, almost toylike nature of the Mac interface was intended to make using the computer an easy, immediate experience (further demolishing the wall of expertise that so forbiddingly surrounded more complex machine surfaces) while hiding away the complex inner workings of machine language and program listings. The interface was also interesting for its indebtedness to gaming: the icons resembled avatars, and the visual layout of the desktop embodied a spatial metaphor very much like the on-screen worlds of video games.

Many of the Mac's features, which also included a suite of built-in applications like MacPaint and MacWrite, were later appropriated by other software designers. Despite Apple's protests and attempts to legally protect its designs, the WIMP interface (for windows-icon-menu-pointer) formed the core of other GUIs (graphical user interfaces). The greatest such "appropriation" was undoubtedly Microsoft's: In 1985, the company introduced Windows as a module for MS-DOS. It followed up with Windows 3.0 in 1990, Windows 95 and 98 in 1995 and 1998, respectively, Windows XP in 2001 and Windows Vista in 2006—amid a host of other versions targeted at both professional and home users. With each iteration, Windows became a more fully featured GUI and operating system, paralleling but never exactly mimicking the Macintosh OS. To this day, the Mac and PC worlds exist in a curious state of detente, establishing reluctant dialogue like two global superpowers, aware that they have to share the same planet but resisting, on a core level, each others' basic ideology.

Throughout the 1990s and into the first decades of the twenty-first century, the personal computer has continued to grow in capability and flexibility. In general, PCs have enjoyed access to a wider field of video game software, with the hardcore gaming community investing much time and money in building ever more powerful and elaborate "rigs"—often outfitted in neon-lit "case mods"—to showcase the latest games in both solo and multiplayer competition. The advent of the World Wide Web in the early 1990s and its exponential growth in the years that followed was a direct result of a broadly installed base of computers in the home, networked together over first phone lines, then cable—another medium in which gamers have thrived. The contemporary personal computer takes on many forms, from home-built PCs to all-in-one Macs to packages put together by companies such as Dell. In the roughly 30 years that personal computers have been in existence, they have continued to multiply in power—as measured by microprocessor complexity, memory and storage capacity, and graphics capability—and drop proportionately in price. The personal computers of today have long surpassed the monsters of yesteryear, and the trend does not seem destined to let up. As high-end computing machinery reaches casual home users, the cultural meaning of computers will continue to evolve, fitting ever more intimately into our daily existence.

CHAPTER 15

GENRE PROFILE: ADVENTURE GAMES

Mark J. P. Wolf

The adventure genre, what it is and what makes it unique, can be described as follows:

> Games which are set in a "world" usually made up of multiple connected rooms, locations, or
> screens, involving an objective which is more complex than simply catching, shooting, capturing,
> or escaping, although completion of the objective may involve several or all of these. Objectives
> usually must be completed in several steps, for example, finding keys and unlocking doors to other
> areas to retrieve objects needed elsewhere in the game. Characters are usually able to carry objects,
> such as weapons, keys, tools, and so on. Settings often evoke a particular historical time period and
> place, such as the Middle Ages or Arthurian England, or are thematically related to content-based
> genres such as science fiction, fantasy, or espionage. This term should not be used for games in
> which screens are only encountered in one-way linear fashion, like the "levels" in *Donkey Kong*,
> or for games like *Pitfall!*, which are essentially limited to running, jumping, and avoiding dangers.
> Nor should the term be used to refer to games like *Dragon's Lair*, *Gadget*, or *Star Trek: Borg*, which
> do not allow a player to wander and explore its world freely, but strictly limit outcomes and possible
> narrative paths to a series of video sequences and linear progression through a predetermined
> narrative.

Attempting to define the genre in such a way as to be distinct from other genres, it appears
that the game's world and the player's use and experience of it are at the core of the
adventure game. Many adventure games, while they have monsters and other characters
opposed to the player's character, often do not have an antagonist in the classic sense.
The game's world itself takes on that role, as players attempt to learn its geography and
the navigation of it, to gain access to its hidden, closed, and locked areas, and learn to
use the various objects and devices within it. Exploration, navigation, areas to which access
is initially withheld, and tool usage are found in many other genres, but in the adventure
genre they occupy a central position, and are often the sub-goals necessary to the achievement of the main objective; the discovery of how such sub-goals contribute to the overall
objective is itself also a part of the experience and essence of the adventure game.

The evolution of the Adventure genre, then, relied on the development of navigable
space (space is so crucial to the genre that solutions of adventure games are often referred
to as "walkthroughs"). In the mid-1970s, William Crowther, a computer programmer,

combined his interest in cave exploration and mapping, the role-playing game *Dungeons & Dragons*, and his background in programming to produce what would come to be known as the first computer game in the adventure genre, *Colossal Cave Adventure* (or sometimes just *Adventure*).[1] The all-text game consisted of descriptions of a series of connected rooms through which a player moved by typing responses such as "n" for "north" or "d" for "down." Several objects, like keys or a lamp, were also needed by the player during the game. The game's geography was based on Bedquilt Cave in Kentucky and mentions many of its features. The game's description of the cave and its layout was accurate enough that one first-time visitor to the cave was able to find her way around based solely on her knowledge of the game.[2] In 1976, programmer Don Woods found Crowther's program and with his blessing, expanded the program, adding fantasy touches influenced by the writings of J. R. R. Tolkien. From there the program was ported onto various computer systems and spread to universities and across computer networks.

Crowther and Woods's *Adventure* was the first in a long line of text adventure computer games, now referred to as "interactive fiction." These games are still being produced today, although no longer commercially.[3] The innovations introduced by text adventures, particularly the concepts of rooms joined together into a navigable space, characters with which one could have brief conversations or interactions, and objects (like keys) which gave players access to new areas, would soon revolutionize the related field of video games. Video games before 1977 consisted of single screens of graphics in which the action of the game took place. Kee Games's arcade game *Super Bug* was the first game to feature a screen that could scroll in all four directions, revealing off-screen space as it scrolled up and down, or right and left, but the space was still a single area, albeit one larger than the screen.

That same year, Warren Robinett developed the first graphical adventure game for the Atari 2600, also called *Adventure*. After playing Crowther and Woods's *Adventure* at Stanford, Robinett decided that it could work as a home video game and took on the challenge of translating such a game into a 4096-byte Atari cartridge, a task that Robinett's boss at Atari thought was impossible. Various problems that had to be solved included how to represent such aspects as rooms and their connectedness, usable objects that could be carried around, picked up, and dropped, and autonomous creatures that could be encountered during gameplay.[4]

Released in 1979, *Adventure* featured 30 interconnected screens that used the cinematic convention of cutting one to the next rather than scrolling, making it the first video game to use multiple screens. The game also had "disjoint regions" which the player could only access with the use of certain tools (the keys to open castle gates, and the bridge to pass into walled areas), and even off-screen actions the player could encounter later (for example, the bat could pick up and drop objects while the player was elsewhere). The game was far more sophisticated and detailed than any of the other home video games available at the time and a commercial success as well, selling over a million copies at $25 each.[5]

Robinett's *Adventure,* while not a literal translation of Crowther and Woods's program, successfully did bring the format of the adventure game to video games. Robinett's work was followed by other graphical adventure games for the Atari 2600, many of which brought further innovations to the idea of a graphical navigable space. *Superman* (1979) featured a subway that was entered from doorways located near the center of the screen rather than at its edge, like *Adventure*'s castle gates, and the subway screens, when exited, could not be reached by going back the way you came, resulting in one-way connections between screens. *Haunted House* (1981) had staircases (in top view) which connected identical looking floors that differed in color, so that the player-character did not disappear and reappear elsewhere but stayed visible in place while the screen changed behind it. *Raiders of the Lost Ark* (1981) mixed top-view screens with side-view screens of its mesas depending on the action occurring and also had an inventory strip at the bottom of the screen and 13 different objects that could be picked up and used. *Venture* (1982) showed its scenery at two different scales, depending on where the player was; the four rooms of the game appear together on one screen while the player is outside them, but each room is shown on a full screen, with its interior visible, as soon as the player enters. *E.T.: The Extraterrestrial* (1982), *Krull* (1983), *Dark Chambers* (1988), and the *Swordquest* series of games also featured variations on the way their spaces were depicted and connected, although all of them relied on cutting from screen to screen, or two-way scrolling.

In 1980, Richard Garriot's computer game *Ultima* was the first home computer game to feature scrolling in both horizontal and vertical directions, resulting in a very large playing field of which only a portion was seen at once. *Ultima*'s four-way scrolling screen technique, using tiled graphics which were added or removed from the edges of the screen as it scrolled, was developed by Garriot with his friend Ken Arnold, who was one of the programmers that developed the computer game *Rogue* the same year (*Rogue* was another adventure game with a graphical display made of ASCII characters; for example, the player's character was represented by an "@" that could be moved around the screen).

From the late 1970s and throughout the 1980s, adventure games generally fell into two camps: graphical adventure games and text adventure games. The first, represented mainly by home video games, relied mainly on graphics that had an on-screen character the player could control and spaces that were navigated graphically. The graphics were simple, and often mixed perspectives, showing the playing field itself in top view, while the characters and objects were shown in side view (the practice of mixed perspectives existed long before video games, and appeared in a variety of places including maps, medieval drawings, and chess diagrams). What the games lacked in visual richness and narrative depth they attempted to make up for in direct, on-screen action which was more immediate than verbal descriptions and typed responses.

The other type of adventure game, the text adventure or interactive fiction described above, relied on words for description and interaction, which enabled it to have much larger worlds with hundreds of room and character responses, although the player's inter-action with the world was more indirect, even if it was more in-depth conceptually. From 1980 onward, beginning with Roberta Williams's *Mystery House,* these games began to include graphics which acted as illustrations for the game's text. Although very low resolu-tion by today's standards, these illustrations were much more detailed than the typical graphical adventure games of the time, but they were for the most part little more than slides in a slide show with which players could not directly interact. These images did introduce a first-person perspective into the games, which helped to engage the player more and compensate for the lack of a graphical user interface.

The reason for the bifurcation of the adventure genre is due mainly to the technologies of home video game systems versus home computers during the late 1970s and 1980s. Home computers (like the Apple II) had keyboards and could display more text, and they had more memory, which allowed for more detailed graphics and a larger world, while home video game systems (like the Atari 2600) had smoother movement and were capable of fast action.

Advances in graphics display standards also made better quality graphics possible. Prior to 1984, the CGA (color graphics adaptor) standard, which allowed image resolutions of 320 by 200 pixels with a four-color palette (or 620 by 200 with a two-color palette), was used by DOS computers for graphic displays. Such harsh graphical restrictions made representational imagery difficult, and it was not until the 1984 release of the EGA (enhanced graphics adaptor) standard, which allowed image resolutions of 640 by 350 with 16 supported colors from a 64-color palette, that images began to dominate the screen in what were still mainly text-based adventure games. In 1987 graphics improved again when the VGA (video graphics array) standard appeared with images of 640 by 480 pixels and a 256-color palette. Later, SVGA (super VGA) would increase image resolution to 800 by 600 pixels. Figure 15.1 shows examples of three different graphics standards: the top screen, from *Déjà Vu 1: A Nightmare Comes True* (1985) is CGA; the center screen, from *King's Quest III: To Heir is Human* (1986) is EGA; and the bottom screen, from *Mean Streets* (1989) is VGA.

During the 1980s, and especially after the appearance of the graphical user interface, home computer adventure games began to add features originally found in console video games, making them less like the early all-text adventures. Roberta Williams's *King's Quest* (1984) introduced the idea of the animated walking character that walked over the background graphics, and *King's Quest III: To Heir is Human* had a clock on the titlebar (see the second screenshot in Figure 15.1), with events occurring at specific times, adding an element of time pressure to the game. ICOM Simulations, Inc.'s *Déjà Vu 1: A Nightmare Comes True* had an inventory box (see the first screenshot in Figure 15.1), similar to video games like *Raiders of the Lost Ark* for the Atari 2600. It also was one of the earliest home computer games to use a mouse and cursor, giving it point-and-click capability similar to home video games using joysticks with firing buttons, although it used point-and-clicking mainly for the selecting of objects from an inventory window or choices from a menu, rather than avatar control or spatial navigation. Despite these advances, however, the images used in many of these games were still more or less illustrations of what was essentially still text-based interaction.

A more user-friendly and graphically oriented interface came in 1987 with the introduction of the SCUMM (script creation utility for *Maniac Mansion*) engine written by Ron Gilbert and Aric Wilmunder of Lucasfilm Games (now LucasArts). Used (and named) for the game *Maniac Mansion* (1987), the engine was described in detail in the game's manual:

> The large top portion, The Animation Window, is the largest part of the screen where the animated world of the mansion is displayed. It shows the "camera's eye view" of the room that the currently active character is in. The Sentence Line is directly below the Animation Window. You use this line to construct sentences that tell the characters what to do. . . . Each character has his or her own Inventory. It is empty at the beginning of the game; the name of an object is added to a character's Inventory when the character picks the object up during game play. There is no limit to the number of objects a character can carry. You may need to scroll up or down to see all items in your inventory. . . . To move a character around, select "Walk to" from the Verbs by positioning your cursor over it and clicking. Then move your cursor into the Animation Window, point it where you want the character to go, and click. If you point to an open door and click, the character will walk through it.[6]

Lucasfilm Games would go on to use the SCUMM engine (and updated versions of it) for their games into the 1990s (see Figure 15.2). Although characters could be directed by

Figure 15.1 Examples of different graphics standards: CGA (top), EGA (center), and VGA (bottom). Even in these black and white reproductions, differences in spatial resolution and color resolution show the improvements from one standard to another.

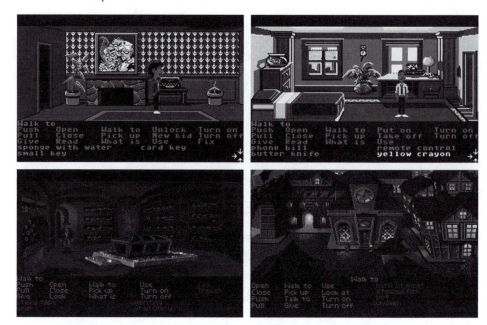

Figure 15.2   An advancement in interactivity. Examples of Lucasfilm Games using the SCUMM engine, *Maniac Mansion* **(1987) (top left),** *Zak McKracken and the Alien Mindbenders* **(1988) (top right),** *Indiana Jones and the Last Crusade* **(1989) (bottom left), and** *The Secret of Monkey Island* **(1990) (bottom right).**

clicking in the "Animation Window," the interface did not allow direct avatar control, as was found in even the earliest home video games, but it did provide, along with cut-scenes, on-screen action that the earlier graphically illustrated games lacked. After the release of the Nintendo Entertainment System (NES) in 1985, home video game systems had improved to the point where home computer games could be ported to them, resulting in the cross-platform release of many home computer adventure titles. Likewise, more adventure titles were originating in home console systems, such as the *Legend of Zelda* series, which first appeared on the NES in 1987.

As the 1990s began, many cross-platform games were available, and after the appearance of VGA a number of early games were rereleased with updated graphics (see Figure 15.3), especially those which were a part of ongoing series (1990 and 1991, for example, saw the rerelease of *King's Quest I* along with *King's Quest V, Space Quest I* along with *Space Quest IV,* and *Leisure Suit Larry I* along with *Leisure Suit Larry V*).

After 1987, an increasing number of games began to be released on CD-ROM (beginning with Rand and Robyn Miller's *The Manhole* in 1987) for both home computers and home console games, like the NEC Turbografx-CD expansion for the Turbografx-16 console system, and later CD-ROM game systems from Sega, Sony, and Nintendo. Adventure games, because they featured navigable environments, typically needed more memory than single-screen or scrolling-screen games, and the CD-ROM, at roughly 650 megabytes, encouraged the use of better graphics, better sound, and even integrated video clips.[7] Advances in computer animation meant more photorealistic graphics, and full-motion video (FMV) began appearing in games, beginning with Trilobyte's spring 1992 release,

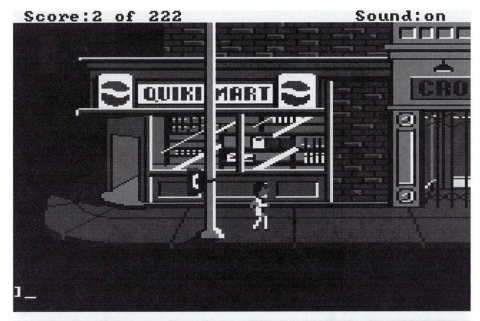

Figure 15.3   The Quiki-Mart in 1987 and 1991. Two incarnations of The Quiki-Mart from the original 1987 version (top) and 1991 update (bottom) of *Leisure Suit Larry 1: Leisure Suit Larry in the Land of the Lounge Lizards.*

The 7th Guest, which was over a gigabyte in size (due to its video clips), and the first CD-ROM game to require two discs.

In September 1993, another game was released which would surpass *The 7th Guest* as the best-selling game of all time; Rand and Robyn Miller's *Myst*. *Myst* brought with it new twists on familiar ideas, innovating and developing existing traditions and conventions of the adventure genre, especially in regard to creating an integrated and seamless experience for the player. Like *Maniac Mansion,* the player's character cannot die in *Myst,* keeping players from being ejected from the game before they want to leave. Graphically, *Myst* is designed to keep players as much within the diegesis (the world in which the story takes place) as possible. This is in keeping with the development of the adventure genre; whereas many early games featured nondiegetic (outside of the story world) informational graphics, such as explanatory text, titlebars with score counters and clocks, inventory boxes or lists, and lists of response choices, later games had an increasing amount of emphasis placed on the image, which directly linked the player into the diegesis. *Myst* would eliminate almost all nondiegetic informational graphics, containing all its player interaction within the image, with objects held by the cursor (like the pages or the match) and only one object held at a time, so that no inventory box was needed (although *Riven* and *Myst III: Exile* would represent the books a player was holding as icons below the screen). The few informational graphics *Myst* did have were integrated directly into the diegesis itself, for example, the map on the wall in the library, the backstory text in the books found on the bookshelf, the note lying on the grass, and so on. *Myst* also had to overcome the sometimes slow loading times of early CD-ROM drives and did so by reducing its images to around 57 Kb each and reducing its sounds to 8 bits, 11 kHz. The separation into various ages also gave the game natural breaks. A transitional sound effect and cinematic fade-out and fade-in helped to retain the continuity of the experience which could have been ruined by the "Loading..." screens sometimes found in other games. [By the time of *realMYST* in 2000 and *Uru: Ages Beyond Myst* in 2003, loading would again take awhile, and bars showing the progress of the load would briefly (and occasionally not-so-briefly) appear on the bottom of the screen.]

Exploration and navigation play an important role in *Myst.* In most games before *Myst,* the areas of the game were one at a time, with entrances and exits indicated on the screen, and only by moving screen to screen could a sense of the game's geography and layout be obtained. Examples of this would include moving from chamber to chamber in a cave system, or room to room in a house, or simply from one game location to another, with a minimal sense of the spatial connection between locations. Occasionally there might be a locked room or blocked passageway that could be opened and explored later, once a key was found, or monster guardian killed, or some other condition fulfilled that granted access. *Myst*'s approach to geography was quite different. As Myst Island and each of the game's images were computer-generated models, the resulting game images could be staged in depth; one could see locations in the distance that might be several moves away, and the same objects and locations could be viewed from different angles and directions (some of these ideas appeared to a lesser degree in the Miller Brothers's 1989 game *Cosmic Osmo*). Likewise, the background ambience also changed gradually from one location to another; near the shore, the sound of the waves lapping was louder, but as the player moved up the hill the sound of the waves grew fainter while the sound of the wind grew stronger. The result was an experience of deep, integrated three-dimensional space which was less segmented and isolated, inviting the player inward into the world and pulling the player's curiosity in multiple directions simultaneously.

Nor were *Myst*'s puzzles standalone and isolated, as they were in other games; instead, they were set into the game's geography and intermixed in such a way that it would not be clear at first which clues went with which puzzles (and one could encounter and solve them in any order), and the sorting and connecting of these clues added another layer

Company Profile:
Electronic Arts

Alison McMahan

Electronic Arts (EA) (originally known as Amazin' Software) was started in 1982 by Trip Hawkins, a veteran of the earliest days at Apple Computer, with an unusual goal: to make stars out of its computer game designers. For example, game boxes were designed as colorfully as album covers and game designers were named and promoted in the marketing. He attracted key talent and in their first year they published three now-classics: *Hard Hat Mack* (1983), *Archon* (1983), and *Pinball Construction Set* (1983).

Console game makers, starting with Nintendo in the mid-1980s, began to approach EA about designing games for their consoles. But Hawkins found their licensing structure oppressive and did not think the 8-bit consoles were powerful enough for EA games. By the late 1980s, EA worked out a favorable licensing deal with Sega and in 1990 released *Populous, Budokan: The Martial Spirit,* and *Zany Golf* for the Genesis. Their Genesis version of *John Madden Football* (Hawkins was the first to license star athletes' images for his games) was phenomenally successful. Hawkins's innovative sales strategy entailed selling directly to retailers, something no other game developer had done. Within 12 years, Hawkins's initial investments of $200,000 had grown into a billion-dollar business.[8] Hawkins left Electronic Arts in 1991 to form 3DO, leaving Larry Probst, who had originally joined the company in 1984 as vice president for sales, as chairman and CEO of EA.

Following Hawkins's departure, the company took a new direction with EA making exclusive deals for sports licenses with the NFL, ESPN, the Collegiate Licensing Company (for college football content), and NASCAR. EA now has exclusivity on so many sports franchises that critics contend that the quality of sports video games as a whole is dropping due to reduced competition.

EA's innovative treatment of game designers evolved to a Draconian work policy in which employees were expected to work 80-hour weeks (9 a.m. to 10 p.m. seven days a week), even during non-crunch time, without additional compensation. As a result, game artists brought a class-action lawsuit in 2004 which was settled for $15.6 million,[9] and many of the lower-level artists are now working at an hourly rate. A similar suit brought by programmers in 2006 was settled for $14.9 million.[10]

EA is most often criticized for its lack of support and follow-through on its own games, especially from European players, and for forcing current players to pay full price for the next upgrade, without which continued play is impossible.[11] Nevertheless, at the end of 2005, EA was one of the world's largest third-party publishers, best known for its EA Sports label, games based on popular movie licenses and games from long-running franchises like *Need for Speed, Medal of Honor,* and *The Sims.* In its original tradition of supporting creativity, EA supports the Game Innovation Lab at the University of Southern California.

of enigmas. An understanding of the game's geography was also crucial, not just for navigation as it was in most other games, but for the solving of the puzzles themselves (an idea which would also be central to the *Rhem* series of games). A grasp of the layout of the islands is needed to comprehend the puzzles involving alignment, both visually (as in Myst Island's map and rotating tower) or aurally (as in the Selenitic Age's dish antennas which had to be aligned to the transmitters of various sounds around the island). These ideas would appear in the later games of the series as well, for example, *Riven's* map room on Survey Island or the rotating pentagonal room on Temple Island, or *Exile's* rotating reflectors which reflect a beam of light around the island, the rotating plant which picks up sounds depending on where it is aimed, or the cameras that must be aligned with the symbols found on other parts of the island.

Myst's puzzles also used geography in another way. Often the machinery used to power other machines or to gain access to new places was spread out over different locations, rather than being localized in a single place, making the connection of cause and effect, or even an understanding of what the player needed to do, more difficult to figure out. Power lines, pipes, gear systems, and so forth stretched consequences of actions out across the landscape, requiring the player to move about the island to see where they led. (Some connections, like those between the sunken ship in the harbor and the sunken ship model in the fountain, or the large gears and the small gears in the clock tower, did not have visible physical connectors like wires or pipes, but rather symbolic connectors that relied on visual resemblance.) These ideas as well would be further elaborated on in later games, especially *Riven,* where physical connections and symbolic connections would extend between islands as well as across them.

While *Myst's* innovations set new standards for the adventure genre and inspired a number of games that followed, including such games as *The Lighthouse* (1996), *Rhem, Rhem 2* (2005), and *Alida* (2004), as well as *Myst's* own sequels, *Riven, Myst III: Exile* (2001), *Uru: Ages Beyond Myst, Myst IV: Revelation* (2004), and *Myst V: End of Ages* (2005). Other games like those in the *Shenmue, Tomb Raider,* and *Grand Theft Auto* series included developed narratives with cut-scenes and interacting characters and three-dimensional worlds that the player moved through in real time, unlike the still images of the earlier games. Nonplayer-characters in the games became more interactive, due to a degree of artificial intelligence programming that responded to the player-character's actions.

Finally, alongside the single-player games mentioned above, MMORPGs took the adventure genre in a new direction, with large, persistent (24 hours a day, 7 days a week) worlds that featured hundreds of thousands of players within them. As descendents of the multiplayer online text adventure games from the mid-1980s (like the 16-player *Sceptre of Goth*), these games offer an experience so different from single-player adventure games that they arguably constitute their own genre; they are an extension and development of the worlds developed in the single player adventure games whose history is described above. Many single-player games have also incorporated elements from other genres and influenced the design of their game worlds. Due to such overlapping, the boundaries of the adventure genre have become rather blurred, but we can still ask whether the exploration, navigation, and tool use so central to the genre are present in a game's main focus, as these will always remain at the heart of the adventure genre.

CHAPTER 16

ARCADE GAMES OF THE 1980S

Mark J. P. Wolf

By the end of the 1970s, video games had become the main type of game found in arcades. Arcade video games of the time had graphics that were two dimensional, and many were still black and white or monochrome (a single color). Those games that were color generally featured brightly colored figures on a black background and were typically space-themed shooting games or sports games with an overhead view (blue backgrounds for some sky and sea shooting games). Shooting games typically featured shooting on the vertical axis, and unlike home video games, most arcade games positioned their monitors vertically, so the video image was taller than it was wide. Namco's *Galaxian* was the first game to have 100 percent of its graphics in RGB color (a standard used for color video using red, green, and blue signals), and by the end of the 1980s virtually all games would be full color. Raster graphics would become the standard, and the mid-1980s would see the end of arcade games using vector graphics (see Chapter 12, "Vector Games"). Many of the ideas behind vector games would appear in raster games; for example, Venture Line's *Space Force* (1980) was basically a raster version of Atari's *Asteroids* (1979), in which the player must blast away objects floating around the player's ship while avoiding crashing into them.

According to *Play Meter* magazine, by 1981 there were 24,000 full arcades, 400,000 street locations, and 1.5 million arcade video games in operation.[1] The 1980s would be the decade that the video game would come of age, bridging the gap between the simpler, two-dimensional games of the 1970s and the more detailed and three-dimensional graphics of the 1990s. During the 1980s, many conventions of video games would become established, allowing players to be familiar with games they had never played before, due to their similarity to other games. While the 1970s produced some hit games like *PONG, Space Invaders,* and *Asteroids,* the next decade would cement video games' position as a commercial success and a cultural force. By 1980, arcade games were well established but were now finding competition from other gaming industries; home console games, home computer games, and even handheld computer games, which threatened to keep players home from the arcade and forced arcade games to offer unique experiences that home games could not provide.

The decade opened with many games inspired by *Space Invaders* and *Galaxian,* many of which were nearly identical in design and gameplay (in fact, several were actual bootleg versions of the games, released in other countries). The 1980s also saw its own trends in games; many wrestling games and racing games, and during Olympic years, Olympic sports games. In Japan, dozens of Mahjong games appeared, though these were not as popular in the United States. The popular games of the early 1980s, among them *Pac-Man, Defender, Frogger* (1981) and *Donkey Kong* (1981), also had many imitators in the years following their appearance. *Pac-Man* and *Defender,* in fact, would go on to earn over a billion dollars each.[2] Games of the decade, then, would represent a careful balance between innovation and imitation, as each company tried to produce the next hit game that would be different yet familiar enough to attract a large number of players.

The Early 1980s (1980–1982)

Probably the best-known game of the 1980s was *Pac-Man* (discussed in detail in Chapter 13, "Video Game Stars: Pac-Man"). *Pac-Man* was one of the early great crossover games, a nonviolent game that appealed to both men and women and a wide range of age groups, and perhaps the game that attracted the most newcomers to the arcade and brought public notice to video games in general. It was released in Japan in 1979, and in North America in 1980.

Other popular games of 1980 were Williams's *Defender* and Atari's *Missile Command,* both variations on the standard shooting game which purported to be defensive rather than offensive, in an attempt to justify the games' violence. In *Defender,* the player had to rescue astronauts while shooting at enemy ships, while in *Missile Command* players shot down incoming missiles, protecting three bases at the bottom of the screen. *Defender* and another game of 1980, Atari's *Battlezone,* would be the first to depict off-screen events that the player had to monitor in order to be successful in the game. *Battlezone* showed enemies approaching the player from behind on a radarscope on the side of the screen, while *Defender* depicted off-screen events in miniature in a box at the top of the screen, alerting the player as to what was coming or what remained to be done.

Atari's *Battlezone* was also the first video game that generated a 3-D polygon-based environment, and one of the early ones with a first-person perspective.[3] Game events took place in front of and around the player, who was situated in the center of the playing field.A version of *Battlezone* known as the "Bradley Trainer" was produced for the military, who planned to use the game for tank training.

Other innovative games of 1980 included a variety of advances in video game hardware and software. Three games, Stern's *Berzerk,* Taito's *Stratovox,* and Karateco's *Taskete,* included synthesized speech among their sound effects. Cinematronics's *Star Castle* featured moving enemy mines that could home in on the player's ship. Another new device that added time pressure to a game was the idea of limited resources. In Universal's *Space Panic* (a platform game) the player had a limited amount of oxygen, Nichibutsu's *Moon Alien Part 2* had an energy bar timer, and Sidam's *Condor,* an Italian bootleg of Centuri's *Phoenix,* was the first shooting game to feature a fuel system with a fuel gauge that would limit the game's playing time. Midway's *Rally-X,* a racing game, also had a fuel supply bar, and had four-way scrolling similar to Kee Games's *Super Bug,* which implied a large plain of racetrack of which the player was seeing only a small portion at a time (*Ultima,* 1980, was the first home computer game with four-way scrolling). One last game from 1980 worth noting is *Radar Scope,* a submarine game which did not do well commercially but was the Nintendo Company's first entry into the U.S. arcade video game market released under the Nintendo name.

Nintendo did find success with a game they released in 1981. *Donkey Kong* became one of the year's hit games, and the game's "Jumpman" character, later given the name Mario, became the symbol of the Nintendo Company itself. Other popular games of 1981 included Sega's *Frogger,* Namco's *Galaga,* Konami's *Scramble,* Exidy's *Venture,* Taito's abstract game *Qix,* and Midway's *Ms. Pac-Man* (a strange title; why not *Pac-Woman?*). The use of synthesized speech was growing and could be found in several games, including Century Electronics's *Space Fortress* and Sega's *Space Fury,* and one game, Pacific Novelty's *Shark Attack,* even used a cassette tape loop of recorded screams as a sound effect. Gottlieb's *Caveman* was their first and only pinball and video game hybrid machine, an experimental combination of the two types of games. Electro Sport's *Quarter Horse,* a horse racing game, was the first video game to incorporate a laserdisc, though its video imagery was not interactive; players bet on horses on one screen and watched the races on another. Sega's *Eliminator* was a rare, four-player vector graphics game.

In the area of game design, Exidy's *Venture* and Centuri's *Route 16* both featured games whose spaces alternated between maps showing large areas and close-ups of those areas that were displayed when the player entered them, an innovation that helped players keep track of where they were in spaces that, when seen at full resolution, were much larger than the screen. Other games, including Exidy's *Mousetrap,* Centuri's *Loco-Motion,* and Nihon Bussan's *Lock 'N' Chase* were variations on maze games, following the popularity of *Pac-Man.* Finally, the competition between game companies resulted in some hidden references within at least one game of the time. Williams produced *Stargate,* a sequel to *Defender* which is sometimes known as *Defender II,* which featured enemies named "The Irata" and "Yllabian Space Guppies," which were Williams's competitors' (Atari and Bally) names spelled backwards.

The year 1981 also saw the appearance of Atari's *Warlords, Tempest,* and *Centipede* (the first arcade game designed by a woman, Dona Bailey), all three of which it would later try to port to its VCS 2600 home console.[4] Whereas *Asteroids, Warlords, Battlezone, Centipede,* and a number of Atari's other arcade games did come out in home versions, *Tempest* never made it beyond the prototype stage. Part of the reason was that vector games had to be adapted into raster versions before they could appear on the 2600, and games like *Tempest* in which objects were continually being resized did not adapt well at all. *Battlezone,* which did appear as an Atari 2600 cartridge, only did so in a much changed form. Throughout the 1980s, the growing popularity and number of home game systems had an interesting effect on the production of arcade games; the arcade games had to be able to provide an experience that could not be found in home games, usually that of fast action and better graphics, yet arcade titles might see less profit if they could not eventually be ported to home systems.

The ease with which cartridge systems could change games was something arcade owners did not have. In 1981, game company Data East introduced the DECO Cassette System, which allowed new games to be uploaded into an arcade cabinet from tape cassettes. The magnetic tapes, however, proved to be unreliable and easily demagnetized, and the games released on the tapes were not popular. The system met with some success in Japan but was a failure in the United States, and after producing around 40 games for the DCS, Data East ended it in 1985. Other systems, like Sega's Convert-a-Game, saved the price of a new cabinet, but was still expensive due to the replacing of the printed circuit board which contained the game.

In 1982 a variety of games were being produced. Among the usual science fiction shooting games like Irem's *Moon Patrol,* Atari's *Space Duel,* and Williams's *Robotron: 2084,* there were games like Bally/Midway's *BurgerTime,* which involved the building of hamburgers, and Sega's *Pengo,* the title character of which was a little penguin who pushed ice blocks around. Both games revealed game design possibilities outside of the typical activities of shooting and getting shot at.

Atari had several games of note that year. *Dig Dug* featured characters that dug the paths they wandered through, *Joust* had flying, jousting knights which alternated between cooperative and competitive play, *Quantum* was an abstract game inspired by particle physics, and *Pole Position* (made by Namco, but released by Atari in the United States) had sprite-based scaling foreground and background objects which gave the racing game a three-dimensional feel even though it did not involve any real 3-D computation.

Other games of the year included Gottlieb's *Q*bert,* Centuri's *Time Pilot,* which featured enemies taken from different time periods from 1910 (biplanes) to 2001 (UFOs), and Cinematronics's *Jack the Giantkiller,* which had six different screens or stages that the main character Jack had to pass through to complete the game, each from a different part of the story *Jack and the Beanstalk* on which it was based. Two games were tie-ins to movies, Nintendo's *Popeye* (1980) and Bally/Midway's *Tron* (1982), which actually outgrossed the movie it was based upon.

But many of the games released in 1982 were sequels, including *Baby Pac-Man, Pac-Man Plus, Super Pac-Man, Donkey Kong Jr., Missile Command 2, Frenzy* (a sequel to *Berzerk*), and *Millipede* (a sequel to *Centipede*). Although innovative games would continue to appear throughout the mid-1980s, the presence of so many sequels suggests that the industry was beginning to rely more on the familiarity of past hits. And by late 1982, signs of stagnation began to appear in the arcade video game industry.

The Crash and Afterward (1983–1985)

While the number of video game arcades more than doubled from 1980 to 1982, reaching a peak of about 10,000 arcades, over 2,000 would close in 1983.[5] In the two years that followed, the video game industry would undergo a crash (see Chapter 18, "The Video Game Industry Crash"). During the mid-1980s, the arcade industry would try to reinvent itself and reorganize, but the times and technology were changing, and the arcade would never be the same again. Around 1983 and 1984, one attempt to rejuvenate the industry came in the form of laserdisc games (see Chapter 17, "Laserdisc Games") the best known of which was probably Cinematronics's *Dragon's Lair* (1983), but laserdisc games proved to be twice as expensive as other games and failed to live up to the hype surrounding them.

Another game of 1983 introduced a technology that would eventually find great success, but was well ahead of its time. Atari's *I, Robot* was the first raster-graphics arcade video game to use filled polygons and true three-dimensionally generated graphics, both of which represented the direction most games would go in the 1990s and beyond (another game, Sega's *Subroc-3D,* was 3-D in that it delivered different images to each eye; but it had sprite-based graphics). *I, Robot* featured a somewhat abstract setting in which the player controlled a robot that had to move around a blocky, 3-D structure, turning the surface it passed over from blue to red. The game also featured the first camera controls that allowed the player to view the action from different angles, and a "doodle" mode outside of the game. But in 1983, the three-dimensional graphics were too new and confusing to players, and the game was unfortunately a financial failure, discouraging any more experimentation in that direction for years to come.

Other important games of the mid-1980s included Atari's *Crystal Castles* (1983) and *Star Wars* (1983) (a vector game based on the film), Atari Games's *Gauntlet* (1985) (which had an interactive environment that multiple players could experience simultaneously (see Chapter 11, "System Profile: The Atari Video Computer System [VCS]," for the difference between Atari and Atari Games), Irem's platform game *Lode Runner* (1984), Capcom's *Ghosts 'N Goblins* (1985), Gottlieb's *Q*bert* (1982), and Nintendo's *Mario Bros.* (1983), *Punch-Out!!* (1984), and *Super Mario Bros.* (1985). After Pac-Man, the title character of *Q*bert* was one of the more popular and most merchandised characters, with a board game, card game, action figures, plush figure, lunchbox, books and coloring books, wristwatch game, wastepaper can, and even a short-lived TV show. But on the whole, the period of 1983 to 1985 saw few hit games produced, and a large number of sequels hoping to cash in on their predecessors' successes: *Discs of Tron* (1983), *Donkey Kong 3* (1983), *Jr. Pac-Man* (1983), *Pac & Pal* (1983), *Pac-Man & Chomp Chomp* (1983), *Pole Position II* (1983), *Professor Pac-Man* (1983), *Galaga 3* (1984), *Pac-Land* (1984), *Return of the Jedi* (1984), *Dig Dug II* (1985), *Pitfall II: The Lost Caverns* (1985), *Return of the Invaders* (1985), and *Super Punch-Out!!* (1985). While game designers retrenched in an effort to find something new, game producing companies turned to game hardware in an attempt to revive the industry and cut costs.

The Late 1980s (1985–1989)

One way arcade game companies tried to improve business was to become more sensitive to the needs of arcade operators, who leased the games. To a small extent, the games were already customizable. Arcade games often came with DIP (dual in-line parallel) switches that would let operators set some game parameters like difficulty levels, the number of points needed for extra lives, the number of players, the number of quarters the game would charge players per play, and so forth. During the 1980s, some interesting use of these switches was made; for example, GAT's *Dambusters* (1981) had a DIP switch that could filter out swear words that players might leave on high-score tables on the game. A 1983 game, Bally/Midway's *Domino Man,* had a DIP switch that could set the skin color of the game's main character to either black or white, depending on what the operator thought would be better for business. Other games, like Toaplan's *Demon's World* (1989) had DIP switches to change between an English title screen and a Japanese one, or change the game's legal warnings or licensing information for different regions.[6] Midway's *Mortal Kombat* (1992) would even use DIP switch settings to set the level of violence and blood displayed in the game's graphics, and a 1998 game, *Dead or Alive++,* a fighting game with buxom female fighters, had an operator control which could turn "breast bounce" on or off.

But as players got tired of games, income fell, and replacing arcade games was not only expensive but cumbersome, since the typical standalone upright cabinets were about the size of refrigerators. Data East's DECO Cassette System had seemed like a good idea, but its tapes were neither as durable nor as reliable as arcade operators had hoped.

Home consoles were advancing and narrowing the gap between arcade games and home video game systems, and the Nintendo Entertainment System helped close the gap. In 1985, Nintendo began using its "Vs. System" (also known as the UniSystem [single-player games] or DualSystem [for two-player head-to-head games]). The system was a version of the NES with some additional arcade game hardware. Many of the games had two video screens, one above the other; one screen for text and game instructions and the other for the actual gameplay. Some NES home video games were ported to arcade machines, perhaps the first time that games from a home system were adapted into arcade games.

Almost all of the Nintendo "Vs. System" games ran on the same hardware and used the same controls, so games could be changed simply by changing their circuit boards. The following year Nintendo released the PlayChoice system, which had games on extension cards that plugged into the main circuit board of the game and allowed players to choose from up to 10 different games in the same cabinet. (Although the games were NES games, the cartridges from the NES were not compatible with the arcade game hardware.) Other companies also developed their own arcade game systems, including Atari Games's Atari System 1 in 1986, Capcom's CP System 1 in 1988, SNK's Neo•Geo MVS in 1989, and Sega's Mega Tech System in 1989. These interchangeable systems also changed the look of arcade games; because a variety of different games would use the same cabinet, the cabinets were often bland and lacked the colorful artwork that appeared on dedicated cabinets.

An industry-wide standard for interchangeable hardware was also in place by the mid-1980s. With the decline of Atari and the rise of Nintendo, Japan became a center of video game production, and in 1982 the Japanese Arcade Machine Manufacturers' Association (JAMMA) was founded. Around 1985, JAMMA introduced a wiring standard for arcade machines, known as the JAMMA conversion class, which would become the main one used in Japan for the next decade or so, and many American game companies also conformed to this standard. All games using the JAMMA standard could be converted from one to the other by changing the printed circuit boards inside. These standards also have been helpful to arcade video game collectors, who can plug a large variety of printed circuit boards (PCBs) of games into the same cabinet, so long as the cabinet uses the JAMMA standard.

While the arcade systems kept arcade operators from the expense of having to buy new cabinets, some game companies limited the lifespan of their games through the use of what are now referred to as "suicide batteries." Presumably installed to fight piracy, these batteries supplied power to a small amount of RAM which holds a decryption key. The decryption key is used to decode the program code in the game's ROM, so when the battery dies, the RAM is erased, and with out the decryption key, the game can no longer run. Several companies used suicide batteries in their arcade games, the largest two being Sega, who began using them around 1987, and Capcom, whose system used them from 1989 onward.[7]

In the late 1980s, the industry failed to return to the heights of its glory days before the crash. Fewer games were produced that are today acknowledged as classics, but there were some, including Sega's *Outrun* (1986), Bally/Midway's *Rampage* (1986), Taito's *Arkanoid* (1986), *Bubble Bobble* (1986) and *Double Dragon* (1987); Nintendo's *R-Type* (1987), Capcom's *Street Fighter* (1987) and *1943: The Battle of Midway* (1987); and *Tetris* (1988), which was originally written in the Soviet Union in 1985 and made its way around the world as it was ported to a wide variety of systems. By the end of the decade, the arcade game's biggest competition came from home video games on console systems and home computers.

Home consoles were improving and catching up to arcade games, and arcade games had to find experiences that it could provide that home games could not. This may account for an increased interest in cockpit games which players sat inside of and driving and racing games with seats built into them, games like *Space Harrier* (1985) or *Outrun* (1986) with their hydraulic systems that could shake players as they played, or *After Burner* and *After Burner II*, both from 1987. Other sit-in games included Sega's *AB Cop* (1989), Namco's *Winning Run* (1988), and Taito's airplane simulator game *Top Landing* (1989). Some games, like Taito's *Darius* (1986) and Data East's *Round Up 5 Delta Force* (1988) connected three video screens together into one wide panorama. Sega's *Heavyweight Champ* (1987) had unique controls that simulated the physical activity of boxing.

Game graphics was another area awaiting innovation. Gottlieb's *Exterminator* (1989) was the first game to use all digitized imagery for its backgrounds, apart from laserdisc games which used digitized video for their backgrounds (see Figure 16.1). Although the 3-D graphics of *I, Robot* had been ahead of their time, the time of 3-D was approaching fast. Three-dimensional dungeons with a first-person perspective could already be found in home games like *Phantasy Star* (1988) for the Sega Master System, only a year after they had debuted in *Xybots* (1987) at the arcade. For much of the decade, arcade games had achieved a three-dimensional look through the use of scaling sprites, which are small images or parts of images which are enlarged or shrunk to give the appearance of moving closer or farther into the distance. *Space Harrier,* for example, could scale 32,000 sprites quickly, creating its illusion of 3-D. But filled polygons and true three-dimensionally generated graphics were used in a few games like Atari Games's *Hard Drivin'* (1989) and *S.T.U.N. Runner* (1989) by the decade's end and stunned players with their graphics.

By the end of the 1980s, 3-D polygonal graphics began to reach the limits of what was possible within the JAMMA standard, which had not been designed for such games, and in the 1990s the industry would undergo changes again as the era of 3-D gaming began.

Figure 16.1 Gottlieb's *Exterminator* (1989). This game was among the first to have backgrounds made from digitized imagery. Image from www.klov.com.

The 1980s, then, now stands as the peak of sprite-based graphical games, most of which involved fighting, shooting, or driving. The 1980s also saw the end of the golden age of arcade video games, with many hit games, like *Pac-Man* and *Defender,* that were introduced at the beginning of the decade and enjoyed their heyday throughout it, and in some ways it is these games from the 1980s that represent the height of the arcade video game experience.[8]

CHAPTER 17

LASERDISC GAMES

Mark J. P. Wolf

The era of laserdisc games was only about a decade and a half long, lasting from the early 1980s to the mid-1990s. The laserdisc, a type of optical storage disc technology, was first commercially available in 1978 and used mainly for movies, as an alternative to videotape. Laserdiscs had several advantages over videotape, including better horizontal resolution and sharper images and the ability to jump from one point to another for instant access. Both of these capabilities would allow laserdisc technology to be adapted to arcade video games, and laserdisc games would be the first appearance of full-motion video in video games.

In 1981, David H. Ahl, the founder of *Creative Computing* magazine, wrote a program for the Apple II computer that could control a laserdisc and play scenes from the movie *Rollercoaster* (1975), demonstrating that the new technology could be used in games. The first time a laserdisc was used in an arcade video game was in 1981, in Electro Sport's *Quarter Horse*. The game had two screens, one for computer graphics and one for video. Players placed their bets and interacted on the screen with the computer graphics, and then the game would randomly select a winning horse and play a video clip from the disc on the video monitor. While the game used a laserdisc, the use was not very interactive, but others were conceiving ways laserdiscs could be incorporated into games.

Laserdisc games typically fell into two categories. The first used laserdisc imagery as a background and placed computer-generated vehicles or characters over it (including the player's character, enemy characters, and objects like projectiles and laser shots); in such cases the background imagery is a prerecorded sequence to which players must coordinate their movements, for example, racing games in which players must steer their vehicles and avoid crashing. The video clip is the same each time, and players try to fly or drive as far as they can without crashing and ending the game. One such game, *Astron Belt,* was manufactured by Sega and licensed to Bally/Midway and introduced at the 1982 Amusement and Music Operators Association convention and then perfected for its release in arcades in 1983. In it, the player steers a spaceship through space, over land, through tunnels, and other locations seen in the video backgrounds, while shooting at enemy ships and avoiding computer-generated mines. Other games with overlaid graphics that came out in 1983 included Bally/Midway's space shooting game *Galaxy Ranger,* Funai's space shooting game *Interstellar Laser Fantasy* (also known as *Interstellar*), Mylstar's flying game *M.A.C.H. 3,* and Williams's *Star Rider,* a racing game in which computer-generated competing racers could appear on-screen either in front of you or in your rearview mirror. The laserdisc imagery used in these games was typically live-action video, or prerendered computer animation.

The other kind of laserdisc game used the technology's random access capability to create branching narratives which were steered by the player's input at crucial moments in the game. Instead of controlling overlaid characters, players played by making quick decisions and interacting with precise timing to avoid sequences ending in the player-character's death. This type of game is also sometimes called an Interactive Movie (see Chapter 22, "Genre Profile: Interactive Movies").

The most famous of these types of games was one of the first ones released; *Dragon's Lair* (1983) by computer consultant Rick Dyer, who had teamed up with the game company Cinematronics and former Disney animator Don Bluth to create the game. *Dragon's Lair* featured a knight, Dirk the Daring, who fought various creatures and had adventures the outcomes of which were partially determined by the player. With hand-drawn cel animation from Bluth, the game's graphics were far better than the usual arcade game imagery. The novelty interested players and arcade operators alike, and there were hopes that laserdisc technology could revive interest in arcade gaming and raise income after 1982's crash-related sagging profits (see Chapter 18, "The Video Game Industry Crash"). According to one *Newsweek* article from August 1983, while the average arcade game's take per week was $140 in 1981 and $109 in 1982, the *Dragon's Lair* machine discussed in the article was taking in up to $1,400 a week.[1] Other games with hand-drawn animation appeared in 1983; two *animé*-based games, Nihon Bussan/AV Japan's *Bega's Battle* and Stern's *Cliff Hanger* both had action-packed narratives with branching storylines. Two other games of 1983 added another element of player choice; Bally/Midway's *NFL Football* and Stern's *Goal to Go,* both football games with live action video, allowed players to select plays and then showed the teams running them.

By the end of 1983, the video game industry crash was affecting home games as well as the arcades and profits were falling. But the industry was still hopeful about laserdisc games, and over a dozen more appeared in 1984, with over a dozen different companies producing games. Cinematronics, Dyer, and Bluth returned with *Space Ace,* a science-fiction-themed game, and Dyer's own company, RDI Systems, also produced *Thayer's Quest,* an adventure game that was a conversion kit for *Dragon's Lair* and *Space Ace* machines. A few more adventure games appeared: Funai's *Esh's Aurunmilla,* Universal's *Super Don Quixote,* and Taito's *Ninja Hayate,* and the only abstract laserdisc game, Simutek's *Cube Quest,* which featured some of the best computer animation in video games of the day. Other releases of the year included shooting games (Laserdisc Computer System's *Atomic Castle,* Konami's *Badlands,* Nihon Bussan/AV Japan's *Cobra Command,* Atari's *Firefox,* and Mylstar's *Us Vs. Them*), racing games (Taito's *Cosmos Circuit* and *Laser Grand Prix,* Sega's *GP World,* and Universal's *Top Gear*), and one sports game (Stern's *Gold Medal With Bruce Jenner*).

Because of derivative games and expensive technology that frequently broke down, laserdisc games failed to revive the arcade as people had hoped. As *Electronic Games* magazine's Dan Persons put it,

To say that the predictions have not come true is an understatement. Laser machines that once commanded a hefty price of three and four thousand dollars are now being sold off at a thousand dollars apiece, so eager are distributors to clear out their inventory.[2]

Another reason for failure of laserdisc games was the nature of the games themselves. Due to the use of prerecorded imagery, the games could only vary slightly from one playing to another, if at all. Once players had played through to the end of a laserdisc game and seen everything, they lost interest; so the games had little replay value and no staying power.

For all these reasons, it is no surprise, then, that home video game systems using laser-discs also failed. In January 1985, Rick Dyer's company RDI Systems released the Halcyon home system, which cost over $2,000 and had only two games for it, *Thayer's Quest* (which actually had more animated footage than the arcade version did) and the football game *Raiders Vs. Chargers* which used real NFL game footage. Four more games were in the planning stages, but the company went bankrupt before they could be released. In Japan, Microsoft's MSX home computer (released in Japan in 1983) could use certain laserdisc players from Pioneer and Sony to play laserdisc games, and 11 games (*Astron Belt, Strike Mission, Badlands, Starfighters, Umi Yakuba, Interstellar, Cosmos Circuit, Esh's Aurunmilla, Rolling Blaster, Mystery Disc 1: Murder, Anyone?,* and *Mystery Disc 2: Many Roads To Murder*) were released for the MSX and available only in Japan (they are also sometimes referred to as "Palcom" games, after Pioneer's laserdisc player).[3]

In the mid-1980s, only a few more games were released, including Sega's space game *Albegas* (also known as *Cybernaut*), Status's *Casino Strip,* Nihon Bussan/AV Japan's *Road Blaster* (also known as *Road Avenger*), and Taito's *Time Gal,* all from 1985, and Millennium Games's *Freedom Fighter* from 1986. Around the end of the 1980s and into the early 1990s, raster games with 3-D graphics were improving and offering more variety than the limited prerendered sequences of laserdisc games in which the player could not control their point of view.

But laserdisc technology attempted a comeback during the first half of the 1990s. Namco produced two games, *Galaxian 3* (1990) and *Attack Of The Zolgear* (1994), both space shooting games that sat six players in front of an enormous image stretching across three giant projection screens placed side by side in an enclosed booth, giving players a unique arcade experience. *Dragon's Lair II: Time Warp,* a sequel that had begun produc-tion in 1984, was finally released in 1991 by Leland Interactive. Nova Games released a driving game, *Street Viper* in 1993, Atari Games released a driving and shooting game *COPS* (1994) based on the television series of the same name, and Sega released, *Time Traveler* (1991), which reflected its laserdisc imagery in a parabolic mirror to attempt to give it a 3-D effect (the game's marquee had the word "Hologram" on it in large letters, even though no holograms were involved). A Spanish company, Web Picmatic, produced a few games, including *Zorton Brothers (Los Justicieros)* (1993) and *Marbella Vice* (1994), and in 1993, Pioneer Corporation even released the Pioneer LaserActive home laserdisc game system, though by this time CD-ROM games were replacing laserdisc as the tech-nology for games using full-motion video.

The company most responsible for the attempted revival of the laserdisc game industry was American Laser Games. Started in the late 1980s, American Laser Games would use better computer technology and produce a series of laserdisc games that used light guns and live action video, including *Mad Dog McCree* (1990), *Who Shot Johnny Rock?*

(1991), *Gallagher's Gallery* (1992), *Mad Dog II: The Lost Gold* (1992), *Space Pirates* (1992), *Crime Patrol* (1993), *Crime Patrol 2: Drug Wars* (1993), *Fast Draw Showdown* (1994), *The Last Bounty Hunter* (1994), and *Way of the Warrior* (1994). A tenth game, *Shootout At Old Tucson* was a prototype that did not make it to the arcade as they decided to release it on CD-ROM instead.

Technologically speaking, the efforts behind the revival were too late. By 1992 CD-ROMs were starting to incorporate full-motion video into computer games, and in 1997 the first consumer DVD equipment would become available. Smaller, more compact discs and more reliable technology which was less expensive pretty much sounded the death knell for laserdisc technology. Movies were moving over to DVD and by 2001 would no longer be released on laserdisc. Probably the last arcade video game to use a laserdisc was Nihon Bussan/AV Japan's *Burning Rush* (2000), which only used it for its opening and closing sequences and cut-scenes, while the rest of the game used interactive computer-generated graphics.

Games using full-motion video, however, continued to be made and played on home computers and systems (see Chapter 22, "Genre Profile: Interactive Movies"). In 1997 the company Digital Leisure, Inc. was formed for the purpose of rereleased laserdisc games on DVD. They bought the rights to *Dragon's Lair, Space Ace,* and *Dragon's Lair II: Time Warp,* which they released over the next couple of years on CD-ROM, DVD-ROM, and for the PlayStation 2. In 2000 Digital Leisure bought the rights to Sega's *Time Traveler,* and in 2001 it acquired the rights to all nine arcade games made by American Laser Games, rereleasing them as well. Today a number of laserdisc games can be played on emulators, like Daphne, which are specially designed for laserdisc games.[4]

Laserdisc games had a brief history due to the quickly changing technology of optical storage media, but they introduced full-motion video into video games and are now fondly remembered by collectors, while the games themselves are still sold and played on other media.

CHAPTER 18

THE VIDEO GAME INDUSTRY CRASH

Mark J. P. Wolf

By the end of 1981, the arcade video game industry was booming with an estimated income of $5 billion.[1] The production of home games and their systems was also at an all-time high, with its market tripling in 1981, and it looked as if it would reach $2 billion by the end of 1982.[2] The largest video game company of the time, Atari, saw revenues of about $415 million in 1980, and even its competitors were doing well. According to *Time* magazine,

> Whatever the future holds, just now the game manufacturers require earth-moving equipment just to clear away the coin. In 1981 Bally's sales jumped to an estimated $880 million from $693 million in 1980. Williams, which makes Defender, saw nine months' gross sales go from $83 million in 1980 to $126 million in last year [1981], and it has just opened a new plant in Gurnee, Ill., capable of producing 600 to 700 Defenders a day.[3]

Not only was the growth phenomenal, but more was expected. An article in *Business Week* in May 1982 supposed that the home market "will continue to expand at least until 1985, at which point nearly half of all U. S. homes with television sets will own a video game machine," and CBS Inc., the television network which itself was getting into game production, predicted that the European market for video games "will explode from $200 this year to $800 million by 1983."[4]

Besides CBS, there were a flood of new cartridge-producing companies flooding the market with games, many of which were derivative, substandard, and cheaply produced. Many new startup companies appeared, hoping to cash in on the video game craze, and some, like Imagic, were started by former employees of Atari and Mattel. Board game makers like Parker Brothers and Milton Bradley, and companies from other industries, like 20th Century Fox, and even Quaker Oats, had game divisions and published games hoping for a hit. With so many companies producing hundreds of games, many of which were poor, and home computers coming down in price while more software was becoming available, the video game industry was heading for another crash.

An Earlier Crash

The video game industry crash of the early 1980s would not be the first the industry had seen. In 1976, electronics manufacturer General Instruments produced the AY-3-8500 chip, which had all of the circuitry necessary for a video game on a single chip, making the production of video games much easier. According to a 1980 article in *Popular Electronics,*

> For companies thinking about going into the TV-game business, the GI chip was the convincer....
> It promised total system costs of $25 to $30 and retail prices in the $60 to $75 range....The GI
> chip made it possible for companies to establish simplified production lines and build lower-cost
> games.[5]

By January of 1977, GI had shipped over 7,000,000 AY-3-8500 chips and planned a new series of chips that could do even more. Cartridge-based game systems were slowly taking off around this time; in August of 1976 the Fairchild Camera and Instrument Company introduced the Video Entertainment System, the name of which was soon changed to the Channel F, and the following year Atari released its VCS 2600 game system. But the surge of all the new games entering the market proved to be too much:

> Despite the shortage of TV games during the Christmas 1976 season, the market collapsed in
> 1977....One by one, most of the video game manufacturers dropped out. The casualties included
> the three semiconductor companies who were building games with their own chips: Fairchild,
> National Semiconductor, and RCA.[6]

Even the new cartridge-based systems were unable to stave off a crash. Fairchild, Atari, Bally, Coleco, and RCA all produced cartridge-based systems, but none of them caught on immediately, leaving a lot of leftover inventory in 1978.

Although Bally and Fairchild got out of the home game system market, Atari started a $6 million advertising campaign in 1978, and Mattel introduced its Intellivision system in 1979. Eventually, with better games and less competition, the industry recovered, and in a few years was booming again.

Warning Signs at the Arcade

By 1982, the video game industry was doing better than ever. Sales of home games had returned, and arcade games were pulling in billions of dollars, with hit games like *Space Invaders, Pac-Man,* and *Defender* (1980) each pulling in hundreds of millions of dollars on their own. Despite all the optimism, the earlier crash led some industry observers to have doubts. In a November 1982 article for *Fortune* magazine entitled "Why the Craze Won't Quit," writer Peter Nulty began by asking,

> Can the home video game boom continue much longer? Softening prices last summer and an
> advertising blitz this fall are raising speculation that there's trouble ahead for game makers. If the
> kids are getting tired of blasting space blobs, won't the manufacturers be left blasting each other
> for shares in a stagnant or shrinking market? Anxiety is clearly written in the stock prices of the
> two industry giants. Warner Communication, which owns Atari, is selling for about eight times
> earnings and Mattel for only four. Some observers even talk of a collapse similar to those suffered
> by CB radios, digital watches, and pocket calculators.[7]

Competition between game-producing companies, poor products, consumer and retailer doubts, as well as improved home computer systems all began to hurt the video game industry, with some of the first effects appearing in arcade game sales. Some hints of a drop in interest came rather early; Atari's Coin-Op $50,000 World Championship, held in Chicago in October 1981, drew only 250 players, when more than 10,000 were expected.[8] Less than a month after Nulty's article, *Business Week* had an article entitled "Arcade video games start to flicker," which reported,

> Except for companies that make the most popular arcade games, the players in the coin-operated video game business are finding themselves stymied by an unexpected halt in their explosive growth.
>
> Sales of arcade video game machines grew from $50 million in 1978 to about $900 million this year. But manufacturers expect equipment sales to be flat next year. Distributors are overstocked, and few operators foresee a repeat of the action in 1981, when players slid an estimated $7 billion worth of quarters into arcade game machines. A shakeout among operators, whose ranks grew by the thousands with the lure of easy money, is already underway.[9]

Just like the new companies that would soon go bankrupt and distributors who ended up with leftover inventory, many arcades would close and those that remained open would buy fewer new arcade games.

The End of an Era

While the number of video game arcades more than doubled from 1980 to 1982, reaching a peak of about 10,000 arcades, over 2,000 would close in 1983.[10] By the year's end the home video game market was oversaturated and consumers were disappointed with the products. Overall, the video game industry's profits in 1983 amounted to $2.9 billion, down about 35 percent from 1982.[11] Industry-wide losses totaled about $1.5 billion.

Mattel, who had once been the third largest video game maker and had $250 million in revenue from its Intellivision system in 1981, left the market in 1983. Even Atari, with a majority share of the market and among the few companies producing games for both the home and the arcade as well as home computers, lost over half a billion dollars in 1983. In 1984, the home video game system market dried up and only one new system appeared, Rick Dyer's Halcyon home laserdisc game system, and it was a failure.

The Halcyon system appeared because the year before, laserdisc games were seen as possibly rescuing the arcade game industry. Laserdisc games used video graphics stored on laserdiscs, either as background the player flew over, as in Mylstar's *M.A.C.H. 3* (1983), or as animated segments representing a player's actions during the game, as in Cinematronics's *Dragon's Lair*. While the graphics were improved, gameplay was severely limited since the graphics were already rendered and stored on the discs. In *Dragon's Lair*, for example, there were only a few choices a player could make in any given situation, all of them ready as animated scenes that the player would play next once a player had made a choice. The games also cost twice as much as standard arcade games, and charged players 50 cents a play. In the end, laserdisc games failed to catch on, due the lack of interesting game play and higher expenses for both players and arcade operators.

The crash finally ended in 1985 when a new system appeared that advanced home video games to a new level. The Nintendo Entertainment System already was a success in Japan, where it had been released in 1983 as the Nintendo Famicom, and it, along with its large library of games, helped revive the American video game industry and helped to bring an end to the problems it was suffering.

PART III

THE INDUSTRY REBOUNDS (1985–1994)

The Nintendo Entertainment System (NES), released in North America in 1985, was a success and proved that the video game industry was still viable. Computer games were also growing as an industry, as home computer technology improved. CD-ROM technology appeared in the mid-1980s, and within a few years both home computer games and home console games would begin using them, the increased storage capacity opening up new possibilities for games. Shareware games, developed outside of the industry, were also appearing and making their way from computer to computer.

Around the late 1980s and early 1990s, mobile gaming was becoming more popular, as handheld games and game systems grew more advanced. The Atari Lynx and Nintendo Game Boy were both released in 1989, and the Sega Game Gear in 1990. All three were cartridge-based systems. The Game Boy was extremely successful, selling around 70 million units, and lead to the consoles Game Boy Color and Game Boy Advance.

The arcade was also recovering from the crash, and now it had to compete with home game systems and computer games as they improved. Although some new technologies, like laserdisc games, failed to pull the industry out of the crash, more emphasis was placed on game experiences that were more difficult to duplicate in the home. More ride-on and sit-in games were produced into the 1990s, and a variety of new interfaces were tried, some of which eventually made their way into home video game systems.

Online gaming also began to grow more popular, as home computers connected first to Bulletin Board Systems (BBSs) and the Internet, playing early games like *Xtrek* and *Mtrek* from 1986, or *Gemstone II* from 1988. Later, around 1993, multiplayer games moved to the World Wide Web and soon would be played by hundreds of thousands of players.

By the end of 1994, the video game industry had reinvented itself, had evolved new forms, and had spread to a variety of new media. The industry was booming again, providing the revenue to invest in new technological advances, like 32-bit home game systems, that were just around the corner.

CHAPTER 19

System Profile: The Nintendo Entertainment System (NES)

Dominic Arsenault

The Famicom (a contraction of "family computer") console was released in Japan by Nintendo in 1983. After a slow start due to hardware and programming instabilities, the then-newcomer to the home video game console market ordered a product recall and replaced the device's motherboard. This significantly improved reliability and boosted sales of the Famicom up to over 500,000 consoles sold in the first two months.[1] Nintendo thus set its sight on the rest of the world and prepared its console for export.

The world's second biggest market, the United States, had collapsed in the video game crash of 1983 (sometimes referred to as "the crash of 1984" since its full effects would not be seen until then). This meant that any home video game console would have a hard time gaining acceptance from the consumers and retailers, who were convinced that video games had been a passing fad. On the other hand, it also meant that if the system succeeded, it would virtually have the whole market for itself. The Famicom had conquered Japan; this gave Hiroshi Yamauchi, Nintendo's president, good reasons to believe it could work just as well in the United States.

The Famicom, however, had to change its name and appearance to make a splash in a country allergic to "video games." Nintendo of America's president Minoru Arakawa and senior vice president Howard Lincoln opted for the Advanced Video System name and demonstrated it at the January 1985 Consumer Electronics Show. People who played it liked the games, but retailers were not willing to try selling video games after the crash. Nintendo thus developed the Zapper light gun and a robot named R.O.B. (for Robotic Operating Buddy), two peripherals that were to be used with a handful of games but whose true purpose was to change the perception of the console from a "video game console" to a system that would allow people to play arcade shooting hits like *Wild Gunman* (1984) or *Hogan's Alley* (1984), or a technological robot toy. A final name was given to the console: the Nintendo Entertainment System. The NES was test marketed in New York, the toughest place in the United States since the competition for entertainment products was very high. (Yamauchi's reasoning was that if the NES managed to sell there, it would sell anywhere.) Fifty thousand units were sold.[2] The NES caught on and was soon for sale through the whole country and eventually around the globe, thriving until the 16-bit consoles' arrival on the market. Nintendo tried to prolong its life by releasing an updated, stylish version known as the "New NES" or "NES 2" in 1993, but many consumers had moved on to the Super NES or Sega Genesis by then, and it was a commercial failure. Nintendo officially stopped supporting the NES in 1994; today, the company claims to have sold over 60 million units worldwide.

Licensing Terms

One of the reasons behind Atari's demise was the flood of poor-quality titles that glutted the market because the company had lost exclusive control of the content developed for its console. Nintendo wanted to make sure this would not happen with the NES, but also realized the importance of having a huge library of games, which could not be large enough with only Nintendo's own games. The company thus approached many successful Japanese publishers—such as Bandai, Taito, and Namco—and arranged partnerships to have them develop games for the NES. Nintendo's conditions, however, proved to be Draconian;

> Yamauchi protected [the NES] with a security chip that locked out unauthorized cartridges. This meant that the only way to make games for the NES was to allow Nintendo to manufacture them, and Nintendo maintained final authority in deciding which games would be manufactured and in what quantities.[3]

In addition, third-party licensees were restricted to publishing a maximum of five games per year, and every one of them had to be exclusive to the NES for two years. (As a matter of fact, Nintendo circumvented this rule when Konami and Acclaim, two developers that produced hit games, asked for more than five games per year. They were allowed to create subsidiaries, and thus Konami published five additional games under the Ultra Games label, and Acclaim did the same with the LJN subsidiary.) Atari—who had the resources to afford legal battles with the Japanese giant—sued Nintendo for monopolizing the home video game market, but lost. Many companies simply agreed to the terms. As Steven L. Kent puts it,

> Nintendo controlled somewhere between 86 to 93 percent of the market by the end of 1987. By the time Sega [Nintendo's only serious competitor] had sold 100,000 Master Systems, Nintendo had already sold more than 2 million NES units and the gap was widening.[4]

While Nintendo claimed these regulations existed to ensure that games made for the NES were of sufficiently high quality, many developers saw them as strong-arm tactics, often citing Nintendo's censorship policies in particular. Conscious of the importance of keeping a clean image, especially in the United States where the NES's primary target audience consisted of kids, Nintendo had set up an "NES Game Standards Policy" to prevent the appearance and bad publicity of games like *Custer's Revenge,* an infamous game developed and published by Mystique in 1982 for the Atari 2600 console, in which the player controlled a naked man who had to dodge obstacles in order to reach a Native American woman tied to a pole and rape her. (Predictably, the game caused controversy and tarnished Atari's reputation, even though the latter had no involvement in this game.)

Every game developed or translated for a North American release had to be sent to Nintendo's censors first, who would review the content and request that the developer make any number of changes to "meet the concerns of the members of [Nintendo's] target age group and their parents."[5] Some of the forbidden things included illegal drugs, explicit or suggestive sexuality, alcohol, smoking materials, graphic depictions of death, gratuitous or excessive violence, foul language, and ethnic, religious, nationalistic, or sexual stereotypes of language or symbols. As a result, many games had to be significantly altered from their original versions, sometimes for things as seemingly unwarranted as removing all crosses from hospitals or tombstones (the cross being recognized as a symbol of Christianity).[6]

Many licensees thought Nintendo of America's inflexible enforcing of these regulations was disproportionate and stymied their creativity and freedom in making games. Douglas Crockford may speak for many in "The Untold Story of *Maniac Mansion*," an account of his relationship with Nintendo's censors when he converted *Maniac Mansion* for the NES: "They insist that their standards are not intended to make their products bland, but that is the inevitable result."[7] Nintendo kept enforcing these policies rigorously until the home version of *Mortal Kombat* flopped in 1994 (due to censorship, much of the violence players expected was gone from the game), at which point it released its grip a little. But it was too late: by then, many developers were disgruntled with the company. When rival Sony offered in 1995 a viable alternative with its PlayStation console and liberal licensing policies, these developers flocked out. Nintendo's dominance over the home video game market had ended.

Games Library

It should first be noted that while the hardware of the NES and Famicom were essentially the same, one important difference makes their games library very distinct. The NES was fitted with the 10NES lockout chip, which acted as a software "lock" that would scan a game cartridge's code for a "key." Upon recognizing the specified code needed (which was inputted into the cartridge directly by Nintendo when it manufactured the cartridges), the NES would proceed to launch the game. If the code was not found, the game would not start. This made it difficult to create games without becoming an official Nintendo licensee. Some developers worked around the chip itself, selling their game cartridges with special adapters that would bypass the 10NES chip, and others managed to reverse-engineer the system to figure out the needed authentication code. Nintendo actively prosecuted any known offender to further discourage such enterprises. Thus unlicensed games for the NES were probably fewer in number when compared to the Famicom, which was not equipped with a lockout chip; in Japan and the Far East, Famicom piracy proved to be rampant, significantly increasing the number of games available for the system.

Another factor that further divides the Famicom and the NES's libraries is the Nintendo of America licensee regulations. Since the video gaming culture in Japan was well established among all layers of society, the Famicom had as much success with adults as with kids, and its market could accommodate a very large offering of games without fear of collapse. Therefore, there was no need for Nintendo to monitor the games made by third-party developers. The censorship reviews, limit on the number of published titles per year, and centralized manufacturing and pricing of cartridges by Nintendo were all absent from the Japanese licensing agreements. Most developers released many titles for the Famicom, and translated five of their best for a North American release.

According to a Nintendo of America representative Joel Hochberg, the amount of published NES games is difficult to establish with certainty: over 650 North American titles are confirmed, but if unlicensed games are to be included, that number would probably reach over 900. This indicates that even with the 10NES chip and legal actions by Nintendo, piracy was still a serious issue. Nintendo of America estimates that internationally, the total number of games released for NES and Famicom is well over 1,000.[8] This number, however, seems rather conservative, considering the NES was victim to an estimated 250 unlicensed games; since the Famicom had no lockout chip, it is reasonable to expect that it saw many more unauthorized games, in addition to various "adult" and pornographic games which were systematically refused entry into the North American market. A closer estimate of the total number of NES and Famicom games would probably be higher than that, though how high exactly is difficult to tell.[9]

Identifying the most successful games of the library proves to be much easier. The Video Game Chartz website[10] hosts a chart of video games whose worldwide sales have surpassed one million copies. Of the 64 NES games listed there, Nintendo has published 41, with Capcom, Enix, and Square sharing the responsibility behind the other platinum hits. Nintendo's *Super Mario Bros.* series, *Donkey Kong* (1989), *Metroid* (1986), *The Legend of Zelda* series, *Mike Tyson's Punch-Out!!* (1987), *Kirby's Adventure* (1993), and *Kid Icarus* (1986) all became franchises that churned lucrative sequels in the following years. Other Nintendo games such as *Tetris* (1988), *Duck Hunt* (1984), *F1 Race* (1984), *Gyromite* (1985), and the sports games [*World Class Track Meet* (1986), *Ice Hockey* (1988), *Pro Wrestling* (1987), *Golf* (1984), *Tennis* (1984), and *Baseball* (1983)] sold extremely well, but did not develop into sequels. Capcom was one of the major third-party developers for the NES, with its *Duck Tales* (1990), *Ghosts 'N Goblins* (1986), and *Chip'n Dale Rescue Rangers* (1990) all selling over a million copies; but Capcom's greatest contribution to the NES library undoubtedly lies in the *Megaman* series, which has spawned over 50 games to this day. Other games and series of note include Square's *Rad Racer* (1987) and *Final Fantasy* series, Konami's *Teenage Mutant Ninja Turtles* (1989), *Contra* (1988), and *Castlevania* series, Capcom's *Bionic Commando* (1988), Enix's *Dragon Warrior* series, and Tecmo's *Ninja Gaiden* series. While this list is far from exhaustive, it showcases the biggest advantage the NES had over its competitors: a huge library of high-quality games.

Technical Specifications

The NES is known as an 8-bit console, which means it can access 8 bits of data in a single operation.[11] The CPU has access to 2KB of RAM and 48KB of ROM, though various multi-memory controllers (MMCs) can increase those numbers. MMCs were chips designed by game developers and included in their cartridges to expand the features of the NES. For instance, Nintendo's MMC1 chip allowed the player to save his progress in *The Legend of Zelda*, and the MMC2 chip was used in *Myke Tyson's Punch-Out!!* to portray the boxers using bigger sprites than normally allowed by the console hardware. The CPU also is responsible for the console's audio playback. The NES supports five sound channels: two square pulses, one triangle pulse, one noise channel, and a DPCM (differential pulse code modulation) channel. The square pulses can be set to different

COMPANY PROFILE: NINTENDO

Dominic Arsenault

The foundations of Nintendo (whose Japanese name can be roughly translated as "leave luck to heaven") in the entertainment industry were established as early as 1889, starting as a manufacturer of Hanafuda playing cards. (Hanafuda is a gambling card game, something of a cross between traditional Japanese and Western games.) The company attempted to penetrate a handful of other markets during the 1960s including toys, a taxi service, and a "love hotel" before deciding to explore the avenue of electronic games, a choice that would prove most beneficial as today Nintendo is one of the world's most successful video game companies.

Nintendo's first worldwide large-scale success came in 1981 in the form of the arcade game *Donkey Kong,* in which players had to rescue a princess from a stubborn gorilla. The colorful graphics, cartoon characters, and efficient story all appealed to people, but more importantly, the game had varied gameplay. *Donkey Kong* was one of the first games to feature multiple levels, in which the player's goal was alternately to jump over barrels or pans of cement, ride elevators, and remove rivets to make a structure collapse. In 12 months, the company sold 60,000 units, bringing revenues of U.S. $180 million.[12] This, along with the release of *Mario Bros.* (in which players had to kick enemies using the platforms on the screen), firmly established Nintendo's position in the video game industry. Being based in Japan, the arcade manufacturer avoided the crash of 1983—in which home video games were proclaimed "dead" in the United States by the press (see Chapter 18, "The Video Game Industry Crash")—and launched its Famicom console in Japan, where it was a huge hit. Nintendo then marketed the console for the United States in 1985, and eventually the rest of the world, under the Nintendo Entertainment System name. Industry experts agree today that the NES did nothing short of single-handedly resurrecting home video game systems.[13]

Nintendo maintained its dominance on the home video game console market with the release of the Super NES in 1990–1991, but began losing ground when Sony released its PlayStation console in 1994–1995. Its position further eroded with the future generations of home consoles, with the Nintendo 64 and GameCube progressively losing market shares to their competitors from Sony and Microsoft. Nintendo's Game Boy, on the other hand, seized the handheld video game console format when it launched in 1989, and its successive iterations (Game Boy Color/Pocket/Light/Advance/Micro) further tightened the company's grip on the handheld market. As of 2004, the various Game Boys had sold for a combined total of 168 million units,[14] earning Nintendo a 94 percent market share, according to Reuters news service.[15]

The success of Nintendo can be attributed to two key strategies. The first consists of developing franchises based on distinctive characters, the most popular having each spawned a lengthy series of games (as evidenced by the various *Mario, Zelda, Metroid,* and *Donkey Kong* titles, among many others) as well as extensive merchandising gear such as plush dolls, hats, T-shirts, toys, and so on. The second is an emphasis on making games fun and playable for everyone. This has earned Nintendo a somewhat negative image among mature gamers, who may feel its games are aimed at children. (Sega, Nintendo's top competitor from 1985 to 1995, played that card by marketing its consoles to teenagers.) This choice of consumer demographics also led to important censorship issues in the past (as described in Chapter 19) and is reflected by Nintendo's advertising for its 2006 console, the Wii.

As of 2006, Nintendo has offices in Australia, Austria, Belgium, Brazil, Canada, Denmark, France, Germany, Italy, Japan, Mexico, the Netherlands, Norway, Sweden, the United Kingdom, Ireland, and the United States. Its consolidated net sales in fiscal year 2005 were ¥515 billion (approximately U.S. $4.81 billion), with a gross margin of ¥217.4 billion (approximately U.S. $2.03 billion).[16] The company is headquartered in Kyoto (Japan) and employs 2,977 people worldwide according to recruitment website WetFeet.com (http://www.wetfeet.com/). Satoru Iwata succeeded Hiroshi Yamauchi as the fourth Nintendo president in 2002.

levels of saturation in an attempt to simulate different instruments such as a piano or guitars; the triangle pulse's main function is as a bass line, but it can also serve as a flute with higher notes; and the noise channel's primary use is simulating percussions. Each of these channels can be assigned different values of reverberation, vibrato, delay, and sustain to increase their expressiveness. The DPCM channel can play heavily compressed samples, such as digitized speech in JVC Musical Industries's *Super Star Wars: The Empire Strikes Back* (1983), or sampled drum sounds (one notable example is the bass drum sound in *Super Mario Bros. 3*).

A dedicated graphics processor relieves the CPU of its most demanding operations, allowing the NES to process complex graphics (for the time at which it was released). At a resolution of 256 x 240 pixels, up to 64 sprites (moving characters or objects) can be displayed simultaneously, at a maximum of 8 per line. These sprites can be 8 x 8 or 8 x 16 pixels in size, and have up to 4 colors. The NES's palette has 52 colors, and up to 16 of them can be displayed on-screen at a time.

CHAPTER 20

A New Generation of Home Video Game Systems

Leonard Herman

Before the great crash of 1983, the home video game industry was predominantly American. The major systems were all exported to Japan and Europe (Magnavox was owned by Philips, which was a Dutch company). The Odyssey^2 was sold as the Videopac in Europe and was much more popular there than it was domestically. In 1983 the Japanese companies decided to get in on the action too. Sega released a pair of consoles, the SG-1000 and Mark III, and Nintendo released the Famicom. All these systems were originally intended to be released solely in Japan.

The Famicom became a huge success in Japan and it was not long before Nintendo began setting its sights upon selling the console worldwide. The only problem with this plan was the fact that Atari dominated the video game industry and Nintendo felt that it just could not compete against Atari. So Nintendo approached Atari with the opportunity to license the Famicom for worldwide distribution outside of Japan. After taking a look at the Famicom, Atari's executives were very interested in the deal. Agreements were made and the final signings would be made at the Consumer Electronics Show (CES) in June 1983.

Something funny happened at that CES. Coleco unveiled its Adam computer system. But was it a computer or was it a video game system?

There is a distinct difference between video game consoles and home computers that played games. Back in 1983, Coleco had the exclusive license to produce and distribute Nintendo titles for home video game consoles. On the other hand, Atari had the license to produce and distribute Nintendo games for home computers.

So when the Atari executives visited the Coleco booth at the summer 1983 CES, and saw *Donkey Kong* proudly playing on the Adam, they were deeply concerned. Coleco was touting the Adam, which was an inexpensive home computer, so therefore it should have been Atari's *Donkey Kong* playing on it. On the other hand, the game-playing capabilities of the Adam made it a Colecovision in sheep's clothing and the Coleco camp contended that since the Colecovision was a game console, then Coleco's *Donkey Kong* could play on it. Atari did not buy that logic. After all, the Adam was clearly a computer. Atari representatives told Nintendo to clear it up with Coleco, or else they would not sign the agreement to market the Famicom.

Nintendo cleared up the mess but it took a little time. In fact by the time the mess was cleared up, Atari posted substantial fourth quarter losses for 1983 and the video game crash had occurred in the United States. Atari was no longer the mighty power that it had been just a year earlier and it was no longer in any position to license the Famicom from Nintendo. In fact, Atari was no longer the threat that Nintendo feared. The Japanese company was free to distribute the Famicom worldwide on its own.

Of course, that was contingent upon anybody even caring about a new video game system any longer.

Nintendo unveiled the Famicom to the American public at the Winter (January) 1985 CES under the name Nintendo Advanced Video System (NAVS). The system was able to generate 52 colors and was totally wireless. Its controllers used infrared light to send signals to the console. The controllers were also different in another respect. Instead of the popular joystick, the NAVS's rectangular shaped controller featured a touchpad that could move in one of eight directions. A light gun was also going to be sold with the unit for target games such as *Hogan's Alley* and *Duck Hunt.*

Despite the fact that video games were selling so poorly everywhere, Nintendo received much attention at the Consumer Electronics Show. Nintendo promised that the NAVS would be available by the late spring of 1985. Naturally that deadline came and went without any sign of the NAVS. However, in June the company again had a booth at the CES. This time the console on display was called the Nintendo Entertainment System.

The wireless controllers were gone but a 10-inch-high robot called R.O.B. (Robotic Operating Buddy) accompanied the system. Although R.O.B. was used to play some games, its basic purpose was that of a Trojan horse. Since electronic retailers did not seem to want anything to do with video game systems any longer, Nintendo promoted R.O.B. as a toy to get the system into toy stores.

Nintendo successfully test marketed the system, thanks partly to a game called *Super Mario Bros.,* finally in mid-October 1985 in the New York metropolitan area, proving that people still wanted to play video games. The $159 system was released nationally in February 1986.

Nintendo displayed the NES at the Consumer Electronics Show in January. Alongside the main booth were satellite booths that housed third-party companies who were also releasing games for the NES. However, unlike the third-party companies that manufactured games for the early American systems, the companies producing the games for the NES did it with Nintendo's blessing. In fact, to prevent a glut of games on the market, Nintendo licensed the right to produce games to the third-party companies. Further, to make sure that the companies indeed went to Nintendo for licensing, Nintendo alone manufactured all of the cartridges for every one of the third-party companies. To prevent companies from manufacturing their own game cartridges, Nintendo designed a "lockout" chip into the NES. If any rogue company decided to avoid paying for a license and manufactured games themselves, they still could not bypass the lockout chip and the games would not play on the NES. Each game sold by a licensed company had Nintendo's "seal of quality" on the box to assure consumers that the game had been approved by Nintendo.

But the NES was not alone in 1986. Following Nintendo's success, Sega decided to do likewise and released an American version of the Mark III, which they called the Sega Master System (SMS).

The SMS was very similar to the NES. Both consoles came with similar-looking controller pads and both were sold with light guns for target shooting games. Although the NES came with R.O.B., the robot was not supported after a short while. The SMS utilized game cards in addition to the standard game cartridges. The cards could contain games that were the size of the games available on the cartridges and were therefore less expensive to manufacture and sell.

Although many in the industry declared that the SMS technology was superior to the NES, the buying public favored the NES. The SMS simply did not have any stand-out games that made people rush out and buy the system, as Nintendo had with its *Mario*-based games.

In addition to Nintendo and Sega, Atari also released two game consoles in 1986. This was surprising because the company's then chief executive claimed that Atari would no longer be involved with video games.

In May 1984, Atari announced a new console, the 7800. Despite the crash, Atari believed that the industry was still alive since 20 million game cartridges had been sold between January and April 1984 and over half of them had been sold at their full retail price. The company commissioned a market study to determine exactly what the public wanted in a new console. With this information in hand, Atari worked with General Computer Corporation of Massachusetts and came up with the $140 Atari 7800, a system that would be 100 percent compatible with the 2600 library. However, before the console could be released, Warner Communications sold the consumer division (the division which produced the video games and computers) of Atari Inc. to Jack Tramiel, the founder of Commodore. The new company was called Atari Corp. Tramiel's intention was for Atari to market computers that would compete against his former company. Tramiel had no interest in game consoles, and the 7800s, which had been manufactured already, were banished to warehouses.

After Nintendo proved successfully that there was indeed an interest in video game consoles, Tramiel decided to make some money off of the 7800s that were languishing in the warehouses. In 1986 he released the two-year old system along with the seven game cartridges that had been designed for it. To the surprise of very few, Atari could not compete with Nintendo or Sega.

But the 7800 was not the only surprise that Tramiel had in store for video game fans. The company released a newly designed 2600 that resembled a small 7800 and retailed for less than $50. The console was targeted for lower income households that could not afford the higher-priced consoles. During the following years, Atari released seven new games for the 2600. Although it never regained the popularity it had enjoyed during the early 1980s, the 2600 remained on the market until 1991. This 14-year run remains a record to this day for a console. Only the Nintendo Game Boy, in one incarnation or another, has remained on the market longer (17 years).

When Atari Inc. was sold in 1984, Jack Tramiel only purchased the consumer division of the company. The arcade division was retained by Warner Communications and was renamed Atari Games. A year later a controlling interest in the company was sold to Japanese arcade company Namco, which turned around and sold its interests in Atari Games to a group of Namco employees. In 1988 Atari Games started a subsidiary called

Tengen, which would market cartridge-based games for the NES. Tengen quickly became a licensed publisher for the NES but it was not long before the company became a problem for Nintendo.

In late 1988 Tengen took Nintendo to court, claiming that Nintendo had an unfair monopoly on the video game industry that it achieved through illegal practices such as price fixing and the use of the computer chip lockout technology that prohibited unlicensed development of NES software. Tengen then discovered a way to get around the lockout chip and produce NES compatible games without Nintendo's approval. Tengen quickly announced that it would develop, manufacture, and distribute NES compatible games without obtaining Nintendo licensing.

Among the titles that Tengen released for the NES without Nintendo approval was *Tetris,* an enormously popular game designed in the Soviet Union by Alexey Pajitnov in 1985. The object of the game was to keep blocks from piling up to the top of the screen.

Robert Stein, the founder of a European software company called Andromeda, discovered *Tetris* while in Hungary and he quickly negotiated with Pajitnov for the worldwide rights to the game. Once acquired, Stein quickly licensed them to Mirrorsoft, a British software company, and Spectrum Holobyte, its American subsidiary. Mirrorsoft then licensed the Japanese arcade game rights to Sega and the North American arcade game, home console, and handheld rights to Atari Games. An NES version of *Tetris* was released quickly from Tengen.

But while Mirrorsoft was doling out rights to the game, Nintendo also was interested in getting home console rights to the game, particularly for their new handheld Game Boy. Nintendo's Howard Lincoln and Minoru Arakawa flew to Moscow to deal directly with the Soviet Foreign Trade Association where they learned that Robert Stein had only obtained the *computer* rights to *Tetris.* Nintendo quickly obtained both the console and handheld rights to *Tetris* and churned out copies of the game. Since Tengen did not have the legal right to distribute the game, it had to recall all of the *Tetris* cartridges that were still on store shelves. In all, 268,000 cartridges were returned and destroyed.[1]

Rise of the 16-Bit Consoles

In 1989, readers of video game magazines began seeing a new term appear: 16-bit games. In computer jargon, a bit, which is the contraction of the words "binary digit," is a fundamental unit of information having just two possible values, 0 or 1 (or two states: on and off). All of the video game systems, from the mid-1970s through the late 1980s, were 8-bit systems. This meant that the system processed, and sent data to the screen in units of bytes that consisted of 8 bits each. Since each bit could be either turned on or off, each byte represented a total of 256 different combinations. These buzzwords were suddenly important because in 1989 the news came out that 16-bit systems were going to be released. A 16-bit system processed and delivered information in 16-bit words that allowed for over 65,000 different combinations, thus allowing more information to be processed by the system in the same amount of time, resulting in faster speeds.

The first console to be advertised as a 16-bit system was the PC-Engine, released in Japan by computer company NEC. Technically, this was only slightly true. The PC-Engine did indeed have a 16-bit processor—a *graphics* processor that could display up to 256 colors on the screen at once at a number of resolutions. However, its CPU was 8-bit as were all of the systems that preceded it. When NEC released the PC-Engine in the United States, it chose a name that more honestly reflected its processing power: The TurboGrafx-16.

Games for the TurboGrafx-16 came on small plastic cards very similar to the ones that were used in the Sega Master System. The cards themselves were packaged in plastic jewel-cases similar to the type that housed audio CDs. Although NEC did not make history by releasing the first true 16-bit console, it claimed its place in history for another reason.

In 1989 NEC released a CD player for the console that gave it the ability to read data from compact discs. While the CD player could be used to play standard audio discs, it had been designed especially for video game use. CDs were a great breakthrough in video game technology. Prior to their introduction, the maximum amount of code that a game could utilize was 256 kilobytes. A compact disc was able to contain 550 megabytes of code; or 2,000 times that of the most powerful cartridge. Since the CD could be accessed randomly and quickly, the console was able to load new information without the gamer being aware that such input was taking place. Because the disc could hold so much information, CD-based games offered the ultimate in complexity, detail, and sound.

Despite its claim to history, the Turbografx-16 was not the runaway best-seller that NEC had hoped for, even with the addition of the optional CD player. That claim went to Sega.

Shortly after the release of the PC-Engine in Japan, Sega announced its intentions to release a true 16-bit console. That promise became a reality in the United States when Sega shipped the first Genesis units in late August 1989 to stores in the New York and Los Angeles areas. Nearly everyone who bought one was pleased with the console's high resolution and crisp stereo sound. The unit was quickly compared to the Turbografx-16 and while many felt that NEC's console offered better graphics, most gamers were impressed by the Genesis's speed.

Sega also offered exciting peripherals for the Genesis. One was the Telegenesis modem, which allowed gamers to compete against one another online via the telephone. For Sega Master System owners, Sega released a power base converter that plugged into the Genesis and played Master System games. Finally, Sega released a CD player for the Genesis, which it simply called the Sega CD. Sony manufactured the CD-ROM player that sat beneath the Genesis and the two units worked in tandem to produce outstanding games. The Sega CD contained its own processor that ran at 12.5 MHz—much faster than the 7.5 MHz speed at which the Genesis's processor ran. Together, the two CPUs eliminated any game pauses while the system loaded new information from the CD.

In addition to the 68000 CPU, the Sega CD also had two custom graphics chips. These chips allowed the CD player to add more colors and sprites to the TV screen than the Sega Mega-Drive (released in North America as the Sega Genesis) could do by itself. The two chips also added scaling and rotation to Sega games. Along with the custom Sega CD games, the unit also could play standard music CDs and the new CD+G discs (CD plus graphics). In Japan this was a big deal because it meant that gamers could play karaoke discs.

Nintendo was expected to respond and release its own 16-bit console following the release of the Genesis, and eventually the Super Nintendo Entertainment System (SNES) was released in 1991, nearly two years after the first appearance of the Genesis. But before that occurred, a new type of gaming console was released.

SNK was a manufacturer of arcade games. Its Neo•Geo looked like any other arcade upright except that players had a choice of five different games to play. As in previous home video game systems, each game was stored on a cartridge. In the case of the Neo•Geo, each cartridge was the size of a VHS videotape and could store 330 megabits of data. When a game began to lose its appeal, the arcade operator simply had to change the cartridge instead of the entire machine. Players also could purchase 4K memory cards from the arcade operators which could be inserted into the machine to save games.

Following a successful introduction of the unit in Japan in 1989, SNK released a home version of the Neo•Geo in the United States a year later. The home version utilized the same cartridges as the arcade machines so gamers could play exactly the same games in the arcades or at home. It also accepted the memory card which allowed gamers to save their games in the arcades and then play them at home.

Although SNK flaunted the Neo•Geo as a 21-bit machine, it actually used the same 16-bit processor as the Genesis. It also had an additional 8-bit processor that was the same as the one in the Sega Master System. The dual processors allowed the Neo•Geo to display 4,096 different colors on the screen at one time (as opposed to the TurboGrafx-16 which could only display 512 simultaneous colors). The Neo•Geo also produced sounds from 15 different channels (the Genesis used only 10 separate channels).

Unfortunately, all of the features that the Neo•Geo offered came at a separate price. SNK sold the Neo•Geo in two different packages. The basic Green System retailed for $399 and included a console and one controller. For an additional $200, a consumer could purchase the Gold Set, which came with an additional controller and one game cartridge. The cartridges themselves carried a suggested list price of $199. While the system attracted hardcore gamers who liked the type of games that SNK was known for, it was in no way any competition for the Genesis.

That competition would be provided by Nintendo. With the eight-year-old NES beginning to show its age, Nintendo knew that it had to have a more advanced system on the market. Nintendo planned a September 1, 1991, release for the $200 Super NES which would boast a 16-bit processor. Many NES owners quickly wondered how much support their 8-bit machine would continue to receive. Nintendo announced at the Summer CES that the SNES would be backward compatible with the NES via a plug-in.

With the release of the SNES, Nintendo again had a serious contender in the home console race. However, despite the popularity of the SNES and Nintendo's reputation, during the 1991 Christmas season, the company lost its position as the top-selling video game company to Sega, which had taken control of 55 percent of the 16-bit market. In many cases, the Genesis had outsold the SNES by as much as two to one.[2] Many of the sales were in part due to a new game that Sega released called *Sonic the Hedgehog*, a *Super Mario*-type game that played at lightning speeds.

Despite Sega's slight dominance, their success would be short lived. Even as they fought it out with Nintendo over the 16-bit machines, the console designers were already looking into the following generation of machines. And along with the 32-bit machines would come new competition.

CHAPTER 21

CD-ROM GAMES

Carl Therrien

While it became a standard relatively recently, disc-based storage goes a long way back in the history of video game distribution. The term encompasses a wide range of technologies, from magnetic floppy discs, analog laserdiscs, and a variety of digital optical media. Of the latter, the CD-ROM enjoyed the strongest following and the longest life span; as of 2006, a significant number of PC games are still burned on CDs. When it became the most common video game distribution format in the mid-1990s, the compact disc was already a standard in the music industry. In contrast to the magnetic tapes used for the distribution of albums and movies, optical discs allowed relatively fast, random, nonlinear access to the content. But these features were common already in the realm of cartridge-based video game systems; the ROMs in the Atari 2600 or Super Nintendo game cartridges were directly connected to the systems' working memory and could be read instantly. The CD drive optical head could not compete; as a matter of fact, optical discs introduced the infamous "loading" screen to the console gamer. Video games benefited first and foremost from the storage capabilities of the CD-ROM. While the CD format shares its core technical principle with the more recent DVD standard (found in the Xbox and PlayStation 2) and other dedicated formats (such as the Dreamcast's GD-ROM and the GameCube optical disc), the integration of CD-ROM technology and its consequences on game design and development are beyond the scope of this chapter.

In 1980, Sony and Philips agreed upon the specifications of the audio CD format. This agreement, known as the "red book" standard, was followed in 1985 by a "yellow book" specifying the data structure of CD-ROM technology. In 1986, a single 12-cm diameter disc could hold 550 megabytes of data; as of 2006, the same disc could hold up to 700 megabytes. In the mid-1980s, even the biggest players in the industry could not possibly produce enough content to fill the extra space. By comparison, cartridge sizes for home consoles were commonly referred to in megabits; converted back to megabytes, the storage space available to what is known as the 16-bit generation appears relatively meager: up to 2.5 megabytes for the Turbografx-16's TurboChip (or HuCard), 4 megabytes for the Sega Genesis cartridge, and 6 megabytes for the Super Nintendo Entertainment System's cartridge. On the personal computer side, the largest games at the beginning of the 1990s required a handful of high-density floppy disks (1.44 megabytes per disk). Of course, these sizes were adequate for most of the games produced in that generation. But at the same time, new ways of producing game assets were emerging: digitization of sound/picture/video and computer-generated imagery (CGI), for example. The ability to integrate this variety of assets defines one of the most salient buzzwords of the CD era: "multimedia." In reality, multimedia was associated first and foremost with the development of full-motion video. This fascination for a cinema-like illusion of motion actually led to a multitude of video compression techniques, typically specific to a given developer, with no actual norms in terms of image quality, frame rate, and proportion of the animation on the screen. The introduction of the CD-ROM format created a need to expand the content, and many different strategies emerged.

CD-ROM-Based Gaming Systems

For the personal computer user, CD-ROM gaming began in 1987, with the release of Cyan's *The Manhole*. However, the high cost of CD-ROM drives resulted in a smaller user base for the technology during the first generation of CD-based gaming systems. In 1989, NEC was the first to bring CD technology to the console world. Its Turbografx-16/PC-Engine CD-ROM peripheral could transfer data at a rate of 150 kilobytes per second, a feature known as the 1X standard. Since there are 1024 kilobytes in one megabyte, and considering the total storage on a CD (about 650 megabytes), this transfer rate might appear insufficient. But this would not be the system's worst performance bottleneck. Being an add-on, the Turbografx-CD depended on the original console's display and processing capabilities. The Turbografx-16 could handle typical 2-D gaming tricks (such as sprites and parallax scrolling) with ease and display most of the 512 available colors on screen at once with a few technical tweaks, but its work and video memory (8 and 64 kilobytes, respectively) were not suited to the multimedia ambitions of the CD era. The same could be said of Sega's CD add-on for the Genesis/Mega Drive, introduced in 1992 to the American market. While it provided a faster CPU and a significant increase in memory, the display was limited to 64 on-screen colors in most situations. Graphic adapters on IBM PC and compatible systems were more capable: cards compliant with the 1987 VGA standard, for instance, could display 256 simultaneous colors from a palette of 262,144. In 1989, Fujitsu released the FM Towns computer in Japan. Built with cutting-edge PC technology (but incompatible with PC software), its most touted feature was indeed the integrated 1X CD-ROM drive. Back in the United States, the Software Publishing Association (including Microsoft, Dell, and Creative Labs) was also working on a standard dedicated to multimedia applications and games. In 1990, the association established the Multimedia PC (MPC) norm, which consists of a configuration guideline for PC CD-ROM users. Finally, the Commodore CDTV and Philips CD-i (both released in 1991) introduced a third category of products, in between home computers and game consoles, designed to bring a larger array of multimedia applications to the living room.

Interestingly, many of these first generation CD-based gaming systems were upgraded one way or another: NEC issued various system and memory upgrades on TurboChips and some Sega CD games would take advantage of the 32X Genesis add-on. Fujitsu released many versions of the FM Towns, including the FM Towns Marty in 1991, the first console with an integrated CD drive. NEC would soon follow with its Turbo Duo in 1992, a new design for a system essentially equivalent to the Turbografx-CD with the latest system card. The MPC norms were reevaluated in 1993, the same year the 3DO Company and Commodore launched their CD consoles. Featuring a 2X CD-ROM drive, the 3DO and Amiga CD^{32} could be upgraded to read the MPEG-1 movie standard developed by the Motion Picture Expert Group. With the U.S. releases of the Sega Saturn and the Sony PlayStation in 1995, developers now had the technical means to integrate good quality FMV in their CD games: 2X transfer rate, sufficient work/video memory, and graphical processors that could display millions of colors. The multimedia capabilities of CD gaming matured, but at the same time, these systems were among the first to hardwire real-time 3-D manipulation. It is interesting to note that, notwithstanding their relative abilities, FMV games appeared on most of the CD systems mentioned here.

Extended Games, Extended Play?

The real advantage of CD-ROM technology resides in its massive storage space. The actual quality of gameplay-related assets depends on the global competence of any given system. Of course, from the Turbografx-CD to the PlayStation, these assets constantly grow richer with detail and thus become more data intensive; while this evolution can be addressed by the CD format, it cannot be seen as a direct consequence of its introduction.

Two tendencies in game design can be directly associated with the advent of CD-based gaming systems. The expression "extended game" aptly identifies the first tendency. From a production standpoint, the examples in this category follow two distinct ideas: add extra content around the game spaces or add "more of the same" game spaces. Considering the roots of CD-ROM technology as an audio-playback device, the addition of CD-quality musical pieces "around" the game world was no surprise. Audio tracks were read directly from the CD as the player progressed through the levels, with no additional cost in terms of system resources. Consequently, this feature could be easily integrated in any game. CD music became the main attraction of early CD games (such as Cyan's *The Manhole,* the first game distributed on CD-ROM in 1987) and the most frequent addition to preexisting games converted to a CD system. Memorable examples include *Gate of Thunder* (a shooting game, HudsonSoft, 1992, Turbografx-CD), *The Terminator* (platform game, Virgin, 1993, Sega CD), *Fighting Street* (HudsonSoft/Capcom, 1989, Turbografx-CD), *Loom* (graphic adventure, Lucasfilm Games, 1991, FM Towns), and *The Secret of Monkey Island* (graphic adventure, LucasArts, 1992, PC CD-ROM).

The second frequent CD-related addition "around" the game world also prospered in a great variety of game genres. While cut-scenes beween game levels were already common in the early 1990s and surfaced quite early in the history of video games (most notably with *Pac-Man* in 1980), CD-ROM technology quickly became an incentive to include full-motion video cut-scenes created with computer-generated imagery, live-action video, or both. Minimally, developers would add an animated introduction sequence to action-oriented games. On the other hand, extensive use of this feature eventually came to be associated with certain genres and series; Japanese role-playing games, most notably *Final Fantasy VII* (SquareSoft, 1997, PlayStation) and the *Command & Conquer* series (*Red Alert,* Westwood Studios, 1996, PC CD-ROM) are noteworthy examples.

The third strategy to "extend" games obeys a different logic, since it provides more game spaces and variety. Typically, developers would include extra levels for a game previously available and/or integrate more variety from one level to the other (*The Terminator,*

Virgin, 1993, Sega CD; *Zool,* Gremlin, 1993, Amiga CD[32]). At first glance, the seminal CD-ROM adventure game *Myst* (Cyan Worlds, 1993, PC CD-ROM) appears to follow the same logic. By the nature of its gameplay, the graphic adventure genre had a different representational economy than action-oriented games; the game world is usually depicted through a series of fixed, but very detailed, game screens. While *Myst* oriented the adventure genre into its "brain-teaser" branch, its most striking feature resides in the multiplication of completely unique game screens. From this perspective, *Myst* is clearly part of what we have called the "extended games" tendency; it adds content to an existing game genre without affecting the gameplay fundamentals. But at the same time, this particular extension affects how we perceive the game world in a way the narrative load of adjacent cut-scenes, the beauty of an orchestral score, and the extra thrills of additional levels do not. *Myst* does not increase the actual size of this world, but rather its density. It is also devoid of the repetition that usually plagued games with first-person exploration such as the *Eye of the Beholder* (Westwood Studios, 1990) or *Ishar* (Silmarils, 1992) role-playing game series, while retaining the same continuity. In *Myst,* the world becomes saturated with detail; it partially achieves a certain representational variability that is at the heart of the second tendency associated with CD-ROM gaming.

Contemporary to *Myst's* release, Trilobyte's *The 7th Guest* (1992, PC CD-ROM) made a statement about what CD-ROM technology could achieve. In the game's haunted house, the player assumes the role of a floating point of view whose identity constitutes the notorious final revelation. One may argue that the depiction of this point of view floating from one exploration node to the other is a first clue to the mystery, but it is obviously the technical aspect that deserves our attention here. Trilobyte managed to develop a system capable of streaming intensive graphical information (high-resolution 256 color prerendered animations, with more than 10 frames per second) directly from the CD. In the gaming industry, there might have been as many FMV techniques as there were developers, but one thing is certain: the more-or-less convincing illusion of motion is indeed a central element of the "saturated world" tendency. By saturated, we refer to a significant increase in verisimilitude, an illusion abstracted from the typical shortcomings of video game representation such as repetition and rigidity of motion. Another early feature of CD-gaming complies with this definition: digitized voices. "Talkie" versions of popular adventure games were edited on CD, including *Indiana Jones and the Fate of Atlantis* (LucasArts, 1993, PC CD-ROM) and *King's Quest V: Absence Makes the Heart Go Yonder!* (Sierra On-Line, 1992, PC CD-ROM). Like FMV, digitized sound proposes an illusion forever changing as it evolves through time. Both illusions would come together in the ideal of interactive cinema. Many clones built on the *Myst* and *The 7th Guest* models had no significant human presence to speak of. But the explosion of live-action FMV games shows that the human figure could only linger backstage for so long. Games such as *Under a Killing Moon* (Access Software, 1994, PC CD-ROM), *The Beast Within: A Gabriel Knight Mystery* (Sierra On-Line, 1995 PC CD-ROM), and *Ripper* (Take-Two Interactive, 1996, PC CD-ROM) rely on character interaction as much as the typical graphic adventure game; as a matter of fact, these games required up to 6 CDs to store all the live-action sequences. Earlier examples include *Sherlock Holmes Consulting Detective* (ICOM Simulations, 1991, released on PC CD-ROM, Turbografx-CD, and Sega CD) and *It Came from the Desert* (Cinemaware, 1991, Turbografx-CD).

The fascination for gameplay-integrated FMV spread way beyond the predictable graphic adventure enclave. American Laser Games brought their arcade laserdisc titles to home gaming systems (*Mad Dog McCree,* 1993; *Crime Patrol,* 1994) and many other live-action shooters were produced for the Sega CD (*Surgical Strike, Tomcat Alley,* Code Monkeys, 1993 and 1994, respectively). Shooting courses using CGI were also common, with key titles appearing in the major formats (*Rebel Assault,* LucasArts, 1993, PC CD-ROM; *Sewer Shark,* Digital Pictures, 1992, Sega CD; *Microcosm,* Psygnosis, 1994, Amiga CD^{32}; *Cyberia,* Xatrix, 1996, 3DO). Some racing games also had prerendered courses whose display would be affected by the player's speed (*MegaRace,* Cryo Interactive, 1993, PC CD-ROM). Even platform games were produced; side-scrolling 3-D levels integrated slight point-of-view modifications at specific moments (*Bram Stoker's Dracula,* Psygnosis, 1993, Sega CD; *Time Commando,* Adeline Software, 1996, PlayStation). However, the most unlikely genre to undergo FMV treatment is undoubtedly the fighting game. In *Supreme Warrior* (Digital Pictures, 1994, 3DO) and *Prize Fighter* (Digital Pictures, 1994, Sega CD), live-action sequences depict street fights and boxing as seen through the eyes of the protagonist.

In the global production landscape, however, action games were clearly outnumbered, and few actually acquired critical or popular recognition. This failure can be explained partially by a gameplay discrepancy between FMV CD-ROM games and contemporary prime examples in any given genre. As the industry began its transition towards real-time 3-D mechanics, and as the virtual worlds' visual representation could be affected more by the user's manipulations, the worlds depicted by FMV appeared fixed and rigid even compared to most 2-D games of the time. In FMV shooters, the player would typically control a simple crosshair on top of the movie sequence, and exploding targets were presented on separate shots, whereas any 2-D side-scrolling shooter could dynamically integrate the player's animated avatar and the havoc it created in a single, continuous scene. Movie sequences could not be altered and manipulated with ease, and many action games ended up relying on *Dragon's Lair* gameplay mechanics (hit the right key at the right moment). Even adventure games eventually frustrated players; live-action conversation sequences could not be assimilated and skipped as easily as their text-based predecessors, changing the typical pacing of the genre. Ultimately, these worlds were not only saturated with detail, but also with authorship, and the creators' authority over the experience was a reflection of the authority exerted by the technology itself.

In the end, CD-ROM technology did affect the face of gaming for a few years. Its massive storage capabilities led developers to embrace the latest visual attraction, and this emphasis on FMV favored slow-paced genres and/or simpler gameplay mechanics. With the CD-ROM, the quality of in-game assets increased but at the expense of gameplay itself. This regression of game language in favor of verisimilitude evokes the introduction of sound in filmmaking technology. And just as film language eventually integrated the new expressive resources more seamlessly, the gaming industry found a way to develop the ideal behind FMV through techniques more suited to the nature of games. Nowadays, the assets incorporated in a real-time 3-D world are so data intensive that many games nearly fill up the 8.5 gigabytes available on a double-layer DVD. Already, a new generation of optical media is available; a single PlayStation 3 Blu-ray disc can store up to 50 gigabytes of information. Even though the increase factor is nowhere as significant as it was when CD technology was integrated in the early 1990s, this storage space exceeds the needs of most current productions. It remains to be seen if and how this extra storage will affect production strategies, favor certain types of contents and genres, and, ultimately, if it will play the same decisive role as the CD-ROM did in the tendencies that defined its generation.

CHAPTER 22

GENRE PROFILE: INTERACTIVE MOVIES

Bernard Perron

The interactive movie as a genre holds a place in the history of video games for one main reason: its well-known failure. Made possible by the increased storage capacity of laserdisc and CD-ROM, the idea was to take "video game" literally by combining full-motion video of live-action footage and cinematic techniques with a gaming experience. Considered to be at the cutting edge of technology at the beginning of the 1990s and seen as the future of the industry (mainly by those who were making them), interactive movies were no longer made by the end of the decade, despite the introduction of DVDs, which had greater storage capacity and greatly improved the use of movie clips. They came to have a very bad reputation due to the limited possibilities of their branching structures, their lack of interactivity, the bad acting of their cast, and, in the case of the earlier interactive movies, their low-resolution pictures and the dismal quality of their playback. Yet despite such a general discrediting, this phenomenon should not be overlooked.

Because of the reference to movies, it is in the genre's best interest to be viewed in the light of the "cinema of attractions," a concept introduced to better understand the specificity of the early cinema by comparison with the institutional narrative cinema that is more familiar (according to film theorist Tom Gunning, the "cinema of attractions" is in fact opposed to the cinema of narrative integration which subordinates film form to the development of stories and characters).[1] The term "cinema of attractions" refers to the exhibitionist nature of early cinema, a cinema willing to display its visibility and to rupture the self-enclosed fictional world to get the attention of the spectator or, in this case, of the gamer. While the cinema of attractions was more interested in the film's ability to show something rather than the telling of stories, the interactive movie was more concerned with questions of nonlinear storytelling and photorealistic imagery than the development of innovative gameplay. During the early 1990s, full motion video was a novelty in games, just as the cinema was a novelty at the end of the nineteenth century. It is thus understandable that interactive movies appeared at a particular period of technological progress. And some interactive movies had quite an impact at the time they were produced.

Although the genre came to be associated with live-action video, its first occurrence is an animated interactive movie now displayed in the Smithsonian Institution alongside the only two other video games there, *PONG* and *Pac-Man*. *Dragon's Lair* was the first analog laserdisc-based coin-op video game to be released. The idea became clear to designer and programmer Rick Dyer at a 1982 coin-op trade show when he saw *Astron Belt* (which was finally released by Sega/Bally in 1984), the first arcade game ever created with a laserdisc generating the background footage (computer graphics where used for the foreground ship and lasers). Dyer then approached former Disney animator Don Bluth, who the previous year had created the acclaimed film *The Secret of NIMH* (1982) (and who teamed up with Gary Goldman and John Pomeroy for Dyer's project), in order to create a game based on the new laserdisc machine. The production cost of *Dragon's Lair* was 10 times the average budget of the era ($1.3 million), but it grossed $32 million in its first eight months. This was due to the 22 minutes of prerecorded full animation that really stood out in comparison to the computer-generated graphics displayed on the screens of other arcade games. It was so impressive that it cost 50 cents instead of 25 cents to play, and some arcade owners even installed a monitor over the cabinet so people could watch the game as it was played. *Dragon's Lair* was not just another game; as Bluth said in September 1983, "We've combined the unique capabilities of both computer and animation and formed a new style of entertainment—participatory movies."[2] The gamer was indeed invited to play his "own" cartoon, to embark in a fantasy adventure by becoming Dirk the Daring, a valiant knight gone to rescue the fair and voluptuous Princess Daphne from the clutches of Singe the Evil Dragon. His actual participation consisted of making decisions by using a joystick to give Dirk directions or hitting an action button to make him strike with his sword. If the direction chosen was good or the "sword" button pushed at the right moment, the obstacle was overcome or the monster slaughtered. If not, Dirk died in horrible and funny ways. This decision-tree branching gameplay would attract a following and remains the basic design model of interactive movies. Indeed, the popularity of *Dragon's Lair* saw the release of similar games like *Space Ace* (Cinematronics/Magicom, 1983), *Cliff Hanger* (Stern/Seeburg, 1983) and *Badlands* (Konami/Centuri, 1984). In the 1990s, Sega TruVideo Productions like *The Masked Rider: Kamen Rider ZO* (Sega, 1994) and *Mighty Morphin Power Rangers* (Sega, 1994) even recreated a similar experience using footage from the popular TV series. Nevertheless, those games never achieved the same success. If *Dragon's Lair* "proved to be a milestone in the history of videogames," it is because "its debut not only served as a window to the future of interactive entertainment, but also represented the industry's last great hurrah before it came to crashing down in 1984."[3]

Sports games, such as *Goal to Go* (Stern/Seeburg, 1983), which were composed of real sports sequences, were made at the same time as *Dragon's Lair*.[4] In the same vein as *Astron Belt*, 1980s arcade laserdisc games using video footage also had short lifespans, due to the unreliability of the technology. Shooting games akin to *M.A.C.H. 3* (Mylstar/Gottlieb, 1983) and *Us vs. Them* (Mylstar/Gottlieb, 1984), and racing games like *Laser Grand Prix* (Taito, 1983) and *GP World* (Sega, 1984) gave more continuous control to the gamer. The company American Laser Games revived the use of live action in the arcade at the beginning of the 1990s with its nine laserdisc games. A flyer underlines what distinguished its first-person shooters from the other ones made at the time: "The player is part of a true-to-life movie...combining laser technology with player interaction!" Formerly designed to train police officers, the games offered the player "realism never seen in the amusement game industry."[5] In games such as *Mad Dog McCree* (1990), *Who Shot Johnny Rock?* (1991), *Space Pirates* (1992), *Crime Patrol* (1993), and *Fast Draw Showdown* (1994), which was the first laserdisc game to film its imagery in "portrait" mode instead of the usual "landscape" mode, the gamer had first and foremost to draw his light gun before his rivals did. The plot lines of the games—rescuing the mayor and his daughter from the lowdown dirty sidewinder Mad Dog McCree, trying to discover who shot Johnny, searching for energy crystals to save the galaxy, joining the force to fight crime, or competing to be the fastest gunfighter in town—were of course a pretext to stage many shoot-outs which took place in different locations. If the gamer stayed alive or did not kill an innocent bystander, he gathered clues and the story unfolded a bit more. If not, he lost a life and funny comments were made about his death. This was not very different from *Dragon's Lair.*

With the advent of CD-based home systems, movie-like gaming experiences arose. The introduction of the Multimedia PC in 1990 and the release of the peripheral Turbografx-CD in 1989, the Philips CD-i system in 1991, the Sega CD add-on in 1992, and the 3DO console in 1993 marked the increased use of live-action video. Compared to cartridges, the amount of information the CD could hold allowed the storing of movie sequences (that were even called "cinemas" at the time). *Dragon's Lair,* its clones, and the American Laser Games first-person shooters (available with a game gun for the Sega CD and 3DO or a peacekeeper revolver for the Philips CD-i) thus made their way into the home. The laserdisc game *Us vs. Them* (1984) had filmed cut-scenes of frightened citizens and military command personnel between missions, and many other games had such "cinematics" (the real-time strategy game series *Command & Conquer* from Westwood Studios, for instance, was known for its live-action cut-scenes). The attraction of cinema drove all types of games to be associated with the interactive movie genre.

Available only on CD-ROM (since it was too large for floppy disks), *The 7th Guest* (Trilobyte/Virgin Games, 1992/1993[6]) was one of the three "killer applications" that launched, according to Steven L. Kent, the multimedia revolution (along with *Myst* and *Doom* released in 1993). As a showcase for technology, it was, claimed Kent, "a masterpiece."[7] To Microsoft's founder Bill Gates, it was "the new standard in interactive entertainment."[8] Designers Rob Landeros and Graeme Devine formed their own company, Trilobyte, to create "the first interactive drama in a terrifying real virtual environment complete with live actors," according to the game's box. Inspired by the board game *Clue* and by David Lynch's television series *Twin Peaks* (1990–1991), the game revolves around an investigation to identify an unknown guest that would join six ghostly visitors invited to a spooky mansion owned by the evil toy maker Henry Stauf. Through the eyes of Ego, a disembodied consciousness, the gamer moves in widescreen through the rooms of the high-resolution prerendered 3-D house to solve puzzles that unfold in part of the story. Although *The 7th Guest* is mainly a puzzle-oriented game, it was not meant to be only that. In the second version of the design document, Landeros and Devine stated: "We at Trilobyte have coined the phrase 'Hyper Movie' to describe the medium in which we work." The entire product was "to be regarded as one big audience-participation cinematic production."[9] Indeed, thanks to innovations in digital compression and full-motion video playback, the game is peppered with short film clips showing the actors superimposed over the 3-D image with a transparency and aura effect (due to a technical error that fortunately contributed to the look of the game). Contrary to their arcade game background (film footage based laserdisc games which used computer graphics in the foreground), it now became the norm to stage the actors in virtual settings. By solving the brainteasers, exploring the house, and clicking on objects, the gamer of *The 7th Guest* is rewarded with sequences which uncover the desires of the ghostly visitors, expose their relationships, and unravel their roles in Stauf's malevolent machinations. As this plot line is puzzling, it also contributes to the overall appeal of the game.

The huge success of *The 7th Guest* saw the release of similar games and of a sequel, *The 11th Hour* (Trilobyte/Virgin Games, 1995) which was difficult to develop and did not sell as well. Landeros teamed up with filmmaker David Wheeler, who had directed the film parts of *The 11th Hour*, to produce two of the last interactive movies on DVD: *Tender Loving Care* (Aftermath Media/DVD International, 1999) and *Point Of View* (Digital Circus/DVD International 2001). The first, starring John Hurt, relates the weird links which form between a husband, his lovely but sick wife, and the sensual but devious nurse/therapist who comes to live with the couple in order to take care of the wife. The second tells the story of a young and reclusive artist named Jane who spies on her musician neighbor. The interactivity works the same in both cases. The movies are divided into chapters, and each chapter ends with exit poll questions about the action and the secret thoughts and desires of the player. The answers to those questions influence the way the following chapter will be selected.

While mature themes and some violence are found in *Tender Loving Care* (which had nudity as well) and *Point Of View,* the scenes were not that problematic at the end of the 1990s since the games were rated. But this was not the case at the beginning of the decade. For a start, many of the Sega games were based on live-action sequences. TruVideo Productions like *Fahrenheit* (Sega, 1995) and *Wirehead* (1995) exploited a decision-tree branching gameplay akin to *Dragon's Lair* by putting the gamer in the shoes of a fireman rescuing people and of a father with a wireless controller in his brain who has to escape evil clutches. A company like Digital Pictures developed titles for the Sega CD such as the create-your-own-music-video series *Make My Video: INXS/Kriss Kross/Marky Mark & the Funky Bunch* (1992), the first person shooter *Corpse Killer* (1992), the rail shooter *Sewer Shark* (1994), the fighting game *Supreme Warrior* (1994) and the basketball game *Slam City with Scottie Pippen* (1995). Digital Pictures made *Night Trap* in 1992, one of the first live-action video games released on the Sega CD. Tom Zito, founder of the company, was thinking about merging movies and video games in the mid-1980s. He believed, Kent reports, that controlling real people instead of cartoons would give games impact.[10] Although such an idea remains questionable, his game was indeed to become famous for the controversy it sparked. Inspired by the idea of an interactive movie based on the film *A Nightmare on Elm Street* (1984), *Night Trap,* shot on location in 1986 and starring the television celebrity Dana Plato, was not a typical video game. Playing an agent of the S.C.A.T. (Sega Control Attack Team), the gamer has to protect a group of five girls at a weekend house party from the vampires. By closely monitoring, through hidden cameras, eight rooms displayed at the bottom of the film screen, the gamer needs to capture the hooded intruders with traps concealed in the house and accessed with a code that could be changed anytime during the game. If the gamer clicks on an operable trap at the right moment, he captures an intruder. If he does not, the intruder leaves the room or a victim is attacked with a weird drilling device or hangs on a meat hook. Although the action is far from gory, the girls do not run naked everywhere in the house, and the goal is to save, not to kill, the young ladies, *Night Trap* was, with the fighting game *Mortal Kombat* (Midway/ Acclaim, 1993), at the origin of a Congressional investigation about violence in video games. Encouraged or not by Nintendo in order to undermine Sega's commercial success, the December 1993 hearings were commissioned by Democrat Senator Joseph Lieberman. Along with the fact that any young person could buy the game, a main concern of the first session was the realistic look of the live actors in *Night Trap*.[11] The hearings lead to the development of a ratings system, at first Sega's own Videogame Rating Council (VRC) in 1993, and the video game industry's Entertainment Software Ratings Board (ESRB) the following year. *Night Trap*'s clone, "the cinematic mystery" *Double Switch* (Digital Pictures/Sega, 1993) was rated as a teen game (ages 13 and over) by Sega VRC.

As *Night Trap* came under fire, the release of Philips CD-i *Voyeur* (POV Entertainment Group/Philips Interactive Media, 1993/1994) did not bring as much political controversy. And yet the gameplay was similar and the content was adult oriented enough to receive an "18" certificate by the British Board of Film Classification. *Voyeur* shows women in lingerie, simulates sex scenes right from the start, and has lesbian relationships. Living in front of the Hawke's Manor where family members and guests are gathering for a last weekend before the father decides to run for the presidency of the United States, the gamer is contacted by the police at the beginning of the game. He is to spy on the Hawke in order to get incriminating evidence on video and audio tapes about the aforementioned father who wants to hide a secret which could compromise his political career. The gameplay consists of clicking on windows of the manor to read information, look at personal belongings, hear conversations, or witness some scenes between the characters staged in digital settings. Created by the Hollywood production company that made the film *Madonna: Truth or Dare* (1991), *Voyeur* was a "true hybrid" as it showed, and *Time* magazine reported how this coming "attraction" had "real motion pictures on the screen while the player control[led] which of hundreds of twists and turns the plot [would] take."[12] The number of twists and turns is obviously not that many, but the game runs differently every time its one weekend game time sessions are played. *Voyeur II*, the sequel, banked on the same formula in 1996.

Interactive movies centered on mystery or detective stories are numerous and are better described as adventure games where the gamer works along with the investigator, as opposed to the voyeuristic distance of *Voyeur* that leaves the gamer out of the action. *Sherlock Holmes Consulting Detective* (ICOM Simulations, 1991; three volumes were released), originally developed for home computer CD-ROMs, is the first of this kind and the earliest use of live-action video in a small window at the center of the screen. To solve (in the desired order) the three "Full-Motion Color Video Whodunits" (according to the box) introduced by Sherlock Holmes and Dr. Watson, the gamer has to consult editions of *The Times* to lean on the insights of the Baker Street Irregulars and to look at Holmes's files. The gamer is mostly able to choose from Holmes's notebook or the London directory to travel to places so as to meet with the Regulars, the witnesses, and the suspects. The movie clips filmed with professional actors in real sets show the detective with or without his acolyte talking to people.

Whereas the exchanges of *Sherlock Holmes Consulting Detective* occur without interruption, conversations are rendered interactively and the gamer is given a choice of answers through dialog boxes in the graphic adventure game tradition. The second of the five titles of the Tex Murphy series (Access Software, 1989–1998), *Martian Memorandum* (1991), had small, low-resolution talking heads to answer questions. However, even if the gamer was supposed to "experience interactive cinema" (according to the box), it is with the third and classic *Under a Killing Moon* (1994) that the gamer would see the

Philip Marlowe-type detective portrayed in live-action video. With this "interactive 3-D experience that [set] a new standard for realism" (according to the box), creator Chris Jones, who also plays Tex Murphy, reversed the idea behind the film *The Purple Rose of Cairo* (1985), so that the spectator is participating in the virtual world[13] (an idea, predictably enough, shared by the other designers of interactive movies). This world, far from being realistic in regard to movie standards, is a 2042 futuristic San Francisco where the hardboiled private investigator has to accomplish nothing less than to save the world in seven days. A paradigm of the genre, the navigation in the 3-D computer graphic environment is made through a first-person perspective (to save production cost). Film clips come into view upon clicking on objects and by interacting with people through dialog boxes. *The Pandora Directive* (1996) and *Tex Murphy: Overseer* (1998, released on CD and DVD), with widescreen imagery, ended the series. Various adventure mysteries and detective movie games have been developed, such as *The Dame Was Loaded* (Beam Software/Philips Interactive Media, 1995), the singular *Psychic Detective* (Colossal Pictures/Electronic Arts, 1995), *In the First Degree* (Brøderbund/Brøderbund, 1995), *Ripper* (Take Two Interactive/Take Two Interactive, 1996), *Spycraft* (Activision/Activision, 1996), *Black Dahlia* (Interplay/Take Two interactive, 1997) (with a record eight CDs), *Dark Side of the Moon* (SouthPeak Interactive/SouthPeak Interactive, 1998) and *The X-Files Game* (Hyberbole Studios/Fox Interactive, 1998). As for the latter company, Hyperbole Studios made two early examples of "VirtualCinema movies": *Quantum Gate* in 1993 and *The Vortex: Quantum Gate II* in 1994.

The attraction of live-action video inspired celebrated game designers such as Chris Roberts, Roberta Williams, and Jane Jensen to move in this direction. Chris Roberts's *Wing Commander* series was successful right from the start in 1990, depicting a galactic war between a Confederation of human systems and the Empire of Kilrathi, a race of warlike, feline extraterrestrials. However, *Wing Commander III: Heart of the Tiger* (Origin Systems/Origin Systems, 1994) became more than just a space combat simulation. Roberts made one of his dreams come true: he shot a (interactive) movie. (He later also directed the film adaptation of his series in 1999.) While all the games with live-action video were expensive, *Wing Commander III* was marketed as a multimillion dollar production ($3.5 million) and, above all, as "professionally scripted and filmed in Hollywood" (according to the box). With a cast led by Mark Hamill (the Luke Skywalker of *Star Wars*), Malcolm McDowell, and John Rhys-Davies, the game lived up to expectations. In order to succeed in the combat sequences, the main goal of Colonel Christopher Blair (Hamill) is to keep up the morale of his troops. Through conversations, he has to choose between two options regarding a character or an event. The decision the gamer takes will have an impact on what will happen next; a wingman always fights better with his morale high. The interactive video sequences therefore serve to add depth to the characters. They also help to further the story, a story told in the same way in *Wing Commander IV: The Price of Freedom* (1995, which had an impressive budget of $12 million) and *Wing Commander: Prophecy* (1997).

Carrying on the Sierra On-Line tradition of point-and-click adventure, Roberta Williams and Jane Jensen created two classics of the interactive movie genre. Co-founder of the company and designer of the famous *King's Quest* series, Williams wanted to try something new. She decided to make a horror game and thought it was necessary to use real actors to truly scare people.[14] The third-person perspective *Phantasmagoria* (Sierra On-Line/Sierra On-Line, 1995) takes place in a digitally rendered manor and town (whereas *Phantasmagoria II: A Puzzle of Flesh*, not designed by Williams, would be shot in real sets). Adrienne, the main character, has to discover the mystery of the manor and to fight an evil spirit she ill-advisedly released and who comes to possess her husband. The game contains a rape and several violent death scenes. Controversial enough, it was banned by the Australian government. Nonetheless, it was considered at the time a masterpiece and was part of the "Hot Ten List" (along with *The 11th Hour*) in the September 1995 *Electronic Gaming Monthly.* Jane Jensen's *The Beast Within: A Gabriel Knight Mystery* (Sierra On-Line/Sierra On-Line, 1995) was also well received. Alternating between Gabriel Knight and his assistant Grace Nakimura, the goal is to solve the mysterious existence of a werewolf. Praised as a great adventure, it was also considered to be one of the few successful examples of live-action video used over photographed back-drops. What is more, Jensen's series is in itself very representative of the evolution of genre. It goes from 2-D with *Gabriel Knight: Sins of the Fathers* (1993) to full-motion video with *The Beast Within: A Gabriel Knight Mystery* and to 3-D with *Gabriel Knight 3: Blood of the Sacred, Blood of the Damned* (1999).

Upon the release of *Dragon's Lair* in 1983, associate editor Telka S. Perry underlined in a epigraph of her article "Video Games: The Next Wave," that although interactive disk technology lent reality to arcade games (and home video games, we should add), purists still believed the ultimate video game evolution lied in real-time computer-generated graphics.[15] This actually turned out to be true. As real-time 3-D engines grew in image processing power during the mid-1990s and delivered a much more truly interactive experience, the production cost and the lack of malleability of the filmic image, coupled with limited gameplay, became less appealing for both designers and gamers. Just like the early cinema of attraction, the making of interactive movies would give way to other practices. The interlude of the interactive cinema experiment in the 1980s and 1990s would have shown that, indeed, video games are not the movies.

CHAPTER 23

ARCADE GAMES OF THE 1990S AND BEYOND

Mark J. P. Wolf

When the 1990s began, arcade video games faced growing competition from home console video games, which were slowly catching up to them as technology improved. Several games had already appeared that had three-dimensional filled-polygon graphics, which was something arcade games could do that home games could not, at least at the time. A number of unusual interfaces and controllers that were not available in the home appeared and helped to redefine the arcade experience throughout the decade. Eventually even the arcade itself would be redefined as a game center, amusement center, or cybercafé, as operators tried to lure players back.

But along with technological innovations came a cautious retreat to the more tried-and-true genres that had always been a staple of the medium, including vertically oriented shooting games (in which the action occurs along the vertical axis), fighting games, and driving games. The number of games produced in these genres expanded, while other genres shrank, and fewer innovative game designs were produced. More sequels and series games were made, relying on their predecessors' successes for instant recognition and acceptance. Even the move to three-dimensional graphics was done with apparent reluctance, until it seemed that home games would soon be making the jump; sprite-based games continued throughout the decade, growing ever more elaborate graphically while gameplay remained relatively unchanged.

The decline of arcade video games would come in the 1990s, despite attempts to redefine the arcade experience and attract players back to the arcade. According to a survey in the trade publication *Vending Times,* there were approximately 1,000,000 video games in arcades in 1988, but by the year 2000 that number had shrunk to 450,000.[1] Few, if any, arcade games from the 1990s became household names that even nonplayers would recognize. Perhaps only *Mortal Kombat* (1994) was widely known among the general public, and infamously at that, due to the controversy surrounding the game's extremely violent fatality moves. And as interest in new arcade games declined, older arcade video games were becoming objects of nostalgia and even collectibles as their glory days passed further into history and the children who grew up with them became adults who could afford to purchase the old games.

The Early 1990s: Sequels, Variants, and Series Games

The first third of the 1990s saw a plethora of vertically scrolling shooting games, fighting games, *Tetris* imitations, and in Japan, mahjong games. Vertically oriented shooting games had been popular and a staple of arcade video games since *Space Invaders*, the first game of the genre. During the first half of the 1990s, Taito released three *Space Invaders* sequels: *Super Space Invaders '91* (1991), *Space Invaders DX* (1993), and *Space Invaders '95* (1995). While 1990s games featured more detailed graphics, new power-ups, and extra options for players (such as the split screen for a two-player game found in *Space Invaders DX*), gameplay basics remained the same and many derivative games were produced.

Fighting games were also popular, with continuations of 1980s franchises, including three new Fatal Fury games from SNK [*Fatal Fury: King of Fighters* (1991), *Fatal Fury 2* (1992), and *Fatal Fury Special* (1993)], and five versions of Capcom's *Street Fighter II* [*Street Fighter II—Champion Edition* (1991), *Street Fighter II—The World Warrior* (1991), *Street Fighter II—Hyper Fighting* (1992), *Street Fighter II—Rainbow Edition* (1993), and *Street Fighter II—The New Challengers* (1993)]. New franchises of fighting games included Midway's *Mortal Kombat* series [*Mortal Kombat* (1992), *Mortal Kombat II* (1993), *Mortal Kombat 3* (1995), *Ultimate Mortal Kombat 3* (1995), and *Mortal Kombat 4* (1997)] and Namco's *Tekken* series, which would appear in the mid-1990s, along with still more *Street Fighter* games.

Several dozen puzzle games were produced in the early 1990s, though the majority were very similar to *Tetris*, and involved arranging falling blocks either into rows or into groups of three of the same color, with rows or matches disappearing as the screen filled up with blocks. In 1990 alone there was Philko's *Atomic Point;* Sega's *Bloxeed* (which featured backdrops of digitized imagery); *Columns* and *Columns II: The Voyage Through Time*, both from Sega; Semicom's *Cookie and Bibi 2*, Nintendo's *Dr. Mario*, SNK's *Puzzled*, Taito's *Palamedes*, Video System Co.'s *Hatris* (which used stacking hats instead of blocks), and Jaleco's *Tetris Plus*, among others. Some puzzle games did feature innovative play, such as Video System Co.'s *Pipe Dream* (1990) which was a variant of a home computer game, Leland's *Ataxx* (1990), which was almost like a board game, and Sega's *Borench* (1990) and Kaneko's *Magical Crystals* (1991) which were both unique in their gameplay. Finally, in Japan, mahjong games were popular, with over a dozen a year produced until 1994, when their numbers decreased somewhat. The games varied in their visual trappings and their themes included war, baseball, fantasy quest, horse racing, and striptease (even with animated characters). There was even one Japanese game, *China Town* (1991) which was described on http://www.klov.com/ as being "a cross between mahjong and *Tetris*."[2]

While the early 1990s extended popular genres and saw many sequels and derivative games, more innovation could be found when it came to games' interfaces and interaction. Arcade games had been competing with home systems since the mid-1980s when the Nintendo Entertainment System appeared, but the mid-1990s would step up that competition considerably.

Innovative Interfaces

Just as movies tried to win audiences back into theaters after the appearance of television, arcade video game producers searched for ways to provide experiences that most home consoles of the time could not. Arcade games that four players could play simultaneously had been around since the release of *PONG Doubles* in 1972, and were made throughout the

1970s and 1980s, but during the 1990s the number of three- and four-player games increased dramatically. There were even some six-player games, like Sega's *Hard Dunk* (1994), Atari Games' *T-Mek* (1994), Konami's *X-MEN* (1992), and Namco's *Galaxian 3* (1990) and *Attack of the Zolgear* (1994); and racing games like Namco's *Final Lap 2* (1991), Sega's *Daytona USA* (1994) and *Manx TT Superbike Twin* (1995) which could accommodate up to eight players when the cabinets were networked together; and one game, *Daytona USA 2: Power Edition* (1999), could network up to 40 players.

Although specialized interfaces had been around since the earliest days, for example, the steering wheel and foot pedals used in Kee Games's *Formula K,* or the two mounted guns used in Sega's *Balloon Gun,* arcade video games of the 1990s abounded in specialized interface devices. The most common ones were cockpit games, with sit-in car seats and steering wheels found in a wide variety of driving or racing games, such as Konami's *Over Drive* (1990), Sega's *Rad Rally* (1991) and *Sega Super GT* (1997), and Namco's *Driver's Eyes* (1990) which had a panoramic image spread over three video monitors extending into the player's peripheral vision. Namco's *Lucky & Wild* (1993), a two-player cooperative game, combined interfaces and had a steering wheel, foot pedal, and two mounted guns.

Other vehicle interfaces could be found, including motorcycle handlebars in Atari Games' *Vapor TRX* (1998) and *Road Burners* (1999), Namco's *Suzuka 8 Hours* (1992), Sega's *Super Hang-On* (1992), *Motor Raid* (1997), and *Harley Davidson & L. A. Riders* (1998). Taito's *Landing Gear* (1995) was an airplane simulator with a throttle lever and joystick interface, and Sega's *Airline Pilots* (1999) was a commercial Boeing 777 aircraft simulator made with the help of pilots and engineers from Japan Airlines.[3] Players drove an excavator in Taito's *Power Shovel Simulator* (1999), a motorboat in Stricor's *Powerboat Racing* (1998) (which also used three adjacent screens for a widescreen effect), a train in Taito's *Densha De Go! 2* (1999), a pedaling bicycle in Namco's *Prop Cycle* (1996), a hang glider in Konami's *Hang Pilot* (1997), a water scooter in Namco's *Aqua Jet* (1996) and Sega's *Wave Runner* (1996), and even rode on a saddle in Namco's *Final Furlong* (1997).

Instead of sitting, some interfaces were designed for players to stand on and steer with foot movement. Sega's *Top Skater* (1997) featured a skateboard interface, while Namco's *Alpine Surfer* (1996) featured a snowboard. Namco also produced two skiing games, *Alpine Racer* (1995) and *Alpine Racer 2* (1997), which had skis to stand on and ski poles for the player to hold. Sega's *Ski Champ* (1998) also had a similar interface.

Other sports games also had specialized interfaces. Gaelco's *Football Power* (1999) had a soccer ball that the player kicked to move the ball about the field, while Global VR's *Kick It!* (1997) had a tethered soccer ball that the player kicked into a miniature goal area while an on-screen goalie attempted to stop it. Namco's *Family Bowl* (1998) used a small bowling ball which the player rolled down a small bowling alley where sensors then used the ball's position to determine which on-screen pins were knocked down. Another bowling game, Stern's *Super Strike* (1990), used a cue ball and a table-top alley. Grand's *Slick Shot* (1990) used a cue ball and a full-sized pool cue on a miniature pool table and infrared sensors to detect the ball's movement. Taito's *Sonic Blast Man* (1990) was a boxing game with real boxing gloves, a punch target, and on-screen opponents who reacted to the punches (players were only allowed three punches per game). Jaleco's *Arm Champ* (1988) and *Arm Champ II* (1992) had a robotic arm that players arm-wrestled. There were even a number of fishing games, including Namco's *Angler King* (1990), and Sega's *Sport Fishing* (1994), *Sport Fishing 2* (1995), *Get Bass* (1998), and *Sega Marine Fishing* (1999), each of which featured a fishing pole interface.

New interfaces occasionally spawn new genres of games, and the 1990s saw the rise of "rhythm and dance" games, in which players had to coordinate their movements to music. Konami produced so many of these games that it had a separate division, Benami Games, to produce them ("Benami" is a combination of "Beatmania" and "Konami").[4] Devecka's *Drumscape* (1990) and Konami's *DrumMania* series (five games over the period 1999 to 2001) all had a set of miniature drumheads that the player played on with tethered drumsticks. Konami's *Beatmania* series (34 games over the period 1998 to 2007) had games featuring a five- or seven-key piano and a DJ turntable interface which the player used interactively in time with the music playing. Namco's *Guitar Jam* (1999), SCEI's *UmJammer Lammy* (1999), and Konami's *GuitarFreaks* series (14 games over the period 1998 to 2006) were two-player games with two full-sized guitars that were used as an interface to play along with the music, although players pressed buttons on the guitars instead of strumming strings. Some *DrumMania* and *GuitarFreaks* games could even be networked together so that two guitarists and one drummer could play a song together.

Other interfaces required physical movement that involved the player's whole body. The most famous of these, Konami's *Dance Dance Revolution* (1998) had players follow a series of on-screen dance steps, dancing on a pressure-sensitive dance floor interface. The game began a popular series of games (16 versions over the period of 1998 to 2006) and it was even used in a physical education class in California.[5] These games eventually became available for home console systems, and in 2003, three of the top seven best-selling PlayStation 2 games were variations of *Dance Dance Revolution.*[6] Konami also produced several *Dance Maniax* games in 2000 and 2001, in which infrared motion sensors detected the movements of players' arms and legs. A few other companies produced motion-oriented games. Andamiro, a Korean company, released *Pump It Up* (1999), which had a dance floor interface, and was sued by Konami for patent infringement. Namco's 1998 game *Jumping Groove* had a much smaller interface, with one position for each foot, requiring a player to hop on one or the other in sequence. Namco also released *Balance Try* the same year, which had a rocking bar that the player tried to remain standing on while it moved.

Other unique games of the time include SNK/Saurus's *The Irritating Maze* (1997), which had air jets that blasted the player suddenly when mistakes were made (the game even had an advisory warning that people with epilepsy and pregnant women should not play the game); Virtuality's *Dactyl Nightmare* (1992) featured a three-dimensional world seen through head-mounted displays, where players could see and shoot at each other's avatars, as well as get carried off by the pterodactyl flying around in the game's simple world; VR8's *Virtual Combat* (1993) was a one-player game, and its head-mounted display hung from its game cabinet for the player to wear; and finally, there was even a game which used a computer keyboard as its input device: in Sega's *The Typing of the Dead* (1999), players typed words quickly and accurately to kill the zombie coming at them.

While the 1990s saw some innovative hardware in arcade video games, it was changes in software and in particular game graphics, where home console systems were catching up and raising players' expectations, which would have to be met if the arcade was to continue.

The Move to Three-Dimensional Graphics

Three-dimensionally generated computer graphics had been in the arcade since the wireframe graphics in Atari's *Battlezone* and the filled-polygon graphics of Atari's *I, Robot,* but the former looked like line drawings and were limited in detail, and the latter was also relatively bland due to the lack of textures and smaller details. Atari would occasionally try 3-D graphics again, for example, in 1989's *Hard Drivin'* and *S.T.U.N. Runner*. But not until sufficient computing power was available could three-dimensional objects and environments be generated that were detailed enough to compete graphically with the best sprite-based graphics of the day. This was not only a matter of programming but of hardware issues as well; Namco's *Cyber Sled* (1993), which generated filled-polygon graphics, required cooling fans to keep it from overheating.[7] And many games simply did not seem to require the extra dimensionality of 3-D graphics, such as vertically scrolling shooting games with top-down views, which continued to be typically sprite-based even into the late 1990s.

Another way that three-dimensional graphics were created was through the use of video clips, consisting of either live action or hand-drawn animation. Laserdisc games began in the 1980s, and continued into the 1990s, with games like Leland's *Dragon's Lair II: Time Warp* (1991) which had been completed in 1984 but was not released due to the crash (see Chapter 18, "The Video Game Industry Crash"), American Laser Games' *Mad Dog McCree* (1990) and *Mad Dog II: The Lost Gold* (1991) which both included two optical guns for firing at on-screen targets, and Sega's *Holosseum* (1992) and *Invaders 2000* (1992), which both used a parabolic mirror to give a more dimensional look to each game's imagery. With their optical guns and mirrors, these games also provided an experience hard to duplicate in the home, but once home computers and home console systems began using CD-ROMs and incorporating full-motion video, many laserdisc games would be able to be adapted into home games (there was one home laserdisc game system released in 1984, Rick Dyer's Halcyon, but the system was expensive and was not widespread).

Like video imagery, there were other forms of graphics that looked three dimensional but did not involve any actual 3-D computation. Atari's *Xybots*, for example, had a three-dimensional perspective looking down a hallway, but not one which the player could move about freely. Some games like Taito's *Light Bringer* (1993), Seta's *Twin Eagle II* (1994), and Atlus's *Princess Clara Daisakusen* (1996), used an isometric perspective that alleviated the flatness of the plan without requiring any 3-D computation. Other games like Irem's *Dream Soccer '94* (1994) and SNK's *Super Sidekicks 3—The Next Glory* (1995) used an oblique perspective, which, while appearing flatter than the isometric perspective, still managed to give a more dimensional feel to sprite-based games. Some sprite-based games, like *Konami GT* (1985) used scaling sprites to create an illusion of 3-D movement.

A few games appeared in the early 1990s that did use true three-dimensional graphics. In 1992, Virtuality released *Dactyl Nightmare* (described above), and Catalina Games released *Cool Pool,* a pool game which had a three-dimensional pool table that could be rotated and seen from different angles, allowing the player to set up shots.

By 1993, when *Myst* and *Doom* were released, home computer games began catching up to arcade game graphics. *Myst*'s graphics were prerendered stills but looked beautiful, while *Doom*'s were less detailed but interactive and generated in real time. That same year, more games with true 3-D graphics began appearing in the arcade, including Sega's two fighting games *Dark Edge* and *Virtua Fighter,* Namco's *Cyber Sled,* VR8 Inc.'s *Virtual Combat,* Alternate Worlds Technology's *Wolfenstein VR,* Konami's *Polygonet Commanders,* and Atari Games's *Hard Drivin's Airborne.* A new company, Virtual World, also produced two eight-player games, *Battletech* (1993) and *Red Planet* (1993), though they were limited to the Virtual World sites and not found in arcades.

During the next two years, 1994 and 1995, more 3-D games were released, including Namco's *Soul Edge* (1995) and the first two games of its *Tekken* series, Sega's *Virtua Striker* (1994), Semicom's *Hyper Pac-Man* (1994), Strata's *Driver's Edge* (1994), Namco's *Ridge Racer 2* (1994), and Taito's *Real Puncher* (1994). During most of the 1990s, 3-D graphics mainly appeared in fighting and racing games. Fighting games typically had two characters attacking each other with a variety of moves, so the 3-D computation was usually limited just to the two characters (although some later games, like *Tekken 3* (1997) did have three-dimensional backgrounds). In racing games, the race course was a 3-D landscape that the player drove through with a first-person perspective, so possible points of view were limited by the roadway itself.

In 1995, home games made another leap into 3-D graphics, with the release of two 32-bit home console systems, the Sega Saturn and Sony PlayStation (both had appeared first in Japan at the end of 1994, but were released in North America in 1995), and a 64-bit system, the Nintendo 64, was released in 1996. The new generation of home console systems could do three-dimensional computation, more specialized controllers were available, and home games in many ways had finally caught up to arcade games. In the coming years as even more powerful home consoles appeared, the arcade would find itself in decline.

The Decline of the Arcade

Just as video games displaced pinball games in the 1970s and early 1980s, video games were starting to become displaced by redemption games during the 1990s, as operators began to believe that they would be more profitable. Redemption games involved some sort of skill (like Skee-ball) and paid out in tokens or tickets that players could redeem for prizes. Some, like crane-drop games, allowed players to access prizes directly, if they had the skill needed to obtain them. Redemption games typically had shorter play times than video games and were more family oriented since they did not have the reputation for being violent that many video games had. Restaurants sometimes featured separate rooms for redemption games, and mall arcades often had them as well. Just as there were a few hybrid pinball/video games, there were hybrids combining video games and redemption games, including Namco's *Golly! Ghost!* (1991), Kaneko's *Bonk's Adventure* (1994), Game Room's *Frantic Fred* (1998), and Capcom's *Mallet Madness* (1999). Like the interfaces discussed above, these games, with their payouts, provided an experience that home games could not.

As the old style of arcade declined, the arcade changed into game centers, video game lounges, and "location-based entertainment" centers which in addition to games offered dining and socializing. During the 1990s, Namco opened a chain of Cyberstation Amusement Zones and produced game theatres which were small rooms in which a team of six people sat playing a game with large images projected on the walls by over a dozen projectors. Namco's *Ridge Racer Full Scale* (1994) featured a full-sized car that the players sat in, which was housed in a room in front of an 18-foot screen on which the game's backgrounds were projected. The car's steering wheel, brakes, clutch, gears, and other controls all affected what was happening on-screen.[8] In 1990, Virtual World opened a game center in Chicago, and more would open across the country over the next few years; and as of 2007 they are still in business. At each center, eight players can enter networked cockpits and compete in two games, *Battletech* (1990) and *Red Planet* (1992). Besides the cockpits, each center also has a lounge and snack bar where players can relax, watch replays of the game, and receive sheets with scores and accounts of game events. Other merchandise like jackets and plastic figures are also available.

In 1997 several well-known media companies began opening chains of location-based entertainment centers, including Disney, Sony, Viacom, and Sega, whose GameWorks was a joint venture with DreamWorks and Universal Studios. Nolan Bushnell, the founder of Atari, opened the uWink Media Bistro, a restaurant with video games at every table. In some ways, however, some of the new game centers have distanced themselves from the image that arcades once had. For example, despite trying to be a place where people could meet and socialize, GameWorks initially attracted more young male video gamers than they expected and decided to change their emphasis to games like bowling and skee-ball instead, looking for a different image and demographics. According to Maureen Tkacik writing for *The Wall Street Journal,*

> Instead of singles in their 20s running up big bar and food tabs, GameWorks was attracting a mostly male, mostly underage crowd that was deeply obsessed with video games and not much else. Same-store sales, or sales at locations open at least a year, began to plummet, the expansion stopped and earlier this year DreamWorks sold out as a partner.
>
> Now, the company, jointly opened by Sega and Vivendi, is in the midst of a turnaround effort led by Chairman and Chief Executive Ron Benison....Benison has settled on...diversions like bowling, skee-ball, bingo and billiards.[9]

In Japan as well, the 1990s saw arcades being transformed into *amyuuzumento sentaa* (amusement centers) that were more family oriented and untainted by the seedy image that arcades sometimes had.[10]

On the other end of the spectrum, there are still places where games are the central focus. At game centers like Cyberglobe and Cyberglobe 2, both in the Bay Area surrounding San Fransisco, California, players sit at tables lined with networked computers which offer groups a chance to compete together in games like *Counter-Strike* (1999) or compete on home game systems like the Xbox. By 2003, the number of such game centers was growing rapidly. According to Mark Nielsen of iGames (http://igames.org/), an organization helping game centers work together, "What we're seeing now is the very beginning of a trend that is just beginning to explode. There are easily 1,000 legitimate centers in the United States today. I expect this number to continue to grow for years and years."[11]

The future of game centers will depend on the sense of community they can generate, to give players a place to go and a reason to play outside of their homes, where both networked games and some of the most advanced video game technology now resides, sometimes along with the old arcade video games themselves.

The Return of the Old Arcade Games

Although the early twenty-first century saw the passing of the video game arcade, the games themselves were enjoying a comeback as collectibles and nostalgia. As arcades closed, their games were sold, and many of the people who grew up with the games were now grown up and in a position to buy them for their basements.

By the end of the 1980s, collectors were already starting to buy games, and in 1990 they started the Video Arcade Preservation Society (VAPS), which by late 2006 had grown to almost 2,000 members who collectively owned around 27,000 games. Pooling their collective knowledge, they began the "Killer List of Videogames," and later in 2002, the International Arcade Museum, of which the KLOV became a part. Today, www.klov.com stands as arguably the greatest online resource for arcade video game information, with information and images from thousands of games. Many other websites, such as www.gamespot.com, www.basementarcade.com, and www.gamespy.com, are also sources of video game news, reviews, and other game information for collectors.

During the 1990s, museums also began looking at arcade video games as historical artifacts. From June 1989 to May 1990, the American Museum of the Moving Image (AMMI) in Astoria, New York, ran the exhibition "Hot Circuits: A Video Arcade," which included selected arcade video games from *Computer Space* (1971) onwards.[12] The 1990s saw a number of other museum exhibitions of video games, including a traveling collection, Keith Feinstein's Videotopia, which also maintains a presence on the Internet (www.videotopia.com). Magazines have catered to collectors as well; in 1997 *GameRoom Magazine,* which covered the collecting of jukeboxes and arcade machines, widened its scope to include arcade video games, and in 2001 they published *The Arcade Video Game Price Guide,* one of the first guides of its kind.[13]

Even some of the arcade games released in the 1990s were themselves retro games. Along with 3-D updates of older games, like Namco's *Xevious 3D/G* (1996) and Taito's *G-Darius* (1997), machines were released containing the old games themselves, like *Namco Classic Collection Volume 1* (1995) and *Volume 2* (1996), Braze Technologies' *Double Donkey Kong* (1999), and Two-Bit Score's *Pac-Man Super ABC* (1999), each of which had multiple games in their original versions.[14] Versions of home games also appeared in collections for home computers, and downloads of some of them appeared on the Internet for emulators like MAME, which tried to digitally recreate the games on personal computers.

Though the arcades have all but vanished, the games themselves have not. They are now firmly a part of late twentieth century culture and nostalgia, and their legacy continues to influence the video game industry which they began and introduced to the public, paving the way for all the other branches of the industry to come.

CHAPTER 24

HANDHELD VIDEO GAME SYSTEMS

Leonard Herman

By the mid-1970s, video games had become an everyday part of life. Although they would not become "must have" items in the home until 1980 when Atari released *Space Invaders* for the Video Computer System (VCS), they were no longer the curiosity that they were in 1972 when the Odyssey was released. It would only be a matter time before someone would transfer the electronic gaming experience to a portable device.

Early Electronic Handhelds

By 1976 video games were slowly making their impact on the world. While still not a household word, they were gaining momentum thanks to Atari Home PONG in 1975. Mattel, the world's largest toy company, felt that the time was ripe to jump on the bandwagon. Their initial goal was not to create a video game system that would compete against the Atari VCS (which had not been released yet). They wanted to create their own niche market.

They succeeded with the 1976 release of *Auto Racing,* the world's first handheld electronic game. As simple as the consoles were at the time with their ball-and-paddle graphics, *Auto Racing* was even simpler. The console itself was roughly the size of a handheld calculator. Along the right side of the screen ran a vertical LED display. The idea of the game was that the player controlled a red LED blip (car) at the bottom of the display and had to avoid the descending blips (oncoming cars) by steering left and right to avoid crashing into them.

Auto Racing was not an overnight success. But fortunately for Mattel Electronics, it did garner enough interest for the company to continue. The company's next handheld release came out in 1977. *Football* also used an LED display which ran horizontally at the top of the console. As in *Auto Racing,* the football players were portrayed as red LED blips. Still, people playing the game found that it resembled the real thing as close as the technology of the time could depict it. And the idea that they could play this game on the go, rather than in front of a television set, made it even more attractive.

Between 1976 and 1978 Mattel released several handheld games, many of them based on sports, such as *Baseball* and *Basketball*. In 1978 Coleco followed Mattel's lead and released its own series of handheld sports games under the name *Head-To-Head*. Unlike the Mattel games, Coleco's *Head-To-Head* series could be played by two people, in addition to one against the computer. The units themselves looked like two of the Mattel handhelds fused together with one common screen in the center. Players sat across from one another.

In 1974 Atari released an arcade game called *Touch Me*. The machine consisted of large buttons which had lights that randomly flashed. The player had to press the buttons in the same order that the machine flashed them to stay in the game. And when a person lost, the machine would sound off an annoying rasping noise. The game was a flop. However, when it was on display at the Music Operators of America (MOA) show in November 1976, Ralph Baer, the inventor of home video games, noticed it. Although he liked the game itself, the package did not impress him

A few months later Baer decided to build a handheld game based on the children's game *Simon Says*. Using *Touch Me* as a model, he and his partner Howard Morrison, discarded the things they did not like about the game such as its annoying sounds, which they replaced with four pleasant-sounding bugle tones. The finished product was sold to Milton Bradley who named the unit *Simon* and released it in time for the 1978 holiday season. It also became the top-selling electronic game of all time.[1]

Coincidentally, Atari decided to release a handheld version of *Touch Me*. The handheld *Touch Me*, which resembled a yellow calculator, was released in 1978 prior to *Simon* but it failed to attract an audience. After *Simon's* release *Touch Me* joined a long list of electronic games that were referred as *Simon* clones.

Programmable Handhelds

In 1979, Milton Bradley followed *Simon* with another handheld unit which it called *Microvision*. Designed by Jay Smith of Smith Engineering, the Microvision had a two-inch square LCD screen and a dial controller. The graphics were small and blocky but they allowed more movement than the light emitting screens that were found on the previous handheld.

The Microvision system was programmable in the sense that is used interchangeable game cartridges. Milton Bradley released a series of cartridges that were challenging, despite the small screen. Unlike the programmable consoles that were on the market, the Microvision did not have its own CPU, the central processor that processed all data. Instead, each of the Microvision cartridges had their own 4-bit microprocessors that allowed the system to be easily upgradeable as new cartridges came with more powerful CPUs.

The Game Boy Dynasty

Surprisingly, the world was not ready for a programmable handheld system and the Microvision disappeared from store shelves around 1981. While new dedicated handhelds continued to be developed and released, the next programmable handheld would not be released until 1989.

By that time, Nintendo was the leading producer of video game consoles so it was only naturally for the company to develop a handheld. Like the Microvision, the Nintendo

Game Boy featured a monochrome LCD screen and interchangeable game cartridges. The Game Boy was smaller than the Microvision, roughly the size of a Sony Walkman, which made it easier to fit into pockets and make it more portable. Contributing to the success of the Game Boy was the fact that Nintendo adapted many of its hit games from the NES to the Game Boy. One game in particular was so hot that people bought Game Boys just to have it.

Tetris had already been a success on every console and computer that it could be played on. Nintendo realized that with its game complexity and simple graphics it would be a natural for the Game Boy. They even packaged *Tetris* with the Game Boy and this marketing strategy sold millions. The Game Boy was successful right from the beginning and the popularity still continues although the Game Boy itself has changed over the years.

In 1996 Nintendo released the first major change to the Game Boy with the *Game Boy Pocket*. This unit was smaller than the original Game Boy although it featured a larger screen.

In Japan the following year, Nintendo released a Game Boy that contained a backlight. The *Game Boy Light* was scheduled to be released outside of Japan in 1998 but Nintendo's development suddenly went in a different direction. Instead of releasing a Game Boy Light, Nintendo released something people had been waiting for, the Nintendo *Game Boy Color,* which featured a color screen.

The Game Boy Color was backwards compatible. This meant that it could play all the games that had been introduced for the prior Game Boys. However, these games would not play in true color on the Game Boy Color. Instead, the Game Boy Color would substitute each monochrome shade into a color. However, Nintendo introduced new games that would play in color on the Game Boy Color and in monochrome on the earlier units. The games came in different colored cartridges so people could tell them apart. The original monochrome games came in gray cartridges and the color games came in black cartridges. Before long, though, companies began producing color games that could only be played on the Game Boy Color and could not be played on the earlier units. These games were housed in clear cartridges.

The year 2001 brought the *Game Boy Advance,* a 32-bit system that had Super NES quality graphics and which was completely compatible with all of the prior Game Boy cartridges. The cartridges themselves were half the size of the original Game Boy cartridges and would not fit any system except the Advance. Unlike the previous vertical units that had the screen at the top and the controls at the bottom, the Advance was a horizontally oriented system. The screen was in the center with controls on both sides of it.

Nintendo returned to vertically oriented handhelds with the *Game Boy Advance SP* in 2003. This system had a clamshell design that allowed the screen to fold over the controls to close it and keep dust out. It also featured a backlit screen and was completely compatible with all previous Game Boy games.

In 2004 Nintendo introduced a new handheld which they simply called the *DS,* which unofficially stood for *dual screen.* The DS had two screens, which were not backlit, one on the top and one on the bottom, and the two closed together like the Advance SP. The top screen represented a standard game while the bottom allowed the use of a stylus. Although the DS was never officially part of the Game Boy line, it did accept all of the Game Boy Advance cartridges, along with its own games that were housed on flash memory cards.

Nintendo released a new Game Boy in 2005. The *Game Boy Micro* was a tiny, horizontally oriented unit with a large screen in the center. This was the first Game Boy that was not 100 percent compatible with previous models. Like the DS, it would only accept Game Boy Advance cartridges.

Nintendo's 2006 entry in the handheld market was the *DS Light*. The system is a redesigned DS with a backlight.

Other Handhelds

Although Nintendo dominated the programmable handheld market for over 15 years, other companies have continually tried to compete. Most have failed for one reason or another.

Atari released a handheld unit in 1989 at approximately the same time as the original Game Boy. The Lynx was a 16-bit color system, originally designed by Epyx, a leading gaming software company at the time. Unfortunately, Atari priced the unit at $189, whereas the Game Boy only cost $109. Unlike the Game Boy, the Lynx also contained custom chips. Nintendo was easily able to supply enough Game Boys during Christmas while Atari was not able to keep up with the demand.

Atari redesigned the Lynx and in 1990 released the Lynx II, a smaller version of the original color handheld. Atari was able to drop the price of the new unit to $99, which improved sales, although by that time the Game Boy dominated the market.

In May 1991, Sega joined Atari in the color handheld market by releasing the Game Gear. Despite costing more than the Lynx, being larger in size, and having a lower battery life, the Game Gear outsold the Lynx. The Game Gear was also compatible with Sega's Master System, which helped sales. By 1994, Atari focused its attention on the Jaguar, its final console, and the Lynx faded into obscurity.

In 1995 Sega decided to release the *Nomad,* a handheld version of its popular Genesis system. This portable system accepted all Genesis games and marked the first time that a console was released as a handheld system. But the unit drained batteries rapidly, and although an AC adaptor was available, the use of an adaptor meant the loss of portability, making it simply a more expensive version of the Sega Genesis.

Additional Handhelds

In 1992 a Hong Kong based company called Watara released a handheld unit called the Supervision. Its monochrome LCD screen, the largest on any handheld system available, was built into a pivoting base which allowed players to tilt the screen if there was too much glare. The buttons on the unit were larger than those on the Game Boy and spaced a little farther apart.

The Supervision initially sold for $50 and included one game with additional cartridges selling for between $8 and $18. The games themselves were simpler than those available for the Game Boy. The system itself had limited distribution and was not known by the general public. It disappeared from the few stores that sold it in 1992.

Tiger Electronics released its first entry into the programmable handheld market in 1997. While the $69.99 game.com had a monochrome LCD screen like the Game Boy, it also employed a few built-in extras such as a solitaire game, a calculator, address and phone number database, and a calendar. One unusual feature of the game.com was the inclusion of a stylus and touch-screen technology, seven years before Nintendo decided to include this in the DS. While the stylus could be used to select menu choices, its main purpose was to compose messages. This was extremely important because the game.com could connect to the Internet and users could sign up for an online text-based e-mail service. But the system was not able to store data so users could not save or print their messages.

Thanks to a combination of poor distribution, a small game catalog, and limited marketing, the game.com could not compete against the Game Boy. Tiger redesigned the system and released the smaller game.com Pocket Pro in 1998 with a retail price of $50. However, by then it was too little too late and the game.com faded into oblivion in 2000.

In 1998, SNK, the company behind the Neo•Geo console, decided to release a mono-chrome handheld system, and curiously the company chose the name of its old console for it. The *Neo•Geo Pocket* lasted approximately a year when it was replaced by the *Neo•Geo Pocket Color.* The older system was able to play most of the color games made for the newer system although they naturally did not appear in color on the monochrome sets.

In 2000, SNK was purchased by a Japanese company called Aruze. At the time, North American and European sales of the handheld system were dropping and the remaining stock was returned to Asia for repackaging. Surprisingly, this stock returned to the United States in 2003 where the system was bundled with six cartridges. With a lack of promo-tion and a large catalog of games, these repackaged systems did not sell very well.

Japanese toy company Bandai, which had tried to break into the video game business several times, finally got its chance in 1999 when it released the *Wonderswan.* The system was released only in Japan. Some critics felt that it had a good chance of competing against Nintendo's formidable system because it had been developed by Koto, a company founded by Gunpei Yokoi, the man who originally designed the Game Boy.

Like the Neo•Geo that came out before it, the Wonderswan initially was monochrome but it was replaced by the Wonderswan Color a year later. Although at first the Wonder-swan held its own against the Game Boy Color, Nintendo's system eventually pulled ahead and knocked it into anonymity.

Playable Memory Cards

In 1998, Sega and Sony both released memory cards for their respective systems, the Dreamcast and PlayStation. While these units cannot be considered handheld consoles in the truest sense, they were indeed self-sufficient units that could play individual games.

Sega touted its Visual Memory System (VMS) as the "world's smallest portable game card." Unlike memory cards that preceded it, the VMS could be used as a standalone aming unit, in addition to storing game data. The unit had action buttons, a directional pad, and its own small LCD screen. Two VMSs could be docked together allowing gamers to transfer data between the two. But Sega did not support the VMS as it had planned. Although the company announced that graphically primitive standalone games would be available, they never were released and the VMS died along with the Dreamcast in 2001.

Sony's Personal Digital Assistant (PDA) was announced in February 1998 and was similar to Sega's VMS. The PDA could plug into the PlayStation like a standard memory card and gamers could then load characters from a PlayStation game into the PDA. They could then train these characters even when a PlayStation was not available. When the gamer had access to the PlayStation, the character could then be downloaded back into the game. The PDA contained an infrared function so gamers could trade characters with one another easily.

But the PDA was not meant to be merely a PlayStation peripheral. Sony planned to release simple games that would play only on the PDA. Software would be available on standard PlayStation discs that could be loaded into the PDA via the game console. Sony planned to have 12 titles available upon the PDA's release and at least one third party company, Square, also planned to support the PDA.

Sony changed the name of the PDA to *PocketStation* and released the unit only in Japan on January 23, 1999. The tiny handheld system sold out immediately and Sony soon claimed that because the demand for the PocketStation was so high in Japan, it would have to postpone the U.S. and European launch so it could meet the demand adequately.

When the PlayStation 2 became official, Sony announced that it was going to revamp the PocketStation so it could be used with the new console. This decision effectively cancelled all plans for the PocketStation to be released outside of Japan. Sony planned to upgrade the PDA by adding more memory and increasing the battery power.

Unfortunately for people who bought the PocketStation, Sony never supported it. Instead, the company abandoned the playable memory card, concentrating entirely on the PS2.

Sony PlayStation Portable

Sony announced in 2003 that it was going to break into the handheld gaming market. Released in Japan in December 2004, and in North America three months later, the PlayStation Portable (PSP) could play games, videos, MP3, and provide Internet support. All this did not come cheap. The PSP retailed for $250.

The PSP's color screen was the largest ever available on a handheld system: 4.3 inches with a 16:9 widescreen ratio. But battery life had not been drastically improved since the days of the Lynx. While the PSP could provide 10 hours of MP3 playback with the screen off, users could only get about three hours of power if they were accessing the wireless network with the screen turned to its highest brightness setting.

Instead of using cartridges, Sony released its software on a small, proprietary optical disc called a UMD (universal media disc), which was 2.5 inches wide and stored 1.8 gigabytes of data. Because the PSP could play videos as well as games, major movie studios began releasing movies on the UMD format.

By 2006, Sony sold 24.7 million PSPs around the world, the most successful handheld system ever that was not manufactured by Nintendo. However, that number was far below the 35 million DS units that Nintendo sold over roughly the same time period.[2] It is safe to assume that Nintendo still has not relinquished the handheld crown after nearly 20 years on top.

To the Future

Where will the future of portable gaming lead? It is hard to say. Some companies such as Sony and Microsoft believe that the future of portability lies in shrinking the consoles to portable size. Nintendo seems to be following its path of simplicity. And other companies believe that the future of portable games are in cell phones and PDAs. Whichever idea is correct in the end, it is safe to assume that portable games will be around for a long time to come.

COMPANY PROFILE: SEGA

Alison McMahan

One of the larger video game companies and Nintendo's main competitor for many years, Sega is among the few companies to find success for both their arcade video games and home game console systems. The company began in 1951 when the United States passed laws regulating slot machines, which led Marty Bromley, who managed game rooms at military bases in Hawaii, to buy some of the machines that were now not allowed on the continent and open Service Games (SEGA), to provide entertainment for American servicemen. In 1964 Rosen Enterprises, Japan's largest amusement company, merged with Sega, becoming Sega Enterprises. In 1966 Sega released *Periscope,* an electromechanical arcade game that became such a hit in Japan and then in the United States and Europe, that it became Japan's first amusement game export. High shipping costs led U.S. arcade owners to charge a quarter per play, thereby setting the standard price for playing arcade games for years to come.

To compete with Nintendo's NES released in North America in 1985, Sega released its first home console Master System in 1986, and in 1987 unveiled its 16-bit Mega Drive game console. Sega released the Mega Drive in the U.S. as the Genesis in 1989, and in 1991 the company recreated itself with a new mascot—Sonic the Hedgehog. By 1994, now starting to fall behind Nintendo in sales, Sega shipped a Sega CD peripheral for the Genesis game console, the Sega 32X, which increased its power from 16x to 32x. That same year Sega released the Saturn in Japan and met new competition in the form of the Sony PlayStation. By 1997 it was clear that the Saturn could not compete and it was discontinued.

In 1999 Sega released its Dreamcast game console in the United States with record prerelease sales. In 2000, the Sega Internet Service for the Dreamcast was added, leading to sales of 10 million consoles by 2001.[3] The Dreamcast was now leading the industry: it had a one-year jump on Sony's PlayStation 2; it started out with some excellent games, most notably *Sonic Adventure* (1998) and *Shenmue* (2000); it moved from 16 bit to 32 bit; and the Dreamcast was designed in such a way that it was easy to recode PC games for the Dreamcast. Clearly, Sega expected players to buy a Dreamcast instead of a computer for online gaming and take advantage of the well-designed Dream Arena portal and the system's low price. But developers were hesitant, preferring to wait for the PlayStation 2, and no online games were offered through Sega's Dream Arena portal during that crucial year before the PS2 was released.

Shenmue proved that Sega's strength was in game design. Players take on the role of Ryo and walk through his world, alternating sleuthing with fighting. Time passes in *Shenmue;* characters in the embedded story lead their own lives even when the player is not interacting with them, and the whole is packaged with incredibly realistic and beautiful 3-D graphics. An online version of the game appeared, which was discontinued in spring 2002, around the same time Sega withdrew from the hardware race, choosing instead to develop games for other consoles and arcade games. Sega's transition, as many of its earlier transitions have been, is a sign of a sea change in industry, where battle is not over console capability, but content, and Sega remains among one of the world's biggest game companies.

CHAPTER 25

SHAREWARE GAMES:
BETWEEN HOBBYIST AND PROFESSIONAL

Brett Camper

With the arrival in the early 1980s of personal computers—the IBM PC, Apple II, Atari 400/800, Commodore 64, and others—home computer games became a bourgeoning commercial industry. It was an acutely entrepreneurial period, and many hobbyist programmers were curious about selling their games, or showcasing them in an effort to land a full-time job in the new industry. Several groundbreaking games of the period that we know as commercial titles actually began as amateur efforts, including: *Rogue,* the archetypical "dungeon crawler" that helped pioneer the statistical role-playing genre and use of randomly generated environments; *Lode Runner,* the fast-paced single-screen gold-collecting game in which digging holes is the player's only means of avoiding capture; and *Zork,* a canonical text adventure set as a sprawling fantasy-comedy. But at the same time that such movement from "amateur" to "professional" developer was common, an alternate, third category that blurred these lines was also developing.

"Shareware" is a distribution method that attempts to preserve some of the communal aspects that characterized game development on university mainframes, while harnessing the monetary benefits of commercial software. A shareware program is often released in two variants: the "free" version, which is available without payment and encourages its own copying and redistribution by users (thus a kind of word of mouth or "viral" marketing); and the "registered" (or "paid") version, which usually improves upon the free with additional features or documentation. Shareware's free distributions often exhort the user to register for the "full" version by sending payment directly to the author. In the pre-World Wide Web 1980s and early 1990s, most shareware (both games and more general applications) could be registered for anywhere between $10 and $40, a fee commonly delivered as a check or even cash via regular postal mail. Diskettes, a manual, or a registration code for the full program could then be expected in return.

Shareware's messages can be ambivalent, a mixture of salesmanship promising more advanced capabilities, an appeal to the user's desire to contribute to a community of grassroots software development, and outright guilt-tripping pleas for compensation.

The related term "freeware" usually indicates that the "full" version of the program is available without a registration fee, and as such payment, while often requested for goodwill, is even more discretionary. Though shareware and freeware are often discussed together, freeware retains a greater association with hobbyists, while shareware is considered entrepreneurial—in the terms of the late 1990s Internet boom, shareware is analogous to "dot-com startups," with freeware closer to user-run community websites. The shareware concept is generally attributed to a trio of developers, each of whom created important early business programs: Jim Knopf's database software *PC-File* (1982); Andrew Fluegelman's *PC-Talk* (1982), a networking program for using dial-up modems; and Bob Wallace's *PC-Write* (1983), a word processor. Despite its office-software roots, however, PC game programmers quickly took up the form and began releasing shareware and freeware in the mid-1980s.

Classic IBM-PC Shareware and Freeware

An early highlight is *Beast* (1984), developed by Dan Baker, Alan Brown, Mark Hamilton, and Derrick Shadel, an elegantly simple yet surprisingly deep action game in which the player manipulates a dense playing field of green blocks viewed top-down, pushing and pulling wall formations in an effort to crush the enemy "beasts" between them. *Beast* borrows from *Sokoban* (1982), the quintessential "block pushing" game, but whereas that game focuses on careful step-by-step puzzle-solving configuration, *Beast* offers a frantic freeform, real-time spatial control. Despite comparative obscurity, the gameplay has inspired a cult following even today, and suggests well-known contemporaneous commercial classics such as *Lode Runner,* with its use of negative space to lure and snare the player's computer-controlled hunters. The "beast eggs" that hatch particularly intelligent and powerful adversaries on later stages recall the arcade hit *Joust* from Williams Electronics. From a technical perspective, *Beast* is innovative in that its gameplay, though highly visual, is constructed entirely using ASCII text characters. [The American Standard Code for Information Interchange (ASCII) was largely responsible for the standardization of methods for representing and communicating text between computers. ASCII allows for standard letters and numbers, as well as common mathematical symbols and related characters.]

The earlier, wildly popular role-player *Rogue* had already firmly established this technique of "text graphics," in which letters, numbers, and symbols (familiar and obscure) coarsely represent the characters and objects of the game world. But *Beast* takes this mode from a turn-based to an action format, maintaining a level of fluidity that is unexpectedly effective for an early PC with limited graphics hardware. *Beast's* title screen includes a typical freeware announcement: "This is a free copy of BEAST. You may copy it and give it away. If you enjoy the game, please send a contribution ($20) to Dan Baker."

David Clark's *Sopwith* (1984–1986) is a World War I-themed game that was influential in establishing the side-scrolling aviation subgenre. While the premise is straightforward— your plane must attempt to destroy enemy flyers and ground targets either by shooting or bombing—there is an unusual level of nonlinearity and conceptual sophistication to the gameplay. For instance, unlike most arcade or action-oriented flying games, the player must achieve and maintain sufficient speed to get the plane off the ground and keep it airborne. Players cannot pursue a pure shoot-'em-up strategy, as the danger of stalling the aircraft can be equal to that posed by the enemy targets. And while most other flying games

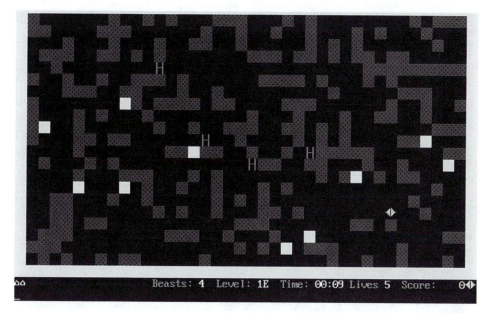

Figure 25.1 Deceptively simple. Abstract, text-based, but frighteningly intelligent "H"-shaped adversaries in *Beast* (1984).

in the horizontal scrolling format reveal the landscape at a fixed, steady pace from left to right (or in the unusual case of Namco's *Sky Kid*, from right to left), *Sopwith* allows (and often requires) the player to roam the map at will, doubling back until all targets have been destroyed.

Historically, one of the most interesting aspects of *Sopwith* is the tenuous position it occupied between hobbyist freeware and commercial business software. When he wrote the game, Clark was a programmer at BMB Compuscience, a Canadian database and networking company. He included a multiplayer mode in order to demonstrate BMB's just-developed PC networking technology, Imaginet. But while for-profit, BMB was not a game company, and *Sopwith* was given away for free to promote Imaginet at tradeshows. Twenty years later the game has maintained a devoted following—Clark released a definitive "author's edition" in 2000—while needless to say, the proprietary Imaginet is an obscurity known only from the history of the game. *Sopwith* is a lesson in the difficulty of technological prediction, and the influence of programmers' personal interests on the products of their employers.

Probably one of the best loved PC shareware games is the turn-based tank fighter *Scorched Earth* (1991–1995) by Wendell Hicken. At first glance a simplistic hit-or-be-hit series of cannon volleys, *Scorched Earth*'s increasingly exotic ammo (homing missiles, vaporizers, "dirt bombs," and other concoctions), randomly generated landscapes and weather conditions, and social play style create a deep replayability. Particularly well known is its "hot seat" multiplayer mode, in which players alternate turns in front of a single computer. The precision physics ultimately have more in common with video game adaptations of sports such as pool or golf than with most "war" games per se. Like many popular shareware and freeware titles, *Scorched Earth* succeeds by limiting its ambitions, catering to the particular (and often restrictive) capabilities of the early PC, opting for a stripped down graphical style: a single-screen, side-view mountain range done up in a

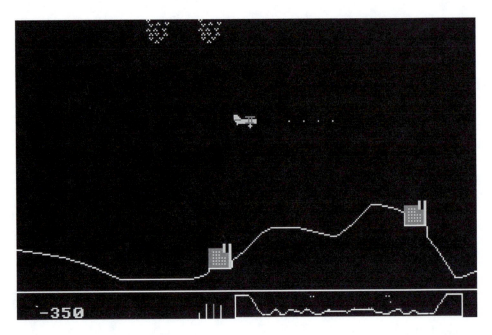

Figure 25.2 *Sopwith* (1984–1986). This game appears simple, but it is a surprisingly sophisticated flying game.

Figure 25.3 Tiny turn-based tanks with a big bang. A war game that doesn't take itself too seriously, *Scorched Earth*'s bright colors and precise missile aim are reminiscent of billiards or miniature golf.

handful of bright, saturated colors. *Scorched Earth*'s instantly addictive appeal is infamous, and its strong influence is evident in the commercial *Worms* franchise, a success across several game platforms.

Bulletin Board Systems and Door Games

Without the structure and inventory provided by commercial exchange, independent games have always been more reliant on the informal, word-of-mouth trading provided by networks, both digital and social. For PC shareware and freeware, the predominant distribution channel was the dial-up modem BBS, or bulletin board system. These pre-Web communities typically resided on individual home computers, which other PCs could then "call into" over a standard phone line by modem. This reliance on the phone system made most BBSs local in scale, though some did have regional or national reach. As the name indicates, BBSs began as places where users could have discussions and share knowledge and software. Due to the modem's speed limitations, these BBSs were almost always presented as text rather than images. However, color and visual representations were often added through special non-alphanumeric ASCII and ANSI characters— a technique of "text art" that had already been established in games like *Rogue* and *Beast*. [The American National Standards Institute (ANSI) provided additional capabilities that allowed ASCII text to be colored and, to a limited degree, animated.]

Because they were usually hobbyist projects themselves, the BBS phenomenon always had a natural affinity with shareware and freeware games. And in addition to acting as way-stations for the trading of game files, many BBSs also hosted their own games locally. These "door games" as they were known (the name refers to the manner in which the BBS software ran additional programs "on the side") are important to the history of gaming because many pioneered multiplayer networked play long before other platforms. Since most BBSs only allowed one person to log in at a time (as connecting to the BBS required exclusive use of the attached phone line), door games were by and large turn-based. But having the BBS serve as a "home base" for the game meant that its world could be maintained indefinitely, tracking and remembering each player's actions from day to day, across weeks or even months—much like today's popular massively multiplayer online games (MMOGs). *Solar Realms Elite* (1990), written by Amit Patel, was particularly advanced for its time. Each player manages a colony of planets, balancing factors from economic development, trade and taxation, natural resources, military alliances and diplomacy (including espionage), and ecological health. The range of evaluative axes allows players to explore a variety of strategies unseen even in most current titles in the genre. Other popular door games include the similarly themed *Trade Wars 2002* (1986), and medieval action-RPG (role-playing game) *The Pit* (1990).

The Shareware Climax

In the 1980s, most shareware was created and distributed by individual programmers at home, on evenings and weekends, or on borrowed time from work or school. Registration fees were a friendly way for players (themselves sometimes hobbyist developers) to support one another, even if modestly. By the early 1990s, however, shareware had spawned its own "big business" wing, enterprising companies that assisted with payment collection (adding conveniences such as toll-free ordering by phone), large-scale floppy diskette duplication, and postal exchange. The two most prominent of these full-service shareware publishers were Apogee Software and Epic MegaGames. Initially each company simply extended the reach of its founders' own games: Scott Miller of Apogee's *Kingdom of Kroz* (1987), and Tim Sweeney of Epic's *ZZT* (1991). Both games offered a mix of adventure and puzzle play in a light fantasy theme, and both evolved the ASCII text graphics mode of *Rogue* and *Beast* to new levels of complexity with expansive, colorful maps interconnected across screens. *Kroz* eventually developed into an eight-game series, while *ZZT*'s level editor allowed users to extend the game with their own worlds, carrying its appeal to the current day.

With these early successes—*ZZT* is said to have garnered over 30,000 registrations for Sweeney[1]—Apogee and Epic began ramping up their publishing operations, providing a regimented distribution framework far more organized than solo developers previously had. Apogee released side-scrolling platform games like its in-house creation *Duke Nukem* (1991), and *Commander Keen* (1990) from id Software, an up-and-coming shareware developer founded by four friends from Texas and a client of Apogee's distribution services that would go on to create the blockbusters *Doom* and *Quake.* Epic countered with the *Jill of the Jungle* series in 1992. But while popular on the PC by shareware standards, these action games lacked in innovation, and none could hold a technological candle to *Super Mario Bros. 3* on the NES, or *Super Mario World* (1991) on the SNES, the pinnacle of platformers by which all comers were judged. The IBM PC, intended more for business applications than games, simply did not have the dedicated graphics hardware found on game consoles from Nintendo and Sega.

One game published by Apogee in May 1992 changed all that, however: *Wolfenstein 3D,* id Software's World War II-themed, Nazi-hunting, verging-on-camp breakthrough single-handedly popularized modern three-dimensional gaming and established the first-person shooter (FPS) genre that has been a staple in the 15 years since. While *Wolfenstein 3D* and its successor *Doom* are without a doubt the most widely known and successful games ever to use the shareware model, they were not the only advances to show that PCs could compete with and occasionally rival the flash of the console systems. 1994 in particular was a bumper year for Apogee and Epic, bringing a stream of releases with top-notch coding, graphics, and gameplay: Arjan Brussee, a skilled Dutch graphics programmer, finally made PC side-scrollers respectable with *Jazz Jackrabbit* from Epic; *One Must Fall: 2097* (also Epic), was a highly capable 2-D fighter, offering some tweaks to the genre by employing robots as characters; and the vertical shoot-'em-up genre, long the province of the arcade and consoles, was tackled by Apogee's *Raptor: Call of the Shadows,* and Brussee's next effort *Tyrian,* from Epic (1995).

Tellingly, these games were almost exclusively published, but not developed, by Epic and Apogee. That such "middlemen" companies could not only support themselves but indeed thrive through the shareware method signaled a continuing loss of meaningful distinction between shareware and the mainstream commercial games industry. One final example in this transition was *Descent* (1995), a unique 3-D action game that had players piloting a small craft through futuristic mining tunnels in outer space. The engine expanded upon the 3-D capabilities of predecessors in the first-person shooter genre by introducing a full six degrees of freedom, facilitated by the zero-gravity space theme—allowing the player to seamlessly look and move in all directions rather than remain confined to the ground. *Descent* was as technically sophisticated as any commercial PC game of the time, and while developed by the small company Parallax, it was published as shareware by Interplay, a traditional, fully commercial house that did not arise from

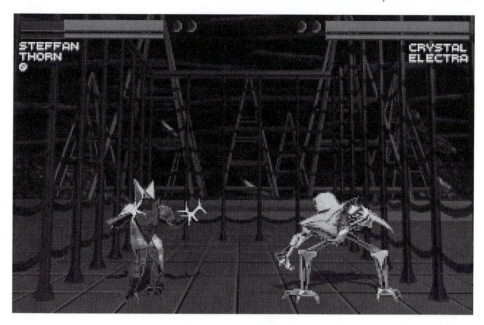

Figure 25.4 *One Must Fall 2097* **(1994). This was one of the few successful action fighting games on the PC.**

the same independent development community as did Epic and Apogee. The latter publishers themselves drifted from their shareware associations and became fully integrated into the larger industry, where they remain prominent today: Apogee changed its brand name to 3D Realms in 1996 and subsequently developed the successful *Max Payne* games (2001), while Epic is responsible for the *Unreal* series (1998) and technology engine that underlies many of today's most popular 3-D games. As home Internet access rapidly increased in the mid-1990s, commercial game companies began offering extensive "demos" of upcoming or newly released games, a free source of entertainment that drew attention and viability away from the remaining shareware developers who had not already gone to larger distribution houses. By the final years of the decade, the shareware model had fallen from favor.

The "shareware era" of the 1980s and 1990s was neither the beginning nor the end of games produced and distributed by individuals. As far back as the 1960s, programmers on university campuses across the country were trading and tweaking their own games, and "freeware" games (even if the term has lost much of its popularity) continue on many platforms today, with Web-based games the most notable. Yet for many curious users, shareware and freeware were the first chance to find and play video games—commercial or otherwise—on the new personal computers. Shareware flourished not only on IBM PC compatibles, but also on practically all home computer platforms of the day, including the Commodore 64, Atari 400/800 and ST, Spectrum ZX, and others. These games made many contributions to the evolution of gameplay and genre conventions, while the do-it-yourself spirit and economic experiments of what Jim Knopf (one of the original shareware founders) called "user-supported software"[2] help to provide us with a richer social context for understanding video gaming's establishment as a media industry, one of the largest and most important of our time.

PART IV

ADVANCING TO THE NEXT LEVEL (1995–PRESENT)

By 1995, three-dimensional gaming was in full swing both in the arcade and the home. That year, three new home game systems were released in North America, the Sony PlayStation, the Nintendo 64, and the Sega Saturn, bringing a new level of sophistication to home video games. Home computer games as well had 3-D graphics, and they were now typically released on CD-ROM, as were the games for the PlayStation and the Saturn (the Nintendo 64 still used cartridges, and would be the last major home console to do so).

Arcade games found it difficult to compete with home games, and despite a number of unusual interfaces that would be expensive to duplicate in the home (like movable skis that the player stood on, a bicycle interface, or a moving cockpit), they were losing their audience to home video games. But the arcade had something else the home didn't; it was a public space where people could gather, so by emphasizing the social aspects of gaming, the arcade would transform itself into game centers, amusement centers, and cybercafés, in an attempt to lure players back.

A social element was also present in online gaming, which became a booming industry during the late 1990s and early 2000s. Games like *Everquest, Ultima Online, Asheron's Call, Star Wars Galaxies,* and *World of Warcraft* attracted millions of players from around the world.

And by the latter half of the 1990s, video games were being played all around the world, in North and South America, Europe, Asia, and Australia. While the video game industry took on different forms in other countries, it managed to find success in most of them.

What had began as a novel form of arcade game machine with simple graphics had now grown into a worldwide industry bringing in billions of dollars every year. And even those old games, with their relatively unsophisticated graphics and simple play, were now being re-released in various forms, as the generations that grew up with them experienced a wave of nostalgia for the early games that began it all.

CHAPTER 26

THE LATER GENERATION
HOME VIDEO GAME SYSTEMS

Leonard Herman

During the years 1977 to 1991, coinciding with the birth and death of the Atari 2600, video game console design seemed to stagnate. Graphics improved with each new generation of systems, but processing power seemed to be at a virtual standstill. Roughly all consoles introduced during those years had 8-bit processors, until the release of the SNES and Sega Genesis which had 16-bit processors.

The 16-bit systems are commonly referred to as fourth generation video game consoles. The first generation consoles (1972–1975) were nonprogrammable systems, while the second generation consoles (1976–1984) were early 8-bit programmable systems, and the third generation consoles (1985–1991 [approximately]) were more advanced 8-bit systems.

With the release of fourth generation systems, visionaries began seriously looking at the future of video game consoles. As newer and more powerful systems were introduced, and the entire concept of "bit processing" disappeared, the blur between one generation of systems and another seemed to fade. By this time the new systems were all lumped into one category: next generation machines.

Once Nintendo released the SNES in 1991, Nintendo was once again on solid ground to compete against Sega, which was by then leading the popularity contest with its Genesis console. Although the Genesis had a year's head start on the SNES, the Nintendo caught up quickly. No sooner was the SNES on store shelves that Nintendo announced that it was going to release a CD drive for the 16-bit console. Although NEC's Turbografx-CD player attachment was not breaking sales records, both Nintendo and Sega saw opportunities for the new medium. A compact disc could contain 550 megabytes of code; or 2,000 times that of the most powerful cartridge. CD-based games offered the ultimate in complexity, detail, and sound.

Nintendo had partnered with Sony to create a $700 CD add-on for the SNES. Part of the deal allowed Nintendo to use characters from movies by Columbia Pictures, the movie company that Sony owned. Sony in turn would develop a standalone unit called the

Play Station which would have a cartridge slot for SNES cartridges and play games designed for the SNES CD. However, the deal also gave Sony complete control of all the titles that would be developed for the CDs. When Nintendo president Hiroshi Yamauchi learned this he immediately ceased all partnerships with Sony and signed Philips to create the CD format.

Philips's approach was to make the SNES CD format compatible with its own CD-i format, which it planned to release as a standalone multimedia unit in 1991. Philips also obtained the right to use Nintendo characters such as *Zelda* and *Mario* in CD-i applications.

In the end, Nintendo's marriage with Philips dissolved, along with its plans to release a CD player for the SNES. In hindsight this may not have necessarily been a bad thing considering what happened to Sega.

Sega's CD player, an add-on for the Genesis, was released in Japan in late 1991 and in the United States nearly a year later under the name Sega CD. Unfortunately it was not the hit that the Sega executives expected it to be. This may have been due to the games that Sega released for the system. Rather than using the expanded storage to use for more sophisticated games, Sega used it mostly for full-motion video. At the time FMV was a novelty for games, but it really did not add anything to the play and consumers simply were not willing to spend money on games that simply were not fun.

Despite the apparent failure of CDs, nobody was giving up on them. In 1991, Trip Hawkins, the founder of software giant Electronic Arts, started a new company called 3DO. Hawkins's aim was to create a universal console using the CD as the medium to deliver games. Rather than calling it a video game console, Hawkins sold the idea as a multimedia device similar to Philips's CD-i and Commodore CDTV systems, both of which were introduced in 1991. A multimedia device is simply a computer without a keyboard or a mouse which played interactive software (not necessarily games) that were supplied on CDs. The units were touted as educational devices since much of the software was of the encyclopedic variety.

The CDTV and CD-i systems were not commercial successes, mainly because the public was not exactly sure what they were. Were they computers? Were they game consoles? The distinction was not clear, and the systems were not heavily promoted or explained to the public.

Commodore tried to better define the line between video game console and multimedia console when it released the Amiga CD^{32} in September 1993. The company specifically touted the system as a CD-based, 32-bit game machine. Priced at $400, the system came onto the market with a lot of readily available software since it was compatible with the nearly defunct CDTV system.

Although the CD^{32} was fairly successful in Europe, it could not make an impact in the North American market. And its success in Europe was short lived as well. Commodore could not meet the demand for new units because of component supply problems. When Commodore International filed for bankruptcy in April 1994, the CD^{32} was discontinued.

The 3DO was released in October 1993, one month following the CD^{32}. The system, which was manufactured by several companies including Panasonic and Sanyo, enjoyed a major publicity campaign. Kiosks set up in shopping malls allowed people to experience the system hands-on. Unfortunately this was not enough to make "3DO" as common a word as "audio" and "video" (Hawkins's original idea was that his console was the third logical component after *aud-DO* and *vi-DO*, hence, *3DO*). Although there were many educational titles available for the 3DO, there also were many games which gave consumers the impression that the 3DO was just another gaming console. And its $700 retail price did not exactly make it affordable for most households.

If the 3DO was a multimedia console that pretended to be a video game, then the Atari Jaguar was just the opposite. Atari's final console was released in late 1993 and cost $250. Although Atari touted the system as a 64-bit machine, purists claimed that this was inaccurate, much in the same way that the Turbografx-16 was not a true 16-bit machine. Regardless, the system was more powerful than the other gaming consoles on the market at the time and it sold pretty well initially. But developers found the system hard to program, and despite Atari's claim that over 20 third-party developers had signed on, software was never abundant for the console. When the newer 32-bit consoles arrived from Sony and Sega, they pretty much sealed Atari's fate.

Sega Systems

The new 32-bit consoles would not be available until late 1994 in Japan. In the interim, Sega released a curious device called the 32X, an add-on adaptor that turned the Genesis into a 32-bit gaming console.

Sega's purpose for the 32X was to get a jump over Nintendo into the 32-bit market. The unit plugged into the cartridge slot of the Genesis and could accept any standard Genesis game where it would act merely as a pass-through. However, it could also accept special 32-bit cartridges that took advantage of the 32-bit processor. In addition, the Sega 32X could be used in conjunction with the Sega CD, and a new line of 32X-CD games were released.

The 32X never caught on with the public. Its $150 price tag, and the fact that Sega had a true 32-bit console coming out within the year, resulted in the unit's failure.

Exactly when Sega's 32-bit console, the Saturn, was going to be released was a matter of speculation. The system had been in development for over two years to make sure that it met the exact needs of both the Japanese and American markets. Sega rushed out the final specifications in order to get the system on the market before Sony, who was also going to release a console that year. The design itself, with eight processors, including two CPUs, made it very difficult for third party companies to make the best use out of all its power. In addition, the system used "off the shelf" components rather than custom chips, which meant that a lot of the power had to be handled through programming, instead of letting the system do much of the work. Another road block for third party design was the lack of useful development tools. Programmers had to use difficult assembly language to obtain decent performance and in most cases this difficulty only led them to use only one of the dual CPUs.

Like the Sega systems before it, the Saturn featured a cartridge slot; but software was only being offered on CDs. The slot was for additional future add-on peripherals.

The release of the Saturn was set for fourth quarter 1994; the actual release date depended on Sony. Following the 1991 Consumer Electronics Show surprise in which Nintendo announced it was dropping Sony in favor of Philips, Sony first considered dropping all of its plans for its Play Station (the name was originally two words instead of one) console which would play CD games as well as SNES cartridges, but decided to continue with the development that had already started. When Nintendo learned that Sony was still planning a console that would accept SNES cartridges, it filed a lawsuit against Sony claiming that Nintendo owned the "Play Station" name. As 1992 came to a close, Sony and Nintendo settled their differences stemming from the agreement for Sony to make a CD player for the SNES, as well as its own Play Station, which would be compatible with the CD player and SNES cartridges. By this time, Nintendo permitted Sony to go ahead with its SNES-compatible Play Station as long as Nintendo controlled the rights to all of the CD games that were designed for it.

Sony PlayStation

At this point Sony questioned the future of the SNES and realized the system was beginning to show its age. Although Nintendo had not announced any new systems, it was apparent that the SNES was old technology. Sony decided to go ahead with a stand-alone console but one that would not be compatible with the SNES. The new 32-bit system was to be called the *PlayStation*.

In April 1994, Sony officially announced that the PlayStation would be released in Japan by year's end and in North America and Europe in the following September. The delay outside of Japan was to give developers in the foreign countries enough time to create extraordinary games. Sony also demonstrated the capabilities of the PlayStation. The custom chips within the PlayStation featured an R3000A 32-Bit RISC CPU that was supported by three high-performance subsystems. This let the PlayStation create sophisticated 3-D geometric graphics that would rival workstations costing tens of thousands of dollars. The system could also play full-motion video. And while the PlayStation was completely CD-driven, gamers could plug in, for the first time ever, external memory cards that would allow them to save game data.

Sega had 170,000 Saturns available for sale in Japan on November 22, 1994.[1] Among the games that were available for the Saturn at its launch was *Virtua Fighter,* the world's first 3-D-based fighting game. Sony's Japanese launch of the PlayStation followed 11 days later. Sony only had 100,000 units available at the onset so sales of the PlayStation were limited to one per customer. By year's end all of the original Saturns sold out while a few PlayStations remained on store shelves. Critics felt that the PlayStation was the superior machine but it did not yet have any popular titles like *Virtua Fighter.*

The American releases of the two consoles followed in 1995. Both were shown at the CES in January and release dates were announced. Saturday, September 2, was set for the Saturn and in a publicity move, Sega called it *Saturnday.* Sony announced that the American PlayStation would arrive 20 days later on September 22. The $299 price for the PlayStation was announced several months later at the very first Electronic Entertainment Exhibition (E3), which was held in May. Sega did not believe that Sony could deliver a console at the caliber that Sony claimed for that price. And Sega had its own bombshell of an announcement at E3. It was there that Sega told the E3 crowd that the Saturn's promised September 2 launch date had simply been a decoy to throw Sony off. To everyone's surprise 30,000 Saturns were released that very day in four retail chains: Toys 'R' Us, Electronics Boutique, Babbage's, and Software Etc. Each system carried a $399 retail price and was packed with *Virtua Fighter.*

Unfortunately, this plan backfired on Sega. Third party companies were caught by surprise so the only games available at launch were those released by Sega. Retailers who were not included in the launch, like Wal-Mart, were upset with Sega for not including them. Executives at KB Toys were so upset that they refused to carry the Saturn or its successor, the Dreamcast, in their stores. Shelf space that would have been used for the Saturn was instead allocated to the PlayStation.

Sony released the American PlayStation on September 9. By that time, nearly 100,000 consoles had already been sold through pre-orders, a new record for any console. By the end of 1995, Sega dropped the price of the Saturn to $299. But by then the PlayStation had a leading edge which it refused to relinquish.

Nintendo 64

Adding to Sega's woes was Nintendo's 1996 release of a 64-bit console, simply called the Nintendo 64 (N64). The system was launched in Japan on June 23 and was followed in North America in September 1997.

Going against the trend, Nintendo opted to continue using cartridges rather than CDs. The company received flack for this because not only were cartridges more expensive to produce (and therefore to sell), but the lead time to manufacture them was much longer than with optical media. And while left unstated, critics knew Nintendo wanted to retain its stringent control of everything associated with the N64 from licensing to manufacturing. Nintendo stood by its decision, claiming access time was quicker with a cartridge. In an effort to please its customers, Nintendo announced that it would release a magnetic disc drive, called the 64DD, in 1997. In addition to using the 64DD to save games, games would be sold in the disc format beginning with an N64 version of *The Legend of Zelda*. Nintendo also planned to release a memory expansion pack which would add an additional four megabytes of main memory to the console.

When the first 300,000 N64s were launched in Japan along with three games, 80 percent of them already had been pre-sold, breaking the pre-order record set by Sony. Few retailers received systems that they could sell to people who had not pre-ordered it. All of the launch consoles sold out on the first day and Nintendo shipped an additional 200,000 systems three days later which also sold out in one day. June ended with the release of another 200,000 units and Nintendo released one million more during the summer. The company then concentrated on its American launch. The biggest surprise occurred a month before the September date when Nintendo announced that the American system would retail for $200. This last-minute announcement had been designed to prevent Sony and Sega from planning competitive price cuts.

The N64 sold 500,000 pre-orders in North America despite the fact that only two titles were available (*Pilot Wings* and *Super Mario 64*). This was the same amount that Sony had sold in three months and which Sega had sold in an entire year. Because the console sold well, Nintendo decided to double the amount of available consoles, taking the additional supply from units allocated for Japan and Europe. Despite this success, critics still wondered if the cartridge-based system could really compete against CD-based systems in the long run. Nintendo was certain it could as long as their cartridge-based games were high quality. *Super Mario 64* apparently was. The Video Software Dealers Association reported that *Super Mario 64* generated $52,000 in rental fees during its first week of release. On the average, one copy of *Super Mario 64* was being rented every minute for an entire week straight!

Sega Dreamcast

With the success of the N64, Sega of America's president, Bernie Stolar, saw that the Saturn was languishing in third place. In early 1997, Sega of Japan agreed with Stolar that the company needed a new console and, for the first time, the company went outside its own development team and hired a consultant from IBM who spearheaded a development team set up at Sega of America's headquarters. The existing development group in Japan was not happy about this and they independently worked on their own system. A competition between the two groups arose, with the Japanese group settling on a Hitachi SH4 processor manufactured by NEC, and the U.S. group going with an IBM/Motorola PowerPC 603e processor. Unfortunately, in April 1997 when 3dfx attempted to go public, in its initial public stock offering it mentioned that it was developing Sega's next console. At the time, Sega did not want this information disclosed and in July Sega chose to go with the system developed by the Japanese team. The new system, named Dreamcast, was released on November 27, 1998, in Japan and on September 9, 1999, in North America. The Dreamcast was an immediate hit among hard-core gamers and was the first console to embrace online gaming. The system was sold with a built-in 56k dial-up modem (a first), and a broadband Ethernet modem was available optionally. The system also came with a disc that included Web browser software which allowed dial-up Internet access. Sega started SegaNet, an online service that allowed gamers to play against others via the Internet. Among the first online titles available were *ChuChu Rocket, NFL 2K1,* and *Phantasy Star Online.*

Unlike previous consoles which used CDs, games for the Dreamcast came on discs that Sega called *Gigadiscs* (GD). The GD-ROMS were proprietary formats that allowed for increased storage capacity. While the GDs were not compatible with any other system, the Dreamcast could also play standard audio CDs.

The Dreamcast also was closely related to personal computers, and even used the Microsoft Windows CE operating system. This was touted as a benefit to PC game developers since they could then convert their existing PC games to the Dreamcast with relative ease. While most developers found the Dreamcast's native operating system superior to the Windows one, it gave Microsoft much needed insight to the world of designing video game hardware.

Sega released several unique accessories for the Dreamcast. Among them was the virtual memory unit (VMU) which acted as a memory card and had an LCD screen. Some titles, such as *Sonic Adventure,* had the ability to load mini-games into the VMU. The screen also could be used to view the data stored on the VMU.

A keyboard was released to make Web browsing easier. This was the first time a first-party keyboard was available for a console. A fishing rod controller was available for fishing games. Again, while this type of controller also was available for other consoles, the one for the Dreamcast was released by Sega itself. A unique controller not available for any other system was a special maraca that Sega released for its *Samba de Amigo* music game.

Initially, sales for the Dreamcast were respectful and Sega's console moved into second place, ahead of the N64. However, sales began to stall in March 2000 when Sony announced it was releasing the PlayStation 2 (PS2) later that year. When people learned what Sony planned to offer, and that the new console would be backwards compatible with the original PlayStation, many casual gamers decided to wait and see before committing themselves to a new console.

New PlayStations

Hype surrounded the PS2 long before its actual Japanese release on March 4, 2000. Unlike the Dreamcast which used the proprietary GDG format, PlayStation 2 games were going to be released on DVD, a format that was introduced in late 1995 but still had not received worldwide acceptance. The benefit of the DVD format was that it could store six times as much data as a CD. Because it was utilizing DVDs, the PS2 would have the capability to play back DVD movies, something that no other console at the time could do. The system was attractive to movie buffs because with a $300 retail price, it cost much less than standalone DVD players at the time. Current PlayStation owners were excited that the PlayStation 2 would be completely compatible with Sony's original system.

Within a matter of days after the Japanese release, Sony broke new records by selling over one million units. The initial supply of consoles was sold with defective memory cards. Since the drivers that ran the DVD software resided on the memory card, users found that their Japanese systems could play DVDs from any region of the world. Sony fixed this bug in time for the American launch on October 26, 2000, by hard-coding the DVD drivers directly into the consoles themselves.

Because of the huge demand, stores sold out quickly and Sony was unable to resupply the consoles. People who were lucky enough to obtain a PS2 during the launch turned around and sold their systems on eBay and other online sites for as high as $1,000 each. Robberies were reported as people stood in line waiting for systems. Never before had so many instances of violence been reported during a launch of a system. Still, the launch was considered a success by Sony.

Sony did not discontinue the original PlayStation upon the release of the PS2. Instead, the company redesigned the system so it was almost as small as a portable CD player and lowered the price to under $100. The unit was renamed the PSOne. By offering an optional screen for the system, Sony marketed the PSOne as a portable unit that could be played in the car. After its release on July 7, 2000, the system went on to outsell all other competing consoles, including the PS2.

Microsoft Xbox

After Microsoft played a part in the development of Sega's Dreamcast, the company had aspirations of releasing its own game console. That goal was reached in March 2000. Less than three weeks after the PS2 was launched in Japan, Bill Gates officially announced to the crowd assembled at the Game Developer's Conference that Microsoft was indeed developing a game console.

Ironically, that announcement indirectly led to the death of the Dreamcast. With sales of the Dreamcast lagging substantially behind the PS2 around the world, Sega felt that the introduction of another console would only hurt sales of the Dreamcast even further. Sega stopped production of the Dreamcast in March 2001. The company stayed in the video game business as a software developer for competing systems.

Microsoft's system, called the Xbox, became a reality when it was launched in November 2001 in North America. The first American console in nearly a decade contained an Intel 733 MHz Pentium III CPU, an Nvidia NV2a 250 MHz graphics processor, 64 MB of unified RAM, broadband Internet support, and for the first time, an 8 GB hard drive. Although the $299 system utilized a Windows 2000 operating system, it was not merely a PC without a keyboard.

Like the PS2, the Xbox could play DVDs. However, while the PS2 could play DVDs off the shelf using the game controller for the DVD functions, the Xbox could only be used as a DVD player if an optional $30 remote control was purchased. This was done so Microsoft could avoid paying DVD licensing fees if it had been sold as a DVD player.

Nintendo GameCube

Nintendo launched the GameCube, its first non-cartridge system in North America just three days after the Xbox was released, and only two months following its Japanese release. Unlike its competition, Nintendo chose to use a proprietary storage medium, an optical-disc that was three-fourths the size of a standard DVD. Because of this, the $200 GameCube was incapable of playing DVDs (and prevented Nintendo from paying DVD licensing fees).

The GameCube was not as powerful as its two competitors, but it was not meant to be. Nintendo was banking that its stable of familiar characters such as Mario, Zelda, and Pokemon, would keep the system afloat. Nintendo also designed the system to be compatible with its portable Game Boy. A link cable was released and certain games could be played using both the Game Boy and the GameCube. Acting as controllers, up to four Game Boys could be connected to one GameCube. Nintendo also released a Game Boy adaptor which allowed gamers to play their Game Boy games on their TV sets. The GameCube also could connect directly to up to seven other GameCubes for LAN (local area network) play, although individual TVs were needed for each console.

System Competition

In November 2002, Microsoft introduced Xbox Live, a subscription-based service that allowed players to compete against one another over the Internet. Although the PS2 was outselling the Xbox, Sony executives realized that online gaming was a sector that they could no longer ignore. Games that incorporated an online component began to be released. However, unlike Microsoft's Xbox Live where Microsoft provided the network server for online gaming, it was the responsibility of Sony's third-party vendors to provide servers for their respective online games. However, since this was mainly transparent to the gamers, it did not affect Sony's goal to make the PS2 the *de facto* console for online gaming.

PS2 gamers did not have to pay for a subscription service like Xbox Live to play online games. They did have to purchase an optional Network Adaptor. Sony also released a 40 GB hard drive that could be used to download content such as extra levels, maps, weapons, and so forth. The hard drive was also sold with the game *Final Fantasy XI* already installed on it. As gamers ventured further into the virtual world, the system constantly downloaded additions to the playing environment that were in turn saved on the hard drive.

Nintendo also provided online gaming when it released optional online adapters at the end of 2002. But Nintendo did not aggressively promote the online capabilities of the GameCube, and very few games supported it.

In the end, Sony's PS2, with over 120 million units sold worldwide, was the uncontested leader in the console wars. Microsoft sold 24 million[2] Xboxes and while that was only a fraction of what Sony sold, it was still a momentous number considering it was Microsoft's first console. Nintendo came in third with 21 million units sold, leading to speculation that it was going to abandon the hardware market just as Sega had done. Nintendo merely denied this rumor as it worked on its next system which would replace the GameCube.

XaviXPORT

In 2003, Sony released a new, unique accessory for the PS2. The Eye Toy was a camera that plugged into the PS2 via a USB connection. Initially, the camera was sold with software called *Eye Toy: Play* which consisted of a series of mini-games that used the player's on-screen image input live through the Eye Toy camera. The player then had to maneuver his body so his on-screen image could perform different tasks such as popping balloons. The games themselves were not very interesting but the idea of being in the game was unique.

Games involving bodily movements were not new. In *Dance Dance Revolution,* players danced to music and had to respond to on-screen arrows using their feet. The Dance Pad people danced on was merely a large controller which responded to players' feet in the same way that traditional controllers responded to fingers. The Eye Toy marked the first time in which a home system actually responded to a player's movement in a nontraditional manner.

In 2004, a Japanese company called SSD Company Limited took this idea one step further and released a unique gaming system called the XaviXPORT. The XaviXPORT was not a standard gaming console and was not meant to compete against the systems already available. Only a handful of cartridges were available for the system and they all shared a similar theme: sports.

The XaviXPORT employed wireless controllers and the unique aspect of the console was that the controllers were sold with each of the game titles and actually looked like equipment for the games. For instance, the controllers packaged with *Xavix Golf* looked like a putter and a driver. The controller that accompanied *Xavix Bowling* was a bowling ball. Using the special controllers, users could simulate the movements of the sport being played. In *Xavix Baseball,* a player could watch the on-screen pitcher toss the ball and then swing the bat controller at the appropriate time.

Only six games were released for the system, but it was enough to show that playing video games did not mean merely sitting on a couch and pushing buttons. And while the system was not a commercial success, it gave the public a glimpse of what the future of video games held.

Microsoft Xbox 360

When Sony released the PS2 in 2000, it got a one-year head start on the competition. In late 2005, it was Microsoft's turn. Microsoft launched the Xbox 360 on November 22, 2005, and it sold out completely. The system sold in two configurations. The standard system, which cost $399.99 in the United States, came with a detachable 30 GB hard drive, an Ethernet cable, an Xbox Live headset, a remote, and a wireless controller. The "core" system, which cost $100 less, did not have any of these accessories, although a wired controller was included.

Many people who bought the Xbox 360 with preconceived ideas about it were quickly disappointed. While the system was able to produce high-definition graphics, they could only be displayed on high-definition television sets. For those who did not own an HDTV, the graphics displayed were similar to the original Xbox.

Another problem was that the Xbox 360 was not really backwards compatible with games from the original Xbox. In order to play Xbox games on the Xbox 360, emulation software first had to be loaded onto a CD from Xbox Live. Then the software had to be installed from the CD onto the Xbox 360's hard drive. Yet those who purchased the Xbox 360 core system did not get hard drives. And even with the emulation software, there were too many technical differences between the two systems to render 100 percent compatibility. Only approximately 30 percent of the entire Xbox library can be played on the Xbox 360. Although Microsoft regularly updates the emulation software so that more games can be played, the company has announced several times that it is doubtful that all Xbox games will ever be compatible.

Sony PlayStation 3

The PlayStation 3 (PS3), released in Japan on November 11, 2006, and a week later in North America, did not suffer from the incompatibility problems that haunted the Xbox 360. Sony has assured the public that if a PS2 game adhered to Sony's Technical Requirements Checklist, it would be playable on the PS3. Approximately 3 percent of the 1,500 PS2 games are incompatible with the new system, and Sony is working on patches for this.

Still, the launch of the PS2 echoed that of the Xbox 360 a year earlier and the PS2 in 2000. People lined up for hours outside stores before the official launch, only to be turned away due to a shortage of consoles. Many who were fortunate to obtain systems quickly turned around and sold them on eBay, where prices as high as $2,300 were recorded.

The pricing structure of the PS3 was also similar to the Xbox 360. A premium system featuring a 60 GB hard drive sold for $599. A system with a 20 GB hard drive sold for $499. Another similarity between the two systems was that they both played video games with high-definition video, for those who had an HDTV set. People who hooked the PS3 up to standard televisions would not see any difference between the new console and its predecessor.

Despite Microsoft's one-year head start, Sony still figured the PS3 would eventually outsell its competition. But as of early 2007, that lead was not apparent. For one thing, in the months following the launch, the system was in short supply. Sony announced that it would have 400,000 units available worldwide before the end of 2006. And even when it was available, its high price had limited appeal to those who did not own HDTVs.

Surprisingly, the PS3's main competition did not come from the Xbox 360. Instead it came from Nintendo's newest console, one that could not compete with the PS3 or the Xbox 360 in pure processing power. But it did offer something innovative that even appealed to non-gamers.

Nintendo Wii

During the development of a new console Nintendo was going to call Revolution, Nintendo's goal was not to compete against Sony and Microsoft, but to attract as many gamers as possible. The company knew that they had to come out with something really revolutionary to do so. While the final console was not as revolutionary as most people thought, it did gain the attention of most. By the time the system was launched on November 19, 2006, in North America and two weeks later in Japan, the name of the console had been changed to Wii, a word that sounded like the English word "we," meaning that the system was for everybody.

What Nintendo delivered was a system that at first glance acted amazingly like the XaviXPORT. Packed with a title called *Wii Sports,* the system allowed gamers to play sports such as virtual baseball and golf while using a wireless controller that acted as the baseball bat or golf club. While the controller did not actually look like the sports equipment, Nintendo kept the controller amazingly simple. Unlike the current trend in controllers in which seven buttons were the norm, Nintendo's Wii Remote only had two buttons.

But as simple as the Wii Remote was, it led to trouble from the first day of launch. The Wii Remote came with a wrist strap that attached to the remote and looped around the player's wrist. While involved with the sports games, many players got caught up in the action and let go of the controller. The wrist strap came apart and sent the remote flying, sometimes straight into TV sets. Nintendo quickly rectified the problem by making the wrist band more secure and offering them free of charge to all Wii owners.

The Wii made great use of wireless technology, including using a wireless connection to hook up to the Internet. The system allowed players to obtain news and five day weather forecasts. Players could also use the Internet to access the Virtual Console, an online service that allowed players to download earlier Nintendo games which played on all previous consoles from the NES to the N64. Games from the Genesis and Turbografx-16 could also be downloaded. In addition, the Wii was completely compatible with the GameCube, although it used standard 5-inch discs.

System Wars

The North American launches of the PS3 and Wii were only a few days apart. Both systems were in short supply for the 2006 holiday season. Nintendo announced that four million units would be available with the majority of them allocated to the United States. Sony's response to the shortage was that only 400,000 units were available on the entire planet. Still, after only one full month of availability, the Wii seemed to be the favorite among the three systems. Whether it was idle curiosity that led to interest in the system, or the sheer innovativeness of the physical interaction, or even its lower price, the Wii appeared to be the system of choice.

Of course it may be too soon to determine a clear winner in the console wars. If Nintendo fails to deliver more innovative titles that take advantage of the Wii Remote, then its popularity could fall quickly. If the number of HDTVs in homes continue to rise, the popularity of the PS3 could increase.

One thing that is certain is that the popularity of any system is fleeting. In a few years new systems will replace the Xbox 360, PS3, and Wii. Or a new company may jump into the fray as Microsoft did in 2001, leading a current company to abandon its console market as Sega did the same year. The industry players will constantly revolve, but the game players will always be there.

CHAPTER 27

ONLINE ROLE-PLAYING GAMES

Kelly Boudreau

Online role-playing games have a diverse and rich history extending from the dorm room to corporate boardroom. Through technological developments, online role-playing games have progressed from obscure text-based adventures to richly intricate graphical worlds inhabited by millions. As multiple versions of history often coexist, especially in the case of online role-playing games, origin stories are often contested and open for debate.[1]

It is important to bear in mind that, technologically, one game does not necessarily build upon another in a cumulative manner. Because early multiplayer networked computer games were created on often closed university networks, game developments often occurred in isolation; as a result, simultaneous, conceptual development occurred. In this sense, the history of online role-playing games is more weblike than linear.

Word Play: 1977–1989

In the late 1970s, the first group of multi-user networked role-playing computer games were created for the PLATO system at the University of Illinois. *Mines of Moria* (1977) was created by Chuck Miller and was one of the first graphical games "composed of a detailed line drawing of the scene ahead...including monsters, doors and corridor walls, along with status charts for...character's current strength and powers."[2] Although the game could support up to 200 players at one time, communication was very limited and the game world was not persistent (available 24 hours a day). The second and more interactive game on the PLATO system was *Oubliette* (1977), a group-based dungeon exploration game, but like its predecessor, the game world was not persistent and communication between players remained limited.[3]

In 1978 at Essex University, Roy Trubshaw wrote the first formal text-based multi-user dungeon (MUD) game for the DEC PDP-10 system. The game world was small and consisted of only a few different locations that the player could navigate through and have conversations with other players who were in the same space at the same time. Working with Trubshaw, Richard Bartle introduced a combat system and *MUD1,* and the first goal-oriented interactive MUD was born.

MUD1 is a fantasy-based role-playing game where might and magic entice players to cooperate and battle towards the goal of immortality. In order to play *MUD1*, players would log into a remote server and connect to a bulletin board system that hosted the game. Once inside the game, players were confronted with text-based descriptions of the player's location, character description, and other relevant information. In order for players to navigate and interact within the game space and with other players, they would type and enter commands that would then be processed within the game to initiate play. What was revolutionary in comparison to the PLATO-based games was that the game world was persistent and character specific information, such as the player-accumulated experience, levels, and in-game items, was stored within the system. *MUD1* is the longest running MUD and is still playable today through a web browser.[4] As *MUD1* grew in popularity, expanding beyond the UK, other MUDs began to appear.

When the games shifted from BBS-supported systems to ones using modem connections, players were able to connect to locally supported games. By 1983, MUDs began to commercialize with the release of the fantasy role-playing game, Alan Klietz's *Sceptre of Goth*. Designed around a traditional *Dungeons & Dragons* role-playing system, *Sceptre of Goth* bore typical fantasy role-playing elements including magic-users and character classes such as clerics and rangers, along with the accumulation of experience points and levels for up to 16 simultaneous players who connected to the game via a modem. *Sceptre of Goth* followed the same command-driven text-based gameplay of earlier MUDs, as players navigated through various types of puzzles, group combat adventures, and merchant interactions.

The game was released as franchises in several locations, operated and owned by individuals who would run the system independently. Each franchise owner was given a relatively simple "world editor" in order to create in-game events, handle world resets, and alter attributes of any in-game object, often acting as the game's dungeon master (DM). As individual DMs had the ability to manipulate gameplay elements and alter content, *Sceptre of Goth* offered a unique dynamic game play experience, influencing other games such as Mark Peterson's *Swords of Chaos* (1984) and Brett Vickers's *Quest of Mordor* (1993). Other commercial MUDs that began to appear around this time included titles such as *Dragon's Gate* (1984), *Mirrorworld* (1985), *AberMUD* (1988), and *TinyMUD* (1989). *TinyMUD* has since become a most influential game since it combines gameplay with world creation for the players, influencing the game *Avalon* (1989), among others, which was the first MUD to be released live on the Internet in 1994 via its own Windows telnet client; it is still available today under the title *Avalon, the Legend Lives.*[5]

Playing with Pixels: 1990–2007

The shift from text-based gameplay to graphical user interfaces first began with Lucasfilm Games's *Habitat* (1985) which boasted "a real-time animated view into an online simulated world in which users can communicate, play games, go on adventures, fall in love, get married, get divorced, start businesses, found religions, wage wars, protest against them, and experiment with self-government."[6] Although not truly three dimensional or fantasy based like many of the MUDs of the 1980s, for many, *Habitat* was the first and most influential predecessor of today's highly successful aesthetically complex massively multiplayer online role-playing games.

Often considered the first modern graphical MMORPG, *Neverwinter Nights* (1991) was released by Quantum Computer Services (later to become AOL) and was co-developed with the companies SSI and TSR as the first Advanced Dungeons & Dragons (AD&D) online game. The game server hosted a persistent world and at its peak supported up to 500 players at one time. *Neverwinter Nights* was unique in that it combined real-time first-person graphical gameplay with an interactive chat engine and a turn-based combat system. It was also the first online role-playing game to introduce organized player-versus-player (PvP) gameplay and player clans.

Two years later, *The Shadow of Yserbius* was released in 1993 on the Sierra Network. Another classical fantasy role-playing game, *The Shadow of Yserbius* offered players the opportunity to create their characters by selecting their race, class, and combat skills as well as their guild alliance, which influenced their gameplay once inside the game world. Combat was turn based and adventures were played in groups of four. Travelling through dungeons, confronting pixelated monsters, and amassing treasures, skill points, and other attributes, players could increase their character's abilities and power, while immersing themselves in challenging puzzle-solving and social interaction.

Inspired by *Sceptre of Goth,* the game *Meridian 59* was released in 1995 by 3DO as the first commercial online game. It was also the first online role-playing game to be developed on a fully 3-D engine offering the player a 3-D playing perspective. Presenting players with meaningful player-versus-player combat as well as guild-versus-guild action, players must protect not only their in-game property, but their guild mates as well. Gameplay was unique in that it was not based on the traditional fantasy role-playing game framework of character progression through the accumulation of levels and classes. Rather, players developed different skills and attributes independently of each other based on different types of play such as combat and exploration. In order to increase a spell's strength the player had to increase its use, and in order to augment combat skills the player had to enter battle more often. Despite being closed down in 2000, *Meridian 59* has since reopened and maintains an active and loyal fan base.

Origin Systems released *Ultima Online* in 1997 and within weeks it had a registered player base of almost 46,000 players.[7] With so many players, the game's system often had difficulty supporting simultaneous play, often causing the game to crash, forcing everyone out of the game. Regardless of this initial bug (among others), *UO* was a revolutionary game experience for many. Players were now able to build persistent houses on land they had to purchase, requiring players to commit more time and energy to gameplay, which for some created the feeling of an immersive game world. The game also boasted an intricate skill system that followed *Meridian 59*'s example, moving away from a strict character-class level system. PvP was also a significant part of gameplay, and unlike past online games, could occur in all areas of the game, removing any safe zone from PvP.

Shifting away from more traditional turn-based combat systems, *UO* had a dynamic reactive combat system allowing the players to experience combat in real time. The graphics were a significant upgrade from previous titles as well, while maintaining an isometric three-quarter-view perspective consistent with other online games at the time. This player perspective enabled players to see the action all around them, which in a PvP environment became an added benefit. *Ultima Online* was under recent redevelopment by Electronic Arts, resulting in the summer 2007 release of the overhauled *Ultima Online: Kingdom Reborn.*

With the rapid increase in technological development, widespread Internet access, and a growing interest in online role-playing games, *EverQuest* (EQ) was released in March 1999 by Verant Interactive with subscription numbers rising steadily until 2001 and then settling to approximately 450,000 subscribers by 2004. Following a Tolkien-esque aesthetic and traditional fantasy role-playing game progression model, players created their characters before entering the game by selecting their gender, race, class, and deity, and distributed skill points across several different attributes. Character customization continued throughout gameplay, as players increased in levels, attaining new armor and raising skill sets. Once in the game-world, players were able to choose their player perspective from first-person, third-person from behind, or the conventional isometric three-quarter view from earlier games. Graphics aimed to push the limits of technology, and the user interface was designed to be simple and effective. Encouraging a more cooperative play style than past titles, some in-game events required up to 80 players to coordinate their efforts in order to win an epic battle. Player-versus-player gameplay was a minimal part of the game, contained in special arena combat areas and specially dedicated PvP servers. With new content introduced over the span of 13 expansions, including one in early 2007, *EverQuest* maintains a large dedicated player base in an increasingly expanding market.

As the market broadened with an increasing number of competitive releases such as *Anarchy Online* (2001), *Dark Age of Camelot* (2001), *Shadowbane* (2003), *Star Wars Galaxies* (2003), *Horizons* (2003), *City of Heroes* (2004), and *Lineage II* (2004), the game that would demarcate the complete commercial success of the genre was Blizzard's *World of Warcraft* (*WoW*), released in fall 2004. Based on the popular real-time-strategy (RTS) computer game of *Warcraft*, *WoW* had players lined up and waiting before the game was even released. Gameplay shifted from the socially dependent multiplayer style of earlier games such as *Ultima Online, EverQuest,* and *Dark Age of Camelot* to a more independent, solo style, allowing players to level their characters in shorter amounts of time with less help from other players.

World of Warcraft's graphics were crisp and colorful, and player movement was smooth and agile. Gameplay was designed around a questing system to alleviate the repetitiveness of level progression found in other online role-playing game titles. Unlike the mass numbers required for epic battles in *EverQuest, World of Warcraft*'s epic battles were based on smaller numbers (around 20 to 40 players). *World of Warcraft* is also credited with introducing "instances," which were essentially individualized, duplicate dungeons for small groups. This lowered the competition level for quest monsters, in-game items, and experience points, allowing all players to experience the same content regardless of server population. By spring 2006, *World of Warcraft* boasted international subscription numbers as high as 6.5 million, and by August 2007 the number had grown to 9 million subscribers.[8]

Over the years, other titles have been released with significant success and influence over the development of online role-playing games, specifically *The Realm Online* (1996), which is often credited as being the longest continuously running MMORPG. As Western culture becomes increasingly digital, and the MMORPG market continues to expand into popular culture, we are seeing an increase in online games aiming at particular demographics, such as pre-teens and teens, with titles such as *Toontown Online* (2003) and *Rose Online* (2005) as well as an increased interest in adult-oriented virtual social worlds like *Second Life* (2003).[9] As online role-playing games continue to develop at an increasing rate, each genre and demographic contribute to a global billion-dollar industry that currently shows little sign of slowing down.

CHAPTER 28

System Profile: Sony PlayStation

Dominic Arsenault

Sony had been working on a project that would eventually become the PlayStation—the first console to sell over 100 million units and that would end Nintendo's dominance over the video game market—as early as 1988. At the time, the company had a partnership with Nintendo in the form of licensed technology: Nintendo was using Sony's SPC-700 processor (designed by Ken Kutaragi) for the playback of sound and music in their upcoming Super Nintendo Entertainment System, to be released in 1990. Nintendo, the top video game company at the time, saw the rising CD-ROM technology as an opportunity to gain a technological advantage over its competitor Sega and match NEC's offering, which represented a growing threat to its market clout. (Sega's console, the Sega Genesis, was competing in Europe and North America with Nintendo's NES and SNES.) NEC's PC-Engine was released in Japan in 1987 and soon became very popular, outselling both Sega's Genesis (Mega Drive) and Nintendo's NES (Famicom). The PC-Engine CD-ROM add-on hit the Japanese market in 1988. The system was subsequently exported to North America in 1989 and Europe in 1990 under a different name: the TurboGrafx-16, with the Turbografx-CD soon following.

Nintendo and Sony reached an agreement in which Sony would develop an add-on for Nintendo's Super NES which would use CD-ROMs (much like the Sega CD that was added to the Genesis a few years later). In exchange for this, Nintendo would let Sony develop its own "Play Station" platform, a gaming and multimedia CD-ROM machine fitted with a port for SNES cartridges. Both the SNES-CD add-on and the Play Station console were to be announced at the 1989 Consumer Electronics Show. However, Nintendo did not realize that the CD-ROM format to be used was under development by Sony, which meant the company would hold licensing rights over all games produced with its proprietary technology (it is unclear whether this was due to Nintendo not interpreting the contract correctly or because of subtle legal wording from Sony's part). Needless to say, this was in complete opposition to Nintendo's business practices of the time. Though Sony demonstrated their Play Station at the CES, the next day Nintendo announced that they would be working with Philips, Sony's rival in CD-ROM technology, to develop an add-on for the SNES. The leading video game company had inked a similar deal with Philips with one notable difference: Nintendo would hold the licensing rights to all CD-ROM games produced for the SNES.

Sony decided to keep working on their project and make their entry in the video game market. Since Nintendo still used their sound chip in the Super NES and had broken their contract by allying themselves with Philips, Sony managed to negotiate the right to keep the port for SNES cartridges on their console, although Nintendo would keep most of the profits from the games licensed. Sony unveiled its Play Station at the 1991 Tokyo International Electronics Show, with a scheduled release date in the summer of 1992— six months before the launch of the SNES CD-ROM add-on. Then Nintendo broke off their agreement, Sony created the Sony Imagesoft subsidiary to develop and publish games for the Sega CD and the SNES, and Nintendo slowly postponed and eventually cancelled their CD-ROM add-on after observing the blunders of Sega and Philips's CD-based game consoles.

In 1993 Nintendo struck a deal with Silicon Graphics to develop a 64-bit console based on 3-D graphics, essentially leapfrogging the 32-bit CD-ROM hardware generation. As the industry was reaching the end of its current life cycle that had started with the release of the Sega Genesis, Sony decided to wait for the next cycle to make their entry in the market. The Play Station was completely redesigned and the SNES cartridge port removed, and Sony's PlayStation (now one word) was released to consumers on December 3, 1994, in Japan, and in September and November 1995 to the rest of the world. The Sega Saturn, released in November 1994 in Japan, outsold the PlayStation for the first six months. Sega attempted to gain a head start over it with a surprise U.S. launch in May 1995, but lack of third-party support and software production delays resulted in a drought of games that nullified this edge in timing. By contrast, the Play-Station's excellent selection of launch titles and large stable of third-party developers provided ample opportunities of showcasing the system's strengths. It also retailed for $299 in the United States, $100 less than the Saturn. By the time Nintendo released their next console in June 1996 in Japan, the PlayStation already had attracted many gamers and game makers alike.

The PlayStation conquered the world of gaming and ended Nintendo's decade of dominance over the home video game consoles market. By December 1999, Sony had sold 70 million units, compared to a meager 28.7 million Nintendo 64s.[1] Nintendo survived thanks to its amassed wealth from the past and its Game Boy's monopoly over the handheld market, which accounted for 31 percent of the total market share for video games (handhelds and consoles included). The winner of the 32-bit and 64-bit home consoles era is clear: at the dawn of the next hardware generation in 2000, the Sony PlayStation held 34 percent of the market, almost twice as much as the Nintendo 64's 17.5 percent.[2]

According to Sony's March 2006 figures, the company shipped 102.49 million Play-Station units. The console was the first to break the 100-million mark in the home video game market, a feat that is, as of March 2007, only equaled by the PlayStation 2. These figures are due in part to Sony's release in 2000 of a smaller, redesigned version called the PSOne, much as Nintendo's earlier "New NES." Contrary to Nintendo's failure, however, the PSOne successfully kept consumer interest in the aging PlayStation: it was a great success and outsold even Sony's own new PlayStation 2 for the first six months following its release. With the original hardware and the PSOne combined, Sony produced Play-Station units for 11 years, an unusually long time for a home video game console. Production officially ended on March 23, 2006.

Licensing Terms

The system gained favor among game developers over the Nintendo 64 and Sega Saturn for a number of reasons. First, most of them were burned out by Nintendo's strict licensing policies and found Sony's terms extremely attractive: according to Steve Kent, "Sony's licensing structure was built around a $10-per-game arrangement that included manufacturing disks, manuals, and packaging."[3] Second, they saw in CD-ROMs the double advantage of low production costs and increased storage capacity that multiplied their creative possibilities. According to Kent,

> Compared to the cost of pressing CDs, manufacturing cartridges for Project Reality [development codename for the upcoming Nintendo 64 console] would be prohibitively expensive. At the time, it cost more than $20 to manufacture an 8-megabyte cartridge, compared to less than $2 to press a 640-megabyte CD. And the additional storage space on CDs could be used for video clips, animations, audio files, music, and larger games.[4]

Finally, programming for the PlayStation was much easier than for the Sega Saturn, the architecture of which was based around two processors. This proved to be a challenge for most programmers, and those who worked on Saturn projects ultimately seldom used the console's power to its fullest. This was especially true on the U.S. production side, as Sega's four-month advance launch took developers by surprise and did not give them time to appropriately familiarize themselves with the system.

Games Library

According to Sony's official March 2006 figures, the PlayStation is host to 7,888 titles which shipped a cumulative total of 961 million units to consumers worldwide. Like the NES and Super NES before it, the PlayStation's success is attributable to its vast library of high-profile games. Sony's system featured most of the biggest franchises and series of its time (with the exception of Nintendo's first-party *Zelda* and *Mario* titles), including *Grand Theft Auto, Madden NFL Football, Tony Hawk's Pro Skater, Need for Speed, Tomb Raider,* and *Mortal Kombat.* While these games were also available for other systems (the Sega Saturn, Dreamcast, and Nintendo 64 in particular), Sony could rely on a large number of exclusive titles which went on to become video game classics, including the *Gran Turismo* series, whose first namesake entry became the PlayStation's best-selling game with over 10 million copies worldwide. Other exclusive series include *Legacy of Kain, Syphon Filter, Twisted Metal, Tekken,* and *WWF SmackDown. Crash Bandicoot,* developed by Naughty Dog, was published by Sony Computer Entertainment America and its character was used in Sony's marketing as a mascot to combat Sega's trademark hedgehog Sonic and Nintendo's Mario. *PaRappa the Rapper,* a game in which the player had to press certain buttons at the right time to make its title character rap along to music, helped popularize the genre known today as "rhythm games." The *Resident Evil* and *Silent Hill* series were born on Sony's console and spawned numerous sequels, eventually across many gaming platforms, along with movie adaptations.

Many franchises that originated elsewhere were either moved to or resurrected on the PlayStation. The most notable example of this is Squaresoft's iconic *Final Fantasy* series. The company's exclusive relationship with Nintendo was threatened both by the latter's content policies and decision to continue with cartridges in the CD-ROM era; Square wanted to develop more mature themes and on a higher-capacity storage media, which were both possible by going with the Sony PlayStation. When Square released *Final Fantasy VII* in the United States in 1997, the game became a huge mainstream gaming success and redefined the role-playing game genre, which up until then had been only a niche market outside Japan. Square thrived on the PlayStation platform with its eighth and ninth *Final Fantasy* installments, *Chrono Cross* (the successor to the highly praised *Chrono Trigger* that appeared on Nintendo's Super NES), and a spin-off game that would later become a series, *Final Fantasy Tactics.* Konami resurrected its *Metal Gear* franchise with the release of *Metal Gear Solid* exclusively on the PlayStation in 1998. It was the first release in the series since 1990, and it established the roots of the stealth-based action game genre with its 3-D graphics and intricate storyline. Konami also brought its long-standing *Castlevania* series to the PlayStation with *Symphony of the Night,* a 2-D platform game that showed such games were still viable in the 3-D era and redefined the nature of the series by emphasizing open-ended exploration, character development, and item collection rather than the usual level-based progression. Capcom also joined the fray by releasing *Mega Man 8, Mega Man X4,* and *Mega Man X5* on the PlayStation.

Without a doubt, the migration of well-known franchises to the PlayStation seduced many gamers to adopt Sony's console. Another incentive was Sony's establishment in 1997 of a "greatest hits" selection in the United States, which regrouped all titles that had sold a high number of copies and been on sale for more than a year.[5] Popular games were repackaged with a different label and sold at a discounted price ($24.99 was suggested, but many retailers offered them for $19.99). This provided gamers with a selection of successful games at a more budget-conscious price and soon became an industry standard with Nintendo and Microsoft reproducing the concept with their "Player's Choice" and "Platinum Hits" titles.

Technical Specifications

The Sony PlayStation is a 32-bit console, designed to compete against Sega's 32-bit Saturn (released a week and a half earlier in Japan) and the 64-bit Nintendo 64 (that would enter the market a year and a half later). It is generally considered less powerful than the Sega Saturn, but as it was a lot easier to program, the actual quality of most games on the PlayStation is usually higher than on the Saturn. Similarly, while the Nintendo 64 had more raw processing power, the higher precision allowed by 64-bit processing was seldom required in 3-D games, and ultimately did not compensate for the lack of storage space on the N64 cartridges when compared to the PlayStation's CD-ROMs. As such, while the theoretical power of Sony's console was lower than its competitors, it did not readily appear as an inferior console.

The PlayStation marks the beginning of "modchips" in video game console history. By soldering a "modification chip" into the system, gamers could bypass or alter Sony's program code for verifying disc authenticity or regional lockout. This allowed them to burn a CD-R copy of a game and play it on their console or to play games belonging to a different commercial zone. Because of modchips, the piracy of PlayStation games was widespread: people could rent games at their local video club and burn a copy for themselves and their friends, and with the growing usage of the Internet, games could be downloaded from dedicated websites or peer-to-peer networks by millions of users.

Company Profile: Sony

Mark J. P. Wolf

Sony Corporation is one of the leading manufacturers of electronics, communications technology, televisions, computer monitors, video games, movies, music, and other entertainment. In the video game market, it is best known for its PlayStation series of home game console systems.

The company began as the Tokyo Telecommunications Engineering Corporation in 1946, and changed its name to "Sony" in 1958, taking its name from a combination of the words "Sonus" (Latin for "sonic") and "Sonny" ("denoting small size, or a youthful boy," according to Sony's website). The company produced the first magnetic tape, tape recording equipment, and transistor radios in Japan during the 1950s, and established Sony Corporation of America in the United States in 1960. Although it did not invent the transistor radio, Sony was the first company to successfully market transistor radios, bringing in profits that would allow Sony to develop other products.

Some of Sony's technical innovations over the next decades included the Betamax video cassette format in 1975, the Walkman portable tape player in 1979, the Discman portable CD player in 1984, the Video8 format in 1985, DAT (digital audio tape) in 1987, and the MiniDisc format in 1992. The company produced the MSX home computer in 1983, and found success with its home video game consoles, the PlayStation (1994), PlayStation 2 (2000), PlayStation 3 (2006), and the PlayStation Portable (PSP) (2005) which was a handheld unit. All of these products continued to add to the company's growth and funded expansion into new areas over the years.

Today Sony is a vast multinational company, with corporate branches in China, Spain, France, Canada, South Korea, and elsewhere, and it is among the largest media conglomerates in the world, with interests in many different media. In 1988 Sony acquired CBS Records, renaming it Sony Music Entertainment in 1991, and in 2004 it merged with BMG Records to become Sony BMG Music Entertainment. Sony acquired Columbia Pictures in 1989, renaming it Sony Pictures Entertainment, and in 2005 Sony led a consortium that acquired The MGM Company. In 1993 the company also established Sony Computer Entertainment, which produces its video games and console systems. Sony continues to innovate, and as of 2007 it was developing high-definition equipment and formats, computer technology, video display systems, digital cameras, robots, audio equipment, broadcast technology, and recording media.

The PlayStation contains five separate components: a CPU, a graphics processing unit (GPU), a sound processing unit (SPU), some onboard memory, and a CD-ROM drive. The CPU is a 32-bit chip manufactured by LSI Logic and runs at 33.8688 MHz. It allows 30 million instructions per second (MIPS), has a bus speed of 132 megabits per second, an instruction cache of 4 KB, and a data cache of 1 KB. It also houses the geometry transformation engine (GTE) and the data decompression engine (DDE). The former serves as extra processing power for the calculation of 3-D graphics: it can handle 66 MIPS and render 360,000 "flat," or 180,000 light-sourced or texture-mapped, polygons per second.

(Sony originally claimed the PlayStation could display 1.5 million polygons per second, but this estimate was given without taking into account artificial intelligence processing and other operations that commonly limit the amount of resources that can be allocated to graphics in video games.) The DDE's function is to decompress images and video files. It has been used extensively in games like *Final Fantasy VII* to playback high-quality, prerendered, cut-scenes.

The GPU is responsible for drawing the 2-D graphics on-screen (this includes the calculated 3-D polygons). The SPU features 24 channels at a sampling rate of 44,100 Hz (standard audio CD quality). The PlayStation's onboard memory consists of 2 MB of RAM with an extra MB dedicated to video processing and 512 KB for sound. The operating system is allocated 512 KB of ROM.

The CD-ROM is a double-speed drive with a maximum data transfer rate of 300 KB per second. It is compatible with both the CD-DA (for playback of audio CDs) and the XA Mode 2 (for increased CD storage capacity) standards. The first production run of PlayStation units sported an interior design that caused the laser unit to slightly go off-balance after extended usage, preventing the correct reading of CD-ROMs. This was due to the laser unit being made of plastic and being too close to the power supply; overheating slightly distorted the plastic alloy and altered the beam's angle. Sony corrected this problem in subsequent manufacturing runs.[6]

CHAPTER 29

VIDEO GAME STARS: LARA CROFT

Alison McMahan

In 1996, Eidos's game *Tomb Raider* introduced Lara Croft, the female adventurer who would go on to become one of the most recognized video game stars of the 1990s. Core Design Europe, who designed the game, originally had a male character but decided to change the character to a female because the game was more about puzzle-solving and stealth than action.[1] Lara was created by designer Toby Gard, who admitted in an interview that her large breasts occurred by accident when his mouse slipped, expanding them 150 percent instead of just 50 percent. Others thought they were a good idea, and according to Gard, "The marketing men just saw them as the easy route to take with their campaign."[2] Lara continued to be marketed using her sex appeal, to the point where Gard even left Core Design over the way she was being portrayed and marketed because he felt they were misrepresenting the character.[3] *Tomb Raider* went on to become a franchise with over a dozen games released on a variety of platforms, a series of 50 comic books from Top Cow Productions, three novels, and two feature films, *Lara Croft: Tomb Raider* (2001) and *Tomb Raider: The Cradle of Life* (2003), both starring Angelina Jolie as Lara Croft.

Who Is Lara Croft?

According to information surrounding the game, Lara has her favorite music (U2, Nine-Inch Nails), her favorite food (Beans on Toast), her favorite cities (Atlantis, Venice, and London), and her favorite weapons (Uzis—one in each hand—and the M-16 automatic). Her birthday is given as Valentine's Day 1968, in Wimbledon, London. She's 1.70 m tall, weighs 55 kg, with brown hair, brown eyes, and the famous 75DD bust. Her education is given as "private lessons (3–11 years old), Wimbledon High School for Girls (11–16 years old), Gordonstoun Boarding School (16–18 years old), and Swiss Finishing School (18–21 years old)." Her hobbies are rock-climbing, extreme skiing, and sharpshooting.

From the first screenplay for the Hollywood film *Tomb Raider* we learn that Lara's parents died in a plane crash when they were taking her mountain climbing in the Himalayas; Lara survived, was sheltered by a Tibetan monk, who taught her all of her fighting skills and now acts as her personal valet. Though it is not mentioned, we are encouraged to assume that the monk also taught her numerous ancient languages, how to read ancient maps, and the value of ancient tomb treasures. Lara is also assisted by three techno-nerds (reminiscent of the computer geeks/conspiracy theorists that help Agent Mulder of *The X-Files*) that design and build her weapons and worship her from afar. By the time the film was made, Lara had one techno-geek on her staff, and everything worth learning was taught to her by her late father.

Lara's history continues to change. In 2006, the game *Tomb Raider: Legend* appeared, along with a whole new backstory for Lara that conflicted with her earlier one. Her legend continues to grow.

Goddess

Like all deities, Lara has her priestesses, her look-alikes that represent her in "meat-space" (that is, in the real world). Eidos employs models to play the "real" Lara at trade shows and store openings (over half a dozen, including model Rhona Mitra; Nell McAndrew who went on to grace the cover of U.S. Playboy; Lara Weller, erstwhile swimwear model; and British actress Karima Adebibe). When a new actor in Hollywood is turned into a movie star, the process is partly due to the publicity machine of the studio, which constructs a certain image for the actor; partly due to the choices the actor makes, either by choosing certain kinds of roles or by "playing" their star persona in public, or both; and by what the star's movie fans want to see (Marilyn Monroe's gay fans see a different Marilyn than do the straight men who desire to possess her). Lara Croft represents a step forward in star making in that she is not a construct built up around a real person but a star construct built up over a digital character who lets different people, from Rhona Mitra to Angelina Jolie, inhabit her.

Where Did Lara Come From?

According to the Eidos literature, a company called Core had merged with U.S. Gold a year before U.S. Gold combined with Eidos. Lead Core artist Toby Gard had the original concept for Lara as a female Indiana Jones in a background of temples and pyramids. Adventure games like *Prince of Persia* were the primary models. "We wanted it to be a game where the player has more of an affinity for the character, and that's where the third-person view came from, so that you could always see her. We wanted her to be as real a person as possible, so that people could really identify with the character," said Adrian Smith, head of product development for Core, in the company literature.

"We wanted someone who was coy and agile," he continues. "Almost a fantasy object... Lara borders all those attributes." Since there were already so many 3-D *Doom*-style shooter games, it was agreed that Lara's world needed to provide something more. Combat would be part of it, but adventuring was to remain the center of the game. This meant that each digital terrain to be traversed is its own puzzle. This was not radical either, but "the way Lara pursued her quests that set her far apart—with style and athleticism, and within a very strict set of parameters that allowed for incredible freedom of movement."

It is clear that Eidos has succeeded in creating a star. Like most stars, Lara Croft has an appeal that crosses boundaries, that works on females as well as males, on adults as well as on the young. The fact that she is a digital character hardly seems to matter to her fans.

But it does make a difference: we do not adore Lara Croft in the same way that we adore our favorite movie star on the big screen. In other words, because we partly control Lara, we relate to her in a different way than we do our favorite movie stars.

In many games, such as *The Sims,* although players influence the Sim environment, they do not have that much control over the Sim characters, who often shake their head "no" if their programming impels them in a direction other than where you want them to go. In other words, their behavior is unreliable. Gameplay with digital characters offers a similar feel of unreliability. In the case of a single-user game such as *Tomb Raider,* the avatar—Lara Croft—comes to us already formed, with her appearance and personality in place; a whole cult of stardom has developed around this persona. But each new player of *Tomb Raider* has to learn to make Lara move—how to walk, jump, swim, avoid deadly obstacles. With each failure, Lara dies, and the player must begin again, with the hope that this time he and Lara will get a little further ahead in the game. In other words, with an avatar, both forms of spectator identification are working at once: the player identifies with the avatar—in this case Lara Croft—but also has to be constantly aware of the computer interface, of the "gaze" or way of gazing that is built into the program. In this sense, computer games represent a solution to some of the stresses and quandaries raised by the classical cinematic apparatus. At the same time it creates new problems: the interface and gameplay take commitment and time to be learned. Perhaps it is just this that has led to Lara Croft's stardom. Our pleasure comes not just from identifying with her but also from the fact that it is we who give her the breath of life, like Rabbi Loew gave it to the Golem and God gave it to Adam.

CHAPTER 30

GENRE PROFILE:
FIRST-PERSON SHOOTING GAMES

Bob Rehak

Doom, Quake, Unreal, Half-Life, Medal of Honor, Halo: among the most popular video games ever released, these are all examples of the first-person shooter or FPS. Combining graphic sophistication and violent content for a powerful immersive effect, the FPS also has been a lightning rod for controversy about the moral and psychological impact of video games, triggering debates about whether such games function as training simulators for aggressive and even homicidal behavior, and if so, how they should be regulated. The roots of the FPS extend back to the mid-1970s, when creators in several different corners of the game industry began developing computer graphics up to the task of immersing players in three-dimensional (3-D) space. Throughout the 1980s, these experiments continued, placing players in ever more detailed and explorable worlds. Along with the evolution of the Internet, the FPS exploded in the early 1990s as the "killer app" of networked personal computers, enabling players to fight each other in arena-style death-matches and spawning new forms of team-based gameplay such as *Capture the Flag*. Nowadays, high-end shooters, with their steep processing and memory demands, drive users to upgrade their computers and buy new gaming consoles. Each generation of shooters has pushed the limits of computer hardware and clever programming to become one of the most widely recognized and globally lucrative families of interactive electronic play.

First-person shooters are played from a subjective perspective—as though the player is embodied in three-dimensional space, directly perceiving a game world that recedes real-istically into the distance. Action unfolds in a more-or-less continuous "tracking shot," mimicking the point-of-view cameras of Hollywood but extending that concept to its logical extreme: rather than gazing on the player's stand-in from the outside, the camera *becomes* the avatar and vice versa. With its emphasis on presence, the FPS is highly immer-sive and sensorially immediate, and, at its most successful, almost overwhelmingly visceral. Perhaps more than any other game genre, FPSs address the player at the level of the body. In this sense they are like the "body genres" of cinema—melodrama, horror, pornography, gross-out comedy—and have drawn condemnation in equal measure to those stigmatized cultural forms. But the controversial status of the FPS involves more than immersive graphics. Just as essential is the third term in its name—*shooter.* In its purest form, the FPS is relentlessly aggressive, its action driven by shooting and being shot at. As the primary means of interacting with opponents, ranged weapons provide the genre with its defining iconography: a gun barrel (as of a shotgun, plasma rifle, or rocket launcher) jutting from the bottom of the frame and pointing toward a real or implied crosshairs at the center of the screen. This gun, along with the hand holding it, bridges the space of the player and the space of the game, combining with 3-D graphics to create the shooter's key illusion: *you are here.*

The experience of playing an FPS is that of exploring an endlessly unfolding environment (sometimes a claustrophobic maze, sometimes vast open areas) through the eyes of another, often enjoying scenery rendered in relatively lush detail. In its visualization of a detailed world, centered on a player who acts as an embodied agent, the shooter literalizes a fundamental conceit of computer gaming—one present even in games that consist solely of text, such as the seminal *Adventure.* Written by William Crowther in 1973 and subsequently modified by Don Woods at the Stanford Artificial Intelligence Laboratory (SAIL), *Adventure* allowed players to explore a large space composed of outdoor and indoor spaces, houses and underground caves populated by creatures, objects, and puzzles. In a process that might best be described as "second person," players type commands and receive descriptions in order to navigate and interact with the world. The game's opening block of text, for example, reads: "You are standing at the end of a road before a small brick building. Around you is a forest. A small stream flows out of the building and down a gully."

The "you" in *Adventure* is functionally equivalent to the "I" of the avatar, in that it designates both the human player and his or her emissary within the game world. More importantly, it emphasizes the importance of embodiment in video games' address to their players, inviting human beings to imagine themselves as fully present and participatory inhabitants of a world contained within the machine. Graphics of the mid-1970s were incapable of representing players visually as anything more than crude blocks of color. The abstract domain of the all-text *Adventure,* paradoxically, embodied players in high *mental* resolution by drawing on their novelistic training: seeing a personal pronoun on the page (or the screen), readers equate the literary character with their own.

Early 3-D Gaming

In the years since *Adventure,* the dream of exploring virtual worlds with virtual bodies has expanded with advances in computer technology. Associated with high-end equipment such as specialized hardware for 3-D acceleration, spacious memory, and speedy processors, as well as elaborately clever software to calculate line-of-sight perspective, remove hidden walls, paint surfaces with convincing textures, and generate light and shadow, the FPS epitomizes the cutting edge of video gaming. Each new generation of releases drives users to upgrade their computers or purchase new systems. The FPS thus plays a special role within the video game industry, reflecting the significant historical function of games and their graphics in popularizing and democratizing information technology.

Three-dimensional perspective has long been a goal of game designers. While the early days of arcade gaming in the 1970s were dominated by top-down and side-view displays in blocky resolution and limited color palettes, certain game forms, such as racing games and flight simulators, placed viewers behind windshields and viewports, gazing out at train tracks that converged on vanishing points, eye-level horizons, and objects that appeared small far away but grew larger as they approached. An early experiment in 3-D gaming was the tank combat simulator *Panther,* developed in 1975 at Northwestern University for a multi-user computer system known as PLATO. Many attributes of *Panther* showed up five years later in the first commercially successful implementation of 3-D gaming, Atari's *Battlezone* (1980). *Battlezone* placed players behind the controls of a tank on an arid landscape, firing away at enemy vehicles. When an enemy missile hit, jagged cracks appeared across the field of view, and many gamers of that generation can recall the reflexive spasm that would jerk them back from the cabinet's periscope and twin joysticks.

Rather than laboriously painting in game space with blocky pixels, *Battlezone*'s vector graphics merely drew lines connecting vertices, resulting in wireframe worlds and models that moved with the fluidity of pure mathematics. But *Battlezone*'s graphics were convincing only in their smoothness and dimensionality. The obstacles on the battlefield were primitive pyramids, blocks, and cylinders. All consisted of transparent wireframes; there were no textures, only a skeletal dance of vectors. Another 3-D game released soon after, Atari's *Tempest,* devoted its much more colorful wireframes to a simulation of combat in terms of abstract art: boomerangs, lightning bolts, and whirling spirals. *Tempest* was definitely perspectival—players peered into receding tunnels, a well up the walls of which climbed enemy shapes as superzaps rained down upon them.

Throughout the 1980s, arcade video games continued to extend the boundaries of subjective-viewpoint graphics. Atari's *Pole Position* was a fast-moving, visually rich racing game, but—like earlier racing games such as Vectorbeam's *Speed Freak,* or for that matter, *Tempest* with its angular C-shaped figure—these games lacked a visible, organic avatar with which players could identify better than with a machine or vehicle. Another arcade game, Nintendo's *Punch-Out!!,* was more effective in this regard, simulating a boxing match in which players peered through a wireframe body into the eyes of their pugilistic opponent. But it was in the home, on personal computers, that the groundwork for the FPS was laid in the form of maze games. A series of releases from Med Systems for the Apple II and TRS-80 featured simple 3-D renderings of mazes loaded with secret doors, puzzles, treasures, and perils. These included *Rat's Revenge* (1980), *Deathmaze 5000* (1980), *Labyrinth* (1980), *Asylum* (1981), and *Asylum II* (1982). In 1984, a version of *Asylum II* came out for the Atari 800 and Commodore 64. Many of these titles were coded by William F. Denman, Jr., making him something of a pioneer in first-person gaming. In 1986, Lucasfilm Games released *Rescue on Fractalus!,* which represented a high-water mark in the fluid animation of 3-D space of the time. Another 3-D game for home computers that enjoyed great popularity was Acornsoft/Firebird's *Elite* (1984), a spaceflight-and-trading simulation.

First-Person Shooters: The First Wave

But it was not until the early 1990s that the FPS exploded onto the scene, bringing together several new developments in game design and hardware. Powerful new processors, expanded memory capacity, and storage media, and the nascent World Wide Web, made possible the 3-D graphics, spacious yet labyrinthine game spaces, and networked multiplayer action that quickly came to define the genre. During this period—in a story as old as the technology itself—multiple inventors working independently of each other were pursuing the same goal of an immersive 3-D maze exploration game. Only one company, id Software, would emerge as the breakthrough "originator." But there was competition.

Developed by Looking Glass Technologies and published by Origin Systems in 1992, *Ultima Underworld* grew out of Richard Garriott's long-running *Ultima* series, a franchise of role-playing games whose first incarnation—*Akallabeth*, released for the Apple II in 1980—actually featured rudimentary first-person graphics, providing players with a window through which they gazed at a simple wireframe maze in 3-D. Twelve years later, *Ultima Underworld* texture-mapped colorful patterns of stone and wood onto walls, floors, and ceilings, a substantial leap forward in the creation of immersive environments. At the other end of the first-person spectrum, Robyn and Rand Miller's *Myst* plunged players into an interactive puzzle-mystery set on a mysterious island. *Myst's* near-photorealistic rendered artwork unfolded as a series of still frames, accented with subtle animation and a rich envelope of sound effects; playing it was like clicking through a slide show.

Clearly there was an idea floating around in the first part of that decade, waiting to be plucked from the ether: a vernacular virtual reality (VR), employing sophisticated audiovisual aesthetics to embed real human beings in unreal spaces. The advent of the first-person shooter turned home computers and consoles into pint-sized reality simulators, delivering on speculative technologies of science fiction that ranged from the nightmarish nursery in Ray Bradbury's short story "The Veldt" (1951) to the neural recordings in *Brainstorm* (1983), cyberspace in William Gibson's *Neuromancer* (1984), and the holodeck in various incarnations of *Star Trek* from *Star Trek: The Next Generation* (1987) onward.

But it was the novel *Snow Crash,* published in 1992, that most directly foreshadowed the shooter's emergence both as practical technology and cultural fantasy. Author Neal Stephenson's *Metaverse,* a networked virtual environment populated by computer users wearing digital bodies called avatars, evoked the FPS as well as later evolutions of graphically intensive—though not necessarily first-person—video gaming like the massively multiplayer online role-playing games *EverQuest* (1999) and *World of Warcraft* (2004). The Metaverse portrayed virtual reality as *fun,* full of action, conflict, contest, and masquerade. Rejecting the abstract data structures and sterile visualizations that had up till then characterized VR research in science and business, *Snow Crash* recast VR as an essentially playful space, implementable on personal computers and a perfectly worthwhile use of technology.

This combination of pop irreverence and flamboyant invention was precisely the spark missing from *Ultima Underworld,* with its *Dungeons & Dragons* nerdiness, and *Myst,* with its chill and cryptic air of the museum. In order to win a wide audience, desktop VR had to be not just technically proficient but a bit vulgar: fast-moving, carnivalesque, accessible. id Software's profane products were all three. A small software company based in Texas, id Software brought together two talented young men who, like John Lennon and Paul McCartney, achieved in their partnership a magic that neither has quite been able to reproduce in later solo work. John Carmack was a programming genius with impressive technical skills; John Romero, a designer and conceptual artist whose tastes tended toward heavy metal music, twisted humor, explicit gore, and potent firepower. The pair grew up in the 1980s playing arcade games like *Asteroids* and *Defender,* games whose instantly graspable rule set ("shoot anything that moves") formed the kernel of their first forays into

3-D gaming, *Hovertank 3D* and *Catacombs 3D,* both released in 1991. These were not just games but technology tests—trial runs for Carmack's specialized code for rapidly and fluidly rendering 3-D spaces. Both were basically maze-navigation puzzles: rolling down corridors, players would round a corner to find a monster or evil machine ready to attack.

Even in these proto-shooters, with what now seem like absurdly limited graphics, the basic appeal of embodied combat simulation shines through. By virtue of its perspective, even the most rudimentary shooter generates ongoing suspense and surprise from the simple fact that players can see nothing that is not directly in front of them, or at least nearby: the radius of visible action shrinks literally to one's line of sight. Shooters thus mark a profound change in the relationship among perception, knowledge, and strategy in game play. While a game like Stern Electronics's *Berzerk* presents the same basic situation as that faced in *Hovertank 3D*—the player guns his or way through a maze, pursued by a converging swarm of enemies—*Berzerk*'s screen is a combination of top-down and side views. One can take in, at a glance, the entire space of a given screen, including the robots waiting in other areas of the room which would, to an embodied viewpoint, be blocked by walls. (Exiting one side of the screen, of course, would bring up a new map, populated with new opponents.) By contrast, id Software's early shooters radically reined in player knowledge, so that nearly every "step" forward carried with it the thrill of the unexpected.

This certainly was true of id's *Wolfenstein 3D,* released in 1992—an update of *Castle Wolfenstein* (1981), an Apple II game by Muse Software in which the player explores a castle populated with Nazi soldiers, growling attack dogs, and treasure chests full of loot and ammunition. Again, the 2-D graphics of the original game, in which multiple rooms were visible to the player, gave way to a ground-level view of receding hallways and shut doors. No longer was there a split between what the player could see and what the avatar could (in theory) perceive; the two points of view merged to create a fully "inhabited" avatar, and by the same token a more fully immersive game world.

Wolfenstein 3D was popular, but it was id's next game, *Doom,* that launched the FPS craze and came to define the genre (for better or worse) in the public mind. Certainly its storyline—a space marine facing down hordes of demonic beasts unleashed on a Martian base by a transdimensional portal—was not particularly groundbreaking, echoing the flamboyantly pulpy science-fiction setups of countless games that had come before. *Doom*'s most profound innovation, apart from its graphics, had to do with its exploitation of an increasingly interlinked computing environment (modem-to-modem connections, local area networks or LANs, the emerging architecture of the World Wide Web). Released online, *Doom* became an immensely popular shareware download, its handful of demo levels serving as an invitation to buy the full version of the game.

A second way in which *Doom* exploited connectivity was in allowing players to meet in networked "deathmatches," firing at and dodging each other rather than computer-generated opponents. The idea of networked environments as playspaces dates back at least to the multi-user dungeons (MUDs) of the 1970s. Like the early *Adventure,* the MUDs were text-based, their interactions involving words rather than graphics, and play within them was a sophisticated collective spinning of fantasy identities serving as a matrix for interaction: social interaction as gaming. A more direct ancestor of the networked FPS was the 3-D game *Mazewar* and its numerous variants. Developed for the IMSAI PDP computer in 1974, and realized thereafter on a host of different networked platforms, *Mazewar* let players face off against each other (or alternatively against computer-controlled "robots") in a wireframe labyrinth. The graphics were in one sense extremely simple: players appeared to each other as a single disembodied eyeball. But in another sense, that of an inhabited environment in which *seeing* involved *being seen* and thus risking enemy fire, *Mazewar* stands as the most direct prefiguration of the shooters that would follow 20 years later.

Doom also made history through changes to the underlying architecture of video game software—changes that affected how games would from then on be conceived, designed, and marketed. The amount of code devoted to rendering a 3-D world, populating it with objects and characters, and animating it all in response to player actions, was substantial enough that it split off conceptually from the rest of game content. The *game engine,* consisting of that world-creating code and its various components (sub-engines for physics, sound, lighting, artificial intelligence [AI], and so on), became as much a product as the game itself. Carmack's work at id consisted of crafting ever more sophisticated engines, while Romero created data to plug into those engines. Hence id was able to license the *Wolfenstein 3D* engine to Apogee Software, also known as 3D Realms, to produce *Rise of the Triad* in 1994, while *Doom's* engine went into Raven Software's *Heretic* (1994).

The advent of the engine/data architecture, and the potential for world creation that came with it, also opened up new possibilities for building franchises. Sequels or "expansion packs" such as *Doom II: Hell on Earth* (1994) consisted of new data for the existing engine. Engines contributed to what might be called the "levelization" of gaming, dividing large game experiences into discrete chapters, each taking place on a different map, which in theory could be crafted by multiple designers (one reason for the tonal shifts between demonic medieval imagery and chromed science-fiction surfaces in id's output). Another important outgrowth of the shooter's architecture was the involvement of player-programmers in producing their own levels and modifications (or "mods"), customizing the game to their own ends.

The Shooter Matures

Throughout the 1990s, id Software dominated the first-person shooter market, both with its genre-defining flagship titles and with the successively more complex 3-D engines it licensed to other software developers. *Doom* and *Doom II* were followed by *Quake* (1996) and *Quake II* (1997), each of which featured an improved generation of engine and several mission-pack expansions (*Scourge of Armagon* and *Dissolution of Eternity* for *Quake* in 1997; *The Reckoning* and *Ground Zero* for *Quake II* in 1998). All of these shooters and their offshoots were bound to straightforward narrative frames—generally involving dimensional gates and battle scenarios merging cyborgs and satanic beasts—but with *Quake III: Arena* in 1999, id largely did away with story. *Arena,* true to its name, was more or less a virtual coliseum in which players fought each other, or computer-controlled "bots." The commercial viability of *Arena* reflected the importance of the deathmatch within the FPS genre, which by that point had separated into two distinct modes: single-player story-dominated play, and networked multiplayer team-based play (exemplified in game subgenres like "Capture the Flag").

id Software, from which Romero departed in the late 1990s, continues to produce shooters that grab media attention and market share, but Carmack's remarkable technical innovation seems to come at the cost of narrative sophistication. *Return to Castle Wolfenstein* (2001) was basically a remake of *Wolfenstein 3D* using the *Quake III* engine; similarly, *Doom 3* (2004) and *Quake 4* (2005) revisited the pleasures of previous id titles with updated graphics. For the most part, it has fallen to id's competitors to use the first-person mode as an interface for more cognitively and emotionally involving game experiences. The earliest of these was the company Bungie, whose *Marathon* series for the Macintosh [*Marathon* (1994), *Marathon 2: Durendal* (1995), and *Marathon Infinity* (1996)] blended sober science fiction with innovative deathmatch modes. Even darker in its sci-fi stylings was Looking Glass's *System Shock* (1994), which, like its sequel, Electronic Arts's *System Shock 2* (1999), hybridized RPG and FPS elements with horror. Other generic blendings included *Duke Nuke'em 3D* (1996) and *Shadow Warrior* (1997), both from 3D Realms. The FPS also proved adaptable to media and gaming franchises such as *Star Wars* (*Dark Forces* in 1995, *Jedi Knight* in 1997, and a host of *Jedi Knight* expansions and sequels from 1998 to the present) and *Star Trek* (*Elite Force* in 2000 and *Elite Force 2* in 2003).

If 1992 marked the birth of the FPS, 1998 saw its maturation, with the release of several watershed games that redefined the shooter experience: Epic Games/GT Interactive's *Unreal* and Valve Software/Sierra Studios's *Half-Life*. Both had complex storylines, while Looking Glass Studios's *Thief: The Dark Project* substituted sneaking for shooting. In each, objectives could be accomplished through multiple paths, encouraging player agency and a sense of realism within the game world. Shooters set in World War II proved particularly popular, with series such as DreamWorks Interactive/Electronic Arts's *Medal of Honor* (1999) and Digital Illusions CE/Electronic Arts's *Battlefield 1942* (2002). Finally, a string of games preserved the spirit of the original id shooters, like Croteam's *Serious Sam* (2001), People Can Fly/DreamCatcher Interactive's *Painkiller* (2004), and Monolith Productions/Vivendi's *F.E.A.R.* (*First Encounter Assault Recon*) (2005).

Recent years have seen the emergence of "superstar" games—released amid much fanfare, trumpeted for their technical achievements in graphic and sound, and quickly becoming the core of devoted gaming communities. The first of these was probably *Halo* (2001), a return to prominence by Bungie and the heart of the Xbox console line. Offering a sci-fi adventure drawn in equal parts from James Cameron's *Aliens* (1986) and Larry Niven's novel *Ringworld* (1974), and rumored to be a sequel to Bungie's own *Marathon* (1994), *Halo* successfully bridged single- and multiplayer gaming. In 2004, Valve's *Half-Life 2* and id's *Doom 3* demonstrated contrasting poles of shooter play, with *HL2*'s bleak and complex play versus *Doom 3*'s extremely simplified creep-and-shoot gameplay. Both, however, were showcases of graphics, *Doom 3* in particular receiving attention for the engine developed by John Carmack—for the first time rendering all lighting from within the game, calculating it on the fly rather than relying on pre-set "lightmaps."

But it should also be noted that the same characteristics that make shooters stand out—their graphical sophistication, immersive power, and visceral "you are here" impact—are what have brought the form in for much criticism over the years. In large part because of id Software's early influence on the form, shooters are often associated with the worst and most culturally corrosive effects of gameplay: desensitization to violence, inability to tell fantasy from reality, and training and drilling in combat perception and reflexes. Some critics have gone so far as to call the FPS a "murder simulator," and this charge is perhaps not far off. Certainly it is hard to deny in light of school shootings in which the killers reportedly were heavy players of first-person shooter video games. But as critics of this view have pointed out, there are other explanations for the correlation: the social ostracism experienced by tormented teenagers coincides with a number of suspect subcultural affiliations, including goth, heavy metal, comic books, and horror movies. (There is also the

RETROGAMES

Bob Rehak

If you have ever found an old computer or gaming console in a closet, plugged it in, and found to your joy that it still worked, then you are part of the retrogame movement. If you have ever used an emulator to play a game designed for an older computer, or stopped at an arcade to partake of the nostalgic pleasure of a cabinet-style game from the 1970s or 1980s, then you are part of the retrogame movement. If, while standing in line at an electronics superstore, you were tempted to buy a specially designed joystick that plugs into your TV set and allows instant access to beloved titles from yesteryear such as *Tetris, Pac-Man, Pole Position,* or *Galaxian,* then you are part of the retrogame movement—a movement that revisits the history and evolution of classic or "old school" video and computer games, appreciating the innovations of the past. Retrogaming can take many forms, as the list above suggests. What unifies the various activities is their enshrining of old technologies and interactive art forms, treating classic video games both as past history and as playable present, a kind of living museum.

Apart from actually finding and buying the old games themselves, there are three primary ways in which retrogames are played: emulation, commercial products, and small-platform devices. Emulators are programs that simulate a "virtual computer" in an actual computer's memory, allowing current technology to mimic the actions of an older machine. By resurrecting a phantom version of the Z80 or 6502 processor, emulators such as MAME (multiple arcade machine emulator) can imitate arcade games like *Asteroids, Donkey Kong,* and *Mortal Kombat* on contemporary personal computers. Because they are usually unauthorized, emulators frequently run afoul of copyright, forcing this wing of the retrogame movement into a kind of "data underground" in which ROM files (snapshots of the original software architecture, often ripped directly from the chips in old game devices) circulate illicitly online. While the emulation software itself is legal, the games played on them are not. By contrast, commercial products enable consumers to legitimately purchase and play prepackaged versions of older games. This can take the form of the chip-containing joystick mentioned above: a combination computer and controller that usually contains multiple games to choose from. Collections of old games, such as *Capcom Classics Collection, Sega Classic Collection,* and *Namco Museum 50th Anniversary,* are available for consoles like the PlayStation 2 and Xbox 360. Finally, small-platform devices such as cell phones, iPods, and PDAs—like the handheld Nintendo DS or PSP—are ideal for retrogames.

Retrogames keep history alive and raise intriguing questions about the evolution of the video game medium. They spawn subcultures of appreciation for the music and graphic design of older games. Retrogaming is particularly interesting in light of the high-tech aura around video games, which have usually been received (regardless of their year of release) as examples of "state of the art," the latest and greatest use of available technology. Retrogames would seem to puncture that aura, reminding us that, thanks to Moore's Law (which says that the transistor density of integrated circuits doubles every 24 months), games date quickly and cruelly—much more so than media such as film, which evolves at a glacial pace by comparison. Yet the appeal of classic

sts, perhaps as a way of appreciating the aesthetic design of programs
ited memory and graphics into elegant solutions (the heart of the "hack"),
a critical response to current mainstream games, many of which have
uge proportions, requiring DVD-ROMs worth of storage and expensive
and computers to run.

incontrovertible evidence that most people who play violent video games do not commit such crimes.)

Nevertheless, cultural responses to the FPS are interesting for what they reveal about our reactions to our own recreational technologies, a way of measuring our suspicions about simulation and immersion—the dark side to the hyperbolic and exhilarating fantasies of the virtual. This quintessentially "state of the art" genre, then, actually builds on several trends that have characterized video games from the very start. The medium has always relied on a certain "first-personness" to involve players in dynamic environments whose moment-to-moment action depends on input from keyboard, mouse, or controller. Taken with other aspects of digital entertainment—branching narratives, iterative or "looping" formal structures, and the adaptive behaviors known as artificial intelligence, video games' inherent responsiveness and distinctly personal address anchor a host of criteria—immersion, interactivity, presence, and flow—by which we sort "new" media from ancestors like print, film, and television.

CHAPTER 31

INDEPENDENT AND EXPERIMENTAL VIDEO GAMES

Brett Camper

As home Internet access became common through the mid to late 1990s, websites dedicated to the exchange of free independent games evolved from the shareware trading communities of local area dial-up bulletin board systems. Enabled by affordable and technologically accessible platforms such as Flash from Macromedia (now Adobe), indie developers could craft simple, compact and elegant games, creating the equivalent of short films, charcoal sketches, or poetry. Founded in 1995, one of the first and longest-standing indie gaming sites is Newgrounds (www.newgrounds.com), a Flash portal that allows users to upload and instantly publish their own games (and other media).

Especially in the 2000s, such sites have participated in the rise of social networking and word of mouth propagation that drives open and amateur media communities like YouTube and Flickr, as captured succinctly by Newgrounds's slogan: "Everything, by everyone." Well before the practice became commonplace, Newgrounds offered a user-driven voting system for featuring each day's top submissions. But Tom Fulp, the site's founder, also proved he was more than just a tastemaker, using Newgrounds as a launching pad for *Alien Hominid,* a Flash game he co-authored in 2002. *Alien Hominid* garnered such popularity as a free download that it was "picked up" by a commercial publishing company and ported to the PlayStation 2 and GameCube consoles. While such a transition continued a pattern long established in the history of amateur games, it was a first for those created with Flash and a milestone for the platform. Other prominent websites dedicated to promoting independent games include Jay Is Games (http://jayisgames.com/) and Game Tunnel (www.gametunnel.com).

The field of today's indie games is wide, with designers challenging how we make and play games, why we do so, and what subject matter they can portray. Indie gaming is far more than a niche. Rather, it is fully engaged in our attempt to understand the history of gaming and the current state of gaming as a whole.

Indie Physics Games

Freedom from corporate constraints allows indie games to play with our expectations. Indie designers can quickly prototype their ideas and receive feedback from players in a matter of days, a fundamental shift from the 18-month or longer development cycles of most commercial titles. Such experimentation has been particularly fruitful in incubating new kinds of "game mechanics"—a game's rules, the building blocks of the player's interactions with its world. Players of established gaming genres (role-playing, first-person shooter, and so on) have certain expectations of how a game will respond, bred by familiarity. Frustrating and foiling these expectations expands our understanding of games as a medium, and here indie games have excelled. One case in point is their significant contribution to the 2000s trend of "physics-based" games, abandoning Mario's rigid, predictable jump for tricky bounces, wobbles, and twists, perhaps best described as a more "tactile" style of gaming.

Finnish development group tAAt's series of "dismount" games is a prime example. In 2002, they released *Porrasturvat* (or *Stair Dismount*), described by the game preservation website Home of the Underdogs, www.the-underdogs.info, as "simple but weirdly cruel: fall down a flight of stairs and try to hurt yourself as much as possible." Simply choose where and how hard to push the hapless hero. Set to a laid back, jazzy soundtrack, the game is an absurd extension of the "rag doll physics" model increasingly popular in action games such as *Half-Life,* in which characters' bodies act as if attached loosely with string at the joints. *Porrasturvat* succeeds via a strategy rightfully described as avant-garde: moving a marginal artifact of gameplay to the center of attention, highlighting its artificiality. *Porrasturvat* also retains (self-consciously) the sort of bizarre, extraneous storyline one could only expect from a video game; as a superhero seeking damage claims on an insurance policy, you must fake the "evidence" of your battles against the forces of evil to make a convincing case. tAAt created the sequel, *Rekkaturvat* (*Truck Dismount*), in 2003, this time placing the anti-hero inside a vehicle located in a kind of nightmarish skate park. The dismount games have built a cult following because they emphasize the "accidents" of games, turning a traditional game goal on its head.

Shifting the emphasis of gameplay does not necessarily mean defining entirely new genres. Many indie developers have grafted physics-based experiments similar to those of *Porrasturvat* onto more traditional game structures. Csaba Rozsa's *Elasto Mania* (2000) is like a parody of a motocross game, with a ridiculously sensitive, molasses-slow bike that feels as if it is held together by heavy rubber bands. No racing opponents are necessary, as you will be lucky just to survive a deceptively simple obstacle course right-side up. As with the "dismount" series, the game recontextualizes conventions, in this case those of the driving genre, by substituting extreme precision for speed. It also reminds us of the selective, constructed nature of gameplay. If "acceleration" correlates to a mere button press in the traditional arcade driving game, *Elasto Mania* confronts the player with an unusual level of realism and complexity, even in this most straightforward action. Indeed the game's overcompensation appeals on multiple levels: as an immediately fresh approach for the player in a recognizable setting and a quiet exemplar of alternate possibilities for game representation in the longer view.

In the commercial market, games are often judged by their graphics. Aesthetic evaluation is hopelessly tied up with technology, and publishing companies (and too often the gaming press) consider the "best" graphics to be those that use the newest hardware,

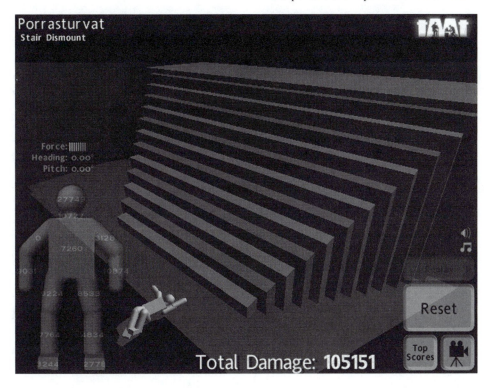

Figure 31.1   Falling downstairs. The protagonist suffers a hard fall in *Porrasturvat* (*Stair Dismount*) (2002).

push the most polygons, and have the highest resolution. Naturally, indie development teams comprised of one, two, or a handful of designer-programmers lack the access and resources to compete with this commercial standard and the hundred-plus person production pipelines that maintain it. But by working to their technological and personal limitations, designers have explored new aesthetic territory for games, continuing a tradition of independent media in music, film, underground comics, and other fields. Take the physics-action game *N* (2004), best described as marrying a wiry rag doll ninja character with single-screen, puzzle-heavy levels reminiscent of the gold-collecting classic *Lode Runner.* Action is concentrated in the player, with a physics model that gives a high degree of control and an otherwise quiet environment. Unlike the few stock animations assigned to most game characters, in *N* one feels that the same scenario could not possibly occur twice in the same manner. The character feels alive, despite its monochromatic stick figure depiction. Raigan Burns and Mare Sheppard, the game's developers, cite an explicit desire for a minimalist gaming style as motivation, both paring and vivifying visuals and gameplay. Such an approach is borne equally from technical constraints, gaming nostalgia, and independent artistic vision.

Another pair in this minimalist vain includes *Spout* (2003) and *TUMIKI Fighters* (2004), both by independent Japanese developers. In *Spout,* the player pilots a vehicle a mere one pixel in size through sparse black, white, and gray caves. *TUMIKI Fighters* continues Kenta Cho's colorful rejuvenation of the classic scrolling shooter genre with an elegant, additive gameplay mechanic in which players "catch" the falling pieces of

Figure 31.2   **Building up a makeshift ship in** *TUMIKI Fighters* **(2004). In** *TUMIKI Fighters,* **the player's ship is an ever-growing amalgamation built from the salvaged remnants of defeated enemy crafts.**

debilitated enemies, haphazardly accumulating extensions that eventually fill near half the screen, done up in pastels. The game shares this incremental effect with the offbeat commercial breakout title *Katamari Damacy* (2004), where players roll an ever-expanding adhesive ball of objects around the game world, steadily taking all in its path. The two games were released within weeks of one another, but while the marketplace sees *Katamari* as an oddball, the independent experiments described in this chapter show us the family of exploratory gameplay from which both arose.

Thus independent games often innovate by revisiting earlier genres, styles, and technologies no longer considered part of the mainstream. For instance, indie physics games heavily favor 2-D graphical representation, eschewing the 3-D "state of the art." The horizontal shooter (*TUMIKI Fighters*) and fighting game (*Alien Hominid*) genres belong in the heyday of the 16-bit console era, on the Sega Genesis or Super NES, and are anomalies in today's market. Yet despite these apparent "retro" tendencies, indie games are often as equally facilitated by advances in technology as those in the commercial sector—indie designers have simply opted to harness different technical opportunities, focusing on those that tweak and evolve gameplay (for example through computational physics models) rather than only graphics. In an industry on a relentless, hardware-defined march "forward," where entire platforms are abandoned in a short matter of years, independent games take both the historical and the true aesthetic look sideways and ahead. Only the briefest reflection on our cultural understanding of film history is needed by way of comparison: imagine if we viewed black and white movies as "obsolete" or inferior, rather than an artistic choice, with objective visual effects but also subjective historical evocation.

Unauthorized Game Development: Homebrew Communities

If indie physics games seek formal experimentation through gameplay, another community of independents challenges the industry on the level of intellectual property, branding, and economics. Enterprising, technically savvy, and by necessity a touch audacious, these programmers create unauthorized "homebrew" games for dedicated consoles, old and new. There are homebrew communities, or "scenes," revolving around virtually every major console in game history. Popular targets include the Atari 2600 of the late 1970s and early 1980s, the Sega Dreamcast of the late 1990s, and the more recent Sony PSP.

Nintendo's extremely popular Game Boy Advance (GBA) handheld system has one of the largest such followings. Unlike, for example, online Flash-based games—which anyone can make and play on a PC or Mac—the GBA is a proprietary system that only plays Game Boy-specific games. And Nintendo keeps that system "closed": the coding and access to GBA game design tools is kept secret and revealed only to select development teams, official licensees who must purchase development kits for thousands of dollars. Nintendo controls every aspect of the GBA market, from the initial green-lighting of projects, to approval of artwork and packaging, to stringent pre-order requirements which put the burden of economic risk on the developer while reserving substantial royalty rates for themselves, the corporate parent. Homebrew GBA development operates underground, without Nintendo's consent.

Homebrew is also a legal grey area. Because GBA games are distributed (like all game consoles) on physical, dedicated game cartridges, simply getting an unofficial program to boot on the machine is a first hurdle. Amateur developers and fans purchase third-party "flash cards" from Hong Kong-based stores online, special hardware devices that allow game files to be transferred between the GBA and standard personal computers. But because they are just conduits for data, flash cards are not limited to legal homebrew uses: they also enable game piracy. For Nintendo, focused on intimidating techniques for protecting its own high margins, it is easiest to ignore this nuance and simply label these devices illegal, sweeping legitimate, independent homebrew developers quietly under the rug with the pirates.

Whether it is a case of Nintendo's corporate convenience, close-mindedness, or open hostility, hobbyists in the homebrew scene are left to reverse engineer and tinker with the system's hardware to get at the knowledge and equipment they need, technical internals such as ROM layout (which determines which areas of memory within the machine perform what functions) and BIOS (or basic input/output system—the code which starts up the system and provides access to built-in features like advanced mathematical calculations). Websites like www.gbadev.org, the hub of unofficial Game Boy Advance development, are crucial for the exchange of such "hacked" technical information. Homebrewers are in fact partly driven by the desire for the forbidden, by Nintendo's close guard, but also by the system's inherent technical limitations in comparison to today's "modern" computers, the challenge of getting such a small machine to get up and go. And those who demonstrate their technical mastery are the tastemakers of the scene. GBA homebrew development is simply one of the latest in a long tradition of hands-on, young male-dominated pastimes: early twentieth century amateur "radio boys,"

Figure 31.3   Scenes from experimental games. Make way for the egg in *ClacQ* (left); rock-paper-scissors RPG battle in *Tragical Historie of Rodion and Rosalind* (right).

the garage rock and hot-rodding movements of the 1950s and 1960s, and the creation of the original Apple computer in the mid-1970s via the Homebrew Computer Club (the terminological origin of today's "homebrewers").

Though they generally have less experimental gameplay, scores of highly original and polished homebrew games (and other kinds of programs) have come out of the GBA scene, with hundreds released online in total. Spanning all major genres, standouts include the puzzle game *ClacQ,* in which players build elaborate bridges to ensure safe passage for a rolling egg; *The Tragical Historie of Rodion and Rosalind,* an over-the-top medieval side-scrolling adventure-RPG in 16-bit Super NES style; and *Llamabooost,* a top-down action shooter in the *Robotron* tradition. Homebrewers' interest in highly precise technical challenges also has led to the popularity of programming pixel-perfect remakes of classic 8-bit computer games, such as the slow-paced, physics-based *Thrust* and action-scroller *Nebulus.*

As with many of the PC-based indie physics games, there is that special retro appeal: the GBA's 2D-based graphics give it an older visual and gameplay style reminiscent of the *Metroid* and *Zelda* adventures homebrew developers grew up with. Not to mention the cultural resonance of Nintendo, a brand identity so successful that in the 1980s it was once (and for many non-gamers still is) synonymous with the medium of video games. Homebrew GBA developers are left in the paradoxical position of transgressing against the closed nature of Nintendo's corporate and technological system in order to feel that they legitimately participate within it. This amounts not to a traditional brand "loyalty," nor to anti-corporate brand "hijacking" or Adbusters-style "culture jamming," but rather a lateral repurposing of the system's commercial intent.

While homebrew developers may exploit weaknesses in Nintendo's technical and legal regime of control, they remain parasitic to it. Yet by insisting—through technical force of will—on access to hardware for independent, noncommercial developers, the tactics of the homebrew scene have yielded a protest that is, perhaps surprisingly, anything but apolitical. In our digital society, in which intellectual property debates such as those over DRM (digital rights management) for online music have become a crucial battleground, homebrewers comprise a peaceful, non-pirate, non-infringing movement to equalize media production that is indeed at the heart of American political debate.

CHAPTER 32

Video Games in Europe

Lars Konzack

Many European releases of video games have been later than those in the United States and Japan. Still, Europe has made an impact on the global scene as well. As a moderate ludologist and game researcher I feel the need for European video games to be acknowledged as an influential part of the video game development both culturally and aesthetically. The European video game scene may not have the fancy new consoles, but what they lack in technology they have in video game content.

The Rise and Fall of Sinclair Computers

Perhaps the most promising example of a European computer standard came from Sir Clive Sinclair in the UK. A company by the name of "Sinclair Computers," later renamed "Sinclair Research Ltd.," launched the ZX80 in February of 1980. The price was an inexpensive £79.95 in kit-form and £99.95 as a ready-build. This was followed up by the ZX81 in March 1981 with an even lower price tag: £49.95 (kit) and £69.95 (ready-built). In February of 1982 Timex obtained a license to manufacture and market Sinclair computers in the United States under the name of Timex Sinclair.

In April 1982, the ZX Spectrum came out, costing £125 for the 16 kilobytes version and £175 for the 48 kilobytes version. Unlike the older machines, the ZX Spectrum was in color, with eight different screen colors. The sound was from a built-in loudspeaker that sounded like a bad telephone connection. External storage of games was usually on cassette tapes and was not always easy to fine-tune, and large amounts of data were lost due to this unreliable storage system. Another difficulty was the rubber keyboard (it was later replaced by a real keyboard). Most games were keyboard controlled and consequently hitting the button right proved to be a problem. Furthermore, the letter on the key tended to fade away. Fortunately, it was possible to buy a joystick.

Many of the games for the ZX Spectrum were actually code from magazines such as *Your Spectrum* (later *Your Sinclair*) or *Sinclair User*. The user would key in all the code from the game magazine, hopefully without a single error, and finally when all this was done, with a bit of luck, the user could play the game, and save it on a cassette for later use.

There were, of course, commercial games too, many of which were well-known games from the arcade scene, rewritten for the ZX Spectrum and launched under a new title to avoid paying tribute to the owners of the intellectual property. Other games had original content. There were games of all genres, from the common action-oriented arcade games to adventure and strategy games like Firebird Software's *Elite* (1985), Imagine Software's *Target Renegade* (1988), Ocean Software's *The Great Escape* (1986) and *Where Time Stood Still* (1988), Electric Dreams Software's *R-Type* (1988), Hewson Consultants's *Zynaps* (1987) and *Exolon* (1988), Bug-Byte Software's *Manic Miner* (1983), Microsphere's *Back to Skool* (1985), Ultimate Play the Game's *Atic Atac* (1983), Durell Software's *Saboteur* (1986), and The Edge Software's *Fairlight: A Prelude* (1985). Many games were cracked, illegally copied, and distributed freely among gamers from the gaming community, undermining the commercial benefit of game titles.

During the 1980s, Sinclair computers had an important market share. Because of this success Sir Clive Sinclair himself was knighted in 1983. However, in 1985 he decided to make a battery-powered electrical vehicle called C5 and in 1992 the Zike, which was an electrical bicycle. Both attempts at transport innovation were commercial failures and in the end the company suffered from the lack of success.

Presumably as some sort of tribute, in 1990 Soviet Russia released a computer called *Hobbit* with 64 kilobytes of RAM, based on the ZX Spectrum hardware. The *Hobbit* was briefly marketed in the UK for ZX Spectrum fans willing to lay their hands on a better computer compatible with familiar architecture.

The British Invasion

Ian Livingstone founded the British game company Games Workshop in 1975 together with his flatmate Steve Jackson (not to be confused with Steve Jackson from the U. S. game company Steve Jackson Games). The company was originally an importer of the U.S. role-playing game *Dungeons & Dragons*. Livingstone and Jackson also made the famous *Fighting Fantasy* books, beginning with *The Warlock on Fire-Top Mountain* (1982) and ending with *Curse of the Mummy* (1995). In 1983 they released their own miniature game *Warhammer Fantasy Battle* with its own fantasy world. This fantasy world later grew into several original computer games: *Warhammer: Shadow of the Horned Rat* (1995), *Warhammer: Dark Omen* (1998), *Warhammer: Mark of Chaos* (1998), and *Warhammer Online: Age of Reckoning* (due to be released in 2008). It is widely believed that the Warhammer fantasy world is the direct inspiration for *Warcraft* (1994) and *World of Warcraft* (2004) by Blizzard Entertainment. Likewise, *StarCraft* (1998) resembles the miniature game *Warhammer 40,000* (1987) that is Games Workshop's science fiction equivalent to Warhammer Fantasy.

During the 1980s, Livingstone did some design work for the video game company Domark, where he designed the adventure game *Eureka!* (1984). Domark actually offered £25,000 to the first person who completely solved the game. In 1995 Domark merged with Eidos Interactive.

In 1987, Les Edgar and Peter Molyneux founded the British video game company Bullfrog Productions. They became popular with the innovative god game *Populous* (1989) and *Dungeon Keeper* (1997), the latter of which was an ironic comment as to why the dungeons exist in games like *Dungeons & Dragons*. (A "god game" is a computer simulation that casts the player in the position of an entity with divine or supernatural powers and places them in charge of a game setting containing autonomous mortals to guard and influence.) In 1995, Electronic Arts (EA) acquired Bullfrog Productions. Two years later Molyneux left EA and founded Lionhead Studios together with Jackson. Lionhead Studios has become famous for three game series: the god game *Black & White* (2001), the role-playing game *Fable* (2004), and the simulation game *The Movies* (2005).

The two biggest British video game distribution companies, SCi (founded in 1988) and Eidos (founded in 1990), merged into one in 2005 when SCi acquired Eidos. In the 1990s, however, this scenario seemed very unlikely. Between 1993 and 1999, Eidos was the fastest-growing company in the world with its share price rising over 400 times,[1] and with the distribution of game series started by games like Core Design's *Tomb Raider*, IO Interactive's *Hitman* (2000), Pyro Studios's *Commandos* (1998), Ion Storm's *Deus Ex* (2000), Silicon Knights's *Legacy of Kain* (1996), Kronos's *Fear Effect* (2000), and Looking Glass Studios's *Thief* (1998). The Danish game developers from IO Interactive created *Hitman,* and the Spanish game developers from Pyro Studios made *Commandos,* showing the influence Eidos had on European game development.

Tomb Raider alone points to the fact that this game company was highly influential on popular culture. The game character Lara Croft designed by Toby Gard, based on a female version of Indiana Jones, has on several occasions been discussed as a postmodern feminist icon. It may be noted that indeed Livingstone has contributed to the latest version of Lara Croft in *Tomb Raider: Anniversary* (2007). *Tomb Raider: Anniversary* was co-developed by Crystal Dynamics and Buzz Monkey Software for Sony's PlayStation Portable, PlayStation 2, Nintendo's Wii, and Windows. Eidos announced June 1, 2007, as the European release date for the PS2 and Windows versions, with the North American release to follow on June 5, 2007. Additionally the subscription PC gaming service Game-Tap has announced that the game will be available on their service on the same day the game is released at retail. The game will also be available on Steam. The PSP version will be released soon thereafter, with the Wii version to be released at a later date. An Xbox 360 version was officially announced on June 18, 2007. In 2006, SCi/Eidos Interactive was the sixteenth largest video game publisher in the world.

The French Connection

Some French video game publishers are rated even higher than SCi/Eidos. Vivendi Games (owner of World of Warcraft) and Ubisoft both rank among the largest video game publishers. Furthermore, Infogrames owns controlling interest in Atari which is rated the nineteenth largest video game publisher in the world. These three companies comprise the influential French video game scene.

Infogrames was founded in June 1983 by Bruno Bonnell and Christophe Sapet. The name of the company was supposed to have been Zboub Système, but their legal advisor advised them against it. Instead they decided on the brand name Infogrames, which was a combination of "informatique" and "computer programme." The company logo is an armadillo, chosen when the company moved to Villeurbanne. Bonnell explained this, saying, "This dinosaur is our symbol. The armadillo always survives to the changes of his environment, from the thawing of the ices, to the worst of the heat waves."

The company is not only a distributor but a developer as well. Infogrames is known for famous video game titles such as *Passengers on the Wind* (1986), *North and South* (1989), *Alone in the Dark* (1992), *Mission Impossible* (1998), and *Rollercoaster Tycoon* (1999).

[*Passengers on the Wind* is based on a French comic series from the 1980s by François Bourgeon, and the game follows the series very closely. Likewise, *North & South* is an offshoot of the Belgian cartoon *Les Tuniques Bleues* (by Dupuis) which is based on the American Civil War.]

Ten years after the founding of the company, Infogrames went public on the French stock exchange with great success. Six years later, in 1999, Infogrames purchased GT Interactive, renaming the company to Infogrames, Inc., and in 2001 they acquired Hasbro Interactive, including MicroProse, Atari, and Game.com. Following this line of events, they rebranded their own game company, renaming it Atari. In this new millennium many *Dungeons & Dragons* licensed computer games have been launched as Atari titles, such as *Temple of Elemental Evil* (2003), *Baldur's Gate: Dark Alliance* (2004), and *Neverwinter Nights 2* (2006). This is due to the fact that Hasbro owns *Dungeons & Dragons*, which was purchased in 1999 when Hasbro acquired Wizards of the Coast, who previously had acquired TSR, Inc. (the inventors of *Dungeons & Dragons*) back in 1997.

However, in September 2006, Atari announced that its stock faced delisting from NASDAQ since its price had fallen under $1.00. A few days later, David Pierce was appointed the new CEO of Atari, replacing Bruno Bonnell. Pierce had worked previously as an executive at Universal Pictures, Metro-Goldwyn-Mayer, Sony Pictures Entertainment, Sony Music Entertainment, and Sony Wonder. In April 2007, Bonnell left the company that he had founded more than 20 years earlier.

Ubisoft was founded in 1986 by five brothers of the Guillemot family, and Yves Guillemot remains the chairman and CEO. Their first game was *Zombie* (1986) and it was followed by great titles such as *Rayman* (1995) and *POD* (1997), Tom Clancy's *Ghost Recon* (2001), *Myst: Trilogy* (2002), *Prince of Persia: The Sands of Time* (2003), *Beyond Good and Evil* (2003), *Far Cry* (2004), and *Brothers in Arms* (2005).

Ubisoft started out in France as a distribution company for games made by MicroProse and EA, and soon they were engaged in distributing games to the UK and Germany as well. In 1996, the company was publicly traded, which led to a failed attempt at a hostile takeover in 2004 when EA acquired close to 20 percent of the stock. Today, the company has offices around the globe.

Vivendi has an odd history. An Imperial decree by Napoleon III led to the formation of a company named Compagnie Générale des Eaux (CGE) in December 1853. This might have remained only a company to this day had it not been for Guy Dejouany, who was appointed CEO in 1976. During the 1980s he began investing in waste management, energy, transport services, and construction and property, diversifying the interests of the old company. In 1983 they participated in the foundation of Canal+, which was the first Pay-Television channel in France, and this naturally led to investments in communication media during the 1990s.

The company changed its name to Vivendi in 1998, and in 2000 they split into Vivendi Universal (later renamed Vivendi) and Vivendi Environnement (later renamed Veolia Environnement). Vivendi Games (formerly known as Vivendi Universal Games) owns the rights to such franchises as *Warcraft* (1994), *Diablo* (1996), *StarCraft* (1998), and *World of Warcraft* (2004) from Blizzard Entertainment as well as others like *Leisure Suit Larry* (1987), *Crash Bandicoot* (1996), *Spyro* (1998), *Ground Control* (2000), and *Empire Earth* (2001).

The games developed and/or distributed by these companies are not really any different from games from other parts of the world. There seems to be no distinct French hallmark or style for video games, as there is in other arts, for example, in French cinema. However, a game like *Fahrenheit* (2005) (known as *Indigo Prophecy* in the United States and Canada) published by Atari and developed by the French game studio Quantic Dream shows that there may indeed be a move towards style-conscious games with complicated story construction. Quantic Dream and their game designer David Cage are also credited for the critically acclaimed *Omikron: The Nomad Soul* (1999) published by Eidos.

Other European Countries

England and France may have the leading video game publishing houses in Europe, but there are big financial and artistic successes elsewhere in Europe. What is interesting here is that games are produced in many different European countries for global player communities; they are not just coming from Hollywood. However, since games are produced for a global market, it is often difficult to tell which country produced them. It is not that these games are all the same global "McGame," but they are often produced in a fashion that goes beyond national boundaries. One reason for this may be that most games are action oriented rather than language oriented, and that language is more culturally loaded nationalistically than action is. This does not mean that there isn't any cultural diversity at all; it is just not always present.

Turning towards Russia, we find an interesting game from the mid-1980s quite different from the games produced in the West and in Japan. It was, of course, *Tetris*. *Tetris* was designed by Alexey Pajitnov (Pazhitnov), who was assisted by Dmitry Pavlovsky and Vadim Gerasimov. The game rights were first sold to Mirrorsoft (UK) and Spectrum Holobyte (United States) in 1986. By 1988, the Soviet government began to market the rights to *Tetris* via an organization named Elektronorgtechnica ("Elorg" for short), and within a few years the game turned into a massive success. Pajitnov did not get much money from the deal, even though, for example, Nintendo got an advantageous return from selling the game.

Looking at Germany, we find a country with a remarkable tradition for game design. There is even a style of board games that is simply referred to as German-style board games; they are a broad class of easy-to-learn family games for a few players that take a modest length of time to play. One might expect that the German video game industry would be very much focused on such games, but it seems as if the crossover between the old board game industry and the new video game industry has not been easy.

The growth of the German video game industry comes from new companies rather than the old board game industry. Companies like Ascaron, Piranha Bytes, Synetic, Funatics, Crytek, Sunflowers Interactive Entertainment, and Blue Byte Studio are examples of this new development. Video games such as Ascon's *The Patrician* (1992) and *Pole Position* (1996), Blue Byte Studio's *The Settlers II*(1996), Piranha Bytes's *Gothic* (2001), and Crytek's *Far Cry* (2004) are some of the prestigious German video games.

That said, there are links between the good old German-style board games and the video game industry. *The Patrician* and *Settlers* are games that resemble this tradition of game design. They are, in a way, both fairly simple strategic games based upon family game concepts. *The Patrician* is furthermore an example of how a game can use the historical background of German culture, focusing as it does on the trading efforts of the Hanseatic League during the late medieval period. *Gothic,* even though it sounds very German, is just another sword and sorcery role-playing game, and *Pole Position* is a racing game about managing a Formula 1 team, which could have been done anywhere in the world. The same goes for the popular shooting game *Far Cry*.

Scandinavian game design has worked wonders in recent years. For example, the game *Hitman: Codename 47* (2000), developed by the Danish game company IO Interactive, is a high-concept 3-D first-person stealth game in which the player simply plays a hitman with the codename 47 on several missions, discovering his hidden past. Other Danish-produced games worth mentioning are *Total Overdose* (2005) by Deadline Games, and the interactive television game *Hugo the TV Troll* (1990) by ITE. *Hugo the TV Troll* was based on an interactive television game *OsWald* (1988) and has aired in more than 40 countries worldwide. In Sweden we find games such as *Europa Universalis* (2000) by Paradox and *Battlefield 1942* (2002) by DICE. Finland is known for the innovative shooting game *Max Payne* (2001) by Remedy Entertainment, which introduced the concept of slowing down movement in video game action scenes, similar to the "bullet-time" scenes from the film *The Matrix* (1999). Funcom is an interesting Norwegian game development company. They not only made the video game *The Longest Journey* (1999) but also the popular MMORPG *Anarchy Online* (2001), a science fiction game set on the world of Rubi-Ka and its extra-dimensional twin, the Shadowlands. And their long-awaited fantasy game *Age of Conan: Hyborian Adventures* MMORPG opened its beta-testing in April 2007 and is due to be released later this year. Another intriguing MMORPG known as *EVE Online* (2003) was designed by the Icelandic game company CCP. It is a science fiction game set in a futuristic galaxy that deals with intergalactic trading and warfare.

Mediterranean video game development has been increasing over the last few years and includes efforts like the previously mentioned *Commando* series from the Spanish company Pyro Studios. In the 1980s, Dinamic Software (later Dinamic Multimedia) made games for ZX Spectrum, Amstrad, and Commodore 64 home computers, most notably, *Don Quijote* (1987) and *After the War* (1989). Today they are famous for the PC Fútbol series of games made from 1992 to 2006. Other Spanish video game companies include Effecto Caos (later renamed Xpiral), who designed the innovative game *Vital Light* (1994) for Amiga, and Pendúlo Studios who created the adventure game *Runaway: A Road Adventure* (2001). Italian game development company WaywardXS Entertainment is known for sport games, and another company, Milestone, has made several racing games.

Much is going on in game development all over Europe, although many games only exist in non-English European languages and have not been translated for a wider audience. However, the European game industry focuses primarily on game software development, and many new game concepts have originated from the European video game industry.

Organization, Control, and Support

The British video game industry founded ELSPA back in 1989 as an organization to take care of their interests. Today ELSPA stands for Entertainment and Leisure Software Publishers Association, but up until 2002 it stood for the European Leisure Software Publishers Association (the name changed probably because they realized that they dealt with domestic British issues rather than Pan-European issues). From 1994 to 2003, ELSPA voluntarily rated computer and video games released in Britain, because the British Board of Film Classification did not want to rate video games. The system put games into the following age categories: 3–10, 11–14, 15–17 and 18+. A red X would mark which age group a title was not appropriate for, while a check mark in the categories above would indicate the suitable ages. The age categories were later changed to 3+, 11+, 14+, or 18+ as the suitable ages. In April 2003 this system was replaced by the Pan European Game Information system, also known as the PEGI-system. Today, ELSPA is concerned with promoting the game industry through government lobbying both at a national level and at an international level, commissioning market research and gathering information, sales charts for video games sold in the UK, and protecting the industry through anti-piracy activities spearheaded by their anti-piracy unit.

As mentioned, PEGI (nicknamed Piggy) is a European video game content rating system. It was established in 2003 to help European parents make informed decisions when buying video games. The PEGI age bands are 3+, 7+, 12+, 16+, and 18+. As a supplement to this, there are seven different game descriptors presented as icons that can be attached next to the appropriate age marking: bad language, discrimination, drugs, fear, gambling, sex, and violence. The system has been accepted in more than 20 European countries. Contrary to what some believe, the PEGI-system does not relate to the difficulty level of the game but only how appropriate the content of the game is considered to be for a certain age group. The system is also not associated with the European Union; for example, Germany is not part of the system because their censorship is stricter than the standards of other European nations. The German system, known as the *Unabhängige Selbstkontrolle* (Independent Self-Control), does not allow red blood or public displays of Nazism and the swastika. As a consequence, anti-Nazi games like id Software's *Wolfenstein 3D* or Pyro Studios's *Commandos: Behind Enemy Lines* (1998), involving Allied soldiers on missions to kill Nazi soldiers, have been banned. Unlike the PEGI-system, which is voluntary, the German USK-system has become obligatory.

Other European countries have a different way of dealing with video game censorship. Poland will supposedly leave the PEGI-system, because the Catholic Conservative government wants stricter laws. The Greek parliament passed the Greek law number 3037, banning electronic games in general, in July 2002. Even though the law was meant to ban gambling, it did indeed target all video games as well. In December 2003 the law was restricted to only affect Internet cafés in accordance with an official letter from the European Union, explaining that the law might have been in conflict with European legislation; in which case, the European Court of Justice could, in fact, take action against Greece. This controversy was followed closely by the video game industry not only in Greece and the rest of Europe, but also in the United States, fearing that this ban of electronic games would lead to some sort of precedent.

The European Union has been supportive of the video game industry, financing innovative multimedia projects and video game entrepreneurship. In the 1980s the European national broadcast media faced strong competition because the development of a European industry would be compromised by competition from cheap, non-European television programs, which are perfectly adapted to the programming of new, private broadcasters. And domestic film production was also experiencing a downturn. All this led to the establishment of the European MEDIA programme, which has been operating to encourage the development of the European audiovisual industry since January 1991. MEDIA is a support programme of the European Union meant to strengthen the competitiveness of the European film, TV, and new media industries and to increase the international circulation of European audiovisual products. There have been four multiannual programmes since 1991: MEDIA I (1991–1995), MEDIA II (1996–2000), MEDIA Plus (2001–2006), and MEDIA 2007 (2007–2013).

The MEDIA programme was not meant to support video games; nonetheless, between 1996 and 1998 there was a platform for innovative multimedia projects, from 1999 to 2000 they supported first- and second-stage slate funding, and from 2001 to 2007 they supported single development projects and slate funding. In the latest MEDIA program it will be possible for the first time to apply directly for financial support for video game production. A video game project can apply for up to 100,000 Euros, whereas before it was only possible to get 50,000 Euros, and it was meant for all kinds of project development.

Another attempt at promoting the video game industry in Europe is the European Game Developer Federation (EGDF). This organization was formed in November of 2006 to represent more than 500 European game development studios in Austria, Belgium, Germany, Great Britain, Italy, the Netherlands, and the Nordic countries that together employ more than 15,000 people in their video game industries.[2] The EGDF, which is based in Malmö, Sweden, has the goal of promoting and supporting the video game industry. It is too soon to say whether or not this organization will prove successful in the years to come, but it shows that video game development is receiving an increasing amount of serious attention in Europe.

A different angle on video games has resulted from video game studies and research. In early March 2001, Jesper Juul and Lisbeth Klastrup held a conference called Computer Games and Digital Textualities at the IT-University in Copenhagen, Denmark. It was the first conference worldwide to look at computer games from an academic perspective. This conference led to a new conference called Computer Games and Digital Cultures in Tampere, Finland, the following year. At this conference Frans Mäyrä founded the Digital Game Research Association, which again led to the first DiGRA conference in Utrecht, the Netherlands, in 2003. Today the conference is held biannually, each time in a new city around the globe.

Following this third millennium trend for video game research, the need for video game education became apparent, and as a consequence video game education initiatives have been launched in many European countries. An example of this is the National Academy of Digital, Interactive Entertainment in Denmark. The Academy is an interdisciplinary educational institution based on collaboration between art and design schools and Danish Universities. They have two joint productions over a two-year period in close collaboration with the video game industry. Hopefully, all of this will lead to the development of an even more interesting European game industry in the future.

CHAPTER 33

VIDEO GAMES IN ASIA

Benjamin Wai-ming Ng

Japanese popular culture[1] is an integral part of global culture, and of all of its forms, the video game is perhaps the most globalized due to its strong universal appeal and ability to cross cultural boundaries.[2] Japanese video game makers, such as Nintendo, Sega, and Sony, and game series, such as *Mario Bros., Street Fighter,* and *Final Fantasy* have dominated the video game world market since the mid-1980s. Regardless of their global popularity and impact, Japanese video games are relatively neglected in game studies. Although there are some basic studies[3] of Japanese video games in the Western world, their impact in Asia is largely unknown.

Arcade Video Games: From Simple 2-D Games to 3-D Online Games

In Asia, in the late 1970s and early 1980s, most young people in Hong Kong, Taiwan, and Singapore first came to know video games by playing such simple, early games as *PONG, Pac-Man, Galaxian, Breakout, Asteroids,* or *Space Invaders,* on coin-operated arcade machines introduced by American video game companies such as Atari and Midway, although the software was often designed by Japanese companies like Namco and Taito.

During the 1980s and 1990s, video game arcades mushroomed and reached the peak of their popularity. Going to game arcades became one of the most popular forms of entertainment among young generations in Hong Kong, Taiwan, and Singapore. The most popular genre was that of fighting games. In particular, *Street Fighter* and *The King of Fighters* created a commotion throughout Asia. Long lines for these two games were common and they influenced the language and behavior of game players and the entertainment industry in Asia. For example, the *Street Fighter* and *The King of Fighters* series of games were extremely popular in Asia in the 1990s and were adapted into movies, comics, dramas, and pop songs in Hong Kong and Taiwan, influencing the behaviors and vocabulary of Asian youths.[4] In Singapore, due to the popularity of *Street Fighter II,* the game's hero, Ryu, became an object of worship and imitation. Kids in Singapore learned to leap and punch the way Ryu does. "Ha do ken," a phrase uttered by Ryu when he delivers a fireball, was picked up by children to mean punching.[5]

The number of video game arcades in Asia has been decreasing since the 2000s mainly due to the strong competition from online game centers. During the last decade, the mushrooming of small-size online game centers where customers buy time to play computer games with others interactively at affordable prices has forced many video game centers to shut down. Online technologies have had an impact on arcade games, many of which can now be played online. As a result, Asian players can challenge their Japanese counterparts in cyberspace. For example, Hong Kong players do well in car race and mahjong games among online arcade game players in Asia.

In Mainland China and Taiwan, game centers have a very bad public image and are subject to regular security checks and official crackdowns. In the last decade, most of the game centers in Taipei were forced to shut down. Since the centers have an image problem, many people shy away from them and parents discourage their children from frequenting them. In Hong Kong in the past, the majority of game centers were small (less than 50 coin-operated machines) centers that were usually smoky, dirty and dim. Associated with drug trafficking and gang activities, they became a target of regular raids by the police and criticism by teachers, social critics, and parents. In the past few years, many small game centers closed down and the remaining centers are relatively large and clean.

Game centers in Singapore have a much better image. They are clean, bright, smokeless, spacious, lively, and are accepted by the public as entertainment centers for families and friends. The majority of game arcades are located in shopping malls which can provide the huge space required by the government. Many young people go there to play, and players are usually in their late teens and early twenties. Parents also take their kids to play non-video amusement games, such as mini bowling and basketball. Many big game centers also have photo-sticker machines (*purikura* in Japanese) made by video game makers such as SNK, Sega, and Namco. Because of these characteristics, video game centers in Singapore are also called amusement arcades.

If Sony has an upper hand in the home video game market and Nintendo controls the handheld video game market, then Sega is a major player in the arcade video game market in Asia. Sega provides a large number of machines and their software. Other major manufacturers of arcade video game machines and software are SNK, Namco, and Capcom. Sega game software for coin-operated machines is the most expensive. Big game arcades can afford these, whereas medium-sized game centers have fewer Sega games. SNK poses a great challenge to Sega by offering software at very competitive prices. Popular game genres include combat games (such as the *Street Fighter, The King of Fighters* and the *Gundam* series), car games (such as the *Daytona* and the *Initial D* series), shooting games (such as *Virtua Cop* and *Time Crisis*), sports games (such as the *Winning Eleven* and the *Virtua Striker* series) and dancing games (like *Dance Dance Revolution*).

Hong Kong and Taiwan import Japanese original versions of the games, whereas Singapore prefers to wait for the English versions because players in Hong Kong and Taiwan understand Chinese characters used in Japanese, whereas many Singaporeans feel more comfortable with English. In Singapore, the percentage of English versions of games is the highest in Asia. There are some games in Japanese and a few in Mandarin, but they are less popular.

Differences in arcade game centers can also be seen from the perspective of players who play Japanese games in their own ways. In Hong Kong, some skillful players invite challengers for their favorite games. Sometimes, the losers lose not only face but also some money. Gambling is indeed quite common among game players in Hong Kong. In addition, Hong Kong players have many unwritten but common rules among themselves. For instance, putting a token on the top of the machine is a symbol of booking for the next game. In certain games such as *Street Fighter,* Hong Kong players also have rules to make the game more fair or exciting. For example, in a three-round combat game, the winner of the first round must give in the second round, so that both players can play the third round. This rule makes both players (usually strangers) play longer and avoid conflicts or losing face. These practices are not commonly found among players at game centers in other parts of Asia.

Home Consoles: From Nintendo Famicon to PlayStation 3

The Americans opened the doors of the Asian video game market to the Japanese. In the early 1980s, the U.S. video game giant Atari introduced the Atari 2600 to Asia. Despite its success in the United States, the Atari 2600 failed to create a video game revolution in Asia. During this time, most first-generation game players in Asia played at game centers and home video game systems were something too new to catch on and too expensive to buy. It was Nintendo which created the first video game boom and a video game culture in Asia. Nintendo came to Hong Kong, Taiwan, and Singapore in 1985, the same year it launched its products in the U.S. market. It soon dominated the Asian market with its 8-bit game console, the Nintendo Entertainment System (NES, also called "Famicom" in Asia). Thanks to games such as *Donkey Kong, Contra,* and *Mario Bros.,* it was the most popular game in Asia during the 1980s. By mid-1980s standards, the NES was not considered very affordable, and only well-to-do families in major Asian cities could afford to buy it for their children. Hence, video games began as a group activity; children and their classmates got together to play video games in the house of a friend who owned an NES. During this period, video game shops in Hong Kong and Taiwan offered rental service of Nintendo's console and software at affordable prices.

The popularity of the NES reached its peak in the late 1980s. (The popularity of video games in Asia in the 1980s should not be exaggerated. The number of players was not very large, and many families did not have a second TV set for video games. The NES was much more popular in Japan and the United States than in the rest of the world.)[6] A flood of unauthorized NES-compatible machines (the so-called "red and white machine" in Asia, made in Hong Kong in 1985) and pirated Nintendo cartridges (mostly made in Taiwan and Thailand, one cartridge carried hundreds of games) played an important role in popularizing the NES.[7]

Sega was the archrival of Nintendo in the late 1980s and early 1990s. The Sega Master System lost the battle to the NES in the 8-bit game console market, but turned the table in 1989 by introducing the first 16-bit game console in Asia, the Sega Genesis. It was a huge success, because Asian players were already tired of the 8-bit games. Nintendo was slow to develop its 16-bit game console, which did not enter the Asian market until 1991. Hence, 1989 to 1991 was the golden age of Sega in Asia when the Sega Genesis captured about half of the video game market share. It introduced popular games such as *Sonic the Hedgehog, Super Shinobi, Herzog Zewei,* and *Rambo.*

Nintendo made an impressive comeback in 1991 by launching the long-awaited 16-bit game console, the Super Nintendo Entertainment System (SNES, also called the "Super

Famicom" in Asia) which featured better graphics, sound, and software than the Sega Genesis. SNES conquered the lion's share of the video game market in Asia in just a few months. SNES included many superb and now-classic games designed by Nintendo or released exclusively for SNES, such as *Final Fantasy* (versions 4, 5, and 6), *Dragon Quest* (versions 4 and 5), and *Super Mario World*. As the most successful product that Nintendo ever made, the SNES dominated the market for about five years, until it gave way to the new 32-bit game consoles, the Sony PlayStation and the Sega Saturn, released in 1996. Ironically, beyond its superb technology and excellent games, the availability of pirated hardware (such as "Super UFO" and "Doctor," made in Hong Kong and Taiwan) and software also boosted its sales. "Doctor" had a TV commercial in Hong Kong and its makers were later sued by Nintendo for copyright infringement.

Introduced to Asia in 1996, the Sony PlayStation and the Sega Saturn used CDs instead of cartridges, providing a completely different level of graphics and sound effects. The PlayStation quickly caught up and became the biggest winner in the history of the video game industry in Asia, with all the top software companies developing games for it, including the *Tekken* series, *Ridge Racer* series, *Parasite Eve,* and *Time Crisis*. The PlayStation was the number one game console in Asia in the late 1990s and early 2000s. Why was the Sony PlayStation so successful in Asia? Ironically enough, the most decisive factor was the availability of cheap, pirated CD software made in Taiwan, Hong Kong, Malaysia, and Thailand. In Hong Kong, Taiwan, and Singapore, almost all PlayStation consoles could be modified to use pirated CD software by inserting a special chip. A pirated CD could be 20 to 30 times cheaper than the original. The PlayStation also had more games than its competitors, and hundreds of them had pirated versions.

The other reason was that Sony put more emphasis on the Asian market than Sega. Sony set up regional offices in Hong Kong, Taiwan, and Singapore to promote and monitor PlayStation sales, and they provided repair services for PlayStation consoles. They even made Sony PlayStation consoles specifically for Asian nations and games for English and Chinese speaking nations. For instance, their Asian machine used 200–220 voltage instead of 100–110 voltage and came with an English manual. Game instructions were also in English instead of Japanese. Sony selected software for promotion in Taiwan, Hong Kong, Singapore, and Malaysia.[8] (Sony is famous for applying a business strategy called "global localization" (coined by Roland Robertson to refer to global companies that are sensitive to local preference) to relatively immature markets. Sony applies this strategy in Singapore and Southeast Asia in promoting video games.) Sony understands the cultural differences in Asia and makes localizing marketing strategies accordingly. For example, in line with the family values promoted by the Singapore government, the Sony PlayStation Office in Singapore introduces games which can be played by the entire family to promote family values. On Father's Day 1999, Sony organized a video game tournament made up of father-son teams. In addition, Sony produced Chinese games for the Chinese-speaking communities. For example, *The Condor Hero* (2000), a PS Chinese game adopted from a famous martial arts novel by Jinyong, was well-received in Taiwan and Hong Kong.[9]

The Sega Saturn was the distant second. Despite its initial success, it fell behind the Sony PlayStation. One reason was that there was less pirated CD software for the Sega Saturn; it was also higher in price. Unlike Sony, Sega did not have a good marketing network and its products could only be found in video game shops. Sega made a short comeback by launching its 32-bit game console, the Sega Dreamcast, in Hong Kong,

Taiwan, and Singapore in November 1998. Representing a breakthrough in video game technology, the Dreamcast met with overwhelming response in Japan, Taiwan, and Hong Kong, but its reception in Southeast Asia was lukewarm due to high price and limited software.

Nintendo, the former champion in the Asian market, dropped to third place. After the SNES, Nintendo moved directly to develop a 64-bit game console. As a result, it left the lucrative 32-bit game console market entirely to Sony and Sega. It took Nintendo five years to introduce its 64-bit game console, the Nintendo 64, to Asia. Unfortunately, the Nintendo 64 was launched at the worst possible time. It appeared in mid-1996 when most players had just bought their first Sony PlayStation or Sega Saturn. They had not yet digested the 32-bit technology and were thus less interested in investing in 64-bit game consoles. Nintendo also made a miscalculation in the way they designed and marketed the Nintendo 64, and the adoption of the cartridge format and the high price of its software also hurt its sales. Its games were generally very good (for example, *Pikachu* and *Legend of Zelda 64*), but the number of software titles for the Nintendo 64 was relatively small, and the system had only moderate success in Japan, Taiwan, and Hong Kong. Even a pirated console (the Taiwanese "Doctor V64") that arrived in Hong Kong and Singapore in early 1998 could not boost its sale because its software was so expensive.

In early 2000, Sony launched the PlayStation 2 in Japan and its reception was overwhelming. It was introduced to Hong Kong, Taiwan, Singapore, Thailand, and Malaysia in December 2001, a month after the launch of Microsoft's Xbox in Asia. From 2001 to the present (as of September 2006), the PS series and Xbox series have been the two major competitors in Asian home video game console market. The winner is the PS2, because it can use old PS software, has more games (both authorized and pirated) in the market, and has better advertising and customer service.[10] Microsoft's Xbox is the distant second. With the exception of China due to its piracy problem, Microsoft set up Xbox offices in major Asian nations. Adopting a "glocalization" policy (in which products made for a global market are customized to fit local laws and culture), the Xbox has introduced hundreds of games in Asia with English or Chinese instructions and even Mandarin or English dubbing. However, many Asian players find Xbox games too Western.

Asia has been a battlefield for the next-generation home game consoles. The Xbox 360, launched in Japan in December 2005 and in Hong Kong and Taiwan in March 2006, only met with moderate success in Asia. Until the end of 2006, Sony's PlayStation 2 had been in the lead. With the introduction of Sony's PlayStation 3 in November 2006 and the Nintendo Wii in December 2006, the Japanese have regained their dominance in home video game consoles in Asia. As predicted by game industry experts, the Nintendo Wii is the winner of the next-generation home console competition, thanks to its revolutionary remote control device and attractive price (only about half the price of the PS3).

Handheld Games: From Game and Watch to Nintendo DS and PlayStation Portable

Pocket-sized electronic games have been popular in Asia for about three decades. In the late 1970s and early 1980s, most of the games were very simple (such as *Western Bar, Boxing,* and *Submarine*) and the players were mostly primary and secondary school students. In the 1990s and 2000s, handheld electronic games have become more popular, the games more sophisticated, and the players more diversified.

Before the 1990s, the handheld electronic game market was wide open to minor toy and electronic companies. Small factories in Taiwan, China, Hong Kong, Malaysia, and South Korea made a lot of handheld electronic games. They were cheap enough for children to buy, and the games were very simple, so they had little appeal for adults. Each unit was programmed to play one game, and even kids could master the game in a few days and they quickly became bored. Casio also incorporated car race and shooting games into some of its digital watches. The computer puzzle game *Tetris* created the first handheld electronic game fever in Asia in the late 1980s. Some calculators could also play *Tetris*. Nintendo was perhaps the only major Japanese manufacturer that made an impact on handheld electronic games in the 1980s. Its first generation non-cartridge electronic game device, Game and Watch, was quite popular in Asia.

Big names in the industry, such as Sega, Sony, and Bandai, finally entered this lucrative market in the 1990s, and handheld electronic games became a popular toy and a form of entertainment for both children and adults. Nintendo's Game Boy and Sega's Game Gear were the first generation of cartridge-based handheld game consoles, and Nintendo's Game Boy became the most successful handheld console ever made in the history of video games. Nintendo launched its Game Boy in Hong Kong, Taiwan, and Singapore in 1989 and it was a tremendous business success. It could play popular Nintendo games, such as *Tetris, Arkanoid, Mario Bros.,* and *Donkey Kong,* and it dominated the handheld game console market in Asia from 1989 to 2005. A large number of unlicensed Game Boy accessories, such as a speaker, magnifier, and joystick, were made in Hong Kong and widely circulated in Asia. Sega was a latecomer which introduced its Game Gear in Asia only in 1991, posing a challenge to Game Boy in the early 1990s. Unlike the monochrome Game Boy, Game Gear had a color LCD screen. Game Gear had very few pirated cartridges, which made it less popular in Asia.

Part of the success of Game Boy was related to the availability of cheap pirated cartridges. Most of these pirated cartridges were made in Taiwan. Each carried 10 to 30 games, but only cost the price of an original cartridge. *Pokemon,* a Game Boy game, became a smash hit in Japan in 1997. Its spin-off software, *Pikachu,* was made into a game for the Nintendo 64 in 1998 and a popular handheld electronic game, *Pocket Pikachu.* However, *Pokemon* did not create a craze among Game Boy fans in Singapore, Hong Kong, or Taiwan. Game shops in Asia usually recommended Taiwan-made 30-in-1 pirated cartridges rather than original software like *Pokemon* for getting a higher profit. In October 1998, Nintendo launched the fourth generation Game Boy, Game Boy Color, that had an attractive body design and could play some sophisticated games on its color LCD screen. It was a hot product in Japan, Taiwan, and Hong Kong. A strange phenomenon was that many Game Boy Color players in Asia did not buy software designed for Game Boy Color and instead played with their old pirated cartridges initially made for older versions of Game Boy. In 2003, Nintendo introduced its last and most powerful Game Boy model, Game Boy Advance, that dominated the market for about two years, until the next-generation handheld consoles, the dual-screen Nintendo DS, which was cartridge-based, and Sony's PlayStation Portable (launched in Hong Kong, Taiwan, and Singapore on May 12, 2005), which was Universal Media Disc (UMD) based and entered the Asian market in 2005. Since then, the NDS and the PSP have been competing head to head. It seems that the NDS has an upper hand by a small margin and its *Nintendogs* (a dog simulation game similar to a virtual pet) for the NDS was a very hot handheld game in late 2005 in Hong Kong, Taiwan, and Singapore. The PSP also has a strong following, in particular among young people who see it as a multifunctional and trendy electronic device instead of just another handheld game console.

Aside from the cartridge-based handheld game console market, the old-style non-cartridge handheld electronic games also have their market in Asia. The Tamagotchi is an electronic virtual pet housed in an egg-shaped and egg-sized console. Invented in 1996 by Bandai, the Tamagotchi created a great commotion among high school girls in Japan and soon became a national and then international craze. It later created a fever in many cities such as New York and Hong Kong, as well as in Taiwan and Singapore in early 1997.[11] For example, in Singapore, when Takashimaya Department Store declared its plan to sell this electronic pet on April 8, 1997, hundreds of people lined up outside and bought up the entire stock of 1,000 units in less than two hours. Toys 'R' Us encountered a similar reaction. All Tamagotchis sold during this time were Japanese versions imported from Japan. Buyers even had to read the Japanese manual to learn how to take care of it.[12] More than a dozen imitations, including cat, dog, monster, frog, and dinosaur ones made in Japan, Taiwan, Hong Kong, and Mainland China flooded the Asian market. A Hong Kong-made imitation, Tamahonam, a game in which players train a gangster by teaching him to drink, smoke, and fight, created controversy and was banned in Singapore because it contained excessive violence.

The Tamagotchi soon became a national craze in Taiwan, Hong Kong, Singapore, and Thailand, which lasted for about six months. Both students and adults were crazy about it, some playing it day and night. Bandai launched a number of Tamagotchi products in Asia, such as key chains, lunchboxes, stationary, books, T-shirts, and even socks. The Tamagotchi was adapted into a Nintendo Game Boy game and Sony PlayStation software. The mass media featured stories about it, and some schools, offices, and factories banned it.[13] People set up cyber-graveyards for their deceased electronic pets. Even the Singapore government made use of this fad, introducing in 1997 the "Tamagotchi War Hero," educational software using a virtual animal to teach Singapore history at school. Unlike its long popularity in Japan, the Tamagotchi was "game over" after a few months in Asia.

When people were tired of the Tamagotchi, a new sensational product, Digimon (digital monster), was developed by the Tamagotchi team at Bandai in 1997. The player cultivates the virtual pet into a monster which can fight with another monster when two consoles are linked. Unlike the Tamagotchi, Digimon was mainly popular among small children, particularly primary school pupils in Asia. Introduced to Asia in early 1998, Digimon became the most popular electronic toy among children in Hong Kong, Taiwan, and Singapore for about 4 or 5 years and more than 10 generations of Digimon were introduced during this period.

Compared with the Tamagotchi, Digimon was relatively expensive because many of them were parallel imports. "Parallel imports" are genuine (non-counterfeit) consoles or games placed on the market in one country, which are subsequently imported into a second country without the permission of the owner of the intellectual property rights the products have in the second country. In Asia, before the importation of licensed editions, consumers relied on parallel imports that were usually more expensive than the licensed editions.

The size of all Digimon units were small (4 cm by 6 cm) and portable. During its heyday in the late 1990s and early 2000s, it was a must for kids in major Asian cities.

Digimon was banned by some schools because it made noises and promoted a fighting spirit. For example, one school in Singapore suggested the following tips for parents to help cope with this problem: "(1) Only allow the children to play with it after they finish their homework. (2) Only allow the children to play for up to two hours a day. (3) Encourage children to do other more meaningful things, such as reading and chess. (4) Do not overreact. This is after all a fad and it will die down soon."[14] It was common for Digimon players to gather at public places like subway stations, playgrounds, shopping malls, and game centers to have their Digimon fight against each other. Jumping on the bandwagon, some organizations including community centers, churches, and voluntary organizations included Digimon in their activities.

Non-cartridge-based handheld electronic games have become less popular these days, because many Asian youths use their mobile phones for games and music. The new generations of Tamagotchi and Digimon launched in the mid-2000s have failed to make an impact in Asia. Non-cartridge-based handheld games are losing ground to their cartridge-based counterparts and other electronic devices that can play games.

The Making of an Asian Game Culture

How can we locate the video game culture in Asia within a larger context of the globalization of Japanese popular culture? What are its distinctive characteristics? How does East Asia differ from Southeast Asia in consuming and domesticating Japanese video games?

In order to understand the characteristics of Japanese video games in Asia, it is useful to identify the differences between East Asia and Southeast Asia in their game culture. In terms of the percentages of players and consoles per capita, the sale of games, and the degree of knowledge and enthusiasm, East Asia is leading Southeast Asia in consuming Japanese games.

The home video game system is considered a household necessity like the television and the rice cooker in Hong Kong and Taiwan, but in Singapore, less than half of the families own one. The same condition can be found in major cities in Southeast Asia, such as Kuala Lumpur, Bangkok, and Manila.

The attitudes of players throughout Southeast Asia are not the same. East Asian players take the games more seriously. They form game clubs, visit game fairs, read game magazines, line up to buy new games, write articles or have discussions about games on the web, and burn the midnight oil to find ways to win. Taiwan and Hong Kong even have their own video game magazines.

Southeast Asian players, on the other hand, lack the true fan (*otaku*) spirit. Regarding games as a kind of entertainment, they usually neither read game magazines nor research games. Southeast Asian players are slow to follow new developments. Game dealers import new games slowly, usually six months to one year later than in Taiwan or Hong Kong. The number of games imported is fewer. Players prefer waiting for the English version of the games. Games in Japanese are few and less popular. For instance, *Graduation* is a popular game in Taiwan and Hong Kong but has not been well received in Southeast Asia because it contains too much Japanese dialogue. Games such as *World's First Soccer* and *Oda Nobunaga's Den* are popular in Taiwan and Hong Kong, buy they are virtually unavailable in Southeast Asia because they do not have English versions.

In Taiwan or Hong Kong, many video game players are interested in Japanese history, culture, and language, because they want to understand more about their favorite games.

For instance, after playing J-League's and Nobunaga's games, they might look for information about J-League and the life of Oda Nobunaga. Taiwanese and Hong Kong game players are also interested in knowing some Japanese. Almost all game magazines have a corner to teach readers game terminology in the Japanese language. Southeast Asian players care less about Japanese history, culture, and language related to the games they play. To them, the video game is a source of entertainment without a national boundary, and they do not necessarily see it as a springboard to learn about Japan.

In Hong Kong and Taiwan, video games are a must in children's TV programs and youth magazines. For instance, the Asian channel in Hong Kong broadcasts news about video games and organizes competitions in its children's programs on a regular basis. In contrast, in Singapore, none of its local magazines or newspapers has a game corner. In Hong Kong, popular weeklies such as *East Touch* and *Easyfinder* and leading newspapers such as *Apply Daily* and *Oriental Daily* have a video game corner. In Hong Kong, the mass media and press report stories about game shows and game competitions, whereas the mass media and press in Southeast Asia are less interested in reporting game-related activities. For instance, although video games are popular among children, they are not included in children's TV programs. Although quite a number of game shows and tournaments have been organized in Singapore, Bangkok, and Kuala Lumpur by Japanese companies or local organizations, the mass media show little interest in these events. If they report them, they usually focus on cosplay ("costume-play," dressing up as comic or game characters) rather than the games.

Many Japanese hardware and software companies have set up offices in Hong Kong, Taiwan, and the United States, but very few of them have offices in Southeast Asia. (Sony, Bandai, Konami, and SNK all have set up offices in Singapore, but it seems that only the Sony office is active. The Bandai office covers mainly Digimon and merchandise, and Konami and SNK offices are small liaison offices.) Konami has a branch in Taiwan to create Chinese game software, and a number of Taiwanese companies have acquired licenses from Japanese software makers to make Chinese versions of Japanese video games. Taiwanese and Hong Kong software companies also have begun to write and sell games for Japanese makers. Japanese game developers also recruit talents from South Korea, Taiwan, Hong Kong, and Mainland China. For example, *The Condor Hero* was developed by a team which consisted of Japanese, Mainland Chinese, Hongkongers, and Taiwanese who worked for Sony in Tokyo. This kind of collaboration is missing in Southeast Asia. For example, although Singapore has many software companies, most of them focus on online games in English and have little interaction with the Japanese.

With the regional difference in Asian game culture in the backdrop, we can examine some similarities in Asian game culture as compared with their Japanese counterpart. First, piracy is prevalent and has played an important role in jumpstarting Japanese video games in Asia. Piracy has been a major form of game consumption in Asia. From the early 1980s to the present, unlicensed software has dominated the Asian market. These unlicensed games include pirated games, unlicensed new games (such as *Street Fighter II* and *The Fourth Generation*), and unlicensed Chinese versions of Japanese games (such as *Shining Force*). Asia is a big manufacturer and importer of pirated games.[15]

All nations have some regulations against pirated software, but whether they are forceful in exercising them or not is another matter. There is little pirated software in Japan, because Japanese consumers are willing to pay for the original game software, which is much cheaper than in Taiwan, Hong Kong, or Singapore. Also, the secondhand market for original software is very large, and the Japanese government is very forceful in suppressing piracy.

Taiwan, China, and Malaysia are major manufacturing and distribution centers of pirated games, whereas Hong Kong and Singapore are major importers of pirated games. In Malaysia, Mainland China, and Thailand, many players buy and many game shops sell pirated software exclusively. As a matter of fact, it is much easier to buy pirated than original software. Many game titles are only available in pirated software. Game shops also suggest their customers buy pirated software in order to acquire a higher profit margin. Piracy popularizes video games in the short term but hurts the video game industry and culture in the long term. The Microsoft Xbox does not have offices or release games in Mainland China because of the piracy problem there. For the same reason, Japanese game developers show little interest in developing Chinese games.

Governments in Asia have tried to crack down on pirated software but to no avail. Game shops have smart ways to beat the system. Inspectors can hardly find any pirated game software in their shops, because they are stored in hidden compartments or in locations outside the shops. Usually they show game folders to the customers and allow them to choose, and then get the pirated software for them from other locations. Some shops sell pirated software only at night or on certain days. Some employ ex-convicts to operate the shops and to take the legal responsibility when caught. Shops form an intelligence network and inform each other on things such as police raids and suspicious persons. In 2006, the Hong Kong government made the reworking of the PS2 to read pirated software and the uploading or downloading of unlicensed game software on the Internet illegal. Many other places also have made similar measures to enhance copyright protection.

Second, legal control of and the social prejudice against video games are strong. Most Asian nations exercise some kind of censorship of video games, directly or indirectly. However, perhaps with the exception of Mainland China, the censorship of video games in Asia is not as strict as that of movies, comics, and TV programs. Most Asian governments only screen certain video games when they receive complaints from teachers or parents. If the games are found problematic, the importer will be punished severely. Hence, game importers and distributors in Asia usually exercise self-censorship and do not import games with excessive sex or violence. East Asia is more liberal than Southeast Asia in this respect. For example, mahjong and card games are popular in Japan, Taiwan, and Hong Kong, but they are not introduced to Singapore because they contain sexual materials (for example, when the player wins, a sexy girl on the screen will take off her clothes piece by piece).

Problematic games such as *Mortal Kombat,* a game of bloodshed and torture, have been banned in Hong Kong and Singapore. In Taipei City, the city government once closed all game centers and later only allowed several big ones to reopen. In China, the official control of video games has been very tight. All kinds of games, including arcade games, home computer games, home console games and online games are subject to censorship and a large number of them have been banned for containing sex, violence, gambling, or unwanted political messages. The Singapore government has basically banned all games with sexual content. In Hong Kong, policemen regard game centers as the hotbed for crime and keep them on surveillance. In South Korea, for political and historical reasons, Japanese game consoles by Nintendo, Sega, and Sony had been officially banned for more than two decades, and the ban was only lifted in June of 2000. As a result, Korean players play mostly home computer games and online games. Most people in Asia, in particular, educators, social critics, politicians, and parents, hold negative opinions about video games. The mass media report negative news about game addiction or game-related crime. For instance, there was a recent TV advertisement by the Hong Kong government to discourage gambling, using online game addiction as an example.

Finally, Japanese video games have been popular and have had an impact on Asian cultural industries. Compared with other forms of Japanese popular culture in Asia, the video game culture is quite unique in many ways.

First, it came to Asia later than Japanese comics, animated series, character goods, TV dramas, and pop music, but it made a very strong impact. Introduced to Asia in the mid-1980s, Japanese video games became an instant success, and since then have been one of the most popular forms of Japanese popular culture. Only comics and animation can match their popularity. The video game culture has been growing strongly and in general it has shown no signs of decline. Japanese video games have few competitors of their kind. In comics, animation, TV dramas, music, food, fashion, and merchandise, Japanese popular culture is competing with its Western, Asian, and local counterparts. However, the entire video game market in Asia, until the rise of the Xbox and American and Korean online games in the past few years, had been largely dominated by the Japanese.

Second, playing video games is mainly a children's and young men's culture. For other forms of Japanese popular culture, the main patrons are teenagers and those in their early twenties, mostly high school and university students.

Third, video games have caused an "entertainment revolution,"[16] stimulating the consumption of other forms of Japanese and Asian popular culture in Asia. Popular video games, such as *Mario Bros., Pokemon, Samurai Spirits, Final Fantasy, Street Fighter,* and *The King of Fighters,* have given rise to comics, films, animation, CDs, VCDs, merchandise, and other spin-offs. Asian films, games, comics, TV dramas, and pop music have borrowed considerably from Japanese video games. For example, there are at least 65 Hong Kong comics adapted from the *Street Fighter* and *The King of Fighters* series.[17]

Through a historical overview of the global popularization and local consumption of Japanese video games in an Asian context, we have seen that East Asia and Southeast Asia are consumption centers of Japanese games and Japan is leading the market in arcade games, home consoles, and handheld games. Playing Japanese games has become an integral part of Asian youth culture and has an impact on Asian entertainment industry. Japan's Achilles' heel, however, is the online game, an area in which it is outperformed by South Korea, the United States, and Taiwan.

This investigation indicates that Asian players are not passive consumers and they are indeed, in John Fiske's terminology, "active readers."[18] They consume and interpret Japanese video games in their own ways, following their cultural backgrounds. Because of this, Japanese video games have acquired Asian dimensions and become a kind of hybrid culture. This hybridity of video games challenges two influential but somewhat old-fashioned ideas. First, the old notion of seeing Japanese video games as a form of cultural imperialism[19] does not fit in an Asian context, because Asian players have domesticated Japanese video games. Various degrees of localization of Japanese video games still can be found in Asia due to reasons that are political (censorship which makes the games relatively "clean"), economic (it is less expensive to buy pirated software), social (background of the players), and cultural (preference for games in English or Chinese). Finally, the cultural "odorless" theory[20] that sees Japanese video game as largely a technology without a strong ideology and cultural identity is not always true. Japaneseness can be a major attraction rather than a problem to most Asian players; the more advanced they are in playing Japanese video games, the more they ask for Japaneseness.

CHAPTER 34

VIDEO GAMES IN AUSTRALIA

Thomas H. Apperley

Looking at video games in Australia, there appears to be a trend towards a political under-standing of video games: the notion that there is something at stake that is more than simply play. This has led to several situations where the creative and artistic elements of video games have come under pressure from the Australian federal government. While Australia has a long-standing local video game production industry for both international and local markets, the laws governing the regulation of video games have led to a number of international releases being denied distribution in Australia because the Office of Film and Literature Classification refused to give them a rating. Among these games was The Collective's *Marc Ecko's Getting Up: Contents Under Pressure* (2006). Despite this restrictive environment, the government also has funded politically motivated artistic game design projects, like Escape from Woomera Project Team's *Escape from Woomera* (2004). Both of these examples, and the controversies that surround them in part stem from the video games having a—more or less—artistically motivated political agenda.

Australia's Video Game Industry

The history of the video game industry in Australia begins with the 1980 establishment of Beam Software in Melbourne, Victoria. They are remembered for their innovative series of text adventures, including *The Hobbit* (1982). Beam Software was soon followed by two influential Australian companies, both based in New South Wales: Strategic Studies Group (SSG) founded in 1982 and Microforte founded in 1985. The Australian industry increased in size during the 1990s when many companies started up in both Melbourne, Victoria, and in Brisbane, Queensland. Torus Games and Tantalus Interactive were founded in Melbourne in 1994, followed by IR Gurus in 1996. In Brisbane, Queensland, Auran was founded in 1995, and Krome Studios was established in 1999. While Australia can hardly be considered an industry hub, it now has a long-standing export tradition, worth 110 million Australian dollars in 2006, with over 40 operating development studios.[1] The oldest video game company in Australia, Beam Software, became Melbourne House, and having passed through the hands of Atari/Infogrames, the purchase of Melbourne House by Brisbane-based Krome Studios was announced in November 2006, making them Australia's largest independent game development studio, with over 300 employees. This gives them significant status in the Australian gaming industry, which in 2006 employed approximately 1,600 people.[2] Krome Studios, the developers behind the *Ty the Tasmanian Tiger* series that sold over two million units worldwide, has renamed the studio Krome Studios Melbourne. Having recently completed the multi-platform *Legend of Spyro: A New Beginning* (2006), the company is now focused on developing its own intellectual property and completing *Hellboy*, scheduled for publication by Konami in 2007.

The games industry in Australia is focused almost exclusively in the cities of Melbourne, Victoria, and Brisbane, Queensland. Like Krome Studios, Auran is another globally prominent studio that is also located in Brisbane. Widely known for the development of the *Trainz* series of railroad simulators, Auran's innovative business practices have been extensively discussed elsewhere.[3] Currently, they are developing an MMORPG, *Fury: Unleash the Fury*, that focuses on player-versus-player style play; they also have in recent years moved into publishing PC games for the Australian, New Zealand, and Asian markets. Other companies of note include three Melbourne based businesses: IR Gurus Interactive, who specialize in local sports games; Tantalus Interactive, who are developing games for handheld systems; and Torus, who have recently branched out from their focus on developing titles for the Game Boy Advance, to release the multi-platform *Shrek Smash N' Crash Racing* (2006). Also prominent, but catering to a niche market, is the New South Wales-based Strategic Studies Group, who are the developers of the *Decisive Battles of WWII* series, turn-based strategy games for the PC. Microforte, with studios in Sydney and Canberra, has moved away from game development and is now making development software for Massive Multi-player Online Role Playing Games (MMORPGs), an endeavor in which—with Big-World Technology—they have met a degree of success with Chinese MMORPG developers.

Despite the industry's evidently healthy state, the Game Developers' Association of Australia acknowledges that several major challenges face it in the coming years; in particular, maintaining independent Australian studios. There has been an increase in foreign buyouts of Australian development studios, as the high-waged centers of the video game industry—USA, Japan—ship projects offshore to reduce costs. This has been accompanied by another practice that takes advantage of the Australian industries' reputation for achieving respectable results on tight budgets; the development of games based on licensed products for overseas publishers.[4] While 85 percent of gaming companies in Australia claim to develop their own intellectual property, 90 percent of the industry's output has been based in licensed products.[5] Initiatives by the State Government of Victoria's Film Victoria Digital Media Fund have focused on giving developers access to the high-tech skills and equipment that they need to compete internationally, and—as the Minister for Information and Communication Technology emphasizes—develop local IP and "initiate their own concepts."[6] While several Australian video game companies have developed their own concepts and intellectual property, video games have also been significantly deployed by an artistic collective to demonstrate a new conceptual understanding of the political role of video games.

Escape from Woomera

Escape from Woomera was designed by a collective calling itself the Escape from Woomera Project Team, which was made up of journalists, artists, game designers, and programmers. The game was developed with a political agenda in mind; to highlight the dreadful conditions in the Woomera Immigration Reception and Processing Centre, located in South Australia. The role of the center—and various others around the country—was to hold illegal immigrants while their details and asylum applications were processed; it was operational from 1999 until its closure in 2004. By 2000 the Woomera center, in particular, had become the subject of widespread allegations of overcrowding and human rights abuses towards the detainees. The subsequent media attention about the Woomera center and the plight of the detainees brought the highly divisive issue of detaining illegal immigrants into the public sphere.

Escape from Woomera was eventually released as an almost-finished downloadable online version in May 2004 after the Woomera center had been closed, although the practice of detaining asylum seekers continues in other centers. The game was actually a "mod" (modification) for Valve Software's *Half-Life* (1998). For the project, the Escape from Woomera Project Team received 25,000 Australian dollars from the Australian Council of the Arts (ACA) through the New Media Arts Board (NMAB).[7] Philip Ruddock, the Federal Minister for Immigration, heavily criticized this move; his colleague Ron Kemp, Federal Minister of Arts, demanded an explanation from both the ACA and NMAB. Michael Snelling, Chairman of the NMAB, attempted to diffuse the situation, claiming that the project was awarded funding based on its artistic merit, and that in any case the project members were "not attempting to offer a political or ethical solution to the plight of the refugees."[8] Other parties were soon drawn into the fracas. Advocates for refugee groups argued that the game "trivialized the plight of asylum seekers," while the Australian Human Rights Commissioner, Dr. Sev Ozdowski, stated that the game was "at best... insensitive."[9] When the ACA dissolved the NMAB in 2004 in the wake of the furor, many believed that the funding of *Escape from Woomera* was the cause.[10] Certainly, considering that *Escape from Woomera* was a modestly funded mod project, its impact in Australia has been tremendous and has been used in several scholarly texts—Jon Dovey and Helen Kennedy's *Game Cultures: Computer Games as New Media* (New York: Open University Press, 2006), and Geoff King and Tanya Krzywinska's *Tomb Raiders & Space Invaders: Videogames Forms & Contexts* (New York and London: I.B. Tauris, 2006)—as an example of the ways that video games may be deployed by activists to broaden the scope of political debate.

While the governmental response to a locally produced artistic game project might appear astonishing, when placed in the context of a rigidly enforced strategy of arresting the global flows of video games that are imported from elsewhere, the heavy-handed response to *Escape from Woomera* is appreciable. Video games, in order to obtain commercial distribution in Australia, must obtain a classification from the Australian Government Office of Film and Literature Classification through a written application that requests a rating (either G, general; PG, parental guidance recommended; MA, recommended for mature audiences; MA15+, not suitable for people under 15) and includes a written description of gameplay as well as a video of any contentious parts of the game.[11] Notably, in the case of video games, the classification of R18+ (restricted to adults only) may not be granted. The classification of a game is established according to six categories: themes, violence, sex, language, drug use, and nudity. While the R18+, if interpreted liberally, only goes so far as to refuse classification to pornography (explicit, non-simulated sexual acts) and to sexual violence, it also includes a caveat on interactive media that make use of "incentives and rewards."[12] This feature is enough to allow an automatic refusal if the rewards include sex, sexual violence, or drug use.

Refusals of classifications for video games, for whatever reason, are the subject of much controversy among the video game industry and consumers in Australia. High profile refusals of classification—that include Rockstar North's *Manhunt* (2003), *Grand Theft Auto: San Andreas* (2004), and most recently Blitz Games's *Reservoir Dogs* (2006)—have led to an outcry among the game-playing public that the R18+ classification be extended to include video games.[13] When laws governing the classification of games were last reviewed in 2002, South Australia blocked a proposal to allow an R18+ rating category for games.[14]

Marc Ecko's Getting Up: Contents Under Pressure

The Collective's game *Marc Ecko's Getting Up: Contents Under Pressure* (2006) is set in a dystopian future world where graffiti is the key way of mobilizing the masses against the strictures of the authoritarian police state—a theme not entirely dissimilar to that of Smilebit's *Jet Set Radio Future* (2002), which has an MA15+ rating, as did *Getting Up* when Atari first applied for a classification. However, the game's rating was appealed by the Queensland Local Government Association, a collective of local governing bodies in the tourist region of Queensland known as the Gold Coast. The association's representative, Ron Clark, argued that: "*Getting Up* promoted graffiti on public property, train-surfing, fighting and other anti-social behavior."[15] The association believes that the decision to refuse the game classification has the potential to prevent the escalation of these activities. The irony of the situation was not lost on local journalists. While Atari was outraged and issued a statement that the banning of *Getting Up* was compared to book burning, Marc Ecko was reported to be disappointed.[16]

The decision to deny the game classification was contentious among the members of the review board. As the four members were split 2–2 over the decision, the convener of the board, Maureen Shelley, had a second tie-breaking vote that she used to vote in favor of the appeal to reclassify the game. Shelley reported that the bottom line of the board's decision was that *Getting Up* promoted the crime of graffiti.[17] This was the first time a video game had been refused classification in Australia because it promoted crime. While the only acts mentioned which the board considers criminal are sexual violence and drug use, unspecified general crimes could be—and in this case were—examined as "themes." In the official report of the review board's decision, the board's examination of the game covers three pages, of which two and a half are devoted to themes and the remaining half to the other five categories potentially under consideration.[18]

In the report there was an emphasis on two related themes that the board believed make the game undesirable: the notion of graffiti as a legitimate form of art and the use of graffiti as political protest.[19] Also of concern to the board, was the game's fluency and familiarity with graffiti subculture.[20] They stated, "The objective purpose of the game is to encourage or enable the likely audience of the game to undertake graffiti or participate in the graffiti culture."[21] In their opinion the game, as a whole, incited the crime of graffiti; it "encouraged a disposition towards crime."[22] This encouragement was exacerbated by the video game's interactivity, which the board believed, like commercial training simulations, could be used to "train" a person in crime.[23] They disapproved of *Getting Up*'s portrayal of graffiti as a legitimate form of art, by using the biographies of real graffiti artists within the game, which they argue serves to both glamorize and normalize the crime of graffiti.[24] The dissenting opinion of the minority poignantly states their reason why the game should retain the MA15+ classification: "The tone of the game is escapist and has been designed as entertainment."[25]

The Australian games industry is a burgeoning area of local growth. However, a key problem facing the game development companies in Australia revolves around the issue of intellectual property. The Victorian government, at least, has acknowledged this problem. However, the attitude of the state government is evidently unsupportive of video games as anything other than a childish diversion. Once they are deployed artistically to make a political point, or recontextualize a criminal act as artistic and political, the limits of the government's perception and appreciation of the medium are exceeded. While many countries, and smaller local jurisdictions, have had issues with violence and sex in video games, which stem from a concern that games made for adults might be played by children, in Australia it appears that video games must also be detached from any suggestion or possibility of artistic or political critique.

PART V

A Closer Look at Video Games

A look through video game history often reveals areas which call for more explanation or raise questions which require different lines of inquiry to answer. Following these lines provides us with a richer understanding of video games, and a greater appreciation for their development.

The last section of this book explores some of the topics and questions that might arise during a study of video games beginning with the video game development process, which itself has grown from a one-man activity to a large team effort which can cost as much as several millions of dollars per game. Other aspects of video games which have been touched upon in earlier chapters are discussed in greater detail here. Separate chapters are devoted to video game graphics and sound and their development over the years. A list of video game genres charts the wide variety of games that have been produced and attempts to classify them according to the kinds of activity they embody. Video games have occasionally been the object of controversy, and their moral and ethical dimension is also explored. The relationship that video games have with other media is examined, and finally, some speculation is given regarding the future directions of video games.

CHAPTER 35

THE VIDEO GAME DEVELOPMENT PROCESS

Feichin Ted Tschang

The video game development process has changed dramatically over the past 30 years, though the same basic structure still remains. In part, the increasing complexity of the video game as a product has shaped the way in which games are developed. The industry has advanced from its initial beginnings as students' larks or fun things to play on university mainframe computers in the 1960s, through an era of innovation on consoles and early personal computers in the 1970s and 1980s, to the maturity and focus of the 1990s, accompanied by a reduction of innovation according to some industry participants. This was partly aided by the increasing use of three-dimensional (3-D) graphics hardware in consoles and personal computers as well as the increasing focus on "photorealistic" and immersive gaming experiences, which some observers claim are dominating the industry.

The video game development process binds together many activities, including game design, content production, and the programming of code. These may be done at the individual or group level. They may be creative in nature or rational, that is, requiring problem-solving within fairly well-defined domains. While most of the process involves an internal team that may work on a game for two or more years, there is also the need to interact with publishers, and the hiring of temporary staff and outsourcing of work is increasingly common.

The video game industry is for the most part composed of independent studios and publishers, with the studios being funded by the publishers to develop games. Publishers sometimes carry their own development efforts, focusing a considerable amount of resources to ensure that the content and quality of the games meets consumers' expectations of them. Sometimes, an independent studio will initiate a game idea and contract with a publisher at an early stage of a game, while at other times, a more innovative studio might try to develop alternate sources of funding (sometimes another publisher) to proof out the concept in a demonstration or prototype, before seeking funding from the same or another publisher for full-scale development.

The Video Game Product Development Process

Because of the substantial amount and variety of input typically incorporated into games, it is often necessary to plan out the game development process. Many studios hire specific personnel to be producers in charge of scheduling development tasks and for ensuring that resources (such as team members' time) are allocated efficiently. However, the creative side of game design also has led to an unplanned form of development process, with adaptation to unforeseen circumstances (or design) being the order of the day.

The atypical game development process can be said to consist roughly of three or four stages: idea conceptualization, preproduction, and production (a fourth period of postproduction is normally not discussed as a distinct stage but is brought in here for the sake of completeness). These stages can be considered to be somewhat arbitrary delineations in a single continual process that ensues as the artifact takes shape. Each stage incorporates milestones that correspond with significant decisions, but at the same time, the stages may also blend into one another. It is necessary to recognize that the various components of a game—particularly the software, art, and design—will be developed at varying speeds along this developmental process.

Idea Conceptualization

The vision or core concepts that differentiate the game from other games are created during the idea conceptualization stage. This integral first stage provides a broad creative sketch of the whole game and often involves more the design of the "core mechanics" of the gameplay (the thinking and actions by which players interact with the game in a repeated manner) and the context within which it is enacted, rather than any actual coding (programming) or art, although some concept art may be put to paper to help clarify the vision.

Many factors can influence the initial idea or concept of the game, either in a creative manner including acts such as inspiration or brainstorming, or through a rationally defined need, that is, the desire to improve on an existing game, or an outside-defined need, like a publisher's desire and specification for a particular type of game.

The idea conceptualization phase may also involve a single person having creative thoughts or a group brainstorming session where ideas are built on one another ("riffing" or reshaping of an idea that passes through different group members' minds). This might begin with an initial sparking of the idea of what the game would be about and be followed by an elaboration of how the game would work and how gameplay would ensue. Designers may draw on a variety of sources, including other video games, board games, reading, movies, and so on in their idea conceptualization effort. This process also would include the determining of what differentiates the game from other games and makes it interesting. In some studios, this process might involve a further aspect of "feature construction," where a list of desired features is brainstormed and agreed upon.

The initial game concept may be summarized in a concept or proposal document that is anywhere from one to a dozen or more pages long. This details the basic idea of the game, including any distinguishing characteristics, such as the core mechanics or style of the gameplay (how the player interacts with the game), the background story or context, and the visual style. While this would appear to be a simple matter to do, in many cases, the designer also should have enough knowledge of existing and future capabilities of the technology and anticipated development effort so as to ensure that this vision can be realized. Because the very nature of games makes them difficult to understand without actually having played them, developers might even find themselves verbally pitching their ideas to prospective sources of funding in the way of "it's like [that game], except with...." Naturally, the more innovative the game, the harder it is to gain acceptance.

Preproduction

The preproduction stage involves concretizing the game, both in a formal and informal way. In the formal sense, preproduction (in the sense of producing prototypes and setting the groundwork for production and implementation) becomes a key stage for ensuring a smooth process. Informally, the idea is fleshed out by an individual or a group.

There is an argument that preproduction (including prototyping) helps in "managing chaos" in the development process, and subsequently, aids in lessening developmental errors downstream (a point also supported by a number of *Game Developer* magazine postmortems). In one essay, authors Mark Cerny and Michael John point out that preproduction is essentially a chaotic creative process that "is about creating a canvas on which to find the core concept or feature that will set the game apart," and therefore, will necessarily mean "throwing out good work."[1] They believe that preproduction will save time and avoid costly mistakes downstream and should be scheduled in as a specific phase, with prototypes being made. While most developers might agree with the general benefits, others do not agree with whether preproduction is even a definable stage with clear cutoffs. For some projects, the stages of preproduction and production tend to blend into one another, while for others, especially ones comprised of veteran developers making similar products (such as sequels), the gameplay is already well understood. Hence, this model is not true for all successful projects. Another myth that Cerny and John seek to debunk is that of the need to have a "100 page design document" up front, despite the fact that many teams do create detailed design documents up front in their development process—often for a variety of reasons, which are discussed later.

One of the more common models for preproduction is that of a lead designer/programmer working alone, or small core team led by the lead designer, setting up the vision and the details underlying it, then focusing on developing a prototype and some displayable assets to secure buy-in from company executives or, if developed independently, attract funding from publishers or other organizations.

The most important activity of preproduction may be the creation of a prototype or early version of the game that is playable. This playable sequence is comprised of the code, initial sequence of art and animation, and simple game rules, to show how a player might step through a sequence of the game. This allows the game to be partially played and experienced. The core visual style may also be established at this stage. This would be done as much to convince a publisher as it might be to help the team to realize what the actual game might look and play like. Since games are interactive products, the actual game experience might be quite different from what was initially envisioned on paper. In an advanced preproduction situation, this might yield what the industry calls the "first playable" version or "the first time all of the major gameplay elements are functional and playable."[2] Preproduction is often punctuated at the end by a proposal, consisting of the prototype (and possibly also a document up to a dozen or more pages long (including accompanying artwork), which is used to convince publishers to accept the game.

How prototyping, preproduction, and conceptualization are related can differ across people and projects. For example, American McGee's *Alice* (2000) had a unique artistic style, but fairly traditional gameplay, so its preproduction took about three months—largely to get the artwork and theme right. Many other teams also have months-long preproduction periods. On the other hand, designers involved in new genres may take even longer. Will Wright spent two or more years researching and reading widely before conceptualizing some of his ideas like *The Sims*.[3]

Production

The third stage of development is that of production, in which the detailed design is implemented. Production often entails a scaling-up of the development effort. The development team at this stage may include more programmers and artists, as well as level designers, writers, audio specialists, and testing personnel, who are all responsible for implementing the design document's specifications. The full range of artistic assets is created at this stage, and a full story may be written. Games usually feature so much dialogue and alternative dialogue (for example, in response to various player decisions) that the full set of text exceeds that of a novel. The game's basic design may continue to be fine-tuned here, to either a minor or major degree. Some projects have junked entire games during production simply because they found the overall game itself to be uninspiring (and thereby making a case for early prototyping). For games that require levels, level design is initiated. For games with first-person perspectives or action games, this involves creating a series of spaces that are designed to provide a player with a navigational challenge. For planning games like real-time strategy games, scenario designs are the equivalent of levels. In many strategy games, there may also be the balancing of the game design, that is, activities that involve quantifying or assigning values to tokens and other objects in the game. [In chess for example, the tokens are the chess pieces. In a video game, tokens could include not only pieces that represent military units or player-controlled characters (avatars), but also buildings that produce output, and other kinds of usable objects.] This helps ensure that there will be equality or at least a balance between opposing players' forces. It is generally difficult to predict the effects of various combinations of tokens on opposing sides without extensively play testing these various combinations. Coding also continues, with the full set of technical and graphical aspects (such as artificial intelligence, user interfaces, etc.) being completed at this stage. Finally, sound effects, music, voice acting, and other content may also be developed.

The production stage is usually accompanied by more formal testing, and punctuated by the release of various versions of the game, such as the alpha, beta, and gold master versions. Some developers consider the alpha version to be the first one with "complete" features, and beta to be the "point at which a game contains no known bugs."[4] The gold master is the final version that becomes the master for commercial production (i.e., the copying or printing of discs) of the final game. While testing might continue throughout the product development life cycle, testing of a beta version might be the most extensive, as it may be released to a user community to ensure that the product is well fitted to their expectations. In the production stage, there is also a winding down phase where software bugs are identified and tracked, and testing is used to further balance or refine the gameplay.

Post-Production

The fourth stage is the post-production stage that occurs following the commercial release of the video game. While there is no post-production stage in video games as there is in film or animation (where the stage typically consists of editing the film to ensure a compact and releasable product), there is a phase just after the product's release when further bugs discovered after shipping are incorporated into "patches," or software code that will repair the most egregious errors.

Game Design and the Design Document

Depending on the maturity and self-assuredness of the team, the creation of a detailed design may take place either during preproduction or during full-scale production. Although designers are responsible for the core concepts of video games, a detailed design is necessary in order for the game to be implemented by the rest of the team.

The detailed design may be described in a design document of a hundred or more pages and may be developed during preproduction or even earlier. There are two different philosophies of game design: "design everything before full development ensues" or "design as we go along (throughout development)." The first type is more likely to have a more fully fleshed out design document. The design document outlines the description of the game's world, including the major types of tokens and objects within it (such as buildings, characters and their characteristics, relationships between objects, and story-line), the rules that operate in that world and which facilitate game play, and the features that distinguish the game.

Game design also needs to go beyond the specification of the basic rules, to the actual quantification of the results of values (in numeric terms) assigned to different tokens (such as the firepower of a military unit) as well as the interactions between the different players' tokens (for example, which token beats which other ones). While this may be specified in the game design document, the final set of values will necessarily require a lot of game balancing or fine-tuning for playability, that is, the redesign of the game, or the more detailed task of optimizing the values assigned to tokens and the relationships between the tokens. This is done in order to improve the playing experience, to provide a challenge, and to make the play fun.

Since the design document details every aspect of the game and its implementation, it will be the primary reference of the team. It fleshes out the whole game and provides a detailed road map for the rest of the game's development. The act of creating it also helps to ensure that the project is feasible. Design documents also ensure communication between team members and help to make sure everyone is on board with the vision or details.

While the design is an integral part of the development effort, designers also note that successful games (whether innovative or not) were ones in which the implementation was properly done. This involves the efforts of the rest of the team over the course of the game's development.[5] The difference between the inspiration for a creative idea and a successful innovative game is a lot of detailed work—both creative work and rational work. All it takes is a single flaw (for example, in the user interface) to render the game unplayable or frustrating for the player. Furthermore, designers have suggested that "ideas are cheap" or "plentiful." In their estimation, any good designer should have been able to come up with a surfeit of good ideas to begin with. Having said that, a compelling or insightful idea would be needed in the first place to start off an innovative game.

Some Problems in the Video Game Development Process

Games have a technological and increasingly rational side, partly due to the large amounts of programming and project management needed.[6] The programming side means that games can face similar issues as software products, since they need to be rationally structured in order to increase productivity and to advance the certainty of their development. Advanced techniques used for such structuring in software development are increasingly mentioned or applied in game development. In fact, since games also involve the design of complex systems and content that players must interact with to have fun, they are arguably more difficult to develop than non-game kinds of software.

There are many issues that can bedevil game development projects. Some have to do with the components themselves, such as the design (which might be unrealistic or unachievable), programming (technical problems or technology that cannot support the goals of the design), and the art. Others are characteristics that are general to game development; some of these may resemble characteristics seen in other high tech products' development.[7] Some of the problems more specific to games include: the pipelining of content with other components like design (that is, the need to develop most of the content after design), the difficulty of testing the entire game until a late stage of development, and feature creep. "Feature creep" is the tendency of designers or teams to add features over time in order to make the game more fun. However, too many features are sometimes added, or the added features may make the game confusing or cause it to lose the focus of the original design. This will require designers and teams to exercise substantial discipline throughout the project, or to have to eventually cut back on features before their implementation.

Many problems have to do with the team itself. For instance, it is possible to lose valuable team members midway through the production and for game development teams to suffer a lack of communication. To manage the latter, designers or producers are increasingly tasked with the function of coordinating the rest of the team. In addition, meetings are held throughout the project (either for the entire team or subgroups within it) to ensure that all of the team's resources are properly allocated, for example, that a programmer is fully tasked and that critical bottlenecks do not form. The actual composition of these meetings will vary by stage of the project, depending on the team's need for communication and coordination. It should also be noted that some teams actually thrive on the chaos caused by not planning out every design detail up front. Instead, these teams will add to or even change the design as production ensues. As games grow increasingly more complex, teams grow inevitably larger, and communication flows become more one-way in nature. In some larger teams, coordination is amongst the department leads and many members may not see the overall picture or how the design is evolving.

Finally, another set of problems that affects game development is the nature of the business environment. Players (that is, customers) may be unhappy with games that are not state of the art, and while tastes may change, they also do not change that much for many people. Managing to meet this dualistic and sometimes fickle nature of many consumers is perhaps one of the most difficult aspects of game development. As the postmortem for one game asked: "When making a sequel, the question that always has to be answered first is, How far do you stray from the original game to make it compelling, yet still familiar?" On top of this, studios have to deal with publishers who usually impose strict deadlines, such as a release date for the Christmas season.

As the industry and technology matures, game development will no doubt become even more rational in nature, catering to more businesslike objectives and productivity issues. This may affect how creativity occurs in game development. The combination of these rational aspects of development with the ostensibly creative aspects can also cause tensions in game development similar to those seen in other creative industries such as film.

Despite the full completion of games, many assets (art, design, and even code) of games might be thrown out at the very end (that is, wastage can occur even beyond prototypes). This could be due to any reason, including the teams' dissatisfaction with their effort, the publisher's change in product strategy, and so on. Prototype code and art may also have been hastily assembled during preproduction and could be thrown out in lieu of a more proper effort. This has occurred in the case of radically innovative games such as *PaRappa the Rapper* (1996) (the first "play to the music" game which was developed for the Sony PlayStation) as well as in cases of more incremental innovations that were seeking a very well-honed user experience (such as the first-person shooter *Half-Life*).[8]

Balancing Creativity and Rationality in Game Development

Game development is often thought to be a highly creative process, but in reality, it is a highly rational process as well. Creative processes may occur throughout the product development process; for instance, idea conceptualization may involve one or more designers or team members riffing or bouncing ideas off one another. Much of the creativity occurs in the idea conceptualization stage. Many types of creativity may be found, with different games illustrating how different designers look at the world and play in very different ways. Peter Molyneux's *Dungeon Keeper* for instance, involves reversing the role of the player, so that instead of controlling the party entering the dungeon as in a conventional fantasy role-playing game, the player controls the dungeon and uses it to attack the party of "heroes" (represented by computer-controlled characters). The concept appears deceptively simple, yet it yields considerably different and refreshing gameplay. Another example, Will Wright's *The Sims* (in which players can live alternate lives with virtual alter egos), also appears as seemingly mundane as a dollhouse simulation, but it was a revolutionary product that required the creator to engage in significant research as well as to convince the team and publisher to come on board the project. It is also one of the most successful games of all time. In the end, all this may relate to another skill in creativity: the ability to recognize good (and implementable) ideas from bad ones.

Creativity can also be exercised at later stages of development (such as during production) albeit at a lower, more detailed level of the design or its implementation. A great deal of creativity is exercised in this detailed way by many members of the development team.[9] For instance, designers can add new features in an inspired fashion, or programmers can use code to express in-game effects more beautifully or in an appealing way. Thus, even programming work requires not only technical sophistication, but also a tacit (even empathic) appreciation of what works, and what the user would enjoy.

A large amount of game development is also rational or problem-solving in nature. This includes a lot of the design work (the design of the system and rules to be effective, playable, and consistent as a set in itself), programming (the overcoming of technical problems), and content (such as the artwork involved). While these may also be creative in nature, they may not necessarily be creative in the usual sense of the term.

CHAPTER 36

GRAPHICS IN VIDEO GAMES

Carl Therrien

So why did polygons become the ubiquitous virtual bricks of videogames? Because, whatever the interesting or eccentric devices that had been thrown up along the way, videogames, as with the strain of Western art from the Renaissance up until the shock of photography, were hell-bent on refining their powers of illusionistic deception.

—Steven Poole[1]

Illusion refining, indeed, appears to be a major driving force of video game evolution. The appeal of evermore realistic depictions of virtual universes in itself justifies the purchase of expensive new machinery, be it the latest console or dedicated computer parts. Yet, one must not conceive of this evolution as a linear progression towards perfect verisimilitude. The relative quality of static and dynamic renders, associated with a wide range of imaging techniques more or less suited to the capabilities of any given video game system, demonstrate the unsteady evolution of visual representation in the short history of the medium. Moreover, older techniques are sometimes integrated in the latest 3-D games, and 2-D gaming still enjoys a very strong following with portable game systems. Despite its short history, a detailed account of the apparatus behind the illusion would already require many volumes in itself. In this chapter, we will examine only the fundamentals of the different imaging techniques along with key examples. However, we hope to go further than a simple historical account of illusion refining and expose the different ideals that governed and still govern the evolution of visual design in games.

In video games, visual representation started from scratch again; a few shapes, a few colors. The first arcade games, *Computer Space* and *PONG,* proposed strikingly abstract universes that could nonetheless be associated with real-world referents (science fiction and table tennis). The popularity of space settings in early games is not surprising; notwithstanding the programmers' interest in science fiction, a black backdrop could depict the emptiness of space with minimal costs in terms of system resources. During the first decade of its history, the appeal of video game entertainment is to be found elsewhere than in its figurative potential. The bitmap display mode, based on the subdivision of the screen in discrete units (pixels) to which individual values are associated, is bound mainly by two sets of restrictions: display capabilities (most notably screen resolution and simultaneous on-screen colors) and processing capabilities (working memory and central processing unit frequency). The two are closely tied: the "blockiness" of early games can be explained by low screen resolution (the maximum theoretical resolution of the Atari 2600, for example, is 192 x 160), but also by the inability to manipulate detailed bitmaps (hence the dominance of large, uniformly colored "blocks"). These restrictions favored frontal or lateral depictions and different points of view were often merged in a single scene. A few simple bitmaps, like building bricks, were assembled and tiled to create the playfield (Figure 36.1).

To prolong the art history analogies set forth by Steven Poole, one could observe that the stacking of space planes and point of view discrepancies found in many pre-Renaissance paintings are also typical of early games.

Through a steady flow of home consoles, arcade games, and personal computers, display and processing technologies evolved rapidly. Higher resolution bitmaps could represent objects from odd angles more easily, thus adding some depth to the game world. The arcade version of *Zaxxon* systematizes these efforts by introducing an isometric perspective, a subtype of axonometric perspective which represents a tridimensional space with no vanishing points, giving all three dimensions equal importance (Figure 36.2).

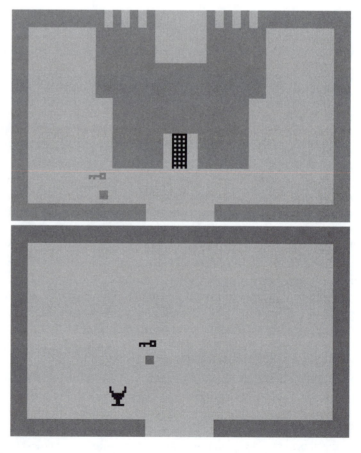

Figure 36.1 **Two screen images from *Adventure* for the Atari 2600. The top image is the Gold Castle exterior, and the image below it is the castle's interior, which is entered by passing through the castle gate when the portcullis is raised.**

Figure 36.2 Isometric perspective. Two screen images showing the isometric perspective in the arcade game *Zaxxon* (1982).

Game worlds expanded beyond the initial one-screen limit, either by displaying multiple adjacent spaces (*Adventure* and *Pitfall!*) or through a technique known as scrolling, first introduced in Kee Games's arcade game *Super Bug*. Flat layers of space appear gradually, in a continuous motion either controlled by the computer [as in *Xevious* (1982)] or in response to user navigation (as in the arcade version of *Defender*). In *Moon Patrol,* three distinct layers of scenery unfold at various speeds, producing a basic illusion of depth. This technique, known as parallax scrolling, was made more convincing by the multiplication of planes and/or the manipulation of discrete objects (sprites, more on this later) in a similar fashion, as seen in the arcade version of *Choplifter* (1985). Through the horizontal and/or vertical parallax scrolling of many action games, a simulated vanishing point emerges, and on its virtual horizon, one can already see the emergence of the virtual camera in the bitmap world.

"It is perhaps due to the desire to measure up to the standards of visual realism set by film and television that the video game has evolved as it has," supposes Mark J.P. Wolf.[2] Incidentally, technological evolution quickly stirred up the game developers' cinematographic ambitions. The development of the graphic adventure genre, associated early on with evermore vivid depictions of settings and characters through the integration of elaborate bitmaps, is the first major manifestation of these ambitions. Close-ups of characters gradually become mandatory during conversation sequences (Figure 36.3), with some games trying to simulate basic shot-linking structures: medium shot/close-up in *King of Chicago* (1987) (Figure 36.4); and shot/counter-shot in Delphine Software's *Croisière pour un Cadavre* (1992) for the Amiga. Early on, developers even use digitized photographic material to produce these detailed bitmaps (as in Access Software's *Mean Streets*). However, all this added detail often accounted for particularly static scenes, with most of the processing resources being dedicated to the data-intensive images. This flaw was even more striking with digitized photography; photo-novels being a rather scarce cultural reference amongst gamers, photographic material inevitably points towards the greater

Figure 36.3   **Close-ups. One in Sierra On-Line's *King's Quest V* (1990) (top) and another in Lucasfilm's *Loom* (1990) (bottom).**

ideal of cinema. The obvious, most sought-after aspect of cinematographic representation is indeed the illusion of motion.

Throughout the first generations of hardware, the dynamic objects of game worlds were called "sprites," a term actually referring to the underlying display mechanics (more or less hardwired depending on the system). Sprites moving on the screen are animated by displaying a series of different bitmaps, or animation "frames." In 1984, Brøderbund Software released J. Mechner's *Karateka* for the Apple II, whose animated characters

Figure 36.4 *King of Chicago* **(1987). Two screen images from** Cinemaware's *King of Chicago* **for the Amiga.**

impressed the gaming community. *Prince of Persia* (1989) for the Apple II, Mechner's latter and most renowned effort, is associated with the advent of motion capture in video games but actually borrowed a well-known animation technique: rotoscoping. Each step of the needed movements is drawn painstakingly from the performance of a model captured on film. The prince's impressive action range (walking, running, jumping, climbing, sword-fighting) is brought to life with unknown fluidity for the time (Figure 36.5).

In 1992, Midway's *Mortal Kombat* attracted a lot of attention in the arcades. Each fighter of this tournament was created from video sequences shot with real actors, key frames being integrated into the sprite animation system. The resulting illusion is still short of cinematographic quality. Laserdisc-based arcade games already integrated filmic material in the early 1980s (like Atari's *Firefox*), but the gameplay was limited and relatively few games were produced. The ultimate attempt to integrate cinema in video games occurs concurrently with the Motion Picture Coding Experts Group's (MPEG) efforts to develop a motion picture compression standard for CD-ROM technology. However, the quality of digitized video sequences (full-motion video) varies greatly from game to game and often pales in comparison to the MPEG-1 standard of 1989. Access Software's

Figure 36.5 Decomposed running animation. An example from J. Merchner's *Prince of Persia* (screenshots from the Amiga version).

Martian Memorandum (1991) introduced FMV to depict some of the characters interrogated throughout the adventure. These sequences are short, restricted to a small window, low resolution, and suffer from erratic frame rates. The advent of CD-ROM technology as a storage medium allowed for better quality FMV along with a more consistent integration throughout the games. The long-running Tex Murphy series perfectly illustrates the evolution of FMV integration (Figure 36.6).

Video games, it is now clear, remediate cinema in a variety of ways: through the integration of conventions and language, animation techniques, up to complete digitization. The concept of remediation, central to Jay David Bolter and Richard Grusin's genealogy of

Figure 36.6 Full-motion video evolves. Evolution of FMV integration in Access Software's Tex Murphy series: digitized photographs in *Mean Streets* (1989) (upper left), windowed live-action sequences in *Martian Memorandum* (1991) (upper right), live-action characters integrated into the scenes in *Under a Killing Moon* (1994) (lower left), and full-screen sequences in *Tex Murphy: Overseer* (1998) (lower right).

new media,[3] is often interpreted in a progressive manner: newer media "remediates" the "defects" of their predecessors. The case of video games is clearly more complex; for all the interactivity offered by the medium, games cannot claim superiority in terms of strict visual realism. One could conceive of remediation in this context not as the reform of older media, but as an assertion of a representational ideal. But what exactly constitutes this ideal? Beyond the lack of detail and/or fluidity, the most obvious shortcoming of visual representation in video games is repetition: tiled bitmaps, reused animations create an undesirable impression of homogeneity. In addition to visual realism, cinema also embodies the ideal of representational variability. The cinematographic quality of *Croisière pour un Cadavre* relies first and foremost on the ability of its game engine (aptly named "Cinématique") to present a variety of points of view. Furthermore, the appeal of FMV lies in the possibility to make any given part of the image evolve into something completely different. How is it, then, that when gaming systems finally acquired the technical means to convincingly remediate cinema, interest towards FMV dissipated so abruptly?

For all its representational qualities, live-action video cannot easily adapt to user input. The so-called interactive movie fell short of living up to its ambitions, production and storage issues hindering the integration of significant variations on the local scale of the event and the global scale of the narrative. But this explanation is insufficient; the then-popular graphic adventure game genre, which served as a mold for interactive movies to a great extent, also proposed highly scripted interactivity. Ironically, part of the explanation is to be found in exactly the same games that relied heavily on live-action sequences. Virtual, computer-generated locations were more suited to the relatively low-budget productions than, say, built sets or expensive on-site shooting. The very principle of the computer-generated imagery seen in those games announced a future where the medium could merge the cinematographic ideal with its own interactive ambitions, affording a representational variability that could constantly be affected by the user.

Beyond Cinema

The principle behind computer-generated imagery is very simple: dedicated computer tools simulate a three-dimensional world where objects and eventually whole scenes are modeled from the combination/manipulation of geometric primitives (cubes, spheres, etc.). Textures (2-D images) are applied to the modeled surfaces, and specific algorithms handle phenomenon like lighting, shadowing, transparency, reflection, liquid and volatile matter, etc. The self-proclaimed ideal of CGI artists is photorealism. To this day, computer-generated images often look too perfect. Getting rid of this hyperrealist impression proves to be difficult; the addition of filth and the simulation of oxidation cannot completely erase the virtual surfaces' homogeneity. A greater challenge than photorealism resides in the animation of virtual scenes, which requires intensive fine-tuning in order to achieve realistic movement or "kino-realism." Virtual skeletons are incorporated into objects, with each joint possessing its own set of attributes. For complex movements such as those of humanoids, animators often rely on the technique of motion capture: a performer executes the needed movements wearing a special suit equipped with a set of captors at key joints. Finally, a point of view on the scene must be selected. The virtual camera materializes at last, endogenously, at the very heart of computer imaging.

With the proper resources, CGI has reached near-cinematographic visual realism. It is integrated seamlessly into live-action films, to a great extent in some projects (like George

Lucas's *Star Wars* prequel trilogy, 1999–2005); and a full-length feature aiming for perfect verisimilitude has already been produced, *Final Fantasy: The Spirits Within* (2001) directed by Hironobu Sakaguchi and Moto Sakakibara. Video games, too, integrated CGI in a variety of ways. In 1993, Trilobyte's *The 7th Guest* and Cyan's *Myst* proposed virtual worlds that could be explored through computer-generated imagery, the former with full-motion video. Most of the assets for Rare's *Donkey Kong Country* (1994) for the SNES, from backgrounds to animated sprites, were prerendered on powerful Silicon Graphics workstations. Thanks to its novelty in the media landscape, CGI became even more of an attraction than the contemporary digitization of live-action sequences. Computer-rendered cinematics were integrated into any genre, but soon became associated with Japanese role-playing games through the success of Square's *Final Fantasy VII* (1997) for the PlayStation. In these examples, CGI does not redefine the fundamentals of visual design in video games; it simply replaces drawn or digitized material. Therefore, how can we associate this imaging technique with the pursuit of a greater ideal?

Philippe Quéau eloquently defines the core principle of CGI: "Digital image synthesis techniques break off with photons. They are completely seized by language." Through these techniques, "we do not seek the 'reproduction' of reality, but the very conditions of its production."[4] 3-D models are mathematically formulated and thus easily manipulated by the computer; a digitally rendered image is but one of many possible actualizations that can be reformulated endlessly. But in order to claim any kind of superiority in the realm of video games, this manipulation has to occur in real time. Even though 3-D gaming became the norm during the 1990s, techniques allowing the reformulation of virtual objects in a 3-D space were developed relatively early in the medium's life. In the arcade parlors at the turn of the 1980s, raster displays cohabited with another technology: vector display. Instead of drawing every pixel of the screen 30 times or so every second, the electron beam in vector displays traces the needed lines directly, the rest of the screen remaining black. In comparison to raster displays, lines could be rendered in much higher resolution and manipulated much more fluidly. 2-D games with sharp images and fluid movement were produced (most notably Atari's *Asteroids*), but most interestingly, vector graphics quickly became associated with the creation of wireframe 3-D worlds.

In 1980, Atari's *Battlezone* arcade game proposed the first three-dimensional game universe in a video game. The world's objects were made of basic geometric solids (cubes and pyramids), their surfaces completely transparent due to the limitations of vector graphics. As they piloted their tanks, players could explore the universe in any direction; the planar surfaces of the objects (or polygons) were reformulated according to their virtual first-person point of view (Figure 36.7).

Earlier games oriented their gameplay on the depth axis, most notably Atari's *Night Driver* in the arcade. But on the pitch-black road, as on the more colorful rides offered by later games such as Konami's *Gyruss* (1983) and Sega's *Space Harrier,* objects coming towards the players are in fact 2-D sprites scaled by the game engine. Even if they offered a convincing illusion of depth, these game engines simply transferred the action on a different axis; in terms of point of view redundancy, they are not more capable than side-scrolling games. Wireframe 3-D gathered interest and was used for Atari's adaptation of the first two games based on *Star Wars* movies (1983 and 1985, respectively). But in order to represent solid 3-D worlds, polygons had to be "filled," something vector displays could not easily achieve. Atari's *I, Robot* is the first foray into such a world (Figure 36.8).

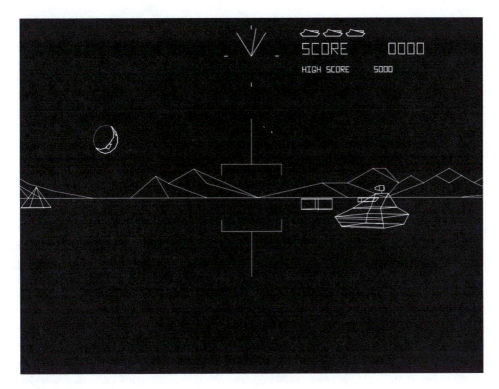

Figure 36.7 Atari's arcade game *Battlezone* (1980). The first arcade game world to make use of true 3-D computation.

Interestingly, the game's controls allowed players to control the position of the camera with two dedicated buttons.

After the commercial failure of *I, Robot,* polygon-based 3-D became associated with the vehicular simulation genre through games such as Sphere's *Falcon* (1987), Lerner Research's *Chuck Yeager Advanced Flight Trainer* (1987) and Microsoft *Flight Simulator* (version 3.0, 1988). Some action/adventure games were produced, most notably those

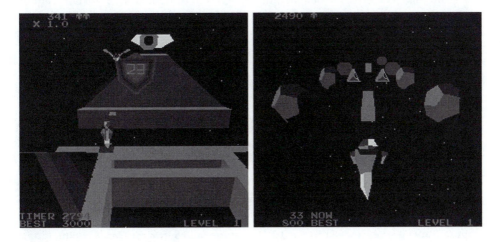

Figure 36.8 Two images from Atari's arcade game *I, Robot.* Images from http://www.klov.com/.

built using Incentive Software's Freescape engine, including *Driller* (1987) and *Castle Master* (1990). Ironically, 3-D gaming became widely popular through the release of id Software's *Doom,* whose game engine is not fully three dimensional. The engine integrated texture maps (2-D images applied to a surface and interpolated according to a set point of view) with some trade offs: the walls, floors, and ceilings of the game world were bound by strict rendering restrictions, thus limiting the first-person point of view, and objects (such as power-ups and enemies) were made of scaled sprites. In 1996, the game engine behind id Software's *Quake* rendered most of its world in textured 3-D, including the various creatures that populated it (see Figure 36.9).

Whereas *Doom*'s sectors had a uniform lighting value, *Quake*'s settings integrated light maps: lighting and shadowing produced by the light sources in a given scene were prerendered and applied on the textures. Along with a few other games, *Quake* became an incentive to buy one of the first-generation 3-D accelerator cards that now replace the standard graphic adapter cards in personal computers. Arcade games and homes consoles, too, had hardwired 3-D capabilities, and many genres began their transition to the third dimension [for example, Tamsoft's *Battle Arena Toshinden* (1994) for the Playstation; Nintendo's *Super Mario 64* (1996) for the N64; and Sega's arcade game *Sega Rally Championship* (1995)].

In today's game worlds, polygons are indeed the most commonly used bricks. CGI artist Alvy Ray Smith once estimated that it would require 80 million polygons per second in order to reproduce reality on the screen.[5] It would be naive, however, to think that the sole challenge of 3-D engines resides in geometrical complexity. Our visual world is populated with phenomenon far less tangible than bricks; water, smoke, fog, fire, and explosions are difficult to mimic with simple textured polygons. Modern special effects in video games convene an impressive array of techniques. Programmable shaders, for instance, affect the display of pixels or vertices (points in space defined by 3-D coordinates), thus contributing to many subsystems of the graphics engine. The particle system reformulates simple primitives (usually small 2-D objects) and coordinates them in order to simulate the subtle behavior of flames, smoke, and so forth. Bump mapping and normal mapping add the shading values of an uneven surface to a regular flat polygonal surface; the values adapt to the position of light sources in the scene, thus creating bumps with no additional geometry. Incidentally, the integration of light-related phenomenon in

Figure 36.9   Light maps and textured 3-D creatures in id Software's *Quake* (1996). (http://planetquake.gamespy.com, used by permission.)

interactive environments constitutes a decisive aspect of visual realism. Light dispersion, reflections, transparency, various material refraction values, and shadowing need to be calculated in real time in order to dynamically adapt to the player's actions. To this day, few games have been able to fully simulate these aspects, considering the amount of moving light sources that arise in game settings such as weapon fire and explosions.

Beneath the Surface

Even with the addition of ever more complex special effects, 3-D game worlds are still prone to repetition; tiled textures and reused animations account for the same homogeneity impression that came to be associated with 2-D gaming. No doubt the medium will continue refining its illusions until it rivals cinematic visual realism. This ideal might be reached sooner than expected; recent examples such as Valve Software's *Half-Life 2* (2004) suggest that virtual actors, in many ways the ultimate challenge of video game visual design, may not sojourn in the valley of the uncanny for much longer (Figure 36.10).

With its ability to reformulate a virtual world around the performance of a player, the medium is also perceived as a step towards the greater ideal of virtual reality. VR seeks to fully reproduce our corporal relation to the world and make computer-mediated interaction as natural as possible. 3-D game engines can indeed simulate a first-person point of view, and some developers are trying to integrate symbolic visual feedback (such as health and ammo meters) more seamlessly as well. Supposing that the interactive entertainment medium will strive towards this "greater" ideal seems like a natural assumption. Alison McMahan, for example, already sees most game genres adopting the first person point of view.[6] But such an assumption tells only half of the story. Most interestingly, 3-D engines are now used to create striking cinematic presentations. Virtual cameras are designed to momentarily frame the player's performance from spectacular angles [as in Rockstar North's *Grand Theft Auto III* (2001) for the PlayStation 2 or Ubisoft's *Prince of Persia: The Sands of Time* (2003) for the Xbox]. Popular games reintroduce *Dragon's Lair*-style gameplay (press the right key at the right moment) during computer-generated cinematic sequences [such as those in Capcom's *Resident Evil 4* (2005) for the

Figure 36.10   Valve Software's *Half-Life 2* (2004).

GameCube, Sega-AM2's *Shenmue II* (2001) for the Dreamcast, or Quantic Dream's home computer game *Indigo Prophecy* (2005)], whereas previous generations condemned it for being more "cinema" than "game." Camera-related effects like motion blur, focus, and lens flare are simulated and refined just like any other illusion. Some first-person shooters even introduce third-person segments, such as those found in Bungie's *Halo: Combat Evolved* (2001) or Starbreeze's *The Chronicles of Riddick: Escape from Butcher Bay* (2004), both for the Xbox.

Clearly, the game industry's fascination for the medium of cinema is still strong. The harmonious fusion of cinematic expressivity and interactivity (the ideal of interactive cinema) might very well be a major force driving the evolution of games for years to come. The unsteady character of the evolution of imaging techniques is now more apparent; a given technique sacrifices the gains of another one in order to develop a specific aspect of the illusion or to respond more completely to user input. Visual design in video games goes beyond the obvious graphical technicalities. Beneath the quality and diversity of animations, artificial intelligence determines how characters evolve in the environment and react to the virtual world's other actors. Beneath the appearance of this world, virtual physics simulate gravity and calculate the intensity of deflagrations in real time. As they integrate these dynamic behavior models, virtual game worlds explore a whole new layer of visual realism. It would be naive to assume that the medium will evolve solely to integrate evermore complete and complex simulation models. But as new techniques emerge, as video games strive to refine their illusionistic deception, it is undeniable that these models, too, affect the way we look at games.

CHAPTER 37

SOUND IN VIDEO GAMES

Eric Pidkameny

The origin of video game sound design can be traced to one of the most popular video games of all time, Atari's *PONG*. The game's signature sound effect, the "sonar ping" of the ball ricocheting off the paddles (created by Atari engineer Al Alcorn, from an amplified waveform from the game's own circuitry[1]), was the first of its kind. Taito's *Space Invaders* went beyond sound effects and featured an actual soundtrack, a constant, marching background rhythm. Whether its soundtrack was technically music or not is debatable, but *Space Invaders* was the first widely played game with persistent sound that was also interactive (as the player destroyed the invaders, those remaining would move faster, and the soundtrack's tempo would increase). Namco's *Pac-Man* fused all the elements of sound design into a compelling whole. Sound designer Toshio Kai's soundtrack featured constant and varied effects, musical interludes at the start of every level, additional music during the between-level cut-scenes, and a distinctive musical flourish whenever Pac-Man died. In the early days of video games, the computer was still in its infancy; every improvement in hardware or software was a move into uncharted territory, with developers leapfrogging over each other's advances. Several arcade games experimented with digital speech [such as Stern's *Berzerk* and Williams's *Sinistar* (1982)], while Cinematronics's *Dragon's Lair* took advantage of the game's laserdisc format to provide digital audio along with full motion video, though the format's technical sophistication came at the expense of limited interactivity in its gameplay.[2] Synthesized speech and full-motion video may have seemed like mere novelties at the time, but their presence in the world of games contributed to the development of the medium as a whole.

Few early home games had continuous musical soundtracks, largely due to memory and sound output limitations. The first consoles and personal computers [such as the Magnavox Odyssey[2] (1978) and IBM's PC XT (1983)] had less than one megabyte of RAM and could play only one simple tone at a time, with no volume control. Games were programmed in assembly language, which meant that the sound designer needed advanced programming knowledge—the "sound designer" was usually just one of the programmers working on the game's code. The Atari VCS console (1977), also known as the 2600, had two audio channels, but the sound chip's pseudo-random counting procedure meant that the different possible waveforms (square, sine, saw, etc.) were tuned differently; the same note played in two different waveforms could be off by as much as half a semitone.[3] Later machines like the Colecovision (1982) and Commodore 64 (1982) had sound chips capable of three and four sounds at once, along with increased storage capacity, but space was always at a premium. The Atari VCS, for example, had 128 bytes of internal RAM, with a four kilobyte maximum capacity on its cartridges. Compared to the current home consoles (Sony's PlayStation 2, Nintendo's GameCube, and Microsoft's Xbox), with RAM in the 40–60 megabyte range, more than 64 sound channels, and disc storage capacity of several gigabytes, the computers of the late 1970s and early 1980s were extremely constrained in their sound capabilities.

Beyond purely technical limitations, the music and sound effects of early video games were also hindered by the nature of the games themselves. The first arcade games were designed to appeal to a public who knew nothing about video games or computers. As designer Richard Rouse III explained,

> The thought was to get players to easily understand a game, so that by the end of their very first game they had a good sense of how the game worked and what was necessary for success. Second, the players' game, even the game of an expert, could not last very long, since any one player had only paid a quarter, and if the game only earned a single quarter in a half hour, it would not be profitable to operate.[4]

Players were impressed primarily by the technology. As video games grew in popularity, however, players began to expect a higher level of innovation from their gaming experiences. A game with the newest sound chip or the most realistic effects would not succeed over a less advanced game if the newer game lacked compelling gameplay. By the mid-1980s, home consoles and personal computers had brought video games out of the arcade and into the living room, and with this transition the emphasis of the games shifted. Rather than designing games primarily to catch a player's eye and ear, developers began to use sound to expand the scope of their games' narratives. Whereas arcade games were intended to be played repeatedly for an average of 2.5 minutes per quarter, home console and computer games could take hours, days, or months for the player to fully experience once.[5] As the storytelling aspect of games became more integral to the player's experience, the musical accompaniment became more closely entwined with the story; the composers aspired to make music an essential part of the game, rather than something extra or unnecessary.[6]

Two home gaming platforms in particular were at the heart of game sound development in the 1980s: the Commodore 64 and the NES. The Commodore 64 computer contained a dedicated SID (sound interface device) chip, designed by engineer Robert Yannes. The SID chip could produce three channels of sound with four available waveforms and multiple filters.[7] Compared with the other 8-bit consoles (such as the Atari 2600 and 5200, the Colecovision, and the Intellivision) and home computers (such as the Atari 800, Apple II and ZX Spectrum) available at the time, its sound capabilities were unmatched. Both the Commodore 64 and its successor, the Amiga (one of the first computers that utilized sampled sounds instead of standard waveforms), remain popular today as a platform for chiptune and demoscene composers. (Composers of chiptune and demoscene music practice the art of game music *in vitro,* with no particular commercial endeavor, writing instead to show off their skill and to pay tribute to the games of the past. Using programs that emulate the sound quality of old consoles and computers, they produce original works and covers that are at once both nostalgic and futuristic.)[8]

When the NES was first released in the United States in 1985, its five-channel sound system was unprecedented in home consoles, and its cartridges (up to 512 kilobytes in capacity, more if memory management chips were used) allowed more space to be devoted to sound. The success of the system's flagship game, *Super Mario Bros.*, ushered in a new era of video game sound, thanks in no small part to the game's composer, Koji Kondo. Kondo's innovative sound design, both laid-back and energized at the same time, was unique in the extent of its adaptation to the gameplay; it followed the player's movement through the game's environments (becoming low and percussive in an underground area or light and bubbly when underwater) and reflected changes in the player's status (increasing in tempo when the player's time was about to run out or playing a special melody while an invincibility power-up was in effect), making it a precursor to the adaptive soundtracks of later games such as LucasArts's *Star Wars: X-Wing* (1993) and Nintendo's *The Legend of Zelda: Ocarina of Time* (1998).[9] Kondo, along with fellow composer Hirokazu "Hip" Tanaka [composer for Nintendo games *Metroid* (1987), *Dr. Mario* (1990), and *Earthbound* (1994)], provided the music for the earliest iterations of some of Nintendo's most popular franchises.[10]

With the arrival of *Super Mario Bros.* and games like it, the compositional complexity of video game music grew considerably, even if the sounds themselves were still relatively primitive. In 1986, Sega released the Master System, with sound capabilities comparable to the NES; however, it was not until the release of the Sega Genesis (1989), Super Nintendo (1991), and other 16-bit consoles that game sound design truly began to resemble what it is today. With six sound channels in the Genesis and eight in the SNES, game soundtracks had the potential to have twice the texture and depth of their predecessors. Waveform synthesis was replaced by FM (frequency modulated) and wavetable (sample) synthesis, both of which sounded more realistic and could be tweaked easily by a composer for volume and effects (such as vibrato, reverb, panning, and fade). With larger memory capacities (SNES cartridges had from 0.25 to 6 megabytes of space), games could be of much greater length; they became more cinematic in their presentation, and they began to have soundtracks that changed to reflect the mood of the story. A well-known example of this trend is Square's *Final Fantasy 3* (1994), whose composer, Nobuo Uematsu, was one of the first game sound designers to achieve international recognition for his work.[11] In *Final Fantasy 3*, each hero and villain in the game had his or her own musical leitmotif, which played whenever that character became the focus of the story. The musical accompaniment was a form of wordless narration, giving insight on the game's characters and events in a way that text alone could not.

At the same time as console game sound was evolving, home computer games were also undergoing a major transformation. Prior to the advent of compact discs in the mid-1990s, game sound designers pioneered the widespread use of the versatile MIDI format. MIDI (musical instrument digital interface), proposed as a protocol in 1981 by engineer David Smith, published as a standard in 1983, and standardized as "General MIDI" in 1991 by the MIDI Manufacturers Association, was inspired by electronic musicians' interest in linking together banks of synthesizers to simplify the logistics of live performances.[12] MIDI files were relatively high quality compared to consoles of the time (boasting a sound bank of 128 possible "instruments" playing in up to 16 separate channels) but still compact enough to meet the size restrictions of 3.5-inch floppy disks (1.44 megabytes apiece). The release of Roland's General MIDI-compliant sound card Sound Canvas in 1991 allowed game composers to embrace MIDI as a viable format.[13] Since MIDI files only contained instructions for what notes were to be played, rather than the actual synthesized instruments themselves, and their size was a fraction of what it would be in other formats, such as WAV or AIFF files. MIDI's strength was its universality, since the files could be read by any computer with MIDI capability, a feature which became ubiquitous in computers of the early 1990s and which has since remained so. This strength, however, has also proven to be a liability; since a MIDI file depends on the computer's sound card to perform the sound synthesis, the music quality of a MIDI soundtrack will vary from computer to computer according to the sound card installed, sometimes drastically so. According to Aaron Marks, "Internal instruments gradually became better as sound card manufacturers included high-grade synthesizer chips, but because this quality differed greatly between manufacturers, what sounded good on one card sounded like a train wreck on another."[14] Despite this drawback, MIDI remains in use as a compositional format because of its versatility; a piece of music is often composed with a MIDI sequencer or keyboard, and then translated to a more sophisticated file format using a sample library.[15]

As data storage technology progressed beyond floppy disks, the technology of home computers and consoles began to merge. The CD-ROM format, first used in 1985, became the vehicle of choice for computer games of the mid-1990s.[16] In the field of home consoles, the Sega CD (1992), Panasonic 3DO (1993), Atari Jaguar (1993), Sega Saturn (1995), and Sony PlayStation (1995) all stored their games on CD-ROMs, allowing them to utilize Red Book digital audio, the format of a standard music CD. (The Red Book format, first released in 1980 by Philips and Sony, has a sample rate of 44.1 kHz, compared to the SNES's 32 kHz, or the 28 kHz of the NES's pulse waves.) Both the PlayStation and Nintendo 64 (1996) could produce up to 24 sound channels. The Nintendo 64 was cartridge based, which meant less storage space (4–64 megabytes) compared to the PlayStation's CDs (650–700 megabytes). In 1998 Konami released the arcade game *Dance Dance Revolution,* notable for its incorporation of music and rhythm-based dancing into its gameplay mechanic. With the increased capacity of CDs and DVDs, it was perhaps inevitable that the next generation of consoles would all feature disc-based games. Sega's Dreamcast (1999), Sony's PlayStation 2 (2000), Nintendo's GameCube (2001), and Microsoft's Xbox (2001) were the new faces of gaming at the start of the twenty-first century, each with channel and sound bank capabilities many times greater than those of the 1980s consoles. In 2000, the National Academy of Arts and Sciences allowed video game soundtracks to compete for Grammy awards; as of 2007 no game has yet won an award. With the release of the next generation of consoles in 2005 and beyond, and the implementation in games of user-designated soundtracks [such as in EA's *The Sims 2* (2004) and Rockstar's *Grand Theft Auto: San Andreas*], the line between what is and what is not game music has been all but erased.

Music and Narrative—Adaptive Audio

Most games released today contain a mixture of diegetic and nondiegetic sound; the character of a game's sound can vary widely between the two extremes throughout the course of its narrative. This difference can be seen in comparing an earlier game like Williams's *Defender,* with its cacophony of laser blasts and explosions, and one like Square's *Chrono Trigger* (1995), which features a persistent soundtrack that abstractly reflects both the game's various locales throughout time and space and the emotional arc of the story. Almost all modern games have some degree of nondiegetic sound, just as most modern films have some kind of musical score, though diegetic sound still plays a large role, both as short sound effects (gunfire, character voices) and as prolonged, ambient ones (wind in the trees, a roaring fire). In Valve's *Half-Life 2,* for example, diegetic sound makes up nearly the entire soundtrack, except for short musical cues when the player reaches a new area. The designers chose to forego the traditional use of cut-scenes, instead telling the story in-game through character dialogue and events that unfold with no significant pause in the action. The game's sound design reflects this choice, heightening the immersion with ambient sound that matches the game's dystopian battlefields.

The process of sound design for a video game can vary greatly from game to game, depending on what kind of game is being made, but it typically follows the course of game design process as a whole. A composer or sound design team is hired or assigned, based on the needs of the game and the resources available. As the cost of making games has grown in size, the budgets for game sound design have also increased proportionately, with some games incorporating soundtracks performed by classical ensembles and popular recording artists. However, the majority of game sound design is still done by small in-house teams or by freelance composers, and most games' music features synthesized instruments rather than real ones, for reasons of storage space and budget. After meeting with the rest of the design team, which can include artists, programmers and writers, the sound designer learns what is expected for the game and begins composing. Depending on the game's complexity, the sound design required can be no more than a handful of sound effects, or it can be several hours of fully orchestrated soundtrack. There may be a team of foley artists, composers, voice actors, and musicians, or one designer may perform all these roles himself. Whatever the scope of his work, the sound designer attempts to match the vision of the programmers while adhering to strict deadlines and hardware constraints. Throughout the process, the sound designer remains in constant contact with the rest of the design team to stay apprised of any changes. As in film scoring, video game sound designers are often tasked with doing a great deal of work near the end of a project's timeline, after most or all of the game's visuals have been finalized; last-minute alterations to the game can necessitate the reworking or rewriting of its soundtrack. No single aspect of a game can necessarily ensure its success, but high-quality sound design is fast becoming essential for any video game that hopes to do well, regardless of genre, system, or audience.[17]

Though film and game music share certain similarities, there is still a vital difference between them: interactivity. Films are viewed passively, and thus their scores must be passive. Video games are played interactively, and thus have the potential for interactive music. A game's story cannot progress without the player's input, and for that reason a game's music is inevitably tied to the player's actions. Game music must match the style of play: if a game allows a player a great deal of freedom to act and explore, the game's music must be able to keep pace with whatever use of that freedom the player makes. Fully interactive music (or adaptive music) has long been the goal of many designers in the games industry, and while some games have achieved various levels of success, the question of how to respond to and even anticipate a player's actions still remains. As author Alexander Brandon explains,

> Interactive music is audio that happens when a user does pretty much anything with any kind of device, whether it be to click a mouse or hit a key. Adaptive music refers to something that happens…when the user influences the audio, and the audio influences the user.[18]

The issue becomes increasingly complicated in light of the open-ended format of more recent games, sometimes referred to as sandbox games (the term "sandbox" is used to mean a playing environment that encourages experimentation and creativity, sometimes to the exclusion of any set narrative). The somewhat rigid nature of Red Book audio (i.e., the tempo and pitch cannot be modulated, only one track can be played at a time, etc.) makes its use in adaptive music problematic. Simpler, more modular sound file formats, such as MIDI, are better suited to the task, a fact capitalized on by LucasArts in the 1990s with their development of the iMUSE system, which permitted smooth transitions between pieces of looped music in several of their games.[19] Microsoft's Direct-Music interface (introduced in 1999 and still widely used today) allows composers to pair MIDI with more advanced sound formats.

Most games feature some level of adaptation in their music; often, it is no more compli-cated than changing melodies whenever the player reaches a new level or location, or when the player's status in the game changes. Even the "game over" music that accompanies player death or defeat in any given game can be said to be adaptive, since it is the player's action or inaction that causes it. The style of game often dictates how much adaptivity a game's soundtrack can employ. Role-playing games, for example, focus more closely on character development than any other genre; they have the most potential for an extensive story and, therefore, an extensive soundtrack. However, since RPGs are the most narrative-dependent genre of games, their interactivity potential is thereby limited; most of them do not allow significant deviation from the preprogrammed storyline and the music that accompanies it. Thus, though the soundtrack of an RPG can be beautifully written (and often is); at its heart it is most like film music. First-person shooters have a high potential for adaptive music, since the player's environment has a high interaction potential; enemies appear suddenly, passageways open and close, and the player is con-stantly updating his playing style, moving slowly through the shadows when avoiding ene-mies, and then charging out with guns blazing to take them by surprise. A truly adaptive soundtrack would tailor itself closely to the player's style while still providing atmosphere and audio cues; for example, the appearance of an enemy would cause an "enemy theme" to play for both a cautious player and an aggressive player, but the cautious player would hear the theme played in a different style than the aggressive player—in a minor key, for example, as opposed to a major one, or with slurred notes rather than sharply articulated ones.[20] As games become more complicated and allow for even greater levels of player freedom, game music will have to adapt to an ever-increasing number of scenarios and narrative moods. Most video games are still primarily combat-oriented, but as game technology begins to allow for player interaction that goes deeper than pure antagonism, the need for effectively nuanced game sound design is greater than ever. As video games continue to evolve in scope and detail, their music must necessarily evolve with them.

The importance of music in games has become increasingly apparent since its inception in 1972, both to game players and game developers. Game sound design has progressed to the point where the music is no longer considered secondary to graphics or gameplay, but rather part of a dynamic whole that succeeds or fails as a single unit. The works of celebrated sound designers and composers have been elevated in status to the point where today gamers and non-gamers alike listen to game music entirely separated from the games that contained them, on soundtrack CDs and at live performances in concert halls.[21] In 2005, companies EA and Square-Enix began offering music from their games through the online music service iTunes. Video game music ringtones for cell phones have also grown in popularity (on May 6, 2006, the ringtone "Super Mario Bros. Theme" was No. 2 on *Billboard*'s "Top 10 Ringtones" after 80 weeks on the list.).[22] The May 19, 2005, *Business Week Online* article, "From Beeps to *Billboard*" puts the phenomenon into perspective:

> The soundtrack for *Halo 2,* a game in which a genetically enhanced supersoldier battles evil, has sold more than 90,000 copies since its release last November. Peaking at No. 162, it marked game music's first entry into the Billboard 200 chart. (A typical movie soundtrack, on the other hand, sells only 10,000 copies and never comes even close to the chart.).[23]

Game sound has grown from the looped beeps of its beginnings to fully realized digital audio that rivals the output of the traditional music industry in fidelity and originality—well on its way to being recognized as a true genre of music in its own right.

CHAPTER 38

VIDEO GAME GENRES

Mark J. P. Wolf

The idea of categorization by genre, and the notion that there are certain conventions present in each genre, has been used in the studies of literature and film and has proven to be a useful way of looking at both. The idea of genre has not been without difficulties, such as the defining of what exactly constitutes a genre (or a subgenre), overlaps between genres and hybrids of them, works occurring in multiple genres simultaneously (and thus what the criteria are for genre membership), the role of the audience's experience in determining genre, and the fact that the boundaries of genres and even genres themselves are always changing as long as new works are being produced.

Video game genre study differs from literary or film genre study due to the direct and active (in a physical as well as mental sense) participation of the audience. In some ways, player participation is arguably the central element used in describing and classifying video games, moreso even than iconography. From the earliest times when video games were classified into genres, first by the companies that made and marketed them and game reviewers, and later in works like Chris Crawford's 1982 *The Art of Computer Game Design,* the player's experience and the activities required for gameplay (commonly referred to as "interactivity") have largely provided the basis for video game genre delineation.[1]

Imagery Versus Interactivity

Just as different forms of dance (foxtrot, waltz, ballet, jazz) are defined by how the dancers move rather than how they look, it is the forms of interactivity, rather than imagery, which we must use when classifying video games. While some video games can be classified in a manner similar to that of films (we might say that *Outlaw* is a Western, *Space Invaders* is science fiction, and *Combat* is a war game), classification by imagery ignores the fundamental differences and similarities which are to be found in the player's experience of the game. *Outlaw* and *Combat,* both early games for the Atari 2600, are very similar in that both simply feature player-characters maneuvering and shooting at each other in a field of obstacles on a single, bounded screen of graphics, with cowboys in one game and tanks in the other. In a similar vein, Activision's *Chopper Command* for the

Atari 2600 is essentially a version of *Defender* with helicopters replacing the spaceships. Conversely, an analysis of the content of *Space Invaders, Spaceward Ho!, Defender,* and *Star Wars,* as well as many other games, would consider them all "science fiction" even though they vary widely in player experience. As narrative games grow more complex and cinematic, image-based and thematic generic classifications from film will be able to be applied more usefully, but interactivity will always be an important factor in the way the games are experienced.

The kind of interactivity present in a game will depend on the game's main objective. In a video game, there is almost always a definite objective that the player strives to complete (or find and complete, as in the case of *Myst*), and in doing so very specific interactions are used. Thus the intention, of the player-character at least, is often clear and can be analyzed as a part of the game. The game's objective is a motivational force for the player, and this, combined with the various forms of interactivity present in the game, are useful places to start in building a set of video game genres. The object of the game can be multiple or divided into steps, placing the game in more than one genre, just as films can be placed in multiple genres (the film *Blade Runner,* for example, fits both science fiction and hardboiled detective genres). The main objective in *Pac-Man* by which a player gains points and advances levels, for example, is the eating of the yellow dots. In order to do so successfully, the player-character must avoid the pursuing ghosts, and also navigate a maze. Thus while *Pac-Man* may be primarily classified as a "Collecting" game, we may also classify it as an "Escape" or "Maze" game, albeit secondarily. By beginning with the interaction required by the game's primary objective, we can start to divide the wide variety of video games into a series of interactive genres.

Interactive Genres for Classifying Video Games

The following list of genres based on interactivity take into consideration the dominant characteristics of the interactive experience and the games' goals and objectives, and the nature of the game's player-character and player controls. Also, certain genres listed here (Diagnostic, Demo, Educational, Puzzle, Simulation, and Utility) contain programs which are arguably not "games," but since they appear as cartridges or discs in a form similar to game cartridges and discs (and are treated as such by many game collectors), and because they sometimes contain gamelike elements (such as *Mario Teaches Typing*), they have been included here for the sake of completeness. As genres grow and expand, they inevitably begin to break up into a series of subgenres (for example, the Shooting genre could include subgenres like the First-Person Shooter, Third-Person Shooter, Side-Scrolling Shooter, Vertical Shooter, and so on). A list of all the subgenres contained in each genre, however, is beyond the scope of this chapter, and would more than double its length.

In the culture surrounding the video game, certain generic terms are already established and in use among players, and these terms and distinctions are reflected in the proposed list of terms below. Some of these genres overlap commonly used genres of moving imagery (such as Adaptation, Adventure, Chase), while others, such as Escape, Maze, or Shooting, are specific to video games and reflect the interactive nature of the medium. These genre terms regard the nature of interactivity in the game itself rather than ask whether the game is single-player, multiple-player, or designed to be playable over a network. Due to the different types of action and objectives that can occur in a single game, games can often be cross-listed in two or more genres. Also, some games, like *M*A*S*H* or *Rebel Assault,* feature different sequences or scenarios each of which can be categorized into different genres. Video games used as examples here include arcade video games, home video games, home computer games, and in a few cases, networked games. The format of this list is patterned after the Library of Congress *Moving Imagery Genre-Form Guide* compiled by Brian Taves (chair), Judi Hoffman, and Karen Lund, whose work was the inspiration and model for this list. The decision was made to use their list as a model not only because it was rigorous enough to be accepted and used at the Library of Congress, but also due to the way in which it attempts to articulate the genres it describes by examining the differences that demarcate individual genres relative to one another, seeking to divide the field of moving imagery forms in such a way so as to be as inclusive and exhaustive as possible, rather than setting up finite and absolute criteria for genre membership. Thus the following genres below tend towards inclusion, with some genres (i.e., Demo, Diagnostic, Utility) which are arguably not "games" as noted above.

Genres covered in the following list Abstract, Adaptation, Adventure, Artificial Life, Ball-and-Paddle, Board Games, Capturing, Card Games, Catching, Chase, Collecting, Combat, Demo, Diagnostic, Dodging, Driving, Educational, Escape, Fighting, Flying, Gambling, Interactive Movie, Management Simulation, Maze, Obstacle Course, Pencil-and-Paper Games, Pinball, Platform, Programming Games, Puzzle, Quiz, Racing, Rhythm and Dance, Role-Playing, Shooting, Simulation, Sports, Strategy, Table-Top Games, Target, Text Adventure, Training Simulation, and Utility.

Abstract

Games which have nonrepresentational graphics and often involve an objective which is not oriented or organized as a narrative. Often the objective involves construction or visiting or filling every part of the screen (as in *Tetris, Qix, Pipe Dream,* or *Q*bert*), or destruction or emptying of the screen (as in *Breakout* or *Pac-Man*). Characters appearing in abstract games may even resemble people or animals but usually do not attempt to represent real world animals or people or their behaviors. Abstraction is, of course, a matter of degree, though it is usually possible to discern whether or not the game was intended to be deliberately representational. For example, despite their simple, blocky graphics, early Atari 2600 games such as *Basketball* or *Street Racer* attempt to represent people and race cars, which is reflected not only in their design but in their interaction within the game. Nor should the term be used for games which are adaptations of games existing in different media, such as *Checkers* or *Othello,* which are abstract in design and play, but which are nonetheless adaptations and thus representations of games from other media.

EXAMPLES: *Arkanoid; Amidar* (with Collecting); *Ataxx; Block Out* (with Puzzle); *Breakout; Marble Madness; Pac-Man* (with Collecting, Escape, and Maze); *Pipe Dream; Q*bert; Qix* (with Collecting); *Super Breakout; Tempest* (with Shooting); *Tetris* (with Puzzle).

Adaptation

Games based on activities adapted from another medium or gaming activity, such as sports, table-top games, board games, card games, or games whose action closely follows a narrative from a work existing in another medium, such as a book, short story, comic book, graphic novel, or play. This involves such questions as how the original work is changed to allow for interactivity and the completion of an objective, or in the case of adapted games, how the original activity changes as a result of being adapted. This term should not be used for games which use the same characters as existing works in another medium but make no attempt to even loosely follow plots or imitate activities found in those works. Home video games and computer games may also be adaptations of arcade video games, in which case they are usually reduced in graphic detail, complexity, or speed when compared with the original. In a few cases, arcade games, such as *Computer Space,* are adaptations of mainframe computer games. This term should only be applied to Simulation games when they are adapted from games or gaming activities in other media.

NOTE: See Sports, Table-top Games, Board Games, Card Games, Pencil-and-Paper Games, and Simulation.

EXAMPLES: Adapted from card games: *Casino; Eric's Ultimate Solitaire; Ken Uston Blackjack/Poker.* Adapted from cartoons: *Spy Vs Spy; The Simpsons.* Adapted from comic books: *Spiderman, X-MEN, Teenage Mutant Ninja Turtles.* Adapted from film: *Tron; Star Wars; Krull; Muppet Treasure Island.* Adapted from pencil-and-paper games: *Hangman; Tic-Tac-Toe.* Adapted from sports: *American Football; Atari Baseball; Hot Shots Tennis.* Adapted from table-top games: *PONG; Sure Shot Pool; Virtual Pool.* Adapted from television game shows: *Family Feud; Jeopardy; Joker's Wild; Password; The Price is Right; Tic-Tac-Dough; $25,000 Pyramid; Wheel of Fortune.*

Adventure

Games which are set in a "world" usually made up of multiple, connected rooms or screens, involving an objective which is more complex than simply catching, shooting, capturing, or escaping, although completion of the objective may involve several or all of these. Objectives usually must be completed in several steps, for example, finding keys and unlocking doors to other areas to retrieve objects needed elsewhere in the game. Characters are usually able to carry objects, such as weapons, keys, tools, and so on. Settings often evoke a particular historical time period and place, such as the middle ages or Arthurian England, or are thematically related to content-based genres such as Science Fiction, Fantasy, or Espionage. This term should not be used for games in which screens are only encountered in one-way linear fashion, like the "levels" in *Donkey Kong,* or for games like *Pitfall!* which are essentially limited to running, jumping, and avoiding dangers (see Obstacle Course). Nor should the term be used to refer to games like *Dragon's Lair, Gadget,* or *Star Trek: Borg,* which do not allow a player to wander and explore the game's "world" freely, but strictly limit outcomes and possible narrative paths to a series of video sequences and linear progression through a predetermined narrative (see Interactive Movies).

NOTE: For adventure games which are primarily text based, see Text Adventure. For related games similar in theme to adventure games, see also Obstacle Course and Interactive Movies.

EXAMPLES: *Adventure* (for the Atari 2600); *E.T.: The Extraterrestrial* (with Adaptation); *Haunted House, Krull* (with Adaptation); *Myst* (with Puzzle); *Raiders of the Lost Ark* (with Adaptation); *Spy Vs Spy* (with Adaptation); *Superman* (with Adaptation); games in the *Tomb Raider* series; *Venture*; games from the *Daggerfall* series; games from the*Ultima* series.

Artificial Life

Games which involve the growth and/or maintenance of digital creatures of some sort, which can "die" without the proper care by the player. Often growth and the "happiness" or "contentedness" of the characters are the goals of the game. (Whether or not all such programs constitute "games" is debatable.) The term should not be used for games which deal with the allocation of resources or games which are primarily concerned with management (see Management Simulation).

EXAMPLES: *AquaZone; Babyz; Catz; Creatures; Dogz; The Little Computer People; The Sims* (with Management Simulation).

Ball-and-Paddle

See Table-top Games.

Board Games

Games which are an adaptation of existing board games (see Adaptation) or games which are similar to board games in their design and play even if they did not previously exist as board games. Games of this genre include either classic board games like Chess, Checkers, or Backgammon, or trademarked ones such as *Scrabble* or *Monopoly*. This term should not be used for games adapted from games such as pool or table tennis, in which physical skills are involved (see Table-top Games), nor for games adapted from games which require only paper and a pencil to play, such as *Hangman* or *Tic-Tac-Toe* (see Pencil-and-Paper Games), nor for games adapted from games which are primarily card based and do not use a board (see Card Games). Three games made by Philips/Magnavox, *Conquest of the World, Quest for the Rings,* and *The Great Wall Street Fortune Hunt,* required a board game to be used along with the video game itself.

NOTE: Not necessary to cross-list with Adaptation as this is implied in Board Games. Most Board Games can also be cross-listed with Strategy.

EXAMPLES: *Backgammon; Battleship; Clue; Conquest of the World; The Great Wall Street Fortune Hunt; Monopoly; Othello; Quest for the Rings; Scrabble; Stratego; Video Checkers; Video Chess.*

Capturing

Games in which the primary objective involves the capturing of objects or characters that move away from and try to evade the player-character. This may involve stopping the object or character (as in *Gopher* or *Keystone Kapers*), or closing off their access to an escape route (as in *Surround* or in the light cycle section of the arcade game *Tron*). This term should not be used for games in which objects or characters do not move (see Collecting) or do not actively try to avoid the player-character (see Catching), nor should it be used for Strategy games (such as Chess and Checkers) involving the capturing of pieces which are controlled by the player, but which are not player-characters directly representing the player in the game.

NOTE: Not necessary to cross-list with Chase as this is implied in Capturing. Many games with more than one player can be cross-listed with Escape, as game play often involves player-characters alternately trying to capture one another and escape from one another. Capturing objectives also occur briefly in some games; for example, in *Pac-Man* after eating a power pill when the ghosts can be chased and eaten, or the capturing of criminals in *Superman*.

EXAMPLES: *Gopher; Hole Hunter; Keystone Kapers; Surround* (with Escape); *Take the Money and Run; Texas Chainsaw Massacre;* the light cycle game in *Tron*.

Card Games

Games which are adaptations of existing card games, or games which are essentially like card games in that they are primarily card-based (such as various solitaire computer games). While most Card Games use the standard four-suit deck, some games use specialized cards (such as *1000 Miles,* a shareware game which is an adaptation of Parker Brothers's *Milles Bornes* racing card game). This term should not be used for Trivia Games which are primarily question-and-answer games.

NOTE: Not necessary to cross-list with Adaptation, as that is implied in Card Games. Many card games which involve betting can also be cross-listed with Gambling.

EXAMPLES: *1000 Miles* (with Racing); *Blackjack* (with Gambling); *Casino* (with Gambling); *Eric's Ultimate Solitaire; Ken Uston Blackjack/Poker* (with Gambling); *Montana; Video Poker* (with Gambling).

Catching

Games in which the primary objective involves the catching of objects or characters that do not actively try to evade the player-character. If the objects or characters are in motion, it is usually along a predetermined path and independent of the movements of the player-character. In some cases the player-character can affect the motion of the objects or characters (such as in *Stampede,* where the player-character can nudge the cattle forward), but at no time do the objects or characters try to actively avoid the player-character. This term should not be used for games in which objects or characters do not move (see Collecting) or games in which they actively try to avoid the player-character (see Capturing). Nor should the term be used for games that require timing in order to use moving objects, such as the moving logs in *Frogger,* or the swinging vines in *Pitfall!,* nor for Sports games with balls which are thrown, bounced, or caught, as these objects are used and reused but not "caught" and removed from the game.

EXAMPLES: *Alpha Beam with Ernie* (with Educational); *Big Bird's Egg Catch; Circus Atari, Fishing Derby; Lost Luggage; Stampede; Quantum;* and games 21 through 27 in *Street Racer.*

Chase

See Catching, Capturing, Driving, Escape, Flying, and Racing.

Collecting

Games in which the primary objective involves the collecting of objects that do not move (such as *Pac-Man* or *Mousetrap*), or the surrounding of areas (such as *Qix* or *Amidar*). Often scoring in these games is determined by the number of objects collected or areas bounded. "Collecting" here can mean simply running over or hitting objects which then disappear (as the dots in *Pac-Man* or the balloons in *Prop Cycle*). This term should not be used for games in which objects or characters sought by the player-character are in motion (see Catching) or games in which they actively try to avoid the player-character (see Capturing). Nor should the term be used for games that require the use of objects (such as keys, currency, or weaponry) which are only indirectly used in the attainment of the game's objective. Some games involve the collecting of pieces of an object which can be assembled once all the pieces are found, such as the bridge in *Superman* or the urn in *Haunted House,* although these games often have objectives that involve more than simply collecting and so should not be considered as belonging to this genre.

EXAMPLES: *Amidar* (with Abstract); *Mousetrap* (with Maze and Escape); *Pac-Man* (with Maze and Escape); *Spy Vs Spy* (with Combat and Maze); *Prop Cycle* (with Flying); *Qix* (with Abstract).

Combat

Games which involve two or more players, or one player and a computer-controlled player, shooting some form of projectiles at each other, and in which all players are provided with similar means for a fairly balanced fight. These games usually emphasize maneuverability and sometimes the outwitting of the opponent. This term should not be used for Shooting games in which the two sides are clearly unequal or not evenly balanced, nor for Fighting games which do not involve shooting. Although these games may range in the appearance of their content, for example, cowboys in *Outlaw,* tanks or planes in *Combat,* or paddles in *Warlords,* the basic play of the game, shoot the opponent while avoiding getting shot, remains essentially the same.

NOTE: For related games, see Fighting and Shooting.

EXAMPLES: *Battletech; Battlezone; Combat; Dactyl Nightmare; Outlaw; Spy Vs Spy* (with Collecting and Maze); *Warlords.*

Demo

Cartridges, discs, or downloads designed to demonstrate games or a game system. Such cartridges were primarily used in store displays to demonstrate games. While they may not contain complete games themselves, these cartridges have the same appearance as game cartridges and are sometimes collected and traded as game cartridges, and they are often included in listings of cartridges. As discs or downloads, Demos allow a player to try out a game for free without buying the full-sized game.

NOTE: Not necessary to cross-list with Utility, as that is implied in Demo.

EXAMPLES: *Adam Demo Cartridge, Dealer Demo* (Bally Astrocade), *Demonstration Cartridge* (RCA Studio II), *Music Box Demo* (Coleco Adam).

Diagnostic

Cartridges designed to test the functioning of a system. While they are not games themselves, these cartridges have the same appearance as game cartridges and are sometimes collected and traded as game cartridges, and they are often included in listings of cartridges.

NOTE: Not necessary to cross-list with Utility, as that is implied in Diagnostic.

EXAMPLES: *Diagnostic Cartridge* (Identification No. FDS100144) for the Atari 5200 system; *Diagnostic Cartridge* (Identification No. CB101196) for the Atari 7800 system, *Final Test Cartridge* (Coleco Adam), *Super Controller Test Cartridge* (Coleco Adam).

Dodging

Games in which the primary objective is to avoid projectiles or other moving objects. Scoring is often determined by the number of objects successfully dodged, or by the crossing of a field of moving objects that must be dodged (as in *Freeway* or *Frogger*). This term should not be used for games in which players avoid getting shot at and are able to shoot (see Combat and Shooting). In many games like *Asteroids* or *Space Invaders* avoidance of objects or projectiles is important for the player to remain in the game, but points are not awarded for merely avoiding them, and players usually have the option of shooting at obstacles, which is not the case in Dodging games.

EXAMPLES: *Dodge 'Em* (with Driving), *Freeway* (with Obstacle Course); *Frogger* (with Obstacle Course); *Journey Escape;* and some games in *Street Racer* (with Driving and Racing).

Driving

Games based primarily on driving skills, such as steering, maneuverability, speed control, and fuel conservation. This term should not be used for games in which racing or the winning of a race is the main objective (see Racing), nor for games which are essentially obstacle courses in which a player's main objective is to hit or avoid touching a series of objects or characters (see Obstacle Course), unless driving skills are essential to play and to the winning of the game. In most cases, Driving games involve vehicles, whereas Obstacle Course games generally do not. Scoring in Driving games is often based on how fast a particular course is completed, rather than whether or not an opponent is beat in a race, and these games are often single-player games.

EXAMPLES: *Dodge 'Em* (with Dodging); *Indy 500* (with Racing); *Night Driver; Pole Position* (with Racing); *Red Planet* (with Racing); *Street Racer* (with Dodging and Racing).

Educational

Games which are designed to teach and in which the main objective involves the learning of a lesson. Rather than being structured as a straightforward set of lessons or exercises, these programs are structured like games, with such elements as scoring, timed performances, or incentives given for correct answers. The degree to which these programs can be considered games varies greatly.

NOTE: Not necessary to cross-list with Utility, as this is implied in Educational.

EXAMPLES: *Alpha Beam with Ernie* (with Catching); *Basic Math; Mario's Early Years: Fun With Numbers; Mario Teaches Typing; Math Blaster: Episode 1; Math Grand Prix; Morse; Number Games; Playschool Math; Spelling Games; Word Games.*

Escape

Games whose main objective involves escaping pursuers or getting out of some form of enclosure. Games can be open-ended, with the game ending when a player escapes from an enclosure or enters a place safe from the pursuers, or closed, in which a player escapes pursuers for as long as possible but always succumbs in the end (as in *Pac-Man*). This term should not be used for games in which the player-character battles the opponent instead of fleeing (see Combat and Shooting), nor for games like *Adventure* or *Haunted House* in which the player-character is only occasionally pursued by characters.

EXAMPLES: *Pac-Man* (with Collecting and Maze); *Maze Craze* (with Maze); *Mousetrap* (with Collecting and Maze); *Ms. Pac-Man* (with Collecting and Maze); *Surround* (with Capturing).

Fighting

Games involving characters who fight usually hand-to-hand, in one-to-one combat situations without the use of firearms or projectiles. In most of these games, the fighters are represented as humans or anthropomorphic characters. This term should not be used for games which involve shooting or vehicles (see Combat and Shooting), or for games which include fighting, like *Ice Hockey*, but which have other objectives (see Sports).

NOTE: Many Fighting games can be cross-listed with Sports. For related games, see also Combat.

EXAMPLES: *Avengers; Body Slam; Boxing* (with Sports); games in the *Mortal Kombat* series; *Soul Edge;* games in the *Tekken* series; *Wrestle War.*

Flying

Games involving flying skills, such as steering, altitude control, takeoff and landing, maneuverability, speed control, and fuel conservation. This term should not be used for games in which shooting an opponent is the main objective (see Combat and Shooting), unless flying skills are essential to game play and to the winning of the game. Flying games can involve airplanes, birds, or spaceships, and movement can take place in the sky (as in *A-10 Attack* and *Prop Cycle*), through caverns (as in *Descent*), or in outer space (as in *Starmaster* and *Star Ship*).

NOTE: See also Combat, Shooting, Sports, and Training Simulation.

EXAMPLES: *A-10 Attack* (with Training Simulation); *Descent* (with Maze and Shooting); *F/A-18 Hornet 3.0* (with Training Simulation); *Flight Unlimited* (with Training Simulation); *Prop Cycle* (with Collecting); *Solaris; Starmaster* (with Shooting).

Gambling

Games which involve the betting of a stake, which increases or decreases the player's total assets in the following round. These games usually involve multiple rounds of betting, allowing a player's stakes or money to grow or diminish over time. This term should not be used for games in which betting does not occur, or for games in which wins and losses do not carry over into the following round.

NOTE: See also Card Games and Table-top Games.

EXAMPLES: *Blackjack* (with Card Games); *Casino* (with Card Games); *Slot Machine; Video Poker* (with Card Games); *You Don't Know Jack* (with Quiz).

Interactive Movie

Games which are made up of branching video clips or other moving images, the branching of which is decided by a player's actions. Players are often called to make decisions at points in the game where the action stalls or loops, or during action sequences that allow player input which can stop or change the course of action while the video clip is running. While the player may be given limited freedom of movement or action, revelation of the story is still largely linear in structure, with little or no variation possible in its overall sequence of events. This term should not be used for games which place a controllable player-character over backgrounds which are video clips, like *Rebel Assault,* nor should the term be used to refer to games like *Myst* which allow a player to wander and explore its "world" freely, but still limit outcomes and possible narrative paths to a series of video sequences and linear progression through a relatively predetermined narrative.

EXAMPLES: *Dragon's Lair; Space Ace; Gadget; Johnny Mnemonic; Star Trek: Borg.*

Management Simulation

Games in which players must balance the use of limited resources to build or expand some kind of community, institution, or empire, while dealing with internal forces within (such as the crime and pollution in *SimCity*) or external forces such as those of nature or chance (such as natural disasters and monsters in *SimCity*, or planets that require various amounts of terraforming as in *Spaceward Ho!*) and often competition from other players as well. Single-player games are often open-ended, where the community or institution grows and is developed over time and continues changing, while multiple-player games usually have the objective of dominating all of the other players, at which point the game ends. In some cases, these games can take on an educational function as well, for example, games found in museum displays which simulate supply and demand or other economic principles.

NOTE: See also Educational and Utility.

EXAMPLES: *Aerobiz; Caesar II; Sid Meier's Civilization; M.U.L.E.; Monopoly; Railroad Tycoon; SimAnt; SimCity; SimFarm; SimTower; Spaceward Ho!*

Maze

Games in which the objective requires the successful navigation of a maze. What can be called a maze is, of course, a matter of degree, though it is usually possible to discern whether a configuration of rooms or hallways was intended to deliberately cause difficulties in navigation (consider, for example, the difference in complexity between the mazes found in *Berzerk, Pac-Man,* and *Doom*). Mazes may appear in an overhead view (as in *Pac-Man*), a side view (as in *Lode Runner*), or first-person perspective (as in *Doom*) or hidden from view (as in certain games in *Maze Craze*). In some cases, the player-character can alter the maze, such as opening or closing passageways (as in *Mousetrap*), or even digging holes or passageways (as in *Lode Runner* or *Dig Dug*). Some mazes, such as those found in *Lode Runner,* focus less on navigation and more on how to gain access to certain portions of the screen in order to achieve certain results or obtain objects. Often the player-character must navigate the maze under the pressure of pursuers, although this is not always the case. Mazes are also often imbedded within other games, such as the Blue Labyrinth in *Adventure,* or the underground maze of the Selenetic Age in *Myst.*

EXAMPLES: *Descent* (with Flying and Shooting); *Dig Dug; Doom* (with Shooting); *K. C. Munchkin* (with Collecting and Escape); *Lode Runner* (with Platform); *Maze Craze; Mousetrap* (with Collecting and Escape); *Pac-Man* (with Collecting and Escape); *Tunnel Runner; Tunnels of Doom* (with Adventure); *Ms. Pac-Man* (with Collecting and Escape); *Spy Vs Spy* (with Collecting and Combat); *Take the Money and Run.*

Obstacle Course

Games in which the main objective involves the traversing of a difficult path or one beset with obstacles, through which movement is essentially linear, often involving running, jumping, and avoiding dangers. This term should not be used for games which do not require more than simply steering down a clear path (see Driving) or avoiding objects or characters without a linear progression of movement (see Dodging), nor should it be used for games which involve chasing or being chased (see Chase), or shooting at opponents or getting shot at (see Combat and Shooting), nor for games with complex objectives (see Adventure), nor for games involving more than traversing a path of obstacles (see Platform).

NOTE: While Obstacle Courses are generally linear in design as far as the player-character's advancement through them is concerned, this degree of linearity can vary somewhat; for example, in games allowing a character to backtrack, or choose an alternate route.

EXAMPLES: *Boot Camp; Clown Downtown; Freeway* (with Dodging); *Frogger* (with Dodging); *Pitfall!; Jungle Hunt.*

Pencil-and-Paper Games

Games which are adaptations of games usually played by means of pencil and paper (see Adaptation). This term should not be used for drawing or doodling programs (see Utility) or for games like those in the *Dungeons & Dragons* series whose adaptations are very different from the version of the game played with pencil and paper.

NOTE: Not necessary to use with Adaptation as this is implied in Pencil-and-Paper Games.

EXAMPLES: *3-D Tic-Tac-Toe; Effacer; Hangman from the 25th Century; Noughts and Crosses; Tic-Tac-Toe;* and *Hangman* which appears as a cartridge in several game systems.

Pinball

Games which simulate the play of a pinball game. Although these games could be considered Table-top Games, there is a tradition of video pinball games and a wide enough variety of them to warrant categorizing them in a genre of their own.

NOTE: Not necessary to cross-list with Table-top Games as that is implied in Pinball.

EXAMPLES: *Arcade Pinball; Astrocade Pinball; Electronic Pinball; Extreme Pinball; Flipper Game; Galactic Pinball; Kirby's Pinball Land; Midnight Magic; Pachinko!; Pinball; Pinball Challenge; Pinball Dreams; Pinball Fantasies; Pinball Jam; Pinball Quest; Pinball*

Wizard; Power Rangers Pinball; Pro Pinball; Real Pinball; Sonic Spinball; Spinball; Super Pinball: Behind the Mask; Super Sushi Pinball; Thunderball!; True Pinball; Video Pinball.

Platform

Games in which the primary objective requires movement through a series of levels, by way of running, climbing, jumping, and other means of locomotion. Characters and settings are seen in side view as opposed to top view, thus creating a graphical sense of "up" and "down" as is implied in "Platform." These games often also can involve the avoidance of dropped or falling objects, conflict with (or navigation around) computer-controlled characters, and often some character, object, or reward at the top of the climb which provides narrative motivation. This term should not be used for games which do not involve ascending heights or advancement through a series of levels (see Adventure), nor for games which involve little more than traversing a path of obstacles (see Obstacle Course).

NOTE: For related games, see also Adventure and Obstacle Course.

EXAMPLES: *Crazy Climber; Donkey Kong; Donkey Kong Jr.; Lode Runner* (with Maze); *Spiderman* (Atari 2600); *Super Mario Bros.* (with Collecting); *Warioland; Yoshi's Island.*

Programming Games

Games in which the player writes short programs that control agents within a game. These agents then compete and react to situations based on the player's programming. This term should not be used for games in which a player must learn to operate a machine, such as in *Riven* (see Puzzle), nor for games in which the player controls the player-characters directly. Depending on what the programmed agents do, games may be able to be cross-listed with other genres.

EXAMPLES: *AI Fleet Commander; AI Wars, CoreWar; CRobots; Omega; RARS* (Robot Auto Racing Simulator); *Robot Battle.*

Puzzle

Games in which the primary conflict is not so much between the player-character and other characters but rather the figuring out of a solution, which often involves solving enigmas, navigation, learning how to use different tools, and the manipulating or reconfiguring of objects. Most often there is a visual or sonic element to the puzzles as well, or at least some verbal description of them. This term should not be used for games which only involve the answering of questions (see Quiz). Many Text Adventures also contain puzzles and use text to describe their sights and sounds.

EXAMPLES: *The 7th Guest; Atari Video Cube; Block Out* (with Abstract); *Dice Puzzle; The Hitchhiker's Guide to the Galaxy* (with Text Adventure); *Jigsaw; Myst* (with Adventure); *Rubik's Cube* (with Adaptation); *Sokoban; Suspended Animation* (with Text Adventure); *Tetris* (with Abstract).

Quiz

Games in which the main objective is the successful answering of questions. Scoring is usually based on either how many questions are answered correctly, or on the amount of money players have after betting on their answers. Some of these games are adaptations of board games or quiz shows from television.

NOTE: Games in which the player can place a bet on their answers should be cross-listed with Gambling.

EXAMPLES: *$25,000 Pyramid* (with Adaptation); *Fax; Jeopardy* (with Adaptation); *NFL Football Trivia Challenge '94/'95; Name That Tune;* (with Adaptation); *You Don't Know Jack* (with Gambling); *Sex Trivia; Trivial Pursuit* (with Adaptation); *Trivia Whiz; Triv-Quiz; Video Trivia; Wizz Quiz.*

Racing

Games in which the objective involves the winning of a race or the covering of more ground than an opponent (as in *Slot Racers*). Often these games involve driving skills and can be cross-listed with Driving. One-player games can be considered Racing if there are other computer-controlled cars or vehicles competing on the race track; however, if they are not competitive and act only as obstacles, use Driving.

NOTE: See also Driving. Not necessary to cross-list with Sports as this is implied in Racing. Although most of these games involve driving skills and can be cross-listed with Driving, some of them, like *1000 Miles,* do not.

EXAMPLES: *1000 Miles* (with Card Games); *Daytona USA* (with Driving); *High Velocity* (with Driving); *Indy 500* (with Driving); *Mario Kart 64* (with Driving); *Math Grand Prix* (with Educational); *Pole Position* (with Driving); *Red Planet* (with Driving); *Slot Racers* (with Dodging);*Street Racer* (with Dodging and Driving); *Super GT* (with Driving).

Rhythm and Dance

Games in which gameplay requires players to keep time with a musical rhythm. These games may employ a variety of controllers beyond the usual video game hardware, including controllers simulating drums (as in *DrumMania*), turntables (as in *Beatmania*), guitars (as in *GuitarFreaks*) or even maracas (as in *Samba de Amigo*); or players may have to dance to a beat following prescribed dance steps (as in *Dance Dance Revolution*).

EXAMPLES: *Beatmania; Bust-a-Groove; Dance Dance Revolution; GuitarFreaks; PaRappa the Rapper; Pop'n Music; Samba de Amigo; Space Channel 5; UmJammer Lammy; Vib-Ribbon* (with Obstacle Course).

Role-Playing

Games in which players create or take on a character with a developed persona that often has a description often including specifics as species, race, gender, and occupation, and may also include various abilities, such as strength and dexterity, to limited degrees usually represented numerically. The games can be single-player, such as *Ultima III: Exodus* (1983), or multiple-player games such as those which are networked. This term should not be used for games like *Adventure* or *Raiders of the Lost Ark* in which identity is not emphasized or important.

NOTE: Many networked games, including MUDs (Multi-User Dimensions), MOOs (MUD, Object-Oriented), and MUSHs (Multi-User Shared Hallucination) fall into this category, although the degree to which they can be considered games may vary depending on the players and system operators, and whether or not objectives are set for the players and competition occurs.

EXAMPLES: *Anvil of Dawn; Diablo; Dragon Lore 2; Fallout; Mageslayer; Phantasy Star; Sacred Pools;* games from the *Ultima* series or *Dungeons & Dragons* series. Networked games include: *Interstate '76; Ivory Tower; JediMUD; Northern Lights; OutlawMOO; PernMUSH; RiftMUSH; Rivers of MUD; Sunflower; Unsafe Haven; VikingMUD; Zodiac.*

Shooting

Also known colloquially as "Shoot 'Em Up" or "Shooters." Games involving shooting at, and often destroying, a series of opponents or objects. As opposed to Combat games which feature one-on-one battles with opponents of roughly equal attributes and means, Shooting games usually feature multiple opponents (the "'Em" is short for "them") attacking at once (as in *Space Invaders* or *Galaga*) or multiple objects which can be destroyed (as in *Centipede*), which are often potentially harmful to the player-character (as in *Asteroids*). In many cases, the player-character and opponents of the player-character have unequal attributes and means and do not even resemble one another (as in *Yar's Revenge*), and the games usually require quick reflexes. Do not use this term for games like *Stellar Track*, in which the player-character and opponents fire at each other, but in such a way that quick reflexes are not necessary (see Strategy). There are three types of Shooting games which are common: in one, the player-character moves horizontally back and forth at the bottom of the screen shooting upward while opponents moving around above shoot downward (as in *Space Invaders*); in the second, the character moves freely about the screen, encountering opponents from all sides (as in *Berzerk* or *Robotron: 2084*), and the third features a first-person perspective (as in *Doom*). This term should not be used for fighting games which do not involve shooting (see Fighting), nor for games in which opponents are fairly evenly matched (see Combat), nor for games in which none of the objects the player-character fires upon can harm the player-character (see Target). In a few cases, the player-character is primarily defending rather than attacking, as in *Atlantis, Commando Raid, Missile Command,* and *Missile Defense 3-D.*

EXAMPLES: *Asteroids; Berzerk; Centipede; Doom; Duckshot; Galaga; Millipede; Missile Command, Robotron: 2084; Space Invaders; Yar's Revenge; Zaxxon.*

Simulation

See Management Simulation and Training Simulation.

Sports

Games which are adaptations of existing sports or variations of them.

NOTE: No need to cross-list with Adaptation as this is implied in Sports. See also Driving, Fighting, Obstacle Course, Racing, and Table-top Games.

EXAMPLES: *American Football; Atari Baseball; Bowling; Boxing* (with Fighting); *Fishing Derby* (with Catching); *Hot Shots Tennis; Golf; Human Cannonball* (with Target); *Ice Hockey; Madden Football 97; Miniature Golf; NHL Hockey 97; PONG* (with Table-top Games); *Skeet Shoot* (with Target); *Track & Field; Summer Games; Video Olympics;*

RealSports Soccer; RealSports Tennis; RealSports Volleyball; SimGolf; Sky Diver; Tsuppori Sumo Wrestling; World Series Baseball '98.

Strategy

Games emphasizing the use of strategy as opposed to fast action or the use of quick reflexes, which are usually not necessary for success in these games.

NOTE: See also management simulation games like *M.U.L.E.* and *Spaceward Ho!,* as well as many Board Games, Card Games, and Combat games.

EXAMPLES: *Ataxx* (with Abstract); *Checkers* (with Board Games); *Chess* (with Board Games); *Monopoly* (with Board Games); *M.U.L.E.* (with Management Simulation); *Othello* (with Board Games); *Spaceward Ho!* (with Management Simulation); *Stellar Track.*

Table-top Games

Games involving adaptations of existing table-top games requiring physical skill or action (such as pool or table tennis). This term should not be used for games involving little or no physical skill or action (see Board Games and Card Games), nor should it be used for games which cannot be played on a table-top of some sort (see Sports). For games which resemble pinball games, see Pinball.

NOTE: Not necessary to cross-list with Adaptation, as this is implied in Table-top Games.

EXAMPLES: *Battle Ping Pong; Electronic Table Soccer!; Parlour Games; Pocket Billiards!; PONG* (with Sports); *Sure Shot Pool; Trick Shot; Virtual Pool.*

Target

Games in which the primary objective involves aiming and shooting at targets. Occasionally the targets may be harming the player-character's property (as in *Wabbit*). This term should not be used for games in which the player-character can be fired upon by opponents (see Combat, and Shooting), or games do not involve shooting (see Catching and Collecting), nor for games in which the objects or characters actively elude the player-character.

EXAMPLES: *Air-Sea Battle; Carnival; Human Cannonball; Marksman/Trapshooting; Shooting Gallery; Skeet Shoot* (with Sports); *Wabbit.*

Text Adventure

Games which rely primarily on text for the player interface, and often for the description of the game's "world" and the action which takes place there as well. Some games may use images, but these are usually noninteractive illustrations which are not central to the play of the game. Games range from allowing free movement throughout the game's "world" (usually by commands such as "north," "south," "east," "west," "up," and "down") with a variety of options for interaction, to more linear, branching narratives. Players often are able to carry objects which are kept track of by an inventory function and are able to converse with computer-controlled player-characters through a very limited vocabulary. Although some games may incorporate text-based informational screens (as in *Stellar Track*), rely on text for description (such as the books in the library in *Myst*), or even use text as a graphic element (such as *Rogue*), this term should only be used for games in which the "world" of the game is primarily experienced through text which describes the world of the game and the events occurring in it.

NOTE: Not necessary to cross-list with Adventure since that is implied in Text Adventure. Multiple-player Text Adventures which are networked are considered to be Role-Playing games (see Role-Playing). Almost all Text Adventures can be cross-listed with Puzzle.

EXAMPLES: *The Hitchhiker's Guide to the Galaxy; Planetfall; Leather Goddesses of Phobos; Suspended Animation; Zork.*

Training Simulation

Games or programs which attempt to simulate a realistic situation for the purpose of training and usually the development of some physical skill such as steering (as in driving and flight simulators). This term should not be used for simulations which focus on management (see Management Simulation) or the employment of strategy (see Strategy). These games can range from realistic simulations used by institutions, such as those used to train astronauts, tank drivers, or airline pilots, to simplified gamelike approximations of them used mainly for entertainment, such as *Police Trainer* or *A-10 Attack*.

NOTE: Not necessary to cross-list with Utility or Simulation, as that is implied in Training Simulation.

EXAMPLES: *A-10 Attack; Comanche 3* (with Flying); *F/A-18 Hornet 3.0* (with Flying); *Flight Unlimited* (with Flying); *Police Trainer;* military and airline flight simulators; and driving simulations used in driver education.

Utility

Cartridges or programs which have a purpose or function beyond that of entertainment, although they may be structured in a manner similar to games (such as *Mario Teaches Typing*) or contain elements of entertainment. While they are often not games themselves, some of these programs have the same appearance as game cartridges and are sometimes collected and traded as game cartridges, and they are usually included in listings of cartridges.

NOTE: See also Demo, Diagnostic, Educational, and Simulation.

EXAMPLES: *Basic Programming; Beginning Algebra; Beginning Math; Computer Programmer; Diagnostic Cartridge* (Identification No. FDS100144) for the Atari 5200 system (with Diagnostic); *Home Finance; Infogenius French Language Translator; Mario Teaches Typing; Music Box Demo* (with Demo); *Number Games; Speed Reading; Spelling Games; Touch Typing, Word Games.*

BEST-SELLING VIDEO GAMES

Mark J. P. Wolf

Video games are big business. The U.S. video game industry alone made $9.9 billion in 2004, $10.5 billion in 2005, and $12.5 billion in 2006.[2]

What are the best-selling video games? There are a number of factors to consider when attempting to answer this question. First, there are several different types of video games, which makes comparisons difficult, or perhaps unfair. Arcade games are played for a quarter a play (although some are 50 cents, or even more), while home games are bought outright, and their systems must be purchased as well. Home computer games are also bought outright, while shareware games are not bought at all but are often freely distributed with no way to measure how many copies of them have been produced. Likewise, pirated copies of games can erode the market for a game, meaning that the number sold may not reflect how many copies are actually being played.

While *PONG* was the first arcade game hit in 1972, followed by *Space Invaders* in 1978, it is *Pac-Man* and *Defender,* both released in North America in 1980, that are usually listed as the most successful arcade games of all time. Each of them has earned more than a billion dollars—a feat that few movies have achieved.[3] Since the decline of the arcade during the 1990s, it is unlikely that any arcade games will ever do that well again.

In the area of home game systems, the Atari 2600 was the best-selling system for nearly a decade, until the Nintendo Entertainment System passed it up. Home game systems often come bundled with games, inflating the number of games sold; for example, the best-selling home video game of all time, *Super Mario Bros.,* has sold over 40 million copies because it came bundled with the NES.[4]

Computer games are often ported to a variety of home consoles, which also help their sales. *Myst* was available for a variety of platforms, including Sony PlayStation, Sega Genesis, Atari Jaguar, and both Macintosh and IBM-compatible computers. Although they both were released in 1993 and had sold over 100,000 copies by the end of the year, *Myst* soon passed up *The 7th Guest* as the best-selling home computer game of all time, a title it would hold until 2002 when *The Sims* would overtake it with 6.3 million units sold.[5]

Finally, there are also online role-playing games, which are subscription based and have hundreds of thousands of players who pay monthly fees. Of these, *World of Warcraft* is the largest, with over 9 million subscribers as of summer 2007, with 2 million of them in North America, 1.5 million in Europe, and 3.5 million in China.[6]

CHAPTER 39

THE VIDEO GAME AS AN OBJECT OF CONTROVERSY

Dominic Arsenault

The appearance of a new form of entertainment is often marked by multiple controversies. Like comic books and television before them, video games have had their share in the spotlight of social debates. As early offerings replicated existing games (like *PONG* or the Magnavox Odyssey *Volleyball* game) or were otherwise aiming at fostering social gatherings and expanding on the traditional idea of "playing," they were perceived as digital embodiments of already-known phenomena, and thus did not generate anxieties or questions, except for a few special cases. (The example of *Custer's Revenge* for the Atari 2600 console is discussed in Chapter 40, "Morals, Ethics, and Video Games.")

The other title of note is the very first video game to have sparked controversy: Exidy's *Death Race,* an arcade game based on Paul Bartel's film *Death Race 2000* (1975) starring David Carradine, Simone Griffeth, and Sylvester Stallone. In the game, players had to drive cars so as to run over "gremlins" (which looked like human stick figures) to score points. When hit, a gremlin would disappear with a scream and was replaced by a tombstone. People found the "gremlins" indistinguishable from human characters, and the term "gremlins" was really just a euphemism coined by the developers to lessen the game's questionable nature, since the game's development title was *Pedestrian.* The fact that a video game asked a player—potentially a child—to engage in violence against ordinary people instead of monsters or spaceships and that this violence took place in a realistic setting (inferred from the blocky graphics with the aid of the game's title, cabinet artwork and so on, rather than portrayed directly using vivid imagery) caused a public outcry. Numerous protests and extensive media coverage gave *Death Race* extra publicity, but not enough to make it a success by any standard: as historian Steve Kent writes, "According to [Exidy founder's Pete] Kauffman, Exidy sold only 1,000 *Death Race* machines, just a fraction of the number of *Sea Wolf* and *Gun Fight* machines Midway placed that same year."[1]

In the later half of the 1980s, Nintendo and its "family friendly" policy succeeded in marketing video games to children, thus prompting their thorough examination to ensure that they were appropriate recreation—or even better, learning tools—for kids. This led to the first wave of investigations, research, claims, counterclaims, and passionate speeches on the subject, the main results of which have entered popular culture and general knowledge.[2] For most people, video games on the one hand developed hand-eye coordination, problem-solving skills, and spatial navigation and comprehension in general, with some particular titles being capable of teaching classic subject matters like geography and history (as in such games as *Where in the World is Carmen Sandiego?* and *Civilization*), and on the other hand video games were thought to be responsible for antisocial or increased aggressive behaviors and health problems ranging from obesity to epileptic seizures (as of 2007, many video games instruction manuals contained a warning that playing video games may trigger an epileptic seizure).[3]

Violence

The aforementioned case of *Death Race* had set the tone for video games' major source of moral debate: the increasingly detailed graphical depiction of violence. In 1992, Midway's *Mortal Kombat* went further down that road. Designed as a response to Capcom's very successful *Street Fighter II,* the game attempted to attract notoriety with excessive, over-the-top content: characters would fly across the screen, throw fireballs, freeze their opponents, or instantly teleport themselves and eventually face a four-armed humanoid and a shape-shifting sorcerer. However, many found these features marginal, due to the exaggerated depiction of blood and gore, with simple jabs causing streams of blood to pour from the opponent's face or body. The one fighting game innovation that caused much of the controversy was the inclusion of gory "fatalities." When an opponent was beaten, instead of dropping to the ground, he or she stood up, stunned and incapable of doing anything. The winner could "finish off" the loser with any move of his choice and had a few seconds to execute a special command. If done correctly, the character would dismember, incinerate, or behead his victim.

Unlike *Death Race,* more realistic graphics were one of the game's strengths. Instead of hand-drawing and animating the characters, the development team filmed real actors, digitized their performance as still photographs, and individually animated them. This made the extreme violence scandalous enough that in 1993 U.S. Senator Joseph Lieberman arranged a hearing on video games, which he claimed were marketing violence to kids.[4] The hearings particularly focused on *Mortal Kombat* and the Sega CD game *Night Trap* (1992), chiefly because these two games featured digitized footage of actors and actresses. The main outcome of these hearings was the creation of the Entertainment Software Rating Board, a self-regulatory body developed by the video game industry.

Numerous controversial games followed in the next years. Some titles deserving special mention include *Doom,* which popularized the first-person shooter genre and was used by one of the boys responsible for the 1999 Columbine High School shooting, and the *Grand Theft Auto* series for bringing violence into a realistic contemporary urban setting and letting the player engage law enforcement officials, civilians, and even prostitutes with a wide array of weaponry.

Sexual Content

Troublesome sexual content in video games appeared rather early. In 1982 Mystique developed and released *Custer's Revenge,* an infamous game for the Atari 2600 console.

The player controlled a naked man, running from a fort and through a plain, who had to dodge obstacles in order to reach a Native American woman tied to a pole and rape her. Predictably, the game caused controversy from all kinds of social groups and tarnished Atari's reputation, even though the latter had no involvement in this game.

A relatively small and marginal production of erotic video games continued in the wake of *Custer's Revenge,* appearing not on video game consoles but rather on personal computers. The most famous of these was Sierra's *Leisure Suit Larry in the Land of the Lounge Lizards* (1987), an adventure game that by 1996 would span five sequels in which the player controlled a middle-aged loser desperately trying to have sex with various women. The visuals were still low-resolution due to the limited graphical power of the time, and the games' main appeal resided in their humor. Aside from *Larry,* most games that featured sexual content or nudity consisted of electronic renditions of various strip poker, pinball, mahjong, and puzzle games. The arrival of full-motion video technology in the 1990s meant that erotic and pornographic video games could now feature live-action videos of real actors and actresses, and a number of titles were produced to test the grounds of "adult interactive entertainment," *Riana Rouge* (1997) and *Michael Ninn's Latex* (1998) being among the higher-profile ones. Erotic video games should not be confused with "interactive adult videos," interactive software pioneered by Digital Playground's *Virtual Sex* series that also appeared in 1997, which are not formally "games."

From the late 1990s and onward, the growing popularity of the Internet coupled with the advent of accessible Web-based development tools like Adobe Flash allowed the production of many erotic games, often by hobbyists, in the *hentai* style (a hand-drawn style popular in Japan) and often belonging to the "dating sim" genre. Pornographic and erotic video games have caused less controversy as they are not handled through any organized distribution channels as standard video games are, and much in the same way that amateur or webcam pornography does not appear side-by-side with mainstream cinema and blockbuster movies.

Rather, it is the presence of objectionable content in otherwise standard, widely distributed video games that caused controversy in the mainstream media. *Night Trap* was one of the first titles to cause a stir for featuring a group of college-aged girls having a slumber party in a typical high-class suburban house. Under scrutiny of the Congressional hearings mentioned earlier, the main content found offensive was that the player could let the girls die instead of saving them. The fact that some of them appeared in nightgowns or were otherwise scantily clothed, however, furthered the game's already precarious position. *Night Trap* was pulled from multiple stores in the United States that refused to be associated with it, but at the same time its sales increased dramatically thanks to the exposure it received. In the next two years, it was remade for multiple platforms and the ESRB rated it "Mature." *Phantasmagoria* followed in 1995 and took the controversy to another level with a simulated rape scene. Even though the camera did not film below waist level and the aggressor—the heroine Adrienne's husband—was clearly shown to be possessed by a demon, the game was banned in Australia and received adult ratings in Germany and the United Kingdom. In the United States the game was rated "Mature" by the ESRB and was not subjected to any particular treatment.

In the following years, Rockstar's *Grand Theft Auto* series caused a stir twice, the first time in 2001 with *Grand Theft Auto III* because the player could pick up a prostitute in his car and have sex with her, and in 2004 with *Grand Theft Auto: San Andreas* for the "hot coffee" incident which received considerable media coverage. In *GTA3* the sexual activity was not represented on-screen, the player only saw his car rocking back and forth for a time. In *San Andreas,* the player's girlfriend would ask him to come in her house "for some coffee," and the camera remained outside the house while some moaning sounds were heard from inside. However, the Rockstar developers had designed a mini-game to govern the intercourse, in which the player had to push buttons in rhythm to fill up an "excitement" bar eventually leading his girlfriend to orgasm in order to improve his relationship with her. This content was disabled upon the game's release, but the data was left on the game disc. Players eventually made it available by modifying the program code for the PC version of the game and using third-party cheating devices for the console versions. As a result, the game had its Mature rating revised to Adults Only by the ESRB, and was pulled from many retailers' shelves in accordance with their policies. Rockstar later re-released the game with the "hot coffee" content removed, thus regaining its former rating.

The same principle of inaccessible, dormant content caused a similar controversy with Bethesda Softworks's *The Elder Scrolls IV: Oblivion* (2006). While characters could not be undressed further than their underwear, some modders (people engaging in game modifications, often as a positive expression of creativity and with the goal of expanding their favorite games) found character art for topless women hidden away in the game data. They released a patch for unlocking it, and the game's rating was increased from Teen to Mature.

Ideology

Some games have sparked controversy because of ideological implications seen as dangerous or subversive, or for the treating of sensitive subject matter. *JFK: Reloaded* (2004) put the player in the shoes of Lee Harvey Oswald, John F. Kennedy's alleged assassin, in order to reenact the assassination attempt. The *Grand Theft Auto* series was condemned not only for sexual content but also for having the player live out a life of criminality. Rockstar's subsequent offering, *Bully* (2006; also known as *Canis Canem Edit* in the UK) similarly had the player becoming a troublemaker kid in a boarding school who is given the possibility of hitting other children, pulling pranks, and generally causing mischief. Additionally, the player's male character could kiss certain boys, in a manner similar to the way the male hero of Lionhead Studios's *Fable* (2004) could marry some men. At the other end of the ideological spectrum, *America's Army* (2002) was developed by the U.S. Army, explicitly to be used as a recruitment tool. (See Chapter 34, "Video Games in Australia," for other examples.)

Rule of Rose (2006) had its release cancelled in the UK, and was subsequently banned in Australia. The game's story revolved around a 19-year old woman being captive to a cast of young, evil girls. David Charter of *The Times* reported that "The game puts the player in the shoes of a teenage girl who is repeatedly beaten and humiliated as she tries to break out of an orphanage. She is bound, gagged, doused with liquids, buried alive and thrown into the 'Filth Room',"[5] a depiction that was rejected by Laurie Hall of the Video Standards Council, the organization that gave the game its original 16+ rating: "I have no idea where the suggestion of in-game sadomasochism has come from, nor children being buried underground. These are things that have been completely made up."[6] And while Charter suggested that "Sony did not release *Rule of Rose* in the United States for fear of an outcry, particularly over alleged overtones of lesbianism and sadomasochism," Hall declared that "There isn't any underage eroticism." Shuji Ishikawa, the game's director, thinks otherwise, as he said in an interview on *Gamasutra:* "There are definitely erotic parts to it, and some things that might make people uncomfortable, but it's not the focus."[7] As the case of *Rule of Rose* demonstrates, most of the video game controversies spawned on grounds of ideology are highly subjective.

As games increasingly strive for photorealistic graphics and start exploring everyday, lifelike environments instead of fantasy or science-fiction settings, controversies are bound to multiply.

VIDEO GAMES RATING SYSTEMS

Mark J.P. Wolf

Following the example of the MPAA (Motion Picture Association of America) rating system used for the rating of motion pictures, the video game industry has several times attempted a form of rating system. The Videogame Rating Council (VRC) was introduced by Sega in 1993 for the rating of its own games, and the 3DO company also had their own rating system for their games. The Recreational Software Advisory Council (RSAC), begun in 1994, rated home computer game software, but not home console games, and was later combined into the Internet Content Rating Association (ICRA). None of these systems found industry-wide use or acceptance.

In 1994 the Entertainment Software Association (ESA) established the Entertainment Software Rating Board (ESRB) to rate home video games and computer games. The ESRB is nonprofit and self-regulating, and the ratings are voluntary, though most games appearing in North America carry them. The ESRB has six ratings which it applies to games: EC (Early Childhood), E (Everyone), T (Teen), M (Mature), AO (Adults Only), and RP (Rating Pending). "Early Childhood" indicates games thought to be appropriate for children age 3 and older. "Everyone" indicates games for people age 6 and older, and these games may contain some mild violence and language. "Teen" games can have violent content and language, and suggestive themes. "Mature" indicates that the content may include sexual themes, intense violence, and strong language. "Adults Only" is for games with graphic depictions of sex and violence, and are not for people under the age of 18. "Rating Pending" means that a rating has not yet been assigned.

Rating video games, however, differs from the rating of movies. Films can be viewed from beginning to end, and reviewers can be certain of having seen all of a film's content. Video games, however, may require playing skills and many hours worth of play to see the game's world and events, and players may not even know for certain that they have seen all there is to see. Game developers and publishers demonstrating their games to the ESRB could very easily hide material in order to get a rating that will give their games a wider audience. To counteract this situation, two bills were introduced into Congress in September 2006. The "Truth in Video Gaming Act" (S.3935) required that the ESRB have full access to game content and time to play the games it would rate, while the "Video Game Decency Act" (H.R.6120) proposed legislation to prohibit deception in the rating and labelling of games.

Other ratings systems outside of North America include the Computer Entertainment Rating Organization (CERO) in Japan, which was organized in 2002 using the ESRB as a model, and Pan European Game Information (PEGI) which was organized by the Interactive Software Federation of Europe (ISFE) in 2003, and is used in over two dozen countries in Europe.

CHAPTER 40

MORALS, ETHICS, AND VIDEO GAMES

Mark J. P. Wolf

Video games, like film and television, are sometimes criticized for having too much violence and sex, stereotypical characters, and an overall lack of edifying content. But when these similarities with other media are stressed, it becomes easy to overlook the new ethical and moral questions raised by video games.

Video Games and Traditional Media

Narratives in traditional media, such as novels, films, and television, often attempt to embody some kind of worldview, idea, or point (the lesson or moral of the story) by attempting to show a causal connection between actions and consequences. In doing so, they simulate situations in which characters' actions become linked to the fates that befall them (i.e., someone commits a crime, is caught and put in jail, or does a good deed and is rewarded—or vice versa, depending on what the author's view is). The narrative which successfully convinces the viewer that the cause-and-effect connections between events are sound, then, can become a kind of surrogate experience for the viewer and may even influence someone's future actions, similar to the way movies can influence a person's behavior.

But *influence* is not the same as *cause*. Certainly advertisers suppose that people who see their ads will be more likely to buy their products (or else they would not advertise), and a number of studies have attempted to link violent films with aggressive behavior, but in either case *influence* always stops short of becoming a *cause*.

Video games, however, *can* be causally linked with certain behaviors for the simple reason that these behaviors are required to play the games. In many shooting games, for example, if one does not play aggressively, the game quickly ends in defeat. The player must learn to act and think a certain way in order to master a game. Player activity, then, is one way video games exert an influence; the player is *performing* actions, not merely watching someone else perform them, and over a long time, new skills and reflexes are learned. Many hours can go into the development of these skills, and many trials and repetitions as well, just like any other form of training. Screens and sequences may be seen dozens of times, unlike other media productions like films, television shows, or books, which are consumed usually no more than a few times. Players may even have to learn to think strategically or analytically when puzzle-solving is involved, or, on the other hand, train themselves to respond with fast, reflex reactions that are automatic and do not involve thinking.

For some time, the influence of video games was overlooked because they were seen as a medium mainly for kids, despite the huge adult market and growing complexity of the games, as well as the adult material and themes found in some games. Part of the reason for this may be the way games first began; early games had relatively simple graphics that were iconic and more abstract in design. Likewise, the actions occurring within the games were also iconic and a far cry from the real experiences they attempted to depict (and thus were seen as harmless). But as video game graphics' sophistication and verisimilitude increased, so did the nature of the player's experience. Graphics that had been mainly *conceptual* (so abstract and blocky that the game's manual had to describe what each was meant to be) became more *perceptual* and looked more like the things they were meant to represent, and the simulation improved. Of course, high-resolution on-screen characters exhibiting complex behavior are certainly no more "real" than low-resolution ones with simple behaviors, but the player's experience of them differs due to the level of detail and complexity of gameplay.

Nor is high resolution necessary to convey violent or pornographic ideas. One of the first games to feature human figures, Exidy's 1976 arcade game *Death Race,* had small, blocky stick people which were used as targets to be run over, and because of this the game became an object of controversy. While a single pink pixel can hardly be called offensive, at what resolution does an image become recognizably pornographic or violent? Even the low-resolution Atari 2600 system had enough pixels to convey such ideas; in 1982, 250 protestors gathered outside the New York Hilton where third-party developer Mystique released the first X-rated game, *Custer's Revenge* (see Chapter 39, "The Video Game as an Object of Controversy"). Atari later sued the company for associating its product with the Atari name.[1]

In video games, graphics are the means of conveying ideas, regardless of their resolution. Higher resolutions allow for a greater and more detailed articulation of these ideas. And as graphics look more and more photographic, these ideas grow more concrete in their visual representation and more like the images produced in other media, including those through which knowledge of the real world is obtained and through which social interaction is conducted. And, in many multiple-player games and especially online role-playing games, social interaction between players becomes an important part of the game.

Social Elements of Video Games

Along with graphics, gameplay itself has developed and grown more complex. Multiple-player video games have existed alongside single-player video games since the beginning, in both the arcade and in the home. Players were physically present together in the room where the game was being played (and most likely knew each other as well). Most of the social interaction that occurred during gameplay took place outside the arena of the game. With networked and online games, however, players are usually not present in the same room, and often do not know each other. Role-playing games like *Ultima*

Online, Asheron's Call, Star Wars Galaxies, EverQuest, and *World of Warcraft* may have millions of players in their online worlds, who meet, converse, and form alliances and guilds without having to meet their compatriots face-to-face outside of the game. Because the player-characters are controlled by real people, the social interaction taking place is real, albeit in a more limited bandwidth than in-person interaction.

Social elements enrich game play, and the fact that most players will only know of each other through their player-characters means that a player may have a greater stake in the character that represents them in a game. Most role-playing games are long term, ongoing over years, allowing player-characters to build up skills, powers, and abilities over time. The time, effort, emotional investment, and even financial investment spent on character development increases identification and the player-character's value, and the character can become a player's alter ego instead of merely an on-screen surrogate.

Character identification also can be strong in console- or cartridge-based games and even single-player games. Players will often say things like "I got killed" or "It got me" even when the on-screen player-character has a name and identity of its own apart from the player. While film audience members watch a character's involvement in various situations provided by the storyline, perhaps imagining what it would be like if they were in a similar situation themselves, in the video game, the player causes on-screen events to happen by acting or reacting, and there is a shift from *simulation* to *emulation*. Within this shift, we can identify three areas in which video games can exert an influence: reflexes and behaviors of players, ethical worldviews, and certain ways of thinking that are promoted and sharpened by the games.

From Simulation to Emulation

The difference between *simulation* and *emulation* is akin to the difference between *sympathy* and *empathy*. While "sympathy" and "empathy" both share the same Greek root *pathos,* meaning feeling (from *paschien,* to suffer or feel), the prefix "sym" comes from *syn,* meaning "together," while "em" comes from *en-,* meaning "in."[2] In the former, one has an experience or feels along with a third party, while the latter is more internalized. Likewise, whereas *simulation* can be limited to passive contemplation, *emulation* involves action. Taken together, they can influence behavior, beliefs, and outlook.

Reflexes and Behaviors

Watching martial films does not help one develop fast reflexes, whereas a video game *can* sharpen hand-eye coordination skills and reflex responses. The fast speed at which game action occurs can often require players to develop reflex responses at the expense of contemplative ones, sometimes resulting in a kind of Pavlovian stimulus-response training in which reflex speed is crucial. These responses can vary widely, from abstract tile manipulation and construction in *Tetris* and *Pipe Dream* (1989), to the exploratory curiosity of *Myst* and *Riven,* to the hair-trigger automatic killing in *Doom* or *Unreal Tournament* (1999). While games can be designed to develop a variety of skills and reflex responses, shooting and killing are unfortunately the skills that most often appear.

Films and television shows may encourage certain types of behavior, but video games require them. And unlike Internet Web-browsing interactivity, video games often contain win-loss scenarios that encourage competitive behavior, which, in many cases, involves aggression. A major study conducted by Craig A. Anderson and Karen E. Dill and featured in the *Journal of Personality and Social Psychology* found that "violent video game play was positively related to aggressive behavior and delinquency," and that "exposure to a graphically violent video game increased aggressive thoughts and behavior."[3] The study considers other factors along with game content, including predispositions of players, delinquency, favorite games, time spent on games, and other data, and it is more extensive in its investigation than many of its predecessors. Still, correlations with such aspects as degrees of graphical resolution, gameplay speed, character identification, narrative involvement, and so on have yet to be explored.

And finally, the context of a player's actions and behavior must be taken into consideration. As in film, the reaction to a violent scene can differ depending on whether the audience's identification coincides with the victim or the aggressor. In video games with a kill-or-be-killed mentality, players may find themselves alternating between both positions though the predominant one is usually that of killer, at least in most shooting games.

Over time, the reflexes and behaviors learned can become deeply ingrained and affect a player's personality. Studies have shown that video games can be addictive, and one study by Griffiths and Hunt suggests that as many as one in five adolescents may be pathologically dependent on them.[4] According to Anderson and Dill,

> When the choice and action components of video games…is coupled with the games' reinforcing properties, a strong learning experience results. In a sense, violent video games provide a complete learning environment for aggression, with simultaneous exposure to modeling, reinforcement, and rehearsal of behaviors. This combination of learning strategies has been shown to be more powerful than any of these methods used singly.[5]

Many psychological studies of video games focus on the relationship between video games and violence and aggression, but, as noted above, skills and reflexes learned in video games do not always involve violent or aggressive behavior. If violent and aggressive games can influence a player's behavior, it seems possible that games could be designed to encourage positive and useful skills. Studies typically do not ask whether contemplative adventure games make players more observant or increase their problem-solving skills, although Anderson and Dill's study did use *Myst* and *Tetrix* (a game similar to *Tetris*) to control for differences between violent and nonviolent games. The existence of educational games for children and others for adults that teach mental skills (such as problem-solving or resource management) or physical skills (such as hand-eye coordination or typing) also suggests that much can be learned through video games. Educational games have also been developed in more academic environments, such as the I.C. Squared Institute in Austin, Texas, or MIT's *Games-to-Teach* program.

Yet most games do not have learning as an objective, and the learning that occurs can be inadvertent. As one colonel in the U.S. military put it in an interview with *ABCnews.com,*

> A flight simulator played on a computer will teach you how to fly, and you can transfer the skill from a simulator to reality. In the same way, a murder simulator played on a computer screen can teach you how to kill, and those skills will transfer over to reality.[6]

And, because video games differ from other types of software in that they are often narrative based and set in an on-screen diegetic world, not only skills, but also certain worldviews[7] may be encouraged or taught which may also transfer over to life outside of the games.

Ethical Worldviews

Stories involving some point or moral often embody them by causally linking actions and consequences. Villains and evildoers are punished at the story's end, and heroes and good characters are rewarded. Consequences and outcomes to character's actions are also explored, and the importance of an individual's actions and their effect on others is a common theme in literature and film. By setting the author's ideas in a narrative context, ideas of how actions and consequences are linked can seem more natural and similar to occurrences in the real world or the audience member's own life than if the lessons involved were stated directly and overtly. Because video games involve the player's own choices and participation and because players can do things differently and explore alternate causal chains of actions and consequences, video games can even more covertly embody a worldview. Player activity and the sense of "live-ness" that it adds to the player's experience make events appear to be happening in the present, rather than in the past, and the opportunity for making choices makes the outcome seem less predetermined even though the game's programming has already determined how actions and consequences will be linked. Games like *SimCity, The Sims* (2000), and other simulation games contain dozens of "rules" by which the simulation advances, and discovering these through trial and error becomes an overall goal of the player who wants to be successful in the game.

The malleability and repeatability of most video game experiences may undermine some of the positive effects of simulated worlds or situations. Nothing is final or irreversible when a game can be restarted or when a player has multiple "lives." Careless actions may end a game but have no lasting effects beyond that. Few video games can elicit deep emotions or feelings, which may be one of the reasons the video game still has not been accorded the status of "art"; however, film and television also had similar struggles when they were young, developing media. Instead of empathy, games with graphic violent content can lead to desensitization, especially when the games frame the violence as humorous or "cool" or promote violence as the solution to one's problems (and as a default response at that). On the other hand, there are games which overturn these default assumptions (for example, in *Ultima IV: The Quest for the Avatar,* ethics became important; indiscriminate killing and looting could work against a player).

Online role-playing games, however, differ greatly from arcade games or home video games and involve on-screen diegetic worlds which in some ways are more like the real world. The worlds of games like *World of Warcraft* or *Asheron's Call* are "persistent"; play continues 24 hours a day, whether players are logged in or not (since these games have several hundred thousand players, there are always at least a few thousand players logged in at any given time). The games cannot be restarted, and players may invest large amounts of time and money in the game, so there is more at stake when player-characters combat to the death. Alliances of player-characters cooperate and compete, and hierarchical social systems exist. While aggressive and violent behavior still exists, the persistent nature of the world, its social elements, and the long-term play make for a rather different gaming experience, and debates over the nature and limitations on violence continue. Too much player-versus-player combat in which players can kill each other results in fewer accounts (and thus corporate income), while too little conflict may also displease players, so a balance between the two must be found. Dr. Simon Carne, a player of *Asheron's Call,* explained it this way:

Asheron's Call has six servers, five of which are "non-player killer" (NPK) (nicknamed "carebear") in which players can opt out of player vs. player combat. On the remaining one (Darktide) you cannot opt out of player vs. player combat. This means that anyone can kill you at any time, even if you are low level (newbie) and they are absurdly powerful. And if they kill you, they get experience points for it, and can steal your stuff (assuming you have any!).

Players on Darktide generally, then, fall into two camps, "PKs," that is, those who kill anyone who is not their friend...(this is known as "RPK" or random player killing) and "Antis" (rather confusingly meaning "Anti-PK") which are those who kill only members of guilds who engage in "RPK"ing. There are also some guilds who do not necessarily kill everyone they run into, but only those guilds they are at war with (these guilds are generally not RPKs, but do not actively kill RPKs, and may be called neutral). The worst RPKs engage in Newbie-killing, trash-talking and trust-killing (i.e., acting friendly until your defenses are down, then killing you "in the back" so to speak)....

I think I played about ten minutes on one of the non-player killer servers once, but I just couldn't see the point. However, they are where most people prefer to play—clearly if there were more demand for another Darktide they (Microsoft, actually) would have opened another PK server.[8]

In virtual worlds where players have invested time and money and built relationships and social structures, ethics takes on greater importance as consequences within the game extend into the real world.

Clearly there is a difference (usually) between the morality of the real world and the "virtual morality" of the diegetic world of the online game. While the "killing" of another player's character may be considered an act of aggression, it still falls within the established rules of play in *Ultima Online,* and players can avoid it by staying off the Darktide server. And even players whose characters are killed off can come back online with new characters. Yet the metaphor of "killing" remains, as does the question of why pretend "killing" is considered fun by so many people. The idea of shooting or "killing" has become so ingrained in video game culture that it seems difficult for many people to imagine it otherwise. The question first arose in 1976 with the game *Death Race,* at a time when video game graphics were so simple that images were little more than very rough iconographic representations; today, as graphics advance toward photorealism, the question is more pertinent than ever.

Graphic violence, killing, lying, cheating, and other ethical issues involving social interactions between player-characters are often the subjects of discussion among players and in the larger debate surrounding video games and even in the courts; families of the children slain in the Columbine High School shooting started a $5 billion lawsuit against big video game companies, arguing that the shooting might not have occurred were it not for the opportunity to practice made possible by the violent games.[9] Yet there are other potential effects which may be more subtle than these, involving the player's default assumptions and ways of thinking about or conceptualizing the world, a kind of inherent philosophical outlook lingering in the background and shaping the player's experience.

Ways of Thinking

Players who vicariously enter the diegetic world of a video game through player-character surrogates must also adapt their thinking to the game's demands if they are to be successful. This is perhaps best illustrated by violent kill-or-be-killed-style video games in which the player-character is constantly in jeopardy. As Anderson and Dill summarize it,

Each time people play violent video games they rehearse aggressive scripts that teach and reinforce vigilance for enemies (i.e., hostile perception bias), aggressive action against others, expectations that others will behave aggressively, positive attitudes toward use of violence, and beliefs that violent solutions are effective and appropriate. Furthermore, repeated exposure to graphic scenes of violence is likely to be desensitizing. In essence, the creation and automatization of these aggression-related knowledge structures and the desensitization effects change the individual's personality.[10]

Not only violent games, but also games that are frustrating due to difficulty level, programming bugs, or poor design, can have similar effects. As psychologist Rebecca Tews writes,

> Gameplay may modify the player's behavior in interpersonal relationships. Game-play, particularly with violent or frustrating games, seems to elicit increased perception of threat, increased physio-logical arousal in game threat situations (which may translate to other perceived threat situations), and less use of traditional problem-solving strategies and appropriately assertive person-to-person conflict resolution.[11]

A player's choices within a game scenario are often very limited, and repetitive gameplay, either as practice in lower levels of a game until higher levels can be achieved, or because of computer crashes and software bugs, may wear on players' patience and agitate them into a frustrated state. Losing a game at home among friends or in a public arcade among strangers may impact a player's ego and self-esteem. And, interestingly, many video games are designed in such a way that they always end with the player's failure and defeat; the Space Invaders always manage to get to the bottom of the screen and crush the player; Pac-Man eventually gets caught by the ghosts chasing him, and a wide variety of fighting and shooting games always end with the player-character's death (or deaths, in the case of multiple lives).

Not all games have such a pessimistic outlook, however, and many, like *Myst, Riven,* and *Ultima III: Exodus* have realizable objectives and storylines that can end with the player's success. Yet even these games each feature their own models of world analysis and promote certain decision-making processes, all of which may influence a player's thinking outside the game. One such effect comes from the way the player's point of view is constructed.

The video game is perhaps the only medium that makes frequent use of the second-person address, particularly in adventure games. Graphically, these games simulate a first-person point of view, but the player is addressed as a participant (second-person mode) as opposed to a close confidant (first-person mode) or merely an observer (third-person mode). Everything is structured around the player and is present to produce an experience for the player. Other characters in the game are usually there either to help or to hinder the player-character, and when they speak it is often in direct address to the player-character (as opposed to other characters in the game). Objects exist in the game for the player to use, take, consume, or destroy. The overall effect can be a self-centered, utilitarian point of view, in which players consider everything in the game's world according to how it will affect them or be of use to them.

Positive effects are also possible. Completing an adventure game's objective, for example, usually requires goal-oriented behavior and single-minded pursuit. Even when they are laden with puzzles and ambiguity, most adventure games' problems and goals are relatively clear-cut and simple relative to the problems and goals typically encountered in real life. The video game may remove the player momentarily from the complex problems of real life and offer solvable, simplified conflicts and goals which can be solved in a few hours (or days) and for which solutions already exist.

In either case, these effects may be subtle, but repeated exposure to situations in which one is required to think a certain way can have gradual, long-term effects. Some may find affirmation outside the games; certain ways of thinking like overcompetitiveness and the accruing of personal wealth and goods are already driving forces in capitalistic society, which may explain the rise and popularity of games with similar themes. On the other hand, video games can have a positive influence, enhancing problem-solving skills, powers of observation, and patience.

While most people can clearly distinguish between video games and real life, ideas learned through the games can spill over to other behaviors in either positive or negative ways. As media becomes more prevalent in people's lives, however, the line between video games and real life can begin to blur. Electronic Arts's game *Majestic* (2001) is an example of a game for people who enjoy blurring the line. Billed as "the suspense thriller that infiltrates your life and leaves you guessing where the game ends and reality begins,"[12] *Majestic* sent its players clues via e-mail, voicemail, and faxes and even made use of AOL Instant Messaging. Gameplay took place in real time over a period of months, with players receiving clues at any time. As *ABCnews.com* columnist Dianne Lynch reported,

> Electronic Arts and its partner Anim-X have gone to extraordinary lengths to make it happen. They've purchased hundreds of telephone numbers all over the country, constructed scores of websites embedded with sophisticated access restrictions and hidden clues, and even set up dummy corporations to confuse you.[13]

For those concerned about the blurring of the line, the game also featured "adjustable realism settings" which identified incoming messages as part of the game. The game could be played alone or with others in the *Majestic* online community, who may or may not be actual players.

While *Majestic* was largely experienced alone, the online RPGs, with their social structures and 24-hours-a-day, 7-days-week persistence, are the ones that most combine fantasy and reality. Some players spend several hours every day on their RPGs, where their friends and compatriots spend their time, sometimes supplanting relationships in the world outside of the game. Friendships and marriages occurring between player-characters can affect real-world relationships. In *Computer Games,* Christine Gilbert writes about such virtual marriages:

> Do some of these cyber-relationships survive into the real world? Yes. Have some individuals lost their spouses to other members of their guild or to an über-level warrior? According to the forums, yes. [Sony Interactive's Scott] McDaniel verifies that *EverQuest* has received complaints from spouses not only regarding the addictive qualities of the game, but also the damage to real world relationships the game is allegedly responsible for. It also turns out that people have actually left their real world spouses for individuals who can take out a Hill Giant without destroying the soufflé.
> But while there are some sad stories, there are considerably more happier ones. There is a multitude of married couples who team together every night and share the fun of seeking new adventures.[14]

As online RPGs develop into new forms of social experience that emulate the real world (at least in rudimentary ways), they become more than just "games." They do not simply influence a player's real life, they can become a significant part of it as players spend several hours a day online. And game complexity, graphical detail, and the numbers of player accounts continue to grow.

A Growing Medium

While it is true that the content of most video games has been less than edifying, there does seem to be hope that the medium is maturing as its possibilities are explored. Shooting games and violent content may always be around just as one can still find slapstick and pratfalls in cinema and television, but a much wider range of content is becoming available. Many past best-selling games, like *Pac-Man, Tetris, Myst,* and *The Sims,* are nonviolent ones with a great crossover audience potential. In an article on the best games of the year 2000, *Computer Games* noted that the "Most Ignored Fact" was that "Most of the best-selling games of the year didn't feature any violent content whatsoever."[15] Game designer Peter Molyneux's epic game *Black & White* (2001) is built around the theme of morality, and the company "actually brought in a team of psychologists to explore the concept of morality, and to relate it to actions that have real-life consequences."[16] Furthermore, one role-playing game from eGenesis, *A Tale in the Desert,* had no player combat in it at all; instead of killing or accruing wealth, character advancement depends on the completion of projects and challenges based on virtues.

That many of the best-selling games are nonviolent should encourage developers to expand the range of the medium and explore its possibilities. Commercial success has driven the technological development of the video game, and technology has revealed the medium's potential for creating vicarious experience and interaction. One hopes that designers and developers will rise to the challenge of meeting that potential as the medium matures.

CHAPTER 41

VIDEO GAMES AND THEIR RELATIONSHIP WITH OTHER MEDIA

Martin Picard

In the 1990s, LucasArts, the game division of the powerful empire set up by director George Lucas, created some of the most narrative and cinematographic video games ever seen with *The Secret of Monkey Island* (1992), *Sam and Max Hit the Road* (1993), *Full Throttle* (1996), and *Grim Fandango* (1998). Conversely, video game industry leaders have gained enough power to control the production of the film adaptations of their games; for example, Microsoft sold the rights for the adaptation of the video game *Halo* (2001) to Hollywood studios by their own terms.

Even filmmakers are starting to share creative interest in both media, such as Steven Spielberg who has always admitted to being a video game enthusiast. In 1995 he founded DreamWorks Interactive, a division dedicated in producing video games, including *Medal of Honor* in 1999, based on an original concept by Spielberg himself. In 2005, Spielberg signed a partnership contract with EA to personally design three new video games.[1]

These examples demonstrate the indisputable bond which has developed between video games and other media, especially cinema and, to a lesser extent, television. The associations between these media have been unfolding in many ways, as we will see. First, the audiovisual likeness and the economic rivalries between video games and films (or television) are the most obvious ones. From an economic point of view, the video game industry maintains a partnership with these media as well.

Since video games have become a huge industry involving a large number of employees working in many specific departments, the production processes and facilities now have many similarities with film and television. Some of these industries merged into powerful multinationals (Sony Corporation) which have interests in all of these media. In some other cases, major film studios have their own division of video game production, like LucasArts and Dreamworks mentioned above.

Video games' exhibition outlets are similar to those of cinema and television: arcade games can be found in multiplex theatres, home systems are hooked to television sets, and major video stores have video games, film, and television series rentals all in one place.[2] All these examples reveal a kin partnership among these industries. The music industry is also becoming an essential player in the video game industry, and video game soundtracks are increasingly popular.[3] Live concerts of video game music (like the Video Games Live tour in 2006) have played to sold-out crowds. Nowadays, the music created for video games is composed in a similar fashion as film music scores. As on television, advertisements in video games have become a common phenomenon. A study by Activision and Nielsen Entertainment was conducted in late 2005 on this issue and found that young gamers felt that the presence of in-game advertisements, if well integrated into the games, increased their enjoyment of the games.[4]

Much video game theory shares a close connection with other media, since many of its basic concepts and thoughts came principally from film and television studies.[5] For media theorist Henry Jenkins, all these associations are consequences, or symptoms, of a much larger manifestation in culture which he calls "media convergence." Such convergence manifests itself in many ways, including technologically, economically, socially, culturally, and globally.[6]

Such relationships between video games and other media go back to the early days of video game history. In the early 1980s, video games already were known for their adaptations of television series and American films, especially on the Atari 2600 console:

> Film and television industries realized the potential of the new medium as early as the mid-1970s, when they sought to have a hand in the video game market; CBS Electronics and 20th Century Fox made their own game cartridges, and several dozen movies and television shows were planned to be adapted into game cartridges for the Atari 2600 alone.[7]

It was not until 1983 that the movie industry stopped showing interest in video games, as a result of the video game crash caused by the saturation of the market and the eager releases of poorly made licensed games for the Atari 2600 like *Pac-Man* or the video game adaptation of the movie *E.T.,* which was a monumental flop and quickly became an icon of the crash. Another reason may be the commercial failure of Steven Lisberger's film *Tron* (1982) (the first movie based on a video game world), which helped push Hollywood away from CGI technology and the whole video game industry for a decade.[8]

Video Games and Cinema

The almost total absence of video games-related themes in Hollywood did not last long. The U.S. importation of the Japanese home consoles from companies like Nintendo and Sega [especially the NES in 1985, the Sega Master System (SMS) in 1986, the Sega Genesis in 1989, and the SNES in 1991] changed the course of video game history. Because of the enormous popularity of these consoles in households, the movie industry regained interest (and economic interest) in video games. In 1989, Universal Studios, in partnership with Nintendo, released Todd Holland's film *The Wizard,* which was mostly a feature-length publicity film for Nintendo products like the NES, the Power Glove, and the forthcoming *Super Mario Bros. 3*. The buzz created by the motion picture among the gaming youth led *Super Mario Bros. 3* to sell "more than 17 million copies...worldwide, setting a lasting sales record for a game cartridge that was not packed in with console hardware."[9]

Since the video game industry continued to release video game adaptations of movies at the end of the 1980s and the beginning of the 1990s (especially for the NES console, where many games were based on movies),[10] it was therefore only a matter of time before Hollywood, in return, adapted a video game. The obvious choice at that time was to adapt one of the biggest video game icons of all time: Nintendo's Mario. In 1993, Hollywood Pictures in association with Nintendo released *Super Mario Bros.* starring Bob Hoskins as Mario. Even though the film was a commercial and critical failure ($20 million gross for a $42 million budget[11]), movie studios saw this as an opportunity to attract gamers into theaters while it gave the video game industry an occasion to have licensed revenues and better media coverage.

Thanks to fighting games like *Street Fighter II, Mortal Kombat, Virtua Fighter* (1993) and many others, arcade games enjoyed a renewal of popularity: from 1990 to 1995 alone, more than 100 arcade fighting games were manufactured by more than 20 companies, most notably Capcom (*Street Fighter* series), Midway (*Mortal Kombat* series) and SNK (*The King of Fighters* series). Movie studios then decided to adapt some of them, these games being well suited for audiences of Hollywood action movies, due to their kinetic combat and stylish graphic violence. In 1994, following *Double Dragon* (directed by James Yukich) based on the 1987 arcade game of the same name, an adaptation of *Street Fighter* (directed by Steven de Souza) was released, but without much success ($33 million gross for a $35 million budget). The first relative success came with *Mortal Kombat* (1995) directed by Paul W.S. Anderson. Made for a budget of $20 million, the film grossed $70 million in the United States and $122 million worldwide. The popularity of the film was sufficient for a sequel, *Mortal Kombat: Annihilation* (1997) directed by John R. Leonetti.[12]

After the box office failure of the film *Wing Commander* (1999) based on the science fiction video game series of the same name, a commercial success even bigger than *Mortal Kombat* followed with the first adaptation of a video game with a female icon: the heroine Lara Croft. With an $80 million budget, *Lara Croft: Tomb Raider* directed by Simon West, grossed $131 million in the United States ($47 million the first weekend), making it the biggest commercial success for a video game adaptation. A sequel followed in 2003, *Tomb Raider: The Cradle of Life* (directed by Jan de Bont), again starring Angelina Jolie as Lara Croft.

Meanwhile in Japan, a company named SquareSoft, who was responsible for *Final Fantasy,* the most popular role-playing game series worldwide, worked on a flamboyant adaptation of its own video game series. Square Pictures (their movie division) in association with Columbia Pictures wanted to make the first entirely photorealistic digital animation movie. Although the film was noted for its technical achievement, thanks to the enormous budget of $137 million, *Final Fantasy: The Spirits Within* (directed by Hironobu Sakaguchi, 2001) was a major commercial failure, grossing only $32 million in the United States, and $85 million worldwide. Ironically, the studio's losses of approximately $123 million (taking the marketing cost into account) eventually bankrupted Square Pictures, leading to the merging of SquareSoft with their longtime rival, Enix.

Back in Hollywood, the major studios decided to take advantage of new interest in popular culture that had begun in Japan a few years before: horror movies and games. As a result, Hollywood studios hastened to produce several remakes of Japanese horror movies rather than to simply import them [for example *The Ring* (*Ringu*), *The Grudge* (*Ju-On*), *Dark Water,* and *Pulse* (*Kairo*)]. Soon after, Hollywood decided to devote their film adaptations of video games to survival horror games. The first one to be adapted to cinema was the *Resident Evil* series, and in 2002, Paul W.S. Anderson directed *Resident Evil,* starring Milla Jovovich. The film had a budget of $32 million and grossed $101 million worldwide. A sequel followed in 2004, *Resident Evil: Apocalypse* directed by Alexander Witt.

Following on the horror craze, the controversial German director Uwe Boll purchased the rights of several horror video game hits and started to make his own adaptations of such games as *House of the Dead* (2003), *Alone in the Dark* (2005), and *BloodRayne* (2005). These adaptations were mostly famous for being the weakest ones, irritating gamers who nevertheless went to see Boll's pictures or purchased the DVDs of his films. (*House of the Dead* grossed $10 million in the United States with a budget of only $7 million, while *Alone in the Dark,* with a budget of $20 million, only grossed $5 million in the United States. *BloodRayne* grossed a mere $3 million worldwide in theaters with a budget of $25 million. Nevertheless, the DVD sales of these films were much more profitable.) The controversy surrounding Uwe Boll continued in 2006 when he decided to organize a boxing event, "Raging Boll," with his most virulent critics. The footage of these fights was used for his next movie, another adaptation of a violent video game, *Postal* (2007).

Another horror movie based on a video game, based on a popular sci-fi first-person shooter, was released in 2005: *Doom* (directed by Andrejz Bartkowiak), starring the wrestling champion The Rock. Despite the common practice of casting celebrities, the adaptation was again a critical and commercial failure (it was shot with a budget of $70 million and grossed $28 million in the United States). At the time of this writing, the last movie adaptation of a video game was *Silent Hill* (2006), based on the critically acclaimed survival horror series of the same name, directed by the French filmmaker Christophe Gans (*Brotherhood of the Wolf / Le Pacte des Loups,* 2001) and written by Roger Avary (director of *Killing Zoe* and writer of *Reservoir Dogs* and *Pulp Fiction*). Even with these big names behind the camera and the fact that Gans was a self-proclaimed gamer and fan of the *Silent Hill* series, the film received bad reviews and did disappointingly at the box office (it was shot with a budget of $50 million and grossed only $72 million worldwide).

Although none of these films became major blockbuster hits, the tendency to adapt video games to cinema is far from over. Considering the large number of video games licensed by Hollywood studios, there will be more adaptations than ever in the years to come. Indeed, almost all video game best-selling hits had their rights bought by a movie studio or a producer. Several projects are already in production, the most anticipated ones (perhaps excluding the ones by Uwe Boll) being *Splinter Cell* (due in 2007), *Halo* [announced for 2008, to be produced by WingNut Films (Peter Jackson's banner)], and finally *Metal Gear Solid* (also announced for 2008, to be directed by the famous designer of the game, Hideo Kojima). To ease the wait, fans can buy the graphic novels adapted from some of these video games, an increasingly popular practice from the game developers. In early 2006, Hideo Kojima released a digital graphic novel based on the *Metal Gear Solid* universe sold exclusively on UMD for Sony's PSP. Another graphic novel, based on the game *Halo* was published by Bungie Studios in the summer of 2006.

Video Games and Comics/Animation (Manga/Animé)

Many video games have been adapted from comic books since the beginning of the console era in the United States. The majority of these adaptations are based on Marvel and DC Comics's super heroes. The MobyGames website has listed more than 100 adaptations of Marvel and DC Comics (67 for Marvel and 39 for DC Comics more precisely). The main characters adapted in this fashion have been Marvel's X-Men and Spider-Man, and DC Comics's Superman and Batman.

In Japan, the list is significantly larger, since video games have always been strongly associated with other Japanese media, especially *animé* and *manga. Manga* is the word in Japanese for comics or printed cartoons. *Animé* are Japanese animated films created according to a distinct aesthetic, influenced almost exclusively by *manga.* Video games, which have such a major importance in Japanese popular culture,[13] appeal to a whole generation, named the "visual generation" (*shikaku sedai*) in Japan.[14] The obsessive fans of these hobbies are called by the Japanese pejorative term *otaku.*

Consequently, almost every popular *manga* and *animé* have been adapted into video games in Japan,[15] with increasing numbers of them being imported into Europe and North America. Although children in countries such as France, Italy, Canada, and the United States grew up with Japanese animation since the end of the 1970s, the craze for all that touches Japanese popular culture truly started with the *manga*-based *animé Akira* (1988) directed by Katsuhiro Otomo and was followed by several others during the 1990s, like Mamoru Oshii's *Ghost in the Shell* (1996) based on a *manga* by Masamune Shirow, and Hideaki Anno's television series *Neon Genesis Evangelion* (1995). These titles have also had their video game adaptations. *Akira* was adapted into a video game in 1988 on the NES, *Ghost in the Shell: Stand Alone Complex* in 2004 on the PlayStation 2, and *Neon Genesis Evangelion* in 1999 on the Nintendo 64, although the latter had never been released outside of Japan.

Not surprisingly, many young people worldwide who are interested in Japanese animation are also gamers and consumers of video games series adapted from *manga* and *animé* (such as *Dragon Ball, Mobile Suit Gundam, Full Metal Alchemist,* and so on), to such a point that even some fans in the United States have been called *otaku.* In the United States, adaptations of animated films and television series was less of a phenomenon, with the notable exceptions of games based on Disney characters (of which there are more than 100) and games based on the immensely popular series *The Simpsons* (of which there are more than 20), until the emergence of movies using 3-D computer animation made by studios like Pixar and DreamWorks. Every feature film from these studios has had a video game adapted from it so far. For this genre, video games have become the obvious tie-in products, since 3-D animation and video games share the same target audiences as well as the same visual style and technology.

Conversely, fewer and less known are the adaptations of video games to comics and animation. Once again, it is necessary to look at what has been done in Japan. With the exception of the recent adaptation of *Metal Gear Solid* into a graphic novel as previously mentioned, the best known example is the *Pokemon* video game series. It was so popular in Japan and then in North America that one could forget that this franchise began as Nintendo Game Boy Advance video games (*Pokemon Blue* and *Pokemon Red,* released in Japan in 1996 and in North America in 1998). Indeed, Pokemon involved a great many tie-in products, such as television series, animated films, figurines, cuddly toys, home furnishings, and practically every piece of clothing for children with an effigy of the characters Pikachu and Ash. Even though the Pokemon franchise is best remembered in North America as a cartoon and may be the most successful adaptation of a video game, it is not the first manifestation of the close relationship between video games and television.

Video Games and Television

Since the emergence of video games as a popular phenomenon, the video game industry has had a relationship with television, while the film industry often considered video games as mere spin-offs. Similar to television, the video game "has played a crucial role in the child's entry into narrative," as well as to the construction of "consumerist subjects."[16]

It is therefore no coincidence that video game settings and characters were first adapted to television in Saturday morning cartoons. The first popular one was the *Pac-Man* series (which ran from September 25, 1982, to September 1, 1984). Based loosely on the original arcade games *Pac-Man, Ms. Pac-Man, Pac-Man Jr.,* and *Super Pac-Man,* the cartoon production company Hanna-Barbera brought all these characters to life for the TV series. The show featured the Pac-Man family (in which "Ms." Pac-Man is actually a "Mrs."), who are in most episodes troubled by the familiar villainous Ghost Monsters from the games. The family usually got out of trouble by munching on power pellets to energize themselves and chomp the Ghost Monsters. Other shows followed over the years, including *Frogger Video Game* (1982), *The Super Mario Bros. Super Show!* (1989), *Sonic the Hedgehog* (1993), and *Donkey Kong Country* (1998).

The video game craze also inspired a television quiz show called *Starcade.* The game show aired on television stations across the United States between 1982 and 1984, generally in a Saturday morning or early afternoon time slot. It consisted of trivia questions regarding video games as well as one-on-one competition between contestants, usually a father and son, on arcade games for electronic prizes and a grand prize of an arcade terminal.[17] While arcade games tended to be popular among both children and adults,[18] home video game systems, with their basic controls and simple graphics, were more typically aimed at children. Moreover, since systems such as the Atari 2600, the Intellivision, and the Colecovision were connected to television sets, they became substitute objects of entertainment for children that competed with television and could offer the feeling of control and direct action that the television could not.

Although Saturday morning cartoons would benefit from the popularity of the video game phenomenon, the video game industry had been adapting games from television shows for some time.[19] However, some licenses were hard to obtain, especially in the arcade sector since the *Death Race* controversy.[20] For example, in Japan, Nintendo's game designer Shigeru Miyamoto wanted to license Popeye for a new arcade game. King Features Syndicate refused to sell the rights to Nintendo, so Miyamoto was then forced to create his own original character for the game. This is how the character Jumpman began, who was later renamed Mario for the arcade game finally entitled *Donkey Kong.*[21] Even the name "Donkey Kong" caused legal issues, because of the strong association with King Kong. Nintendo did eventually obtain the rights and produced the arcade game *Popeye* in 1983, but the game had nowhere near the success enjoyed by the *Donkey Kong* and *Mario Bros.* series.

Exchanges between video games and television (mainly cartoons) became increasingly frequent.[22] Some extremely popular franchises, like *Star Wars* and *Star Trek,* marketed derivative products using a variety of media (film, television, video games, comics, novels, toys, and so on), and have over 100 and over 50 games based on them respectively. This aggressive strategy played on consumers' desire for franchises they liked; once the consumption of a franchise begins, one wants logically and emotionally to obtain other products in the franchise, to obtain a complete vision of the whole, both materially and narratively.

In her book *Playing with Power,* Marsha Kinder called this sort of marketed franchise a "supersystem of entertainment," and cited the huge success of the *Teenage Mutant Ninja Turtles* (TMNT) as a good example of this phenomenon at the end of the 1980s.[23] For Kinder, the success of the TMNT with children was based on the judicious intertextual mixture of animality (Turtles), science fiction (Mutant), and Japanese martial arts (Ninja), and on the expansion of the franchise in several media. The TMNT "supersystem" began with a cult comic book from Mirage and then an enormously popular cartoon series, created in 1987. An arcade game appeared in 1989, followed by many console games, the first ones being on the NES [*Teenage Mutant Ninja Turtles* (1989); *Teenage Mutant Ninja Turtles_II: The Arcade Game* (1990)]. Finally, a feature film directed by Steve Barron was released in 1990, its success spawning a series of sequels. The success of this kind of "supersystem of entertainment" relies enormously on the idea of "transmedia storytelling."

Transmedia Storytelling and Media Convergence

In *Hamlet on the Holodeck: The Future of Narrative in Cyberspace,* Janet Murray acknowledged transmedia storytelling when she introduced the concept of "cyberdrama": "The coming digital story form...will encompass many different formats and styles but will essentially be a single distinctive entity...a reinvention of storytelling itself for the new digital medium."[24]

Henry Jenkins, a few years later, coined the term "transmedia storytelling" which simply means "the movement of [narrative] content across media."[25] The concept is an aspect of "media convergence," which Jenkins described as follows:

> The flow of content across multiple media platforms, the cooperation between multiple media industries, the search for new structures of media financing which fell at the interstices between old and new media, and the migratory behavior of media audiences who would go almost anywhere in search of the kinds of entertainment experiences they wanted.[26]

This type of manifestation was advanced by the *Star Wars* franchise, in which the tie-in products played a central role. During the 1980s, for instance, the accompanying line of action figures and vehicles from *Star Wars* outgrossed the movies themselves,[27] creating a precedent in the marketing of ancillary products. Since then, goods—including video games—have been promoted with almost every Hollywood blockbuster targeting young audiences. The *Star Wars*-related video games have been used for two main purposes: the re-creation of the most memorable scenes from the trilogies (to be played by their fans), and the addition of new storylines and fresh approaches expanding the Star Wars universe. Such effects are not limited to the United States. Recent examples of transmedia storytelling in Japan include such franchises as *Neon Genesis Evangelion* (1995–1997) and *Blood, the Last Vampire* (2001). These franchises consist of many *manga, animé,* novels, and video games, each one telling a different story which adds to the franchise's world.

Inspired by these notable achievements, the Wachowski Brothers, the creators of *The Matrix* film series and declared aficionados of video games, Japanese *animé* and *manga,* and comic book cultures in general, attempted to expand on the concept of transmedia storytelling by creating *Enter the Matrix* (Infogrames, 2003), a video game that could expand the story of *The Matrix Reloaded* (which was released the same day as the *Enter the Matrix* video game, May 15, 2003), and anticipate developments of the third opus of the movie trilogy. Thus, in the game *Enter the Matrix* players can play as two minor characters in the movies, Niobe and Ghost (played by actors Jada Pinkett-Smith and Anthony Wong, respectively). These characters became increasingly crucial (especially Niobe) to the victory of the humans in *The Matrix Reloaded* and *The Matrix Revolutions* (2003). In this way, the game is not a mere spin-off but an integral part of a complex work spanning several media forms and platforms, which fills in blanks in the movies' stories to facilitate the comprehension of the movie trilogy. In addition to the video game, the Wachowski Brothers simultaneously released derivative material such as a series of nine animated films (*The Animatrix,* 2003), two comic books (*Matrix Comics,* Vol. 1 and 2, 2003), and complementary content on the official movie website (http://whatisthematrix. warnerbros.com/).

Two more video games were released with the same objective in mind. In 2005, the Wachowski Brothers released an MMORPG called *The Matrix Online,* which continued the story of the trilogy beginning just after the end of the third film where machines and humans have reconciled thanks to Neo (Keanu Reeves). *The Matrix Online* allowed players to be part of one of three opposing groups (the humans of Zion, the machines, or the exiles of the Merovingian), all of whom strive to achieve control of the Matrix. The game producers released on a regular basis what they called "Live Events" to stimulate players' immersion in the virtual universe. At the end of 2005, Infogrames released another video game based on the Matrix franchise, also written by the Wachowski Brothers, called *The Matrix: Path of Neo.* The game put the player in the shoes of Neo himself, reliving the main adventures of Neo in the movie trilogy, but with new perspectives never seen in the movies.

The marketing strategies of this groundbreaking franchise helped create a unique transmediatic work brought about by the convergence of several media (film, video games, websites, comics, *animé,* etc.). Media convergence and transmedia storytelling are becoming the new trend for creators who do not want to be confined to a unique medium or platform and for producers who want to maximize the profits from a hit, no matter what the original platform. This kind of cultural practice underscores the importance of other media in the emergence and construction of the video game and helps to predict the possible directions that video games may take in the future. The "intermedial" nature of the video game is far from being a mere tendency but instead forms an essential part of the medium.

How to Get a Job in the Video Game Industry

Mark J. P. Wolf

Anyone wishing to work in the video game industry should first decide which area of it suits them best, such as design, development, art, animation, testing, programming, or producing. Game designers initiate ideas and begin their development, while development teams take designs and develop them further into models that can be implemented, built, and tested. Artists design the look and feel of a game, including background art, the game's locations, characters, and objects, and even such things as the lighting and sound effects that occur in a game's world. Animators design the movement occurring in a game, which could include anything from drawing characters and events frame by frame (by hand or digitally), to supervising motion-capture sessions that record the movements of live actors and apply them to computer-generated characters. Quality Assurance people, otherwise known as video game testers, check game play to make sure it is smooth and free of software bugs. Programmers generate the code behind the games, while producers organize the project and make sure things are running smoothly between all of the people in the jobs described above who are working together. There are also subdivisions of each of these areas into very specialized positions, which will vary based on the kind of games being made.

Today, one of the best ways into a career in the video game industry is a college degree from one of the programs or schools (like Digipen or Full Sail) specializing in video game design and production. While background and experience are helpful, luck still plays a part, and location does as well; certain areas like Southern California, the San Francisco Bay Area, Seattle, and so forth have more game development companies than do other areas. Some people transfer in from other careers, where they have honed skills that the video game industry finds useful (for example, filmmakers, graphics designers, artists, or computer programmers). Often getting a job depends on showing that you have done similar work elsewhere. On the other hand, being a well-rounded individual with a wide range of experience and cultural knowledge will give someone an edge over someone with a narrow range of experience limited only to games.

Beyond that, there are game industry websites, like gamesindustry.biz and Gamasutra.com, books[28], and many game development companies have their own websites listing this information as well. If you are targeting a specific company, you can often e-mail them directly with questions. Detailed knowledge of a particular company and what they do will make a job applicant stand out during a job interview, as opposed to those who have only a general idea of what the company is like. And finally, create your games, either games programmed with software like XNA or even mods (modifications) made from existing games. If you really like to do something, you should be doing it long before you are hired to do it.

CHAPTER 42

The Future of Video Games

Mark J. P. Wolf

Video games have been around now for over 40 years and have taken on many forms. Besides being entertainment, some of them tell stories, while others simulate situations and let players explore them. Video games have been used in education, as a teaching tool, and some games even aspire to be artistic and create an interesting experience for their players. Games can be a solitary activity, or one shared by friends, or in the case of online role-playing games, an activity shared by millions of strangers. Finally, games create miniature worlds on-screen which the player enters into, so to speak, during the playing of the game.

To speculate as to what the future of the video game medium might be, we can extend and extrapolate all of these directions in which the video game has already been moving, that is, the video game as *entertainment,* as *narrative,* as *simulation,* as *education,* as *art and experience,* as *communication,* and as *subcreation,* the term coined by J.R.R. Tolkien to describe both the product and process of building an imaginary world.

Video Games as Entertainment

Although it need not be their only purpose or function, video games primarily have been made and used for entertainment to an even greater extent than theater, film, or television, or almost any other type of media. The dominance of entertainment as the main use for the medium has obscured other possibilities, and perhaps this happened because of the rich vein of possibilities existing within this one function. For example, the number of venues for video games keeps increasing. Arcade games appeared outside the arcade in bars, restaurants, movie theaters, shopping malls, and almost anywhere that vending machines might be found. The video game also can combine entertainment with exercise; the game *Dance Dance Revolution* is full-body aerobic exercise, and one California school has even added it to its physical education program, since the game teaches such things as balance, timing, and coordination.[1]

Other games appeared in the home, first on television sets and later in handheld units and home computers (even within operating systems themselves, like the *Minesweeper* game included with Microsoft Windows), and of course, on personal digital assistants, wristwatches, and cell phones. In the future we can probably expect to find games on any interactive electronic device that has a screen.

Games with multiple players may find new places to play as well. Currently games with larger numbers of players are found online, but other configurations are possible, for example, people playing as contestants on a television show via their cell phones. Large gatherings of physically present players also could be explored; imagine, for example, an Imax theater with game controls for every seat in the theater, each controlling a character in a larger projected screen image, allowing several hundred people to play at once all on the same large screen.

Another way the video game is a part of our culture is as an outlet for cross-media franchises, including tie-ins to movies, television shows, board games, card games, table-top games, novels, other video games, and so forth. Today it is not unusual to find franchises developed for a range of media all at the same time. For example, the *Enter the Matrix* video game was developed at the same time as the second and third *Matrix* films and incorporated the same actors, storylines, and effects. Often an entire series of games is produced, as in the *Star Wars* and *Star Trek* franchises. And as game graphics improve and grow more photorealistic, and film imagery becomes more and more computer generated, the appearance of imagery in both media continue to converge.

Entertainment will probably remain the dominant use of the medium, just as it has for film and television. And, just as it is in film and television, the dominant form of that entertainment will likely remain narrative.

Video Games as Narrative

While most video games are oriented around some kind of story (at times very weak ones), the adaptation of narrative to an interactive medium in which players act and make decisions has both placed limitations on storytelling as well as opened up new possibilities. In some cases, techniques little-used in literature are better suited to interaction. Second-person narration, for example, was the typical mode of address found in text adventures. Most games are oriented as first-person experiences, where the player's avatar functions as the main character in the story presented, the outcome of which depends on the player's actions. Story events, then, range from predetermined and unchanging sequences (like many events found in opening sequences), to conditional events (depending on what the player does), to randomized events (for example, the appearance of attackers or obstacles).

Writing for video games means stories with multiple pathways, which at first resulted in simpler narratives or games with a low degree of interactivity. Games with low interactivity, such as games in the genre known as Interactive Movies, have typically been unpopular, allowing simpler storylines to win out. Arcade games, whose success is determined by the number of quarters per hour they take in, will probably always trade complicated storylines for fast action and state-of-the-art graphics, so it is in home games where we find the most interesting narrative innovation.

Home games have expanded narrative potential through the growth in capacity of the storage media used, which moved from cartridges to floppy diskettes to CD-ROMs and now to DVD-ROMs, resulting in better game imagery, more narrative pathways, and a larger game world. Other advances have increased the possibilities for the stories taking place in games: the use of computer-controlled characters driven by algorithms and artificial intelligences helped make more character interaction possible, and in the case of online role-playing games, the other characters in a game are all controlled by other people. Both allow for a greater variety of game events, as well as open-ended games that can go on indefinitely (like the *Sim* series of games or most online games).

An interesting question to consider is how increasing narrative possibilities will impact the scholarly study of the games themselves. The researcher will have to spend more time exploring narrative possibilities, with no guarantee that everything has been seen or experienced. Many games already are designed to take 40 hours or more to complete, compared to the two-hour or so time slot that most movies fit into.

As artificial intelligences and other game structures generate narratives through the use of algorithms, games move into another realm, that of computer simulation, which is where the future of interactive narrative will be found.

Video Games as Simulation

Although many early games had simplified simulations of physical phenomena such as gravity or ricochets, during the 1980s more games began to appear in which simulation was given a central role. Games like *M.U.L.E.* (a home computer game about homesteading) were management simulations in which players had to allocate limited resources while balancing competing needs, modeling simple economic principles. The most successful series of these games began in 1989, with Will Wright's *SimCity*, and *Sim* games are still being produced today. While simulation-based games have objectives, like building a successful city or expanding one's empire, the overall objective from one playing to the next is the understanding of the underlying principles and algorithms governing the simulation. Simulation games, then, can simulate systems, institutions, and even the political ideas behind them.

As simulations grow increasingly complex, a wider variety of phenomena can be modeled; *The Sims,* for example, has moved the genre from economic or political phenomena into the realm of psychology, albeit in a simplified form. Since players may play the games without consciously analyzing what kinds of worldviews are embodied in the underlying rules governing the game, the design of the game may be imparting ideas and ways of thinking which are subtler than those found in surface representations (for example, those of race, gender, ethnicity, and so forth). Such implications may take many hours of gameplay to notice, but they are likely to be necessary for an in-depth analysis of a game.

We might also speculate as to what ever-more-detailed kinds of systems or institutions will be simulated. Already one can play God [in *Black & White I* (2001) and *Black & White II* (2005)], create a world like earth [in *SimEarth* (1990)], become a Latin American dictator [in *Tropico* (2001)], build theme parks, railroads, towers, ant colonies, and ancient empires, or conduct war campaigns. Perhaps someday we will see games simulating HMOs, public school systems, nonprofit organizations, or other areas that could potentially help give some indication of the intricacies involved in social or political problem areas. And the more simulation is able to capture the working of real-life systems and institutions, the more video games move in the direction of education.

Video Games as Education

Even the early home game systems, like the Magnavox Odyssey and the Atari 2600, had programs purporting to be educational for children, though their content was fairly simple. In the home computer, educational software bridged the gap between utility software and games. Some were even spin-offs of games, such as *Mario Teaches Typing*. The closest the arcade ever got to being educational were several puzzle games, quiz games, and a modified version of *Battlezone* that the military wanted to use for tank training.

Today the video game is being seriously considered as a means of education. The Games-to-Teach Project, a partnership between the Massachusetts Institute of Technology and Microsoft, is exploring ways of teaching math, science, and engineering through the use of games. They already have a set of conceptual frameworks for games, several of which are being developed into prototypes which they hope will become marketable products. Among these are *Supercharged,* which teaches principles of electromagnetism and charged particle physics, and *Environmental Detectives,* a game involving environmental engineering investigation and played on handheld PCs. Other proposed games include puzzles in optics, the effects of mass and velocity on levers, pulleys, strings and gears, and engineering principles. Still others involve psychology, viruses and immunology, history, design, and architecture. The project is also exploring educational networked gaming environments.

The Digital Media Collaboratory, an initiative of the I.C. Squared Institute at The University of Texas at Austin, is another program working on video games as education. Two of their projects, EnterTech and Career Connect, involve simulated work environments which are used for the training of individuals entering the workforce who have not had the opportunity for education or the necessary skills for the workplace. The program was begun in the year 2000 and has been successful, and according to an article in *Syllabus,* "More than 67 percent of EnterTech graduates found jobs or enrolled in future education."[2] Another project at the institute, "Valuation Matrices for Learning/Educational Content in Popular Games" is researching "the potential for commercially situated computer games to demonstrate educational utility."[3]

As video game technology expands into areas of virtual reality and augmented reality, new educational possibilities will also appear, and online gaming communities are another area of potential. Some educators may be skeptical of video games as teaching tools, perhaps due to their limited ideas of what a video game is or what it can be. As newer technologies enable students to have new experiences that they could not have had with older technologies, perhaps those educators will change their thinking and begin incorporating their use in curricula.

One question that should be asked in regard to video games and education is, who is doing the educating? Advertisers who want consumers to learn about their products are already producing "advergames." According to *Wired* magazine, an *advergame* is "a downloadable or Web-based game created solely to enable product placements."[4] The ideas and ways of thinking that are incorporated into a game may be hidden in the way the game is designed and programmed and less obvious than, say, the ideas described in a textbook. A game based on the way the economy functions or the way social groups interact will be based on theories which will vary greatly depending on the politics and beliefs of the group designing the game. Students may play such games without ever being aware of the theories that control the simulations being depicted in the game's events, much less question whether or not those theories are sound. Of course, anything used as a tool of education has the potential to become a political tool with a hidden agenda as well.

As video games are used to express certain ideas or points of view, we can see them as becoming forms of artistic expression and experiential art.

Video Games as Art and Experience

Perhaps because entertainment has been the dominant function of the video game throughout its entire history, the potential function of the video game as art and experience has been the most overlooked. As a time-based visual medium, the video game possesses great potential for artistic expression. Although video games have been used for artistic expression, the art has almost always been subject to commercial concerns leaving much of the artistic potential untouched. An important question for future development of video games, then, is how to make the means of production more available to artists and make the technology user-friendly enough that the artist can work directly without having to rely too much on others for technical aspects such as hardware design or the writing of computer code. Similar barriers were encountered when artists first began using computer technology, and it seems inevitable that they will soon begin creating video games as well.

Another area of great untapped potential lies in the graphics of video games. By definition, the video game is a visual medium, and one that combines information processing and interaction, often in such a way that one relies on the speed of the other. A large part of playing a video game involves reading and interpreting the graphics of the game, for navigation and other goal-oriented activities such as collecting or using objects and interacting with the right characters, and so on. Since the earliest games, a tension between abstraction and representation has existed in video game graphics, resulting in games of varying difficulty as far as reading the graphics is concerned. Even the early games, with their severe graphical limitations, usually attempted to be as representational as possible. Games with deliberately abstract graphics are occasionally produced, but their numbers decreased throughout the 1980s and 1990s, as the representational power of the medium grew.

Recently, some abstraction has reappeared in video games, in the textures used for texture-mapping, although even this is arguably a representational use of abstract patterns. As for abstract games, games like *Rez* for the Sony PlayStation and *Tron 2.0* are perhaps a sign that the industry is slowly realizing the possibilities for fresh designs that abstraction has to offer. Games can be abstract not only in appearance but also in behavior, requiring players to learn specific rules and how to interpret events in order to play a game successfully. Abstraction then, in both appearance and behavior, is a major area of potential for future video game design, and one in need of further exploration.

In general, the function of the video game as art and experience has been little explored, perhaps because the industry has been slow to see such possibilities as commercially feasible. Artists, too, must be more willing to explore what the medium can communicate, and how it can be used to express ideas and experiences. Taking this a step further, we can also consider ways in which the video game is becoming a medium of communication.

Video Games as Communication

Once we admit the use of the video game as representation, simulation, and education, we can see that the medium can also be used to communicate moral and ethical worldviews as well, either deliberately or inadvertently. The video game does not merely *show* us things, it asks us to *do* things, to participate, to play. The nature of that play, however, can demand different things; aggressive behavior or cooperative behavior, quick reflexes or contemplation, problem-solving ability or hand-eye coordination, navigational ability, suspicion, strategic thinking, and so forth. The different degrees to which a game requires certain actions and abilities, and how they are combined, will result in certain attitudes being encouraged over others within the game. How players are rewarded or punished for what they do, and the way causes are connected with effects, and actions are connected with consequences, will likewise suggest values for behaviors and suggest moral and ethical worldviews based on those valuations. Also, the presence of level editors and other authoring tools allow players to modify games to personify the messages they embody. Considering that the audience for video games ranges from adults to young children, we might also ask how video games influence and are perceived by different age groups.

In addition to the one-way communication described above, the video game has also become a two-way means of communication, in the form of massively multiplayer online role-playing games. All of the above elements involving morals and ethics are even more influential on a player's thinking when that player is a part of a huge community of players all operating within the same game-world subject to the same rules. In MMORPGs like *Ultima Online, EverQuest, Asheron's Call,* or *Star Wars Galaxies,* community building is a major part of play, as players make friends and enemies, forming alliances and guilds, and compete against each other individually and in groups. Many people form strong friendships with people they will never meet in person, although many online friendships do result in real-world ones, even marriages occasionally. At the same time, the many hours spent in online play may take a person away from real-world friendships and activities.

As online worlds grow in detail, depth, and attractiveness, and as the real world is perceived by many to be more dangerous and unsafe, one might expect social shifts in which online venues grow in importance, and begin to have greater influence and effects on real-world events. With so many players, and events that continue day and night for years on end, the way in which online worlds function becomes different than other games, and grows more like miniature worlds.

Video Games as Subcreation

In 1939, J.R.R. Tolkien proposed the notion of "subcreation," the idea that human beings recombine concepts and elements from the universe of God's creation, "creating under" or "subcreating" to make imaginary worlds of their own; Tolkien's own Arda, in which lies Middle-Earth, is an example of this, and examples in other media include the galaxies of *Star Wars* and *Star Trek.* These worlds are more than simply stories in that they involve their own geography, history, timelines, cultures, languages, and even their own flora and fauna, resulting in imaginary worlds that are as complete and internally consistent as the author wishes to make them.

Larger-scale video games and especially MMORPGs are moving in this direction; some online games have millions of players and the games take place in "persistent" worlds, which means they continue 24-hours-a-day, seven-days-a-week. The geography of these worlds can be enormous; *Ultima Online*, for example, is said to have "more than 189 million square feet" which "would require 38,000 17-inch monitors, nearly enough to occupy a football field."[5] Within these worlds, the buying and selling of objects has blossomed into economies, with the sale of some virtual objects and characters even occurring outside the virtual world on eBay. One researcher looking at Norrath, the kingdom in the online game *EverQuest*, has concluded that "The creation of dollar-valued items in Norrath occurs at a rate such that Norrath's GNP per capita easily exceeds that of dozens of countries, including India and China."[6] As these virtual economies grow, they will no doubt have an increasing impact on real-world economies.

Seeing video games as subcreated worlds is one way that future scholarship will be able to regard the complexity, depth, and sheer size of these kinds of video games, and other games that all take place within the same subcreation, such as the *Myst* series of games, or the *Star Wars* games. As the object of study grows in size, it will also be necessary for researchers to devise new ways of studying video games, and current scholarship has a long way to go to catch up to these quickly expanding worlds.

User-Generated Games

The future of video games will almost certainly continue to include user-created content and games written by users themselves. Dozens of game creations programs, such as Chris Jones's *Adventure Game Studio* (1997, with updates appearing throughout the following decade) or James Paige's OHRRPGCE (Official Hamster Republic Role Playing Game Creation Engine) (1997), allow users to create their own games, and game-creation communities have sprung up around some of these programs. The video game industry as well has begun to encourage user-created games, with the release of programs like Microsoft's XNA (2004, with updates since), and Nintendo's WiiWare program (unreleased as of August 2007). Nintendo even announced in June 2007 that users will be able to buy and sell user-created games on their WiiShop channel on the Wii console.[7]

While the possibility of user-generated games will not level the playing field, as few users have the time, money, and resources to put into a game as a large production studio does, it will open up new possibilities and increase the diversity of games available. Projects too small, too esoteric, or not commercial enough for larger companies to consider will have their chance to reach an audience, and many new, smaller companies may result from the successes of such games. In the end, user-generated games will benefit both users and the game industry alike.

Future Video Game Hardware

Aside from appearing on every electronic device that has a screen, video game hardware may take on new designs that will in turn bring about new kinds of gaming. Playing with ideas in even one area of hardware design yields many interesting ideas, for example, changing the shape of the screen. Imagine, for example, a video game screen that wraps completely around a cylinder; even simple games like *PONG* and *Breakout* become more difficult when the entire screen cannot be seen at once and has to keep on being turned over by the player. Game tablets with screens on two sides, or a game with screens on the six sides of a cube, designed so that game action moves fluidly from screen to screen, could present new challenges for game designers and game players alike (at the time of this writing, only the Nintendo DS features more than one screen). Even older and simpler games could be played in a new way; for example, imagine playing a game like *Pac-Man* on a spherical screen that covers most of a ball. With a mercury switch that, through the use of gravity, tells the game which direction is up, Pac-Man could be made to always appear at the top of the ball, and the player would have to rotate the entire game to move him through the maze. Thin screens with the flexibility of paper would open up even more possibilities for video game hardware design. And for every new hardware design will come a whole series of games that make use of that design, including ones that were simply not possible without the new technologies.

Over the last decade, video games had advanced tremendously in their depth and complexity, and the study of video games has been one of the fastest-growing areas of media studies. The great potential variety of uses and functions of video games is already beginning to be explored, by a wide variety of people including game designers, educators, media theorists, and artists. For many players, video games represent the greatest percentage of media usage in their everyday life, and for a growing number of online players, these games have become a way of life. However one may wish to speculate about the future of media in general, it is clear that the video game is certain to play an increasingly important role.

GLOSSARY OF VIDEO GAME TERMINOLOGY

algorithm — This is the game program which runs the game and determines all the events and responses of the game, and controls gameplay.

attract mode — When an arcade video game is not being played, the game will often be in "attract mode," which demonstrates the game and tries to attract players. This mode keeps motion on the screen and also prevents an image from getting burnt into the screen.

avatar — A player's character or representation with the on-screen world of the video game, and often one which can be personalized in some way so as to be distinctly unique. The word is originally from Sanskrit and refers to a Hindu deity appearing in physical form on earth.

bank-switching — In early 8-bit programming, bank-switching was used to increase the amount of RAM or ROM that could be addressed. The technique involved dividing memory into disjointed sections or banks, only one of which can be accessed at a time. This allowed games requiring larger memory allotments to run on a system that could otherwise not handle them, although the process had its limitations as well and required more complicated programming.

bezel — On an arcade video game, the glass panel through which the monitor is seen. Artwork based on the game usually fills the area around through which the monitor is seen.

bit — A contraction of "binary digit," a bit comes in two states, on or off, which are usually represented as a one or a zero. Bits are the basic building blocks of computer memory.

bitmap — Bitmaps are graphics which are made up of, and stored as, grids of pixels.

byte — A byte is a unit of measurement for information storage, equal to eight bits. Bytes are the "words" used for memory addressing within computer programming.

cabaret — A type of arcade game cabinet that is smaller than a typical upright cabinet.

cabinet — The box, usually made out of wood, that houses an arcade video game.

cathode ray tube — A display device often used for televisions, computer monitors, radar, oscilloscopes, and arcade video games. In a tapering glass tube widening to a screen on one end, an electron beam, varying in intensity, is magnetically scanned across a screen coated with phosphors which glow according to the intensity of the beam, producing an image on the screen.

chip — See *microchip.*

CGI — Short for "computer-generated imagery." Computer graphics used in a variety of media, usually referred to as such in the case of movies or television.

cockpit — A type of game cabinet that a player can sit inside, with a seat and a roof overhead.

cocktail — A type of game cabinet which functions as a small table at which players can sit down. The monitor is seen through a table-top surface, which players can set drinks on, hence the name "cocktail."

coin-op — Short for "coin-operated," this term refers to vending machines, trade stimulators, pinball games, arcade video games, and other coin-operated arcade games.

console — An interactive entertainment computer system designed primarily for the playing of home video games, as opposed to a home computer system designed primarily for other tasks, or arcade video games that are coin-operated.

conversion — Arcade games that are installed, often by means of a "conversion kit," into a modified game cabinet which was not originally used to play them. An arcade operator might use such kits to reuse old game cabinets by installing new games in them.

CRT — See *cathode ray tube.*

cut-scene — A short animated scene which appears between levels of a video game, often involving characters and events related to the game or as part of the background story in which the game takes place.

DECO Cassette System — In 1981, video game company Data East introduced the DECO Cassette System, which allowed new games to be uploaded into an arcade cabinet from tape cassettes. The magnetic tapes, however, proved to be unreliable and easily demagnetized. The system met with some success in Japan but was a failure in the United States, and after producing around 40 games for the DCS, Data East ended it in 1985.

dedicated — Refers to a console system, the main purpose of which is the playing of video games, and it is specifically designed with this end in mind. When referring to arcade games, this means a game is in its original factory cabinet, as opposed to a "conversion" kit which is without a cabinet.

diegesis — The diegesis is the story world in which the characters of a story live and where the story takes place. Dialogue and sound effects which characters can hear are considered "diegetic" whereas a soundtrack that they cannot hear is considered "nondiegetic."

diode — An electronic component that acts as a one-way valve for electricity, a diode allows a charge to travel in one direction, but blocks it from traveling in the reverse direction.

dual in-line parallel (DIP) switch — A set of switches, usually eight, which are typically mounted on the circuit board and used by arcade operators to set game parameters, such as difficulty levels, the score at which an extra life is granted, and other variables. (Players would not have access to these switches.)

Easter eggs — Undocumented and hidden features in a video game that a player can find, often by accident. The first one, a hidden credit for the programmer, appeared in Warren Robinett's *Adventure* (1979) for the Atari 2600.

emulator — A computer program which attempts to replicate the experience of playing a game from an older system. Some like MAME (Multiple Arcade Machine Emulator) can emulate classic arcade video games, while others attempt to reproduce various home systems. Emulators do not always accurately reproduce games, however, and care must be taken if they are used in research.

Gestalt — The word "Gestalt" is a German word translated as a shape, form, guise, or figure, and often refers to the overall effect of the sum of the parts which make up the whole being perceived. Gestalt psychology is the psychology of how the human sensory system perceives parts and wholes, and how the perception of parts and wholes relate to each other.

gigabyte — A gigabyte is a unit of information storage equal to one billion bytes. Used to refer to RAM, a gigabyte (abbreviated GB) equals 2^{30} bytes, or 1,073,741,824 bytes (although to avoid confusion, this is now sometimes referred to as a "gibibyte").

haptic feedback — A device that simulates a force moving the controller held in the player's hands, either providing resistance or vibrations which are synched up with events in the game being played.

indie — "Indie" is short for "independent" and refers to games or films produced and financed outside of the main industrial companies, making them "independent."

interface — An interface is the collection of devices which allow a software program and a user to interact, which may include such conceptual things as menus, cursors, and textboxes, and physical devices such as a screen, mouse, joystick, game controllers, or a microphone and speakers. Interface design usually determines which of these will be used and how they will be used together.

JAMMA — The Japanese Arcade Machine Manufacturers' Association (JAMMA) began in 1982, and in 1985 it introduced a wiring standard, known as the JAMMA standard for arcade video games, which would become one of the main ones used in the video game industry in Japan and the United States during the 1980s and 1990s.

kilobyte — A kilobyte is a unit of information storage equal to one thousand bytes. Used to refer to RAM, a kilobyte (abbreviated KB) equals 2^{10} bytes, or 1,024 bytes (although to avoid confusion, this is now sometimes referred to as a "kibibyte").

kilohertz — A kilohertz is a unit of frequency in electronics. One hertz equals one cycle per second, and a kilohertz (abbreviated kHz) is one thousand cycles per second. In computers, the amount of hertz refers to the computer's processing speed.

laserdisc — An optical disc storage medium used mainly during the 1980s for movies and also used in some video games either for background video imagery, as in *M.A.C.H. 3* or *Firefox* or for a collection of video clips of game events that could be played in a sequence determined by the game's algorithm, as in *Dragon's Lair* and *Space Ace*.

LCD — See *liquid crystal display.*

LED — See *light-emitting diode.*

light-emitting diode (LED) — Light-emitting diode display devices use diodes made with gallium arsenide phosphide, which produces light when a current is applied to the diode. LEDs can come in red, yellow, or green, although red LEDs are the most common. Although many handheld electronic games use LED displays, Nintendo's Virtual Boy is the only pixel-based imaging system to use one.

liquid crystal display (LCD) — A liquid crystal display contains a thin layer of long, crystalline molecules that polarize light, sandwiched between grids of fine wires and polarizers. The polarizers are lined up in such a way so that light passing through the crystals is polarized and reflected back to the viewer, resulting in a bright, clear square. When a current is applied to the grids, the molecules line up together in the same direction and have no polarizing effect, and light is absorbed, resulting in a darkened square.

Early LCD screens were black and white and can be found in games from the early 1980s and game systems such as Milton Bradley's Microvision or Nintendo's Game Boy. Color LCD screens are now common, appearing in game systems like the Atari Lynx or Game Boy Color, as well as in laptop computer screens.

logic circuit — Logic circuits are basic electronic circuits which take one or more inputs (expressed as bits) and produce a single output. The two basic logic gates are the NAND and NOR gates. A NAND gate returns a 0 if both of its inputs are 1 otherwise it returns a 1. A NOR gate returns a 1 only if both its inputs are 0, otherwise it returns a 0. All other logic gates can be built from these two gates.

massively multiplayer online role-playing game (MMORPG) — An online computer role-playing game played by hundreds of thousands of players in a virtual world, usually one which is available 24 hours a day. Examples include *Everquest, Ultima Online, Star Wars Galaxies,* and *World of Warcraft,* which has become the largest MMORPG in the world, with over nine million players.

MMORPG — See *massively multiplayer online role-playing game.*

megabyte — A megabyte is a unit of information storage equal to one million bytes. Used to refer to RAM, a megabyte (abbreviated MB) equals 2^{20} bytes, or 1,048,576 bytes (although to avoid confusion, this is now sometimes referred to as a "mebibyte").

megahertz — A megahertz is a unit of frequency in electronics. One hertz equals one cycle per second, and a megahertz (abbreviated MHz) is one million cycles per second. In computers, the amount of hertz refers to the computer's processing speed.

microchip — A microchip, known technically as a microprocessor, contains many semi-conductors on a single computer chip, which can perform a variety of functions. Before the microprocessor, individual components, often vacuum tubes, would have to be connected together, taking up much more room and power, severely limiting computer power and speed.

multimedia — Short for "multiple media," multimedia is usually used to refer to electronic information technology which integrates audio, video, animation, and interactivity together.

non-player character (NPC) — A character in a video game which is not controlled by any human player but rather by the computer.

NPC — See *non-player character.*

NTSC — A color television standard (adopted by the National Television System Committee, after which it is named) used in North America, Japan, and several other countries. It has 29.97 interlaced frames of video per second, an aspect ratio of 4:3, and 525 scan lines.

PAL — A color television standard (known as phase-alternating line) used in parts of Europe, Asia, Africa, and Australia. It has 25 interlaced frames of video per second, and 576 scan lines.

parallax scrolling — Parallax scrolling involves scrolling graphics in which a foreground plane scrolls faster than a background plane, giving the impression of a three-dimensional space, even though no three-dimensional computation is occurring.

pixel — Short for "picture element," a pixel is the smallest unit of a picture and is a single color or value. Pixels can be round, square, or rectangular in shape, and they represent the smallest unit into which a picture can be divided.

polarizer — A polarizer is a filter which only allows electromagnetic waves (light) with certain properties to pass through it. Some polarizers will absorb the unwanted light which does not have the desired properties, while others will deflect it as a second beam.

PCB — See *printed circuit board.*

player-character — The character in a video game which is controlled by the player.

polygonally based graphics — Graphics which are built from polygons and generated in a three-dimensional space, as opposed to sprite-based graphics which are generated as a series of two-dimensional planes.

port — Used as a verb, "port" refers to the adaptation of a video game from one system or platform to another, which sometimes involves slight changes to a game.

printed circuit board (PCB) — A nonconductive board on which are fastened electronic components which are joined by circuitry etched into the board. The memory chips reside here, where they are joined to the other components of the game. "Printed" refers to the method used to etch the circuitry for the mass production of the board.

RAM — Random access memory, which stores data temporarily and can be changed, but which is erased when power is turned off.

raster, raster scan — A type of scan used by a CRT to produce an image on-screen. The scan pattern goes back and forth, line by line, filling the entire screen, to produce an image with filled areas, as opposed to a vector scan which just draws individual line segments on-screen and does not fill the screen. Television imagery and most video games use raster scanning.

RGB — A color monitor with separate inputs for the red, green, and blue component video signals, which together make up the color image.

role-playing game (RPG) — A game in which the players take on the roles of fictional characters in a game world, and collaboratively undertake adventures there. In many cases, aspects of the characters' identities can be determined by the players controlling them, and characters can change as the game progresses.

ROM — Read-only memory: computer memory which is hardwired into a system and can be read but not changed and which remains when power is turned off. Examples would be the chips in cartridges that hold game programs.

RPG — See *role-playing game.*

scaling — The enlarging or reducing of an image by the changing of its resolution.

scrolling (horizontal, vertical, diagonal, 4-way, 8-way) — The moving of a large image behind a small window which shows only a portion of it at a time. In video games, scrolling first appeared in Kee Games's *Super Bug* (1977).

SECAM — A French color television standard (known in French as *Séquentiel couleur à mémoire* (sequential color and memory) used in parts of Europe, Asia, and Africa. Like the PAL standard, it has 25 interlaced frames of video per second and 576 scan lines.

sprite — A computer graphics entity which is a bitmap (a small grid of pixels used to make an image) that can be moved about the screen and resized, though its surface is always facing the camera. Groups of sprites are used to create larger images and can be moved and resized to give an illusion of depth to a game.

suicide battery — Presumably installed to fight piracy, these batteries supply power to a small amount of RAM which holds a decryption key. The decryption key is used to decode the program code in the game's ROM, so when the battery dies, the RAM is erased, and without the decryption key the game can no longer run. Several companies used suicide batteries in their arcade games, the largest two being Sega, who began using them around 1987, and Capcom, whose system used them from 1989 onward.

terabyte — A terabytes is a unit of information storage equal to one trillion bytes. Used to refer to RAM, a terabyte (abbreviated TB) equals 2^{40} bytes, or 1,099,511,627,776 bytes (although to avoid confusion, this is now sometimes referred to as a "tebibyte").

trackball, track-ball, trak-ball — A type of game controller which uses a housed rolling ball as an input device for moving a cursor around on-screen. It allows for fast action and quick changes of direction and was used in games including Atari's *Football* (1978), *Missile Command* (1980), and *Marble Madness* (1984).

upright — The most common type of arcade video game cabinet which stands upright and which the player stands in front of to play the game.

vector graphics — Vector graphics are produced using a vector monitor, which creates all of its graphics as a series of line segments drawn one after another (see *vector monitor*).

vector monitor, vector scan monitor — A kind of monitor in which the electron beam moves in straight lines that can begin and end anywhere on the screen. Images are drawn from these lines, as opposed to being created by a raster scan. Examples of vector games include *Asteroids* (1979), *Battlezone* (1980), *Tempest* (1980), and *Star Wars* (1983).

wireframe — Wireframe is the name given to graphics in which everything is represented as a series of lines, with no filled areas. Wireframe renderings are used to show spatial locations and interactions of graphical objects, without having to render their surfaces, speeding up the time it takes to create the graphics.

XY monitor — See *vector monitor*.

z-axis — In a three-dimensional space, the direction of movement which is towards or away from the player's point of view.

RESOURCE GUIDE

WEBSITES

Company websites are useful, but do not always list games and are often rather limited beyond advertising themselves and their products. Other sites vary in their reliability and usefulness; below are sites which are useful and reliable. The term "video games" appears sometimes as one word ("videogames"), so web searches often must include both spellings. These websites were all working as of April 2, 2007.

http://fly.hiwaay.net/~lkseitz/cvg/cvglit.shtml The Classic Video Games Literature List is an extensive list of books and published essays relating to video games, although as of April 2007, it only listed books up to 1998.

http://marvin3m.com/arcade/ An excellent source regarding arcade games, particularly electromechanical ones, from before 1977.

http://vgrebirth.org Video Game Rebirth (VGR) is an information source for home video game consoles and includes an online community and a game catalog with profiles of over 34,000 games.

http://www.arcadecollecting.com/dead/dead.html The Dead Battery Society webpage contains information on the "suicide batteries" found in some arcade games from the 1980s and 1990s.

http://www.arcadeflyers.com The Arcade Flyer Archive contains promotional flyers for a wide range of older arcade video games. Useful information about the games, including screen imagery, special features, and cabinet design can be found in these flyers, as well as a sense of how they were marketed by the companies that made them.

http://www.arcade-history.com/index.php?page=detail&id=2623 Another extensive source of arcade game history.

http://www.atari2600.com A place to buy old Atari goods and many other early home video game systems and games as well.

http://www.cooganphoto.com/gravitar/gravitar.html A nice website dedicated to the game *Gravitar* (1982), with a detailed analysis by the game's high score record holder, Dan Coogan.

http://www.dadgum.com/giantlist The Giant List of Classic Game Programmers is useful for establishing game authorship and providing possible contacts for primary research into the creation of the games on the list.

http://www.digipen.edu Digipen Institute of Technology offers degrees in digital interactive entertainment technology, and many of their students are pursuing careers in the video game industry.

http://www.dmoz.org/Games/Video_Games Part of the Open Directory Project, this page lists thousands of websites on video games, neatly arranged and categorized hierarchically by topic and subject matter, making searches easier than a search engine style of search. Includes annotations with listings of websites.

http://www.dragons-lair-project.com/community/related/articles/dl.asp This page features many scans of magazine articles on laserdisc games.

http://www.fullsail.com/game-development/overview.html Full Sail advertises that you can complete its Game Development Bachelor's Degree Program in only 21 months.

http://www.gamasutra.com Gamasutra.com is a source for video game industry news and includes job listings, resumés, product news, and more.

http://www.gamearchive.com A searchable archive of material related to video games.

http://www.gamegirlz.com A magazine-format website with material of interest to women gamers and with connections to women gamers' online communities.

http://www.gameinformer.com These websites are magazine-style formats featuring gaming news, reviews, previews, and some downloads. Though most of the material pertains to newer games, some sites have archives as well.

http://www.gamesindustry.biz/ Gameindustry.biz features industry news, job listings, a company directory, and podcasts on the video game industry.

http://www.gamespot.com Gamespot.com has news, game reviews, previews, cheat codes, downloads, forums, and more.

http://www.gamestudies.com The first online academic journal of video game studies.

http://www.geocities.com/TimesSquare/Lair/9260/labels.html An interesting and in-depth site regarding Atari cartridge labels.

http://www.islandnet.com/~kpolsson/timeline.htm#vidgame Ken Polsson has complied one of the best and most detailed timelines of video game history, complete with source references for every entry.

http://www.klov.com The homepage of the Killer List of Videogames (KLOV) is a growing list of arcade video games including technical information, images, and some video clips of the games. It is perhaps the largest single collection of arcade video game information gathered into one site, with information on over 4,400 games. For a sample of the detailed information available on the games, see http://www.klov.com/game_detail.php?letter=P&game_id=10816 , the page for *Pac-Man*.

http://www.pong-story.com David Winter's pong-story site contains an enormous amount of information on dozens of PONG systems and imitators both in the United States and Europe and some of the history behind them. The site is well organized and features many pictures of these early systems as well as images of their boxes, cartridges, and even their chips.

http://www.retrogames.com A source of information on older video games as well as emulators which run them.

http://www.solvalou.com/subpage/arcade_dips Dual in-line parallel (DIP) switch settings for over 5,000 arcade video games.

http://www.starcade.tv/starcade/episodes.asp Complete episodes of *Starcade,* a TV show about video games.

http://www.system16.com A good source of video game system hardware used by a variety of companies. Good information on games as well; for example, the Sega Museum section has information on over 1,000 Sega games.

http://www.thedoteaters.com/ Video game history with many images.

http://www.vaps.org The Video Arcade Preservation Society is an international group of arcade video game collectors and has a membership of over 2,500 collectors. Contact information is provided for many of these collectors, along with what games they own, which is useful to video game researchers wishing to do primary research or for anyone interested in learning more about arcade games.

http://www.vgf.com Video Gamers Forum features various forums and archives pertaining to video games.

http://www.videogames.org Includes a "Museum" page link to Greg Chance's The History of Home Video Games, a good source for information about home systems, and contains links to lists and photographs of early systems, all collected together in a timeline format.

http://www.videotopia.com Keith Feinstein's Videotopia, based on his traveling museum exhibit of the same name, includes essays on video games, information on The Electronics Conservancy, and assorted video game hyperlinks.

EMULATORS

Emulators are programs that simulate the graphics and game play of video games and video game systems. For researchers trying to track down hard-to-find games, they can sometimes give a good idea what certain early games were like. However, many emulators do not give exact renditions of the games they are emulating; graphics may not appear at their original ratios, and the experience of watching a computer screen is often quite different than that of the kind of monitor on which the games would have been played. While emulators can be useful, users should be aware of the differences and get firsthand experience whenever possible.

http://hive.speedhost.com/ Makers of commercial video game emulators.

http://stella.sourceforge.net/ Stella is an Atari 2600 emulator available for several operating systems, with a large collection of game ROMs for it.

http://www.classicgaming.com/vault/ Scroll down this page for a list of emulators of home game systems, including the Arcadia 2001, Atari 2600, Atari 5200, Atari 7800, Coleco systems, MSX, Neo•Geo, NES, Odyssey², Sega, Genesis, Sega Master System, TurboGrafx16, and Vectrex.

http://www.daphne-emu.com An emulator specifically for laserdisc games. Includes downloads, a forum, FAQ, and screenshots.

http://www.mame.net/ Probably the largest collection of games for one emulator, the Multiple Arcade Machine Emulator (MAME) is able to run over 3,000 arcade games, and its home page shows more than 54 million visitors since May 12, 1997. Also has a good "links" page leading to other emulator sites.

http://www.pong-story.com/odyemu.htm The story and status of ODYEMU, an emulator of the Magnavox Odyssey, can be found on this page.

VIDEO

Game Over: Gender, Race, & Violence in Video Games, 35 min. The Media Education Foundation, 2000. http://www.mediaed.org. An educational documentary which addresses questions of gender, race, and violence in video games.

Lara Croft: Lethal and Loaded, 50 min. West Long Branch, NJ: White Star Video, 2001.

Once Upon Atari, 120 min. Directed by Howard Scott Warshaw. Scott West Productions, 2003. http://www.onceuponatari.com/contact.html.

BOOKS

Aarseth, Espen. *Cybertext: Perspectives on Ergodic Literature.* Baltimore, MD, and London: The Johns Hopkins University Press, 1997.

Adams, Ernest. *Break into the Game Industry: How to Get a Job Making Video Games.* New York: McGraw-Hill Osborne Media, 2003.

Avedon, Elliott M., and Brian Sutton-Smith. *The Study of Games.* New York: Wiley, 1971.

Banks, J. "Gamers as Co-creators: Enlisting the Virtual Audience—A Report from the Netface." In *Critical Readings: Media and Audiences.* Edited by Virginia Nightengale and Karen Ross. Maidenhead, England: Open University Press, 2003.

Bell, A.G. *Games Playing With Computers.* London: Allen and Unwin, 1972.

Bethke, E. *Game Development and Production.* Plano, TX: Wordware, 2003.

Blanchet, Michael. *How to Beat the Video Games.* New York: Simon and Schuster/Fireside, 1982.

Bogost, Ian. *Unit Operations: An Approach to Videogame Criticism.* Cambridge, MA, and London: MIT Press, 2006.

Buchsbaum, Walter H., and Robert Mauro. *Electronic Games: Design, Programming, and Troubleshooting.* New York: McGraw-Hill, 1979.

Buckwalter, Len. *Video Games.* New York: Grosset & Dunlap, 1977.

Bueschel, Richard M. *Guide to Vintage Trade Simulators and Countertop Games.* Atglen, PA: Schiffer, 1997.

Burnham, Van. *Supercade: A Visual History of the Videogame Age 1971–1984.* Cambridge, MA: MIT Press, 2001.

Cassell, Justine, and Henry Jenkins, eds. *From Barbie to Mortal Kombat: Gender and Computer Games.* Cambridge, MA: MIT Press, 1988.

Castronova, Edward. *Synthetic Worlds: The Business and Culture of Online Games.* Chicago and London: University of Chicago Press, 2006.

Chiang, Bor-Yang. *Involvement and Motive in Sports Video Game Playing, Televised Sports Viewing, Live Sports Attendance and Team Sports Participation.* Archival/manuscript material, thesis (M.A. in mass communication). University of Wisconsin–Milwaukee, 1996.

Cohen, Scott. *Zap: The Rise and Fall of Atari.* New York: McGraw, 1984.

Crawford, Chris. *The Art of Computer Game Design.* Berkeley, CA: McGraw-Hill/Osborne Media, 1984. http://www.vancouver.wsu.edu/fac/peabody/game-book/Coverpage.html.

DeMaria, Rusel. *The 7th Guest: The Official Guide.* Rocklin, CA: Prima, 1993.

DeMaria, Rusel, and Johnny L. Wilson. *High Score! The Illustrated History of Electronic Games.* Berkeley, CA: McGraw Hill/Osborne, 2004.

Dovey, J., and H. Kennedy. *Game Cultures: Computer Games as New Media.* Maidenhead, England: Open University Press, 2006.

Fine, Gary. *Shared Fantasy: Role-Playing Games as Social Worlds.* Chicago and London: University of Chicago Press, 1983.

Frasca, Gonzalo. "Ephemeral Games: Is It Barbaric to Design Videogames after Auschwitz?" In *Cybertext Yearbook 2000.* Edited by Markku Eskelinen and Raine Koskimaa. Saarijärvi (Finland: University of Jyväskylä, Research Centre for Contemporary Culture, 2001).

Frasca, Gonzalo. *Videogames of the Oppressed: Videogames as a Means for Critical Thinking and Debate.* Master's thesis. Atlanta, GA: Georgia Institute of Technology, 2001.

Friedman, Ted. "Making Sense of Software: Computer Games and Interactive Textuality." In *Cybersociety: Computer-Mediated Communication and Community.* Edited by Steve Jones. Thousand Oaks, CA: Sage, 1995.

Fromm, Rainer. *Digital Spielen—Real Morden?* Marburg, Germany: Schüren, 2002.

Fuller, Mary, and Henry Jenkins. "Nintendo and New World Travel Writing: A Dialogue." In *Cybersociety: Computer-Mediated Communication and Community.* Edited by Steven G. Jones. Thousand Oaks, CA: Sage, 1995.

Gabriel, Évelyne Esther. *Que faire avec les jeux vidéo?* Paris: Hachette, 1994.

Galloway, Alexander R. *Gaming: Essays on Algorithmic Culture.* Minneapolis, MN: University of Minnesota Press, 2006.

Gieselmann, Hartmut. *Der Virtuelle Krieg.* Hannover, Germany: Offizin Verlag, 2002.

Goldstein, Jeffrey, and Joost Raessens, eds. *Handbook of Computer Game Studies.* Cambridge, MA, and London: MIT Press, 2005.

Goodman, Robert L. *How to Repair Video Games.* Blue Ridge Summit, PA: Tab Books, 1978.

Greenfield, Patricia Marks. *Mind and Media: The Effects of Television, Video Games, and Computers.* Cambridge, MA: Harvard University Press, 1984.

Heiserman, David L. *How to Design & Build Your Own Custom TV Games.* Blue Ridge Summit, PA: Tab Books, 1978.

Herman, Leonard. *Phoenix: The Fall and Rise of Home Videogames,* 4th ed. Springfield, NJ: Rolenta Press, 2007.

Herz, J.C. *Joystick Nation: How Videogames Gobbled Our Money, Won Our Hearts and Rewired Our Minds.* Boston, MA: Little Brown, 1997.

Ichbiah, Daniel. *La saga des jeux vidéo.* Paris: Éditions Générales First-Pocket, 1997.

Jaffe, Martin S. *Regulating Videogames.* Chicago: American Planning Association, Planning Advisory Service, 1982.

Juul, Jesper. *Half Real: Video Games between Real Rules and Fictional Worlds.* Cambridge, MA, and London: MIT Press, 2005.

Kafai, Yasmin Bettina. *Minds in Play: Computer Game Design as a Context for Children's Learning.* Hillsdale, NJ: Lawrence Erlbaum Associates, 1995.

Kent, Steven L. *The Ultimate History of Video Games: The Story behind the Craze that Touched Our Lives and Changed the World.* New York: Three Rivers Press, 2001.

Kinder, Marsha. *Playing With Power in Movies, Television, and Video Games: From Muppet Babies to Teenage Mutant Ninja Turtles.* Berkeley, CA: University of California Press, 1991.

King, Geoff, and Tanya Krzywinska. *Tomb Raiders & Space Invaders: Videogame Forms & Contexts.* London and New York: I.B. Tauris, 2006.

King, Geoff, and Tanya Krzywinska, eds. *Screenplay: Cinema/Videogames/Interfaces.* London: Wallflower Press, 2002.

King, Lucien, ed. *Game On: The History and Culture of Video Games.* New York: Universe, 2002.

Klanten, Robert, and Jaro Gielens, eds. *Electronic Plastic.* Berlin: Die Gestalten Verlag, 2000.

Kohler, Chris. *Power Up: How Japanese Video Games Gave the World an Extra Life.* Indianapolis: Brady Games, 2005.

Kristof, Ray, and Amy Satran. *Interactivity by Design.* Mountain View, CA: Adobe Press, 1995.

Kubey, Craig. *The Winners' Book of Video Games.* New York: Warner Books, 1982.

Kurtz, Bill. *Encyclopedia of Arcade Video Games.* Schiffer Book Farm, PA: Schiffer, 2003.

Lambert, Steve, and Suzan Ropiquet, eds. *CD-ROM: The Current and Future State of the Art.* Redmond, WA: Microsoft Press, 1986.

Lammers, Susan. *Programmers at Work.* Redmond, WA: MicroSoft Press, 1986.

Le Diberder, Alain, and Frédéric Le Diberder. *L'Univers des Jeux Video.* Paris: Éditions La Découverte, 1998.

———. *Qui a Peur des Jeux Vidéo?* Paris: Éditions La Découverte/Essais, 1993.

Lischka, Konrad. *Spielplatz Computer.* Heidelberg: Verlag Heinz Heise, 2002.

Loftus, Geoffrey R. *Mind at Play: The Psychology of Video Games.* New York: Basic Books, 1983.

Marks, Aaron. *The Complete Guide to Game Audio.* Manhasset, NY: CMP Books, 2001.

McGowan, Chris, and Jim McCullaugh. *Entertainment in the Cyber Zone.* New York: Random House Information Group, 1995.

Mertens, Mathias, and Tobias O. Meißner. *Wir waren Space Invaders.* Frankfurt am Main: Eichborn, 2002.

Messaris, Paul, and Lee Humphreys, eds. *Digital Media: Transformations in Human Communication.* New York: Peter Lang, 2006.

Murray, Janet H. *Hamlet on the Holodeck: The Future of Narrative in Cyberspace.* Cambridge, MA, and London: MIT Press, 1997.

Museum für Sepulkralkultur. *Game Over.* Kassel, Germany: Museum für Sepuralkultur, 2002.

Newman, James. *Videogames.* New York: Routledge, 2004.

Perron, Bernard. "Jouabilité, Bipolarité et Cinéma Interactif." *Hypertextes. Espaces Virtuels de Lecture et D'écriture.* Edited by Denis Bachand and Christian Vandendorpe. Québec: Nota Bene, 2003.

Perron, Bernard. *La Spectature Prise au Jeu, La narration, La Cognition et le Jeu dans le Cinéma Narratif.* Ph.D. thesis. Université de Montréal, 1997.

Pias, Claus. *Computer Spiel Welten.* München, Germany: Sequenzia Verlag, 2002.

Poole, Steven. *Trigger Happy: Videogames and the Entertainment Revolution.* New York: Arcade, 2000.

Provenzo, Eugene. *Video Kids—Making Sense of Nintendo.* Cambridge, MA: Harvard University Press, 1991.

Quéau, Philippe. *Éloge de la Simulation. De la vie des Langages à la Synthèse des Images.* Seyssel: Éditions du Champ Vallon, 1986.

Rötzer, Florian, ed. *Virtuelle Welten—Reale Gewalt.* Hannover, Germany: Verlag Heinz Heise, 2002.

Rouse, Richard, III. *Game Design Theory and Practice,* 2nd ed. Plano, TX: Wordware, 2005.

Ryan, Marie-Laure. *Narrative as Virtual Reality: Immersion and Interactivity in Literature and Electronic Media.* Baltimore, MD, and London: The Johns Hopkins University Press, 2001.

Saltzman, Marc. *Game Design: Secrets of the Sages,* 2nd ed. Indianapolis: Brady Games, 2000.

Sanger, George. *The Fat Man on Game Audio: Tasty Morsels of Sonic Goodness.* Berkeley, CA: Peachpit Press, 2004.

Schwartz, Steven A., and Janet Schwartz. *Parent's Guide to Video Games.* Roseville, CA: Prima Lifestyles, 1994.

Sheff, David. *Game Over: How Nintendo Conquered the World.* New York: Vintage Books, 1994.

———. *Game Over: How Nintendo Zapped an American Industry, Captured Your Dollars, and Enslaved Your Children.* New York: Random House, 1993.

———. *Game Over: Nintendo's Battle to Dominate an Industry.* London: Hodder and Stoughton; New York: Vintage Books, 1990.

Skurzynski, Gloria. *Know the Score: Video Games in Your High-Tech World.* New York: Bradbury Press; Toronto: Maxwell Macmillan Canada; New York: Maxwell Macmillan International, 1994.

Smith, Greg M., ed. *On a Silver Platter: CD-ROMs and the Promise of a New Technology.* New York: New York University Press, 1999.

Spencer, Donald D. *Game Playing With Computers.* New York: Spartan Books, 1968.

Sullivan, George. *Screen Play: The Story of Video Games.* New York: F. Warne, 1983.

Tronstad, Ragnhild. "Performing the MUD Adventure." *Innovations: Media, Methods and Theories.* Edited by Gunnar Liestøl, Andrew Morrison, and Terje Rasmussen. Cambridge, MA: MIT Press, 2003.

Uston, Ken. *Ken Uston's Guide to Buying and Beating Home Video Games.* New York: Signet, 1982.

Wolf, Mark J. P. *Abstracting Reality: Art, Communication, and Cognition in the Digital Age.* Lanham, MA: University Press of America, 2000.

———. "On the Future of Video Games." In *Digital Media: Transformations in Human Communication.* Edited by Paul Messaris and Lee Humphreys. New York: Peter Lang, 2006.

———. *The World of the D'ni: Myst and Riven.* Milan, Italy: Costa & Nolan, 2006.

Wolf, Mark J. P., ed. *The Medium of the Video Game.* Austin, TX: University of Texas Press, 2001.

Wolf, Mark J. P., and Bernard Perron, eds. *The Video Game Theory Reader.* New York: Routledge Press, 2003.

Wright, Steve. "Stella Programmer's Guide." Reconstructed online in 1993 by Charles Sinnett from the 1979 original. http://www.classic-games.com/atari2600/stella.html.

Zimmerman, Eric, and Katie Salen. *The Game Design Reader: A Rules of Play Anthology.* Cambridge, MA, and London: MIT Press, 2005.

———. *Rules of Play: Game Design Fundamentals.* Cambridge, MA, and London: MIT Press, 2003.

PERIODICALS

Periodicals devoted to video games include *Videogame Advisor, Arcade, Game Fan, NEXT Generation, Ultimate Gameplayers, Computer Games Magazine, 2600 Connection Magazine, RePlay, Play Meter,* and others like *Computer Graphics World* which feature articles on video games from a graphics standpoint.

Ackerman, Elise. "The Pinball Wizard Blues." *U.S. News & World Report* 127, no. 19 (November 15, 1999): 56.

Adams, Ernest W. "The Challenge of the Interactive Movie." Computer Game Developers' Conference, 1995. http://designersnotebook.com/Lectures/Challenge/challenge.htm.

———. "Three Problems for Interactive Storytellers." *Gamasutra.com*, December 29, 1999. http://www.gamasutra.com/features/designers_notebook/19991229.htm.

Alexander, Charles P. "Video Games Go Crunch!" *Time* 122, no. 17 (October 17, 1983): 64.

Anderson, Craig A., and Karen Dill. "Video Games and Aggressive Thoughts, Feelings, and Behavior in the Laboratory and in Life." *Journal of Personality and Social Psychology* 78, no. 4 (April 2000): 772–90. http://www.apa.org/journals/features/psp784772.pdf.

Anderson, Craig A., and Catherine M. Ford. "Affect of the Game Player: Short-Term Effects of Highly and Mildly Aggressive Video Games." *Personality and Social Psychology Bulletin* 12, no. 4 (1986): 390–402.

Asher, Mark. "Massive (multiplayer) Entertainment: Playing Together Online...Yesterday, Today, and Tomorrow." *Computer Games* (May 2001): 53–68.

Au, Wagner James. "Dispatches from the Future of Gaming, Page 3: Will Wright Speaks...To Arnold Schwarzenegger?" *Gameslice.com*, 2001. http://www.gameslice.com/features/gdc/index3.shtml.

Baba, Y., and Feichin Ted Tschang. "Product Development in Japanese TV Game Software: The Case of an Innovative Game." *International Journal of Innovation Management* 5, no. 4 (2001): 487–515.

Banks, John. "Controlling Gameplay." *M/C: A Journal of Media and Culture* 1, no. 5 (1998). www.uq.edu.au/~webmedia/9812/game.html.

Baumgärtel, Tilman. "Alle Nazis werden Dreiecke." *Die Zeit* 16 (2002). http://www.zeit.de/2002/16/Kultur/200216_computerspielkun.html.

Bayer, Glen. "SNES-CD Profile." *N-Sider. The World's Most In-Depth Nintendo Resource.* http://www.n-sider.com/articleview.php?articleid=279.

Blickstein, Jay, and John Soat. "When it Comes to Sexual Harassment, Play Carefully." *InformationWeek*, no. 774 (February 21, 2000): 29.

Brightman, James. "Breaking: U.S. Video Game Industry Totals $12.5 Billion in 2006." *GameDailyBiz*. http://biz.gamedaily.com/industry/feature/?id=14940.

Buchanan, Levi. "It's All in the Game." *Chicago Tribune*, May 17, 2005.

Bulik, Beth Snyder. "Arcade craze swings into the living room." *Advertising Age* 75, no. 26, midwest region edition (June 28, 2004): 3, 52.

Cole, Vladimir. "World of Warcraft Breaks 8 Million Subscribers." *joystiq.com*, January 11, 2007. http://www.joystiq.com/2007/01/11/world-of-warcraft-breaks-8-million-subscribers.

Collins, Karen. "Flat Twos and the Musical Aesthetic of the Atari VCS." http://www.popular-musicology-online.com/issues/01/collins-01.html.

———. "Loops and Bloops." *soundscaptes.info*. http://www.icce.rug.nl/~soundscapes/VOLUME08/Loops_and_bloops.html.

Crawford, Chris. "The History of Computer Games: The Atari Years." *The Journal of Computer Game Design* 5. http://www.erasmatazz.com/library/JCGD_Volume_5/The_Atari_Years.html.

Croal, N'Gai. "The Art of the Game." *Newsweek* 135, no. 10 (March 6, 2000): 60.

———. "Making a Killing at Quake." *Newsweek* 134, no. 21 (November 22, 1999): 104.

Crockford, Douglas. "The Untold Story of *Maniac Mansion*." *Wired*, no. 1.04 (September/October 1993). http://www.wired.com/wired/archive/1.04/nintendo.html?pg=1&topic=&topic_set.

Dominick, Joseph R. "Videogames, Television Violence, and Aggression in Teenagers." *Journal of Communication* 34 (1984): 136.

Dunford, James. *Playstation Hardware FAQ,* September 26, 1995. http://www.gamefaqs.com/console/psx/file/916392/4701.

Durham, Ken. "History of Pinball Machines." GameRoom Antiques website. http://www.game roomantiques.com/HistoryPin.htm.

Eimbinder, Jerry, and Eric Eimbinder. "Electronic Games: Space-Age Leisure Activity." *Popular Electronics,* multipart essay appearing over several months in 1980.

Elkin, Tobi. "Dreamcast System Brings Sega Back into Contention." *Advertising Age* 71, no. 7 (February 14, 2000): 17.

———. "Sony Blitz Sets Stage for the Next PlayStation." *Advertising Age* 70, no. 45 (November 1, 1999): 24.

Ellis, Desmond. "Video Arcades, Youth, and Trouble." *Youth and Society* 16, no. 1 (September 1984): 47.

Elmer-Dewitt, Philip. "The Amazing Video Game Boom." *Time* 142, no. 13 (September 27, 1993): 43.

Fitzsimmons, C. "Push for 18+ Game Ratings Fails." *The Australian,* November 12, 2002. http://web.archive.org/20021115103906/http://australianit.news.com.au/articles/0,7204,5466570%5e15319%5e%5enbv%5e15306,00.html.

Frasca, Gonzalo. "Ludologia Kohtaa Narratologian." *Parnasso* 3 (1999): 365–71. Also published as "Ludology Meets Narratology. Similitudes and Differences Between (Video) Games and Narrative." http://www.ludology.org/articles/ludology.htm.

———. "Simulation 101: Simulation versus Representation" (2001). http://www.ludology.org/articles/sim1/simulation101.html.

Friedman, Ted. "The Semiotics of Sim City." *First Monday* 4 (1999). http://www.firstmonday.dk/issues/issue4_4/friedman/.

Gagnon, Diana. "Videogames and Spatial Skills: An Exploratory Study." *Educational Communication and Technology* 33, no. 4 (1985): 263–75.

Gallasch, K. "Australia Council Restructures: New Media Arts Wasted." Message posted to the Fibreculture Forum, December 9, 2004. Archived at http://www.fibreculture.org/myspinach/fibreculture/2004-December/004292.html.

Garrity, Brian. "Video-Game Console Makers Eye New Music-Download Applications." *Billboard* 111, no. 42 (October 16, 1999): 3.

Gilbert, Christine. "Virtually Married." *Computer Games,* no. 125 (April 2001): 22–26.

Gillen, Marilyn A. "Sega Bowing 'Backward-Compatible' Game." *Billboard* 106, no. 35 (August 27, 1994): 104.

Gonzalez, Lauren. "When Two Tribes Go to War: A History of Video Game Controversy." *GameSpot.* http://www.gamespot.com/features/6090892/.

Goodale, Gloria. "Inside Video Games." *Christian Science Monitor* 92, no. 20 (May 26, 2000): 13.

———. "Video Games Get Smarter, Good-Looking." *Christian Science Monitor* 92, no. 80 (March 17, 2000): 19.

Graetz, J. Martin. "The Origin of *Spacewar!*" *Creative Computing* (August 1981).

Griffiths, M.D., and N. Hunt. "Dependence on Computer Games by Adolescents." *Psychological Reports* 82 (1998): 475–80.

Guth, Robert A. "Inside Sony's Trojan Horse." *The Wall Street Journal,* February 25, 2000, eastern edition, B1.

———. "Sony Gears Up to Ship One Million Units Of PlayStation 2 for Next Month's Debut." *The Wall Street Journal,* February 3, 2000, eastern edition, A23.

Haddon, Leslie. "Electronic and Computer Games, the History of an Interactive Medium." *Screen* 29, no. 2 (1988): 52.

Hagiwara, Shiro, and Ian Oliver. "Sega Dreamcast: Creating a Unified Entertainment World." *IEEE Micro* 19, no. 6 (November/December 1999): 29.

Hamilton, David P. "Entertainment: Pow Goes Posh as Arcades Zap Old Image." *The Wall Street Journal,* July 2, 1993, eastern edition, B1.

Hara, Yoshiko. "Chip-Supply Kinks May Slow Volume Runs of Playstation 2." *Electronic Engineering Times,* no. 1102 (February 28, 2000): 22.

Hill, J. "Game Industry at the Crossroads." *The Age,* September 7, 2006. http://www.theage.com.au/news/games/game-industry-at-the-crossroads/2006/09/06/1157222139337.html?page=fullpage.

Horton, C. "Videogames See Another Hot Year." *Advertising Age* 62, no. 3 (January 21, 1991): 55.

———. "Zapping the Recession." *Advertising Age* 63, no. 3 (January 20, 1992): 56.

Hosefros, Paul. "Flying the 'Big Iron,' No Experience Needed." *New York Times,* January 13, 2000.

Humphreys, S., B. Fitzgerald, J. Banks, and N. Suzor. "Fan-based Production for Computer Games: User-led Innovation, the 'Drift of Calue' and Intellectual Property Rights." *Media International Australia* 114 (2005): 16–29.

Hutcheon, B., L. Hearn, and D. Braithwaite. "Australia Bans Graffiti Game." *The Age,* February 16, 2006. http://www.theage.com.au/news/breaking/australia-bans-graffiti-game/2006/02/15/1139890798010.html?page=3.

———. "Australia First to Ban Graffiti Game." *The Age,* February 17, 2006. http://www.theage.com.au/news/breaking/australia-first-to-ban-graffiti-game/2006/02/17/1140064210144.html.

Jenkins, Henry. "From Barbie to Mortal Kombat: Further Reflections." Paper presented at the conference *Playing by the Rules: The Cultural Policy Challenges of Video Games.* Chicago, October 2001. http://culturalpolicy.uchicago.edu/conf2001/papers/jenkins.html.

———. "Power to the Players: Why Video Games Need the Protection of the First Amendment." *Technology Review* (June 7, 2002). http://www.technologyreview.com/Infotech/12867/?a=f.

———. "Transmedia Storytelling." *Technology Review* (January 2003): 1.

———. "Welcome to Convergence Culture." *Receiver* (March 2005): 2.

Jones, George, and Ken Brown. "Arcade 2.0: The Future of Public Gaming Doesn't Accept Coins." *Computer Gaming World,* no. 230 (September 2003): 40–44.

Juul, Jesper. "Games Telling Stories?" *Game Studies* 1, no. 1 (July 2001). http://www.gamestudies.org/0101/juul-gts/.

———. "The Open and The Closed: Games of Emergence and Games of Progression." *CGDC Conference Proceedings.* Edited by Frans Mäyrä. Tampere, Finland: Tampere University Press, 2002.

Ko, Marnie. "Mortal Konsequences." *Report/Newsmagazine* 27, no. 2 (May 22, 2000), 47 (Alberta edition).

Koerner, B.I. "How PONG Invented Geekdom." *U.S. News & World Report* 127, no. 25 (December 27, 1999): 67.

Kroll, Jack. "Emotion Engine? I Don't Think So." *Newsweek* 135, no. 10 (March 6, 2000): 64.

Kushner, David. "Care for a Latte with That, Mr. Nukem?" *The New York Times,* September 23, 1999.

Laird, John E. "Research in Human-Level AI Using Computer Games." *Communications of the ACM* 45, no. 1 (January 2002).

Le Diberder, Alain. "L'interactivité, une Nouvelle Frontière du Cinema" (Dossier: Numérique, Virtuel, Interactif. Demain le Cinéma). *Cahiers du Cinéma* 503 (June 1996): 122–26.

Lefton, Terry. "Nintendo Rides Game Boy, N64 Openings with $25M+ in Q4." *Brandweek* 40, no. 37 (October 4, 1999): 4.

Levy, Steven. "Here Comes PlayStation 2." *Newsweek* 135, no. 10 (March 6, 2000): 55.

Lewis, Michael, and Jeffrey Jacobson. "Game Engines in Scientific Research." Special issue, *Communications of the ACM* 45, no. 1 (January 2002).

Lohr, Steve. "Microsoft Plans to Try Its Hand at Video Games." *New York Times,* March 10, 2000.

Maiello, Michael, and Tom Post. "Game Boy." *Forbes* 165, no. 11 (May 15, 2000): 328.

McCullough, J.J. *Nintendo's Era of Censorship* (2004). http://www.filibustercartoons.com/Nintendo.php.

Mehrabian, Albert, and Warren Wixen. "Lights Out at the Arcade." *Psychology Today* (December 1983): 72.

Meloni, Wanda. "Gaming's Golden Age?" *Computer Graphics World* 23, no. 4 (April 2000): 21.

Menez, Gene, Kevin Cook, and Mark Mravic. "All That's Missing Is the Sweat." *Sports Illustrated* 91, no. 23 (December 13, 1999): 32.

Messer, Ian. "Sega's Stock Climbs on Reorganization, Despite Wide Losses." *The Wall Street Journal,* November 29, 1999, eastern edition, B28.

Miller, Skyler. "The History of Square." *Gamespot.com* (2001). http://www.gamespot.com/gamespot/features/video/hist_square/index.html.

Miller, Stephen C. "Most-Violent Video Games Are Not Biggest Sellers." *New York Times,* July 29, 1999.

Moriarty, Tim. "Uncensored Videogames: Are Adults Ruining It for the Rest of Us?" *Videogaming and Computergaming Illustrated,* October 1983.

Nagourney, Adam. "Hillary Clinton Seeks Uniform Sex and Violence Rating for a Range of Media." *New York Times,* December 22, 1999.

Neal, Victoria. "Pac-Man Fever." *Entrepreneur* 27, no. 11 (November 1999): 256.

Newman, James. "In Search of the Videogame Player: The Lives of Mario." *New Media & Society* 4, no. 3 (2002): 405–22.

Nicholls, S. "Ruddock Fury over Woomera Computer Game." *The Age,* April 29, 2003. http://www.theage.com.au/articles/2003/04/29/1051381948773.html.

Nulty, Peter. "Why the Craze Won't Quit." *Fortune* (November 15, 1982): 114.

Office of Film and Literature Classification. "Guidelines for the Classification of Film and Computer Games," 2007. http://www.oflc.gov.au/resource.html?resource=62&filename=62.pdf.

———. "Review Board Decisions, *Marc Ecko's Getting Up: Contents Under Pressure.* http://www.oflc.gov.au/resource.html?resource=794&filename=794.pdf.

Oh, Susan, Danylo Hawaleshka, and Tanya Davis. "An Elaborate Hunt." *Maclean's* 113, no. 4 (January 24, 2000): 9.

Oka, Masaaki, and Masakazu Suzuoki. "Designing and Programming the Emotion Engine." *IEEE Micro* 19, no. 6 (November/December 1999): 20.

Pearce, Celia. "Sims, BattleBots, Cellular Automata God and Go: A Conversation with Will Wright by Celia Pearce." *Game Studies* 2, no. 1 (July 2002). http://www.gamestudies.org/0102/pearce/.

Perry, Telka S. "Video Games: The Next Wave." *IEEE Spectrum* 20, no. 12 (December 1983): 52–59.

Perry, Telka S., and Paul Wallich, "Design Case History: The Atari Video Computer System." *IEEE Spectrum* (March 1983).

Rae-Dupree, Janet, and Irene M. Kunii. "Can Dreamcast Make Sega's Dreams Come True?" *Business Week,* no. 3661 (December 27, 1999): 62.

Rakoff, David. "Let the Games Begin." *New York Times Magazine* 149, no. 51685 (October 24, 1999): 38.

Rash, Wayne. "The Little Graphics Engine That Could Change the Net." *Internetweek,* no. 803 (March 6, 2000): 53.

Ridgeon, Chris. "Planet Lara: Where the World Revolves Around Lara." http://www.planetlara.com/index.asp.

Rubin, Owen R. "Memories of a Vector World." ACM SIGGraph's *Computer Gaming* 32, no. 2 (May 1998). http://www.siggraph.org/publications/newsletter/v32n2/contributions/rubin.html.

Ryan, Marie-Laure. "Beyond Myth and Metaphor—The Case of Narrative in Digital Media." *Game Studies* 1, no. 1 (July 2001). http://www.gamestudies.org/0101/ryan/.

Schmidt, C. James. "Sex-and-Violence Ratings: What's in Them for Libraries?" *American Libraries* 31, no. 4 (April 2000): 44.

Schutte, Nicola S., John M. Malouff, Joan C. Post-Gorden, and Annette L. Rodasta. "Effects of Playing Videogames on Children's Aggressive and Other Behaviors." *Journal of Applied Social Psychology* 18, no. 5 (1988): 454–60.

Selnow, Gary W. "Playing Videogames: the Electronic Friend." *Journal of Communication,* no. 34 (1984): 148.

Skow, John. "Games That Play People." *Time* (January 18, 1982): 58.

Smith, Tracy. "Video Game That's Good for You." *CBSnews.com,* June 13, 2002. http://cbsnews.com/stories/2002/06/13/earlyshow/contributors/tracysmith/main512169.shtml.

Snyder, Beth. "FCB Puts Looking Glass on Kids' Digital World." *Advertising Age* 71, no. 6 (February 7, 2000): 26.

Stevenson, Seth, and N'Gai Croal. "Not Just a Game Anymore." *Newsweek* 134, no. 26 (December 27, 1999–January 3, 2000): 94.

Swalwell, M. "The Meme Game: Escape from Woomera." *RealTime* 55 (2003). http://www.real timearts.net/rt55/swallwell.html.

Swalwell, M., and K. Neil. "'Unaustralia the Game' and the Possibility of Independent Satirical Videogames." Presented at the Annual Conference of the Cultural Studies Association of Australasia, December 2006.

Takahashi, Dean. "How Four Renegades Persuaded Microsoft to Make a Game Machine." *The Wall Street Journal,* March 10, 2000, eastern edition, B1.

———. "The Real Video Game Wars." *The Wall Street Journal,* March 20, 2000, eastern edition, R16.

———. "Sega Console Grabs Big Sales in First 3 Days." *The Wall Street Journal,* September 20, 1999, eastern edition, B8.

———. "'Sonic' Boom Marks Sega's Comeback in Video Games." *The Wall Street Journal,* January 13, 2000, eastern edition, B6.

———. "Video Games Transcend Child's Play as the Industry Broadens Its Appeal." *The Wall Street Journal,* May 12, 2000, eastern edition, B6.

———. "Video-Game Violence Is Under Attack as Issue Heats Up Before Sales Season." *The Wall Street Journal,* November 24, 1999, eastern edition, B14.

———. "With Sony in Its Sights, Microsoft Weighs Entry into Game Machines." *The Wall Street Journal,* October 26, 1999, eastern edition, B1.

Talbot, Ben. "Compete, Command and Conquer: Playing for Space at the International Games Cultures Conference." *Intensities: The Journal of Cult Media* (2001). http://davidlavery.net/Intensities/PDF/talbot.pdf.

Taylor, Chris. "Game Wars." *Time* 155, no. 11 (March 20, 2000): 44.

———. "PlayStation Redux." *Time* 155, no. 21 (May 22, 2000): 156.

Thomson, David. "Zap Happy: World War II Revisited." *Sight and Sound* 11, no. 7 (July 2001): 34–37.

Thorsen, Tor. "Steven Spielberg, EA Ink Three-game Next-gen Deal." *Gamespot.com,* October 14, 2005. http://www.gamespot.com/news/6135746.html.

Tkacik, Maureen. "Back to Bingo: Arcade Firm Shrugs Off High-Tech Flash—GameWorks Thinks It Has a Winner with Classics Like Bowling and Skee-Ball." *The Wall Street Journal,* July 23, 2001, eastern edition, B10.

Townsend, Christian. "Getting the Oh-So-Real Feeling." *Business Review Weekly* 21, no. 44 (November 12, 1999): 206.

———. "Sagging Sega Hopes For a Dreamcast Run." *Business Review Weekly* 21, no. 44 (November 12, 1999): 206.

Traiman, Steve. "Shortages Hurt Video, PC Game Sales." *Billboard* 112, no. 5 (January 29, 2000): 67.

Tschang, Feichin Ted. "Videogames as Interactive Experiential Products and Their Manner of Development." *International Journal of Innovation Management* 9, no. 1 (2005): 103–31.

Wade, Will, Junko Yoshida, Anthondy Cataldo, and Yoshiko Hara. "M'soft Xbox Takes On Sony." *Electronic Engineering Times* 1104 (March 13, 2000): 1.

Waggoner, Ben, and Halstead York. "Video in Games: The State of the Industry." *Gamasutra.com,* January 3, 2000. http://www.gamasutra.com/features/20000103/fmv_01.htm.

Walker, Trey. "The Sims Overtakes Myst: Electronic Arts' Virtual-life Game Has Surpassed the Popular Adventure Game Myst in Terms of Sales To Become the Best-selling PC Game of All Time." *GameSpot,* March 22, 2002. http://www.gamespot.com/pc/adventure/myst/news.html?sid=2857556.

Webb, Marcus. "Arcade-Style Viddies Confront Challenging Future as Market Fragments and Shrinks." *Vending Times* 41, no. 11 (September 25, 2001–October 24, 2001).

Whalen, Zach. "Play Along—An Approach to Videogame Music." http://www.gamestudies.org/0401/whalen/.

Wheless, James W. "Video Games and Epilepsy" (2006). http://www.epilepsy.com/info/family_kids_video.html.

Whitmore, Guy. "Design with Music in Mind: A Guide to Adaptive Audio for Game Designers." *Gamasutra.com,* May 28, 2003. http://www.gamasutra.com/resource_guide/20030528/whit more_01.shtml.

Whitmore, Stuart. "Playing Hardware Hardball." *Asiaweek* 26, no. 12 (March 31, 2000): 43.

Wildstrom, Stephen H. "Boy, Can This Box Play Games." *Business Week* no. 3650 (October 11, 1999): 22.

Wilson, J. "Indie Rocks! Mapping Independent Game Design." *Media International Australia* 115 (2005): 109–22.

Wolf, Mark J. P. "Assessing Interactivity in Video Game Design." *Mechademia 1: Emerging Worlds of Anime and Manga,* of the series *Mechademia: An Annual Forum for Anime, Manga and The Fan Arts* (December 2006).

———. "Book Notes: *Myst." Film Quarterly* 52, no. 1 (Fall 1998): 98.

———. "Game Studies and Beyond." *Games & Culture: A Journal of Interactive Media* 1, no. 1 (2006): 116–18.

———. "Inventing Space. Toward a Taxonomy of On- and Off-Screen Space in Video Games." *Film Quarterly* 51, no. 3 (Fall 1997): 11–23.

———. "The Subcreation of Transmedia Worlds." *Compar(a)ison: An International Journal of Comparative Literature* 2 (Fall 2005).

———. "Virtual Sub-Creation: Two Top Computer Games Were Made by Christians." *World* (December 6, 1997): 23.

Yang, Dori Jones. "Bill Gates Has His Hand on a Joystick." *U.S. News & World Report* 128, no. 11 (March 20, 2000): 54.

Notes

Chapter 2

1. Mark J. P. Wolf, *The World of the D'ni: Myst and Riven* (Milan: Costa and Nolan, 2006), for a detailed comparison.

Chapter 4

1. Richard M. Bueschel, *Guide to Vintage Trade Simulators and Countertop Games* (Atglen, PA: Schiffer, 1997).
2. Ken Durham, "History of Pinball Machines," GameRoomAnitiques.com, http://www.gameroomantiques.com/HistoryPin.htm, (accessed August 14, 2007).
3. J. Martin Graetz, "The Origin of *Spacewar!*" *Creative Computing* (August 1981).
4. Sol Lewitt, "Paragraphs on Conceptual Art," *Artforum* 5, no. 10 (June 1967): 79–83.
5. Gene Youngblood, *Expanded Cinema* (New York: E. P. Dutton, 1970).

Chapter 5

1. See Mark J. P. Wolf and Bernard Perron, editors, *The Video Game Theory Reader* (New York: Routledge, 2003), "Introduction," for a more detailed history of the study of video games.
2. Available online, http://www.klov.com/.
3. Available online, http://gamestudies.org/0601.

Chapter 7

1. See "Vintage Coin Operated Fortune Tellers, Arcade Games, Digger/Cranes, Gun Games and Other Penny Arcade Games, pre-1977," http://marvin3m.com/arcade/ (accessed April 5, 2007); and "electromechanical game," http://www.everything2.com/index.pl?node_id=1242873 (accessed March 27, 2007).
2. According to Steve Fulton, "Atari: The Lost Years of the Coin-Op, 1971–1975," http://www.armchairarcade.com/aamain/content.php?article.101 (accessed March 27, 2007).
3. According to Steve Fulton, "Atari: The Lost Years of the Coin-Op, 1971–1975," http://www.armchairarcade.com/aamain/content.php?article.102 (accessed March 27, 2007).
4. Steven L. Kent, *The Ultimate History of Video Games: The Story Behind the Craze that Touched Our Lives and Changed the World* (New York: Three Rivers Press, 2001), 116.

Chapter 8

1. For more on early home game systems, see David Winter's website, http://www.pong-story.com/.

Chapter 9

1. Leonard Herman, *Phoenix: The Fall and Rise of Video Games* (Springfield, NJ: Rolenta Press, 2007), 4th ed.
2. Herman, *Phoenix: The Fall and Rise of Video Games.*
3. Leonard Herman, "The Baer Essentials," *Electronic Gaming Monthly* (January 2000): 168–76.

Chapter 11

1. Herman, *Phoenix: The Fall and Rise of Video Games.*
2. Telka S. Perry and Paul Wallich, "Design Case History: The Atari Video Computer System," *IEEE Spectrum* (March 1983).

Chapter 12

1. Kent, *The Ultimate History of Video Games,* 130.
2. Although some sources list *Starhawk* as appearing in 1977, the author of *Starhawk,* Tim Skelly, gives 1978 as the year of its creation, in his account at http://www.dadgum.com/giantlist/archive/cinematronics.html (accessed April 10, 2007).
3. According to GameArchive.com, http://www.gamearchive.com/Video_Games/Manufacturers/Atari/asteroids.html (accessed July 27, 2007).
4. According to klov.com, http://www.klov.com/game_detail.php?letter=A&game_id=6939 (accessed April 10, 2007). For the 70,000 units figure, see "Asteroids," *GameArchive.com,* http://www.gamearchive.com/Video_Games/Manufacturers/Atari/asteroids.html (accessed April 10, 2007). Also see http://markn.users.netlink.co.uk//Arcade/aster.html for a history of *Asteroids.*
5. A number of sources give 1980 as the release date for *Red Baron;* however, *GameArchive.com* gives the release date of both the cockpit and upright versions of the game as 1981 (see http://www.gamearchive.com/Video_Games/Manufacturers/Atari/red_baron.html), and the site includes a scan of the original *Red Baron* operator's manual, which also has a copyright date of 1981.
6. Kent, *The Ultimate History of Video Games,* 164.
7. Although 1982 is often given as the year of *Black Widow*'s release, Owen R. Rubin, who programmed vector games at Atari, gives 1983 as the date in his essay "Memories of a Vector World," ACM SIGGraph's *Computer Gaming* 32, no. 2 (May 1998), http://www.siggraph.org/publications/newsletter/v32n2/contributions/rubin.html (accessed April 11, 2007).

Chapter 13

1. Chris Morris, "Game Over: Pac Man Turns 25: A Pizza Dinner Yields a Cultural Phenomenon—and Millions of Dollars in Quarters," *CNNMoney.com,* May 10, 2005. Morris reports on a study undertaken by Twin Galaxies, http://money.cnn.com/2005/05/10/commentary/game_over/column_gaming/index.htm (accessed January 24, 2007).
2. From an interview in Susan Lammers book, *Programmers at Work* (Redmond, WA: MicroSoft Press, 1986), and subsequently posted on the Internet, http://www.geocities.com/SiliconValley/Heights/5874/iwatani.htm (accessed January 23, 2007).
3. See "The Virtual Pac-Man Museum," http://www.zutco.com/pacman.htm, for images of some of these products.

Chapter 14

1. *BYTE Magazine* 3, no. 7 (July 1978): 67

2. According to http://www.economicexpert.com/a/TRS:80.htm (accessed August 25, 2007); and http://indopedia.org/TRS-80.html (accessed August 25, 2007).

Chapter 15

1. The history of *Colossal Cave Adventure* and its various versions can be found at http://www. rickadams.org/adventure/a_history.html (accessed on February 25, 2004).

2. On the connection of the game and the actual cave on which it is based, see "The Real 'Colossal Cave,'" http://www.rickadams.org/adventure/b_cave.html.

3. "A Short History of Interactive Fiction," http://www.inform-fiction.org/manual/html/s46.html.

4. See Mark J.P. Wolf and Bernard Perron, ed., *The Video Game Theory Reader* (New York: Routledge, 2003), foreword by Robinett, for an in-depth look at the problems encountered in adapting *Adventure* into a graphical game.

5. According to http://www.atariage.com/software_page.html?SoftwareLabelID=1.

6. From the Lucasfilm Games manual to *Maniac Mansion*, 1987.

7. Video clips had been used in laserdisc games as early as *Dragon's Lair* (1983), and even in Rick Dyer's Halcyon home laserdisc game system, but the amount of memory needed to store video clips was not available in home computers until the advent of the CD-ROM.

8. According to http://www.greatgamesexperiment.com/user/EA%20Games (accessed July 28, 2007).

9. According to Gamespot.com, http://www.gamespot.com/news/index.html (accessed July 28, 2007).

10. According to Gamasutra.com, http://www.gamasutra.com/php-bin/hews_index.phy?story=9051 (accessed July 28, 2007).

11. Robert Summa, "'No more online gaming for you!' says EA," posted on joystiq.com, http://www.joystiq.com/2006/08/06/no-more-online-gaming-for-you-says-ea/.

Chapter 16

1. According to Kent, *The Ultimate History of Video Games*, 152.

2. Both *Pac-Man* and *Defender* are typically said to have grossed over a billion dollars, for example, see the Gamespot website, http://www.gamespot.com/gamespot/features/all/greatestgames/p-44.html (accessed July 21, 2006).

3. While *Battlezone* had the first 3-D polygon-based environments, Vectorbeam's *Speed Freak* (1978) had the first 3-D polygon-based objects, making it the first arcade game to feature true 3-D computation.

4. Although *Tempest's* title screen gives the copyright date as 1980 (in roman numerals), its release date was in 1981. This is the case for a number of games which are released sometime after their programming is completed, so screen dates do not always coincide with release dates.

5. The numbers here are from Bernstein Research and reported in Albert Mehrabian and Warren Wixen, "Lights Out at the Arcade," *Psychology Today* (December 1983): 72; and Charles P. Alexander, "Video Games Go Crunch!" *Time* (October 17, 1983): 64.

6. DIP switch settings for over 5,000 arcade games can be found at http://www.solvalou.com/subpage/arcade_dips (accessed August 2, 2006).

7. For more information on suicide batteries, see "The Dead Battery Society" website, http://www.arcadecollecting.com/dead/dead.html (accessed on August 2, 2006).

8. Many of the data regarding the arcade games discussed in this chapter came from http://www.klov.com/, http://www.videotopia.com/, and http://www.gamearchive.com/.

Chapter 17

1. Cathleen McGuigan and Peter McAlevey, "Mini-Movies Make the Scene," *Newsweek* (August 8, 1983): 79.

2. Dan Persons, "Laser's Last Stand: Where Have All the Lasers Gone? Can This Be the End of the Road for 'The Saviour of the Arcades'?" *Electronic Games* (July 1984): 78.

3. According to Saku Taipale, "MSX and Laserdiscs," *MSX Computer & Club Webmagazine,* no. 93 (June–December 2000), http://www.mccw.hetlab.tk/93/msxlaserdisc/en.html (accessed April 16, 2007).

4. See www.daphne-emu.com.

Chapter 18

1. The figure of $5 billion for 1981 is found both in *Newsweek* and *Time*. See Lynn Langway *et. al,* "Invasion of the Video Creatures," *Newsweek* (November 16, 1981): 90–94; and John Skow, "Games that Play People," *Time* (January 18, 1982): 50–58.

2. "Video Games Are Suddenly a $2 Billion Industry," *Business Week* (May 24, 1982): 78–83.

3. Skow, "Games that Play People," 58.

4. "Video Games Are Suddenly a $2 Billion Industry," 78.

5. Jerry Eimbinder and Eric Eimbinder, "Electronic Games: Space-Age Leisure Activity," *Popular Electronics,* (October 1980): 55.

6. Ibid.

7. Peter Nulty, "Why the Craze Won't Quit," *Fortune* (November 15, 1982): 114.

8. See *Game Informer* 15, no. 145 (May 2005): 150.

9. From "Arcade Games Start to Flicker,"*Business Week* (December 6, 1982): 39.

10. Albert Mehrabian and Warren Wixen, "Lights Out at the Arcade," *Psychology Today* (December 1983): 72; and Charles P. Alexander, "Video Games Go Crunch!" *Time* (October 17, 1983): 64.

11. "The Trend is Back to Pinball Machines," *Business Week* (May 7, 1984): 37.

Chapter 19

1. Kent, *The Ultimate History of Video Games,* 279.

2. Ibid., 298. Consult David Sheff's book *Game Over: How Nintendo Conquered the World* (New York: Vintage Books, 1994) for more details on the New York NES launch.

3. Ibid., 308.

4. Ibid., 360.

5. See Steven A. Schwartz and Janet Schwartz, *Parent's Guide to Video Games* (Roseville: Prima Lifestyles, 1994). The Schwartzes made an enquiry to NOA regarding their content policies and reproduced the letter they received in their book. The words quoted are taken directly from Nintendo of America's response.

6. For examples of game altering and the official "Nintendo of America's Video Game Content Guidelines," see J.J. McCullough's *Nintendo's Era of Censorship* webpage, http://www.filibuster cartoons.com/Nintendo.php (accessed August 14, 2007).

7. Douglas Crawford, The Untold Story of Maniac Mansion," Wired Magazine, no. 1.04 (September/October 1993), http://www.wired.com/wired/archive/1.04/nintendo.html.

8. These estimates were given personally to this author in response to an inquiry regarding the exact scope of the NES's games library.

9. "International NES/Famicom Cartridge List," *The Nintendo Repository,* http://www.gamers graveyard.com/repository/nes/nesgames.html.

10. The chart is available at http://www.vgchartz.com/worldtotals.php?name=&console=NES&pu blisher=&sort=Total.

11. For more extensive information on the NES hardware, see http://nesdev.parodius.com/.

12. Darrell Hartman, "Life is Like a Game of 'Donkey Kong,'" *The New York Sun,* August 14, 2007, http://www.nysun.com/article/60465?page_no=3 (accessed August 14, 2007).

13. Levi Buchanan, "It's All in the Game," *Chicago Tribune,* May 17, 2005; and Greg Sewart, "Sega Saturn: The Pleasure and the Pain," *1up.com,* http://www.1up.com/do/feature?cId=3142283&did=1 (accessed May 4, 2006).

14. Steven L. Kent, "Nintendo Unveiling a New Portable," *USA Today,* May 11, 2004, http://www.usatoday.com/life/lifestyle/2004-05-11-nintendo-ds_x.htm (accessed May 4, 2006).

15. "Nintendo Unveils Game Boy Micro," *CIOL.com,* http://www.ciol.com/content/news/2005/105051803.asp (accessed May 4, 2006).

16. According to Nintendo's 2005 Annual Financial Report, http://www.nintendo.com/corp/report/NintendoAnnualReport2005.pdf (accessed May 4, 2006).

Chapter 20

1. Herman, *Phoenix: The Fall and Rise of Video Games.*

2. Herman, *Phoenix: The Fall and Rise of Video Games.*

Chapter 22

1. See André Gaudreault and Tom Gunning, "Le cinéma des premiers temps, un défi à l'histoire du cinéma?" in *Histoire du Cinéma, Nouvelles Approches,* ed. J. Aumont, A. Gaudreault, and M. Marie (Paris: Publications de la Sorbonne, 1989), 49–63; and Tom Gunning, "The Cinema of Attractions: Early Film, Its Spectator and the Avant-Garde," in *Early Cinema, Space. Frame, Narrative,* ed. Thomas Elsaesser (London: British Film Institute, 1990), 56–62.

2. From the September 1983 article, "Dragon's Lair: A Marriage of Science and Art" included with the game *Don Bluth Presents Dragon's Lair 20th Anniversary Special Edition* (2003). However, the source is not indicated.

3. Marc Saltzman, "Dragon's Lair," *Supercade: A Visual History of the Videogame Age 1971–1984,* ed. Van Burnham (Cambridge, MA: MIT Press, 2003), 348. As the first game to feature high definition TV graphics, *Dragon's Lair 3D: Return to the Lair* (Dragonstone Software/Ubisoft, 2002) also has its place in history.

4. For information about early laserdisc games, the website http://www.dragons-lair-project.com/ remains the most significant reference.

5. A flyer is available at http://www.dragons-lair-project.com/games/materials/flyers/dl.asp (accessed August 14, 2007).

6. The date on the box set of the game is 1992, but it is known to have been released in 1993. The same is true of the Philips CD-i version of *Voyeur* (1993/1994).

7. Kent, *The Ultimate History of Video Games,* 456–57.

8. Daniel Ichbiah, *La saga des jeux vidéo* (Paris: Éditions Générales First-Pocket, 1997), 208.

9. Rusel Demaria, *The 7th Guest: The Official Guide* (Rocklin, CA: Prima Publishing, 1993), 344–45.

10. Kent, *The Ultimate History of Video Games,* 273.

11. Ibid., 470.

12. Philip Elmer-Dewitt, "The Amazing Video Game Boom," *Time* (Attack of the Video Games) 142, no. 13 (September 27, 1993): 43.

13. Rick Barba, *Under a Killing Moon. The Official Strategy Guide* (Rocklin, CA: Prima Publishing, 1995), 229.

14. Rusel Demaria and Johnny L. Wilson, *High Score!: The Illustrated History of Electronic Games* (Berkeley, CA: McGraw Hill/Osborne Media, 2002), 142.

15. Telka S. Perry, "Video Games: The Next Wave," *IEEE Spectrum* 20, no. 12 (December 1983): 52–59.

Chapter 23

1. David Kushner, "Care for a Latte with That, Mr. Nukem?" *The New York Times,* September 23, 1999, vol. 149, no. 51654; and Marcus Webb, "Arcade-Style Viddies Confront Challenging Future as Market Fragments and Shrinks," *Vending Times* 41, no. 11 (September 25, 2001–October 24, 2001).

2. See KLOV.com, http://www.klov.com/game_detail.php?letter=A&game_id=7331. Many game descriptions and dates in this essay were obtained at http://www.klov.com/.

3. According to the page for *Airline Pilots,* http://www.klov.com/game_detail.php?letter=A&game_id=6835.

4. See http://www.bemani.com/ and http://www.konami.com/ for more information.

5. Tracy Smith, "Video Game That's Good for You," *CBSnews.com,* http://cbsnews.com/stories/2002/06/13/earlyshow/contributors/tracysmith/main512169.shtml (accessed October 6, 2003).

6. Beth Snyder Bulik, "Arcade Craze Swings into the Living Room," *Advertising Age* 75, no. 26 (June 28, 2004): 3, 52.

7. According to the *Cyber Sled* page of *The Killer List of Videogames,* http://www.klov.com/game_detail.php?letter=C&game_id=7466 (accessed November 30, 2006).

8. For more information on Namco's System 16 hardware for their medium-sized attractions, see http://www.system16.com/hardware.php?id=833.

9. Maureen Tkacik, "Back to Bingo: Arcade Firm Shrugs Off High-Tech Flash—GameWorks Thinks It Has a Winner with Classics Like Bowling and Skee-Ball," *The Wall Street Journal,* July 23, 2001.

10. David P. Hamilton, "Entertainment: Pow Goes Posh as Arcades Zap Old Image," *The Wall Street Journal,* July 2, 1993.

11. George Jones and Ken Brown, "Arcade 2.0: The Future of Public Gaming Doesn't Accept Coins," *Computer Gaming World,* no. 230 (September 2003): 40–44.

12. Rochelle Slovin, "Hot Circuits: Reflections on the 1989 Video Game Exhibition of the American Museum of the Moving Image," in ed. Mark J. P. Wolf, *The Medium of the Video Game* (Austin, TX: University of Texas Press, 2001), 137–54.

13. Dan Hower, John Talarico, Tim Ferrante, *The Arcade Video Game Price Guide* (Cleveland, OH: GameRoom Magazine, 2001).

14. Although the sounds in *Double Donkey Kong* are said to have a higher pitch than the original version; see http://www.klov.com/game_detail.php?letter=D&game_id=7618.

Chapter 24

1. According to Aging Hipsters, http://www.aginghipsters.com/blog/archives/000022.php, (accessed July 30, 2007).

2. According to The Gameroom, http://thegameroom1.blogspot.com/2007_03_27_archive.html, (accessed July 30, 2007).

3. According to GamePro.com, http://www.gamepro.com/gamepro/domestic/games/features/111822.shtml, (accessed July 30, 2007).

Chapter 25

1. See Answers.com, http://www.answers.com/topic/zzt (accessed August 14, 2007).

2. Maria Seward, interview with Jim Knopf, http://www.sharewarejunkies.com/invjikn.htm (accessed October 13, 2006).

Chapter 26

1. According to http://www.spiritus-temporis.com/sega-saturn/ (accessed August 25, 2007); and http://info.sonicretro.org/Sega_Saturn (accessed August 25, 2007).

2. Telis Demos, "Ballmer: Xbox Will Capitalize on PS3 Delay," *CNNMoney.com,* March 17, 2006, http://money.cnn.com/2006/03/17/technology/ballmer_fortune/index.htm (accessed August 25, 2007).

Chapter 27

1. See "Plato," *The everyday blog of Richard Bartle,* http://www.youhaventlived.com/qblog/2006/QBlog010206A.html.
2. Marty "Retro Rogue" Goldberg, "The History of Computer Gaming," *ClassicGaming.com,* 2001–2002, http://classicgaming.gamespy.com/View.php?view=Articles.Detail&id=330.
3. Ibid.
4. See Multi-User Dungeon, http://www.british-legends.com/.
5. See http://www.avalon-rpg.com/ (accessed August 14, 2007).
6. Chip Morningstar and R.H. Farmer, "The Lessons of Lucasfilm's Habitat," in ed. Michael Benedikt, *Cyberspace: First Steps* (Cambridge, MA: MIT Press, 1991), 273–301.
7. See Ultima Online Release (Part I), http://www.aschulze.net/ultima/stories9/release1.htm.
8. "World of Warcraft Subscribers Surpasses 9 Million," *Macworld.com,* http://www.macworld.com/news/2007/07/24/wow/index.php (accessed July 31, 2007).
9. See MMORPG Gamelist, http://www.mmorpg.com/gamelist.cfm?gameId=0&bhcp=1.

Chapter 28

1. *Business Week,* no. 3661 (December 27, 1999): 62.
2. *Advertising Age* 71, no. 7 (February 14, 2000): 17.
3. Kent, *The Ultimate History of Video Games,* 511.
4. Ibid., 511.
5. A list of Greatest Hits titles for the PlayStation, PlayStation 2, and PlayStation Portable systems can be found at http://en.wikipedia.org/wiki/List_of_Sony_Greatest_Hits_games. As noted therein, the standard for acceptance was 150,000 copies at first, but was raised to 250,000 later.
6. See "Playstation CD Laser Repair" for a detailed procedure to correct these laser problems, http://www.cyber-mag.com/station/laserPSX.htm (accessed March 30, 2007).

Chapter 29

1. Miranda Sawyer, "Lara Hit in The Face," *The Croft Times* (June 5, 1997), http://www.cubeit.com/ctimes/news0007b.htm (accessed April 30, 2007).
2. "Lara Hit in The Face: Interview with Toby Gard," *The Croft Times* (June 5, 1997), http://www.cubeit.com/ctimes/news0007a.htm (accessed April 26, 2007).
3. "Lara's Creator Speaks," *tiscali.games,* http://www.tiscali.co.uk/games/features/tombraiderlegend/2.

Chapter 32

1. According to http://www.gameskank.net/company-Eidos%20Interactive.html (accessed August 25, 2007).
2. According to the European Game Developers Federation, http://egdf.eu/EGDF_Press_Release_061110.pdf (accessed August 1, 2007). EGDF members are Tiga (UK), APOM (France), GAME (Germany/Austria), BGIn (Benelux), Producentforeningen (Denmark), Spelplan-ASGD (Sweden), and Neogames (Finland). The federation represents about 500 studies based in Austria, Belgium, Germany, Great Britain, France, Italy, the Netherlands, and the Nordic Countries, which together employ over 15,500 people.

Chapter 33

1. The work described in this chapter was supported by a grant from the Research Grants Council of the Hong Kong Government (CUHK4680/05H). Some of the data and analysis about Singapore video

games in this work is modified from "Japanese Video Games in Singapore: History, Culture, and Industry," *Asian Journal of Social Sciences* 29:1 (June 2001, Brill), which the author would like to gratefully acknowledge.

2. Reiji Asakura, *Revolutionaries at Sony: The Making of the Sony PlayStation and the Visionaries Who Conquered the World of Video Games* (New York: McGraw-Hill, 2000); and Chris Kohler, *Power-Up: How Japanese Video Games Gave the World an Extra Life* (Indianapolis: Brady Games, 2005).

3. Michael Hayes and Stuart Disney, *Games War: Video Games, A Business Review* (London: Bowerdean, 1995); J.C. Herz, *Joystick Nation: How Videogames Ate Our Quarters, Won Our Hearts, and Rewired Our Minds,* (Boston, MA: Little Brown, 1997); Marsha Kinder, *Playing with Power in Movies, Television, and Video Games: From Muppet Babies to Teenage Mutant Ninja Turtles* (Berkeley and Los Angeles: University of California Press, 1991); and David Sheff, *Game Over: How Nintendo Zapped an American Industry, Captured Your Dollars, and Enslaved Your Children* (New York: Random House, 1993).

4. Benjamin Wai-ming Ng, "Street Fighter and The King of Fighters in Hong Kong: A Study of Cultural Consumption and Localization of Japanese Games in an Asian Context," *Game Studies* 6, no. 1 (December 2006), http://gamestudies.org/0601 (accessed August 14, 2007).

5. Wui Seng Ng, *Japanese Video Games in Singapore: A Study of Hardware, Software and Players* (Honors Thesis, Department of Japanese Studies, National University of Singapore, 1998): 26.

6. Kinder, *Playing with Power in Movies, Television, and Video Games,* 89–93.

7. Yat-fai Tsang, *A Study of the Game Console Market in Hong Kong* (MBA thesis, Chinese University of Hong Kong, 1991).

8. Koichi Iwabuchi, "Return to Japan: Japan in Asian Audiovisual Markets," in Kosaku Yoshino, ed., *Consuming Ethnicity and Nationalism* (Honolulu: University of Hawai'i Press, 1998), 185–196; and Roland Robertson, "Glocalization: Time, Space and Homogeneity-Heterogeneity," in Roland Robertson, Mile Featherstone, and Scott Lash, ed., *Global Modernities* (London,: Thousand Oaks, 1995), 25–44.

9. Benjamin Wai-ming Ng, "A Preliminary Investigation of the Jin Yong Fever in Japan," *Hong Kong Journal of Social Sciences,* no. 27 (Spring/Summer 2004): 131–46.

10. Brian Underdahl, *PS2: Blow the Lid Off* (New York: McGraw-Hill, 2002).

11. Anne Allison, *Millennial Monsters: Japanese Toys and the Global Imagination* (Berkeley and Los Angeles: University of California Press, 2006), chap. 6.

12. *The Straits Times,* April 9, 1997, p. 8.

13. Suet-Yin Cheng and Cui-Yuk Lo, *Consumer Behavior of Tamagotchi Keepers* (MBA Thesis, Chinese University of Hong Kong, 1998).

14. *Lianhe Wanbao,* December 1, 1998, p. 11.

15. Hodo Suzuki, *Kaizoku Sofuto No Hon* (Book of Pirated Software) (Tokyo, Japan: Sansai Books, 1997): 43–50.

16. Steven Poole, *Trigger Happy: Videogames and the Entertainment Revolution* (London: Little Brown, 2004).

17. Ng, "Street Fighter and The King of Fighters in Hong Kong."

18. John Fiske, *Understanding Popular Culture* (New York: Routledge, 1989), 32.

19. Herz, *Joystick Nation;* and Sheff, *Game Over.*

20. Koichi Iwabuchi, "Return to Japan: Japan in Asian Audiovisual Markets," in Kosaku Yoshino, ed., *Consuming Ethnicity and Nationalism* (Honolulu, University of Hawai'i Press, 1998), 179–183.

Chapter 34

1. J. Hill, "Game Industry at the Crossroads," *The Age* (September 7, 2006), http://www.theage.com.au/news/games/game-industry-at-the-crossroads/2006/09/06/1157222139337.html?page=fullpage.

2. Insight Economics, *Australian Electronic Game Industry Profile,* prepared for the Game Developers' Association of Australia, 2006, page iii, http://www.gdaa.com.au/docs/Industry_Profile.pdf.

3. J. Banks, "Gamers as Co-creators: Enlisting the Virtual Audience—A Report from the Netface," in ed. Virginia Nightengale and Karen Ross, *Critical Readings: Media and Audiences* (Maidenhead, England: Open University Press, 2003), 268–78; and S. Humphreys, B. Fitzgerald, J. Banks, and N. Suzor, "Fan-Based Production for Computer Games: User-Led Innovation, the 'Drift of Value' and Intellectual Property Rights," *Media International Australia* 114 (2005): 16–29.

4. Hill, "Game Industry."

5. For the 85 percent statistic, see "Insight Economics," *Australian Electronic Game Industry Profile,* page 4. For the 90 percent statistic, see Hill, "Game Industry."

6. Hill, "Game Industry."

7. M. Swalwell, "The Meme Game: Escape from Woomera," *RealTime* 55 (2003), http://www.realtimearts.net/rt55/swallwell.html (accessed February 2, 2007).

8. S. Nicholls, "Ruddock Fury over Woomera Computer Game," *The Age* (April 30, 2003), http://www.theage.com.au/articles/2003/04/29/1051381948773.html.

9. Swalwell, "The Meme Game."

10. Keith Gallasch, "Australia Council Restructures: New Media Arts Wasted," message posted to the Fibreculture Forum, December 9, 2004, archived at http://www.fibreculture.org/myspinach/fibreculture/2004-December/004292.html; and M. Swalwell, K. Neil, "'Unaustralia the Game' and the Possibility of Independent Satirical Videogames," unpublished conference paper, presented at the annual conference of the Cultural Studies Association of Australasia, December 2006.

11. Office of Film and Literature Classification, http://www.classification.gov.au/special.html.

12. Office of Film and Literature Classification brochure, *Guidelines for the Classification of Film and Computer Games,* http://www.comlaw.gov.au/comlaw/management.nsf/lookupindexpagesbyid/IP200508205?OpenDocument.

13. For the online petition addressed to the Office of Film and Literature Classification, see http://www.petitiononline.com/oflcr18/petition.html.

14. C. Fitzsimmons, "Push for 18+ Game Ratings Fails," *Australian IT,* November 12, 2002, http://web.archive.org/20021115103906/http://australianit.news.com.au/articles/0,7204,5466570%5e15319%5e%5enbv%5e15306,00.html (accessed January 20, 2007).

15. See B. Hutcheon, L. Hearn, and D. Braithwaite, "Australia First to Ban Graffiti Game," *The Age* (February 17, 2006), http://www.theage.com.au/news/breaking/australia-first-to-ban-graffiti-game/2006/02/17/1140064210144.html (accessed January 20, 2007).

16. Ibid.

17. Ibid.

18. Review Board Decision for *Marc Ecko's Getting Up: Contents Under Pressure,* http://www.oflc.gov.au/resource.html?resource=794&filename=794.pdf, 6–9.

19. Review Board Decision, sections 6.1.1, 6.1.2, 6.1.4, 6.1.5, and 6.1.7.

20. Review Board Decision, sections 6.1.6, 6.1.9, 6.1.10, 6.1.11, and 6.1.12.

21. Review Board Decision, section 7.13.2.

22. Review Board Decision, sections 7.8, 7.9.1, and 7.9.2.

23. Review Board Decision, sections 7.11.1 and 7.11.2.

24. Review Board Decision, section 7.13.4.

25. Review Board Decision, section 7.14.5.

Chapter 35

1. M. Cerny and M. John, "Game Development Myth vs. Method," *Game Developer* (June 2002).

2. E. Bethke, *Game Development and Production,* (Plano, TX: Wordware Publishing, 2003).

3. From an interview with Wright by the author.

4. Bethke, *Game Development and Production.*

5. From interviews done by the author. See Feichin Ted Tschang, "When Does an Idea Become an Innovation? The Role of Individual and Group Creativity in Videogame Design" (Copenhagen: DRUID 2003 Summer Conference, June 12–14, 2003).

6. Bethke, *Game Development and Production.*

7. Feichin Ted Tschang, "Videogames as Interactive Experiential Products and Their Manner of Development," *International Journal of Innovation Management* 9, no. 1 (2005): 103–31.

8. Y. Baba and Feichin Ted Tschang, "Product Development in Japanese TV Game Software: The Case of an Innovative Game," *International Journal of Innovation Management* 5, no. 4 (2001): 487–515.

9. From the author's interviews with various game designers.

Chapter 36

1. Steven Poole, *Trigger Happy: Videogames and the Entertainment Revolution* (New York: Arcade Publishing, 2000), 125.

2. Mark J.P. Wolf, "Inventing Space: Toward a Taxonomy of On- and Off-Screen Space in Video Games," *Film Quarterly* 51, no. 3 (Fall 1997): 12.

3. Jay David Bolter and Richard Grusin, *Remediation: Understanding New Media* (Cambridge, MA: MIT Press, 2000).

4. Philippe Quéau, *Éloge de la Simulation: De la vie des Langages à la Synthèse des Images* (Seyssel: Éditions du Champ Vallon, 1986), 31, my translation.

5. Jay David Bolter and Richard Grusin, *Remediation: Understanding New Media* (Cambridge, MA: MIT Press, 1999), 121.

6. Alison McMahan, "Immersion, Engagement, and Presence," in *The Video Game Theory Reader,* ed. Mark J.P. Wolf and Bernard Perron (New York: Routledge, 2003), 67.

Chapter 37

1. Scott Cohen's *Zap! The Rise and Fall of Atari* (New York: McGraw-Hill, 1984), 28; and Kent, *The Ultimate History of Video Games,* 41–42.

2. See the Video Game History website, *The Dot Eaters,* for more on early uses of speech synthesis and laserdisc technology in arcade games (http://www.thedoteaters.com).

3. Karen Collins, "Flat Twos and the Musical Aesthetic of the Atari VCS" [http://www.popular-musicology-online.com/issues/01/collins-01.html (accessed August 14, 2007)] for more on the Atari VCS's unique sound system, particularly regarding the limitations the system placed on sound designers, and how that may have influenced their compositional style.

4. Richard Rouse III, *Game Design Theory and Practice, 2nd Ed.* (Plano, TX: Wordware Publishing, 2005), 58.

5. Ibid., page 58. Also see Chris Granner, "Tales from the Trenches of Coin-op Audio," *Gamasutra.com,* http://www.gamasutra.com/features/19991118/Granner_pfv.htm, for more on the requirements of arcade game audio versus home games (paper originally published in the 1999 Game Developer's Conference proceedings).

6. Rob Bridgett, "Hollywood Sound: Part Three," *Gamasutra.com,* http://www.gamasutra.com/features/20051012/bridgett_01.shtml.

7. Karen Collins, "Loops and Bloops," *soundscapes.info,* http://www.icce.rug.nl/~soundscapes/VOLUME08/Loops_and_bloops.shtml.

8. Dave Green, "Demo or Die!" *Wired,* no. 3.07 (July 1995), http://www.wired.com/wired/archive/3.07/democoders.html; and *Flat four radio* (United Kingdom), http://www.mcld.co.uk/flatfour/chip tunes/ for the four-part podcast on chiptunes.

9. Zach Whalen, "Play Along—An Approach to Videogame Music," *GameStudies.org,* http://www.gamestudies.org/0401/whalen/. Whalen discusses video game music's relationship to animated film soundtracks (especially in *Super Mario Bros.*), and the role of game music as an enhancement to game-play.

10. *1UP.com,* interview with Koji Kondo, http://www.1up.com/do/feature?pager.offset=5&cId=3140040; and Alexander Brandon's interview with Hip Tanaka at *Gamasutra.com,* http://www.gamasutra.com/features/20020925/brandon_01.htm.

11. Christopher John Farley, "Innovators: Time 100: The Next Wave—Music," *Time.com* (2001), http://www.time.com/time/innovators_v2/music/profile_uematsu.html. In this article, Nobuo Uematsu was named one of the magazine's top innovators.

12. See Jeff Rona, *The MIDI Companion: The Ins, Outs, and Throughs* (Milwaukee, WI: Hal Leonard, 1994), 5–7, for more on the origins of MIDI.

13. See George Sanger, *The Fat Man on Game Audio: Tasty Morsels of Sonic Goodness* (Indianapolis: New Riders, 2003), 187–192, for more on George Sanger and Team Fat's endorsement of Roland's Sound Canvas chip and the subsequent widespread adoption of the chip's sound quality as a further standardization of General MIDI.

14. Aaron Marks, *The Complete Guide to Game Audio* (Lawrence, KS: CMP Books, 2001), 4.

15. Ibid., 200–201.

16. Chris McGowan and Jim McCullaugh, *Entertainment in the Cyber Zone* (New York: Random House Information Group, 1995), 25–29.

17. Marks, *The Complete Guide to Game Audio;* Sanger, *The Fat Man on Game Audio;* Alexander Brandon, *Audio for Games: Planning, Process, and Production* (Berkeley, CA: New Riders Games, 2004); and Jeannie Novak, *Game Development Essentials: An Introduction* (Clifton Park, NY: Thomson Delmar Learning, 2004) for more on the process of game sound design,

18. Alexander Brandon, "Adaptive Audio: A Report," in ed. Sanger, *The Fat Man on Game Audio,* 203.

19. See composers Michael Land and Peter McConnell's 1994 patent for iMuse (U.S. Patent No. 5,315,057) at http://pat2pdf.org/patents/pat5315057.pdf. Pages 21 through 22 in particular discuss the limitations of looped game music and the need for a "dynamic" game sound system. See iMuse Island at http://imuse.mixnmojo.com/.

20. See Guy Whitmore, "Design with Music in Mind: A Guide to Adaptive Audio for Game Designers," *Gamasutra.com,* http://www.gamasutra.com/resource_guide/20030528/whitmore_01. shtml, for possible approaches to adaptive audio in first-person shooters and similarly action-oriented games.

21. In what was previously a Japan-only event, live orchestral performances of video game music are now finding favor with American audiences, in touring venues such as "Video Games Live" (http://www.videogameslive.com/index.php?s=home) and "PLAY!" (http://www.play-symphony.com/).

22. See Billboard.com, http://www.billboard.com/bbcom/charts/chart_display.jsp?g=Singles&f=Hot+Ringtones. See also Elliot Smilowitz, "Ringtone Market Hits a High Note," *UPI Perspectives,* May 27, 2005 http://www.accessmylibrary.com/coms2/summary_0286-6807568_ITM.

23. Olga Kharif, "From Beeps to *Billboard,*" *Business Week.com,* May 19, 2005, http://www.businessweek.com/technology/content/may2005/tc20050519_8337_tc024.htm.

Chapter 38

1. Chris Crawford, *The Art of Computer Game Design* (Berkeley, CA: McGraw Hill/Osborne Media, 1984).

2. "Video Game Set Sales Record in 2005: Game Boy, PSP Lift the Industry, Despite Languid Holiday Season," *CNNMoney.com,* January 14, 2006, http://money.cnn.com/2006/01/13/technology/personaltech/gamesales/index.htm (accessed January 26, 2007); and James Brightman, "Breaking: U.S. Video Game Industry Totals $12.5 Billion in 2006," *GameDailyBiz,* http://biz.gamedaily.com/industry/feature/?id=14940 (accessed January 26, 2007).

3. Jeff Gerstmann, "The Greatest Games of All Time," *GameSpot,* http://www.gamespot.com/gamespot/features/all/greatestgames/p-44.html (accessed January 26, 2007).

4. According to http://www.games4nintendo.com/ and numerous other sites across the Internet.

5. Trey Walker, "The Sims Overtakes Myst: Electronic Arts' Virtual-Life Game Has Surpassed the Popular Adventure Game Myst in Terms of Sales to Become the Best-Selling PC Game of All Time," *GameSpot* (March 22, 2002), http://www.gamespot.com/pc/adventure/myst/news.html?sid=2857556 (accessed January 26, 2007).

6. Vladimir Cole, "World of Warcraft Breaks 8 Million Subscribers," *joystiq.com* (January 11, 2007), http://www.joystiq.com/2007/01/11/world-of-warcraft-breaks-8-million-subscribers/ (accessed January 26, 2007).

Chapter 39

1. Kent, *The Ultimate History of Video Games,* 91.

2. See for instance Craig A. Anderson and Catherine M. Ford, "Affect of the Game Player: Short-Term Effects of Highly and Mildly Aggressive Video Games," *Personality and Social Psychology Bulletin* 12, no. 4 (1986): 390–402; Diana Gagnon, "Videogames and Spatial Skills: An Exploratory Study," *Educational Communication and Technology* 33, no. 4 (1985): 263–75; and Nicola S. Schutte, John M. Malouff, Joan C. Post-Gorden, and Annette L. Rodasta, "Effects of Playing Videogames on Children's Aggressive and Other Behaviors," *Journal of Applied Social Psychology* 18, no. 5 (1988): 454–60.

3. James W. Wheless, M.D., "Video Games and Epilepsy," *epilepsy.com,* http://www.epilepsy.com/info/family_kids_video.html (accessed March 9, 2007). The link between video games and epilepsy is still unclear and subject to research.

4. Kent, *The Ultimate History of Video Games,* 462–80.

5. David Charter, "Torturing This Child is a Game Too Far, Says Appalled EU Boss," *Times Online* (November 17, 2006), http://entertainment.timesonline.co.uk/tol/arts_and_entertainment/article639508.ece (accessed March 19, 2007).

6. Tim Ingham, "505 Games Pulls Rule of Rose Release," *MCV: The Market for Home Computing & Video Games* (November 24, 2006), http://www.mcvuk.com/news/24913/505-Games-pulls-out-of-Rule-Of-Rose-release (accessed March 19, 2007).

7. Brandon Sheffield, "Thank Heaven for Little Girls: Why *Rule of Rose* May Be 2006's Most Controversial Game," *Gamasutra.com.* http://www.gamasutra.com/features/20060607/sheffield_01.shtml (accessed March 19, 2007).

Chapter 40

1. Tim Moriarty, "Uncensored Videogames: Are Adults Ruining It for the Rest of Us?" *Videogaming and Computergaming Illustrated* (October 1983).

2. According to entries for "sympathy" and "empathy" in *Webster's New Universal Unabridged Dictionary,* Revised Edition (New York: Dorset and Baber, 1983).

3. Craig A. Anderson and Karen Dill, "Video Games and Aggressive Thoughts, Feelings, and Behavior in the Laboratory and in Life," *Journal of Personality and Social Psychology* 78, no 4 (April 2000): 772–90, http://www.apa.org/journals/features/psp784772.pdf.

4. M.D. Griffiths and N. Hunt, "Dependence on Computer Games by Adolescents," *Psychological Reports* 82, (1998): 475–80.

5. Anderson and Dill, "Video Games and Aggressive Thoughts, Feelings, and Behavior in the Laboratory and in Life."

6. "The Games Kids Play: Lt. Col. Grossman on Violent Video Games," *ABCnews.com,* March 22, 2001, http://abcnews.go.com/

7. See, for example, Mary Fuller and Henry Jenkins, "Nintendo and New World Travel Writing: A Dialogue," in ed. Steven G. Jones, *Cybersociety: Computer-Mediated Communication and Community* (Thousand Oaks, CA: Sage Publications, 1995), 57–72. Fuller and Jenkins describe how imperialist ideas can be embodied in games featuring versions of colonialism.

8. From an e-mail from Simon Carne to the author, sent March 25, 2001, 8:47 a.m.

9. Ted C. Fishman, "The Play's the Thing," *The New York Times Magazine,* June 10, 2001.

10. From the section "GAMM, Appraisal, and Aggressive Behavior," in Anderson and Dill, "Video Games and Aggressive Thoughts, Feelings, and Behavior in the Laboratory and in Life."

11. Rebecca R. Tews, "Archetypes on Acid: Video Games and Culture," in ed. Mark J.P. Wolf, *The Medium of the Video Game* (Austin, TX: University of Texas Press, 2001).

12. From the *Majestic* website which was online in 2001, http://www.majestic.ea.com, but is no longer available.

13. "Playing the New Game of Life?: In the Upcoming, Cutting-Edge Game *Majestic* It's a Man's, Man's World," *ABCnews.com,* March 7, 2001, http://abcnews.go.com/.

14. Christine Gilbert, "Virtually Married," *Computer Games,* no. 125 (April 2001): 22–26.

15. Tricia Gray, "The Year's Best," *Computer Games,,* no. 125 (April 2001): 46.

16. Tricia Gray, "Shades of Gray: Peter Molyneux's Epic *Black & White* Will Expose Your Morality for the World to See," *Computer Games,* no. 125 (April 2001): 68.

Chapter 41

1. Tor Thorsen, "Steven Spielberg, EA Ink Three-Game Next-Gen Deal," *GameSpot* (October 14, 2005), http://www.gamespot.com/news/6135746.html?q=spielberg (accessed July 22, 2006).

2. Mark J.P. Wolf, *The Medium of the Video Game* (Austin, TX: University of Texas Press, 2001), 2.

3. In Japan, it has been a huge phenomenon since the 1980s. See Chris Kohler, *Power Up: How Japanese Video Games Gave the World an Extra Life* (Indianapolisa: Brady Games, 2005), 131–64.

4. "Activision and Nielsen Entertainment Release Results of Pioneering Research on In-Game Advertising," *gamesindustry.biz* (May 12, 2005), http://www.gamesindustry.biz/content_page.php?aid=13408 (accessed July 17, 2006).

5. Wolf, *The Medium of the Video Game,* 2–5.

6. Henry Jenkins, "Convergence? I Diverge," *Technology Review* (June 2001).

7. Wolf, *The Medium of the Video Game,* 1–2. In the first footnote on page 9, Wolf lists 33 game cartridges for the Atari 2600 based on movies and 23 based on television shows.

8. On the Atari 2600 adaptations, see Kent, *The Ultimate History of Video Games,* 237–39. On *Tron* and its effect on CGI in Hollywood, see Philippe Lemieux, *L'image Numérique au Cinéma* (Montréal, Canada: Les 400 Coups, 2002), 26, 35; and Philippe Lemieux, *Les Images Numériques au Sein du Cinéma Commercial Hollywoodien* (M.A. thesis, Université de Montréal, 1997). Lemieux states that from 1982 to 1989 [ending with the success of *The Abyss* (1989)], CGI in Hollywood movies was almost nonexistent, except for some rare sequences here and there.

9. Kent, *The Ultimate History of Video Games,* 422.

10. For a look at the movie-inspired games on the NES and Sega Genesis platforms, and others, go to MobyGames.com, http://www.mobygames.com/game-group/movie-inspired-games/offset,0/so,1a/ (accessed August 5, 2006).

11. All figures are taken from the Internet Movie Database (http://www.imdb.com/).

12. The controversy surrounding the violence of this game certainly played in its favor at the box office. For more on this subject, see Kent, *The Ultimate History of Video Games,* 461–80.

13. Masuyama, "Pokémon as Japanese Culture?" in ed. Lucien King, *Game On: The History and Culture of Videogames* (London: Laurence King, 2002), 34–35.

14. Kohler, *Power Up,* 6.

15. Often *animé* are adapted from *manga* first, which is why they are so interrelated. MobyGames.com lists about 1,000 games inspired by or adapted from *animé* and *manga,* http://www.mobygames.com/genre/sheet/anime-manga/ (accessed August 17, 2006).

16. Kinder, *Playing with Power in Movies, Television, and Video Games,* 3–4.

17. For more information on *Starcade,* go to http://starcade.tv/starcade/one.asp.

18. Kent, *The Ultimate History of Video Games,* 152; and Kohler, *Power Up,* 52.

19. See note 7.

20. See Chapter 39, "The Video Game as an Object of Controversy."

21. Kohler, *Power Up,* 38–39.

22. MobyGames lists 186 games directly inspired from "cartoon shows" on television. This includes American and European animation and Asian *animé.* See http://www.mobygames.com/game-group/tv-cartoon-inspired-games/offset,0/so,1a/ (accessed August 5, 2006).

23. Kinder, *Playing with Power in Movies, Television, and Video Games.*

24. Janet Murray, *Hamlet on the Holodeck: The Future of Narrative in Cyberspace* (Cambridge, MA: MIT Press, 1998), 271.

25. Henry Jenkins, "Transmedia Storytelling," *Technology Review* (January 2003): 1.

26. Henry Jenkins, "Welcome to Convergence Culture," *Receiver* (March 2005): 2.

27. Stephanie Kang, "A New Way to Use the Force," *The Wall Street Journal,* August 22, 2006. According to Kang, Lucasfilm says sales of *Star Wars* merchandise topped $12 billion since its inception in 1977, about three times the worldwide box office for all six movies combined.

28. Ernest Adams, *Break into the Game Industry: How to Get a Job Making Video Games* (New York: McGraw-Hill/Osborne Media, 2003).

Chapter 42

1. Tracy Smith, "Video Game That's Good for You," *CBSnews.com,* http://www.cbsnews.com/stories/2002/06/13/earlyshow/contributors/tracysmith/main512169.shtml (October 6, 2003).

2. "University of Texas at Austin: Simulated Workplace Builds Skills, Confidence," *Campus Technology* (August 12, 2002), in Syllabus, http://campustechnology.com/articles/39197/ (July 16, 2003).

3. I.C. Squared's website, http://www.ic2.org/; and the Digital Media Collaboratory's website, http://dmc.ic2.org/.

4. See *Wired.com*, http://www.wired.com/wired/archive/9.10/mustread_pr.html.

5. See "Electronic Arts Sets Worldwide Record for Online Gaming; Ultima Online Beta Test Hosts Nearly 3,000 Gamers Simultaneously Playing in the Same Virtual World over the Internet," *Business Wire,* August 21, 1997, http://findarticles.com/p/articles/mi_m0EIN/is_1997_August_21/ai_19683542.

6. Edward Castronova, "Virtual Worlds: A First-Hand Account of Market and Society on the Cyberian Frontier," CESifo Working Paper Series No. 618 (January 14, 2002): 3.

7. Jeff O'Brien, "Nintendo to Sell User-generated Video Games," *CNNMoney.com,* June 27, 2007, http://thebrowser.blogs.fortune.com/2007/06/27/nintendo-to-sell-user-generated-video-games/ (accessed August 3, 2007).

INDEX

3-D computation, xviii, 11, 68, 97, 139–40. *See also* 3-D graphics

3D Crazy Coaster, 70

3dfx (company), 166

3-D graphics, xix, 11–12, 42–43, 70, 74, 91–92, 94, 97, 101, 123, 125, 129, 132–33, 135, 138–40, 142, 149, 156, 159, 164, 175, 178, 180–81, 184, 187–92, 208, 211, 231, 239, 246–49, 297, 315

3D MineStorm, 70

3D Narrow Escape, 70

3DO, 89, 123, 125, 129, 162, 175, 254, 281

3D Realms (company), 157, 192–93

3-D Tic-Tac-Toe, 269

The 7th Guest, xix, 12, 87, 124, 129–30, 246, 270, 275

8-bit systems, 112, 118, 120, 161, 202, 213, 252

8-track audio tapes, 40, 56

10NES lockout chip, 111–12, 116

The 11th Hour, 130, 133

16-bit systems, xix, 110, 118, 121, 146, 149, 161, 163, 200, 202, 213, 253

20th Century Fox, 103, 294

21-bit system, 120

32-bit systems, xix, 107, 120, 140, 145, 149, 162–64, 178, 180, 214

32X Genesis add-on, 122, 149, 163

64-bit systems, 140, 163, 165, 178, 180, 215

65XE computer, 60

130XE computer, 60

1000 Miles, 264, 271

1943: The Battle of Midway, 96

2600jr. *See* Atari 2600jr

6502 processor, 194

6507 processor, 63

$25,000 Pyramid, 262, 271

A-10 Attack, 267, 274

AAMA (American Amusement Machine Association), 21

ABCnews.com, 286, 290

AB Cop, 97

AberMUD, 174

abstract games, 69, 93–94, 100, 261, 307

abstraction, 19, 153, 188, 284, 307

ACA (Australian Council of the Arts), 225

Access Software, 124, 131, 241, 243–44

Acclaim, 110, 130

Acornsoft (company), 189

"active readers," 221

Activision, 33, 58, 65, 132, 294

Adam. *See* Coleco Adam

Adam Demo Cartridge, 265

Adam (first man), 185

Adams, Ernest, xix

adaptations, 260–62, 294–98

adaptive audio, 254–55

Adbusters, 202

Adebibe, Karima, 184

Adeline Software, 125

"adjustable realism settings," 290

Adobe (company), 197

Adobe Flash, 279

Advanced Dungeons & Dragons (AD&D), 175

Adventure (Atari 2600), 64, 82, 240–41, 262, 267, 269, 271, 312

Adventure (text adventure), 34, 82, 188, 191

adventure games, 70, 81–90, 100, 123–25, 131, 184, 202, 204, 241, 245, 247, 260, 262, 279, 286

"advergames," 306

advertisements. *See* in-game advertisements

Aerobiz, 268

Africa, 314–15

After Burner, 97

After Burner II, 97

Aftermath Media (company), 130

After the War, 208

Agent Mulder, 184

Age of Conan: Hyborian Adventures, 208

aggression, 286–89

Ahl, David H., 78, 99

AIFF files, 254

AI Fleet Commander, 270

Airline Pilots, 137

Air-Sea Battle, 41, 273

AI Wars, 270

Akallabeth, 190

Akira, 297

Albegas, 101

Alcorn, Al, 36, 59, 251

algorithm, 24, 37, 74, 245, 305, 311, 313

Alice (video game), 234

Alida, 90

Alien Hominid, 197, 200

Aliens (film), 193

Allen, Paul, 77

Alley Rally, 37

Allied Leisure, xvii, 35–37, 39

Alone in the Dark, 205, 296

Alpha Beam with Ernie, 264, 266

Alpha Denshi, 68

alpha version of video games, 234

Alpine Racer, 14, 137

Alpine Racer 2, 137

Alpine Surfer, 137

Altair 8800, 77

Alternate Worlds Technology, 139

amateur radio, 201

Amazin' Software (company), 89

American Civil War, 206

American Football, 262, 272

American Laser Games (company), 101–2, 124, 128–29, 139

American McGee (company), 234

America's Army, 280

Amidar, 261, 264–65

Amiga, 208, 241, 243–44, 252

Amiga CD^{32} 123–25, 162

Amiga computer, 60

AMMI (American Museum of the Moving Image), 142

Amstrad home computer, 208

Amusement and Music Operators Association, 99

amusement centers, 135, 159, 212

Amutech, 40

amyuuzumento sentaa (amusement centers), 141

Anarchy Online, 176, 208

Andamiro (company), 138

Anderson, Craig A., 286, 288

Anderson, Paul W. S., 295–96

Andromeda (company), 118

Angler King, 137

AnimAction, 70

The Animatrix , 300

animé, 296–97, 299–300, 341 n.15

Anim-X, 290

Anno, Hideaki, 297

ANSI (American National Standards Institute), 155

Anti-Aircraft II, 38

Anvil of Dawn, 272

AOL, 175

AOL Instant Messaging, 290

Apogee Software (company), 156–57, 192

Apollo Moon Shot Rifle, 18

Apple Computers, 59, 78, 89, 201

Apple I computer, 77

Apple II computer, 77–78, 83, 99, 151, 189–91, 242, 252

Apple Macintosh, 79–80, 193, 201, 275

Apply Daily, 219

Aqua Jet, 137

AquaZone, 262

Arakawa, Minoru, 109, 118

arcade game cabinets, 96

arcade games, 13–14, 22, 29, 35–44, 67–71, 73–74, 91–104, 118, 128, 133, 135–42, 149, 159, 189, 194, 204, 211–12, 220, 239–40, 243, 246–48, 251–52, 254, 261–62, 275, 287, 295, 298, 303–4, 306, 311–12, 316

arcade operators, 95, 96, 105, 120, 135, 140

Arcade Pinball, 269

The Arcade Video Game Price Guide, 142

"Arcade video games start to flicker," 105

Archon, 89

Arda, 308

Argentina, 47, 50

Arkanoid, xviii, 96, 216, 261

Arm Champ, 137

Arm Champ II, 137

Armor Attack, 68, 70

Arnold, Ken, 83

artificial intelligence, 192, 195, 250, 305

artificial life genre, 263

artistic expression, 307

Art Master, 70

The Art of Computer Game Design , 259

Aruze (company), 147

Ascaron (company, originally founded as
    "Ascon"), 207

Ascii (American Standard Code for Information
    Interchange), 152, 155

Ascii text graphics, 78, 83, 156

Ascon. *See* Ascaron

Ash (character), 297

Asheron's Call, xx, 159, 285, 287–88, 308

Asia, 211–22, 224, 314–15

Assault, xix

assembly language, 251

Asteroid, 36

Asteroids (arcade version), xviii, 10–11, 44, 61,
    64, 68–69, 74, 91, 190, 194, 211, 246, 266,
    272, 316

Asteroids (Atari 800 version), 60

Asteroids (Atari 2600 version), 59, 64, 93

Asteroids Deluxe, 68

Astrocade Pinball, 269

Astron Belt, 12, 99, 101, 128

Astro Race, 36

Asylum, 189

Asylum II, 189

Atari (company), xvii–xx, 19, 29, 36–44, 45, 50,
    54–55, 57–61, 65, 67–71, 79, 91–96, 100,
    103–5, 110, 115–17, 138–39, 141, 143–44,
    146, 163, 189, 205–7, 211, 213, 224, 226,
    243, 246–47, 251, 275, 279, 284, 315,
    330 n.7

Atari 400 computer, 15, 58–59, 79, 151, 157

Atari 800 computer, 15, 59, 79, 151, 157, 189,
    252

Atari 2600, 4, 13, 15, 23, 25, 29, 36, 40–41, 51,
    57, 59–61, 63–66, 82–83, 93, 104, 110, 117,
    121, 143, 161, 201, 213, 240, 251–52, 259–
    60, 261, 275, 277–78, 284, 294, 298, 306,
    312, 338 n.3 ch.37, 341 n.7

Atari 2600jr, 60, 66

Atari 5200, 58–59, 65, 252, 266, 274

Atari 7800, 59–61, 66, 117, 266

Atari Baseball, 44, 262, 272

Atari Flashback, 61

Atari Flashback 2, 61, 66

Atari Games (company), 60, 70–71, 95–97,
    101, 117, 137, 139

Atari Jaguar, xix, 61, 146, 163, 254, 275

Atari Lynx, xix, 6, 10, 15, 60, 107, 146, 148,
    314

Atari Lynx II, 60, 146

Atari's Coin-Op $50,000 World Championship,
    105

Atari Soccer, 44

Atari ST computer, 60, 157

Atari System 1, 96

Atari Tank (home system), 15

Atari VCS. *See* Atari 2600

Atari Video Cube, 270

Ataxx, 136, 261, 273

Atic Atac, 204

Atlantis, 272

Atlus (company), 139

ATMs, 27

Atomic Castle, 100

Atomic Energy Laboratory, 32

Atomic Point, 136

Attack of the Zolgear, 101, 137

Attract, 48

attract mode, 37, 48, 69, 311

Auran (company), 223–24

Australia, 114, 133, 159, 223–27, 279–80, 314

Australian Government Office of Film and
    Literature Classification, 223, 225

Australian Human Rights Commissioner, 225

Austria, 114, 210

Auto Racing, 143

Auto-Slalom, 49

Auto Test, 37

Avalon, 174

Avalon Hill, 61

Avalon, the Legend Lives, 174

Avary, Roger, 296

avatars, 26, 37, 39–40, 73, 90, 138, 185, 187–
    88, 190–91, 234–35, 285, 288, 304, 311

Avenger, 39–40

Avengers, 267

axonometric perspective, 240

AY-3-8500 chip, xvii, 51, 104

Aztarac, 70

Babbage's, 164

Baby Pac-Man, 74, 94

Babyz, 262

Backgammon, 263

Back to Skool, 204

Badlands, 100–101, 128

Baer, Ralph, xvii, 5, 14, 17, 33, 46, 48, 50,
    53–57, 144

Baker, Dan, 152

Baker Street Irregulars, 131

Balance Try, 138

Baldur's Gate: Dark Alliance, 206

ball-and-paddle games, 37, 39–40, 43, 45–51, 143, 263

Balloon Gun, 38, 137

Bally Arcade, 57

Bally Corporation, 18–19, 35–36, 57, 93, 103–4, 128

Bally/Midway, 41, 43, 94–96, 99–100

Bandai, xx, 6, 110, 147, 216–17, 219

bank-switching, 64, 311

Barrel PONG, 36

Barricade, 40

Barricade II, 41

Barron, Steve, 299

Bartel, Paul, 39, 277

Bartkowiak, Andrejz, 296

Bartle, Richard, 173

basementarcade.com, 142

Bashful (nicknamed "Inky"), 74

Basic (computer language), 33, 78

Basic Computer Games, 78

Basic Math, 266

Basic Programming, 4, 274

Basketball (arcade game), 37

Basketball (Atari 2600 version), 261

Batman (character), 297

Battle Arena Toshinden, 248

Battlefield 1942, 193, 208

Battle Ping Pong, 273

Battleship, 263

Battle Star, 69

Battletech, 139–140, 265

Battlezone (arcade game), xviii, 10, 68–69, 92–93, 138, 189, 246–47, 265, 306, 316

Battlezone (Atari 2600 version), 59, 93

Bazooka, 40

Beam Software, 132, 223–24

Beans on Toast, 183

Beast, 152–53, 156

The Beast Within: A Gabriel Knight Mystery, 124, 133

Beatmania, 138, 271

Bedlam, 70

Bedquilt Cave, 82

Bega's Battle, 100

Beginning Algebra, 274

Beginning Math, 274

Belgium, 114, 210

Bell Labs, 31

Belson, Jordan, 19

Benami Games (division of Konami), 138

Bendix G-15, 32

Benison, Ron, 141

Berzerk, 64, 70, 92, 191, 251, 268, 272

Betamax, 181

beta version of video games, 234

Bethesda Softworks (company), 280

Beyond Good and Evil, 206

bezel, 311

Big Bird's Egg Catch, 264

Bigfoot Bonkers, 40

BigWorld Technology (company), 224

Billboard, 74

Billboard's "Top 10 Ringtones," 257

Bingo Novelty Company, 18

Bionic Commando, 112

Bios (Basic Input/Output System), 201

bit (defined), 311

bitmaps, 311, 315, 239–42, 244

Black & White, 205, 291, 305

Black Dahlia, 132

Blackjack, 264, 268

Blackjack (computer game), 32

Black Widow, 70, 330 n.7

Blade Runner, 260

Blair, Christopher, 132

Blasto, 43

Bletchley Park, 33

Blinky. *See* Shadow

Blinx series, 26

Blitz!, 70

Blitz Games (company), 226

Blizzard Entertainment, xix, 176, 204, 206

Blockade, 40

Block Buster, 39

Block Out, 261, 270

BloodRayne, 296

Blood, the Last Vampire franchise, 299

Bloxeed, 136

Blue Byte Studio (company), 207

Blue Shark, 43

Blu-ray discs, 125

Bluth, Don, 100, 12

BMB Compuscience (company), 153

BMG Records, 181

board games, 61, 136, 207, 232, 261–63

"body genres" of cinema, 187

Body Slam, 267

Boeing 777 aircraft, 137

Boll, Uwe, 296

Bolter, Jay, 244

Bomb Bee, 43

Bomber, 41

Bombs Away, 39

Bonk's Adventure, 140
Bonnell, Bruno, 205–6
Boot Camp, 269
Boot Hill, 40
Borench, 136
Bourgeon, François, 206
Bowling, 272
Boxing, 215, 267, 272
Boxing Bugs, 69
Bradbury, Ray, 190
Bradley Trainer, 68, 92
Brainstorm (film), 190
Bram Stoker's Dracula, 125
Brandon, Alexander, 255
Braun, Ludwig, 33
Braze Technology (company), 142
Brazil, 114
Breakout, xviii, 39, 43, 211, 261, 309
Breakout (Atari 2600 version), 64
Breakout clones, 41, 43
British Board of Film Classification, 131, 208
Brøderbund Software (company), 132, 242
Bromley, Marty, 149
Brookhaven National Lab, 32
Brooklyn Polytechnic Institute, 33
Brotherhood of the Wolf / Le pacte des loups, 296
Brothers in Arms, 206
Brown, Alan, 152
Brown, Bob, 54
Brown Box, 50, 53–54, 57
Brussee, Arjan, 156
Bubble Bobble, xviii, 96
Budokan: *The Martial Spirit*, 89
Bug-Byte Software, 204
bugs (in programming), 234–35
Bulletin Board Systems (BBSs), 107, 155, 174, 197
Bullet Mark, 38
Bullfrog Productions, 204–5
Bully, 280
bump mapping, 248
Bungie Studios (company), xx, 193, 250, 296
Bunker-Ramo Corporation, 33
BurgerTime, 94
Burnham, Van, xiii
Burning Rush, 102
Burns, Raigan, 199
Bushnell, Nolan, xvii, 13, 17, 29, 35–36, 54–55, 59, 141
Business Week, 103, 105
Business Week Online, 257
Bust-a-Groove, 271
byte (defined), 311

C5 (battery-powered vehicle), 204
cabaret cabinets, 14, 311
Caesar II, 268
Cage, David, 207
Cage, John, 19
Cameron, James, 193
Canada, 114, 181, 207, 297
Canal+, 206
Canis Canem Edit, 280
Canyon Bomber, 41
Capcom, xix, 95, 96, 112, 123, 136, 140, 180, 212, 249, 278, 295, 316
Capcom Classics Collection, 194
Capitol Projector Corporation, 37
Capture the Flag, 187, 192
capturing games, 263–64
Car Race, 49
card games, 113, 261–62, 264
Career Connect, 306
Carmack, John, 190–93
Carne, Simon, 287
Carnegie Institute of Technology, 32
Carnegie-Mellon University, 32
Carnival, 273
Carnival Rifle, 35
Carradine, David, 277
Cartoon Gun, 43
cartoons, 262
Casino, 262, 264, 268
Casino Strip, 101
Casio (company), 216
Castle Master, 247–48
Castlevania series, 112, 180
Castle Wolfenstein, 191
Catacombs 3D, 191
Catalina Games (company), 139
catching games, 264
cathode ray tube, xvii, 4–6, 9, 17, 33, 311–12, 315
Catz, 262
Caveman, 93
CBS Electronics, 294
CBS Inc., 103
CBS Records, 181
CCP (company), 208
CD-DA, 181
CD+G format, 119
CD-i, xix, 122, 129, 131, 162, 333 n.6
CD-ROMs, xix, 15–16, 27, 86–88, 101–2, 107, 119, 121–25, 127, 129, 131, 139, 149, 159, 161–67, 170, 177–81, 214, 221, 243–44, 254, 304, 331 n.7 ch.15
cell phones, 148, 304

censorship, 110–11, 114, 209, 220–21
Centipede (arcade version), 61, 93, 272
Centipede (Atari 2600 version), 59, 93
Centuri (company), 70, 92–94, 128
Century Electronics, 93
Cerny, Mark, 233
CERO (Computer Entertainment Rating
    Organization), 281
CGDA (Computer Game Developers
    Association), xix
CGE (Compagnie Générale des Eaux), 206
CGI. *See* computer-generated imagery
Channel F. *See* Fairchild/Zircon Channel F
Chapman, Bob, 31
Charter, David, 280
Chase Game, 48
chase games, 260, 264
Checkers (board game), 263
Checkers (video game), 261, 273
Checkmate, 41
Chess (computer game), 32
Chess (board game), 263,
Chess (video game), 273
Chicago Coin Machine Manufacturing
    Company, xvii, 18, 35–37, 39
China, 181, 211–12, 215–17, 219–20, 224,
    275, 309
China Town, 136
chip (defined), 312
Chip'n Dale Rescue Rangers, 112
chiptune, 252
Cho, Kenta, 199
Choplifter (arcade version), 241
Chopper Command, 259
Christianity, 111
Christmas Comes to Pac-Land, 74
*The Chronicles of Riddick: Escape from Butcher
    Bay*, 250
Chrono Cross, 180
Chrono Trigger, 180, 254
ChuChu Rocket, 166
Chuck Yeager Advanced Flight Trainer, 247
"cinema of attractions," 127, 133
"cinematics," 129
Cinématique (game engine), 245
Cinematronics (company), 40, 42, 44, 67–70,
    92, 94, 100, 105, 128, 251
Cinemaware (company), 33, 124, 243
circularity. *See* recursion
Circus, 41
Circus Atari, 264
Cisco 400, 41
City of Heroes, 176

Civilization, 278
ClacQ, 202
Clancy, Tom, 206
Clark, David, 152–53
Clark, Ron, 226
Classic Gaming Expo, 66
Clay Buster, 39
Cliff Hanger, 100, 128
Clown Downtown, 269
Club Drive, 61
Clue (board game), 129
Clue (video game), 263
Clue VCR Mystery Game, 5
Clyde. *See* Pokey
CMOS chips, 47
Cobra Command, 100
cockpit games, 97, 137, 140–41, 159, 312
cocktail cabinet, 312
Codebreaker, 64
Code Monkeys, 125
Cohen, Kalman J., 32
Cohen, Scott, xiv
Coleco (company), 29, 45, 55, 58–59, 104,
    115–16, 144
Coleco Adam (home computer), 15, 58, 115–
    16, 266
Coleco Telstar, 55
Coleco Telstar Arcade, 57
Coleco Telstar Combat, 57
Colecovision, 58, 65, 115, 252, 298
collecting games (genre), 260, 264–65
Collegiate Licensing Company, 89
color graphics adaptor (CGA), 84
Colossal Cave Adventure, 78, 81
Colossal Pictures, 132
Colossus, 33
Columbia Pictures, 161, 181, 295
Columbine High School shooting, 278, 288
Columns, 136
Columns II: The Voyage Through Time, 136
Comanche 3, 274
Combat, 36, 41, 64, 259, 265
combat games, 265
comic books, 220–21, 261–62, 277, 296–300
Command & Conquer series, 123, 129
Commander Keen, 156
Commando Raid, 272
Commandos, 205
Commandos: Behind Enemy Lines, 209
Commando series, 208
Commodore CDTV, 122, 162
Commodore Computers (company), 60, 64, 78,
    117, 123, 151, 157, 189, 208, 252

Commodore International, 162
Commodore PET, 77–78
Commodore VIC-20, 78
communication, video games as, 303, 307–8
Comotion, 41
compact discs (audio), 253, 256
The Complete Strategyst, 31
computer-assisted instruction (CAI), 33
Computer Games and Digital Cultures (conference), 210
Computer Games and Digital Textualities (conference), 210
Computer Games magazine, 290–91
computer-generated imagery, 11, 122–23, 125, 133, 245–46, 294, 312. *See also* graphics
Computer Othello, 43
Computer Programmer, 274
Computer Quiz, 35
Computer—R-3, 43
Computers and Automation, 17
Computer Space, xvii, 13, 18, 24, 29, 35, 45, 59, 142, 239, 262
Condor, 92
The Condor Hero, 214, 219
Conquest of the World, 5, 263
Consumer Electronics Show (CES), 109, 115–16, 120, 163–64, 177
Contra, 112, 213
controversy, 39, 130–31, 133, 135, 187–88, 193, 209, 217, 226, 229, 277–81, 298
conversion, 312
Convert-a-Game, 93
Conway, John, 33
Cookie and Bibi 2, 136
Cool Pool, 139
COPS (arcade game), 101
Cops 'N Robbers, 39
Core Design (company), 183–84, 205
core mechanics of gameplay, 232
CoreWar, 270
Corpse Killer, 130
Cosmic Chasm, 70
Cosmic Osmo, 88
Cosmos Circuit, 100–101
cosplay ("costume-play"), 219
Counter-Strike, 141
CP System 1, 96
crane-drop games, 140
Crash!, 44
crash, video game industry, xviii, 29, 58, 65, 94–95, 100, 103–6, 107, 109, 113, 115, 117, 139
Crash Bandicoot, 179, 206
Crash Course, 41

Crashing Race, 39
Crash 'N Score, 37
Crawford, Chris, 259
Crazy Climber, 270
Crazy Foot, 36
Creative Computing magazine, 99
Creative Labs (company), 122
creativity, 233–35, 237–38, 256
Creatures, 262
Crime Patrol, 102, 125, 129
Crime Patrol 2: Drug Wars, 102
CRobots, 270
Crockford, Douglas, 111
Croft, Lara. *See* Lara Croft
Croisière pour un cadavre, 241, 245
Cross Fire, 40
Croteam, 193
Crowther, William, 34, 81, 188
CRT. *See* cathode ray tube
Cryo Interactive, 125
Crystal Castles, 95
Crytek (company), 207
Csaba Rozsa, 198
Cube Quest, 100
cultural "odorless" theory, 222
"culture jamming," 202
Curse of the Mummy, 204
Custer's Revenge, 110, 277–79, 284
"cute" games, 43, 74
Cutie Q, 43
cut-scene, 123, 312
CVC Gameline, 65
Cyan (company, also known as "Cyan Worlds"), xix, 122–24, 246
cybercafés, 135, 159
"cyberdrama," 299
Cyberglobe, 141
Cyberglobe 2, 141
Cyberia, 125
Cybernaut. See Albegas
Cyber Sled, 139
cyberspace, 212
Cyberstation Amusement Zones, 140
Cyert, Richard M., 32

Dabney, Ted, 36, 59
Dactyl Nightmare, xix, 14, 138–39, 265
Daggerfall series, 262
Dambusters, 95
The Dame Was Loaded, 132
dance, 259
Dance Dance Revolution (DDR), xx, 138, 169, 212, 254, 271, 303

Dance Maniax series, 138
Daphne (emulator), 102
Darius, 97
Dark Age of Camelot, 176
Dark Chambers, 83
Dark Edge, 139
Dark Invader, 43
Dark Side of the Moon, 132
Darktide server, 288
Dark Water, 295
Dartmouth College, 33
Data Age (company), 58
Data East, 93, 95, 97, 312
Datsun 280 Zzzap, 39–40
Davis Cup, 36
Daytona series, 212
Daytona USA, xix, 137, 271
Daytona USA 2: Power Edition, 137
DC Comics, 297
Dead Eye, 43
Deadline Games, 208
Dead or Alive++, 95
Dealer Demo, 265
"deathmatches," 192–93
Deathmaze 5000, 189
Death Race, 39, 277–78, 284, 288, 298
Death Race 2000, 39, 277
Death Star, 42, 67, 69–70
de Bont, Jan, 295
DEC (company), 76
DEC (Digital Equipment Corporation), 33–34, 173
Decisive Battles of WWII series, 224
DECO Cassette System, 40, 93, 95, 312
Decuir, Joe, 63
dedicated system, 312
Deep Thought, 32
Defender (arcade game), xviii, 10, 22, 29, 64, 92–93, 98, 103–4, 190, 241, 254, 260, 275, 331 n.2 ch.16
Defender II, 93
Déjà Vu 1: A Nightmare Comes True, 84–85
Dejouany, Guy, 206
delinquency, 286
Dell (company), 80, 122
Delphine Software (company), 241
Deluxe Baseball, 40
DeMaria, Rusel, xiii
demo genre, 260–61, 265
Demonstration Cartridge, 265
Demon's World, 95
demoscene, 252
Denki Onyko (company) , 44

Denman, William F., Jr., 189
Denmark, 114, 210
Densha De Go! 2, 137
Descent, 156, 267, 269
Desert Gun, 40
Desert Patrol, 40
designers, 199, 301
design of video games, 207, 231–38, 255, 301, 307
de Souza, Steven, 295
Destination Earth, 44
Destruction Derby, 37
Deus Ex, 205
Devecka (company), 138
development process for video games, 208, 229, 231–38, 301
Devine, Graeme, 129
Diablo, 206, 272
Diagnostic Cartridge (Identification number CB101196), 266
Diagnostic Cartridge (Identification number FDS100144), 266, 274
diagnostic genre, 260–61, 265–66
DICE (company), 208
Dice Puzzle, 270
"dictionary look-up games," 31
diegesis. *See* "world" of video game
Dig Dug, 94, 268–69
Dig Dug II, 95
Digimon (digital monster), 217–19
Digipen, xix, 301
digital audio, 251
digital audio tape (DAT), 181
Digital Circus (company), 130
Digital Games Incorporated, 39
Digital Illusions CE, 193
Digital Leisure Inc., 102
Digital Media Collaboratory, 306
Digital Pictures (company), 125, 130–31
Digital Playground (company), 279
digital rights management (DRM), 202
digital watches, 216
digitized imagery, 97, 136, 241, 244, 246, 278
digitized speech, 114, 124, 251
DiGRA (Digital Games Research Association), 22, 210
Dill, Karen E., 286, 288
Dill, William R., 32
Dinamic Software (company, later renamed Dinamic Multimedia), 208
diode, 312
DIP switch. *See* dual in-line parallel switch
DirectMusic interface, 256

Dirk the Daring, 128

Discman, 181

Discs of Tron, 95

disk operating system (DOS), 78–79, 84

"dismount" games, 198

Disney, 141

Disney characters, 297

Dissolution of Eternity, 192

"Doctor" (pirated system), 214

"Doctor V64," 215

Dodge 'Em, 44, 266

Dodgem, 44

dodging games, 266

Dog Patch, 43

Dogz, 262

Domark (company), 204

Domino Man, 95

Dominos, 41

Donkey Kong, xviii, 58, 81, 92–93, 112–13, 115,
   194, 213, 216, 262, 270, 298

Donkey Kong 3, 95

Donkey Kong 64, xx

Donkey Kong Country, xix, 246, 298

Donkey Kong Country 2: Diddy's Kong Quest, xix

Donkey Kong Jr., 6, 15, 94, 270

Don Quijote, 208

Doom, xix, 11, 129, 139, 156, 184, 187, 191–
   92, 248, 268–69, 272, 278, 285

Doom (film), 296

Doom II: Hell on Earth, 192

Doom 3, 192–93

"door games," 155

Double Donkey Kong, 142

Double Dragon, xix, 96, 295

Double Play, 41

Double Switch, 131

Douchuuki, Yokai, xix

Dovey, Jon, 225

Dragon Ball, 297

Dragon Lore 2, 272

Dragon Quest, 214

Dragon's Gate, 174

Dragon's Lair, 81, 94, 100, 102, 105, 125, 128–
   30, 133, 249, 251, 262, 268, 313, 331 n.7
   ch.15

Dragon's Lair II: Time Warp, 101–2, 139

Dragon's Lair clones, 129

Dragon Warrior series, 112

Dream Arena portal, 149

Dreamcast, xx, 121, 147, 149, 165–67, 179,
   201, 214, 249, 254

DreamCatcher Interactive, 193

Dream Soccer '94, 139

DreamWorks, xx, 141, 297

DreamWorks Interactive, 193, 293

Driller, 247

Drive Master, 35

Driver's Edge, 140

Driver's Eyes, 137

driving games, 37, 39, 98, 101, 135, 137, 266

Dr. Mario, 136, 253

DrumMania, 138, 271

Drumscape, 138

DS. *See* Nintendo DS

dual in-line parallel (DIP) switch, 95, 312

DualSystem, 96

Duck Hunt, 35, 112, 116

Duckshot, 272

Duck Tales, 112

Duke Nuke'em 3D, 193

Duke Nukem, 156

Dungeon Keeper, 204, 237

Dungeon Master (DM), 174

Dungeons & Dragons, 82, 174, 190, 204, 206,
   269, 272

Dupuis, 206

Durell Software, 204

DVD International (company), 130

DVD-ROMs, 16, 102, 195, 304

DVDs, 102, 121, 125, 127, 130, 132, 167–68,
   254, 296

Dyer, Rick, 100–101, 105, 128, 139, 331 n.7
   ch.15

Earthbound, 253

Easter eggs, 23, 25, 65, 312

East Touch, 219

Easyfinder, 219

eBay, 167, 170, 309

Ecko, Marc, 226

Edgar, Les, 204

Edtris, 66

educational games, 260, 266, 286

education, and video games, 210, 217, 268,
   277–78, 303, 305–7

Effacer, 269

Effecto Caos. *See* Xpiral

EGDA (European Game Developers'
   Association), 335 n.1 ch.32

EGDF (European Game Developer Federation),
   210

eGenesis (company), 291

Eidos (company), 183–84, 204–5, 207

Eimbinder, Eric and Jerry, xiii

Elasto Mania, 198

The Elder Scrolls IV: Oblivion, 280

Electra (company), 38–40

Electric Dreams Software, 204

electromechanical games, 35, 149

Electronic Arts (company), 89, 132, 162, 175, 193, 205–6, 254, 256, 290, 293

Electronic Entertainment Exhibition (E3), 164

Electronic Games magazine, 100

Electronic Gaming Monthly magazine, 56, 133

Electronic Pinball, 269

Electronics Boutique, 164

Electronic Table Soccer!, 273

Electro Sport (company), 93, 99

Elektronorgtechnica ("Elorg"), 207

Elepong, 36

Elevator Action, 66

Elimination, 36

Eliminator, 69, 93

Elite, 189, 204

Eliza, 31, 78

ELSPA (Entertainment and Leisure Software Publishers Association), 208

ELSPA (European Leisure Software Publishers Association), 208

Empire Earth, 206

Empire of Kilrathi, 132

The Empire Strikes Back (arcade game), 71

emulators, 16, 22, 71, 102, 142, 170, 194, 252, 312–3

England, 207

enhanced graphics adaptor (EGA), 84

ENIAC, 76

Enix (company), 112, 295

EnterTech, 306

Enter the Matrix, xx, 61, 300, 304

Environmental Detectives, 306

Epic Games (company), 193

Epic MegaGames (company), 156–57

epileptic seizures, 278

Epyx (company), 146

Eric's Ultimate Solitaire, 262, 264

ESA (Entertainment Software Association), 281

Escape from the Devil's Doom, 6

Escape from Woomera, 223, 225

Escape from Woomera Project Team, 223, 225

escape games, 260, 267

Esh's Aurunmilla, 100–101

ESPN, 89

ESRB (Entertainment Software Ratings Board), 131, 278–81

Essex University, 173

Ethernet, 166, 169

ethics. *See* moral and ethical dimension of video games

E. T.: The Extraterrestrial (Atari 2600 game), 83, 262, 294

Eureka!, 204

Europa Universalis, 208

Europe, 45–51, 60–61, 89, 103, 115, 118, 147–49, 159, 162, 164–65, 177, 203–210, 281, 297, 314–15

European Media programme. *See* Media programmes

European Union, 209

Evans & Sutherland, 33

EVE Online, 208

EverQuest (EQ), xx, 16, 159, 176, 190, 285, 290, 308–9, 314

Exidy, 37, 39, 41, 44, 68, 71, 93, 277, 284

Exodus, 43

Exolon, 204

Expanded Cinema, 20

expansion packs, 192

experimental games, 197–202

Exterminator, xix, 97

The Exterminator, 6

Extreme Pinball, 269

Eye of the Beholder, 124

Eye Toy, 169

Eye Toy: Play, 169

F1 Race, 112

F/A-18 Hornet 3.0, 267, 274

Fable, 205, 280

Fahrenheit, 130, 207

Fairchild Camera and Instrument Company, 56, 63, 104

Fairchild/Zircon Channel F, xvii-xviii, 15, 56–57, 63, 64, 104

Fairlight: A Prelude, 204

Falcon, 247

Fallout, 272

Famicon. *See* Nintendo Famicon

Family Bowl, 137

Family Feud, 262

Fantastic, 35

Far Cry, 206–7

Fast Draw Showdown, 102, 129

Fatal Fury: King of Fighters, 136

Fatal Fury 2, 136

Fatal Fury Special, 136

Fax, 271

F.E.A.R.. (First Encounter Assault Recon), 193

Fear Effect, 205

"feature construction," 232

"feature creep," 236

Federmeyer, Ed, 66

Feinstein, Keith, 4, 142
Fighting Fantasy books, 204
fighting games, 98, 125, 130, 135–36, 139–40, 156–57, 164, 200, 211, 267, 289, 295
Fighting Street, 123
filled-polygon graphics, 71, 94, 97, 135, 138–39, 246–48
film, 21, 28, 125, 136, 195, 221, 232, 235, 241, 250, 255, 259, 262, 268, 281, 283–85, 287, 291, 293–94, 294, 296, 298, 299, 300, 303, 304
film history, 200
film scoring, 255
Film Victoria Digital Media Fund, 224
Final Fantasy, xix, 23, 112, 179–80, 211, 214, 221, 295
Final Fantasy 3, 253
Final Fantasy VII, 123, 180–81, 246
Final Fantasy XI, 168
Final Fantasy Tactics, 180
Final Fantasy: The Spirits Within, 246, 295
Final Furlong, 14, 137
Final Lap 2, 137
Final Test Cartridge, 266
Finland, 208
Firebird Software, 189, 204
Firefox, 12, 100, 243, 313
Fireman Fireman, 6
Fire One!, 41
Fire Power, 39
Fire Truck, 42
first-person perspective, 43, 68, 74, 83, 97, 129, 132, 140, 175–76, 190, 193, 195, 208, 246, 249, 272, 289. *See also* first-person shooter (FPS)
first-person shooter (FPS), 78, 156, 187–93, 195, 237, 250, 256, 260, 278, 296
Fishing Derby, 264, 272
Fiske, John, 221
Flash, 197
Flashback. *See* Atari Flashback
Flashback 2. *See* Atari Flashback 2
Flash-based games, 201
Flickr, 197
flight simulators, 78, 97, 137, 189
Flight Unlimited, 267, 274
Flip-Out, 39
Flipper Game, 269
Flowers, Tommy, 33
Fluegelman, Andrew, 152
flying games, 152, 267
Flying Shark, 40
FM Towns computer, 122–23

FM Towns Marty, 122
foley artists, 255
Fonz, 39
Football (Atari), xviii, 40, 42, 44
Football Power, 137
Foozpong, 43
"formula games," 31
Formula K, 36–37, 137
For-Play, 36
Fortress of Narzod, 70
Fortune magazine, 104
The Fourth Generation, 219
Fox and Hounds, 53
Fox Interactive, 132
France, 49, 114, 181, 206, 207, 297
Frantic Fred, 140
Freedom Fighter, 101
Freescape engine, 247
freeware, 152–53, 155, 157
Freeway, 266, 269
Frenzy, 94
frequency modulation (FM), 253
Frogger, 61, 92–93, 264, 266, 269
Frogger Video Game, 298
Frogs, 43
"From Beeps to *Billboard*," 257
frustration, 289
Frye, Tod, 64
Fujitsu (company), 122
Full Metal Alchemist, 297
full-motion video (FMV), 86, 99, 101–2, 122–25, 127, 129, 139, 162–64, 243–46, 251, 279
Full Sail, 301
Full Throttle, 293
Fulp, Tom, 197
Funai, 100
Funatics (company), 207
Funcom (company), 208
Fun Games (company), 39
Fun With Numbers, 4
Fury: Unleash the Fury, 224
future of video games, 229, 303–310

Gabriel Knight: Sins of the Fathers, 133
Gabriel Knight 3: Blood of the Sacred, Blood of the Damned, 133
Gadget, 11, 81, 262, 268
Gaelco (company), 137
Galactic Pinball, 269
Galaga 3, 95, 42, 74, 93, 272
Galaxian, xviii, 42–43, 70, 91–92, 194, 211
Galaxian 3, 101, 137
Galaxian Part X, 43

Galaxy Ranger, 100
Galaxy Rescue, 44
Gallagher's Gallery, 102
gallium arsenide phosphide, 313
Gamasutra, 280, 301
gambling games, 213, 220–21, 267–68
"game" (as a term), 3
Game and Watch, 216
Game Boy, xix-xx, 5–6, 10, 15, 60, 66, 107, 113, 117–18, 144–47, 168, 178, 216–17, 314
Game Boy Advance, 107, 113, 145–46, 201, 216, 224, 297
Game Boy Advance SP, 145
Game Boy Color, xx, 10, 15, 107, 113, 145, 216, 314
Game Boy Light, 113, 145
Game Boy Micro, xx, 113, 145
Game Boy Pocket, 113, 145
game centers, 135, 140–41, 159, 212–13, 220
game.com, 146–47, 206
game.com Pocket Pro, 147
GameCube, xx, 113, 121, 168–69, 171, 197, 249, 252, 254
Game Cultures: Computer Games as New Media, 225
Game Developer magazine, 233
Game Developers' Association of Australia, 224
Game Developers' Conference, xx, 167
game engines, 192, 245, 248–49
Game Gear. *See* Sega Game Gear
gameindustry.biz, 301
Game Innovation Lab, 89
gameline, 65
Game of Life, 33
Game Room (company), 140
GameRoom Magazine, 142
Games and Culture, 22
gamespot.com, 142
gamespy.com, 142, 248
Games-to-Teach, 286, 306
Game Studies, 22
Games Workshop, 204
gametunnel.com, 197
GameWorks, xx, 141
Gans, Christophe, 296
garage rock, 201
Gard, Toby, 183–84, 205
Gardner, Martin, 33
Garriot, Richard, 83, 190
GAT (company), 95
Gate (computer language), 32
Gates, Bill, 77, 129, 167
Gates of Thunder, 123

Gauntlet, 95
gbadev.org, 201
GCE/Cinematronics, 70
GCE/Milton Bradley, 70
GCE/Milton Bradley Vectrex. *See* Vectrex
G-Darius, 142
GDG format, 167
GD-ROMs, 121, 166
GE 255 system, 33
Gemstone II, 107
General Computer Corporation, 117
"General midi," 253
generations of home video game consoles, 161
Genesis. *See* Sega Genesis
genre, 229, 234, 249, 256, 259–61
Gerasimov, Vadim, 207
German-style board games, 207
Germany, 47–49, 114, 206–7, 209–210, 279
Gestalt, 313
Get Bass, 137
Ghost in the Shell, 297
Ghost in the Shell: Stand Alone Complex, 297
Ghost Recon, 206
Ghosts 'N Goblins, 95, 112
Gibson, William, 190
gigabyte (defined), 313
"gigadiscs," 166
GI (General Instruments) (company), xvii, 51, 55, 104
Gilbert, Christine, 290
Gilbert, Ron, 84
Gizmondo, xx
"global localization," 214
Global VR (company), 137
"glocalization," 215
Goal IV, 37
Goal to Go, 100, 128
god games, 204–5
Godzilla, 19
Gold Coast, 226
Goldman, Gary, 128
gold master version of video games, 234
Gold Medal With Bruce Jenner, 100
Golem, 185
Golf, 272
Golly! Ghost!, 140
Gopher, 263–64
Gordonstoun Boarding School, 183
Gotcha, 36
Gothic, 207
Gottlieb, xviii, 19, 35, 93, 95, 97, 128
GP World, 100, 128
Graduation, 218

Graetz, J. Martin, 13, 19, 33
graffiti, 226–27
Grammy awards, 254
Grand (company), 137
Grand Theft Auto, xx, 90, 179, 278–80
Grand Theft Auto III, 249, 279
Grand Theft Auto: San Andreas, 226, 254, 279–80
Gran Trak 10, 36–37
Gran Trak 20, 37
Gran Turismo series, 179
graphical user interfaces, 79, 174
graphics, 6–7, 24, 37, 39, 43, 47, 63, 67, 70–71, 73, 78–79, 83–88, 91, 93–98, 102, 105, 114, 118–19, 122, 124, 129 , 135–36, 138–39, 143, 156, 161, 164, 174–76, 187–88, 191, 193, 198, 200, 202, 214, 229, 239–50, 256, 268, 284, 288, 291, 298, 304, 307, 315. *See also* 3-D graphics; raster graphics; sprites; vector graphics
Gravitar, 69–70
Great Britain, 210
The Great Escape, 204
The Great Wall Street Fortune Hunt, 5, 263
The Great White Buffalo Hunt, 40
Greece, 209
Greek law number 3037, 209
Greenberg, Arnold, 55
Gremlin (company), 69, 124
"gremlins," 39, 277
Gridiron, 41
Griffeth, Simone, 277
Griffiths, M.D., 286
Grim Fandango, 293
Ground Control, 206
Ground Zero, 192
The Grudge (Ju-On), 295
Grusin, Richard, 244
GT Interactive (company), 193, 206
GUI (graphic user interface), 79, 174
Guided Missile, 41
Guillemot, Yves, 206
GuitarFreaks, xx, 138, 271
Guitar Jam, 138
Gun Fight, xvii, 39, 73, 277
Gunman, 40
Gunning, Tom, 127
Gun-O-Tronic, 48
Gypsy Juggler, 43
Gyromite, 112
Gyruss, 246

Habitat, 174

hackers, 76
hacks, 195, 201
"Ha do ken," 212
Halcyon home laserdisc game system, xviii, 15, 101, 105, 139, 331 n.7 ch.15
Half-Life, xx, 16, 187, 193, 198, 225, 236
Half-Life 2, 193, 249, 255
Hall, Laurie, 280
Halo, 187, 193, 293, 296
Halo 2, xx, 257
Halo: Combat Evolved, xx, 250
Hamill, Mark, 132
Hamilton, Mark, 152
Hamlet on the Holodeck: The Future of Narrative in Cyberspace, 299
Hammurabi, 34
Hanafuda playing cards, 113
handheld games, 15, 91, 107, 113, 118, 143–48, 201, 211–12, 215–17, 221, 224, 313
Hangman, 262–63, 269
Hangman from the 25th Century, 269
Hang Pilot, 137
Hanna-Barbera, 298
Hanseatic League, 207
"happenings," 19
haptic feedback, 313
Hard Drivin', xix, 97, 139
Hard Drivin's Airborne, 139
Hard Dunk, 137
"hard-edge" painting style, 19
Hard Hat Mack, 89
Harley Davidson & L.A. Riders, 137
Hasbro Interactive, 61, 206
Hatris, 136
Haunted House (Atari 2600), 82, 262, 265, 267
Hawke's Manor, 131
Hawkins, Trip, 89, 162
HDTV, 170–71, 181, 333 n.3
Head On, 44
Head-to-Head series, 144
Heavy Traffic (arcade game), 39
Heavyweight Champ, 40, 68, 97
Heiankyo Alien, 44
Hellboy, 224
hentai style, 279
Heretic, 192
Herman, Leonard, xiii
Herzog Zewei, 213
Hewlett-Packard, 34
Hewson Consultants, 204
Hex, 31
Hicken, Wendell, 153
hidden room, 64

high-score table, 44
High Velocity, 271
Higinbotham, William, xvii, 32
Hilton, New York284
Hitachi SH4 processor, 166
The Hitchhiker's Guide to the Galaxy, 274
The Hitchhiker's Guide to the Galaxy (text adventure game), 270
Hitman, 205
Hitman: Codename 47, 208
Hit Me, 40
Hi-Way, 37
Hobbit (Soviet computer), 204
The Hobbit (text adventure game), 223
hobbyists, 46, 77, 151–53, 155, 201, 279
Hochberg, Joel, 112
Hoff, Marcian E., 18
Hoffman, Judi, 261
Hogan's Alley, 109, 116
Hole Hunter, 264
Holland, Todd, 294
Hollywood Pictures, 295
Holmes, Sherlock, 131
holodeck, 190
Holosseum, 139
homebrew communities, 201–2
Homebrew Computer Club, 77, 201
home computer games, 220–21, 261, 275, 281, 306, 315
home computers, 75–80, 97, 103, 105, 107, 115–16, 122, 136, 139, 142, 151, 157, 162, 166, 189–90, 194, 231, 240, 249–50, 251–54, 303–5
home console games, 45–58, 96–97, 101, 103, 107, 118, 120–21, 125, 133, 135–36, 138–40, 149, 159, 161–71, 178, 180–81, 190, 201, 211–13, 215, 218, 220–21, 231, 240, 248, 251–54, 261–62, 275, 281, 287, 298–99, 304, 312, 331 n.7 ch.15
Home Finance, 274
Home of the Underdogs, 198
Home T.V. Game, 46–47, 49
Hong Kong, 146, 201, 211–20
Horizons, 176
horror movies, 295
Hoskins, Bob, 295
"Hot Circuits: A Video Arcade" (exhibition), 142
"hot coffee" incident, 279–80
hot-rodding, 201
Hot Shots Tennis, 262, 272
House of the Dead, 296
Hovertank 3D, 191

HuCard, 121–22
Hudsonsoft (company), 123
Hugo the TV Troll, 208
Human Cannonball, 272–73
Hungary, 118
Hunt, N., 268
Hunt & Score, 64
Huntington Computer Project, 33
Hunt the Wumpus, 78
Hurt, John, 130
Hustle, 41
Hutspiel, 32
Hyberbole Studios, 132
hybrid redemption/video games, 140
Hyperchase, 70
"Hyper Movie," 129
Hyper Pac-Man, 140

IBM (company), 31–32, 76, 166, 275
IBM/Motorola PowerPC 603e processor, 166
IBM PC, 79, 122, 151–52, 156–57
IBM PC XT, 251
Ice Hockey, 112, 272
Iceland, 208
Icewind Dale, 23
ICOM Simulations, Inc. (company), 84, 124, 131
iconography, 188, 259–60
ICRA (Internet Content Rating Association), 281
I.C. Squared Institute, 286, 306
idea conceptualization, 232, 237
ideology in video games, 223–27, 280–81
id Software (company) , xix, 156, 190–93, 209, 248
IEEE Spectrum, 64
iGames, 141
IGDA (International Game Developers' Association), 22
iMacs, 75
Imagic (company), 65, 103
Imagine Software (company), 204
Imaginet, 153
imaging technologies, 9–12, 239–40
Imax theater, 304
"imitation game," 31
IMSAI PDP computer, 191
iMUSE system, 256
Incentive Software (company), 247
independent games, 153, 157, 197–202
Independent Games Festival, xx
India, 309
Indiana Jones (character), 184, 205

Indiana Jones and the Fate of Atlantis, 124
Indiana Jones and the Last Crusade (game), 86
indie games. *See* independent games
indie physics games, 198, 200
Indigo Prophecy, 207, 250
industry earnings, 275
Indy 500, 41, 266, 271
Indy 800, xvii, 37–38
influence and cause, 283–84
Infogenius French Language Translator, 274
Infogrames Inc. (company), 61, 205–6, 224, 300
Infogrames Interactive, 61
in-game advertisements, 294
Initial D series, 212
Inky. *See* Bashful
"instances," 176
integrated circuit (IC), 76
Intel Corporation, 18
Intellivision, 29, 57–58, 65, 104–5, 252, 298
Intel's 8008 "computer on a chip," 76
interactive fiction, 82–83
interactive movies, 100, 127–33, 245, 250, 262, 268, 304
interactive music, 255
interactivity, 24–27, 86, 127, 133, 136, 139, 173, 175, 190, 195, 208, 227, 233, 245, 249–51, 255–56, 259–74, 285, 304
interface, 22, 24, 37, 79, 83, 86, 107, 135–38, 140, 159, 176, 185, 193, 235, 256, 313
International Arcade Museum, 142
Internet cafés, 209
Interplay (company), 132, 156
Interstate '76, 272
Interstellar Laser Fantasy, 100–101
Interton Video 2000, 47–49
In the First Degree, 132
Invaders 2000, 139
Invaders of the Mummy's Tomb, 6
inventory box, 84, 88
IO Interactive (company), 205, 207
Ion Storm (company), 205
iPods, 74, 194
Irata, 93
Ireland, 114
Irem (company), 94–95, 139
IR Gurus Interactive (company), 223–24
I, Robot, xviii, 11, 71, 94, 97, 138, 246–47
irreversibility, 26
The Irritating Maze, 138
ISFE (Interactive Software Federation of Europe), 281
Ishar, 124

Ishikawa, Shuji, 280
isometric perspective, 139, 175–76, 240–41
Italy, 43, 114, 208, 210, 297
It Came from the Desert, 124
ITE (company), 208
ITT-Océanic, 45
ITT Schaub-Lorentz, 45
iTunes, 256
IT-University in Copenhagen, Denmark, 210
Ivory Tower, 272
Iwata, Satoru, 114
Iwatani, Toru, 73

Jack and the Beanstalk, 94
Jackson, Peter, 296
Jackson, Steve, 204–5
Jack the Giantkiller, 94
Jaguar. *See* Atari Jaguar
Jakks Pacific, 66
Jaleco (company), 136–37
JAMMA (Japanese Arcade Machine Manufacturers' Association), 96, 313
JAMMA conversion class, 96
Japan, 43–44, 61, 73, 92–93, 96, 101, 106, 109, 111, 113–15, 118–20, 122, 136, 140–41, 145, 147–49, 162–68, 170–71, 177–78, 180, 203, 207, 211–13, 215, 217, 218–21, 224, 246, 279, 281, 294–95, 297–99, 312–14, 339 n.21, 341 n.3
Japan Airlines, 137
Japanese popular culture, 218, 221
Jaws (film), 39
jayisgames.com, 197
Jazz Jackrabbit, 156
JediMUD, 272
Jenkins, Henry, 294, 299
Jensen, Jane, 132–33
Jeopardy, 262, 271
Jet Set Radio Future, 226
JFK: Reloaded, 280
Jigsaw, 270
Jill of the Jungle series, 156
Jinyong, 214
J-League, 219
Jobs, Steve, 59, 77
John, Michael, 233
John Madden Football, 89
Johnny Mnemonic, 12, 268
Joker's Wild, 262
Jolie, Angelina, 183–84, 295
Jones, Chris, 132
Journal of Personality and Social Psychology, 286
Journey Escape, 266

Joust, 94, 152
Jovovich, Milla, 296
Joyboard (by Amiga), 65
Jr. Pac-Man, 74, 95
JT Storage (JTS), 61
Judd, Donald, 19
Jumping Groove, 138
Jumpman (character), 93, 298
Jungle Hunt, 269
Juul, Jesper, 210
JVC Musical Industries, 114

Kai, Toshio, 251
"Kanal 34" clone, 45
Kaneko (company), 136, 140
Kaprow, Allan, 19
karaoke, 119
Karateco, 92
Karateka, 242
Kasparov, Garry, 32
Katamari Damacy, 200
Kauffman, Pete, 277
KB Toys, 165
K.C. Munchkin, 269
Kee Games, xvii, 36–37, 39–40, 82, 92, 137, 241
Keenan, Joe, 36
Kelly, Ellsworth, 19
Kemeny, John, 33
Kemp, Ron, 225
Kennedy, Helen, 225
Kennedy, John F., 280
Kent, Steven, xiii, 67, 110, 129–30, 179
Kentucky, 82
Ken Uston Blackjack/Poker, 262, 264
Keystone Kapers, 263–64
Kick It!, 137
Kid Icarus, 112
Killer List of Videogames (KLOV), xiv, 22, 136, 142, 247
Killing Zoe, 296
kill-or-be-killed mentality, 268
kilobyte (defined), 313
kilohertz (defined), 313
Kinder, Marsha, 299
King, Geoff, 225
Kingdom of Kroz, 156
King Features Syndicate, 298
King Kong, 298
King of Chicago, 241, 243
The King of Fighters, 211–12, 221, 295
King's Quest (also known as *King's Quest I*), 84, 86

King's Quest III: To Heir is Human, 84–85
King's Quest V: Absence Makes the Heart Go Yonder!, 86, 124, 242
King's Quest series, 132
"kino-realism," 245
Kirby's Adventure, 112
Kirby's Pinball Land, 269
Kister, James, 32
Klastrup, Lisbeth, 210
Klietz, Alan, 174
Knight, Gabriel, 133
Knights in Armor, 40
Knopf, Jim, 152, 157
Kojima, Hideo, 296
Konami, 93, 110, 112, 128, 137–39, 180, 219, 224, 246, 254
Konami GT, 139
Kondo, Koji, 253
Koto (company), 147
Kotok, Alan, 33
Krome Studios (company), 223–24
Krome Studios Melbourne, 224
Kronos (company), 205
Krull (Atari 2600 game), 83, 262
Krzywinska, Tanya, 225
Kurtz, Bill, xiv
Kurtz, Tom, 33
Kutaragi, Ken, 177

Labyrinth, 189
Lammers, Susan, 73
Landeros, Rob, 129–30
Landing Gear, 137
Lara Croft (character), 183–85, 205, 295
Lara Croft: Tomb Raider (film), 183, 295
Laserdisc Computer System (company), 100
laserdisc games, xviii, 10, 12, 70, 93–94, 97, 99–102, 105, 124, 128–29, 139, 243, 251, 331 n.7 ch.15
laserdiscs, 121, 127
laserdisc technology, 313
Laser Grand Prix, 100, 128
Lasonic 2000, 49
The Last Bounty Hunter, 102
Lawson, Jerry, 56
LCD. *See* liquid crystal display
Leader, 36
Leather Goddesses of Phobos, 274
LED. *See* light-emitting diode
Legacy of Kain, 179, 205
Legend of Spyro: A New Beginning, 224
The Legend of Zelda, xviii, 112, 165
The Legend of Zelda: Ocarina of Time, 253

The Legend of Zelda series, 86, 113, 179, 202
Legend of Zelda 64, 215
Leisure Suit Larry V, 86
*Leisure Suit Larry in the Land of the Lounge
    Lizards*, 86–87, 206, 279
Leland (company), 136
Leland Interactive (company), 101
Lennon, John, 190
Leonetti, John R., 295
Lerner Research (company), 247
Les Tuniques Bleues, 206
"levelization" of gaming, 192
Levy, Jim, 65
Lewitt, Sol, 19
Liberman, Alexander, 19
Library of Congress Moving Imagery Genre-
    Form Guide, 261
Lieberman, Joseph, 131, 278
Light Bringer, 139
light-emitting diode (LED), 5–6, 10, 143, 313
light guns, 101
The Lighthouse, 90
lightmaps, 248
light pen, 70
LINC, 76
Lincoln, Howard, 109, 118
Lineage II, 176
Lionhead Studios, 205, 280
liquid crystal display (LCD), 5–6, 10, 145–47,
    166, 216, 313–14
Lisberger, Steven, 294
The Little Computer People, 262
Livingstone, Ian, 204–5
LJN (subsidiary of Acclaim), 110
Llamabooost, 202
local area network (LAN), 16168, 191
Lock 'N' Chase, 93
Loco-Motion, 93
Lode Runner, 95, 151–52, 199, 268–70
Loew, Rabbi185
logic circuits, 314
The Longest Journey, 208
Looking Glass Studios (company), 193, 205
Looking Glass Technologies, 190
Loom, 123, 242
looping formal structures, 195. *See also*
    circularity
Lost Luggage, 264
"love hotel," 113
LSI Logic (company), 181
Lucas, George, 245–46, 293
LucasArts, xix, 123–25, 253, 256, 293
Lucasfilm, 70, 242, 341 n.27

Lucasfilm Games (now LucasArts), 33, 84–85,
    123, 174, 189
Lucky & Wild, 137
Lunar Lander, xviii, 44, 68–69
Lunar Rescue, 44
Lund, Karen, 261
Lynch, David, 129
Lynch, Dianne, 290
Lynx. *See* Atari Lynx
Lynx II. *See* Atari Lynx II

M-4, 40
M-79 Ambush, 40
M.A.C.H. 3, 100, 105, 128, 313
Macintosh. *See* Apple Macintosh
MacPaint, 79
Macromedia (company), 197
MacWrite, 79
Madden Football 97, 272
Madden NFL Football, 179
Mad Dog McCree, 101, 125, 129, 139
Mad Dog II: The Lost Gold, 102, 139
Madonna: Truth or Dare (film), 131
Mageslayer, 272
Magical Crystals, 136
Magicom (company), 128
Magnavox (company), 5, 14, 17, 33, 36, 45–46,
    50–51, 54–55, 57, 59, 115, 143, 277, 306
Magnavox Odyssey^2, 57–58, 115, 251
Magnavox Odyssey 200, 55
Magnavox Odyssey 300, 55
Magnavox Odyssey 400, 56
Magnavox Odyssey 500, 56
Magnavox Odyssey 2000, 57
Magnavox Odyssey 3000, 57
Magnavox Odyssey 4000, 57
Magnavox Odyssey 5000, 57
Magnavox Odyssey clones, 45
mahjong games, 92, 136, 279
mainframe computer games, 13, 17, 29, 31–34,
    40, 44, 68, 151, 231, 262
Main T.T. , 41
Majestic, 290
Major Havoc, 70
*Make My Video: INXS/Kriss Kross/Marky Mark &
    the Funky Bunch*, 130
Malaria, 33
Malaysia, 211, 214–16, 220
Mallet Madness, 140
The Management Game, 32
management simulation games, 268
Maneater, 39, 73
manga, 296–97, 299, 341 n. 15

The Manhole, xix, 86, 122–23
Manhunt, 226
Maniac Mansion, 84–85, 88, 111
Maniac-1, 32
Manic Miner, 204
Manx TT Superbike Twin, 137
Marathon, 193
Marathon 2: Durendal, 193
Marathon Infinity, 193
Marbella Vice, 101
Marble Madness, 261, 316
Marc Ecko's Getting Up: Contents Under Pressure, 223, 226–27
Mario (character), 162, 168, 179, 295, 298
Mario Bros., 95, 113, 211, 213, 216, 221, 298
Mario Kart 64, xx, 271
Mario's Cement Factory, 15
Mario's Early Years: Fun With Numbers, 266
Mario series, 179
Mario Teaches Typing, 4, 260, 266, 274, 306
Mark III (console system), 115, 117
Marks, Aaron, 254
Marksman/Trapshooting, 273
Martian Memorandum, 131, 244
Marvel Comics, 296–97
M*A*S*H, 260
The Masked Rider: Kamen Rider ZO, 128
Massachusetts Institute of Technology (MIT), 13, 17, 31, 33, 67, 286, 306
massively multiplayer online games (MMOGs), 155
massively multiplayer online role-playing games (MMORPGs), xx, 23, 26, 90, 174–176, 190, 208, 224, 300, 308
Math Grand Prix, 266, 271
The Matrix (film), 208
Matrix Comics, 300
The Matrix films, 299, 304
The Matrix Online, 300
The Matrix: Path of Neo, 300
The Matrix Reloaded, 300
The Matrix Revolutions, 300
Mattel Electronics (company), 57–59, 65, 103–5, 143–44
Mattel Electronics Baseball, 144
Mattel Electronics Basketball, 6, 144
Mattel Electronics Football, 143
Maxis Software, xx, 4
Max Payne, 157, 208
Mayer, Steve, 63–64
Mäyrä, Frans, 210
Maze Craze, 267–69
maze games, 44, 73, 93, 189–91, 260, 268–69

Mazewar, 191–92
McAndrew, Nell, 184
McCartney, Paul, 190
McDaniel, Scott, 290
McDowell, Malcolm, 132
"McGame," 207
McMahan, Alison, 249
Meadows Games, 39–41, 43
Meadows Lanes, 41
Mean Streets, 84–85, 241, 244
Mechner, J., 242, 244
Mecstron, 47
Medal of Honor, 89, 187, 193, 293
Media I, 210
Media II, 210
media convergence, 294, 299–300
Media Plus, 210
Media programmes, 209–10
Media 2007, 210
Med Systems, 189
megabyte (defined), 314
Mega Corp, 6
Mega Drive. *See* Sega Mega Drive
megahertz (defined), 314
Mega Man 8, 180
Megaman series, 112
Mega Man X4, 180
Mega Man X5, 180
MegaRace, 125
Mega Tech System, 96
Melbourne House, 224
Melody Master, 70
Meridian 59, 175
Merlin, 6
Merovingian, 300
Metal Gear series, 180
Metal Gear Solid, 180, 296–97
Metaverse, 190
Metro-Goldwyn-Mayer (MGM), 181, 206
Metroid, 112–13, 202, 253
Mexico, 114
Michael Ninn's Latex, 279
microchip (defined), 314
Microcosm, 125
Microforte (company), 223–24
MicroProse Software (company), 61, 206
Microsoft (company), 79, 101, 113, 122, 129, 148, 167–71, 180, 215, 220, 252, 254, 256, 288, 293, 306
Microsoft Flight Simulator, 247
Microsoft Windows, 304
Microsphere, 204
Microvision, 5–6, 10, 15, 144–45, 314

Middle-Earth, 308

Midi (Musical Instrument Digital Interface)
    format, 253–54, 256

Midi Manufacturers Association, 253–54

Midnight Magic, 269

Midway Games, xvii

Midway Games West, 60

Midway Manufacturing, 35, 37, 39–41, 43, 69,
    73, 92–93, 95, 130, 136, 211, 243, 278, 295

Mighty Morphin Power Rangers, 128

Mike Tyson's Punch-Out!!, 112

Milestone (company), 208

Millennium Games, 101

Miller, Chuck, 173

Miller, Rand, 86–88, 190

Miller, Robyn, 86–88, 190

Miller, Scott, 156

Milles Bornes, 264

Millipede, 94, 272

Milner, Ron, 63

Milton Bradley, 61, 65, 103, 144, 314

Milton Bradley Microvision. *See* Microvision

Mindlink (by Atari), 65

Mind Magazine, 31

Mines of Moria (game), 173

Minestorm, 70

Minesweeper, 303

Miniature Golf, 272

MiniDisc format, 181

Minor, Jay, 63

Mirage (company), 299

Mirco Games (company), 39

Mirrorsoft (company), 118, 207

Mirrorworld, 174

Missile Command (Atari 2600 version), 59, 64

Missile Command 2, 94, 61, 79, 92, 272, 316

Missile Defense 3-D, 272

Missile Radar, 36

Missile-X, 41

Mission Impossible, 205

Mitra, Rhona, 184

MITS (company), 77

Miyamoto, Shigeru, 298

MMC1 chip, 112

MMC2 chip, 112

MMOGs. *See* massively multiplayer online
    games

MMORPGs. *See* massively multiplayer online
    role-playing games

MOA (Music Operators of America), 144

mobile phones, 218

Mobile Suit Gundam, 297

MobyGames, 297, 341 n.22

modchips (modification chips), 180

Model Racing (company), 39–40

modems, 152–53, 166, 174

mods (modifications), 192, 225, 280, 301

Molyneux, Peter, 204–5, 237, 291

monochrome, 145

Monolith Productions, 193

Monopoly, 263, 268, 273

Monroe, Marilyn, 184

Montana, 264

Moon Alien Part 2, 92

Moon Patrol, 11, 94, 241

Moore, E. F., 31

Moore, Omar K., 33

Moore's Law, 194

Moo (Mud, Object-Oriented), 271

moral and ethical dimension of video games,
    187, 229, 283–91, 308. *See also* controversy

Morrison, Howard, 144

Morse, 266

Mortal Kombat, xix, 95, 111, 130, 135–36, 179,
    194, 220, 243, 267, 278, 295

Mortal Kombat II, 136

Mortal Kombat 3, 136

Mortal Kombat 4, 136

Mortal Kombat: Annihilation, 295

"Most Ignored Fact," 291

motion capture, 243, 245

Moto-Cross, 39

Motor Raid, 137

Mousetrap, 93, 264–65, 267–69

The Movies, 205

MP3, 148

MPAA (Motion Picture Association of America),
    281

MPEG (Motion Picture Experts Group), 123

MPEG (Motion Picture Coding Experts Group)
    format, 243

MPPDA (Motion Picture Producers and
    Distributors Association), 21

Ms. Pac-Man, 74, 93, 267, 269, 298

Ms. Pac-Man Plus, 74

MSX home computer, 101, 181

Mtrek, 107

Mud (Multi-Use Dungeon, or Multi-User
    Dimension), 173–74, 191, 271

MUD1, 173–74

M.U.L.E., 268, 273, 305

Multimedia PC (MPC), 122–23, 129

Multi-Memory Controllers (MMCs), 112

Multiple Arcade Machine Emulator (MAME),
    22, 142, 194, 312

Mush (Multi-User Shared Hallucination), 271

Muppet Treasure Island (video game), 262
Murphy, Tex, 132
Murray, Janet, 299
Muse Software (company), 191
Music Box Demo, 265, 274
Mylstar (company), 100, 105, 128
Myst, xix-xx, 4, 11, 87–88, 124, 129, 139, 190,
    246, 260, 262, 268–70, 274–75, 285–86,
    289, 291
Myst III: Exile, 88, 90
Myst IV: Revelation, 90
Myst V: End of Ages, 90
Myst Island, 88, 90
Myst series, 309
Myst: Trilogy, 206
Mystery Disc 1: Murder, Anyone?, 101
Mystery Disc 2: Many Roads To Murder, 101
Mystery House, 83
Mystique (company), 110, 278, 284

N (video game), 199
Nakimura, Grace, 133
Namco (company), xviii, 43–44, 60, 73, 91, 93–
    94, 97, 101, 110, 117, 136–40, 142, 153,
    211–12, 251
Namco Classic Collection Volume 1, 142
Namco Classic Collection Volume 2, 142
Namco Museum 50th Anniversary, 194
Name That Tune, 271
NAND gate, 314
Napoleon III, 206
NARC, xix
NASCAR, 89
NASDAQ, 206
National Academy of Arts and Sciences, 254
National Academy of Digital, Interactive
    Entertainment, 210
National Semiconductor, 104
Naughty Dog (company), 179
Nebulus, 202
NEC (company), 118–19, 122, 161, 166,
    177
NEC Turbografx-CD. *See* Turbografx-CD
Need for Speed, 89, 179
Nelsonic, 6
Neo•Geo, xix, 119–20, 147
Neo•Geo MVS, 96
Neo•Geo Pocket, xx, 147
Neo•Geo Pocket Color, 147
Neon Genesis Evangelion, 297, 299
NES 2, 110
NES Game Standards Policy, 110
Netherlands, 114, 210

networked arcade games, 137–38
networked games, 16, 140–41, 155, 173, 187,
    189, 191, 261, 272, 284–85
Neuromancer, 190
Neverwinter Nights, 175
Neverwinter Nights 2, 206
Newell, Allen, 32
newgrounds.com, 197
Newman, Barnett, 19
New Zealand, 224
NFL, 89, 101
NFL 2K1, 166
NFL Football, 100
NFL Football Trivia Challenge '94/'95, 271
N-Gage, xx
NHL Hockey 97, 272
Nichibutsu (company), 43–44, 92
Nielsen, Mark, 141
Nielsen Entertainment, 294
Night Driver, xviii, 39, 67–68, 246, 266
Night Driver (Atari 2600 version), 59
A Nightmare on Elm Street, 130
Night Trap, 130–31, 278–79
Nihon Bussan (company), 93
Nihon Bussan/AV Japan, 100–102
Nim, 31
Nine-Inch Nails, 183
Ninja Gaiden series, 112
Ninja Hayate, 100
Nintendo (company), xviii-xx, 43, 58, 86, 93–
    96, 109–117, 120, 131, 136, 144–45, 147–
    49, 156, 161, 163–65, 168–71, 177–79, 189,
    201–2, 207, 211–14, 216, 220, 248, 252–54,
    275, 277, 294–95, 297–98, 313
Nintendo Advanced Video System (NAVS),
    109, 116
Nintendo DS (dual screen), xx, 145–46, 148,
    194, 215–17, 309
Nintendo DS Light, 146
Nintendo Entertainment System (NES), xviii,
    29, 60, 86, 96, 106–7, 109–114, 116–18,
    120, 136, 145, 149, 156, 171, 177–79, 213,
    252–54, 275, 294–95, 297, 299
Nintendo Famicon system, xviii, 29, 106, 109,
    111–13, 115–16, 177, 213
Nintendo Game Boy. *See* Game Boy
Nintendo GameCube. *See* GameCube
Nintendogs, 216
Nintendo of America, 109, 112, 332 n.5 ch.19
Nintendo Revolution, 170
Nintendo 64 (N64), xix, 11, 113, 140, 159,
    165–66, 171, 178–80, 215–16, 248, 254,
    297

Nintendo 64DD, 165

Nintendo Ultra 64. *See* Nintendo 64

Nintendo Virtual Boy, xix, 5–6, 10, 14, 313

Nintendo Wii, xx, 114 , 170–71, 215

Niven, Larry, 193

NMAB (New Media Arts Board), 225

Nokia, xx

Noll, A. Michael, 33

Nomad. *See* Sega Nomad

nondiegetic sound, 254–55

non-player character (NPC), 314

"non-player killer" (NPK) server, 288

NOR gate, 314

normal mapping, 248

Norrath, 309

North and South, 205–6

Northern Lights, 272

Northwestern University, 68, 189

Norway, 114, 208

Noughts and Crosses, 269

Nova Games (company), 101

NSF (National Science Foundation), 33

NTSC (National Television System
    Committee), 314

NTSC standard, 314

Nulty, Peter, 104–5

Number Games, 266, 274

Nutting, Bill, 35

Nutting Associates, 19, 35–37, 59

oblique perspective, 139

obstacle course games, 269

Ocean Software, 204

Oda Nobunaga, 219

Oda Nobunaga's Den, 218

"Odyssee," 45

Odyssey. *See* Magnavox Odyssey

off-screen events, 92

Olympic Home T.V. Game, 47

Olympic Tennis, 36

Olympic TV Football, 36

Olympic TV Hockey, 36

Olympics, 92

Omega, 270

Omega Race, 69

Omikron: The Nomad Soul, 207

One Must Fall: 2097, 156–57

online games, 90, 107, 149, 155, 159, 166, 168,
    171, 173–76, 201, 211–12, 220–21, 284–85,
    287, 290, 304–6, 308, 314. *See also*
    MMORPGs

Orelec (company), 49

Oriental Daily, 219

Origin Systems (company), 132, 175, 190

Oshii, Mamoru, 297

OsWald, 208

Oswald, Lee Harvey, 280

otaku, 218, 297

Othello, 261, 263, 273

Otomo, Katsuhiro, 297

Oubliette, 173

Outlaw (arcade version), 39, 259, 265

Outlaw (Atari 2600 version), 41, 59

OutlawMOO, 272

Outrun, 96–97

Over Drive, 137

Ozdowski, Dr. Sev, 225

Pac & Pal, 74, 95

Pace Car Pro, 37

Pachinko!, 269

Pacific Novelty, 93

Pac-Land, 74, 95

Pac-Man, xviii, 11, 22, 29, 44, 73–74, 78, 92–
    93, 98, 104, 123, 128, 194, 211, 251, 260–
    61, 264–65, 267–69, 275, 291, 294, 298,
    309, 331 n.2 ch.16

Pac-Man (Atari 2600 version), 65

Pac-Man (character), 73–74, 95, 251, 289, 309

Pac-Man (television series), 298

Pac-Man & Chomp Chomp, 74, 95

Pac-Man Collectibles, 74

"Pac-Man Fever" (song), 74

Pac-Mania, 74

Pac-Man Jr., 298

Pac-Man Plus, 74, 94

Pac-Man Super ABC, 142

Pac-Man 25th Anniversary Model, 74

Pac-Man VR, 74

Pac-Man World, 74

Pac-Man World 2, 74

Paddle-Ball, 36

Paddle Battle, 36

Painkiller, 193

Pajitnov (Pazhitnov), Alexey, xviii, 118, 207

paku paku, 73

Palamedes, 136

Palcom games, 101

Palicia, Deborah, 74

Panasonic, 162, 254

The Pandora Directive, 132

Pan European Game Information (PEGI), 281

Pan European Game Information (PEGI)
    system, 209

Panther, 68, 189

parabolic mirror, 101, 139

Paradox (company), 208
"Paragraphs on Conceptual Art," 19
Parallax (company), 156
parallax scrolling, 11, 241, 314
parallel imports, 217
Paramount Studios, 70
PaRappa the Rapper, 179, 237, 271
Parasite Eve, 214
Parker Brothers, 61, 103, 264
Parlour Games, 273
particle systems, 248
Passengers on the Wind, 205–6
Password, 262
Patel, Amit, 155
The Patrician, 207
Pavlovian stimulus-response training, 285
Pavlovsky, Dmitry, 207
PCB. *See* printed circuit board
PC-Engine, 118, 122, 177
PC-File, 152
PC Fútbol series, 208
PC-Talk, 152
PC-Write, 152
PDP-1, 13, 33
PDP-8, 76
PDP-10, 34
PDP-10 system, 173
Pedestrian, 277
pencil-and-paper games, 269
Pendúlo Studios, 208
Pengo, 94
People Can Fly (company), 193
Periscope, 18, 35, 149
PernMUSH, 272
Perry, Telka S., 133
persistent worlds, 287, 308
personal digital assistants (PDAs), 15, 147–48, 194, 304
Persons, Dan, 100
Petaco S.A. (company), 43
Peterson, Mark, 174
Phantasmagoria, 132, 279
Phantasmagoria II: A Puzzle of Flesh, 133
Phantasy Star, 97, 272
Phantasy Star Online, 166
phase-alternating line (PAL), 314
Philips CD-i, xix, 122, 129, 131, 162, 333 n.6
Philips Electronics (company), xix, 49, 115, 121, 162–63, 177, 254, 333 n.6
Philips Interactive Media, 131–32
Philips/Magnavox, 263
Philips Videopac, 5
Philko (company), 136

PhillyClassic, 66
Phoenix, 92
photo-sticker machines, 212
physics games. *See* indie physics games
Pierce, David, 206
Pigeon-Shooting, 49
Pikachu, 215–16
Pikachu (character), 297
Pilot Wings, 165
pinball and video game hybrid, 93
Pinball Challenge, 269
Pinball Construction Set, 89
Pinball Dreams, 269
Pinball Fantasies, 269
pinball games, 18–19, 21, 35, 140, 269–70, 279
pinball industry, 36
Pinball Jam, 269
Pinball Quest, 269
Pinball Wizard, 269–70
Ping-O-Tronic, 46, 48
Pinkett-Smith, Jada, 300
Pinky. *See* Speedy
Pin-Pong, 37
Pioneer Corporation, 101
Pioneer LaserActive CLD-A100, xix
Pioneer LaserActive home laserdisc game system, 101
Pipe Dream, 136, 261, 285
pipelining of content, 236
piracy, 111–12, 180, 201, 204, 213–16, 219–21, 275, 315
Piranha Bytes (company), 207
The Pit, 155
Pitfall!, 81, 241, 262, 264, 269
Pitfall II: The Lost Caverns, 95
Pixar, 297
pixels, 6, 248, 284
pizza, 73
Planet, 68
Planetfall, 274
plastic overlays, 50, 70
platform games, 92, 95, 113, 123, 125, 156, 180, 270
Plato, Dana, 130
PLATO system, 173–74, 189
PLAY!, 339 n.21
playable memory cards, 147–48
PlayChoice system, 96
player-characters. *See* avatars
player-versus-player (PvP), 175–76, 224, 287–88
Playing with Power, 299

Play Meter Magazine, 91

Playschool Math, 266

"Play Station" (two words), 162–64, 177–78

PlayStation, xix, 11, 16, 61, 111, 113, 123, 125, 140, 147–49, 159, 164–66, 177–82, 214–15, 217, 237, 246, 248, 254, 275, 307, 335 n.5

PlayStation 2 (PS2), xx, 102, 121, 138, 148–49, 166–70, 178, 181, 194, 197, 215, 220, 249, 252, 254, 297, 335 n.5

PlayStation 3 (PS3), xx, 125, 170–71, 181, 213, 215

PlayStation Portable (PSP), xx, 148, 181, 194, 201, 216–17, 296

Pocket Billiards!, 273

Pocket Pikachu, 216

PocketStation, 148

POD, 206

point of view, 184, 187, 245–46, 248–49, 289. *See also* first-person perspective

Point Of View (game), 130

Pokemon, 216, 221, 297

Pokemon (character), 168

Pokey (nicknamed "Clyde"), 74

Poland, 209

polarizers, 313

Pole Position, 11, 70, 94, 189, 194, 207, 266, 271

Pole Position (Atari 2600 version), 59

Pole Position II, 95

Police Trainer, 274

political side of video games, 223–27

polygonally-based graphics, 315. *See also* filled-polygon graphics

Polygonet Commanders, 139

Pomeroy, John, 128

PONG (arcade game), xvii, 18, 29, 36, 50–51, 59, 61, 63–64, 91, 128, 211, 239, 251, 262, 272, 273, 275, 277, 309

PONG (home console system), 15, 54–55, 63, 143

PONG clones, 45, 48

PONG Doubles, 36, 45, 136

Pong Tron, 36

Pong Tron II, 36

Poole, Steven, 239–40

Popeye (arcade game), 94, 298

Popeye (character), 298

Pop'n Music, 271

Popular Electronics, 104

Populous, 89, 204

pornography, 112, 226, 279, 284

Porrasturvat (Stair Dismount), 198–99

port (verb), 315

Postal, 296

Post Office, United States, xx

post-production processes, 235

POV Entertainment Group, 131

Powerboat Racing, 137

Power Glove, 294

Power Module (by Amiga), 65

Power Rangers Pinball, 270

Power Shovel Simulator, 137

PP 2000, 49

Practical Wireless, 46

preproduction processes, 233–34

The Price is Right, 262

Prince of Persia, 184, 243–44

Prince of Persia: The Sands of Time, 206, 249

Princess Clara Daisakusen, 139

Princess Daphne, 128

printed circuit board (PCB), 96, 315

priority, 11

Prize Fighter, 125

problems in video game development process, 236–37

Probst, Larry, 89

production processes, 233–34

Professor Pac-Man, 74, 95

Programmers at Work, 73

programming, 301

programming games, 270

Pro Hockey, 36

Project Reality, 179

Project Support Engineering, 39–40, 73

Prop Cycle, 14, 137, 265, 267

Pro Pinball, 270

Pro Tennis, 36

prototypes, 233, 237

Pro Wrestling, 112

PSOne, 167, 178

Psychic Detective, 132

psychology, 285–86

Psygnosis (company), 125

pterodactyl, 138

Puck-Man, xviii, 44

Puck-man (character), 73

Pulp Fiction, 296

Pulse (Kairo), 295

Pump It Up, 138

Punch-Out!!, 95, 189

Puppy Pong, 36

purikura (photo-sticker machines), 212

The Purple Rose of Cairo (film), 132

Pursuit, 37

Puzzled, 136

puzzle games, 136, 188, 190–91, 199, 202, 216, 260, 270, 279, 306
PvP. *See* player-versus-player
Pyro Studios (company), 205, 208–9

Q*bert, xviii, 95, 261
Q*bert (character), 95
Q*bert watch, 6
Qix, 93, 261, 264–65
Quadrapong, 36, 37, 43
Quake, 156, 187, 192, 248
Quake II, 192
Quake III: Arena, 16, 192
Quake 4, 192
Quaker Oats, 103
Quantic Dream, 207, 249
Quantum, 69, 94, 264
Quantum Computer Services, 175
Quantum Gate, 132
Quarter Horse, 93, 99
Quéau, Philippe, 246
Queensland Local Government Association, 226
Quest for the Rings, 5, 263
Quest of Mordor, 174
Quiki-Mart, 87
Quinn, Tom, 55
quiz games, 270–71, 306
Quiz Show, 40
Qwak!, 37

race (biological), 95
Racer, 37
racing games, 37, 39, 41, 92–94, 100, 125, 128, 137, 140, 189, 207–8, 212, 216, 271
Radar Scope, 93
Radio Shack, 77
Rad Racer series, 112
Rad Rally, 137
"Raging Boll," 296
Raiders of the Lost Ark (Atari 2600 game), 83–84, 262, 271
Raiders Vs. Chargers, 101
Railroad Tycoon, 268
Rally, 36
Rally-X, 92
RAM (defined), 315
Rambo, 213
Rampage, 96
Ramtek, xvii, 36, 40, 43
Rand Air Defense Lab, 31
RAND Corporation, 31
random scan, 9

Raptor: Call of the Shadows, 156
Rare (company), 246
RARS (Robot Auto Racing Simulator), 270
raster graphics, 10, 67, 70–71, 91, 93–94, 101, 246, 315
raster scan, 315
ratings, 131, 209, 225, 279, 281
Rat's Revenge, 189
Raven Software, 192
Rayman, 206
RCA, 33, 50, 57, 104
RCA Studio II, 57
RDI Halcyon. *See* Halcyon home laserdisc game system
RDI Systems, 100–101
The Realm Online, 176
realMyst, 12, 88
Real Pinball, 270
Real Puncher, 140
RealSports Soccer, 273
RealSports Tennis, 273
RealSports Volleyball, 273
real-time-strategy (RTS), 176
Rebel Assault, 125, 260, 268
Rebound, 36–37
The Reckoning, 192
recursion. *See* looping formal structures
Red Alert, 123
Red Baron, 68, 330 n.5
Red Book digital audio format, 254, 256
"red book" standard, 121
redemption games, 140
Red Planet, 139–40, 266, 271
Reeves, Keanu, 300
regulation, 23
Rekkaturvat (Truck Dismount), 198
remediation, 244
Remedy Entertainment (company), 208
Renaissance, 239
Rene Pierre (company), 40
Rescue on Fractalus!, 189
Research Analysis Corporation, 32
Reservoir Dogs (film), 296
Reservoir Dogs (video game), 226
Resident Evil (film), 296
Resident Evil 4, 249
Resident Evil: Apocalypse, 296
Resident Evil series, 179, 296
retrogaming, 29, 61, 194, 200, 202
Return of the Invaders, 95
Return of the Jedi (arcade game), 95
Return of the Jedi (film), 70
Return to Castle Wolfenstein, 192

Reuters, 113

Rez, xx, 307

RGB color, xviii, 43, 91, 315

Rhem, 4, 90

Rhys-Davies, John, 132

rhythm and dance games, 138, 179, 271

Riana Rouge, 279

ride-on games, 107

Ridge Racer 2, 140

Ridge Racer Full Scale, 140

Ridge Racer series, 214

RiftMUSH, 272

The Ring (Ringu), 295

ringtones, 256–57

Ringworld, 193

Rip Off, 68, 70

Ripper, 124, 132

Rise of the Triad, 192

Riven, xx, 4, 11–12, 16, 23, 88, 90, 270, 285, 289

Rivers of MUD, 272

Road Avenger, 101

Road Blaster, 101

Road Burners, 137

R.O.B. (Robotic Operating Buddy), 109, 116–17

Roberts, Chris, 132

Robertson, Roland, 214

Robinett, Warren, 64, 82, 312

roboprobes, 69

Robot Battle, 270

Robot Bowl, 41

Robotron: 2084, 94, 202, 272

The Rock (wrestler), 296

rock-paper-scissors, 202

Rockstar Games (company), xx, 254, 279–80

Rockstar North (studio of Rockstar Games), 226, 249

Rogue, 83, 151–52, 156, 274

Roland (company), 253

role-playing games (RPGs), 16, 34, 123–24, 155, 173–76, 180, 190, 193, 202, 204–5, 207, 237, 246, 256, 271–72, 275, 284–85, 287, 290–91, 295, 305, 314–15. *See also* MMORPGs

Rollercoaster (film), 99

Rollercoaster Tycoon, 205

Rolling Blaster, 101

Rolling Crash, 44

ROM (defined), 315

Romero, John, 190, 192

Rosen Enterprises, 149

Rosenthal, Larry, 67

Rose Online, 176

Rothko, Mark, 19

rotoscoping, 243

Round Up 5 Delta Force, 97

Rouse, Richard, III, 252

Route 16, 93

RPGs. *See* role-playing games

RSAC (Recreational Software Advisory Council), 281

R-Type, 96, 204

Rubi-Ka, 208

Rubik's Cube (video game), 270

Rubin, Owen R., 330 n.7

Ruddock, Philip, 225

Rule of Rose, 280–81

Runaway: A Road Adventure, 208

Russell, Stephen R., 13, 33

Saboteur, 204

Sacred Pools, 272

Safari Rally, 44

Sakaguchi, Hironobu, 246, 295

Sakakibara, Moto, 246

Sam and Max Hit the Road, 293

Samba de Amigo, 166, 271

sampled sounds, 252

Samuel, Arthur, 31

Samurai Spirits, 221

sandbox games, 256

Sanders Associates, 33, 46, 50, 53, 55

San Francisco Rush 2049, 60

Sanyo, 162

Sapet, Christophe, 205

Saturday morning cartoons, 298

Saturn. *See* Sega Saturn

"Saturnday," 164

Scandinavian game design, 208

S.C.A.T. (Sega Control Attack Team), 130

SCEI (company), 138

Sceptre of Goth, 16, 90, 174

Schwartz, Judah, 33

SCi (company), 205

Sciences Et Vie, 45

Scientific American, 33

Scorched Earth, 153–55

Scourge of Armagon, 192

Scrabble, 263

Scramble, 70, 93

scrolling, xviii, 40, 42, 70, 83, 92, 125, 136, 139, 152–53, 156, 202, 241, 246, 260, 314–15. *See also* parallax scrolling

SCUMM (Script creation utility for *Maniac Mansion*), 84–85

Sears, 54–55

Sea Wolf, 39, 277

SECAM [*Séquentiel couleur à mémoire* (sequential color and memory)] format, 315

Second Life, 176

second-person narration, 289, 304

The Secret of Monkey Island, 86, 123, 293

The Secret of NIMH, 128

Seeburg (company), 128

See-Fun, 36

See It Now, 17

Sega, xviii-xx, 35, 38–41, 58, 68–70, 86, 89, 93–97, 99–102, 110, 113, 115–20, 122, 124–25, 128, 130–31, 136–41, 146–47, 149, 156, 161–67, 169, 171, 177, 179–80, 201, 211–14, 216, 220, 246, 248, 253–54, 275, 281, 294, 316

Sega-AM2, 249

Sega CD, 162–63, 178, 254, 278

Sega Classic Collection, 194

Sega Dreamcast. *See* Dreamcast

Sega Game Gear, xix, 6, 107, 146, 216

Sega Genesis, xix, 89, 119–21, 146, 149, 161–63, 171, 177–78, 200, 213–14, 253, 275, 294

Sega/Gremlin, 41, 44

Sega Internet Service, 149

Sega Marine Fishing, 137

Sega Master System (SMS), xviii, 97, 110, 117, 119–20, 146, 149, 213, 253, 294

Sega Mega Drive, 122, 149, 177

SegaNet, 166

Sega Nomad, 146

Sega Rally Championship, 248

Sega Saturn, xix, 11, 61, 123, 140, 149, 159, 163–66, 178–80, 214, 254

Sega Super GT, 137

Sega 32X, 122, 149, 163

Sega TruVideo Productions, 128, 130

Seleco, 46, 48

Selenetic Age, 90, 269

Semicom (company), 136, 140

sequels, 94–95

Serious Sam, 193

Service Games (company). *See* Sega

Seta (company), 139

The Settlers II, 207

Sewer Shark, 125, 130

Sex Trivia, 271

sexual content, 220, 278–80

SG-1000 (console system), 115

Shadel, Derrick, 152

shaders, 248

Shadow (nicknamed "Blinky"), 74

Shadowbane, 176

Shadowlands, 208

The Shadow of Yserbius, 175

Shadow Warrior, 193

Shannon, Claude, 31

shareware, 197

shareware games, 107, 151–57, 264

Shark, 39

Shark Attack, 93

Shark Jaws, 39

Shaw, J.C., 32

Sheff, David, xiv

Shelley, Maureen, 226

Shenmue, 90, 149

Shenmue II, 249

Sheppard, Mare, 199

Sherlock Holmes Consulting Detective, 124, 131

Shining Force, 219

Shirow, Masamune, 297

shoot 'em up games. *See* shooting games

shooters. *See* shooting games

Shooting Gallery, 273

shooting games, 39, 40, 44, 70, 91–92, 94, 98, 100, 101, 109, 123, 125, 128–30, 135–36, 139, 156, 184, 187–93, 200, 202, 208, 212, 216, 260, 272, 283, 289, 291. *See also* first-person shooter

Shootout At Old Tucson, 102

Shrek Smash N' Crash Racing, 224

Shuffleboard, 43

Sidam (company), 92

Side Track, 44

Sid Meier's Civilization, 268

Sierra Network, 175

Sierra On-Line, 124, 132, 242

Sierra Studios, xx, 193, 279

Silent Hill series, 179, 296

Silicon Graphics (company), 178

Silicon Graphics workstations, 246

Silicon Knights (company), 205

Silmarils (company), 124

SimAnt, 268

SimCity, 4, 268, 287, 305

SimEarth, 305

SimFarm, 268

SimGolf, 273

Simon, 144

Simon, Herbert, 32

Simon clones, 144

Simon Says, 144

The Simpsons, 297

The Simpsons (game), 262

The Sims, xx, 89, 185, 234, 237, 263, 275, 287, 291, 305

The Sims 2, 254

Sim series, 305

Sims Online, xx

SimTower, 268

simulation games, 32–33, 189, 217, 224, 237, 260, 272, 287. *See also* flight simulators

simulations, 274, 283, 286, 303, 305

Simutek, 100

Sinclair, Sir Clive, 203–4

Sinclair Computers (company), 203–4

Sinclair Research Ltd. (company), 203

Sinclair User (magazine), 203

Singapore, 211–20

Singe the Evil Dragon, 128

The Single Wing Turquoise Bird, 19

Sinistar, 251

sit-in games, 44, 107

Skee-ball, 140

Skeet Shoot, 272–73

Sketchpad, 17

Ski, 39

Ski Champ, 137

Sky Diver, 43, 273

Sky Kid, 153

Sky Raider, 42

Skywalker, Luke, 132

Slam City with Scottie Pippen, 130

Slick Shot, 137

Slot Machine, 268

slot machines, 149

Slot Racers, 271

SMASH, 55

Smilebit (company), 226

Smith, Adrian, 184

Smith, David, 253

Smith, E. E., 19

Smith, Jay, 144

Smith, Tony, 19

Smith Engineering (company), 70, 144

Smithsonian Institution, 128

Smokey Joe, 42

Snelling, Michael, 225

SNK (company), xix, 44, 96, 119–20, 136, 139, 147, 212, 219, 295

SNK/Saurus, 138

Snoopy Pong, 36

Snow Crash, 190

social elements of video games, 284–85, 287–88. *See also* networked games; online games

Software Etc., 164

Software Publishing Association, 122

Sokoban, 152, 270

Solaris, 267

Solar Quest, 69–70

Solar Realms Elite, 155

Sonic Adventure, 149

Sonic Blast Man, 137

Sonic Spinball, 270

Sonic the Hedgehog, xix, 120, 213, 298

Sonic the Hedgehog (mascot), 149, 179

Sony BMG Entertainment, 181

Sony Computer Entertainment, 181

Sony Computer Entertainment America, 179

Sony Corporation (company), 86, 101, 111, 113, 121, 123, 141, 145, 147–49, 161–71, 177–82, 201, 211–12, 214–17, 219, 220, 237, 252, 254, 275, 280, 293, 296, 307

Sony Imagesoft (subsidiary), 178

Sony Interactive, 290

Sony Music Entertainment, 181, 206

Sony Pictures Entertainment, 181, 206

Sony PlayStation. *See* PlayStation

Sony's Technical Requirements Checklist, 170

Sony Wonder, 206

Sopwith, 152–54

Soul Edge, 140, 267

sound, 19, 79, 86, 88, 90, 92–93, 112, 114, 123, 177–78, 181, 192, 203, 214, 229, 234, 251–57, 338 n.3 ch.37

Sound Canvas (sound card), 253

sound design, 253, 255–56

sound designers, 251, 256

sound interface device (SID) chip, 252

soundtracks, 251, 253–57, 294

SoundX, 66

South Korea, 181, 211, 216, 219–21

SouthPeak Interactive (company), 132

Soviet Foreign Trade Association, 118

Soviet Union, 96, 118, 204, 207

Space Ace, 100, 102, 128, 268, 313

Space Channel 5, 271

Space Duel, 69, 94

Space Force, 91

Space Fortress, 93

Space Fury, 69, 93

Space Harrier, 11, 97, 246

Space Invaders, xviii, 11, 25, 29, 41–42, 64, 68, 70, 74, 78, 91–92, 104, 136, 211, 251, 259–60, 266, 272, 275

Space Invaders (Atari 800 version), 60

Space Invaders (Atari 2600 version), 58–59, 64, 143

Space Invaders (characters), 289

Space Invaders clones, 43

Space Invaders DX, 136
Space Invaders '95, 136
Space Panic, 92
Space Pirates, 102, 129
Space Quest I, 86
Space Quest IV, 86
Space Race, 36
Space War, 40, 67
Spacewar!, xvii, 13, 18–19, 33, 35, 40, 67, 69
Spaceward Ho!, 260, 268, 273
Space Wars, 40, 67, 70
Spain, 47, 49–50, 181, 208
SPC-700 processor, 177
Special Break, 40
Spectrum Holobyte (company), 118, 207
Spectrum ZX, 157
Speed Freak, 43, 67–68, 189
Speed Race, 37
Speed Reading, 274
Speedy (nicknamed "Pinky"), 74
Spelling Games, 266, 274
Sphere (company), 247
Spiderman (Atari 2600), 262, 270
Spider-Man (character), 297
Spielberg, Steven, 39, 293
Spike, 36–37
Spinball, 270
Splinter Cell, 296
Sport Fishing, 137
Sport Fishing 2, 137
sports games, 91–92, 100, 112, 128, 137,
    153, 169, 171, 208, 212, 261–62,
    272–73
Spout, 199
Springboard, 41
Sprint 4, 41
Sprint 8, 41
sprites, 11, 40, 71, 94, 97–98, 112, 114, 135,
    139, 241–43, 248, 315
Spycraft, 132
Spyro, 206
Spy Vs Spy, 262, 265, 269
Square-Enix, 256
Square Pictures (Squaresoft's movie division),
    295
Squaresoft (company), xix, 112, 123, 179–80,
    246, 253–54, 295
SSD Company Limited, 169
SSG (Strategic Studies Group) (company),
    223–24
SSI (company), 175
Stallone, Sylvester, 277
stamp, xx

Stampede, 25, 264
Stanford Artificial Intelligence Laboratory
    (SAIL), 188
Stanford University, 33, 82
Starbreeze (company), 250
Starcade (television show), 298
Star Castle, 68–70, 92
StarCraft, 204, 206
Starfighters, 101
Star Fire, 44
Stargate, 93
Starhawk, 42, 67–68, 70, 330 n.2
Starmaster, 267
Star Rider, 100
Star Ship, 267
Starship, 41
Starship I, 39
Star Trek (For-Play arcade game), 36
Star Trek (Sega arcade game), 69–70
Star Trek (text adventure), 78
Star Trek: Borg, 12, 16, 81, 262, 268
Star Trek: Elite Force, 193
Star Trek: Elite Force 2, 193
Star Trek franchise, 298, 304, 308
Star Trek: The Next Generation, 190
Star Trek II: The Wrath of Khan (film), 70
Star Wars (arcade game), xviii, 10, 70, 95, 260,
    262, 316
Star Wars (film), 42, 67, 69–71, 132
Star Wars (film series), 246
Star Wars: Dark Forces, 193
Star Wars franchise, 298–99, 304, 308–9
Star Wars Galaxies, xx, 159, 176, 285, 308, 314
Star Wars: Jedi Knight, 193
Star Wars merchandise, 341 n.27
Star Wars: The Empire Strikes Back, 114
Star Wars: X-Wing, 253
Status (company), 101
Stauf, Henry, 129–30
Steeplechase, xvii, 39
Stein, Paul, 32
Stein, Robert, 118
Stella, 63
Stellar Track, 272–74
Stephenson, Neal, 190
Stern Electronics (company), 92, 100, 128, 137,
    191, 251
Steve Jackson Games (company), 204
Stock Car, 37
Stolar, Bernie, 166
Stop Thief, 3
storytelling, 252, 304
Strata (company), 140

Stratego, 263

strategy games, 43, 204, 234, 273

Stratovox, 92

Street Burners, 37

Street Fighter, 96, 211–13, 221, 295

Street Fighter II, xix, 219, 278, 295

Street Fighter II – Champion Edition, 136

Street Fighter II – Hyper Fighting, 136

Street Fighter II – Rainbow Edition, 136

Street Fighter II – The New Challengers, 136

Street Fighter II – The World Warrior, 136

Street Racer, 261, 264, 266, 271

Street Viper, 101

Stricor (company), 137

Strike Mission, 101

S.T.U.N. Runner, xix, 97, 139

Stunt Cycle, 39, 66

Stunt Cycle (console), 57, 63

subcreation, 303, 308–9

Subelectro (company), 41, 43

Sub Hunter, 41

Submarine, 215

Subroc-3D, 94

Subs, 41

suicide batteries, 96, 315–16

Sullivan, George, xiii

Summer Games, 272

Sundance, 44, 68

Sunflower, 272

Sunflowers Interactive Entertainment
    (company), 207

SUNY, 33

Super Bowl, 41

Super Breakout, 261

Super Breakout (Atari 2600 version), 59

Super Bug, xviii, 40, 82, 92, 241, 315

Supercharged, 306

Supercharger (by Starpath), 65

Super Controller Test Cartridge, 266

Super Crash, 41

Super Don Quixote, 100

Super Famicom. *See* Super Nintendo
    Entertainment System

Super Flipper, 39

Super Galaxians, 43

Super GT, 271

Super Hang-On, 137

Super High-Way, 41

Super Knockout, 41

Superman (Atari 2600 version), 82, 262, 264–65

Superman (character), 297

"Superman" module, 47

Super Mario Bros., xviii, 95, 116, 253, 270, 275

Super Mario Bros. (film), 295

Super Mario Bros. 2, xix

Super Mario Bros. 3, xix, 11, 114, 156, 294

Super Mario Bros. series, 112

The Super Mario Bros. Super Show!, 298

"Super Mario Bros. Theme" ringtone, 257

Super Mario 64, 165, 248

Super Mario World, 156, 214

Super Nintendo Entertainment System (SNES),
    xix-xx, 15, 113, 119–21, 145, 156, 161–64,
    177–90, 200, 202, 213–14, 246, 253–54,
    294

Super Pac-Man, 74, 94, 298

Super Pinball: Behind the Mask, 270

Superpong, 37

Super Punch-Out!!, 95

Super Shinobi, 213

Super Sidekicks 3 – The Next Glory, 139

Super Soccer, 36

Super Space Invaders '91, 136

Super Strike, 137

Super Sushi Pinball, 270

"supersystem of entertainment," 299

"Super UFO" (pirated system), 214

super video graphics array (SVGA), 84

Supervision (system). *See* Watara Supervision

Suppes, Patrick, 33

Supreme Warrior, 125, 130

Sure Shot Pool, 262, 273

Surgical Strike, 125

Surround, 40, 264, 267

Surround (Atari 2600 version), 41, 64

Survey Island, 90

Suspended Animation, 270, 274

Sutherland, Ivan, 17

Suzuka 8 Hours, 137

Swarm, 43

Sweden, 45, 114, 208, 210

Sweeney, Tim, 156

Swiss Finishing School, 183

Swordquest series, 83

Swords of Chaos, 174

Syllabus magazine, 306

Symphony of the Night, 180

Synetic (company), 207

synthesized speech, 92–93

Syphon Filter series, 179

System Shock, 193

System Shock 2, 193

tAAt (game development group), 198

Table by Television, 48

Table Tennis, 36

table-top games, 39, 261–62, 273
Tac/Scan, 69–70
Tail Gunner, 44, 68
Tail Gunner II, 68
Taito, xvii-xviii, 36–37, 39–41, 43–44, 92–93,
    96–97, 100–101, 110, 128, 136–37, 139–40,
    142, 211, 251
Taiwan, 211–21
Takashimaya Department Store, 217
Take the Money and Run (video game), 264,
    269
Take-Two Interactive (company), 124, 132
A Tale in the Desert, 291
Talking Typewriter, 33
Tamagotchi, xx, 217–18
Tamahonam, 217
Tamsoft (company), 248
Tanaka, Hirokazu "Hip," 253
Tandy Corporation, 77–78
Tank, xvii, 36–37, 63–64
Tank II, 37
Tank III, 39
Tank 8, 39
Tankers, 39
Tantalus Interactive (company), 223–24
target games, 273
Target Renegade, 204
Taskete, 92
Taves, Brian, 261
Tecmo, 112
Teenage Mutant Ninja Turtles, 112, 262, 299
*Teenage Mutant Ninja Turtles II: The Arcade
    Game*, 299
Tekken 3, 140
Tekken series, 136, 140, 179, 214, 267
Telegenesis modem, 119
Tele-Spiel ES-2201, 49
TeleTenis, 47, 49
television, 17, 21, 28, 136, 143, 195, 208, 209,
    220–21, 241, 262, 277, 283–85, 291, 293–
    94, 297–98, 303, 311, 312, 315
television interface adapter (TIA), 63
Television Magazine, 46
Telstar, 55
Telstar Arcade, 57
Telstar Combat, 57
Tempest, xviii, 10, 68–69, 93, 189, 261, 316,
    331 n.3 ch.16
Tempest (Atari 2600 unreleased prototype), 93
Tempest 2000, 61
Temple Island, 90
Temple of Elemental Evil, 206
Tender Loving Care, 130

Tengen (subsidiary of Atari Games), 118
Tennis for Two, xvii, 32
Tennis Tourney, 36
terabytes (defined), 316
The Terminator (home video game), 123
testing of video games, 234–36, 301
Tetris, xviii, 60, 96, 112, 118, 136, 145, 194,
    207, 216, 261, 270, 285–86, 291
Tetris clones, 136–37
Tetris Plus, 136
Tetrix, 286
Tews, Rebecca, 289
Texas Chainsaw Massacre, 264
Texas Instruments (company), 55, 78
Texas Instruments 99/4a computer, 15, 78–79
Tex Murphy: Overseer, 132, 244
Tex Murphy series, 131, 244
text adventures, 78, 82–83, 90, 151, 173–74,
    188, 223, 262, 273–74, 304
texture-mapping, xix, 248, 307
Teyboll Automatico, 47
Thailand, 213–15, 217, 220
Thayer's Quest, 100–101
The Collective (company), 223, 226
The Edge Software (company), 204
Thief, 205
Thief: The Dark Project, 193
Thrust, 202
Thunderball!, 270
Tic-Tac-Dough, 262
Tic-Tac-Toe, 262–63, 269
Tiger Electronics (company), 146–47
Tiger Telematics, xx
Time Commando, 125
Time Crisis, 212, 214
Time Gal, 101
Time magazine, 103, 131
Time Pilot, 94
The Times, 131, 280
Time Traveler, 101–2
Time-Warner Inc., 60
Time-Warner Interactive, 60
Timex (company), 203
Timex Sinclair computer, 203
TinyMUD, 174
Tkacik, Maureen, 141
T-Mek, 137
Toaplan (company), 95
Toho Films, 19
Tokyo International Electronics Show, 178
Tokyo Telecommunications Engineering
    Corporation, 181
Tolkien, J.R.R., 82, 176, 303, 308

Tomb Raider, 23, 90, 179, 183, 185, 205, 262
Tomb Raider: Anniversary, 205
Tomb Raider: Legend, 184
Tomb Raider: The Cradle of Life, 295
Tomb Raider: The Cradle of Life (film), 183
Tomb Raiders & Space Invaders: Videogames Forms & Contexts, 225
Tomcat, 70
Tomcat Alley, 125
Tony Hawk's Pro Skater, xx, 179
Toontown Online, 176
Top Cow Productions, 183
Top Gear, 100
Top Gunner, 71
Top Landing, 97
Top Skater, xx, 14, 137
Tornado Baseball, 40
Torus Games (company), 223–24
Total Overdose, 208
Touch Me, 144
Touch Typing, 274
Tournament Table, 43
Toys 'R' Us, 164, 217
Track & Field, 272
trackball, 14, 79, 316
Trade Wars 2002, 155
The Tragical Historie of Rodion and Rosalind, 202
training simulation games, 274
Trainz series, 224
trak-ball. *See* trackball
Tramiel, Jack, 58, 60–61, 117
Trampoline, 43
transistor radios, 181
transmedia storytelling, 299–300
"Trash-80," 77
Trick Shot, 273
Trilobyte, 86, 124, 129–30, 246
Triple Hunt, 40
Trivia, 40
Trivial Pursuit (video game), 271
Trivia Whiz, 271
Triv-Quiz, 271
Tron (arcade game), 94, 262–64
Tron (film), 294
Tron 2.0, 307
Tropico, 305
TRS-80 computer, 77–78, 189
Trubshaw, Roy, 173
True Pinball, 270
"Truth in Video Gaming Act" (S.3935), 281
TSR, Inc. (company), 175, 206
Tsuppori Sumo Wrestling, 273

T.T. Block, 41
TUMIKI Fighters, 199–200
Tunnel Runner, 269
Tunnels of Doom, 269
TurboChip, 121–22
Turbo Duo, 122
Turbografx, 161
Turbografx-CD, 86, 123–24, 129, 177
Turbografx-16, 86, 119–22, 163, 171, 177
Turing, Alan, 31
TV Basketball, xvii
TV Flipper, 39
TV Goalee, 37
TV Hockey, 36
TV Pinball, 37
TV Pin Game, 36
TV Ping Pong, 36
T.V. Tennis, 36
Twin Eagle II, 139
Twin Peaks, 129
Twisted Metal series, 179
Two-Bit Score (company), 142
The Typing of the Dead, 138
Tyrian, 156
Ty the Tasmanian Tiger series, 224

U2 (band), 183
Ubisoft (company), 205–6, 249
Uematsu, Nobuo, 253
UFO Chase, 39
Ulam, Stanisław, 32
Ultima III: Exodus, 271, 289
Ultima IV: The Quest for the Avatar, 287
Ultima Online (UO), xx, 16, 159, 175–76, 284–85, 288, 308, 309, 314
Ultima Online: Kingdom Reborn, 175
Ultima series, 4, 83, 92, 190, 262, 272, 315
Ultimate Mortal Kombat 3, 136
Ultimate Play the Game (company), 204
Ultima Underworld, 190
Ultra Games (subsidiary of Konami), 110
Umi Yakuba, 101
Um Jammer Lammy, 138, 271
Unabhängige Selbstkontrolle (Independent Self-Control), 209
U.N. Command, 40
Under a Killing Moon, 124, 131, 244
UniSystem, 96
United Kingdom, 114, 174, 203–4, 206, 279–80
Universal (company), 43, 92
universal media disc (UMD), 148, 216, 296
Universal Pictures, 206

Universal Studios, xx, 100, 141, 294
University of Illinois, 173
University of Southern California, 89
University of Texas at Austin, 306
Unreal, 157, 187, 193
Unreal Tournament, 16, 285
Unsafe Haven, 272
UPL (company), 40–41, 43
upright cabinet, 316
Uru: Ages Beyond Myst, 88, 90
US Billiards, 36–39
"user-supported software," 157
U.S. Gold (company), 184
Us Vs. Them, 100, 128–29
Utah, 64
utility genre, 260–61, 274
uWink Media Bistro, 141

"Valuation Matrices for Learning/Educational
    Content in Popular Games," 306
Valve Software (company), 193, 225, 249, 255
Vapor TRX, 137
VAPS (Video Arcade Preservation Society), 141
VAX, 76
VCDs, 221
Vectorbeam (company) , xviii, 40, 43, 44, 67–
    68, 189
Vectorbeam monitor, 67
vector games, 40, 42, 44, 67–71, 93, 95, 316
vector graphics, 9–11, 67, 91, 189, 246
vector scan, 316
Vectrex, 5, 10, 14, 70
"The Veldt" (short story), 190
Vending Times, 135
Venture (arcade version), 93
Venture (Atari 2600 version), 83, 262
Venture Line, 91
Veolia Environnement, 206
Verant Interactive (company), 176
verisimilitude, 239
Vertigo, 71
VHS videotape, 120
Viacom, 141
Vib-Ribbon, 271
Vickers, Brett, 174
"video" (as a term), 4–5
Video Checkers, 263
Video Chess, 263
Video8 format, 181
Video Entertainment System, 104
"video game" (as a term), 3–7
"Video Game Decency Act" (H.R.6120), 281
video game lounges, 140

video games, 1–342
Video Games GmbH (company), 41
Video Games Live tour, 294, 339 n.21
video graphics array (VGA) standard, 84, 86,
    122
Videomaster, 46–47, 49
Video Olympics, 272
Videopac, 115
Video Pinball, 57, 270
Video Pinball (Atari 2600 version), 59
Video Pinball (console), 63
video pinball games, 36, 39. *See also* pinball
    games
Video Poker, 264, 268
Video Pool, 39
Video Software Dealers Association, 165
VideoSport MK2, 47, 49
Video Standards Council, 280
Video System Co., 136
Videotopia, 4, 142
Video Trivia, 271
VikingMUD, 272
violence, 70, 73, 92, 95, 111, 130–31 , 133,
    135, 140, 167, 187, 193, 195, 209, 220,
    226–27, 277–79, 283, 286–89, 291,
    295
"viral" marketing, 151
Virgin Games (company), xix, 123–24, 129–30
Virtua Cop, 212
Virtua Fighter, xix, 139, 164, 295
Virtual Boy. *See* Nintendo Virtual Boy
"VirtualCinema movies," 132
Virtual Combat, 138–39
Virtual Console, 171
Virtuality (company), xix, 138–39
virtual memory unit (VMU), 166
virtual pet, 217
Virtual Pool, 262, 273
virtual reality (VR), xix, 190, 249, 306
Virtual Sex series, 279
Virtual World (company), 139–40
Virtua Racing, xix
Virtua Striker, 140, 212
Visicalc, 78
"visual generation" (*shikaku sedai*), 297
Visual Memory System (VMS), 147
Vital Light, 208
Vivendi (company) , 141, 193, 205–6
Volkswagen, 77
Volkswagen Bug, 40
Volley (company), 39
Vortex Concerts, 19
The Vortex: Quantum Gate II, 132

Voyeur, 131, 333 n.6
Voyeur II, 131
VR8 (company), 138–39
VRC (Videogame Rating Council), 131, 281
Vs. System, 96

Wabbit, 273
Wachowski Brothers, 299–300
Wagner, Larry, 64
Walden, William, 32
Walkman, 145, 181
walkthroughs, 81
Wallace, Bob, 152
The Wall Street Journal, 141
Wal-Mart, 165
Warcraft, xix, 176, 204, 206
Warcraft II, xix
Warhammer Fantasy Battle, 204
Warhammer 40,000, 204
Warhammer: Dark Omen, 204
Warhammer: Mark of Chaos, 204
Warhammer Online: Age of Reckoning, 204
Warhammer: Shadow of the Horned Rat, 204
Warioland, 11, 270
The Warlock on Fire-Top Mountain, 204
Warlords (arcade version), 93, 265
Warlords (Atari 2600 version), 59, 93
Warner Communications, 59–61, 64, 66, 104, 117
Warrior, xviii, 5, 44, 68
Watara (company), 146
Watara Supervision (system), 146
Watergate Caper, 36
Watson, Dr., 131
Wave Runner, 137
WAV files, 254
wavetable (sample) synthesis, 253
Way Of The Warrior, 102
WaywardXS Entertainment, 208
Web Picmatic (company), 101
Weizenbaum, Joseph, 31
Weller, Lara, 184
Wells, Mark, 32
West, Simon, 295
Western Bar, 215
Western Gun, 39
Westwood Studios, 123–24, 129
whatisthematrix.warnerbros.com, 300
Wheeler, David, 130
Wheel of Fortune, 262
Wheels, 37
Wheels II, 37
Where in the World is Carmen Sandiego?, 278

Where Time Stood Still, 204
Whirlwind computer, 17
Who Shot Johnny Rock?, 101, 129
"Why the Craze Won't Quit," 104
Wii. *See* Nintendo Wii
Wii Remote, 171
Wii Sports, 171
Wild Gunman, 109
Williams Electronics (company), xix, 35–36, 60, 93–94, 100, 103, 152, 251, 254
Williams, J.D., 31
Williams, Roberta, 83–84, 132–33
Wilmunder, Aric, 84
Wilson, Johnny L., xiii
Wimbledon, 37
Wimbledon High School for Girls, 183
Windows (by Microsoft), 79
Windows CE, 166
windows-icon-menu-pointer (WIMP) interface, 79
Windows telnet, 174
Windows 2000, 168
Wing Commander (film), 295
Wing Commander III: Heart of the Tiger, 132
Wing Commander IV: The Price of Freedom, 132
Wing Commander: Prophecy, 132
Wing Commander series, 132
WingNut Films, 296
Winner, 36
Winner IV, 36–37
Winning Eleven series, 212
Winning Run, 97
Wired magazine, 306
wireframe graphics, 11, 40, 67, 71, 138, 189–91, 246, 316
Wirehead, 130
Witt, Alexander, 296
The Wizard, 294
Wizards of the Coast, 206
Wizz Quiz, 271
Wolf, Mark J.P., 241
Wolfenstein 3D, xix, 156, 209, 191–92
Wolfenstein VR, 139
Wonderswan, 147
Wonderswan Color, 147
Wonder Wizard, 15
Wong, Anthony, 300
Woods, Don, 34, 82, 188
Woomera Immigration Reception and Processing Centre, 225
Word Games, 266, 274
World Class Track Meet, 112

World Cup, 40
"world" of video game (diegesis), 28, 81, 88, 90, 123, 125, 127, 138, 173–76, 188, 191–92, 198, 235, 241, 245–46, 249, 254, 262, 273, 286–89, 303–4, 308–9
World of Warcraft (WoW), xx, 159, 176, 190, 204, 206, 275, 285, 287, 314
World Series Baseball '98, 273
World's First Soccer, 218
worldviews in video games, 305, 308. *See also* moral and ethical dimension of video games
World War I, 152
World War II, 156, 193
Worms franchise, 155
Wozniak, Steve, 77
Wrestle War, 267
wrestling games, 92
Wright, Will, 234, 237, 305
WWF Smackdown series, 179

XA Mode 2, 181
Xatrix (company), 125
Xavix Baseball, 169
Xavix Bowling, 169
Xavix Golf, 169
XaviXPORT, 169, 171
Xbox, xx, 121, 141, 167–68, 170, 193, 215, 220–21, 249–50, 252, 254
Xbox 360, xx, 169–71, 194, 215
Xbox Live, xx, 168–69
XE Game System (XEGS), 60
XE series of computers, 60
Xevious, 241
Xevious 3D/G, 142
The X-Files, 184
The X-Files Game, 132
X-Men, 137, 262
X-Men (characters), 297
Xpiral (company, originally named Effecto Caos), 208
Xtrek, 107
Xybots, 97, 139

XY monitor, 67, 316. *See also* vector graphics

Yale University, 33
Yamauchi, Hiroshi, 109, 114, 162
Yannes, Robert, 252
Yar's Revenge, 272
"yellow book" standard, 121
Yllabian Space Guppies, 93
Yokoi, Gunpei, 147
Yosaku, 44
Yoshi's Island, 270
You Don't Know Jack, 268, 271
Youngblood, Gene, 19
Your Sinclair (magazine), 203
Your Spectrum (magazine), 203
YouTube, 197
Yukich, James, 295

Z80 processor, 194
Zaccaria (company), 44
Zak McKracken and the Alien Mindbenders, 86
Zanussi, 46, 48
Zapper, 109
z-axis (defined), 316
Zaxxon, xviii, 11, 240–41, 272
Zboub Système, 205
Zektor, 69
Zelda (character), 162, 168
Zero Time, 43
Zike, 204
Zion, 300
Zito, Tom, 130
Zodiac, 272
Zombie, 206
Zool, 124
Zork, 4, 151, 274
Zorton Brothers (Los Justicieros), 101
ZX80 computer, 203
ZX81 computer, 203
ZX Spectrum computer, 203–4, 208, 252
Zynaps, 204
ZZT, 156

ABOUT THE CONTRIBUTORS

DAVID H. AHL is the author of 22 how-to books, including *Basic Computer Games* (the first million-selling computer book), *Dad's Lessons for Living,* and *Dodge M37 Restoration Guide*. In 1974, he founded *Creative Computing* magazine, the world's first personal computing magazine. In 1967, he devised the first computer model for forecasting the success of new consumer products. He is also the author of more than 500 articles on technology, automotive restoration, marketing, logic puzzles, travel, market research, financial planning, and investment analysis. He created *Lunar Lander, Subway Scavenger, Orient Express,* and 50 other computer games. Ahl holds an MBA from Carnegie-Mellon and an MS and BS in electrical engineering from Cornell University.

THOMAS H. APPERLEY submitted his PhD dissertation in May 2007. His topic focuses on the role of the quotidian in contextualizing the experience of video game play. During his research on this topic he conducted ethnographies, in Venezuela, Australia, and online. He has worked as a sessional lecturer in the Media and Communications Program at the University of Melbourne since 2006.

DOMINIC ARSENAULT is a PhD student at the University of Montreal working on the history and evolution of video game genres. He has published a number of papers and written his master's thesis on the issues of narrative in the video game medium.

KELLY BOUDREAU has written an MA thesis in Sociology at Concordia University in Montreal that worked towards defining the process of identity construction and maintenance in massively multiplayer online games. Her current research focuses on forms of mediated sociality ranging from the dynamics of social identification in online computer games and virtual worlds to the fusion of Internet activity and everyday life.

BRETT CAMPER is interested in the history and practice of independent media production and distribution, with an emphasis on video games. He has spent the past nine years working with digital media both academically and commercially. He is currently a senior product manager at eMusic, the leading Internet download service for independent music. Formerly, he was the research manager at MIT's Education Arcade group, where he served as a designer and technical lead for the multiplayer history role-playing game *Revolution.* Before coming to MIT, he was a program manager for the e-commerce platform of Internet media pioneer RealNetworks. An independent developer himself, he has created games for the PC, Nintendo's Game Boy Advance handheld platform, and Macromedia Flash. He holds an M.S. in Comparative Media Studies from MIT.

LEONARD HERMAN, a.k.a. The Game Scholar, fell in love with video games the first time he played *PONG* at a local bowling alley in 1972. He began collecting video games in 1979 after he purchased his first Atari VCS. A programmer and technical writer by trade, Herman founded Rolenta Press in 1994 to publish his book, *Phoenix: The Fall & Rise of Home Videogames,* the first serious book on video game history. Three editions have been published between 1994 and 2001 and a fourth edition is planned for 2007. Herman has written articles about video games for *Electronic Gaming Monthly, Video-gaming Illustrated, Official US PlayStation, Pocket Games, Classic Gamer Magazine, Manci Games, Video Game Collector,* and *Gamespot.com.* He also edited Ralph Baer's book *Video-games: In The Beginning.* Herman, who has acted as an advisor for *Videotopia* and *Classic Gaming Expo,* resides in New Jersey with his wife Tamar and their children Ronnie and Gregory.

LARS KONZACK is currently an Assistant Professor in Multimedia at Aalborg University in Denmark. He is a game researcher focusing on topics such as ludology, edutainment, sub-creation, experience design, geek culture, and game criticism.

ALISON MCMAHAN, PhD, is a documentary filmmaker (see www.alisonmcmahan.com) and the head producer for Homunculus Productions, a company that produces training films, industrials, and documentaries. Recent films include the training film *Living With Landmines* (2005) (see www.LivingwithLandmines.com) and an industrial film and a PSA for Pensamento Digital, an NGO in Brazil that provides computers and Internet access to poor communities (see www.HomunculusProds.com). Her latest documentary is *Bare Hands and Wooden Limbs* (2006) (see www.FutureofCambodia.com). She is currently in production on a feature length documentary, *The Eight Faces of Jane: The Life and Work of Jane Chambers* (see www.8FacesofJane.com). From 2001 to 2003 she held a Mellon Fellowship in Visual Culture at Vassar College where she built a virtual reality environment with a biofeedback interface for CAVEs. From 1997 to 2001 she was an associate professor, teaching film history and theory and new media at the University of Amsterdam. She is the author of the award-winning book *Alice Guy Blaché, Lost Cinematic Visionary* (2002) and *The Films of Tim Burton: Animating Live Action in Hollywood* (2005).

BENJAMIN WAI-MING NG is currently an Associate Professor of Japanese Studies at the Chinese University of Hong Kong, teaching and researching Japanese popular culture and Japan-Hong Kong relations. He received his doctorate in East Asian Studies from Princeton University in 1996 and was an assistant professor in Japanese Studies at the National University of Singapore from 1996 to 2001. He is working on a research project on the interaction and collaboration between Japan and Hong Kong in ACG (animé-come-game) industry.

BERNARD PERRON is an Associate Professor of Cinema at the University of Montreal. He has co-edited (with Mark J.P. Wolf) the anthology *The Video Game Theory Reader* (2003) and written the analysis *Silent Hill: Il motore del terrore* (2006). His research and writings concentrate on narration, cognition, and the ludic dimension of narrative cinema, and on interactive cinema and video games.

MARTIN PICARD is a PhD candidate in Comparative Literature and Film Studies and part-time lecturer in the History of Art and Film Studies Department at the University of Montreal, Canada. His publications and research interests cover film and digital media, video game culture and theory, Japanese film, and aesthetics. He is currently writing a thesis on the relationship between the aesthetics of video games and cinema.

ERIC PIDKAMENY graduated from Vassar College with a minor in music. He lives in Seattle with his wife, two cats, and an ever-growing pile of video games.

BOB REHAK is a visiting Assistant Professor in Film and Media Studies at Swarthmore College. He received his PhD in the Department of Communication and Culture at Indiana University. He has written on psychoanalysis, video games, and new media fandom in *The Video Game Theory Reader* and the journal *Information, Communication, and Society*. His articles on graphic engines and special effects are forthcoming in *Videogame/Player/Text, Film Criticism,* and the second edition of *The Cybercultures Reader*. He is associate editor of *Animation: An Interdisciplinary Journal,* published by Sage.

CARL THERRIEN is currently pursuing a PhD in semiology at Université du Québec in Montreal. He is also taking part in Bernard Perron's research project, "History and Theory of Early Interactive Cinema." His research interests include immersion in video games and other media, the history of video games, and ludic aspects of contemporary cinema.

FEICHIN TED TSCHANG is an Assistant Professor of Management in the Lee Kong Chian School of Business, Singapore Management University. His research focuses on the growth and development of information technology industries, and he most recently studied the development of the U.S. video game industry over a period of a few years. From this, he has written journal articles on the nature of creativity (in the design and development process), product development, and studio formation in the industry. He is working on a manuscript that he hopes will definitively describe the forces that shaped the video game industry and that are shaping or constraining its creative nature in recent years. He also has done some recent comparative work on the animation and online game industry in the Philippines and China, respectively, as well as on information technology-enabled services and software outsourcing in Asia. He has a PhD in Public Policy Analysis and Management from Carnegie Mellon University and previously worked at the United Nations and the Asian Development Bank where his research was on the digital divide and on virtual universities (*Access to Knowledge: New Information Technologies and the Emergence of Virtual Universities,* 2001).

DAVID WINTER is currently an antiques dealer specializing in vintage audio equipment and records. He is a software engineer by degree and is passionate for classical music, early records, and video games. He started collecting old computer parts in the early 1980s when he was a kid, and old computers and video games in 1994. He then specialized in early video games, built a large collection of over 800 machines, and met important people such as Ralph Baer who helped him greatly in his research. After rescuing a large amount of early video game documents, he realized that the history of early video games was quite incomplete and contained many mistakes. He is now working on a book about early video games, which will feature never-seen-before documents.

MARK J. P. WOLF is an Associate Professor in the Communication Department at Concordia University Wisconsin. He has a PhD from the School of Cinema/Television at the University of Southern California, and his books include *Abstracting Reality: Art, Communication, and Cognition in the Digital Age* (2000), *The Medium of the Video Game* (2001), *Virtual Morality: Morals, Ethics, and New Media* (2003), *The Video Game Theory Reader* (co-edited with Bernard Perron) (2003), *The World of the D'ni: Myst and Riven* (2006), and a novel for which he has begun looking for an agent. He is on the advisory board of Videotopia and several editorial boards including those of *Games and Culture, The Journal of E-media Studies,* and *Mechademia: An Annual Forum for Animé, Manga and The Fan Arts.* He lives in Wisconsin with his wife, Diane and his sons, Michael and Christian.